FAMILIES, RABBIS, AND EDUCATION

THE LITTMAN LIBRARY OF
JEWISH CIVILIZATION

Dedicated to the memory of
LOUIS THOMAS SIDNEY LITTMAN
*who founded the Littman Library for the love of God
and as an act of charity in memory of his father*
JOSEPH AARON LITTMAN
and to the memory of
ROBERT JOSEPH LITTMAN
who continued what his father Louis had begun
יהא זכרם ברוך

'*Get wisdom, get understanding:
Forsake her not and she shall preserve thee*'

PROV. 4: 5

*The Littman Library of Jewish Civilization is a registered UK charity
Registered charity no.* 1000784

FAMILIES, RABBIS AND EDUCATION

◆

Traditional Jewish Society in Nineteenth-Century Eastern Europe

◆

SHAUL STAMPFER

London
The Littman Library of Jewish Civilization
in association with Liverpool University Press

The Littman Library of Jewish Civilization
Registered office: 4th floor, 7–10 Chandos Street, London WIG 9DQ

in association with Liverpool University Press
4 Cambridge Street, Liverpool L69 7ZU, UK
www.liverpooluniversitypress.co.uk/littman

Managing Editor: Connie Webber

Distributed in North America by
Oxford University Press Inc., 198 Madison Avenue,
New York, NY 10016, USA

First published in hardback 2010
First published in paperback 2014

Catalogue records for this book are available from the
British Library and the Library of Congress
ISBN 978-1-906764-53-1

Publishing co-ordinator: Janet Moth
Copy-editing: Kate Clements
Proof-reading: Mark Newby
Index: Christine Headley
Designed and typeset by Pete Russell, Faringdon, Oxon.

Printed and bound in Great Britain by
CPI Group (UK) Ltd., Croydon, CR0 4YY

To the memory of
SIMI AND RUTH DREYFUSS

Acknowledgements

PORTIONS of this work have appeared in the following articles. In every case I have reworked, revised, and expanded the earlier versions. Grateful appreciation is here expressed for permission to reprint the following.

CHAPTER 1. 'The Social Implications of Very Early Marriage in Eastern Europe in the Nineteenth Century' (Heb.), in Ezra Mendelsohn and Chone Shmeruk (eds.), *Studies on Polish Jewry: Paul Glikson Memorial Volume* [Kovets meḥkarim al yehudei polin: sefer lezikhro shel pa'ul glikson] (Jerusalem, 1987), 65–77.

CHAPTER 2. 'L'Amour et la famille chez les Juifs d'Europe orientale à l'époque moderne', in Shmuel Trigano (ed.), *La Société juive à travers l'histoire*, vol. ii: *Les Liens de l'alliance* (Paris, 1992), 435–68.

CHAPTER 3. 'Remarriage among Jews and Christians in Nineteenth-Century Eastern Europe', *Jewish History*, 3/2 (Fall 1988), 85–114.

CHAPTER 4. 'Scientific Welfare and Lonely Old People: The Development of Old Age Homes among Jews in Eastern Europe', *Studies in Contemporary Jewry*, 14 (1998), 128–42.

CHAPTER 5. 'The *Pushke* and its Development' (Heb.), *Katedra*, 21 (October 1981), 89–102.

CHAPTER 7. 'Ḥeder Study, Knowledge of Torah and the Maintenance of Social Stratification in Traditional East European Jewish Society', *Studies in Jewish Education*, 3 (1988), 271–89.

CHAPTER 8. 'Gender Differentiation and Education of the Jewish Woman in Nineteenth Century Eastern Europe', *Polin*, 7 (1992), 63–87.

CHAPTER 9. 'Literacy among East European Jewry in the Modern Period: Context, Background and Implications', in *Transition and Change in Modern Jewish History*, Shmuel Ettinger Jubilee Volume (Jerusalem, 1988), 459–83.

CHAPTER 10. 'Dormitory and Yeshiva in Eastern Europe' (Heb.), in Mordechai Dagan (ed.), *Religious Dormitory Education in Israel* [Haḥinukh hapenimiyati hamamlakhti dati beyisra'el] (Jerusalem, 1997), 15–28.

CHAPTER 11. 'Is the Question the Answer? East European Jews and North African Moslems: Oral Education and Printed Books and Some Possible Antecedents of Israeli Intellectual Life', *Studia Judaica* (Cluj), 8 (1999), 239–54.

CHAPTER 12. 'Hasidic Yeshivot in Inter-War Poland', *Polin*, 11 (1998), 3–24.

*

I should like to thank the following for their work in bringing this book to press: Janet Moth, who had to put up with a terribly disorganized writer; copy-editor Kate Clements; George Tulloch, who helped untangle the tables, and who checked the Slavonic languages; Lindsey Taylor-Guthartz, who checked the Hebrew; Pete Russell, who designed and typeset the book; proofreader Mark Newby; production manager John Saunders; and also of course Ludo Craddock and Connie Webber.

This book would not have been published without a generous grant from the Bollag Stiftung. I hope that the result meets their expectations.

The book is dedicated to the memory of Simi and Ruth Dreyfuss. They accepted their son-in-law with grace, patience, generosity, and great love. I don't think I can ever repay them, but I have not forgotten my debt. Simi was the *parnas* of the Basel Jewish community for almost two decades. Ruth was not the *parnas*'s wife but a woman in her own right who spoke her mind—but who gave her children the freedom to grow in their own way. Together they exemplified the best of the life of Jewish householders in Europe.

Contents

Tables

Note on Transliteration and Conventions Used in the Text

THE transliteration of Hebrew in this book reflects consideration of the type of book it is, in terms of its content, purpose, and readership. The system adopted therefore reflects a broad approach to transcription, rather than the narrower approaches found in the *Encyclopaedia Judaica* or other systems developed for text-based or linguistic studies. The aim has been to reflect the pronunciation prescribed for modern Hebrew, rather than the spelling or Hebrew word structure, and to do so using conventions that are generally familiar to the English-speaking Jewish reader.

In accordance with this approach, no attempt is made to indicate the distinctions between *alef* and *ayin*, *tet* and *taf*, *kaf* and *kuf*, *sin* and *samekh*, since these are not relevant to pronunciation; likewise, the *dagesh* is not indicated except where it affects pronunciation. Following the principle of using conventions familiar to the majority of readers, however, transcriptions that are well established have been retained even when they are not fully consistent with the transliteration system adopted. On similar grounds, the *tsadi* is rendered by 'tz' in such familiar words as *barmitzvah*, *mitzvot*, and so on. Likewise, the distinction between *ḥet* and *khaf* has been retained, using *ḥ* for the former and *kh* for the latter; the associated forms are generally familiar to readers, even if the distinction is not actually borne out in pronunciation, and for the same reason the final *heh* is indicated too. As in Hebrew, no capital letters are used, except that an initial capital has been retained in transliterating titles of published works (for example, *Shulḥan arukh*).

Since no distinction is made between *alef* and *ayin*, they are indicated by an apostrophe only in intervocalic positions where a failure to do so could lead an English-speaking reader to pronounce the vowel-cluster as a diphthong—as, for example, in *ha'ir*—or otherwise mispronounce the word.

The *sheva na* is indicated by an *e*—*perikat ol*, *reshut*—except, again, when established convention dictates otherwise.

The *yod* is represented by *i* when it occurs as a vowel (*bereshit*), by *y* when it occurs as a consonant (*yesodot*), and by *yi* when it occurs as both (*yisra'el*).

Names have generally been left in their familiar forms, even when this is inconsistent with the overall system.

The transliteration of Russian follows that of British Standard 2979:1958, without diacritics. Except in bibliographical and other strictly rendered matter, soft and hard signs are omitted, and word-final -й, -ий, -ый, -iй in names are simplified to -y.

Introduction

THERE is an element of self-discovery in looking at a collection of one's own articles which is missing when one looks at a monograph that one has written. The steps taken to write a scholarly book are standard. One defines a topic, conducts the relevant research, thinks, thinks some more, analyses the data systematically, and comes to conclusions. The structure is set from the start, and so is the goal. But articles are different. They are written over a period of time, in a variety of circumstances, and in response to different stimuli. Generally they are not written as part of a long-term plan, but in response to current interests and thoughts. Looking back over articles one has written over time therefore provides an opportunity to notice themes and consistent patterns that, at the time of writing, may not have been so evident or obvious.

The chapters in this volume all deal with aspects of east European Jewish life in the modern period. This was a time of transition from a society in which tradition was a key force to one in which models of the past no longer significantly determined behaviour and thought. This shift took place rapidly and under conditions that were not obviously conducive to a quick and smooth transition, and the consequences are still very evident today. I have long been fascinated by this change, and here I explore and try to explain its different aspects, describing the lives of significant individuals, looking at intellectual responses to change, and sometimes going on to consider broader questions including the social consequences of such change. I am not alone in this latter interest, but it has not been the usual approach to the study of east European Jewry.

Not surprisingly my articles reflect attitudes that I consciously espouse. The first is an interest in examining developments that took place not only among the male elite, but also among broader elements of the Jewish community. This has led me to consider the role of women and the nature of their lives in traditional east European Jewish society in a variety of settings, and I will return to this issue below. However, the majority of east European Jewish men—those who were poor—have also been ignored, and I have included them for consideration too. Even in dealing with the elite, such as rabbis, I have concentrated on the general group and not on leading rabbis.

The approach I have developed is to respect people of the past, my working assumption being that these people were easily as intelligent as we are today. Therefore, if their behaviour appears to us as odd or counter-productive, then we are probably missing an important point; there must have been good reasons for how they behaved. I have found that this approach, common to the study of social science, is a very useful tool for the historian. It is precisely the behaviour that seems the least rational or self-defeating that can serve as a means to understand the workings of Jewish communities in the past. In short, modesty and respect for others are useful qualities for research.

I have employed common sense to my collection of data. I have found it useful to examine sources not only in the light of other evidence but also for the degree to which they make sense. As a working hypothesis I usually start with common sense and then try to explain deviations from it. I have done my best to include every possible source relevant to a topic I am dealing with; indeed, much of the actual work of a historian is the search for sources. However, somewhat to my surprise, I have found that very often the con-clusions I have come to on the basis of these sources could have been reached even without them by considering well-known facts and analysing their implications logically. Very often the new sources were a trigger for a new understanding, but they were not the only possible source for an insight.

At times, my findings have led me to conclusions that do not fit with an idealized or stereotypical view of the past. I found less equality, less sensitivity, and less holiness than I would have hoped to have found, then—or now. There are those who wish to distort the image of the past in order to have a useful model for the present. Of course a false model is not useful because the attempt to achieve the impossible is doomed from the start and is more likely to cause harm than to be harmless. Equally serious is the fact that the truth is the truth, and if out of ideology one distorts the truth in one area, it will probably end up being distorted in others. In retrospect, the achievements of the society I have studied—east European Jewish society—are more impressive in light of the grim reality in which that society functioned than are imaginary achievements that took place in a world where there was no human weakness.

Many years ago I gave my doctoral adviser, Professor Jacob Katz, the first draft of the first chapter of my doctoral thesis. I invested a great deal of effort and thought in writing the chapter and I was crestfallen when I received his comments and reactions. He did not like it. What he objected to was my use of academic jargon and pretentious vocabulary. I cannot recall his exact words but his point was that if someone has something to say, it can be said clearly and with regular words. If there is nothing to say, all the jargon and multisyllabic words will not cover up for it. Simple language is, of course, no guarantee of quality; for that, one has to work. However, in my writing I have tried to follow my teacher's good counsel.

This collection is divided into three sections, each containing a number of chapters in which I analyse what I consider to be basic issues. Each section ends with an examination of one or two case studies that illustrate some of the points raised in the other chapters of the section. However, these chapters also stand alone.

The first section deals with family formation, family reformation, and family maintenance. The chapters are grouped in roughly chronological order, from marriage to old age. Although much attention is given to women in these papers, I have tried to give equal attention to men. There is no doubt that the history of Jewish women has been ignored. However, to focus solely on women would be to trade one distorted vision for another equally inaccurate one. Therefore, I have considered both men and women wherever possible. In these chapters, as well as in the other chapters in this volume, I have tried to correct widely held myths about the east European Jewish family and to provide a more nuanced and realistic description and analysis. At times it seems that misconceptions of the past are of more than academic interest. When there are individuals who feel a need to live in the way their ancestors lived in the past but they have an inaccurate vision of what was in the past, they can end up trying to live in a way that their ancestors never lived. In some cases, this creates impossible demands that can only lead to tragedy. The penultimate chapter in this section deals with the history of the *pushke* or the home charity box and relates it to the changing frameworks of women's roles and yeshiva finances.

The second section deals with education. First I deal with elementary education for boys and education in general among women. I then discuss the consequences of this reality with regard to literacy. The section ends with discussions of two specific issues—dormitory housing for yeshiva students and the place of questions in Jewish education and society. These are narrow topics, but they illustrate many of the issues that are not so self-evident. In considering education I was far less interested in stated goals and objectives than with realities. What people did was far more interesting to me than what they said they wanted to do. Similarly I think that values are best determined by looking at deeds and not at statements. In education, as with the family, there is a huge gap between idealized views of the past and realities.

The last section deals with the rabbinate—not with specific rabbis but with the institution. Here as well I give attention not only to the exceptional rabbis but also to the broader circles of rabbis and try to trace changes in the rabbinate in eastern Europe. The changing roles and positions of the rabbis not only reflect the shift to modernity that I mentioned above, but also illustrate a great deal about the day-to-day operation of the Jewish community. Little in this topic lends itself to simple explanations. The prominence of rabbis in Jewish communal life was growing at the same time that rabbinical authority was in general decline and fewer and fewer Jews were availing themselves of rabbinical counsel. Where once lay leaders had led communities, rabbis began to play increasingly prominent roles. One of the first to take steps in this direction was Eliyahu ben Shelomoh Zalman, better known as the Vilna Gaon (1720–97), who played an important role in Jewish society both in his lifetime and through the impact of his image, even after his death. This is explored in detail. The final chapter deals with a halakhic (legal) controversy that divided the two most important groups of east European Judaism, hasidim and mitnagedim, and then suddenly dissipated. The analysis of the dispute over *sheḥitah*, ritual slaughter, sheds significant light both on the values of the two camps and also on the openness of each to modernization in the framework of halakhah, Jewish law. In all of the issues regarding the rabbinate, looking at what was done is a key to understanding what people truly felt.

Almost all of these chapters were published previously in articles and edited books. However, I have revised all of them and in many I have made major changes. I have tried to improve my style, update the bibliographies, and to take into consideration criticism as well as new sources that have become available. My conclusions have not changed a great deal, but I hope they are more convincing in their present state. By bringing these studies together I hope that they will help to provide a clearer picture of a recent past that has been quite successfully misunderstood.

In some respects readers may find elements that appear more relevant than they would have anticipated. I would consider such a reconsideration to be a success. The same readers or others may discover that some elements, which they had assumed were relevant to their current realities, were actually not so. I would consider that to be a success as well. It is unreasonable to imagine that readers are not interested in what is linked and what is not. However, my goal has been to help understand the past and not to provide relevancies or irrelevancies. What is done with what I have written is up to you—the reader.

PART I

FAMILY AND
GENDER

ONE

The Social Implications of
Very Early Marriage

I N T H E E I G H T E E N T H and early nineteenth centuries, many east European Jews married off their children at the age of 13, 12, or even younger. Many saw this practice as a typical characteristic of traditional east European Jewish society. As Avraham Ber Gottlober (b. 1810) wrote in his memoirs: 'Fathers would say: "our son, may the Lord bless him, will soon be 11 years old and if we do not hurry to find him a good match, how will we be able to celebrate his wedding along with his bar mitzvah?"'[1] The phenomenon has been well documented, but not the logic behind this behaviour. After all, these young couples were not yet of childbearing age, nor were they able to set up independent households, even though this is commonly regarded as one of the central functions of marriage. Marriage at such ages sometimes led to extremely unpleasant legal complications, and if the young wife became pregnant quickly, there could be equally unpleasant medical complications. Indeed, not only does marriage at this age appear abnormal today, it also seemed odd to many in the past. Therefore, it is understandable that marriages of this type, when both the bride and groom were just at the age of puberty or even younger, have been termed 'premature marriages' (nisu'ei boser in Hebrew). However, there was also logic to the practice, and uncovering the rationale behind the behaviour can explain not only the phenomenon itself but also contribute to our understanding of the history of Jewish society. The first step towards this goal is to determine the scope of premature marriage.

*

It is not easy to reconstruct marital patterns in the Middle Ages or even in the early modern period because of the limited resources at our disposal. There are few external sources and the most promising internal sources are found in texts related to Jewish law. However, the responsa literature—the body of

[1] See Gottlober, 'Memoirs and Essays' (Heb.), 85–9.

written decisions given by rabbis in response to questions addressed to them—and other Jewish legal writings give only a partial picture of the scope of premature marriage and attitudes to such marriages. The issue did not often get attention because according to halakhah, or Jewish law, early marriage was generally not a legal problem. Jewish law authorized fathers or guardians to contract marriage for female minors. The situation was only a little more complicated with regard to males. According to Jewish law, marriages contracted when the groom was 13 years old or older were unquestionably valid. In his classic legal code, the *Shulḥan arukh*, Rabbi Yosef Karo (d. 1575) wrote: 'A man is commanded to marry at the age of 18 and he can marry at the age of 13, but before 13 a man should not marry.'[2] In his view, premature marriage was legal but not a *mitsvah*—that is, not a halakhic requirement. The words 'should not' left the question open as to whether such a marriage, if carried out, was valid. For this reason, the responsa literature usually discussed the validity of marriages only when the groom was less than 13 years old, whereas marriages involving brides and grooms in their early teens, even though they would be regarded today as very early, generally got little legal attention and were usually not discussed in the responsa literature. As a result, rabbinic sources give us only a partial picture of early marriage and cannot be relied upon as an indication of its scope.

Premature marriage was known in medieval Ashkenazi, that is, central or eastern European Jewish, communities. However, the incidence of such marriages is not clear. Irving Agus claimed that very early marriage was the standard in the tenth and eleventh centuries. According to him, early marriage was practised in order to prevent extra-marital sexual activity, because the financial resources were available, and from a desire to solidify social relationships between families.[3] However, he reached this conclusion on the basis of a limited number of cases without being able to prove whether these cases were typical or not.[4] Some of the cases he cited involved orphans, but one cannot generalize from such cases because orphans were often treated differently from other young people whose parents were alive. It is also important to distinguish between engagement or betrothal and marriage itself. Avraham Grossman pointed out that the sources do not prove Agus's points and he felt that Agus was exaggerating somewhat.[5] Nonetheless, in Grossman's opinion, very early marriage became more common in the tenth and eleventh centuries, and reached a high point in the twelfth and thirteenth centuries. According to the medieval tosafists (the authors of critical and explanatory glosses on the Talmud):

[2] *Shulḥan arukh*, 'Even ha'ezer', 1: 30.
[3] Agus, *The Heroic Age of Franco-German Jewry*, 284–5.   [4] Ibid. 278–9.
[5] See Grossman, *The Early Sages of France* (Heb.), 108 n. 1; id., 'Premature Marriage' (Heb.).

... and now that we are accustomed to marry off our daughters even when they are little, that is because every day the exile imposes itself on us and if a man has the means today to give his daughter a dowry [he marries her off now and gives her a dowry] lest in the course of time he will no longer have means.[6]

This is the clearest statement on the topic that I know of in the Hebrew sources, but even it is not clear. The statement 'even when they are little' does not mean that early marriage was always the case. While there were certainly many cases of very early marriage in the twelfth and thirteenth centuries, it is still debatable whether such marriages were the standard among Ashkenazim or just an acceptable option. This can only be determined after a systematic analysis of all the Ashkenazi sources from the Middle Ages and this has not yet been done. It does seem clear, however, that early marriages were regarded then as acceptable.

There may have been a shift in later centuries. It appears that Ashkenazi Jews in the late Middle Ages did not generally practise premature marriage. However, the average age of marriage among Jews appears to have been lower than among other population groups in Europe.[7] If there was criticism among Jews about age at marriage, it was of those who delayed marriage and not those who married too early. The average age of males was apparently about 18 and about 16 for females.[8]

By the end of the eighteenth century, there were clear differences between Jewish marital patterns in the German-speaking lands and in the Polish–Lithuanian Commonwealth. In the West, there was an especially steep rise in the age of grooms among Jews and a more limited rise in the age of brides. This may have been due both to increased acculturation to the surrounding society and perceptions of increased economic security.[9] There are relatively few sources on marriage patterns among Polish Jewry at the end of the Middle Ages and the beginning of the modern period. Aaron Arbeli claimed that very early marriage was not customary in Poland at that time,[10] though the precise grounds on which he made this statement are not clear. Rabbi Moses Isserles, also known by his acronym 'Rema' (d. Kraków 1572), made one of the few recorded references to early marriage in early modern Poland. In his comments on the *Shulḥan arukh* he cited the tosafists and commented:

---

[6] Tosafot on BT *Kid.* 41*a*, *asur le'adam*.

[7] One of the many difficulties with the claim that early marriage was standard in the early or high Middle Ages is that if that was the case, then there was a rise in the age of marriage at some point before the situation that Jacob Katz described in *Tradition and Crisis*, ch. 14. Such a change has not been documented and it is not clear what might have been the cause of such a change.

[8] A number of studies have been written on marital patterns among Ashkenazi Jews. For a study in English, see Katz, *Tradition and Crisis*, ch. 14.

[9] See Schofer, 'Emancipation and Population Change', 84–5.

[10] Arbeli, 'Polish Jewry in the Eighteenth Century', 135.

'and some say that today we are accustomed to marry off our daughters at a young age because we are in exile and we do not always have the means for a dowry. Moreover, we are few in number and it is not always possible to find a proper mate and thus our custom.'[11] This is evidence that the practice existed, but it says nothing about the scope of the custom or about the customs with regard to boys. Isserles himself seems to have been married in his late teens.[12]

Premature marriage in the Polish–Lithuanian Commonwealth in the modern period is well documented, and it apparently became more and more common during the eighteenth century. Rabbi Aryeh Yehudah Leib Teomim-Fraenkel (d. 1771), the rabbi of Brody in the mid-eighteenth century, wrote a responsum that dealt with the consequences of a very early marriage. However, he also noted that the marriage was contracted under exceptional circumstances. The father of the groom wanted to travel to Palestine, and there was concern that he might not be able to carry out his responsibilities to his children and would not fulfil his duty to marry them off.[13] This suggests that had there not been such special circumstances, such an early marriage would not have taken place. A Polish contemporary of his, Rabbi Shimshon Zelig ben Ya'akov Yehosef Halevi, wrote a responsum in the same period that dealt with the question of 'the contemporary custom of marrying a young boy to a young girl'. He opened it with these words:

I actually recall that a few years ago, when I was young, there were cases of premature marriage in the town of Radzin. There were learned judges in that town and they did not separate the young couples nor did they criticize the matches. However, I did hear that in some communities the couples were told to wait until they were older and only then to live together.[14]

In yet another collection of responsa from this period, by Rabbi Shemuel of Amdur (d. 1771), it was stated that 'In some communities it is customary today to be lenient and to allow the marriage of young boys already before the beginning of their thirteenth year even though according to the Talmud this is clearly forbidden'.[15] The 'lenient' rabbis who allowed premature marriages based their views on those of the medieval tosafists. Statements such as that of Rabbi Shimshon Zelig Halevi clearly indicate that premature marriage was practised in Poland, but they also suggest that it was not the standard everywhere.

[11] Isserles, *Hamapah*, 'Even ha'ezer', *Hilkhot kidushin*, 36: 8.
[12] Siev, *Rabeinu Moshe Isserles* (Heb.), 12, 15, says that Isserles was apparently born around 1530 and married for the first time around 1549. Even if the dates are not precise, he clearly was not a child groom.
[13] Teomim-Fraenkel, *She'elot uteshuvot gur aryeh yehudah*, 'Even ha'ezer', 89*b*.
[14] Zelig, *Teshuot ḥen*, p. 26.
[15] Shemuel of Amdur, *Teshuvat shemuel*, 26*a* (Hilkhot Kidushei Katan).

The first autobiographies we have of east European Jews also date from the eighteenth century, and some document the practice. Solomon Maimon (b. Poland 1753) wrote in his autobiography of his broken first engagement and his subsequent marriage at the age of 11.[16] References to very early marriage can also be found in communal records. In the *Recordbook of the Lithuanian Jewish Council*, the following enactment from 1761 was recorded:

It is absolutely forbidden for a male to marry before the age of 13 years and a day and for a female before the age of 12 years and a day . . . This enactment will come into effect on the first day of the [Jewish] month of Shevat in the year [= 1763]. Even until that date, such marriages cannot be made unless one of the parties, either the male or female, has reached maturity.[17]

The fact that it was necessary to make such an enactment suggests that there were Jews who married off their children at a younger age.

Observers of Jewish society found premature marriage one of the striking characteristics of the Jewish community. The issue came up in discussions that took place in the eighteenth century regarding the cultural and economic 'improvement' of the Jews in Poland. Both Jewish and non-Jewish participants in these discussions felt that the raising of the minimum age of Jews at marriage was a requirement for ameliorating the situation of the Jews. Non-Jewish doctors in Poland saw very early marriage as a health issue, and one such doctor thought that early marriages led to health problems among Jews. Another doctor suggested prohibiting marriage before the age of 16 for males and 14 for females.[18]

Mordekhai Aaron Guenzburg (b. 1795) made a very clear claim for the ubiquity of premature marriage among east European Jews in the first half of the nineteenth century. In his autobiography, he described his marriage at the age of 14 and its unfortunate consequences. In his opinion, early marriage distinguished east European Jews both from western Jews and from the general east European society among whom they lived. Guenzburg wrote:

Who, like the wise man, understands and knows the reason for the custom of the house of Israel and that of the nations with regard to this issue? Our Polish brethren have strongly tipped the scales far from the mid point in this matter . . . [while] our German brothers have gone to the other extreme and have followed the path of the nations of the world like a cow in that they do not marry until they are on the threshold of old age.[19]

---

[16]　Maimon, *An Autobiography*, 59–64.

[17]　Dubnow, *Recordbook of the Lithuanian Jewish Council* (Heb.), 266, no. 968.

[18]　Goldberg, 'Jewish Marriages in Old Poland in the Public Opinion of the Enlightenment Period' (Heb.), 31.　　　　　[19]　Guenzburg, *Avi'ezer* (Heb.), 75.

When historians began to deal with Polish Jewish history, they naturally dealt with the phenomenon of early marriage and also concluded that very early marriage had been characteristic of Jews. Emanuel Ringelblum devoted an article to the topic and wrote: 'Jews at that time would marry at a very early age, much younger than the general population.'[20] Yitshak Schipper took it for granted that in traditional Polish Jewish society, most Jews were married by the time they reached the age of 16.[21] According to Israel Hailperin (Halpern), under normal circumstances in Jewish society 'a 13-year-old boy and a 12-year-old girl were considered ripe for marriage. In fact, it was common to marry off 12-year-old boys and 11-year-old girls.'[22] At times there were panics that swept through the Jewish communities when a rumour spread that limitations would be put on marriage among Jews. Many Jews rushed to marry off their children at an age which even contemporaries thought was exceedingly young—at the ages of 7, 6, and even less. Adolf Landau even claimed that popular romantic love songs in Yiddish were a modern innovation because until the mid-eighteenth century, Jews married at a very early age—before there were opportunities for romantic attachments.[23]

*

In reality very early marriage among Jews was limited in scope in the eighteenth and nineteenth centuries. Most Jews did not marry in their early teens and many did so only in their twenties. In determining the facts and the reasons why so many erred in seeing early marriage as typical of Jews, it is necessary to understand the reasons for those early marriages.

Jacob Goldberg made a major contribution to the clarification of Polish Jewish marital patterns in a study published in 1983.[24] This was the first systematic attempt to analyse archival material on marriage from the late eighteenth century. The picture Goldberg portrayed was radically different from that presented by scholars who had dealt previously with marriage. He found that in the population he examined, only about 20 per cent of the males who were under the age of 20 were married and only 40 per cent of the women. Of the several hundred youths in his population who were between the ages of 12 and 15, only five women and one male were married. There

---

[20] Ringelblum, 'Early Weddings amongst Polish Jews' (Yid.), 145.
[21] Schipper, 'Die galizische Judenschaft', 225.
[22] Hailperin, *Jews and Judaism* (Heb.), 291. He brings many sources and has a valuable critique of Schipper's views. Additional relevant material can be found in Freiman, *The Arrangement of Betrothal and Marriage* (Heb.), 238.
[23] See Landau, 'Das jüdisches Volkslied in Russland', 68, cited by Kahan in his article 'How Old are Our Love-Songs?' (Yid.), 73.   [24] Goldberg, 'Die Ehe bei den Juden'.

may be questions about the precision of the data and the size of the sample, but this certainly contradicts the image of general early marriage.

A study of data on some Latvian Jews from the year 1784 apparently corroborates Goldberg's picture. Andrejs Plakans and Joel Halpern,[25] who analysed the data, found that there were a few cases of early marriage, but that not all of the couples they studied had married young. More significant is that they found that half of the women in the 15–19 age group were unmarried. This is similar to Goldberg's findings. However, Plakans and Halpern also stated that almost 85 per cent of the mothers in their population had delivered their first child before the age of 20. The two statements do not seem to fit well together. In theory, one could claim that many children were born out of wedlock to young mothers, but while theoretically possible, pregnancy before marriage was not common in any known east European Jewish society. It could also be claimed that most women who married after the age of 20 were childless. However, this is also not very reasonable and perhaps there is a problem with the data they used. In a personal communication, Plakans suggested that the data on births might have come from only part of the population and perhaps it was not available for the entire population of women.[26] Despite all the questions their study raised, in general their conclusions fit those of Goldberg.

In 1764 a census of Polish–Lithuanian Jewry was carried out. Marital status was often recorded, but not the age at marriage. However, Raphael Mahler, who studied the raw data of the census, found a record of the ages of single males and females in the community of Modliborzyce in the region of Lublin.[27] In this community 350 Jews were enumerated. Among them were four single women aged 16 and nine aged 18. Among the males, there were eight single males aged 18; two aged 19, one aged 20, and one aged 26. It is difficult to reconstruct the total population of young people aged between 18 and 20 on the basis of Mahler's data. However, given that the total population was only 350, it seems unlikely that the unmarried youths enumerated were a minority of the young people and that the majority of their peers were married.[28] Here as well, premature marriage seemed to have been uncommon.

In almost every case of very early marriage the young couple was supported by the parents of the bride. This support was called *kest* in Yiddish. Therefore, data on *kest* can shed light on early marriage. Mahler found that in

---

[25] Plakans and Halpern, 'A Historical Perspective on Eighteenth-Century Jewish Family Households', 26–8.   [26] In a letter from Plakans to the author, 21 Sept. 1984.

[27] Mahler, *Statistics about Jews in Former Poland* (Yid.), 33.

[28] Had this been the case, the cohort of 18–20-year-olds would have consisted of at least 50 individuals (since we know of 24 singles in this cohort), or about 15% of the total Jewish population. This does not appear to be reasonable.

the Lublin region, almost two-thirds of the *kest* givers (men who were supporting sons-in-law) in villages were *arendators*, or tax farmers,[29] and a quarter were innkeepers. However, he also reported that tax farmers made up less than half of the village population, while a third were innkeepers. In other words, the innkeepers were under-represented among the *kest* givers and the *arendators* were over-represented, even though both groups married off their sons and daughters. This was apparently related to the economic conditions of each group. Tax farmers made up three-quarters of the employers of a single servant and they were the only ones to employ more than one servant, whereas among innkeepers, only a quarter of the employers had a servant. Here as well, the patterns of over- and under-representation were maintained. It may be that the working conditions of tax farmers made it necessary for them to have servants, whereas innkeepers could dispense with them. However, it seems logical that innkeepers could also have found servants useful. The simplest explanation for the differences is that tax farmers were financially better off than innkeepers, which is why they had more servants and also why they could support more sons-in-law.[30] The daughters of innkeepers apparently married at a later age and without getting *kest* support from parents because of economic reasons.

In other words, the limited statistical data on Jewish populations suggest that very early marriage was not universal among Jews in the early modern period despite all of the statements to that effect. This is corroborated by an unlikely source—Yiddish folk songs. One can hardly term Yiddish folk songs a quantitative source, but they certainly can inform us about marital patterns. It is not clear when the first were written, but linguistic characteristics and other attributes suggest that they date back to the eighteenth century, if not earlier.[31] Many of these songs deal with the romantic attachments (and woes) of young unmarried men and women. The contexts and the contents do not suggest that the heroes and heroines were 12 or 13 years old and this suggests that early marriage was not the standard in the environment in which these songs were written. After all, it is hardly likely that such songs would be popular in a society where unmarried teenagers were hard to find. This is certainly no proof of the limited scope of early marriage, but it fits well with the other sources cited above.

We have seen that both statistical sources and folklore materials indicate that very early marriage was never universally practised in east European

[29] A tax farmer is a person who rented the right to collect taxes. This was a common practice in pre-bureaucratic regimes.
[30] Mahler, *Statistics about Jews in Former Poland* (Yid.), Tables VII and VIId. Mahler's data indicate that 10% of the Jews were tavern keepers but only 3% of the *kest* givers were tavern keepers. Similarly, only 2% of the employers of servants were tavern keepers. In other words, the correlation holds here as well.   [31] Kahan, 'How Old are Our Love-Songs?' (Yid.).

Jewry. Indeed, it is illogical to assume a reality in which premature marriage was universal. For example, we know that in the past many Jews were employed as servants, and they certainly were not able to marry at the age of puberty. They married after they had saved up enough money to start out in life as an independent economic entity. However, there is no reference in the literature to servants having distinctive marital patterns. This silence suggests that they were not the only ones to wait until their late teens or later to marry.

Perhaps the strongest evidence for the claim that very early marriage was characteristic only of some Jews is the fact, referred to above, that in almost every description of a case of early marriage, the groom is depicted as moving into the house of his young bride's parents. He would live there and the couple would receive financial support from the bride's parents for the number of years stipulated at the time of the marriage. During these years, the young groom would devote most of his time to the study of Talmud—usually in the local study hall (*beit midrash*). In some cases the groom left for study in a yeshiva while his wife remained in her father's house. A young groom of 12 or 13 never set out to earn a living immediately after his wedding. It is obvious that most Jewish fathers of young women were not able to extend support of this scope to all of their sons-in-law, and often not to any of them. The cost of supporting a young scholar who studied all day in the local study hall or yeshiva was not insignificant. If the young bride quickly became a mother, the costs mounted. Supporting a son-in-law and his family was a luxury that only few could afford. Moreover, most young men were not learned enough to study Talmud all day in a *beit midrash*.[32]

At this stage we can conclude that premature marriage was accepted and widespread among east European Jews in the eighteenth and early nineteenth centuries. There is too much evidence to deny this. On the other hand, it was common only in one sector or class of the Jewish community—the upper class—a group that included the wealthy and the learned.[33] This was a distinct class in the Jewish communities and members of the group were termed *di sheyne yidn* (the beautiful Jews). Most of the Jewish community, the *proste yidn*, or the simple masses as they were called, were unable to allow themselves the 'luxury' of early marriage. Their children had to wait and save up until they had sufficient resources to set up a new household and until they were relatively certain that they could support themselves.

To understand the reasons for the popularity of very early marriage among east European Jews in the eighteenth and nineteenth centuries, and for the image of early marriage as characterizing all east European Jews, it is useful to

[32] See Chapter 7 on the *ḥeder*.
[33] On the close links between class and rabbinic scholarship, see Chapter 7.

trace the connections between early marriage and the social needs of the Jewish community.

It would be tempting perhaps, but not correct, to explain very early marriages as motivated mainly by a concern by Jewish parents for the sexual 'purity' of young people. However, although such a concern may appear to be rational, early marriages were often contracted years before the 'evil inclination' could have an influence on the young bride and groom. Indeed, in many cases the young grooms were so young that they were incapable of sexual activity.[34] In this respect, it is important to distinguish between early marriage, shortly after puberty, and premature or very early marriage which was before or concurrent with puberty.[35] It is the latter that needs explanation.

Another possible explanation for very early marriages is that this was a means to achieve maximal utilization of the fertility potential of women. In other words, one could claim that there was a 'biological' benefit to early marriages. However, it is not at all clear that early marriage was desirable from such a point of view. Studies of menarche or age of female sexual maturity in non-Jewish populations in the past have indicated that it was later than it is today.[36] This suggests that early marriage would not make a significant contribution to the birth rate of the Jewish population. Of course, one cannot automatically assume that patterns of menarche among non-Jews applied to Jews as well. Factors such as living patterns, and especially diet, can have a significant effect on menarche and, indeed, in these areas, there were differences between Jews and non-Jews.[37] The only study I know of on menarche among east European Jews was carried out by Samuel Weissenberg in Elizavetgrad in 1909 on a group of 1,273 women.[38] Weissenberg found few differences between Jews and non-Jews. The median age at menarche among Jewish women was 14½, while the average was 14 years and 2 months. In other words, Weissenberg found that Jews and non-Jews were not that different from each other, but that menarche in nineteenth-century Elizavetgrad was about two years later than it is today in western countries.

One cannot simply generalize from Elizavetgrad to the traditional centres of Jewish population in the eighteenth and nineteenth centuries. There were certainly many differences between a southern Russian city in the beginning of the nineteenth century and towns in the Pale of Settlement a century

[34] On this see the interesting material presented by David Biale in *Childhood, Marriage and the Family in the East European Jewish Enlightenment*. His interpretation is very interesting but I do not share all of his views, as will become evident below. [35] See Katz, *Tradition and Crisis*.
[36] See Marcy, 'Factors Affecting the Fecundity and Fertility of Historical Populations', 312.
[37] See Marcy, Sandberg, and Steckel, 'Soldier, Soldier'. This material could profitably be compared with the data of Fishberg, *Materials for the Physical Anthropology of the East European Jews*, 39–49.
[38] Weissenberg, 'Menarche und Menopause bei Jüdinnen und Russinnen in Südrussland'.

before. However, there is no reason to believe that age at menarche was later in 1909 than one hundred years earlier. The reverse was far more likely. In addition, as is well known, there is generally a time gap between menarche and fertility. Thus it seems that early marriages among Jewish women at the beginning of the nineteenth century took place long before the women were able to give birth. In most cases, the onset of fertility among Jewish women at the beginning of the century was probably around the age of 16. Perhaps among the wealthy and better fed it came earlier, but there is no evidence for this.[39] It should also be remembered that pregnancy and delivery were probably more dangerous for a teenage mother than for a more mature woman. Thus, even if young brides were fertile, early pregnancy was not necessarily desirable. Therefore, on the whole, it would seem that early marriage was not beneficial from a biological point of view and contributed little, if anything, to Jewish population growth. Given the fact that early marriage was not desirable from a health perspective, we must look at social factors for an explanation for the popularity of the practice.

One reasonable possibility to consider is that very early marriage among Jews might have been a reflection—or imitation—of marital patterns in the surrounding society. In his classic article on European marital patterns, John Hajnal suggested that one can draw a line from St Petersburg to Trieste that separates populations with a western European marital pattern—delayed age at marriage and high percentages of men and women who never marry—and populations with eastern marital patterns, such as early marriages and low percentages of never married. Early and almost universal marriage was certainly characteristic of east European Jews and non-Jews alike, and one could consider the possibility of influence on Jews of the surrounding society.[40] However, Joan Sklar rightly suggested a refinement of Hajnal's description. In her opinion, the demographic behaviour in Lithuania, Latvia, Estonia, Poland, Bohemia, and Moravia was more similar to the west European model than to the non-European model, and these were the regions where the Jews were concentrated. She found that in 1900, the age at marriage among non-Jews in these countries was between 25 and 30 for males and around 25 for women,[41] and this was significantly higher than among Jews.[42] It is possible

[39] Plakans and Halpern noted in one of their tables that 40% of the Jewish women had given birth by the age of 17. This would suggest a high level of fertility among women aged 16 or less. However, as we saw, there are problems with their data, and in the absence of corroborating evidence it would seem at best to be a statistical fluke, and at worst a problem with the data. See Plakans and Halpern, 'A Historical Perspective on Eighteenth-Century Jewish Family Households', 27, Table 7.   [40] Hajnal, 'European Marriage Patterns'.

[41] Sklar, 'The Role of Marriage Behaviour in the Demographic Transition'.

[42] By the end of the 19th century, Jewish marital behaviour east of Hajnal's line was also distinctive, though in this case Jews married at an older age than their neighbours. Ansley Coale

that in the recent past the marital patterns in these regions had been radically different, but there is no evidence for this. Therefore there is a need to look beyond the influence of neighbouring societies to find reasons for the Jewish pattern of early marriage.

The key to understanding premature marriage among Jews is to pay attention to the behaviour patterns of the young couples. No Jew in the eighteenth century considered that a 14- or 15-year-old male, to say nothing of a younger male, could be the head of an independent household. As mentioned above, it was always the parents of the bride who assumed responsibility for the financial support of the young couple, and the young couple lived in the house of the bride's parents. Residence by the young couple in the house of the bride's parents created temporary multi-generational households. This deviation from the usual pattern of nuclear families (with the addition of a possible live-in servant) was characteristic of the Jews both in medieval Christian Europe and in later years as well. There were, of course, isolated cases of multi-generational families in the modern period, as that of the Yiddish writer Miriam Shomer, but these were exceptional.[43] In almost every description of early marriage, the young couple moved out after the groom was around the age of 20.

The pattern of public study by a son-in-law in a communal study hall seems to have been a crucial factor in the custom of premature marriage. As noted above, almost all young grooms who married near the age of puberty spent the first years following their marriage in the public study of Talmud in *batei midrash* in the cities or towns where their fathers-in-law lived. Relatively few accounts describe young grooms as studying in *batei midrash* in other towns, or as going to yeshivas—though there were cases of this. The young grooms almost never studied at home even though in theory this was often an ideal setting for study. Study in a communal *beit midrash* had one clear benefit—but it was for the father-in-law and not for the young groom.

and co-workers studied these populations. They concentrated on women and came to the conclusion that in Ukraine and Moldavia, where many Jews lived, the average age at marriage for women in 1897 was only slightly above 20, and that the same was true for the interior of Russia, where there were very few Jews. See Coale, Anderson, and Harm, *Human Fertility in Russia*, 136. On changes in age at marriage, see also the collection edited by A. G. Vishnevsky, *Brachnost', rozhdaemost', smertnost' v Rossii i v SSSR*. Significantly lower ages at marriage were recorded in central Russia. Peter Czap found that in two regions in the interior of Russia, the average age at marriage at the beginning of the 18th century was 19 for males and 17 for females. There were some cases of marriage which were close to the minimum age set by the church—15 for males and 13 for women. Czap, 'Marriage and the Peasant Joint Family'. See also Smith, 'Russian Historical Demography'.

[43] On Shomer's household see Shomer-Zunser, *Yesterday*. On *kest* see Gottlober, 'Memoirs and Essays' (Heb.), 507–8.

Study in a *beit midrash* was a public demonstration of the father-in-law's economic stature and also a public demonstration of his commitment to the religious values current in Jewish society. Everyone who entered the study hall and saw the son-in-law sitting and studying knew that the father-in-law was well off and could support a young couple for a long period of time in addition to meeting the needs of his immediate family. The choice of a scholar as a son-in-law and the financial investment in support of Torah study was visible proof of a strong and deep love of Torah. This was in many respects a Jewish version of the conspicuous consumption that was common in other societies in very different ways.[44] It certainly emphasized the membership of the bride's family in the circle of *sheyne yidn* and the differences between them and the *proste* Jews. Lower-class Jews had to delay marriage until the couple was able to support itself.

The parents of the bride and groom who married very young were almost always able to arrange the early marriages without significant interference on the part of the young, dependent, and inexperienced bride and groom. This was an advantage from the affluent parents' point of view, since they were often concerned by the possibility of inappropriate matches. Delaying marriage could only increase the risk of involvement and interference on the part of the bride and groom. Thus early marriage offered greater benefits to the parents than to the young couple.

We can conclude that very early marriages were never common among all the Jews of eastern Europe, but they were widespread within the elite subgroup. In this group early marriage indicated membership in the elite. Therefore, if the subject of a biography was described as having been married around the age of puberty, one can usually assume that his family, and certainly his bride's family, belonged to the elite of the Jewish community. In this respect, early marriage was similar to another indicator of socioeconomic status—the use of a marriage broker (*shadkhan*). According to the enactments of the Jewish Council of the Four Polish Lands, marriage brokers could charge between 0.8 per cent and 2 per cent of the value of the bride's dowry.[45] This, of course, could be quite substantial if the dowry was large. However, such a payment would be close to meaningless in the case of marriages of artisans or poor people. In general, the descriptions of negotiations, contracts, and so on do not fit the lifestyle, as we know it, of the masses. It was in these circles of the poor that there was room for romance and love, and from which came the popular Yiddish folk songs mentioned above.

---

[44] See the classic exposition in Veblen, *The Theory of the Leisure Class*, esp. ch. 14.

[45] Hailperin, *Records of the Jewish Council of the Four Polish Lands* (Heb.), no. 183, p. 68 and no. 888, p. 467; see also Dubnow, *Recordbook of the Lithuanian Jewish Council* (Heb.), nos 34, 36.

If this is the case, how can we explain the development of a widely accepted view according to which premature marriage characterized the entire Jewish community? The reason is related to the nature of the sources commonly employed by scholars. The richest sources of information on Jewish life in eastern Europe are descriptions of individuals' lives—both autobiographies and biographies. Indeed, most biographies of individuals who came to maturity before the middle of the nineteenth century describe early marriage first-hand. However, it should not be forgotten that the individuals who were literate enough to write autobiographies or to merit a biography were usually famous leaders and rabbis from the circles of the *sheyne yidn*. Most Jews could hardly write—as is easily seen from the popularity of letter-writing manuals in the nineteenth century. In other words, it was precisely those who came from the higher circles of Jewish society who were ultimately most likely to leave written records of their lives.

This does not explain why non-Jews found early marriage so typical of Jewish life. With regard to their statements it must be remembered that non-Jews were quite understandably fascinated by what looked odd and exotic—and in need of change. Moreover, in many cases the closest contacts of these observers were with Jewish leaders among whose circles early marriage was indeed common. It was not a big step to generalize from these leaders to the entire Jewish community. This would certainly not be the only case in which behaviour of a subgroup has been ascribed to the group as a whole.

The memoirs of Avraham Ber Gottlober, cited above, are a good example of generalization to the entire Jewish community from patterns of the elite. Gottlober devoted an entire chapter to matchmaking and engagement, and another to marriage. He wrote: 'When a youth of 12 was not yet a groom he was embarrassed in the presence of boys his age who were already grooms and wore *yarmulkes* [skull caps] covered with gold', and he added:

This is what the father of the bride used to give to the groom either directly or via a messenger to his place of residence: a watch of silver or gold, a silver tobacco box, a gold-covered skullcap, and a small Pentateuch bound in silver. These were called 'little gifts'. The big gifts, which were sent as the wedding approached, were a *talit* and a fur hat (*shtreymel*) . . . to the groom and pearls and a *shterntikhl* [bejewelled headdress worn by married women] . . . to the bride.[46]

Of course, not every father who married off a son or a daughter could afford to give such expensive gifts. What tailor, shoemaker, or water carrier could dream of such presents? Why then did Gottlober write 'this is what the father of the bride used to give'? I believe Gottlober simply got swept away in his description. Elsewhere in his memoirs he wrote that he was describing the

[46] See Gottlober, 'Memoirs and Essays' (Heb.), 86–9.

conditions of young Torah students who were regarded as superior students. However, in describing the wedding arrangements themselves, he 'forgot' that they were typical only of a subgroup, and wrote about them as if what he depicted was characteristic of all Jews.[47] Since he himself was from the elite, this was quite natural.

Premature marriage, which had been so common among the Jewish elite early in the nineteenth century, disappeared from the Jewish community in the course of the century. By the end of the nineteenth century, Rabbi Yehi'el Mikhal Epstein (1829–1908) could summarize a discussion on the topic with these words: 'and there is no need to dwell at length on the topic because is it almost unknown (lit. impossible)'.[48]

How quickly was the practice of premature marriage abandoned? It is important to remember that some demographic patterns change very slowly over the course of time while others are transformed very quickly. One can assume the obvious: that the slow changes are the product of factors that are changing slowly themselves. Thus slow shifts in economic patterns could reasonably be expected to slowly influence certain demographic phenomena. Quick changes in living conditions can reasonably be expected to lead to equally quick changes in demographic patterns. This is often the case with disasters, wars, or new laws. This certainly was the case with the 'panic' marriages, which were a direct response to rumours of a change in the law. In our case, the decline of the very early marriage had the characteristics of a rapid development—common in mid century but forgotten by the end of the century, but without a clear and evident cause.

The claim that 'conspicuous consumption' lay behind the pattern of premature marriage makes it possible to explain the timing of the decline of very early marriage. According to this explanation, premature marriage never met real needs but rather was done to win honour and prestige within the Jewish community. The father and mother of the bride were willing to invest substantially in the young couple in return for gaining status in the eyes of people they respected. It was precisely the cost and hardship that such support would involve for most people that made this step attractive.[49] However, without the element of prestige, there were no good reasons for such matches.[50] In other words, it was stylish to marry early, but not necessary.

---

[47] Ibid. 86.   [48] Epstein, *Arukh hashulḥan*, 'Even ha'ezer', 1: 11.

[49] A similar and curious case of maintaining status symbols in the Jewish community was that of the prohibition, enacted in the Lithuanian town of Keidany in the beginning of the 19th century, on the wearing of *shtreimels* (fur hats) or silk *yarmulkes* by tailors. When tailors, who as artisans were considered to be low-class, tried to enter the community synagogue wearing this headgear, there was a major uproar. See Levitats, *The Jewish Community in Russia*, 239.

[50] This is probably why, despite the revival of various customs among the self-consciously traditionalist elements in Jewish society today, this practice has not been revived.

However, style can be fickle and it seems to have been so in this case. The search for prestige rests on an implied hierarchy whose approval is sought. In Jewish society, the rich and the learned occupied the top of society—and of the two, the rich probably set the style. But in the 1840s a new economic elite began to make its mark on Jewish society in eastern Europe. This new elite adopted a 'western' model of behaviour. Members of this elite had new and different ways to demonstrate their status besides having a son-in-law who was a promising talmudist in the communal *beit midrash*. They were interested in young men who had new symbols of achievement, such as university education, or at least a smattering of the manners of European society.[51]

It is difficult to isolate changes in marital patterns among the elite alone. One promising approach would be a group biography (prosopography) of the members of the rabbinic or commercial elites in the first half of the century. However, no such study has been carried out. In the course of a study I made of the Volozhin yeshiva, I tried to collect data on ages at marriage of students of that yeshiva.[52] These data are not a representative sample of the elite since I was able to collect relatively few biographies of yeshiva students in the first half of the century. However, perhaps the data can be seen as an indication or as partial evidence. I was able to find data on thirteen yeshiva students who were born between 1794 and 1825. Of them, ten married before the age of 14, their marriages taking place before the 1840s. In other words, these cases fit the pattern of early marriage. However, I did not find any cases of early marriages taking place after 1840. On the contrary, the median age at marriage was constantly on the rise. This does not prove that there were no cases of early marriage among Jews in Lithuania after 1840, but it suggests that they were no longer the standard in the Jewish elite.

The drop in the 'market value' of yeshiva students led to a sharp rise in their age at marriage. By the end of the century there were 30-year-old Talmud students who had never married—something that would have been unheard of a century before. They simply had no economic base for marriage. Rabbi Yisra'el Meir Kagan (Hakohen) (the Hafets Hayim, 1838–1933) wrote about rich householders in 1881:

Once respectful and merciful to the rabbis . . . had desired with all of their hearts to attach themselves to scholars [e.g. bring them into their families via marriage], to support them for a number of years at their table and to cover all of their expenses

[51] See Golomb, *The Laws of Women* (Yid.), for current 'market values' of grooms. According to Golomb, an optician went for 10,000 rubles, whereas a medical doctor cost three times as much. He does not record values for rabbinic scholars or historians.

[52] The data are presented in detail in a supplement to my doctoral thesis 'Three Lithuanian Yeshivas in the Nineteenth Century' (Heb.).

until they had completed their studies in Talmud and the legal codes. Thus they could become rabbis and great ones in Israel. However, for our sins, they have ceased to do so.[53]

This is what led young talmudists to postpone their marriage—and inspired the Hafets Hayim and others to invent the *kolel* system for the financial support of young scholars as a substitute for rich fathers-in-law. Thus, while we do not have explicit evidence for the rise of early marriage, we do have a plausible explanation for its appearance and for the circumstances of its disappearance.

In the second part of the nineteenth century there was a general rise in the age of marriage among Jews. It is easier to document this rise in the total Jewish population than to document the decline of early marriage in the small subgroup of the elite. Sara Rabinowitsch-Margolin made a thorough study of marriage among Jews in the tsarist empire and some of her data are presented in the accompanying table (Table 1.1), which shows that in the second half of the nineteenth century there was a growing trend among Jews to delay marriage. This rise in the age of marriage until well after the age of 20 undoubtedly led to a decline in the birth rate of Jews in the tsarist empire. It may be that this decline was due to pauperization of the Jewish community, but changes in values may also have been at work.[54] Rabinowitsch-Margolin's data did not enable her to distinguish between very early marriages and all marriages below the age of 20. However, it is clear from her data that early marriage would have been far more an anomaly at the end of the century than in the middle.

Table 1.1 Age distribution of Jews at marriage in the tsarist empire, 1867–1902 (%)

Year	Aged 20 or less		Aged 21–25		Aged 26–30	
	Male	Female	Male	Female	Male	Female
1867	43	61	26	21	11	8
1875	27	55	36	27	16	8
1885	15	47	50	37	18	8
1895	6	29	46	50	30	13
1902	5	24	41	53	36	15

Source: Rabinowitsch-Margolin, 'Die Heiraten der Juden', 180.

There was only one community of east European Jews among whom very early marriage was the standard and not the pattern of a subgroup alone. This

[53] Kagan, introduction to *Ets peri*, 10.
[54] See Weissenberg, 'Der Rückgang der Geburtsziffer'; Binshtok and Novoselsky, *Materialy*, p. xxvii.

was the community of immigrants to Erets Yisra'el from eastern Europe. Early marriages were common among the Ashkenazim of Jerusalem in the nineteenth century. Even up to the end of the nineteenth century it was rare to find a couple who married after the age of 20, and many married around the age of 14.[55]

The exceptional marital behaviour of the Ashkenazi Jews in Erets Yisra'el was tied to the unique characteristics of this community. They saw themselves as obligated and selected to live an ideal life devoted to study of the holy texts and to the fulfilment of divine commandments in the Holy Land. Very early marriage, which they thought or hoped would guarantee sexual purity, was a step in this direction. Parents in Erets Yisra'el in the late nineteenth century did not model themselves on the changing economic elite in eastern Europe or in the West, but rather on what they imagined to have been the ideal past. In their memory, premature marriage had been a badge of success. However —and this is the key—the economic structure of this community also fostered very early marriage. The Ashkenazi Jews of pre-First World War Jerusalem did not generally support themselves by economic activity, but rather they lived off charitable donations sent to them by pious Jews in the diaspora. As recipients of support, there was no need to delay marriage until a young man and woman could earn a living. As a matter of fact, as soon as young people married they became eligible for direct support from the charity funds. Thus it was to the advantage of parents to have children marry as early as possible. Economics and traditions went hand in hand. However, even in Jerusalem, this pattern ultimately changed. It would appear that the abandonment of early marriage was not so much a matter of economic pressure as in eastern Europe, but rather the result of the unconscious adoption of new, and in this case Western, values.

The marital patterns of east European Jewry reflected both the values and the social structure of this community. The pattern of premature marriage influenced not only those who married in this manner, but also the masses who could not afford to—but who could aspire to the behaviour of the elite. It may well have been the case that the model of premature marriage was a stimulus to the general pattern of early marriage that indeed was typical of traditional east European Jewish society. In this way it may have had an indirect but significant role in the high rate of population growth that characterized east European Jewry in the modern period. The adoption of patterns of delayed marriage in the course of the nineteenth century may, in turn, have contributed to a broader decline in the rate of population growth. In any case, it should not be forgotten that the changing behaviour patterns of the elite could have implications far beyond their limited circles. In the case of

[55] Schmelz, 'Some Demographic Peculiarities', esp. pp. 126–33.

early marriage, an analysis of its dynamic provides insights into the links between values and behaviour and Jewish society, its social structure and economic realities. What appeared odd to many had its own logic—but it has to be considered on its own terms.

TWO

Love and Family

IN THE NINETEENTH CENTURY, almost every aspect of Jewish life was transformed in one way or another. The structures of Jewish family life in eastern Europe and the place of love and affection in these frameworks were no exceptions. This is true both for patterns of behaviour and for values. However, to a greater degree than many today realize there was also a great deal of continuity between what was accepted in traditional Ashkenazi Jewish family life and in the lives of their descendants. In some cases the attention given to atypical lives of famous and exceptional individuals has led to a skewed picture of the past. Similarly, superficial views of traditional family dynamics have created a distorted picture of what life was like in traditional east European Jewish society. Looking at love and family life in their fullness and as part of the general social environment is one of the best ways to correct these errors and to arrive at a balanced view of realities and developments.

Love and the family must be considered in a broad context. That is to say, not only love in the context of courtship or the choice of a partner, but also love as a factor in married life as well as love relationships between parents and children. This can be done only by looking at behaviour and not just at images or literary conceptions. The works of contemporary writers are full of descriptions of love and family life, but although they may tell us a great deal about what the authors felt and thought, they do not necessarily tell us about what they themselves did, and certainly not what others did. Even autobiographies are problematic because the authors usually stem from a narrow socio-economic background. The shoemakers and the water carriers were not writers of autobiographies. It was the members of the small intellectual elite who wrote these accounts—and their stories are the stories of the elite and not of the broader elements of the Jewish population.

Little attention has so far been given to many aspects of east European Jewish family life and many topics have not been satisfactorily explored. One very undesirable consequence of this neglect is that it is almost impossible at this stage to point out regional variations in family behaviour—even though it stands to reason that there were significant differences in behaviour between distinct regions such as Lithuania and Galicia. Nonetheless, the information that is currently available makes it possible to reach some broad conclusions with a fair degree of certainty.

Jacob Katz laid out the basic outlines of family life in pre-modern Ashkenazi Jewry in his classic studies on Jewish society.[1] He pointed out that the fundamental structure of the Ashkenazi Jewish family was that of a monogamous nuclear family. At the same time the family unit assumed responsibilities for support of other relatives when circumstances made it necessary. Marriages, or to be precise, first marriages, were usually contracted by parents, and their considerations in making a match were practical and largely economic. Early marriage (well before the age of 20) was the ideal both for males and females, and this occurred largely from a concern for sexual purity. Indeed, Jews tended to marry earlier than their non-Jewish neighbours. A positive byproduct, from the point of view of some parents, was that early marriage helped maintain class differences over the generations. Although sexual activity was seen as a natural and desirable human characteristic, its expression was limited to the marital framework and Katz emphasized that in all circles sexual attraction probably never 'served as a test of compatibility'.[2] Much of his description applies to Ashkenazi Jews in the German-speaking lands as well as those in eastern Europe.

Although the starting point for east European Jewry and that of central Europe may have been the same, by the nineteenth century the characteristics of family patterns among German Jewry were no longer the same as those of east European Jews. This was due in part to differences in the religious, political, economic, and legal environments in the two regions. Family patterns of Jews in the German-speaking lands had altered in many ways. The average age at marriage had risen and the choice of a partner was no longer in the hands of parents.[3] Moreover, 'the erotic experience [was made] the foundation upon which the family was built',[4] or at least that is what people told themselves. In the early nineteenth century many bourgeois German Jews adopted a new model of marriage. It was marked by subservience of the wife to the husband, a sharp decline in the economic role and activity of women, and a repression of acknowledgement of the role of sexual activity in marital life.[5] In many German Jewish families there were attempts to make economic activity the sole responsibility of men and to invest both time and

[1] See Katz, 'Family, Kinship and Marriage', and *Tradition and Crisis*, chs 14 and 15.
[2] Katz, 'Family, Kinship and Marriage', 11.
[3] For a fascinating study of the later stages of these developments in Germany, see Marion Kaplan, *The Making of the Jewish Middle Class*, especially the introduction.
[4] Katz, *Tradition and Crisis*, 231.
[5] See Carlebach, 'Family Structure and the Position of Jewish Women', 170. This paper has an extensive discussion of the development of family patterns among German Jewry. See also his description of attitudes to sexuality on pp. 173–7.

money in the attempt to rise in social status. This took place in the context of the growing integration of German Jewry into the surrounding society and an acceptance by Jews of marital patterns that were standard in the society of bourgeois non-Jews. Upper- and middle-class German Jewish parents continued to influence the choice of a marital partner for their children, and the role of affection in making this decision was limited.[6] Well into the twentieth century pragmatic factors, usually linked to the size of the dowry, played a major role. Lip service was paid to romance, but the reality was quite different. It has been noted that while arranged marriages of this type distinguished rural Jews from their peasant neighbours, they were common among urban non-Jews—despite the widespread perception that Jews were more oriented to financial arrangements than non-Jews.[7] Only after the First World War did arranged marriages stop being the norm.

In eastern Europe non-Jewish populations did not have a strong influence on Jewish patterns of family life. In early modern Poland peasants often postponed marriage until land became available—and for many individuals the postponement was eternal.[8] Some Polish writers from noble and intellectual backgrounds regarded Jewish behaviour as a positive model. They criticized contemporary marital morality in their circles, along with drunkenness and other faults, and held up the Jews as exemplary. In their opinion adultery was less common among Jews than among non-Jews, and Jews were regarded as models of fertility. In addition, Jews were portrayed as modest in their lifestyles with strong bonds of affection between Jewish parents and children.[9] Quantitative data for the nineteenth century also show distinctive patterns for premature marriage among elite Jews.[10] From the qualitative sources it is, of course, difficult to come to any reliable conclusions about the degree of similarity or difference between urban or upper-class non-Jews and Jews. However, the opinions of contemporary observers and the unique characteristics of Jews justify a separate analysis of Jewish family life in eastern Europe.[11]

Marriage and love within the context of family life is, of course, a very broad topic. The varying forms of love and emotional attraction occupied

[6] This discussion on marital strategies is based on the fine study by Marion Kaplan, 'For Love or Money'.   [7] Ibid. 289.

[8] On patterns of peasant marriage, though in a later period, see Sklar, 'The Role of Marriage Behaviour in the Demographic Transition'.

[9] See Goldberg, 'Jewish Marriages in Old Poland in the Public Opinion of the Enlightenment Period' (Heb.).   [10] See e.g. Chapter 1.

[11] Many characteristics of Jewish marital behaviour in eastern Europe in the early modern period were, of course, not uniquely Jewish, nor were they characteristic only of that period. The question of whether specific characteristics were present only among Jews—and even the question of the source of these characteristics—is not crucial for understanding how the marital system operated, or its impact.

important roles in various aspects of marriage and family life. Therefore, the following discussion of love and family life will deal with four major topics: courtship and creating the marriage, marital roles and expectations, parenthood, and remarriage.

∗

Patterns of marriage formation in nineteenth-century east European Jewry were distinctive because in addition to religious differences, the socio-economic characteristics of Jews were not the same as those of their neigh-bours. Most non-Jews were, of course, peasants and not nobles. Among peasants possession of land is necessary for marriage and for bringing up a family. Hence peasants, in many societies, tend to delay marriage until land is available or appears that it will be soon. While waiting, many children continue to live under the parental roof. An old farmer, who has lived off the land all his life and knows no other means of earning a living, will not retire to the city in his old age after he has handed his land over to his child or children. The most natural thing for him to do is to live with his son in a multi-generational household. Therefore, peasant households often remain multi-generational for an extended period.

In eastern Europe, most Jews were either merchants or craftsmen. Most of the merchants were small-scale traders. The craftsmen were usually artisans who worked in small workshops or modest enterprises and only infrequently worked in large factories. Given the limited scope of commerce and the non-industrial nature of the crafts, the incentive for sons to become partners with their father or to take over his business was limited. If a son went into his father's craft there could even be strong grounds for him to move elsewhere so that he would not compete with his father. The Jews were certainly not tied to the land in the way a peasant was attached to a familial plot. It was also far easier for young Jews to start off independently at a young age. These condi-tions meant that, for Jews, there was no reason to defer marriage until a parent aged or until land was acquired. Given the limited physical demands of the typically Jewish occupations, there was little need for an ageing father or mother to rush into retirement and to become dependent on a son or heir. For Jews there was also little advantage to be had from complex and extended family structures that involved a number of married families living under one roof.

Among Jews, the future success of children was as much the result of the training parents gave as it was the product of the capital they could provide. In the Jewish professions family ties were not crucial to the economic activity of individuals, though they could be useful for commercial ties or to serve as a source of referrals for craftsmen. Moreover, in contrast to the situation among farmers, Jewish siblings did not usually compete with each other for limited resources (such as land) which would be crucial for their future success. Upwards (and downwards) mobility among Jews was seen as the result of individual merit and effort. Jews felt responsible in theory for the well-being of parents and siblings, but there were generally limited practical consequences. It was in the interests of Jewish parents for their children to become independent, and in the interests of the children that parents remain independent. In the absence of economic motivations for preserving family ties, and given the ease with which family ties could be weakened by migration, the only way to preserve the ties among Jews was by encouraging love, affection, and a sense of responsibility.

It is important to remember that the Jewish community was made up of different classes. In traditional east European Jewish society, the ideal Jewish man was wealthy, a Torah scholar, and had honoured ancestors.[12] As a result the Jewish elite was largely made up of scholars and wealthy merchants. This group was distinguished from the masses of Jews, who were much poorer and less educated, and who earned a livelihood in small-scale trade and crafts, and from unskilled labour.[13] On the whole, craftsmen had low status, and in many Jewish circles a craftsman in the family stained its honour.[14] In the second half of the nineteenth century a new elite of industrialists, professionals, and government suppliers arose, which was richer than the past elite, more isolated geographically from the Jewish masses since many lived outside the Pale of Settlement, and more integrated in non-Jewish society than east European Jewish elites of the past. Not surprisingly, this elite, as we shall see, tended to adopt behavioural patterns current in non-Jewish elites, which in turn had a significant impact on the behaviour of the Jewish community at large.[15]

During the nineteenth century the Jewish population of eastern Europe grew rapidly—apparently at a higher rate than in the past.[16] Moreover, while all population groups in eastern Europe were growing in size at this time, the Jewish population was growing at a faster rate than that of the non-Jewish population for most of the century. The reasons for this growth—a common phenomenon in many national and ethnic groups in the modern period—are not clear. It seems that the most significant factors were a decline in mortality, especially of children, and the absence of large-scale disorders such as war or

---

[12] Zborowski and Herzog, *Life Is with People*, pt. 4: 'Into Marriage'.   [13] See Chapter 7.

[14] Greenbaum, 'Contempt for Craftsmen' (Heb.), 49–53.

[15] On the development of the Jewish community of St Petersburg see Nathans, *Beyond the Pale*.

[16] The issue of population growth rates has not been carefully studied. I hope to return to this topic in a future study. The issue of the decline in mortality and population growth is dealt with in almost every textbook of demography.

plague, which directly and indirectly contribute to population loss. Whatever the reasons, the consequences were clear. A drop in infant mortality meant that more children survived infancy and, as a result, families grew bigger and the proportion of young people within the total population increased. This development had many consequences. One is that growing numbers of children may have created difficulties in social supervision.[17] The economic consequences were more serious. Jews were traders and craftsmen and depended on non-Jewish clients. Since the Jewish population growth was outstripping that of non-Jews, this meant that earning a livelihood became progressively more difficult for Jews because there was increased competition for clients. This in turn led to growing impoverishment of the Jewish community. All of this had, as we shall see, an impact on how and when individuals marry.

*

Within traditional east European Jewish society there were generally limitations on social contact between males and females, as well as clear gender distinctions with regard to many aspects of life, such as education, religious activity, and social frameworks. However, in some aspects of life, such as economic activities, women often were active in the same areas as men. In this society there was no ideal (as there was in the twentieth century) of the Jewish woman who stays in the home and is supported by the husband. What is not clear is the degree to which there were opportunities for young males and females to meet and to develop a friendship and attraction. In theory such contacts were proscribed, but the reality seems to have been more complex. As we shall see, it seems that the lines were drawn more clearly and enforced more strictly in the Jewish elite than in the lower classes.

The division between the sexes must have had an influence on their attitudes to the other sex, but these are difficult to measure in retrospect. A recent study of strictly Orthodox Jewish communities today pointed out that in marriages following strict sexual separation 'there is poor sex adaptation and little communication between the spouses [and] children embody the real meaning of the marriage', and that such a system creates a potential for tension and obsessive behaviour.[18] However, the author also added that most members of such societies deal successfully with these pressures and function well within these frameworks. It is important to bear in mind that divisions between boys and girls among strictly Orthodox Jews are enforced more

[17] See the thought-provoking article by Hundert, 'The Decline of Deference' (Heb.).
[18] See the important and very level-headed studies of Goshen-Gottstein, 'Courtship, Marriage and Pregnancy in "Geula"' (Heb.), and 'Mental Health Implications of Living in a Strictly Orthodox Jewish Subculture' (Heb.). The quotation is from the English abstract (on p. 1) of the first article.

strictly today than they were in the past. Patterns of elementary education illustrate this. Today it would be unthinkable for boys and girls to study together in ultra-Orthodox societies. However, in the early nineteenth century and even later it was quite common, though certainly not the standard, for little girls to go to *ḥeder* with little boys, and the mixing of the sexes apparently was not regarded as worthy of note or reaction. A century ago, sending a girl to a boys' *ḥeder* was not an ideological statement. There were no co-educational schools among Jews in traditional east European Jewish society, and the decision to send a girl to a *ḥeder* was usually based on convenience and on the fact that *ḥeder* study was less expensive than employing a tutor.[19]

Despite the restrictions on social contacts and on romance, attention was given in Jewish society to physical attractiveness, though the characteristics that defined attractiveness in that society were not the same as those common today. Physical strength and power were not seen as the determinants of a handsome man. Since commitment and scholarliness were valued, slim fingers and slight figure—which suggested an ascetic lifestyle and studiousness—were considered attractive among men. Among women the ideal was different. A full (and not overly slim) body was considered attractive and physical strength was also valued. A full body hinted that a woman had enough to eat and came from a family of some means. Physical strength suggested that a woman would be a child bearer and also able to earn a living. Paleness was valued for both men and women because it suggested that they did not have to work outdoors.[20]

In the early modern period, the road to marriage among affluent Ashkenazi Jews often began with a matchmaker. Parents saw marriage as far too significant a step to be entrusted to children or young adults. Katz writes in his article on the sixteenth to eighteenth centuries that 'The great majority of matches were arranged through the agency of others and every eligible person was open to marriage proposals, particularly from professional matchmakers.'[21] The figure of the matchmaker, or the *shadkhan*, was one of the stock figures of east European Jewish literature.[22] Professional matchmakers, who were usually males, did not have an easy task. They had to

[19] As Weizmann-Lichtenstein wrote in *In the Shadow of our Roof* (Heb.): 'In the town it wasn't customary to send girls to *ḥeder*, rather a rebbe would come to the house for an hour and teach the girls. In this manner they would manage to acquire very little knowledge of the Torah and few of them knew Hebrew. For my older sister Miriam my parents hired a private tutor and he taught her all of the curriculum. However, this was impossible to do for the rest of the daughters because the family was too large. Therefore I was sent to [a boys'] *ḥeder*' (p. 19).

[20] See Zborowski and Herzog, *Life Is with People*, 138, and the interesting materials collected in Somogyi, *Die Schejnen und die Prosten*. On concepts of maleness, see also Boyarin, *Unheroic Conduct*.   [21] Katz, 'Family, Kinship and Marriage', 7.

[22] See Kena'ani, *The Houses that No Longer Exist* (Heb.), 29–44, esp. 29–33.

consider factors such as physical attractiveness, learnedness, wealth, and family background. The effort invested in making a match could be quite remunerative and a successful match yielded a percentage of the marriage gifts to the successful matchmaker.[23] Parents usually had a rather optimistic self-picture of the 'market value' of their child, and a rather jaundiced view of the value of others. In such matches the parents took into consideration objective criteria, often financial, and the personal preferences of the young man and woman were not usually a factor. Arranged marriages of this type were possible only when the couple accepted the authority of their parents. The younger the bride and groom, the more likely they are to be dependent on their parents and accept their authority. Therefore matchmaking fitted very well with the practice of very early marriage and dependence on financial support from parents in the form of a dowry or the like.[24] However, age was not the sole determinant for parents to employ a matchmaker. In cases of remarriage, the match was made with the direct involvement of the bride and groom even if they were quite young. This indicates that once married and out of parental control, an individual did not revert to dependence even if the marriage was not long lived.

Among the less affluent Jews, who were the majority, matchmaking played a more limited role, as we saw in the previous chapter, and the wishes of young men and women had to be taken into consideration. If one of the goals of matchmaking was to prevent mismatches, for the poor this was not a problem. Moreover, children of poor parents were less dependent on their parents as they approached a marriageable age. Of necessity, boys stopped their studies relatively early and had to support themselves at a younger age than the sons of the more affluent. Girls from poor families often worked to save money for a trousseau. Since potential brides and grooms were more independent, they were less likely to be passive participants in the search for a marital partner.

The many love songs in Yiddish folk music are clear evidence for the importance of love and mutual attraction in couple formation among large parts of the Jewish population. These songs describe the yearnings of lovers for each other. These lovers are clearly not married; nor do they sound like 12-year-olds. The songs reflect a society that offered opportunities for young people to meet and to choose partners on the basis of affection. Love was presented as desirable and as a reasonable ground for marriage. To be sure, these songs are similar in character to love songs from other cultures, and in some cases they were apparently borrowed or adapted.[25] This does not detract from their utility as evidence for a social reality because a song can be

---

[23] See Rivkind, *Jewish Money in Folkways* (Yid.), s.v. 'Shadkhanus gelt', 258–62.

[24] Katz, 'Family, Kinship and Marriage', 6.

[25] For a convenient English-language source, see Rubin, *Voices of a People*, ch. 3: 'Love and Courtship', and especially her sources.

borrowed or adapted only if it is meaningful and understandable in its new context. At the same time the existence of love songs does not indicate the extent to which mutual attraction was a factor in marriage.

The evidence of Yiddish love songs seems to contradict the image of arranged marriages familiar from the memoir literature. However, this is only at first glance. Matchmaking was apparently most common among the upper levels of Jewish society rather than the lower. Since matchmakers profited from a share of the wedding gifts, or occasionally of the dowry, making matches for the poor was not very remunerative—though this did not of course deter amateur matchmakers. As noted above, most of the authors of memoirs belonged to the affluent and elite circles of Jews though they were a minority. The popular Yiddish songs seem to have been sung largely by the poorer strata of society. Thus they serve as evidence for the behaviour and values of those members of society who never wrote autobiographies or left other written records of their lives. These songs do not necessarily reflect the patterns of the elite or the values of all the poor, but they do indicate that there were circles that tolerated romance. We can conclude that the different representations of the steps leading towards marriage reflect the socio-economic differences in Jewish society in eastern Europe.

However, it is important to remember that social differences were not sharp or absolute. Many immigrants to America, even those that came from the lowest elements of east European Jewry, could regard matchmaking as a norm to be aspired to even though they had little cash to pay for it.[26] In this highly status-conscious Jewish society, families would not have been eager to openly demonstrate that they were lower-class. However, it does not necessarily contradict the evidence of popular culture for self-selection of partners. Matchmakers operated in a reality in which many individuals chose their partners.

Courtship patterns came under increasing discussion and criticism within the Jewish community in the course of the nineteenth century, though when considering the written sources it is necessary to distinguish between rhetoric and reality. Early marriage planned by parents was presented as one of the most visible shortcomings of Jewish society in eastern Europe.[27] The modernizing Jews claimed that marriage should be postponed until the groom had an occupation, that romantic love should be tolerated to some

---

[26] See Zborowski and Herzog, *Life Is with People*, pt. 4: 'Into Marriage'.

[27] In this study I have tried to concentrate on the realities and developments rather than on images and theoretical discussions. For a discussion of the question of love in the ideology of the Jewish Enlightenment movement in eastern Europe, see Biale, 'Eros and Enlightenment', especially his sources and chapter 2. A more recent and very perceptive study that deals with attitudes to women in the Enlightenment movement is Feiner's 'The Modern Jewish Woman' (Heb.).

degree, and that the wishes of the bride and groom should be considered.[28] Oddly, early marriage was no longer widely practised when many of these attacks on early marriage were penned, and possibly their authors were responding to their own childhood experiences.[29] The critics used attacks on early marriage as a tactic to arouse support among their readers. In other words, 'beating a dead dog' may have been seen as a useful tool in the general critique of traditional society. Some of the critics regarded affection and romance positively, but they did not make a general demand for a radical change in relations between young men and women, and they did not feel that romantic love should be an absolute goal or a precondition for marriage. Such a demand would not have been in keeping with their general concern for rationality and order in all aspects of life, as opposed to the irrational and the unplanned. No systematic study exists of the family behaviour of modernizers or of their personal lives. However, there are a number of recorded cases of modernizers who chose partners for their children, with or without the use of matchmakers.[30] Many of the personal lives of modernizers were marked by marital unhappiness, which they, of course, attributed to the ills of the society in which they lived. Some writers were divorced, and although others may have had satisfactory marital relations, none seems to have had anything like an ideal relationship between two loving equals. In their writing, love and affection between enlightened lovers or between husband and wife were more of a literary convention than a description of a reality with which they were familiar.[31]

Cases of arranged pre-teen marriages in most east European Jewish communities became rare even before the mid-nineteenth century.[32] It does not appear, however, that the propaganda of the modernizers is what led to this change—after all, much of the criticism was publicized after marital patterns had already changed. In general one must be cautious in assessing the influence of the ideology on Jewish society. Since many modernizers wrote in Hebrew, they restricted themselves to a limited audience—members of the intellectual elite. The readership of these modern Hebrew works included both young Talmud students and broadminded parents, but most Jews found it difficult to read unfamiliar material in Hebrew. The Hebrew writers and poets never had real political power and they also had few students. For

[28] See Biale, 'Eros and Enlightenment'.

[29] The problem of an imagined past as opposed to the reality is common in east European Jewish history. The imagined *shtetl* is a typical case. However, this issue will have to be dealt with in a different context.

[30] Biale, 'Eros and Enlightenment', 59.   [31] Zalkin, *A New Dawn* (Heb.), ch. 8.

[32] Some data on age at marriage of yeshiva students can be found in my doctoral thesis 'Three Lithuanian Yeshivas' (Heb.), 220–30. However, the reader should be warned that the sample is small and probably not statistically significant.

example, even though they called on Jews to choose 'productive' professions (such as farming and crafts), there were few attempts to realize the theory. Books can, of course, change the minds and ideals of people, and the younger the reader and the less committed he is to the system, the more they are likely to do so. However, marriage is such a social event that it is highly unlikely that significant numbers of parents would determine their children's lives on the grounds of what they read in a book and not by what they saw about them.

The practice of early marriage was apparently abandoned for a number of factors. The new Jewish economic elite that arose in eastern Europe in the mid-nineteenth century was strongly influenced by surrounding non-Jewish society and took as a model in many respects the behaviour of contemporary German Jews. Members of the new elite began to stop speaking Yiddish and adopted German dress. It was quite reasonable for them to marry off their children at an age that was common in the West.[33] In issues of status and style, when a few wealthy and prominent individuals adopt novel patterns, members of the secondary elite follow. In any case, whether for these reasons or others, a change in age at marriage took place, and by the mid-nineteenth century both sons and daughters of the Jewish elite were marrying near the age of 20.[34] Early marriage as described in the previous chapter was no longer a sign of wealth or social standing, and one of the byproducts of this shift was that arranging marriages became more difficult.

The popular Yiddish press and literature was no doubt one of the main influences on mass behaviour, including marriage formation, in the second half of the nineteenth century, and it probably had a much greater impact on family life than the Haskalah (Jewish Enlightenment) literature. There was a rapid expansion in the number of books published in Yiddish and the number of authors writing in Yiddish, but most readers were not perusing the works of Mendele Moykher Sefarim (Shalom Jacob Abramowitz, 1835?–1917) or Shalom Aleikhem (Shalom Rabinovitz, 1859–1916). They were reading something else.

An entire genre of popular and often trashy Yiddish literature (*shund*) developed and these became best-sellers. Some of these works were original, though even more were translated and adapted. The origins were irrelevant to the readers who bought them in huge quantities.[35] Although many of these stories were set in exotic settings, the message of many stories was clear: love is the goal and the measure of happiness. The popular writer who has been

---

[33] I know of no demographic or prosopographic study of the elite, and the topic of a rise in the age at marriage among the elite was not explicitly discussed in contemporary literature. However, I do not know of any cases of early marriage among the modernizing elite after 1850, and I certainly have found no traces of a general pattern of such marriages in that elite.

[34] For statistical data, see Binshtok and Novoselsky, *Materialy*, esp. pp. xviii–xx.

[35] Shmeruk, 'The History of the *Shund* Literature' (Heb.).

most carefully studied is Yitshak Me'ir Dick (1814–93). Initially his motives in writing were to edify his readers: 'I wrote . . . for the benefit of our women . . . [My stories are written] in a fine style, full of ethical teaching, free of any words of eroticism and blemish and they instruct the women to walk in the paths of righteousness and to turn away from all evil.'[36] In the course of time Dick wrote a large number of romances and David Roskies has carefully analysed his literary output. He noted that Dick's romances can be divided into three categories: romances in remote settings, romances claiming to describe the life of the upper class, and 'the bourgeois exemplar', which was designed as practical examples of how to succeed. Roskies came to the conclusion that:

What all these stories have in common is some kind of romantic intrigue in which the principle of democratic but mutually compatible love is vindicated either by a positive or negative example. Traditional Jewish society, where it figures at all, represents the suppression of love in the name of economic and status considerations. In short, Dick's romances provided their female readers with escapism and wish fulfillment.[37]

The significance of Roskies' observation lies in the fact that while today the best-known Yiddish writers from that period are figures such as Mendele Moykher Sefarim, Shalom Aleikhem, and Yitshak Leib Peretz (1852–1915), these were not necessarily the best-selling authors of their time. The masses of Jewish readers were reading popular literature (*shund*) to the distress of the creators of 'high' Yiddish and Haskalah literature. The impact of this romantic literature cannot be measured in quantitative terms but it certainly played a major role in influencing attitudes, if not behaviour.

Prostitution was one of the less savoury aspects of eastern European Jewish life in the late nineteenth century but, perhaps surprisingly, it can also serve as evidence for the role of romance in couple formation. It is a well-known fact that east European Jews played a major role in prostitution and in the international 'white slave trade' in the latter part of the nineteenth century.[38] Recruitment of prostitutes was simple. Procurers who posed as suitors looking for a wife were the key. They preyed on single women who wanted to fulfil traditional roles as wives and mothers. The true intent of the 'husband' or 'groom' was revealed after 'marriage', or after the woman had gone off with the newly found friend who promised marriage. Recruitment to prostitution was made easier by the fact that the wave of migration to the

[36] In Dick, *Makhazeh mul makhazeh*, cited and translated in Roskies, 'Yiddish Popular Literature and the Female Reader', 853. [37] Ibid.
[38] See Bristow, *Prostitution and Prejudice* for a fine survey of the phenomenon, and Gartner, 'Anglo Jewry and the Jewish International Traffic in Prostitution' for a detailed analysis of a key element of the trade.

United States included more men than women, which led to a shortage of single males in eastern Europe. One consequence of this was widespread desperation among young women looking for husbands.[39] As one memoirist put it:

To be left an old maid . . . [was] the greatest misfortune that could threaten a girl; and to ward off that calamity the girl and her family, to the most distant relatives, would strain every nerve, whether by contributing to her dowry, or hiding her defects from the marriage broker or praying and fasting that God might send her a husband.[40]

In many cases prostitutes came from disturbed family backgrounds, often without a father present,[41] or they were servant girls living away from home.[42] However, this was not always the case, as the following description points out:

[P]rocurers from Buenos Aires sometimes brought along the Jewish marriage contract, the *ketubah* that traditionally was part of the religious betrothal. On these contracts the procurer's name was already filled in, along with those of two witnesses. The schemer would then arrange to meet the daughter of a poor family and explain that there was no time to lose before getting back to his thriving business across the ocean. Or, he would claim to be acting on behalf of the eligible groom who was too busy to leave America. The *ketubah* was usually enough to convince any traditional family that the match was proper.[43]

Prostitution was not simply a result of the disappearance of traditional values. In certain key respects, the opposite was the case—traditional values remained though traditional patterns of behaviour had been abandoned.[44] The procurers could entrap women only in a reality in which young women played a main role in choosing their life partner and where it was regarded normal for a young man to press his suit directly. In a society where parents made all the decisions and children were totally dependent, the task of a procurer would have been impossibly difficult. The victims of the procurers took for granted that they could make decisions, and that mutual attraction was justifiable and acceptable grounds for marriage. At the same time, the victims felt that sexual promiscuity was unacceptable. Contemporary sources do not

---

[39] There were, of course, many women who knew exactly what they were doing, and saw no great virtue in living a life of poverty, or in selling their body to one man through marriage rather than keeping control over their body for their own profit. See Bristow, *Prostitution and Prejudice*, 158–9.   [40] Antin, *The Promised Land*, 35.

[41] Bristow, *Prostitution and Prejudice*, 95.   [42] Ibid. 98.   [43] Ibid. 105.

[44] Much remains to be studied in this area. A great deal of attention has been given to the 'surprising' fact that Jewish girls could become prostitutes; the fact that young Jewish men who had studied in *ḥeder* became pimps was assumed to be natural. Similarly, the fact that young Jewish men were often clients of prostitutes was also seen as so natural as not to need explanation.

discuss attempts to return home by young women who had been enticed into prostitution. Apparently the unfortunate victims of the procurers accepted society's view that as prostitutes they had no value and consequently they lost any sense of self-esteem.[45]

Marital behaviour of Jewish immigrants to America at the turn of the century is well documented and it may serve as indirect evidence of courtship patterns and the role of love in determining marriage in east European Jewish society. Despite the evidence for the increased role of young people in choosing marital partners in eastern Europe, it appears that the immigrant parents continued to regard arranged marriages as desirable for respectable Jews. This view created innumerable conflicts between the generations and the children were not always the winners.[46] Since Jews were employed to a large extent in industry, young adults often earned wages that were no lower than that of their parents. This meant that they were relatively independent.[47] The relatively high income of young workers, together with the influence of romantic values current in America, was regarded as responsible for the tendency of young Jews to choose their own partners—whether out of love or out of other considerations. As a matchmaker in New York put it in 1898:

Once I lived off the fat of the land, and most marriageable men and women in the quarter depended on me to make them happy. Now they believe in love and all that rot. They are making their own marriages . . . They learned how to start their own love affairs from the Americans, and it is one of the worst things they have picked up. How can a Jewish couple expect to be happy in a marriage of their own making when it has been the custom of their fathers and mothers for ages not to see each other until after marriage?[48]

---

[45] A woman with traditional values was more likely to develop a negative self-image after being seduced than was a woman who lived in a society that was tolerant of premarital sexual experience. See Rosen (ed.), *The Maimie Papers*, for the fascinating correspondence of a 'reformed' Jewish prostitute in the USA in the early 20th century and the editor's sensitive introduction, esp. p. xxiv.

[46] See notably Yezierska, *Bread Givers*. In this apparently autobiographical novel three daughters give up their loves for a match chosen by their father. The source of his authority over his daughters lies in the fact that he is a Torah scholar and dependent on their support—hence he can appeal both to traditional values and to feelings of guilt to impose his will. Even if we assume the accuracy of the description, clearly this was an exceptional household in a society where most men were employed in industry or in commerce. Moreover, the clients of the matchmakers are potential grooms themselves, not their parents, and the young couples are involved with each other for a while before the match is final—both innovations from the traditional patterns. The grooms that the matchmaker presented were also failures of one sort or another, and were far from being typical young men.

[47] See Gillis, *Youth and History*, 44.

[48] 'Shadkens Find Business Bad', *New York Tribune*, 9 Jan. 1898; cited in Ewen, *Immigrant Women*, 228.

Environment alone cannot explain the changing pattern, as the experience of immigrants in New York clearly indicates. Italian parents in New York were matching off their children years after their Jewish counterparts had stopped doing so. In addition, after marriage Italian women were more confined to the home than were Jewish women.[49] Economic differences between the two groups do not appear to explain this and it seems that the important variable was cultural. Most of the Italian immigrants came from a peasant society where parents ruled over their children's future because they owned the land. They made significant efforts in America to maintain the patterns with which they were familiar and comfortable. The Jews came from a society in which parents were used to having limited control over their children's behaviour. For them, letting children make key decisions did not involve a radical shift in the family order. It is even possible that unconsciously Jewish parents had been culturally prepared for granting love a role in marriage—if only through the reading of novels. This may have helped the rapid adoption among Jews of the positive 'American' attitude to the role of love in couple formation.

One factor that eased the transition among Jews in eastern Europe to marriage by choice and on romantic grounds was the development of new ways of preventing misalliances—a function matchmaking had traditionally filled. Jacob Katz pointed out that one of the reasons for opposition to marriages based on free choice was because: 'This society was based on rigid class divisions but it lacked adequate means to differentiate between the social status of the various classes . . . Members of the same class, [in isolated communities, who] could be considered suitable marriage partners, were often geographically dispersed.'[50] In other words, while everyone knew, more or less, who was poor and who was rich, there were many opportunities for mingling that could lead to a misalliance.

This situation existed to a much lesser degree in the mid and late nineteenth century, which meant that there was less need for formal barriers. Geographically there were new concentrations of the rich in St Petersburg and Moscow, cities in which only rich Jews or Jews with special privileges were allowed to settle. Once in such a locale, parents could rest assured that their children would mix with the right crowd. The transition to Russian or Polish as a spoken language in the modernizing Jewish elite created linguistic barriers that effectively inhibited 'mismatches' with lower-class Jews, though this transition led to opportunities for mixed marriages with non-Jews. However, antisemitism served as a partial brake on such relationships. Schooling also served to steer contacts towards individuals from similar backgrounds. Since secondary and university education was expensive, most Jewish students in these schools were from comfortable homes. Thus, these

---

[49] Ewen, *Immigrant Women*, 232–50.   [50] Katz, *Tradition and Crisis*, 120.

educational institutions also functioned as social frameworks in which members of the elite could meet each other and form attachments. Education, language, and geography were now filling in for the matchmaker.

*

In many cases, such as arranged marriages, love made its appearance after marriage. A widely accepted view was that 'First you marry, then you love',[51] of which there are many examples.[52] To understand the function of love and affection in the east European Jewish marriage it is necessary to consider the roles men and women had in marriage.

Of course, marriage and marital roles involved more than the bride and groom alone. Marriage bonds linked not only the couple to each other but also established ties between the families of the bride and the groom. Yiddish even had a special term for the relationship between the parents of the bride and groom: they were *mekhutonim*. The term *mekhutonim* is of Hebrew origin (*meḥutanim*) and it was already in use in the medieval Hebrew of Spanish Jews.[53] The fact that a term for this relationship is missing in other European languages suggests that this relationship may have been stronger among Jews than among other peoples.[54] However, there is little evidence for this. In east European Jewish society, both the husband's family and bride's family had a major role in the life of a couple only before the marriage or, when there was *kest* or parental support, during the *kest* period. Their financial responsibilities were defined and limited to the dowry. After marriage, or after *kest*, a couple was expected to be independent. Young couples often lived far away from one or both sets of parents. On a day-to-day basis, many parents had relatively little contact with grown children.[55] In most cases, there were few frameworks for direct contact between the families of the bride and groom. In rich families—the minority—a young couple often spent the first few years of married life in the house of the bride's parents. However, once this period was over they were on their own.

While marital roles probably varied from region to region and from class to class, some generalizations can be made. One is that up until the end of the nineteenth century, east European Jewish women generally worked.[56] At times this was in contrast to the husband, who was sitting and studying the Talmud all day, but such full-time students were a minority. In most families

[51] See Brayer, *The Jewish Woman in Rabbinic Literature*.

[52] See Stahl-Weinberg, *The World of Our Mothers*.

[53] For reference to the early use of the term *meḥutanim*, see Perfet, *She'elot uteshuvot ribash*, no. 193. I owe the reference to the invaluable Ben-Yehuda dictionary.

[54] Silverman-Weinreich, *Kinship Terminology in a Modern Fusion Language*, 17.

[55] On the constant migration of Jews, see my 'Patterns of Internal Jewish Migration'.

[56] Baum, 'What Made Yetta Work'.

husbands contributed to the family earnings and most women also worked in order to supplement the income. This supplement was critical to the economic well-being of the family. In other words, the Jewish wife was not generally only a housewife. She contributed significantly to the family income, and the economic well-being of the household depended on her wages. Most Jews did not own businesses with many employees so, of necessity, the many women who worked did not usually do so within the framework of a family enterprise. This meant that a woman's contribution to the total family income was measurable, visible, and distinct, and was very often large.

If we define a patriarchal society as a society in which the husband/father exercises absolute authority over the family unit, then traditional east European Jewish society was definitely not such a society. The patriarchal model was common in peasant societies. Among farmers women worked in agriculture, but did so as 'adjuncts' to the work of the males in the family. Thus farming societies are usually patriarchal in that males make most of the decisions. However, Jews everywhere in the modern period were not generally farmers. There were Jewish societies, such as those in Islamic lands or in modern central Europe, in which patriarchal patterns existed and even predominated. The Jews of Islamic lands, like their neighbours, regarded the wife who never left the home as the ideal, and it was the husband who was the source of income—and of authority. Similarly, the bourgeois German ideal adopted by many Jews idealized the husband who supported the family single-handedly and enjoyed a dutiful wife and dutiful children. However, this was not the ideal or the reality that characterized traditional east European Jewish society.

In the traditional east European Jewish family, women had a major role in the decisions that affected the family. The income women brought home could not be ignored and therefore their opinions had to be taken into account. In the few households in which males carried out the ideal role of spending time in study and being totally unfamiliar with the material world, most of the decisions were made by women. Even though in most households both husband and wife worked, the ideal of a household in which women supported their husbands and ran the household justified the involvement and authority women had. In the ritual sphere, men unquestionably had a central role, but this did not hold for other spheres of life.[57]

Sexual relations, of course, had an important role in Jewish marital life, and in certain key respects, the wife was the arbiter of this activity. In traditional east European Jewish society, as in all other Jewish societies, the halakhah, or Jewish law regarding sexual relations, was generally accepted

[57] For a more detailed discussion of this issue, see Chapter 7. For a different point of view, see Parush, *Reading Jewish Women*.

and practised. Jewish law sees sexual activity as a natural part of the marital relationship. On these grounds sexual activity is permitted during pregnancy, even when it is clearly not for the purposes of procreation, which is in contradistinction to practices current in many non-Jewish societies. At the same time there is a strict prohibition on sexual activity and even physical contact not only when the wife is menstruating, but also for a week after menstruation and whenever the wife has a vaginal discharge similar to menstruation. Obviously only the wife could check this, which put women in control of the timing of sexual activity and gave them the potential for avoiding unwanted attention from their husbands.

In all circles of traditional east European Jewish society men interacted mainly with men, and women with women. Men and women lived in separate spheres and there were few shared activities. The shift to modernity was marked to a large extent by the breaking down of some of the barriers between them.[58] However, until this took place men and women occupied adjacent but different cultural worlds in eastern Europe. In the early nineteenth century, for example, there were no opportunities in eastern Europe for mixed social activities involving married men and women. There were no evenings of dancing or eating in restaurants which, in some societies, enable men and women to be together casually. Jews ran taverns but did not frequent them. Enjoying food and drink was permissible, of course, but within a meal in honour of a holiday, or at a religious event such as a wedding or circumcision. At these events there was a great deal of social supervision.

Along with the separation between the sexes went a desire to limit public expressions of affection, which does not mean that such affection did not exist, but simply that it was not displayed in public.[59] This led to the creation of curious circumlocutions for the terms 'my husband' and 'my wife', the most common being *mayner* and *mayne* ('mine', masc. and fem.). Even more periphrastic is the term *tsi-herstu* (literally 'do you hear?'), which evolved from a phrase of address like 'listen here!' into a common noun meaning 'wife' or 'husband'—for example, *mayn tsi-herstu* 'my wife (or husband)'. This was matched by behaviour: 'displays of endearment between husband and wife are frowned upon, regarded as vulgar whether in speech or gesture',[60] but affectionate demonstrativeness towards children was accepted. The ties between mother and son were usually among the warmest,[61] with those between father and daughter coming second. In marriage the wife 'inherited' some of the attitudes the male previously directed to his mother, and the

[58] For a very valuable discussion of the changes in the roles of men and women, see Hyman, *Gender and Assimilation in Modern Jewish History*.

[59] Beatrice Silverman-Weinreich, introduction to Weinreich, *Selected Writings* (Yid.), 11.

[60] Landes and Zborowski, 'Hypotheses Concerning the Eastern European Jewish Family', 453.

[61] Ibid.

husband attitudes previously directed to his wife's father. This meant that emotionally preconditions were favourable for an affectionate relationship to develop between husband and wife, if indeed such a relationship had not preceded the wedding. These models of relationships emphasized intimacy and warmth that could carry on into husband/wife relationships.

However, these models were not necessarily characteristic of particular classes. A very perceptive analysis of immigrant Jewish women in the United States noted the following:

In emphasizing intimacy, sharing, and communication, these [immigrant] women, regardless of their actual economic status, resembled middle-class rather than typical working-class women, who wanted above all a husband who worked steadily and did not drink or beat them . . . Perhaps one reason . . . stemmed from child-rearing practices in Jewish homes. Among most non-Jewish working-class families, children were socialized to observe rigid gender distinctions. Boys learned that they were expected to be strong, assertive and unemotional. The sons of middle-class families on the other hand, learned that it was permissible to cry and show emotion; to be thoughtful, at times even passive; to be eager to learn and to express feelings openly. Many Jewish boys, regardless of their parents' origins, tended to be raised with such middle-class attitudes, for the Eastern European ideal of the Yeshiva student emphasized these characteristics, whereas working-class cultures generally associated them only with women. Similarly, Jewish girls were conditioned to value such traits.[62]

The emphasis on middle-class values impacted in various areas. In east European Jewish society a small percentage of the Jewish population was learned, yet even the working class, which was generally quite unlearned, did not see their children as destined to be equally unlearned. Their image of Jews as people of the book contributed to the quick climb up the educational ladder of the immigrants to the United States and their children.

Supportive evidence for the importance of love and affection in the east European Jewish family can be found in—of all places—the surprisingly high level of divorces among east European Jews,[63] but there are good reasons for this. So, how common was divorce among Jews in eastern Europe? According to the 1897 census of the tsarist empire, there were in that year 3,975 divorced Jewish men and 12,589 divorced Jewish women in the empire.[64] These figures are meaningful only in terms of the base population. If we take all males and females over the age of 20, then the result is as shown in Table 2.1.

As we can see, levels for divorced males did not vary significantly, and the share of divorced women was higher in cities than their share in rural areas.

[62] Stahl-Weinberg, *The World of Our Mothers*, 212.

[63] On divorce, see the analysis and data of Freeze, *Jewish Marriage and Divorce in Imperial Russia*.

[64] Troinitsky (ed.), *Obshchii svod po Imperii*, calculated on the basis of tables 15 and 16.

Table 2.1 Divorced Jews in the tsarist empire, 1897 (as % of Jews ever married)

	All Jews		Urban[a] Jews		Non-urban Jews	
	Male	Female	Male	Female	Male	Female
Entire empire	0.4	1.3	0.6	1.6	0.4	1.0
Polish provinces	0.3	0.9	0.4	1.1	0.2	0.6

[a] 'In the 1897 census, cities consisted solely of "official" or chartered urban places, which in turn consisted mainly of administrative centers . . . as well as a few other legal cities . . . The main shortcomings of the definition employed in the 1897 census are that (1) it excluded numerous sizable industrial centers . . . and (2) it included a number of small agricultural villages . . . Despite these deficiencies, the 1897 urban definition is still largely representative of the urban population based on more conventional definitions': Richard Rowland in Clem (ed.), *Research Guide to the Russian and Soviet Censuses*, 115.

Source: Troinitsky (ed.), *Obshchii svod po Imperii*, vol. ii, table 16 (pp. 176–81).

Divorce may have been more common in cities than in rural areas, but it is also possible that the divorced women gravitated to cities. The percentage of divorced men and women was lower in Poland than in other areas of the empire, which may be related to economic or perhaps cultural factors. In general these percentages were far higher than the percentage of divorced people in any other ethnic group in European Russia. However, the differences between Jews and non-Jews might have been even greater because the data from the census only indicate the percentage of people that were divorced on the day the census was taken. Many divorced Jews remarried quickly,[65] probably more quickly than non-Jews remarried, so that the number divorced on a specific date is not a precise indication of the rate or likelihood of divorce.

No systematic survey of Jewish divorce rates in eastern Europe has been published, but there is some information readily available about divorce in two cities, Berdichev and Odessa. In 1870 Alexander Zederbaum published a short monograph on the Jewish community of Berdichev as a case study of a Jewish community, and it included a statistical table containing data on marriages and divorces in that city, which is shown in Table 2.2.[66]

If we compare the numbers of marriages and divorces during these years the result shows a very high rate of divorce—so high as to be hardly believable. Perhaps the data are not exact but there is no reason to suspect that the numbers are exaggerated. Perhaps Jews in small towns and villages tended to marry locally but, if they decided to get a divorce, they went to a city like Berdichev. On the other hand, given the acceptance of divorce under Jewish

[65] See Chapter 3.
[66] Zederbaum, *The Secrets of Berdichev* (Yid.). For a full discussion of the topic see Freeze, *Jewish Marriage and Divorce*.

Table 2.2 Jewish marriage and divorce in
Berdichev, 1861–1868

Year	Marriages	Divorces
1861	384	146
1862	367	142
1863	385	112
1864	344	114
1865	382	125
1866	410	120
1867	385	117
1868	421	128

Source: Zederbaum, *The Secrets of Berdichev* (Yid.), 87.

law there is no need to assume that divorces were made in the big city to avoid shame. After all, the act can be hidden, but not its consequences. Another reason to prefer cities for divorce might be that marriage is a simple step under Jewish law but divorce is not. Therefore it would be preferable to get divorced in a city where there were recognized legal experts on the matter. It may be that in this table we have the number of marriages contracted by residents of Berdichev and the number of divorces for the region. Since we do not know how large a population Berdichev served, it is impossible to determine an exact divorce rate but, at the same time, it is clear that it was far from minimal.

There are also some data from Odessa,[67] which was far from being a typical Jewish community. In 1876 there were 483 marriages among Odessan Jews and 149 divorces. The following year there were 381 marriages and 147 divorces. The propensity of Jews for divorce aroused comment at the time, which suggests that our sources for Odessa are not flawed but, rather, reflect reality. It should be noted that in the vicinity of Odessa, relatively few Jews lived in villages, so that the numbers of divorces could not be explained by village Jews coming to the big city for a divorce.

Qualitative sources also indicate that divorce was common, but do not enable us to compare or determine rates. The issue of divorce is a recurrent theme in rabbinical literature, and the memoir literature also often mentions divorce. Indeed, the biography of a typical maskil (follower of the Haskalah) born in the first half of the nineteenth century would probably include something like the following. He was married at an early marriage (around the age of barmitzvah), as befitted a member of the scholarly elite, and lived with the family of his bride for the first few years after the marriage. His father-in-law found him reading Haskalah literature secretly. In con-

---

[67] Shalkovsky, *Odessa 84 goda tomu nazad i teper'*, 43–4, cited in Herlihy, *Odessa*, 256.

sequence, the father-in-law threw him out of the house, without neglecting to ensure he gave a divorce to his daughter.

That a certain number of marriages will be unhappy is inevitable. In any couple getting married, each has only limited information about their prospective partner. The parties to a marriage also have limited information about themselves. Therefore it is difficult to predict happiness in a marriage. Moreover, happiness of a married couple is influenced not only by their personal interaction but by the degree to which their expectations of a standard of living are met. This is not always predictable and, indeed, in the formation of couples there is often deception—deliberate and unconscious alike.[68] Short of living together for a trial period before marriage, there is no way of obtaining some of the information needed to be able to predict whether a match will lead to happiness or not, and even premarital cohabitation is not a foolproof method, as we know today. Trial marriage was inconceivable in a society where effective contraceptives were unknown and where children born out of wedlock were a potential burden on society. It was certainly unacceptable in the context of traditional Jewish society and values. The impossibility of predicting compatibility or long-term affection applies both to arranged marriages as well as to marriages based on mutual attraction. Indeed, there is no clear evidence as to whether matches made out of romantic attachments provided the parties marrying with a greater amount and more accurate information than matches made by parents which were based on more objective criteria and on a concern for a firm financial basis for the couple. Which type of marriage was more successful in the long run is unknown. Marriage is unpredictable.

Some of the distinctive characteristics of Jewish tradition and society contributed to making divorce common among Jews. In any society, the decision to terminate a marriage is affected by the degree of difficulty in carrying through the divorce. In the Jewish community divorce required mutual consent but getting a divorce was not difficult provided both sides agreed. All that was needed was a qualified rabbi who could write the necessary bill of divorce and for the husband to give the document (the *get* in Hebrew) to the wife. However, the economic role of Jewish women also had an impact on divorce rates.

Economic factors play an important part in any decision to terminate a marriage. As has been pointed out by Gary Becker: 'A husband and a wife would both consent to a divorce if, and only if, they both expected to be better off divorced'.[69] He also pointed out that 'Women with higher earnings gain

---

[68] Becker, *A Treatise on the Family*, 230, points out that 'marriages are more likely to dissolve when realized earnings, health and fecundity exceed as well as fall short of expectations'.

[69] Becker points out that this is a 'natural extension of the argument . . . that persons marry

less from marriage than other women . . . Therefore, women with higher earnings should be more prone to divorce, a conclusion that is supported by several kinds of evidence.'[70] Similarly, the better the chances for remarriage, the greater the incentive to separate and to seek another partner.

This pattern of divorce fits in with the information we have on the socio-economic patterns of east European Jews. As mentioned above, it was standard for Jewish women to work and they often made a major contribution to the family income. For women like this divorce did not necessarily mean a major drop in income. Moreover, as long as mortality in childbirth created a constant supply of widowers, divorcees had reasonably good chances of remarrying. Their chances for remarriage were strengthened by the fact that Jewish law opposed marriage when there was a great age difference between the bride and the groom. Legal loopholes made it theoretically possible to evade this prohibition and they were employed in certain non-east European Jewish communities. However, east European rabbis generally argued that tradition required individuals to choose partners of equal age and marital experience.[71] This maximized the chances of widows and divorcees remarrying. Jewish law also frowned on men of any age being single, taking for granted that a sexual drive in men always existed and should be channelled into marriage. Hence Jewish society in eastern Europe was one in which remarriage was very common both for males and for females, even after the fertile years.

The relative ease in getting a divorce tells us something about the majority of marriages that did not end in divorce. These were marriages in which the husband and wife remained married not for lack of an alternative, but because they were apparently satisfied with the marriage. Satisfaction is, of course, not identical with great happiness or fulfilment. However, it is something. A very low divorce rate, where divorce is not practical—either because it is prohibited by religious law, because it is unacceptable in society, or because women are not trained to be self-supporting—does not prove that marriages were happy or that their home environments were stable. Similarly, a low divorce rate caused by low expectations of happiness and correspondingly low levels of frustration simply indicates that the power of ideological and economic factors overcomes personal desires. It would appear that among Jews the fact that marriages could be dissolved had a restraining effect on the

each other if, and only if, they both expect to be better off compared to their best alternatives' (*A Treatise on the Family*, 226).

[70] Ibid. 231.

[71] *Shulḥan arukh*, 'Even ha'ezer', *Hilkhot periyah ureviyah*, 2: 9. On loopholes and attitudes to their use, see the commentators there. To this day it is common to see on Jewish wedding invitations the abbreviation *ayin bet gimmel*, meaning 'with a woman of his age', between the names of the groom and the bride.

behaviour both of husbands and of wives. The submission and dependence of a wife could not be taken for granted. In the case of east European Jews, expectations seemed to be reasonably high and hence Jews got divorced when these were not met. Love was not only a pleasant possibility in marriage but it played a positive functional role.[72] In short, the divorces of a minority suggest that there were probably warm relationships at work among the majority.

As mentioned above and as discussed in detail in Chapter 3, remarriage among Jews was very common. Widows, widowers, and divorced individuals remarried even in old age. The reason for this was partially to preclude the temptations of sexual activity outside the framework of marriage, but also partially out of an assumption that marriage is not only for procreation but also for companionship. Rabbis went out of their way to lift possible legal impediments to such marriages, giving legal recognition to the need for affective ties between men and women. The fact that people did remarry seems to indicate the general acceptance of this need.

Positive references to love in marriage are often found in rabbinical responsa dealing with the Jewish law of the childless marriage. According to Jewish law,[73] a couple should divorce if they are married for ten years without having a child, and the husband should remarry and try to fulfil the commandment of 'Be fruitful and multiply' with a different wife. Despite this law and the corresponding deep-rooted desire for offspring among Jews, the east European Jewish tradition was not to enforce this law,[74] and courts did not generally instruct infertile couples to separate—though when a husband wanted to divorce a wife on the grounds of infertility this law was used as a proof text.

In the standard commentaries affection is not a basic consideration but it is taken into account. One of the cases cited and regarded as authoritative is one involving a childless couple which apparently took place in Germany in the eighteenth century.[75] The husband did not want to divorce his wife, yet he also did not want to violate the law requiring divorce after ten years of childlessness. In his query as to what he should do, he claimed that it was hard for him to divorce his wife because she was energetic, pious, and supported him in his studies, and that he was sick, which may be the reason that they did not have children. The practical reasons for not wanting to divorce her are clear, yet another woman could probably have met them. It is obvious that he

---

[72] What Stahl-Weinberg, in *The World of Our Mothers*, attributed to middle-class values might well have been the product not only of class values but also of access to alternatives to marriage. To be sure, the power of middle-class models should not be underestimated.

[73] *Shulḥan arukh*, 'Even ha'ezer', 154: 10.

[74] See the glosses of Moses Isserles on the *Shulḥan arukh*. These glosses reflect the Polish and Ashkenazi traditions.

[75] Eisenstadt, *Pitḥei teshuvah*, a standard commentary on the *Shulḥan arukh*.

cites all of his wife's virtues because he wanted to remain married to her, and not just for material reasons. Indeed, the legal response was sympathetic, noting that bearing children is not the only *mitsvah* (religious precept) that he can fulfil. A Hungarian rabbi, who operated in the same tradition, spoke in one of his homilies about his own past.[76] He had no surviving children because the daughters his wife had borne him had died. He recalled considering the possibility of divorcing his wife and emigrating to the land of Israel. Her response, as he put it, was to cry and remind him that she loved him and that the death of the daughters was the divine will. When he asked his rabbi what to do, the answer he got was to do whatever his wife wanted. He saw this response as perfectly reasonable. Jewish law, it should be added, did not see the woman as being legally required to bear offspring and hence she was under less of an obligation to remarry.

The claim that love comes after marriage and not before was—as noted above—a common one. This statement is likely to have been coined when traditional marital patterns were challenged and needed justification. However, even before the challenges of the second half of the nineteenth century, the patterns of Jewish marital life were congenial to the development of a loving relationship between man and wife—even though it was not a precondition or an automatic product of marriage. At the same time, there is a general assumption that the transition to modern marital patterns of Jewish family life was marked by a transition from marriages based on material calculations of parents to marriages based on love or mutual attraction of the parties involved. The degree of truth of such a view is impossible to determine. Many people continued, as today, to marry for very practical considerations as well as love. What seems to have happened is that patterns based on mutual attraction which once were characteristic of the masses of poor Jews began to spread to the elite and this is what attracted attention. Moreover, people felt a need to talk about affection. A reflection of this transition can be found in letter-writing guides which provided models of letters both for young men and women as well as for parents.[77] In the late nineteenth century these guides indicate that a romantic attraction was a significant element in marriage, but material considerations, mainly the dowry, continued to be significant. In other words, romance was an additional factor but it did not simply replace practical elements. Dowries clearly continued to play a major role in the late nineteenth century. A booklet published in Vilna in 1890 listed the 'tariffs' for young grooms in various

[76] Sofer, *Likutei beit efrayim*, 6b.
[77] See the interesting study of Hurvitz, 'Courtship and Arranged Marriages among East European Jews Prior to World War I', 422–30. I thank Mark Kupovetski for this reference.

professions.[78] A lawyer cost 45,000 rubles, a doctor 30,000, an engineer 15,000, and an optician 10,000!

Among the sharpest critics of traditional society at the end of the nineteenth century was the nascent socialist movement. Although it preached revolution in the economic and political sphere, it was much less revolutionary in family relations.[79] It opposed matchmaking and some religious ceremonies, but in many respects it was quite conservative. Jewish revolutionaries called for restraint in sexual relationships among its members, and saw love as much as a threat to the achievement of its goals as a value or goal. In their opinion what was important for a couple was ideological agreement.[80] In many respects this view was not different from that of the Jewish rabbinic elite which saw love of a wife and children as a threat to devotion to Torah study.[81] Of course, both the scholarly circles and the revolutionary elite were a very small percentage of the Jewish population.

*

Within the family framework love was common but not necessarily universal in husband–wife relationships. However, it was standard in relationships between parents and children. The issue of changing views of children and childcare among east European Jewry is one that has only recently begun to attract attention.[82] However, much is clear already. Having a child was usually a source of great happiness.[83] According to the ideology of traditional society it was a religious precept (*mitsvah*) to have children. However, apart from that it was taken for granted that children were wanted and loved. The central role of children in the family was noted by Marvin Bressler thus: 'love in Jewish family life seems to be relegated to a relatively subordinate position in the value hierarchy as compared to the preoccupation with the rearing of children'. At the same time, he also suggested that 'the simultaneous acceptance on the part of many Jews of the dual but conflicting values of romantic love and contractual marriage based on duties might be a source of Jewish neuroses'.[84]

---

[78] Golomb, *The Laws of Women* (Yid.), 18.

[79] See the very important and often overlooked article by Mordekhai Levine, 'The Family in the Revolutionary Jewish Society' (Heb.).

[80] Ibid. 160   [81] Etkes, 'Marriage and Torah Study', 153, 178–9.

[82] See Hundert, 'Jewish Children', 81–94. For attitudes in an earlier period, see Kanarfogel, 'Attitudes toward Childhood', 1–31.

[83] Goshen-Gottstein, 'Courtship, Marriage and Pregnancy in "Geula"' (Heb.), noted that contemporary strictly Orthodox families tend to see procreation as the main function of marriage. It may have been the case that in the past procreation shared the centre of attention along with a desire for independence from parental control, economic independence, and other factors, but this is certainly not a totally new emphasis.

[84] Bressler, 'Selected Family Patterns', 570.

There were views in the traditional literature dealing with child education that emphasized the need to be strict with children and to hide one's love for them. Hence an influential rabbi wrote in his will: 'Beloved son, I bear witness on myself that even though I had many children . . . I never kissed any of them nor did I ever take them in my arms nor did I engage in a non-serious discussion with them, God forbid.'[85] However, he was very proud of having taken great care to ensure that even as very small children they said their blessings carefully. What is really significant in this passage is not the self-denying (and other) behaviour and beliefs of the author, but the fact that he feels it necessary to dwell in detail on this topic in his will. He was well aware that this behaviour was not typical and therefore he felt he had to tell his son what to do. Moreover, in his household all the care of the children was in the hands of his wife; somebody had to feed, clean, and pick them up when they fell, and hopefully she gave them some love. This 'exceptional' father's responsibility was for the formal education of his children.

However, the usual relationship between parents and children was love that was not so hidden and there were good reasons for this—though it should also be noted that the fact the love was common or expected does not mean that there were not cases of child abuse or that this was never a problem. Here we are concentrating on the broader patterns and, as we shall see, the way in which the east European Jewish family fitted into society had a big impact on the way Jewish parents related to children.

Among peasants land is one of the ties that binds parents and children, as mentioned above, but it is also the source of tension. Sons inherited the father's land and each individually worked his own plot.[86] It was not rare for the son of a peasant to delay marriage until his father was willing to turn over his farm to him, since only at that time could children begin to be self-supporting. In a rural setting there was no alternative other than for old parents to live with married children, and therefore this was the accepted practice. A parent could exert power over his child when the child wanted his land, but the same parent was destined to be dependent on that child for his support in old age.[87]

The situation is quite different in a society of small merchants and craftsmen. Young adults can become economically self-sufficient without being partners with their parents or replacing them, and marriage usually

[85] Alexander Suesskind of Grodno (d. 1794) in his will, cited in Assaf, *Sources for the History of Jewish Education* (Heb.), i. 270–1. Hundert, 'Jewish Children', referred me to this source.

[86] See Thomas and Znaniecki, *The Polish Peasant*, i. 161, for details. On the implications of this system for early marriage see Sklar, 'The Role of Marriage Behaviour'.

[87] Even in the most conservative peasant society there is mobility and there are many landless individuals for a variety of reasons. However, these are not the model members of the society.

takes place when they reach this stage of self-sufficiency. At marriage, the bride usually received a dowry from her parents. According to Jewish law, daughters do not have rights of inheritance; on the other hand, in east European Jewish society only daughters received capital from their parents during their lifetimes. In reality the dowry was like a payment in life of the daughter's 'share' of the parental estate or capital. There were several clear advantages to receiving this payment early and before male siblings received their shares, though the amount was often less then the son's share in an inheritance. However, the place of the dowry in the capital of the young couple could certainly strengthen the wife's position in internal family dynamics.

Once married or finished with *kest*, young couples were expected to support themselves. They were not under pressure to wait for elder parents to drop active economic activity or to hand over an inheritance. On the contrary, in an urban environment in which housing space was at a premium, having older parents move in was not desirable. Moreover, due to migration many young couples did not live in the same city as their parents. In such a reality it was clear that children and parents looked forward to mutual assistance and needed each other, but it was not the type of intense dependence and ties that characterized an agricultural society where generation after generation could work the same land and live in the same house. With less dependence than in a peasant society, love—and its corollary guilt—played a major role in binding parents and children together.

Considering various relationships within the family, it has been claimed that in the shtetl setting, the strongest affectionate relations were between mother and son with father–daughter relations second.[88] Father–son relationships are characterized by rivalry, as were mother–daughter relationships. Relations between father-in-law and son-in-law are usually more positive than mother and daughter-in-law ties, both within the framework of co-residence, as in *kest*, and during visits. The warm ties between mother and son in east European Jewish society have been popularized in countless songs and books—as well as jokes. A well-known one is the following: a young man begs his mother for her heart, which his betrothed has demanded as a gift; having torn it out of his mother's proffered breast, he races away with it; as he stumbles, the heart falls to the ground and he hears it question protectively, 'Did you hurt yourself, my son?'[89] In father–son and mother–daughter relationships there appears to be a strong element of fear of being supplanted. Together with this, parents are responsible for preparing the children for their future, and the success (or failure) of the child reflects on the capabilities

---

[88] Landes and Zborowski, 'Hypotheses Concerning the Eastern European Jewish Family'.
[89] Ibid. 453.

of the responsible parent. The child may feel grateful for this preparation, but he can also feel that he is constantly being tested and measured.

The characterization of the Jewish family as united by affective ties fits the socio-economic reality and was necessary for the functioning of the family.[90] As noted above, in the poorer ranks of the Jewish community (and not just among Jews), the economic power of parents over children was limited. Skills were more important for short-term advancement and future success than was starting capital. The ready availability of credit, though in limited amounts, also decreased the dependence of children on parents. Among the more well-to-do, high status and chances for a good match (and a fat dowry) went to the gifted student who succeeded in his studies. In theory, such a student might owe his chances for future advancement to his inherited genes rather than other aid from his parents. He was certainly not dependent on them to make him a match.[91] Under these conditions it was not prudent for parental authority to rest solely on economic dependence. Parent–child affection was not only desirable but almost necessary to the smooth functioning of the family framework.

These ties were emphasized in the earliest stages of a child's life—in infancy—and were expressed in a very prosaic manner in the ways babies were treated. Jewish patterns of swaddling were significantly different from those of their neighbours.[92] Russians swaddled babies very tightly out of a concern that babies are violent and could hurt themselves if they were not restrained. Poles also swaddled tightly, but from a belief that babies are fragile and need support, and from a concern that babies should not touch 'shameful' parts of their bodies. Jewish babies were swaddled loosely on a pillow. Here the concern was for their comfort and warmth. The nature of relations that was taught to Jewish children was not one of dominance and submission, but rather one of nurture and deference. Jewish childcare from the earliest stages taught love and, of course, the need to reciprocate. These swaddling practices were reinforced by the tendencies of Jewish mothers to nurse longer than non-Jews.[93]

The reciprocation expected by Jewish parents was not financial. As noted above, older parents did not live with children. As Ruth Benedict put it: 'Parents provide for all their children's needs but the obligation for the child to the parent does not include support of his aged parents when he is grown and the saying is "Better to beg one's bread from door to door than to be

[90] Landes and Zborowski, 'Hypotheses Concerning the Eastern European Jewish Family'
[91] The size of the dowry determined the type of husband with which the daughters of the well-to-do would be matched. Their personal qualities played less of a role in mate selection. Thus a girl was dependent on her parents' goodwill (and willingness to invest) in order to get a good match.   [92] Benedict, 'Child Rearing'.
[93] Schmelz, *Infant and Early Childhood Mortality among the Jews of the Diaspora*, 79.

dependent on one's son.'"[94] However, Jewish children could provide parents with love and publicly display honour for them, for example, in the daily recitation in the synagogue service of the Kaddish (memorial prayer) during the year after the death of a parent, and thereafter on the anniversary of his or her death (*yahrzeit*). A firstborn son was sometimes called a 'Kaddish' in anticipation of his filling this duty. Since Kaddish was said only after a death of a parent or a close family member, the deceased clearly got no benefit from it in his lifetime. Nonetheless, the knowledge that Kaddish would be said in the future was regarded as being very important. It was a public demonstration of the love and loyalty of a son to his parent, even when they were no longer present to reward him. Moreover, there was a widespread belief that the regular saying of Kaddish could raise a soul into heaven and this no doubt played a major role in the concern that Kaddish be said. Of course, not all Kaddish-sayers were motivated by love: some saw it as a filial obligation and others did so to maintain their status in their community.

In a study of the role of love in the modernization of the Jews, David Biale concluded: 'rather than assuming that arranged marriages were devoid of sentiment and built on cold calculation, we should imagine a society that expected the arranged marriage to be accompanied by love'.[95] He went on to claim that the modernization of Jewish marital values was not the simple product of the imitation of non-Jewish patterns. Both his evidence and our discussion support his conclusions.

Living in urban environments and drawing on traditional attitudes and laws, the dynamic of the Jewish family was more similar to that of contemporary families than might have been expected. Given this situation it is easy to understand how and why the Jewish family adjusted more easily to Western values and patterns of behaviour than might have been anticipated. Ironically, some features of contemporary Jewish family life are closer to traditional patterns than one might have expected, whereas much of the picture of Jewish family life in the past is in part wishful and in part an unconscious incorporation of images of the past held by non-Jewish societies.

[94] Benedict, 'Child Rearing', 347.

[95] Biale, 'Love, Marriage and the Modernization of the Jews', 1–17, 141–4. The citation is from p. 2.

THREE

Remarriage among
Jews and Christians

STUDIES OF JEWISH marital patterns in the past have rarely dealt in detail
with remarriage. Rather, attention has been paid to topics such as age and
age differences at the time of marriage, as well as patterns of selecting a mate
in the first marriage.[1] Patterns of remarriage deserve attention for a number
of reasons: they influenced fertility levels, affected family structure, played a
role in networking, and served as an indicator of the importance of marriage
in a given society. Remarriage is highly revealing of group characteristics and
behaviour but remarriage in late nineteenth-century eastern Europe merits
attention for an additional reason. Patterns of remarriage and their changes
over time significantly diverged among various population groups. Eastern
Europe is thus an excellent context for examining the impact of significant
variables on remarriage by means of a comparative approach.

By examining the phenomenon of remarriage in nineteenth-century eastern Europe I hope to demonstrate its significance in Jewish marital behaviour. This will provide the opportunity to assess the accuracy of some of the
statistical sources available for the period. Comparing the behaviour of different groups clarifies the singular characteristics of each group, making it
possible to test the nature of the influences that generated these differences
and helping us to better understand varying fertility patterns among different
groups. The changes in patterns of remarriage should enable us to time
developments in family structure and document the scope of changes during
this period.

The quantitative part of this study is based mainly on data derived from
statistical yearbooks published by the Ministry of the Interior of the tsarist
empire,[2] which provide detailed information on the number of births, marriages, and deaths in a given year. Unfortunately, they do not specify the size

[1] This does not mean that remarriage has gone unnoticed. See e.g. Bach, *Population Trends*,
and DellaPergola, *La trasformazione demografica*, esp. ch. 5, p. 152. An English translation is
forthcoming. A study that discusses at length remarriage in a Jewish society is Cohen, 'Patterns
of Marriage and Remarriage among the Sephardi Jews of Surinam'. The situation he describes
in Surinam bears some similarity to the situation in eastern Europe.

[2] Tsentral'nyi statisticheskii komitet, *Dvizhenie naseleniya v Evropeiskoi Rossii*.

of the base population; nor is there accurate census data for most of the period covered. Still, much can be learned. The yearbooks make it possible to calculate the total number of marriages for each religious group as well as the prenuptial status of brides and grooms; that is, whether or not they had previously been married. Data from the empire's western provinces for three purposefully selected years[3] are most revealing about modes of remarriage among four major religious-national groups: (1) Russian Orthodox (mainly non-Polish Slavs, such as Russians, Ukrainians, and White Russians), (2) Catholics (mainly Poles and Lithuanians, and some Ukrainians), (3) Protestants (mainly Germans), and (4) Jews.[4] The data are summarized in Table 3.1,[5] which shows that at all times Jews had the highest percentage of marriages involving at least one remarrying partner, as well as of marriages between two remarrying partners.[6]

In 1867 approximately one-third of all Jewish brides and grooms were marrying for the second time. Among Russian Orthodox and Protestants, only a quarter of those marrying did so for the second time; among Roman

---

[3] The years chosen were the first year, one of the last years, and a rough midpoint. The disadvantages to such a small sample are obvious. There are questions about both the statistical significance of the data and their reliability. Work is currently being done to transfer all the material into machine-readable form, which will make it possible to provide more complete information on marriage trends and other vital statistics. In the meantime the picture presented by the quantitative material in our sample 'fits' the evidence from qualitative sources. Thus, our data provide a clear picture and sufficient information to warrant careful analysis and explanation.

[4] In this chapter the focus is primarily on Jews, Orthodox, and Catholics. Describing the Protestant population is complicated by questions of national background, urbanization, and occupational distribution. I hope to return to this population in a future study. Also, the statistical yearbooks do not allow for an easy breakdown of marital patterns between urban and nonurban populations. Such an analysis is, of course, highly desirable, and would be most illuminating.

[5] The data were collected from Bessarabia, Chernigov, Courland, Ekaterinoslav, Grodno, Kherson, Kiev, Kovno, Minsk, Mogilev, Podolia, Poltava, Taurida, Vilna, Vitebsk, and Volhynia. This corresponds roughly to the Pale of Settlement, the area of the tsarist empire to which Jews were confined. Data were not available for Congress Poland. Data were not analysed for all four religions in every western province. In some provinces there were only small Catholic and Protestant populations. Considering data from these populations not only could distort the conclusions, but would not be significant, since they apply to 'odd' communities. Therefore, data were analysed for Catholics in the following provinces: Grodno, Kovno, Minsk, Podolia, Vilna, Vitebsk, and Volhynia. Data were analysed for Protestants in the following provinces: Courland, Ekaterinoslav, Kherson, Kovno, Taurida, Vitebsk, and Volhynia.

[6] Laslett, 'Family and Household', 525, notes that a high level of remarriage of widows is one of the distinctive characteristics of marriage patterns in the West as opposed to a low level in the East. Our data more or less fit this description. The predilection of Jews to remarry held true in 1867 not only when the figures for all the provinces were collected, but also in every individual province; it also held true for both males and females. The difference between Jews and Christians was most dramatic in the case of females.

Table 3.1 Marriage and remarriage in the western provinces of the tsarist empire, by religion, 1867–1910 (%)

Religion	No. of marriages ('000)	First marriage for both partners	Remarriage for			Remarriage to a partner also previously married, as % of all remarriages by	
			Bride	Groom	Both	Women	Men
1867							
Jews	16.0	68.7	3.7	10.8	16.8	81.9	60.9
Russian Orthodox	538.0	77.0	4.3	9.6	9.0	67.7	48.4
Protestants	14.8	75.7	5.8	14.1	4.4	43.1	23.8
Catholics	23.3	71.7	7.6	14.5	6.1	44.5	29.6
1885							
Jews	20.6	77.4	2.9	8.9	10.8	78.8	54.8
Russian Orthodox	572.5	81.9	2.8	8.5	6.8	70.8	44.4
Protestants	21.8	81.8	3.3	10.7	4.1	55.4	27.7
Catholics	26.8	78.2	4.5	12.5	4.8	51.6	27.7
1910							
Jews	27.0	81.1	2.4	8.2	8.3	77.6	50.3
Russian Orthodox	831.9	84.5	2.4	7.4	5.7	70.4	43.5
Protestants	23.4	83.1	3.5	9.0	4.3	55.1	32.3
Catholics	35.1	81.5	3.9	10.1	4.5	53.6	30.8

Note: The western provinces were Bessarabia, Chernigov, Courland, Ekaterinoslav, Grodno, Kherson, Kiev, Kovno, Minsk, Mogilev, Podolia, Poltava, Taurida, Vilna, Vitebsk, and Volhynia.

Source: Tsentral'nyi statisticheskii komitet, *Dvizhenie naseleniya v Evropeiskoi Rossii*, vols. for 1867, 1885, 1910.

Catholics the percentage was somewhat higher.[7] At the end of the nineteenth century the percentage of individuals remarrying in all groups was down to about 20 per cent, and the differences between the groups were much smaller. In other words, the shift among Jews was larger than in other groups.

There were also important differences between Jews and Christians in specific patterns of remarriage. Among all the Christian groups, a man remarrying usually married a woman who had never been married; among Jews, men remarrying usually married women who had also previously been married. Marriage between bachelors and previously married women was almost always rarer among Jews than among others. Among Christian groups the patterns were not the same. The rate of remarriage was generally highest

---

[7] The differences may seem small, but they are important. In all groups, the vast majority of marriages occurred between people who had not previously been married. This limits the possible percentage of remarriages.

among Catholics and lowest among Russian Orthodox, with Protestants in the middle. Catholic men remarrying were more likely to marry a previously unmarried woman than were Russian Orthodox men remarrying. The percentage of marriages between bachelors and previously married women was always higher among Catholics and Protestants than among Russian Orthodox.

In time, the pattern of marriage changed in all groups. The most dramatic change—notably, the drop in the rate of remarriage—occurred among Jews, particularly in the rate of marriages in which both parties were remarrying. In 1885 a Jewish man who was remarrying was less likely to choose a previously married woman as a mate than a remarrying man had been in 1867, and even less likely in 1910. By 1910, marital patterns among Jews were more like those of their neighbours, with the exception of marriages between previously married women and bachelors. These were still far less common among Jews than among Christians.

In 1910, in contrast to 1867, a much lower percentage of marriages in all the groups involved individuals who had previously been married. How and why this change occurred should be clarified. The fact that the trend in all the groups was towards fewer remarriages raises the possibility of mutual or shared influences, but this is difficult to substantiate. Changes in the rate of remarriage diminished but did not erase distinctive patterns. Irrespective of overall trends, in both 1867 and 1910 the highest level of double remarriage (remarriage for both bride and groom) was among Jews and Russian Orthodox, and the highest levels of remarriage in general were among Jews and Roman Catholics. Several of the factors that made for similarities or differences in 1867 apparently still applied in 1910. These factors are not easily pinpointed because the raw data at our disposal are limited and difficult to control for socio-demographic variables. The historian would do best, therefore, to concentrate on documenting the behaviour of the various groups that are observed. But even this is a complex matter. For example, there may or may not be regional variations in patterns of remarriage of a particular group. The data in Table 3.2 allow us to compare the degree of such variation.

In 1867 the marital behaviour of Russian Orthodox and Roman Catholics did not vary much between provinces; Jewish and Protestant behaviour varied greatly. Most Russian Orthodox and Roman Catholics were peasants; most Jews and many Protestants were urban or urbanized. The two factors may be related. The high levels of variation in the marital patterns of Jews and Protestants suggest that differences in living conditions in cities and urban areas were great, while the low levels among Russian Orthodox and Roman Catholics suggest that conditions of peasant life were similar in the various

Table 3.2 Marriage and remarriage: variation among the western provinces of the tsarist empire, by religion, 1867–1910 (standard deviations of percentages)

Religion	First marriage for both partners	Remarriage for		
		Bride	Groom	Both
1867				
Jews	5.6	4.0	2.2	4.8
Russian Orthodox	3.7	2.4	1.7	1.3
Protestants	5.6	2.2	4.3	2.3
Catholics	4.4	2.0	3.1	2.3
1885				
Jews	5.5	1.0	2.3	4.0
Russian Orthodox	2.0	0.9	1.9	1.6
Protestants	5.2	2.1	3.4	2.1
Catholics	2.7	1.1	2.4	1.5
1910				
Jews	3.3	1.3	1.3	1.6
Russian Orthodox	3.0	1.0	2.1	1.9
Protestants	6.2	1.7	3.4	2.7
Catholics	2.3	1.0	2.1	2.0

Source: Calculated on the basis of Tsentral'nyi statisticheskii komitet, *Dvizhenie naseleniya v Evropeiskoi Rossii*, vols. for 1867, 1885, 1910.

provinces.[8] However, levels of variation in marital patterns were not stable. By 1910 levels of variation in the marital behaviour of Jews in the western provinces had declined and were similar to those of Russian Orthodox and Roman Catholics. Only Protestants continued to maintain high levels of regional marital variation. It may be that improved communications, transportation, and migration began to iron out regional differences in Jewish behaviour. On the other hand, cultural values and standards may have become more uniform.[9] Whatever the cause, this development underlines the degree of change in the conditions of Jewish life. Regional variation among Jews was not random, as may be seen from Table 3.3.

The differences between the regions are not great, but they are consistent. The northern provinces have the highest levels of first marriage for both bride and groom (in other words, the lowest levels of remarriage). They also

[8] Since variation from broader patterns of religious/national groups may have been the result of local conditions, the limited variation in peasant population patterns suggests that the process of peasant adjustment to post-emancipation conditions proceeded at a similar rate in the various provinces. The serfs in the Russian empire were emancipated in 1863. Polish peasants had been partially emancipated earlier. See Kieniewicz, *The Emancipation of Polish Peasantry*. Otherwise, variation would have increased among Catholics and Orthodox.

[9] Why similar developments did not occur among Protestants remains unexplained.

Table 3.3 Civil status at marriage of Jews in the western provinces of the tsarist empire, by region, 1867–1910 (%)

	First marriage for both partners			Remarriage for both partners		
	North-West	South	South-West	North-West	South	South-West
1867	73	67	67	12	18	19
1885	80	77	75	8	11	13
1910	84	78	81	7	12	9

Note: The regions comprised the following provinces: North-West: Courland, Grodno, Kovno, Minsk, Mogilev, Vilna, Vitebsk; South: Bessarabia, Ekaterinoslav, Kherson, Tavrida; South-West: Chernigov, Kiev, Podolia, Poltava, Volhynia. Together these constituted the western provinces.

Source: Calculated on the basis of Tsentral'nyi statisticheskii komitet, *Dvizhenie naseleniya v Evropeiskoi Rossii*, vols. for 1867, 1885, 1910.

have the lowest level of double remarriage. Nevertheless, the number of these remarriages declines over time, as does the share of remarriage in all marriages. The range, or the difference between the highest provincial level and the lowest provincial level, was also on the decline during the second half of the nineteenth century, as shown in Table 3.4.

Table 3.4 Marriage and remarriage: variation in the western provinces of the tsarist empire, by religion, 1867–1910 (range of % points)

Religion	First marriage for both partners	Remarriage for		
		Bride	Groom	Both
1867				
Jews	18.4	16.8	7.9	17.5
Russian Orthodox	16.2	9.3	6.0	5.6
Protestants	15.8	5.9	11.3	6.0
Catholics	16.8	6.2	9.6	7.7
1885				
Jews	20.8	3.4	8.3	14.4
Russian Orthodox	8.3	3.6	8.0	6.8
Protestants	14.1	7.0	10.1	5.2
Catholics	8.9	3.2	8.7	5.1
1910				
Jews	13.4	4.9	4.3	5.3
Russian Orthodox	9.1	3.9	7.5	6.3
Protestants	16.2	5.2	10.6	8.2
Catholics	7.6	3.1	8.6	7.1

Note: The table displays the range between the highest and lowest provincial percentage for each category of marriage, over those provinces where there were significant populations of the various religious groups (see n. 5).

Source: Calculated on the basis of Tsentral'nyi statisticheskii komitet, *Dvizhenie naseleniya v Evropeiskoi Rossii*, vols. for 1867, 1885, 1910.

In 1867 Jews had the highest range in three categories; Protestants, in one category. By 1910 the range among Jews had narrowed significantly, while Protestants maintained a high range; in 1910 they had the greatest range in each category. Changes did not occur simultaneously in all groups. The largest shift in range of mutual first marriages occurred between 1867 and 1885 among Russian Orthodox and Roman Catholics, while for Jews it was between 1885 and 1910 that major changes occurred.

We can also examine the degree to which the marital behaviour of the different groups in the various provinces is related. In other words, to what degree does the level of remarriage patterns among a group in a province correspond to the level of other groups in that same province? A high correlation often reflects a strong influence of regional factors on behaviour, as well as mutual or common influences among the groups. Correlation is measured in Table 3.5.

Among Christian groups there was generally a positive correlation between the marital behaviour of members of the different faiths living in the

Table 3.5 Marriage and remarriage in the western provinces of the tsarist empire, 1867–1910: correlation between the marriage patterns of different religious groups

Religion	First marriage for both partners			Remarriage for both partners		
	Russian Orthodox	Protestants	Catholics	Russian Orthodox	Protestants	Catholics
1867						
Jews	–0.522	0.390	0.209	0.534	0.583	0.605
Russian Orthodox		0.297	0.072		0.132	0.304
Protestants			–0.608			0.247
1885						
Jews	–0.261	–0.262	–0.548	0.385	0.041	0.376
Russian Orthodox		0.795	0.125		0.750	0.512
Protestants			0.387			0.497
1910						
Jews	0.167	0.748	–0.010	0.372	0.672	0.334
Russian Orthodox		0.865	0.663		0.706	0.707
Protestants			0.413			0.649

Note: Because of differing distributions of populations, correlations between different groups deal with varying numbers of provinces. Thus, the correlation between Jews and Russian Orthodox covers twelve provinces, while that between Catholics and Protestants covers a mere three. Therefore, correlations between religious groups cannot be combined.

Source: Calculated on the basis of Tsentral'nyi statisticheskii komitet, *Dvizhenie naseleniya v Evropeiskoi Rossii*, vols. for 1867, 1885, 1910.

same provinces. In other words, not only was there increased similarity among the Christian groups on the national level, but developments among the various groups converged in the provinces. The Jews were different. The correlations between Jews and non-Jews varied wildly. This could mean that the process of change among Jews was fuelled by factors different from those that influenced the Christian population.[10]

Timing the changes in Jewish marital patterns is important for studying eastern European Jewry. The last decades of the nineteenth century witnessed many political and cultural developments, such as the growth of the Jewish press and Jewish literature, the expansion of Jewish national movements, and the rise of Jewish socialism. There was also widespread internal and external migration. Accordingly, historians of eastern European Jewry have concentrated on these fin-de-siècle developments. However, the data on marriage show that the greatest shifts in percentages of remarriage and the greatest decline in the levels of regional variation occurred from 1867 to 1885, well before the end of the century. This suggests that the factors that were changing the most intimate aspects of human life were not necessarily the political and cultural ones with which most historians have dealt and they were very possibly economic and demographic.[11]

The accuracy of the data on which these conclusions rest cannot be assumed. Reports on birth, marriage, and death for the Christian groups which were prepared by the Christian clergy and sent to the government seem to be accurate. The clergy's authority and monopoly on marriage, baptism, and burial ensured its access to precise information. Jewish data, however, are problematic. It is likely that they were gathered by the official 'government rabbis', whose status in the community was not high. Jews had long been reluctant to report births, deaths, and marriages, so the statistics concerning Jews cannot be accepted at face value. The high levels of Jewish remarriage could conceivably be the product of distorted reporting and perhaps in reality the percentage of Jews remarrying was no higher or lower than of non-Jews. However, the statistics in the tsarist yearbooks can be validated. Ethnographic and other documentation indicative of the marital behaviour and attitudes towards remarriage espoused by various groups in eastern Europe both confirm and help explain why different marital patterns were established and subsequently modified.

[10] A study of fertility in Russia examined the proportion married in 1897 and found that 'in general the marriage pattern of each nationality group was strongly related to the pattern of other residents of the given province', with the exception of Jews. This fits with our results for remarriage. See Coale, Anderson, and Harm, *Human Fertility in Russia*, 158.

[11] DellaPergola found a similar phenomenon in Hungary in the same period. See his *Trasformazione demografica*, 176–7.

The Jewish attitude to marriage and sexuality is in clear contrast to that of Christians.[12] Marriage in Judaism is a universal ideal. Jewish law obligates all males to procreate, and therefore to marry. A man who does not marry and have children is regarded as committing a sin of omission. According to most authorities, the requirement of procreation is fulfilled upon fathering a son and a daughter. However, most rabbis claim that a man should have children as long as he is able, since there is no guarantee that a son and daughter will survive childhood and themselves procreate. Therefore, there is legal encouragement for a widower or a divorced man to remarry.[13] Moreover, sexual desire is accepted as a normal and permanent aspect of human nature that is to be satisfied in moderation. Sexual relations, even when not for the sake of procreation, are fully accepted within the context of marriage.

Jewish law could have taken another direction. Talmudic literature records a potential precedent for an ambivalent attitude to matrimony and sexuality. This is the case of Ben-Azai, a famous rabbi who never married. He is quoted as saying that one who does not procreate is like a murderer who diminishes the image of God.[14] The Talmud reports that his students asked him why he did not practise what he preached, to which he responded: 'What should I do if my soul yearns for Torah? The world can be perpetuated by others.' In his view, procreation was desirable, but could be outweighed by other religious precepts. Although Ben-Azai's view is noted by the Jewish legal tradition and was mentioned in the standard code of Jewish law, the *Shulḥan arukh*,[15] it is not considered a model for behaviour. Without exception, the commentators on the codes explain that Ben-Azai's precedent is not to be followed.[16]

Marriage is also seen in Judaism as necessary to avoid sin. Chastity is not considered a realistic possibility. Even a widower, or a divorced man who has children, is regarded as subject to being overcome by sexual desire, which can be prevented only by providing an outlet for licit sexual activity. Having fulfilled the commandment of fatherhood, this man is permitted to marry either a fertile woman or a woman who cannot bear children.[17] Women face

[12] An extremely useful discussion on Jewish attitudes toward procreation is Feldman, *Marital Relations*.

[13] *Shulḥan arukh*, 'Even ha'ezer', *Hilkhot periyah ureviyah*, 1: 5, and see commentators there.

[14] BT *Yev.* 63*b*.

[15] 'He whose soul yearns for the Torah as Ben-Azai and cleaves to it all his days and who never married, has not sinned—but this is on condition that his desires did not overcome him', *Shulḥan arukh*, 'Even ha'ezer', *Hilkhot periyah ureviyah*, 1: 4.

[16] This source, which easily could have been used to justify a negative view of matrimony and sexuality, was neutralized, though the inherent conservatism of the Jewish legal tradition meant that the case of Ben-Azai could not be entirely deleted.

[17] See Katz, 'Family Kinship and Marriage', and *Tradition and Crisis*, ch. 14, 'The Family'.

similar predicaments. Thus, although they are not required to bear children and therefore to marry, they are encouraged to both marry and remarry. Indeed, Jewish law assumes that a widow can remarry.

Jewish legal attitudes to remarriage are complicated by a discussion on remarriage in the central work of Jewish mysticism or kabbalah, the Zohar. The following question is posed: what becomes of the spirit of an ordinary man whose widow has married again? The answer is fascinating, and provides grist for the mills of psychologists and historians of religious thought. It also raises a number of legal and practical problems.

The Zohar states that when the second husband's spirit enters into the body of the woman, the spirit of the first husband contends with it and they cannot dwell in peace together, so that the woman is never altogether happy with the second husband because the spirit of the first one is always pricking her; his memory is always with her, causing her to weep and sigh over him. In fact, his spirit writhes within her like a serpent. And so it goes on for a long time. If the second spirit prevails over the first, then the latter goes out. But if, as sometimes happens, the first conquers the second, it means the death of the second husband. Therefore, we are taught that after a woman has been twice widowed, no one should marry her again for the angel of death has taken possession of her, though most people do not know this.

He who marries a widow is like unto one who ventures to brave the ocean during a storm without a rudder and without sails and knows not whether he will cross safely or sink into the depths . . . Now what happens to the spirit of a deceased husband whose widow does not marry again? It dwells in her for the first twelve months . . . in depression and sadness, and after the twelve months it leaves her and stands before the gates of Paradise, but occasionally visits this world, namely the 'vessel' [i.e. the wife] whence it went out.[18]

According to this view, the spirit of the late husband never fully cuts its ties with the widow. While the Zohar cites the case of the twice-widowed woman, the logical conclusion for a student of the Zohar is to avoid marrying a widow. This passage is frequently quoted in rabbinic literature. It influenced attitudes to remarriage and entered the corpus of 'general Jewish knowledge' in eastern Europe. A similar kabbalistic view of remarriage, although apparently less influential than that of the Zohar, stipulates that each man is 'assigned' a partner in heaven. Whoever marries a woman assigned to someone else is doomed to die. Thus, if a woman is widowed from her assigned partner, whosoever subsequently marries her risks his life.[19]

---

[18] Zohar, ii. 310–12. The original is in Zohar, *Mishpatim*, 102a.

[19] Maharshal (Rabbi Shelomoh Luria, 1510–74), cited by Joshua Falk (1555–1614) in his commentary *Sefer me'irat einayim* on *Shulḥan arukh*, 'Ḥoshen mishpat', cited in Pardo (1718–90), *Api zutri*, 47b.

Yet theoretical literature and—in a sense—both halakhah and kabbalah, can be misleading if we want to understand what was generally believed and done. It is the responsa literature, the answers of rabbis to specific legal questions, that is more indicative of reality.[20] Responsa are not always easy to use. Printed collections are usually heavily edited and it is often the case that the full text of the original question has been deleted. By their nature responsa deal with exceptional cases rather than with common ones for which standard answers are available. Still, they are useful. The questions posed shed light on popular values, desires, and what the questioners feel is right. Responsa also serve as an indicator of change, as people tend to ask questions when existing guidelines are perceived as no longer useful or sufficient. Responsa often refer to accepted practice and popular customs, thus providing information on contemporary standards. Finally, the internal logic of responsa reflects how their authors viewed society. In presenting the reasons for a decision, the *posek* (halakhic authority) reveals his willingness or reluctance to balance the conflicting claims of tradition and contemporary reality. Forced legal reasoning and artificial constructions may not be good practice of law, but they are evidence of the existence of strong communal pressures.[21]

There is a specific issue that came up often in the responsa literature that sheds a great deal of light on attitudes to remarriage.[22] Jewish law terms a twice-widowed woman a *katlanit* (slayer), and prohibits her from marrying a third time. Two reasons are given: one is that the woman has a physical characteristic or quality that caused her husbands to die; the other is that she brought bad luck. In either case she is considered a risk to a potential mate. Since Jewish law forbids risking one's life, it is forbidden to marry such a woman. Jewish law does not impose similar restrictions on men who have buried two wives. The *Shulḥan arukh* states that although women should not marry a third time, a man who has lost two wives should not desist from marrying again.[23] Some commentators observe merely that women are dif-

---

[20] The *Otsar haposekim* data base is an invaluable aid in tracking down sources dealing with remarriage.

[21] Since it is in the nature of any casuistic legal system, such as the Jewish one, to rely on precedents, it is important to note not only what is stated but who is quoted and who is not, as well as whether inconvenient precedents are being ignored. However, to do so for this topic would make this study unwieldy.

[22] It should be emphasized that the discussion of remarriage in the responsa literature is based on a topical arrangement; it is not in chronological order.

[23] *Shulḥan arukh*, 'Even Ha'ezer', *Hilkhot ishut*, 9: 1, 2. A sharp Italian rabbi noted that the *Shulḥan arukh* uses an odd expression that a man who has buried two wives should not desist from remarrying, but does not specifically mention remarrying a third time. Citing sources he raised the possibility that just as a twice-widowed woman should not remarry, so a man who was twice a widower should not, but he drew back from taking such a radical step. He did conclude, however, that the author of the *Shulḥan arukh* used the expression 'not desist' because he

ferent from men, without going into detail. Some point out that since men are required to procreate and women are not, men have a greater responsibility to remarry than do women.[24] This opinion troubled one of the more original eastern European rabbis of the nineteenth century, David of Novogrudok (1769–1837). It makes more sense, he said, to see men, not women, as transmitting danger, but halakhah does not limit male remarriage. In addition, he perceived no physiological basis for the law of a *katlanit*, and refused to consider the element of bad luck. He concluded that the source of danger was not the woman herself but the widespread—although, in his opinion, baseless —folk belief that a twice-widowed woman is dangerous. The superstitious fear such a woman engenders is so great that it can kill the man who marries her. Had there been a similar folk belief about men, Rabbi David added, they, too, would not be allowed to marry a third time.[25]

Faced with a twice-widowed woman seeking permission to marry again, most rabbis were lenient. In the sixteenth century, Rabbi Moses Isserles (Rema, 1525–72) wrote in his standard glosses on the *Shulḥan arukh*, which reflect the Polish tradition, that 'many seek to be lenient in the case of the woman who wants to remarry'. Apart from their convictions, many *posekim* (rabbinic legal decisors) may have been responding to the pressures exerted by female petitioners who were eager to remarry. This approach continued in the modern period. According to Rabbi Moses Sofer of Pressburg (1762– 1839), finding a legal loophole for such a woman was actually a *mitsvah* (a religious precept),[26] and a leading hasidic rabbi reassured anxious grooms by citing an oral tradition that if such a match was approved by the holy rabbis, then the husband could be certain of no harm.[27]

Various justifications were given for a lenient approach. One is cited in a responsum dealing with the case of an indigent widow who wanted to marry a fourth time. Her first husband had been murdered, her second had died of old age, and her third had been sick at the time of their marriage. The candidate to be number four was not afraid of her 'bad luck' and turned to a communal

wanted to discourage such marriages, and to imply that although such a man is allowed to remarry, people should not help him find a wife. Nonetheless, he also found that man's responsibility to procreate and avoid 'spilling his seed' might justify such a marriage. See Meyuhas (1738–1805), *Bereikhot mayim*, no. 53, p. 92.

[24] It would be interesting to analyse developments of other laws, such as those limiting the remarriage of a nursing mother, but that would take us too far afield.

[25] David of Novogrudok, *Galya masekhet*, no. 2.

[26] See Sofer, *Sefer ḥatam sofer*, 'Even ha'ezer', no. 24. For this discussion, the responsa of Hungarian rabbis will be used together with responsa of rabbis from eastern Europe proper. In the world of rabbinic scholarship this, in many respects, was one unit.

[27] Hayim Halberstam, also known as Hayim of Sanz (1793–1876), *Divrei ḥayim*, vol. ii, 'Even ha'ezer', no. 26, p. 95.

rabbi for approval. The rabbi could find no legal grounds to permit the marriage, but he did not want to refuse the request. He therefore turned to the well-known Rabbi Shmuel Engel (1853–1935), who felt obligated to find grounds to permit the remarriage because if the widow were to remain unmarried she would live in poverty.[28] Rabbi Shelomoh Leib Tabak of Sighet, Romania (1832–1908), went even further than Rabbi Engel. Contemporary circumstances, he argued, required leniency, because a woman who was not allowed to remarry might indulge in licentious behaviour. 'Everything', he wrote, 'is dependent on the place and in accordance with how the rabbinical courts see the situation.'[29] Other rabbis felt that remarriages should be permitted because it was in the interests of the orphans to have step-parents rather than to live in a single-parent household, although they must have known that this was legally irrelevant.[30] On similar grounds, another *posek* claimed that it is a *mitsvah* for a man to marry his late wife's sister even if she is a *katlanit*, because she will presumably have 'mercy' on her late sister's children.[31]

It should be emphasized that some rabbis advocated a more conservative approach, denouncing artificial excuses for remarriage. Alongside the many responsa permitting remarriage, there are those that forbid it, even under extenuating circumstances.[32] Indeed, a well-known eastern European rabbi present at the wedding in Jerusalem of a twice-widowed woman suggested to the groom that he prepare his shroud.[33]

Perhaps the simplest way for a rabbi to solve the problem of a *katlanit* within the framework of halakhah was to question the basis of the law. Thus, Rabbi David of Novogrudok, who claimed that the laws of *katlanit* were derived from folk beliefs, stated that if the prospective husband rejected these beliefs, then he could marry the *katlanit*—even though such marriages should not be encouraged.[34] Even more radically, another rabbi concluded that *katlaniyot* may exist but are too rare to generate real concern; the slightest extenuating circumstance, therefore, should suffice to allow a twice-widowed woman to remarry.[35] Were the fear of *katlaniyot* justifiable, he said, no man would ever risk marriage, and the rabbis would have prohibited marriage entirely because of the danger involved. However, such radical approaches

---

[28] Engel, *She'elot uteshuvot maharash engel*, pt. 3, no. 117, p. 174. The responsum is dated 1922. [29] Tabak, *Erekh shai*, no. 9.

[30] Twersky (1840–1904), *Emek she'elah*, end of no. 16, p. 198.

[31] Meizlish (d. 1932), *Ḥedvat ya'akov*, no. 50, p. 86.

[32] Twersky, *Emek she'elah*, no. 15; also Toibesh (1825–89), *She'elat shalom*, no. 119.

[33] Cited in Leibowitz, *Shulḥan ha'ezer*, 31a.

[34] David of Novogrudok, *Galya masekhet*, no. 11.

[35] Aryeh Leib ben Eliyahu (Bolechover), *She'elot uteshuvot shem aryeh*, no. 36, p. 50a. The responsum is dated 1864.

were not usually accepted. Rabbis may have been lenient in individual cases, but they hesitated actually to nullify the law. Many apparently felt it preferable to make individual exclusions from this undesirable category rather than to abrogate the category of *katlanit*.

More widespread was the approach that involved searching for and developing loopholes for specific cases to allow a twice-widowed woman to remarry. An important and often-cited responsum of this type was written by Rabbi Ezekiel Landau (1717–93) of Prague in a case involving a rich widow.[36] The woman's wealth, he wrote, was a sign of good fortune, and was clear proof that she did not bear the bad luck that supposedly was the nemesis of the *katlanit*. The argument is not terribly convincing. Luck in wealth is no sign of luck in health and, not surprisingly, one rabbi wrote 'scholars today reject this position'.[37]

However, many of the same rabbis who rejected Rabbi Landau's specific interpretation did permit *katlaniyot* to remarry,[38] but they did so on grounds other than wealth. For example, a husband who died in an epidemic was not to be regarded as the victim of a *katlanit*.[39] Furthermore, a woman was not be regarded as a *katlanit* if she bore her second husband children, since the children were a clear sign that the spirit of her first husband had left her and no longer competed with that of the second.[40] Nor was a widow to be regarded as the cause of her husband's death if he was sick before their marriage or died at an old age.[41] Finally, if the widow intended to support her new husband, allowing him to devote himself to study, the virtue of the Torah would offset any risk involved.[42]

Such patently casuistic grounds for permitting twice-widowed women to remarry reflect that rabbis felt it necessary to permit such marriages.[43] Popular practices alluded to in the responsa testify to a concern to facilitate remarriage as well as to a certain scepticism about the 'dangerous nature' of the twice-widowed woman. A number of responsa refer to dying men

---

[36] Landau, *Noda biyehudah*, no. 9.

[37] Engel, *She'elot uteshuvot maharash engel*, no. 50, p. 94*b*.

[38] See the views cited by Leibowitz in his *Shulḥan ha'ezer*, 30.

[39] Jacob Willowski (1845–1913), also known as Ridbaz, cited in Eisenstadt, *Pitḥei teshuvah*, 'Even ha'ezer', p. 22, n. 5.

[40] Safrin (1806–74), *Notser ḥesed*, 27 (in the Jerusalem 1982 edition).

[41] Leibowitz, *Shulḥan ha'ezer*, 31*a* at the bottom of column A. The claim that death at an old age should not be counted led to some interesting discussions as to how to define old age. Some rabbis defined it as over the age of 80. Other rabbis claimed that because few reached the age of 70, a man of 60 should be considered old and his widow not a *katlanit*. See also ibid. 46–7.

[42] Engel, *She'elot uteshuvot maharash engel*, pt. 3 no. 117, p. 174, at the end of the responsum.

[43] The rabbis apparently felt that such marriages were no longer dangerous. A recent and thought-provoking article on the relation between halakhah and reality is Soloveitchik, 'Religious Law and Change'.

divorcing wives who otherwise would fall into the category of *katlanit*.[44] As one rabbi wrote, although one might view fatal illness as a sign of bad luck brought by the woman,

. . . today, many act as if they are not at all concerned, and don't ask rabbis, and, therefore, if a rabbi is asked, he should not be concerned [and prohibit such a marriage], because even if he does so, she will find someone who does not care, and in such a case luck has no power—so if someone already asks, we should not be stringent.[45]

He went on to suggest that if such a marriage was with holy intentions, no harm would come of it.

Like Jewish law, the kabbalah was interpreted to accord with accepted behaviour. The negative stand on remarriage expressed by the Zohar, which in some circles was no less revered than normative halakhah, had to be reconciled with the fact that many people, including rabbis, had remarried and that remarriage was the norm. One way this was done was through the unconscious adjustment of tradition to realities, which is characteristic of oral and esoteric traditions.[46] An example from the Sephardi tradition, which was popular in some parts of eastern Europe, of such adjustment was transmitted by Rabbi Hayim Azulai (1724–1806), who quoted an oral tradition of unnamed kabbalists that the remarriage of a widow is undesirable only for twelve months, not for her lifetime.[47] Eastern European kabbalists also relied on lenient precedents, as did, for example, the Vilna Gaon (Eliyahu ben Shelomoh Zalman, 1720–97), who was both a halakhist and a kabbalist.[48] To be sure, as was the case with halakhahists, some kabbalists, like Rabbi Azulai, no doubt felt that the prohibition was correct but unenforceable, and therefore should not be imposed on the community at large. What is significant is the willingness of some to bend their interpretations, not the desire of others to avoid change.

The high point of the reconciliation between remarriage and the kabbalah is to be found in a work written by a hasidic rabbi, Tsevi Elimelekh of Dynow

[44] Kahanov (1817–83), *Netivot hashalom*, 7 n. 4. Of course, it can easily be claimed that a deathbed divorce does not prove that the woman was not responsible for the husband's illness in the first place.

[45] Litwin (1842–1903), *Sha'arei de'ah*, 37*b*, no. 126, near the end. That these questions came up before the rabbis indicates that matchmakers and interested parties were willing to consider such a marriage.

[46] See Goody and Watt, 'The Consequences of Literacy'.

[47] Azulai, *Ḥayim sha'al*, pt. 1, no. 19. R. Azulai himself tended to look with disfavour on any marriage to a widow, and he felt one should not discuss the subject too much.

[48] Eliyahu ben Shelomoh Zalman, *Ma'aseh rav heḥadash*, 17–18, and see the interesting note of the editor there.

(1783–1841),[49] who cited a tradition that the soul of the deceased husband does not rise (in the heavenly spheres) until his widow remarries—if she is still worthy of marriage. In this case the soul of the departed not only does not interfere, but actually stands ready to plead the case of the second husband. In other words, remarriage was not only permitted but desirable. This reasoning was ingenious precisely because it was grounded in the tradition that the Zohar was written by Simon Bar Yohai, and thus predated the Talmud. Therefore, he felt that now marrying a twice-widowed woman was acceptable.

The lively discussions about remarriage, the reliance on recent rabbinic predecessors, and the shortage of 'useful' precedents from earlier, classic legal sources testify to the important role of remarriage in nineteenth-century eastern European Jewish marital behaviour. Jewish remarriage was, of course, not a new phenomenon, but the consistent attempt to enable every presumed *katlanit* to remarry suggests that the demand for remarriage was increasing, or that at least there was growing sensitivity to the problem.

*

No doubt rabbinical encouragement of remarriage was intended in part to prevent extramarital sexual activity. Yet, a concern for sexual activity was perhaps not the only factor motivating those who clamoured for permission to remarry. There were other, pragmatic reasons. For centuries, the Jews of eastern Europe constituted an urban population. Even when they lived in the countryside they were not farmers but worked in 'urban-like' occupations. In this context, where more working hands offered little economic advantage, the nuclear family was the standard.[50] Moreover, housing conditions in towns were not conducive to having older parents living with children. At the same time, relatively high mortality rates created many 'premature' widows and widowers.[51] For many the only alternative to remarriage would have been to

---

[49] Tsevi Elimelekh of Dynow, *Benei yisakhar*, cited in Margaliot, *Nitsotsei zohar*, on *Mishpatim*, 102a. He cited it in the name of his father-in-law, who apparently attributed it to Dov Ber, the Magid of Mezeritch.

[50] See Katz, 'Family, Kinship and Marriage'; Stow, 'The Jewish Family'; Schmidtbauer, 'Household and Household Forms of Viennese Jews', 379.

[51] The data we have on mortality are limited, but the responsa literature indicates that many Jews entered the marriage market more than once. The most extreme case I found is that of a woman who had been married five times. Two of her previous husbands had divorced her, a third had died of apoplexy, a fourth committed suicide, and her fifth had died of old age. Aged 70, she wanted to marry for a sixth time. Albeit this was not a typical case, but one does not get to a sixth wedding in a society that rejects multiple remarriages. See Schick (Maharam Shik, 1807–79), *Responsa*, vol. iii, no. 23.

move in with grown children or to live in loneliness. Remarriage, therefore, was an alternative that provided acceptable living conditions.[52]

Remarriage had a significant impact on the Jewish marriage market,[53] which, like any other, worked on the principle of supply and demand. In the eastern European Jewish community of the mid-nineteenth century, almost all adults were married.[54] This was due to a careful balancing of resources and needs, since not all candidates for marriage were equally attractive. In eastern Europe, as in Jewish societies elsewhere, a woman with no marital experience was generally more attractive than a widow. Intangibles, such as superstition, the fear of sexual comparisons, or a male desire to 'mould' an inexperienced wife may have contributed to this. There were also more tangible reasons. Women marrying for the first time were usually younger than widows or divorcees. Marrying them meant greater potential for progeny and greater economic or domestic productivity. Older men who were more financially established may have had a potential advantage over younger men, since in eastern Europe Jewish matches were based on material considerations no less than on emotional attachment. Some means of controlling the marriage market was thus necessary or many young men would have been competing with widowers, and widows with maidens.[55] In many societies such competition is reduced by the existence of religious orders for men and women, or by military service for men. This, however, goes against the grain of Jewish law and society.

Maximal marriage rates were achieved in eastern European Jewish society because, until the end of the nineteenth century and the onset of heavy

[52] The emphasis on marriage predates the demand to allow remarriage. Moreover, the encouragement of marriage is a central element of the Jewish view of man, while the problem of remarriage and widows is, for all its importance, not. What remains to be examined (though beyond the scope of this chapter) is why the same pressure for remarriage did not exist earlier. One possibility is that in previous centuries the same need for remarriage had existed but, because the Jewish communities were smaller, there were fewer potential partners so the question did not arise as much. Population growth and the rise of larger urban centres may also have facilitated remarriage.

[53] Solid information on the size of the base population would allow us to relate our data to mortality rates and to determine what percentage of those who were eligible really did remarry. However, no such data currently exist. Despite this it is still possible to consider the impact of remarriage on the Jewish marriage market.

[54] Contemporary literature from the period gives the impression that few Jews never married and that few male widowers lived on their own. References to such individuals usually regard them as exceptional. The maiden aunt, for example, was not considered a stock literary figure. An unmarried man was referred to as a *na'ar* (Hebrew and Yiddish for 'boy') no matter what his age. He did not wear a *talit* in synagogue, which emphasized his inferior status.

[55] The marriage of bachelors and widows was possible but not common. It went against the concern for progeny. See below on the negative attitudes of Jewish law to marriages involving a significant difference in age between bride and groom.

emigration, Jewish widowers tended to choose widows when remarrying. Religious legislation provided both a stimulus and support for this. Marriage was forbidden by Jewish law when there was a significant age difference between the bride and groom. Admittedly, legal loopholes made it possible to evade this prohibition, and were employed in certain Jewish communities. However, eastern European rabbis usually argued that tradition required individuals to choose partners of similar age and marital experience and these loopholes were not employed.[56] A widower wishing to remarry was encouraged to choose a partner who also had been previously married. The result was a marriage market in which competition was limited and which generated the maximum number of marriages.[57] As may be seen in Table 3.6, the results were that the percentage of widows and widowers in Jewish society was lower than in other groups, despite early marriage among Jews.

Based on the responsa dealing with the problem of the *katlanit*, on the reinterpretation of kabbalistic teachings, and, perhaps most of all, on statistics of behaviour, it seems that the rabbinic admonition to marry was heeded. Theory and practice, in other words, were congruent and mutually influential.

*

The patterns of remarriage practised by most eastern European Christians and the variables affecting these were quite different from the Jewish patterns.[58] Christian attitudes to marriage were often mixed. Indeed, in Roman Catholicism and Russian Orthodoxy, marriage coexisted with the venerable and institutionalized ideal of celibacy. Marriage itself was often viewed more as a concession than as a desideratum. In practice, of course, most Christians married and celibacy was practised only by a small religious elite. Still, celibacy was a respectable and viable alternative to both marriage and remarriage and therefore there was less pressure among Christians to remarry than among Jews. Moreover, the Russian Orthodox Church discouraged third marriages and forbade fourth marriages.[59] Peasant beliefs ensured that this regulation was generally respected. Like Jews, Russian Orthodox peasants considered widows to be dangerous, superstitiously fearing that 'if

---

[56] *Shulḥan arukh*, 'Even ha'ezer', *Hilkhot periyah ureviyah*, 2: 9. On loopholes and attitudes towards using them, see the commentators there.

[57] The low level of widow–bachelor marriages among Jews is in accord with the tendency for widowers to choose widows. Most bachelors who married widows probably did so for material reasons and because there was a shortage of marriageable younger girls. The widows were seeking a husband and found the market for a man of their age restricted. This should have been less of a problem among Jews than among Christians.

[58] Eastern European Protestants are a special case and are not dealt with in depth here.

[59] Pascu and Pascu, 'Le Remariage', 64.

Table 3.6 Marital status in the tsarist empire by mother tongue, 1897 ('000)

Mother tongue	Unmarried		Married		Widowed		Divorced		Unknown		Ratio	
	M	F	M (1)	F (2)	M (3)	F (4)	M	F	M	F	(4)/(2)	(3)/(1)
Russian	23,090	22,224	16,624	16,818	1,520	3,573	14.4	19.8	22.8	28.7	0.21	0.09
Polish	2,384	2,236	1,457	1,451	88.1	306	1.9	3.3	1.6	2.2	0.21	0.06
Lithuanian/Latvian	927	898	536	545	41.9	144	0.9	1.3	0.6	0.8	0.26	0.08
German	543	516	323	327	17.7	60.8	0.8	1.3	0.4	0.6	0.19	0.05
Yiddish	1,513	1,486	908	935	45.0	156	4.0	12.6	1.5	2.1	0.17	0.05

Key: M = male; F = female.

Source: Calculated on the basis of Troinitsky (ed.), *Obshchii svod po Imperii*, vol. ii, table 16 (pp. 176–81).

God punished once, he can punish again'. As a peasant proverb puts it: 'The first wife comes from God, the second comes from man, and the third comes from the devil.'[60] Thus, while Jews were putting their myth of the *katlanit* to rest, Russian Orthodox peasantry was cultivating a similar myth of its own.

Nevertheless, this myth was frequently offset by necessity. Operating a peasant household efficiently required the presence of both a male, responsible for farming activities, and a female, responsible for domestic work. Thus in Russian Orthodox peasant societies remarriage was accepted when necessary for the household.[61] Peter Czap has noted that Russian Orthodox landlords often pressed widowed peasants to remarry and re-form productive households.[62] Similar attitudes and practices were found in Catholic regions.[63] Christian widows also had good reasons of their own to remarry. A contemporary observer of Russian Orthodox peasant life reported: 'Usually the widow's household was the poorest in the village, as a rule without a horse and a cow, and she and her children were forced to hire themselves out all their life.'[64] A widow could even be evicted from her late husband's house, especially if she did not have children. Sula Benet notes the various options with revealing detail:

When the widow was left with children, her husband's share of the family property was held for her and she usually continued to live with her in-laws. If the family separated, she received a share on an equal basis with her brother-in-law. If, however, at the time of separation the widow was childless, her position was more uncertain. She had two choices, either to return to her family, or, given the opportunity, to remarry. On leaving her late husband's family, she was allowed to take her personal possessions and his clothing. When her relations with her father-in-law were good and he treated her well he might give her a sheep as a dowry for her second marriage.[65]

The main point for us, however, is in the continuation: 'On remarrying, a widow lost her right to her late husband's property. All this was sold and the

---

[60] Mironov, 'Traditional Demographic Behaviour of Peasants' (Russian), 93. He notes that the widows who remarried tended to marry widowers.

[61] Thomas and Znaniecki, *The Polish Peasant*, i. 121.

[62] 'Under pressure from landlords, village communities often took marital affairs into their own hands and arranged matches by lot. This method was used particularly for finding mates for widows and widowers. This was, on the one hand, an incentive to remarriage; on the other hand, it indicates a tendency to avoid remarriage that society felt obligated to counter.' Czap, 'Marriage and the Peasant Joint Family', 115, citing Alexandrov.

[63] The landlord was interested in maximizing production and therefore 'required widowers and widows, and especially the latter, either to remarry or to leave the plot'. Kochanowicz, 'The Polish Peasant Family', 162, and see his sources there. See also Kula, 'The Seigneury and the Peasant Family', 195–7.

[64] Benet (ed. and trans.), *The Village of Viriatino*, 103–4.   [65] Ibid. 103.

proceeds of the sale were distributed among the orphans.'[66] Benet also describes the case of a woman who was widowed after twelve years of marriage:

As long as her little boy was alive she continued to live with the family, but after he
also died, her father-in-law threw her out of the house. She appealed to the head of
the village assembly, but was informed that 'she was entitled to nothing' . . . She was
told: 'Look for a husband. You have nothing coming to you and no one to stand up
for you.'[67]

Another case described involved a woman whose

husband was killed in the Russo-Japanese War [and] she was left with a little girl.
Her father-in-law ordered her out of the house as soon as he received the news of
his son's death. [It was] only when the case came up a second time in the country
court that she received an allotment of land for one person, a horse and a hayloft.[68]

It should be noted that this was in a 'typical' village in the Tambov province
(that is, not in the western provinces). However, see Table 3.7 for data in-
dicating that marital patterns were similar over wide geographic ranges.

Still, remarriage was problematic. Most peasant societies avoid remarriage because of the complicated family problems it can create.[69] Eastern

Table 3.7 Marriage and remarriage among the Russian Orthodox in
the tsarist empire, 1867–1910 (%)

Region	First marriage for both partners	Remarriage for		
		Bride	Groom	Both
1867				
Western provinces	77	5	10	9
Other provinces	77	4	10	9
1885				
Western provinces	82	3	8	7
Other provinces	82	3	9	7
1910				
Western provinces	84	3	7	6
Other provinces	85	2	7	6

Source: Calculated on the basis of Tsentral'nyi statisticheskii komitet, *Dvizhenie
naseleniya v Evropeiskoi Rossii*, vols. for 1867, 1885, 1910.

[66] Benet (ed. and trans.), *The Village of Viriatino*, 104.   [67] Ibid. 103–4.   [68] Ibid. 104.
[69] Davis and Blake, 'Social Structure and Fertility', describe the problem of remarriage in an
agricultural setting: 'It is thus understandable why traditional agrarian societies, especially
where the joint household is normally preferred, should exhibit a prejudice against widow
remarriage. Such unions certainly do occur, particularly in the lower classes which cannot carry
out the joint family ideal, but the prejudice may be strong enough to prevent a high proportion
of widows in the upper classes from remarrying' (pp. 228–9).

European peasants were no exception. Remarriages were often *mésalliances* from the point of view of the family, and for good reason. Normally families had a great influence on first marriages in peasant societies. Less control could be exercised over those who, through a previous marriage, had acquired a measure of independence.[70] At the same time, since their 'market value' was lower, they were less likely to find a 'suitable' match. Opposition to remarriage came from children as well as parents, and in Poland even grown children were known to have opposed their parents' remarrying.[71] Remarriage raised the possibility of alienation from previous familial ties and responsibilities.[72] A widow who took in a husband and stepchildren was thus acting 'against the principle of patrilineality'.[73] Also, the possibility of additional offspring was perceived as a threat to the inheritance of existing children. Since, in a peasant household, there was room for expansion, it was accepted and relatively simple for ageing parents to live with married children. Strong pressure was thus often successfully applied for the single parent to enter his children's household. These pressures were most effective if the prospective bride or groom—that is, the widow or the widower—was already advanced in age and in need of the assistance of older children in running the household.[74]

Both Roman Catholic and Russian Orthodox Christians believed that remarriage was appropriate only up to a certain age. August von Haxthausen commented on a peasant household in the Yaroslavl province in the mid-nineteenth century that consisted of two elderly people, an old widower and a distantly related old widow:

---

[70] Thomas and Znaniecki, *The Polish Peasant*, i. 121.

[71] See Fenomenov, *Sovremennaya derevnya*, ii. 27, and Kula, 'The Seigneury and the Peasant Family', 196.

[72] When Thomas and Znaniecki need examples for the extreme case which can justify breaking the familial principle and the bonds of solidarity which unite parents and children in Catholic families, one of the situations they cite is 'if a widower (or widow) contracts a new marriage in old age and in such a way that instead of assimilating his wife to his own family, he becomes assimilated to hers'. They go on to point out: 'A particular situation is created when a widow or widower with children from the first marriage is involved. Here, assimilation is very difficult, because no longer an individual, but a part of a strange marriage-group, has to be assimilated. At the same time the connection with the widow's or widower's family will be incomplete, because the family of the first husband or wife also has some claims. Therefore, such a marriage is not viewed favorably, and there must be some real social superiority of the future partner and his or her family in order to counterbalance the inferiority caused by the peculiar familial situation' (*The Polish Peasant*, i. 95).

[73] Mitterauer and Kagan, 'Russian and Central European Family Structures', 115.

[74] The conditions of Jewish life naturally encourage different attitudes to remarriage. The general acceptance of remarriage of Jews made *mésalliance* less of a threat. The greater geographical mobility of Jews may also have led to less tension after remarriage. The fact that Jews did not work the land or bequeath it was also an important difference.

The Russian cannot live without secure family ties; if he has no family, he creates a substitute . . . One might ask why the old man did not marry the elderly woman, so that at least an outer bond, that of stepfatherhood, could have been established. Custom in these regions does not tolerate this, however, and considers it improper for a widower or a widow beyond fifty to remarry.[75]

Functional equivalents to remarriage were often preferred to remarriage itself. In fact, Russian Orthodox peasants were predisposed to such alternatives, accustomed as they were to complex households made up of many individuals with varied relationships. One way to 'replace' a deceased wife of the head of a household was to marry off a son, even a very young one, and to assign his young wife—who joined her husband's household—the domestic responsibilities previously shouldered by his mother. In Russian Orthodox circles young boys were often matched with much older women. Twenty-four-year-old wives were even known to carry around their 6-year-old 'husbands'.[76] Arrangements like this were not necessarily grim for the young wife, who was frequently better off marrying a motherless boy than risking being dominated by her mother-in-law. However, such extreme solutions were not the norm, and widowers often remarried. Nevertheless, these remarriages are reported to have taken place only in order to have someone 'to light the oven', that is, to serve as housekeeper.[77] Needs for companionship, sexual activity, or fertility were considered irrelevant.[78]

*

As seen above, Roman Catholics and Russian Orthodox did not have identical marital patterns. Marriages where one party was marrying for the first time and the other for a second were more common among Roman Catholics than among Russian Orthodox. On the other hand, marriages in which both parties were remarrying were more frequent among the Russian Orthodox. Explaining these differences is not easy. It is tempting to try to relate differing rates of remarriage to the different frameworks of family and inheritance among Russian Orthodox and Roman Catholics.[79] In post-emancipation

[75] Haxthausen, *Studies on the Interior of Russia*, 67–8.

[76] See the source cited in Mitterauer and Kagan, 'Russian and Central European Family Structures', 118. In the peasant community of Gadyshi (Novgorod province), for example, it was common practice to marry off young sons after the death of a mother/householder. Fenomenov, *Sovremennaya derevnya*, ii. 20. The reader is cautioned that the citations here refer to peasant patterns in the interior of Russia, not in the western provinces, and that regional variations cannot be ruled out. [77] Ibid. 21.

[78] I did not find reports of similar surrogates for remarriage among Catholic peasants, but they may have existed. If not, it is not clear what the alternatives were, if any, to a remarriage undertaken to solve the problems arising after the death of a householder.

[79] Such a possibility was raised in a somewhat different context by Chojnacka, 'Nuptiality

Polish society, sons divided their father's land and each worked his own plot.[80]
It was not rare for peasant children to delay marriage until the father was
willing to turn over his farm to his children, since only then could children
become self-supporting. Russian Orthodox peasant society in the interior of
Russia operated in a very different context, that of the *mir*, a framework for
communal ownership of land that provided for its periodic redistribution.
Haxthausen described it thus:

The forests and pasture land always remain undivided; the plowlands and meadows
are apportioned to the various families in the commune, who, however, do not own
the land but have only the right to use it temporarily. Formerly, the lands may have
been redistributed annually among the married couples of the community, each
receiving a share equal to all the others in terms of quality. Today [mid-19th
century], however, in order to avoid expenses and great inconveniences, the land is
reapportioned after a certain number of years. If, for example, a father should die
and leave six sons who are not of age, the widow generally continues to manage the
farm until her sons marry. Then, however, they do not divide among themselves the
plot which their father had cultivated; instead, this land reverts to the commune,
and all six sons receive a share equal to that held by the other members of the
community. All together, they might hold five to six times the amount of land which
their father had held. If the six sons should marry when their father is still alive, then
he claims for each one of them an equal allotment of the communal land. Since the
sons continue to live in the same household with their father, he does not have to
worry about establishing them. On the contrary, a marriage is fortunate for the
family. Even if she has no dowry, the arrival of a daughter-in-law means an
additional share of the communal property. The marriage and establishment of his
daughters is thus the least of a Russian peasant's worries.[81]

However, relating the *mir* and partible inheritance to remarriage patterns is
problematic. There were many landless peasants in Poland whose marital

Patterns in an Agrarian Society'. The paper is fascinating. A relationship between family and
inheritance was typical of other marriage systems. Holderness, 'Widows in Pre-Industrial Society', 429, writes: 'It is evident that the frequency of second or subsequent marriages was inhibited by customs and attitudes affecting the transmission of property, despite the real needs for
remarriage that were manifest in the overt experience of rural or small-town society in early
modern times.' The data he has from England and France indicate that about 10% of the marriages between the 17th and 19th centuries were remarriages; he sees 15% as an upper limit. In
his sample approximately 13% of the grooms were widowers and 8% were widows (ibid. 431).
This is, of course, a much lower percentage than that indicated by our data. This may be due to
faulty data reporting, but it seems to be more likely that there were different mortality patterns
in eastern Europe. For a precise definition of the term 'household', see Hajnal, 'Two Kinds of
Pre-Industrial Household Formation', 69 n. 7. The Russian term *khozyaistvo* fits his sense
precisely.

[80] See Thomas and Znaniecki, *The Polish Peasant*, i. 161. On the implications of this system
for early marriage see Sklar, 'The Role of Marriage Behaviour'.

[81] Haxthausen, *Studies on the Interior of Russia*, 279.

behaviour was not determined by patterns of land inheritance.[82] Moreover, in the western provinces, Russian Orthodox peasantry was not organized within the *mir*, but passed rights to land or land ownership from generation to generation, just like the Catholics.[83] Had inheritance determined marriage patterns, the marital patterns of Russian Orthodox peasants in the western provinces should have resembled those of their Catholic neighbours and would have differed from those of Russian Orthodox peasants in the other parts of the Russian empire, where the *mir* was more common. Nevertheless, as Table 3.7 shows, the remarriage rates of the two Russian Orthodox peasantries had much in common and were unlike the rates among Catholics.[84]

In the *mir* system, which provided for the redistribution of land and larger allotments for large families, the remarriage of a parent and the prospect of more children did not threaten the interests of grown children. There should have been less of a reason for Russian Orthodox members of a *mir* to oppose remarriage than for Catholics. If inheritance patterns were crucial in determining remarriage patterns, remarriage should have been significantly more common among Russian Orthodox in the non-western parts of the Russian empire than among both Russian Orthodox and Roman Catholics in the western provinces, but this was not the case.[85] Other factors, probably cultural, were at play.

Another likely cause for differences in patterns of remarriage was age at first marriage. Just as patterns of remarriage differed among various groups, so did patterns of age at marriage, as may be seen from Table 3.8. A causal relationship between age at marriage and the rate of remarriage is not outside

---

[82] On landless peasants see, for example, Kieniewicz, *The Emancipation of Polish Peasantry*, 145–6.

[83] Male, *Russian Peasant Organization before Collectivization*, 52, notes that there was no communal organization in Belorussia. In *Rural Russia under the Old Regime*, Geroid Robinson states: 'Among the peasants of Lithuania, White Russia, and Little Russia or Ukraina, equalization by repartition was little known' (p. 35). Volin, *A Century of Russian Agriculture*, 92, discusses the possible impact of the *mir* system as a stimulant for population growth.

[84] Table 3.8 shows that there was much more early marriage among males and somewhat more among females in internal Russia (including Siberia, the Caucasus, and other regions, but not, of course, the western provinces, which were mainly the Pale of Settlement), where the *mir* system was more common. It should be noted that the population of the non-western provinces was mainly Russian-speaking and Russian Orthodox, and living in or stemming from central Russia.

[85] Age at marriage should also have been affected by the availability of land. The *mir* system provided for easier access to land; thus one might expect that marriage would be undertaken at an earlier age in communities where the *mir* system was common. Nonetheless, Orthodox Russians in the western provinces tended to marry at earlier ages than other peasant populations even though they did not live in the framework of the *mir*. See Table 3.8. This also suggests that land was not the only factor.

Table 3.8 Age at marriage in the tsarist empire as a whole and in the western provinces, by religion, 1867 (% of all marriages)

	Total no. of marriages ('000)	Age 20 or less		Age 21–25	
		M	F	M	F
All empire					
Jews	16.0	43	61	26	21
Russian Orthodox	538.0	40	59	32	26
Protestants	14.8	7	27	32	37
Catholics	23.3	8	39	32	33
Western provinces					
Jews	15.9	44	61	26	21
Russian Orthodox	163.1	22	51	43	31
Protestants	4.8	5	26	34	39
Catholics	22.6	8	39	32	33

Key: M = male; F = female.

Source: Calculated on the basis of Tsentral'nyi statisticheskii komitet, *Dvizhenie naseleniya v Evropeiskoi Rossii*, vols. for 1867, 1885, 1910.

the realm of possibility. When mortality of young adults is more than minimal, a low average age at first marriage means that there will be more young widows and widowers who will be prime candidates for remarriage.[86] Among Jews, the high rate of remarriage went along with early marriage; among Protestants, there were lower rates of remarriage with fewer early marriages. However, although Russian Orthodox often married at an earlier age than did Catholics, their remarriage rate was lower.[87] In short, there is no

[86] Statistics from the end of the 19th century for the Orthodox population indicate that the pattern described in the ethnographic literature, of a significant level of remarriage in certain age groups, still held. Of widowed individuals aged 15–25, close to half remarried in 1896–7. Of those aged 26–35, 11% remarried. In the 36–45 age group, only 4% remarried. This is despite that fact that in the older groups, widowers, and especially widows, constituted a large proportion of those marrying simply because few reached those ages still single. Male behaviour was almost the same in towns and villages. In the younger age groups, minimal percentages of the grooms were widowers, and in the older age bracket, 50–59, approximately 10% were widowers. There were significant differences in the behaviour of village and town women. In the older age bracket, half of all urban women marrying were widows, while less then a third of peasant women marrying were widows. This was the case in the younger age groups as well. While this pattern certainly was affected by the numbers of available marital partners, it seems that there was a link between life in the countryside and the choice of partners. See Tolts, 'Marriage Rate of the Russian Population', 148. The data for the percentage of those married among Catholics and Orthodox reflect patterns similar to those reflected in our data on remarriage. In 1897 Poles in the western provinces had consistently lower percentages of married people than did Ukrainians (i.e. Orthodox). See Coale, Anderson, and Harm, *Human Fertility in Russia*, 159.

[87] Why one group marries earlier then another (see Table 3.8), or has a more positive attitude to marriage, is a question for future study. It may be tied to the need for security, to subtle

simple explanation for patterns of remarriage, and probably many factors were simultaneously at work, including cultural and material ones.

The impact of various marital patterns on the wider community was considerable. Patterns of remarriage, like those of celibacy,[88] influence fertility, quality of life, and possibly child mortality. The impact of remarriage on fertility is influenced by its demographic context. This was clearly demonstrated in a sophisticated simulation of human behaviour under varying constraints of mortality and remarriage patterns that was constructed by Henri Léridon. He concluded that whatever affects marital status during the childbearing years has a significant impact on fertility.[89] The higher the life expectancy, for example, the greater was the influence of remarriage on fertility, because remarriage added years to the reproductive cycle.[90] Moreover, early first marriage, which expands the potential for childbearing, even further increases the positive impact of remarriage on fertility.[91] Thus, since the Russian Orthodox married earlier than Roman Catholics, an identical remarriage rate should have had a more positive impact on their fertility rates.[92] Patterns of mate selection should also affect the impact of remarriage on fertility. As Ansley Coale has pointed out: 'The remarriage of widowers (to young girls), when it occurs, does displace what would otherwise be the marriage of younger men. The effect of the remarriage of widowers is to reduce fertility because if often leads to a large difference between husband and wife in age at marriage.'[93] Given the clear correspondence between remarriage rates and fertility rates, remarriage should have had a more positive influence on Jewish fertility than on any other group of the four studied here. Jews

differences in religious thought, or to patterns of inheritance. A valuable study on this topic is Dixon, 'Explaining Cross-Cultural Variations in Age at Marriage'.

[88]   For the effect of celibacy on populations, which is the direct opposite of high remarriage rates, see Weir, 'Rather Never Than Late'.

[89]   Léridon, 'Effets du veuvage et du remariage', 605–14.

[90]   Léridon found that in a model of an early-marrying society with low mortality, the final number of children in a pattern of no remarriage was 6.54; with high remarriage rates it was 7.24. In a late-marrying society with no remarriage the number was 4.08, with high remarriage at 4.52. See ibid., tables 2 and 3 (pp. 611 and 612).

[91]   In the simulation, the absolute rise in fertility due to a high level of remarriage, given a life expectancy of 45 years, was about 10% in both early and late marriage. There were significant variations in the degree to which remarriage compensated for the possible loss in fertility had the surviving spouse not remarried. Under conditions of short life expectancy and late marriage, high rates of remarriage made up for only 20% of the shortfall in fertility caused by mortality (21% loss with remarriage; 27% without). Under conditions of moderate life expectancy, remarriage compensated for about 40% of the potential loss (14% instead of 22%). Under conditions of early marriage, close to 50% was compensated for (9% instead of 18%).

[92]   This is assuming that the mortality rate was similar in both groups. There is no reason to assume otherwise.

[93]   Coale, introduction to Part III of Dupâquier et al. (eds.), *Marriage and Remarriage*, 155.

married earlier,[94] remarried more often, and lived longer[95] than members of other groups. For most of the century, they also had the highest levels of remarriage of widows. This meant that the potential fertility of these widows was realized to a greater degree than that of their counterparts in other religious-ethnic groups. Moreover, with widowers marrying widows, maidens were free to marry bachelors, and their fertility, too, could be fully realized. Accordingly, it seems safe to assume that a high rate of remarriage contributed significantly to the high rate of population growth among Jews in the late nineteenth century.

Remarriage can also be a contributing factor in reducing child mortality.[96] The descriptions of single-parent families, especially those headed by women, suggest that their lives were particularly difficult. The life expectancy of children in such households was less than that of children reared in families with two parents. It seems that the better the chances a widow had of remarrying, the better the chances her children had to survive.[97] Notwithstanding the ubiquitous horror stories about cruel stepmothers, which no doubt reflect real and deep fears in a society that knew high mortality, a step-parent was probably considered to be better than no parent at all. One reason that contemporary rabbis endorsed remarriage even for a twice-widowed woman was their unquestioned assumption that fatherless children are endangered.[98]

Remarriage patterns also affect the quality of life of the ageing. The responsa contain numerous examples of women marrying sick or infirm older men for reasons of mutual succour. A marital partnership can indeed create more interest in life, which in turn can promote greater life expectancy.[99] The positive impact of remarriage should have been most significant for older Jews. In contrast to older Roman Catholics or Russian Orthodox, older Jews usually did not live in the homes of their children. Multi-generation residence patterns that are common in stable agricultural communities are not practical in an urban population, especially in one characterized by high mobility and limited housing space. By remarrying, Jews were saved from becoming burdens on their children or superfluous supernumeraries. They enjoyed independence and its psychological benefits. The Jewish remarriage pattern,

[94] It cannot be claimed that child marriages created more young widows, since such marriages occurred only among a small elite

[95] Of course, if mortality among Jews was higher, which does not appear to be the case at this stage, this would have offset the advantage of the high remarriage rate. For estimates on life expectancy see Bloch, 'Vital Events among the Jews in European Russia'.

[96] On this topic see the standard study of Schmelz, *Infant and Early Childhood Mortality*.

[97] Measuring the correlation between remarriage and child mortality is not easy, given the problematic nature of our data and the difficulty of isolating variables.

[98] See Twersky, *Emek she'elah*, 198, end of no. 16, cited in n. 31.

[99] This, of course, is even harder to measure.

like the non-Jewish ones, almost certainly had an effect on the redistribution of wealth. It also may have helped reinforce the traditionally Jewish symbiosis between wealth and scholarship.[100]

*

Remarriage rates declined during the second half of the nineteenth century in each of the populations studied. Studies for other regions have shown that a declining adult mortality rate may perforce produce a corresponding decline in the rate of remarriage.[101] The adult mortality rate probably decreased in the tsarist empire in the second half of the nineteenth century; if so, this would have been a factor in the decline in the rate of remarriage. Another probable cause was migration. While the shift in remarriage rates began before the heaviest migration occurred, the departure of a great number of young Jewish men from the marriage market no doubt accelerated the process. Indeed, Jewish migration was proportionally higher than in other groups in the tsarist empire. The result was greater competition for husbands among women left behind, and widows were at a disadvantage. The evidence in Table 3.3 suggests such an explanation. Migrants poured out of the northern provinces to other parts of the tsarist empire and to overseas. Other regions had proportionally less emigration, and were even targets for migrants.[102] Another possible factor was a shift in values. A careful study of patterns of remarriage in fourteen German villages in the eighteenth and nineteenth centuries suggests that marriage rates declined not only due to changed market factors but to changing marital ideals and expectations.[103] What characterized German peasants on this point may also have characterized east European Jews.

[100] The following tale, told in a sermon, illustrates this point. 'I know that there are those who mumble about me because I married a woman the *Shulḥan arukh* said I should not [i.e. a *katlanit*], and they think that I did so because she was rich. In truth, she only had three thousand, and the Lord knows the truth that for several years I could not find a wife and I was a fatherless orphan, and the Lord led me upon a woman who was willing to undertake to support me so that I could devote myself to the study of Torah and the service of God; and thank goodness I devoted myself to the Torah from 1848 until 1891, and I had students . . . and two daughters were born to me, although because of my sins they were taken from me. I moved from place to place, and when I saw there was no longer hope for sons I spoke to my wife about getting a divorce, and she cried, saying that she had borne me two daughters, and I went to the great rabbi of Sanz, and he said that since she had borne two daughters and she cried, that I should do whatever she said' (Naftali Sofer, *Likutei beit efrayim*, no. 4, 6a–b). See also his interesting discussion of sexuality. The same function of distributing wealth was achieved by widow–bachelor weddings. These were more common among Christians than among Jews.

[101] Knodel and Lynch, 'The Decline of Remarriage'.

[102] See Stampfer, 'East European Jewish Migration'.

[103] Knodel and Lynch, 'The Decline of Remarriage', 57.

The importance of remarriage, as both a factor and indicator, is clear. Different population groups in the tsarist empire in the late nineteenth century exhibited distinctive patterns of remarriage that cannot be related to material conditions or patterns of distribution of wealth only. The particularly high rate of remarriage among Jews reflected their urban-geographic distribution and economic structure, and also may have played a role in the rapid Jewish population growth at the time. Moreover, parallel to changes in society, in the economy, and in modes of communication and transportation that occurred between 1867 and 1910, Jewish patterns of remarriage gradually were standardized throughout the empire. Roman Catholic and Russian Orthodox patterns of remarriage had standardized long before, which was probably a reflection of centuries of stable agrarian life, fixed customs, and religious beliefs. In the case of the Jews, changing circumstances may have modified religious standards and values. Whatever the stimuli, however, between 1867 and 1910 levels of remarriage among all groups dropped, so that by the first decade of the twentieth century, levels of remarriage among Jews and non-Jews were similar. Although perhaps not a dramatic issue, remarriage is nevertheless an important phenomenon and a useful indicator of behaviour.

FOUR

Scientific Welfare and Lonely Old People: The Development of Old-Age Homes

O N SUNDAY 17 MAY 1846 Moses Montefiore spent a day in Warsaw en route to England after a meeting with Tsar Nicholas in St Petersburg. What sights of the city did the local Jewish leadership choose to show him? According to Louis Loewe, who later published a summary of Montefiore's journals, 'in order to show how desirous the Jews here are, under the most unfavorable circumstances, to promote the welfare of their poorer brethren, Sir Moses gives a long description of the hospital . . . and of Mr. Matthias Rosen's Aged Needy Asylum and speaks in terms of the highest praise of all the arrangements'.[1] Montefiore was clearly impressed by what was considered at the time to be a most innovative institution: a home for the needy Jewish aged. In fact, the old-age home in Warsaw had been founded only a few years earlier, and at the time of Montefiore's visit it was probably the only such Jewish facility in all of eastern Europe. In the course of time, however, more and more such institutions were founded, until the old-age home became a standard component of Jewish communal organization, and even a stock institution in Yiddish literature.[2] By tracing its historical development it will be possible to clarify the place of the elderly in the Jewish family, along with broader issues of communal organization.

THE ELDERLY IN THE TRADITIONAL FAMILY STRUCTURE OF EAST EUROPEAN JEWRY

In traditional east European Jewish society before the mid-nineteenth century the elderly usually neither lived with their children nor resided in institutions. They lived on their own; contrary to common belief, the typical

[1] A few days earlier Montefiore had been in Vilna. There, too, he had visited the Jewish hospital and the orphan asylum, along with the Romm printing house and various schools (he also visited schools in Warsaw). See Loewe (ed.), *Diaries of Sir Moses and Lady Montefiore*, 345, 351.

[2] See the clearest case, Shalom Aleikhem (pseudonym of Shalom Rabinovitz), *Council of Elders* (Heb.), in which he describes the old-age home in the imaginary town of Kasrilivke.

Jewish household consisted solely of a husband, wife, and their young children.[3] When children were old enough to support themselves they usually
married and went off to live on their own, while their parents remained an
independent economic unit. This pattern, which had been typical for many
generations, was one that distinguished east European Jews from the
predominantly agricultural populations among whom they lived.[4]

As noted above, agricultural societies were indeed characterized by multigenerational households, for reasons that were basically economic.[5] There
are times during the year when farmers need many working hands for a short
period. Families which had sufficient parents, children, and grandparents did
not have to hire outside labour (which was not always available at harvest
time) or cut production. Moreover, the framework of the expanded family
answered the problem of land hunger. Young farmers would receive the
family land from parents in return for commitments to support their parents
for the rest of their lives.[6] The accepted practice was for parents to continue
living under one roof with their children and it was not difficult, if necessary,
to expand a farmhouse to accommodate more than one family unit.

Although many Jews lived in villages, they were not peasants and thus
there were few advantages to having parents residing with their adult
children.[7] In the so-called Jewish occupations connected with business,
services, or crafts, there was little to be gained by the involvement of more
than one generation in the family business or workshop (unless the business
was a large trading enterprise, but these were rare).[8] A shoemaker could teach
his son his trade, but there was no economic advantage to having two

[3] See the classic formulation in Katz, *Tradition and Crisis*.

[4] Mahler, *Statistics about Jews in Former Poland* (Yid.), is still the most useful description. A
number of researchers are compiling residence lists of Jews in eastern Europe. When these lists
are finished, our knowledge of family structure will be much more complete.

[5] See e.g. the many discussions of this theme in Wall (ed.), *Family Forms in Historic Europe*.
Farmers do not automatically develop multigenerational families, and it is important to
note that in much of Europe multigenerational families were not the standard even in the pre-
industrial period. See Mitterauer and Sieder, *The European Family*, ch. 2. The authors note,
however, that multigenerational families were common in eastern Europe, and it is this phenomenon that I analyse here.

[6] See the discussion in Stampfer, 'Remarriage among Jews and Christians', the article on
which Chapter 3 above is based.

[7] The practice of early marriage in which a young couple lived with the parents of the bride
was only an apparent exception since it was a temporary arrangement that was formally limited
in time. Moreover, it was designed to provide a framework for a young couple until they were
ready to go out on their own: assistance, in other words, was provided to the young couple
rather than to the parents.

[8] Even the inheritance of the rabbinate, which I have explored in the article on which the
present Chapter 14 is based, 'The Inheritance of the Rabbinate in Eastern Europe in the Modern Period', was a phenomenon that usually took place after the death or disablement of a rabbi
and not usually in his lifetime.

shoemakers working in the same stall rather than in separate stalls. Similarly, a Jewish-run tavern could often support only one family. Additionally, most Jewish trades were not dependent on manual labour, so that older parents could continue to be economically active even in old age without having to transfer some of the more strenuous parts of the work to their children. Finally, since Jews tended to live in cities or towns, often in rented apartments, providing living quarters for an extended family was no simple matter and hence never became the norm.[9]

Differences between the family patterns of Jews and non-Jewish peasants are reflected in the levels of migration to be found in traditional east European Jewish society. High mobility is more characteristic of nuclear rather than of extended families. Whereas peasants in eastern Europe were often tied to the land, the Jews exhibited a high rate of mobility—a consequence, at least in part, of the constant growth in Jewish population that resulted in increased competition in the traditional occupations. Almost every biography of a nineteenth-century east European Jew is built like an itinerary: the subject being born in one place, studying in another, marrying in yet another, and typically moving several times in the course of finding a livelihood. Although biographies naturally tend to be devoted to individuals from the higher socio-economic strata, statistical data back up the impression of high mobility. The 1897 census of the tsarist empire, for example, indicates that about half of the Jews were not living where they were born, and this figure does not take local migration into account.[10]

The pattern of high mobility and nuclear families also found expression in the marked tendency towards remarriage among Jews, as was discussed in Chapter 3. More than any other group in the tsarist empire, Jews were likely to remarry in the event of the death of a spouse. This was not because their mortality was higher, but rather that there was greater social support and acceptance of remarriage among the Jews. Whereas young peasants would often actively oppose the remarriage of a father who was a widower for fear that it might delay transfer of the all-important land, remarriage among Jews was regarded as an excellent means of ensuring parents' continued self-sufficiency.[11] Hence, in the Jewish context, older parents retained their autonomy and self-esteem for as long as possible. Though difficult to measure it

---

[9] Descriptions of multigenerational households such as that provided by Shomer-Zunser in her memoir *Yesterday*, ch. 1, tend to be of affluent families whose sons were groomed to go into the family business.

[10] See Stampfer, 'Patterns of Internal Jewish Migration'. Many peasants also migrated during this period. However, migration for them often precipitated crises in family structure. Migrant peasants were often single or else left their wives at home. Jewish families, who tended to migrate as a unit, were far less affected.

[11] See Stampfer, 'Remarriage among Jews and Christians'.

would seem likely that the independence of parents contributed to their relatively long life expectancy.[12]

Another reflection, both of the absence of extended family structures among Jews and of a readiness to forgo the warmth and support of intergenerational ties, can be found in a somewhat unexpected area—the patterns of higher education among the children of Jewish immigrants to the United States. Jewish immigrants tended to encourage their children to get a higher education, seeing this as a way to speed socio-economic advancement. Among other immigrant groups, however, it was common for parents to discourage their children from aspiring to higher education out of a fear, often justified, that educated children would drift away from their families. The impressive level of higher education among Jews contributed to a rise in the income and status of children of the second generation, albeit at the cost of considerable estrangement from their parents. This cost, however, was not only anticipated, but to some extent accepted. Even back in the old country, east European Jews did not expect to continue living with their parents indefinitely.[13]

The description above is a far cry from the popular, nostalgic image of a multigenerational Jewish family. In a typical description of the modern Jewish family in America, residents of old-age homes at the beginning of the twentieth century were viewed with pity as 'the aged who were lone and childless or too sick to be cared for in their children's homes'. The 'normal' condition, it was assumed, was for dependent parents to live with their offspring; members of that generation 'often recalled grandparents—newly arrived or living with them in three-generation homes—cherished, included, worked with, and supported by the family'. The rise in the number of old-age homes was seen as an indication of 'the urbanization of this mass immigration with the concomitant problems of family change, housing and human needs' as 'the place of the grandparent also shifted. Older Jews began to seek life outside their children's homes as a matter of choice'.[14] In reality, family patterns in America were not very different from those of Europe. So much in America really *was* novel, however, that the pattern of separate residence of parents came to be perceived incorrectly—as a novelty. The reality was that old-age homes in America continued Old World patterns.

Another common and related misconception about Jewish family structure in Europe is that it was patriarchal,[15] in the sense that power and

---

[12] For data on the longer life expectancy of Jews, see Bloch, 'Vital Events among the Jews in European Russia'. [13] See Kessner, *The Golden Door*, 95–9. [14] See Lederman, 'The Jewish Aged', 326–7. I have focused on remarks that are not central to her argument but which are interesting to me as indicative of common assumptions about traditional Jewish family structure. See similar statements in Schlesinger, 'The Jewish Family in Retrospect'. [15] Schlesinger, 'The Jewish Family in Retrospect', 13.

authority were concentrated in the father's hands. This was far from the case for Jewish families in eastern Europe. (See Chapter 6.) What was true was that adult males had a central role in ritual functions and in the synagogue, but when it came to major life decisions—whether to migrate or not, what match to make for children, how children should be educated—wives very often had as much influence as their husbands. Sometimes women had a greater influence, since they often decided how money was to be spent. The ideal, though it was rarely realized, was of a husband who devoted himself to Torah, supported by a wife who made all of the decisions related to the practical world. Thus, whereas there was a ritualistic patriarchy, the real-world reality was far more complex, and in many cases it was close to a matriarchy. This situation, with its attendant social stresses, led to a comparatively high divorce rate within traditional Jewish society.[16]

Modern Jews, in sum, have tended to reconstruct their picture of the past on the basis of models that reflected the wider and predominantly agricultural society. The popular view that most Jews once lived in shtetls, just as non-Jews lived in farm villages, is yet another aspect of this phenomenon. Although most Jews lived in an urban environment, the shtetl image, and the 'memory' of the patriarchal, multi-generational family, remain the most common 'memories' of the east European Jewish past.

The family structure and behaviour patterns did not change overnight in Jewish or general society, though both underwent modernization and urbanization. However, the relative weight of the rural and urban sectors in eastern Europe changed radically in the nineteenth and twentieth centuries. For many, the move to the city was a traumatic change that required several generations to be assimilated. City dwellers of peasant background transmitted traditional rural values to their children. Hence the widespread custom of urban Russians to employ a *nyanya* (nanny) or to turn to a grandmother to take care of the children. This was a continuation of the patterns developed in rural peasant households, just as the old-age home perpetuated traditional Jewish patterns.

CARE FOR THE AGED: TRADITIONAL AND 'MODERN' APPROACHES

Traditionally, the social welfare needs of the indigent or the ill in east European Jewish communities were attended to directly in their homes.[17] Pious women would often bring food to needy individuals and help meet other needs on an ad hoc basis, and neighbours could also help. This was a

---

[16] See Chapter 2 above. See also the fine studies by Freeze, 'The Litigious Gerusha', and *Jewish Marriage and Divorce in Imperial Russia*.   [17] Levitats, *The Jewish Community in Russia*.

practical and uncomplicated approach to social welfare. It maximized the number of recipients and led to the direct involvement of many volunteers, with no overhead or administrative costs. What may seem to be a drawback of this system—the absence of professional medical care—was not significant, given that in general the level of medical assistance in traditional Jewish society was not very high.

In the pre-old-age-home era, some of the indigent or homeless elderly also made use of *hekdeshim*.[18] These were huts or small buildings that were designated to provide housing for travellers and for the homeless. *Hekdeshim* had a negative image and were notorious for their poor and filthy conditions. This may have been the result of limited resources but perhaps there was an implicit assumption that if conditions were too good in the *hekdeshim*, there would be no stimulus for the poor to work. At the same time, there was rarely a time limit placed on residence in a *hekdesh*, perhaps because such regulations would depend on an administrative structure to enforce them. Since *hekdeshim* were generally not legally recognized institutions, they were often not supported by funds from the *korobka*, the Jewish communal tax income. More 'modern' elements of the community regarded *hekdeshim* as antiquated institutions that had no place in the newly budding philanthropic structure of the Jewish community.

A home for the aged was not a *hekdesh*. Whereas almost anyone who wanted to could find refuge, at least for a night, in a *hekdesh*, a home for the aged had a formal procedure for accepting residents. The basic criterion for admission was advanced age, which naturally excluded travellers, the homeless, the insane, and other types who often populated a *hekdesh*. In contrast to the minimalist *hekdesh*, a home for the aged provided not only housing but regular meals and cultural, religious, and medical services. The physical structure was also quite different: a home for the aged had rooms with furniture and a dining facility. Some also had a garden, a room equipped as a synagogue, and an examining room for doctors and patients. Certain old-age homes were quite large, housing hundreds of residents. Whereas the *hekdesh* was seen as traditional in the negative sense of being primitive and outmoded, homes for the aged were regarded as a modern and rational solution to the problem of guaranteeing care for the elderly.

Of course, the home for the aged was not a Jewish invention. Hospices for aged priests of the Catholic Church are known to have existed from the thirteenth century.[19] Neither did the Jewish use of old-age homes originate in eastern Europe: the first Jewish home for the aged may have been the one founded in Rome in 1682; while in Germany from the mid-eighteenth

[18] On the early history of the *hekdesh*, see Marcus, *Communal Sick-Care in the German Ghetto*.
[19] Minois, *History of Old Age*, 188.

century onwards, various Jewish communities opened such homes (for example, Hamburg in 1763, Fürth in 1770, Berlin in 1829, and Frankfurt in 1840).[20] Similarly, Jewish homes for the aged were established in America starting from the mid-nineteenth century.[21]

The first Jewish home for the aged in eastern Europe seems to have been the one visited by Montefiore, which was founded by Matthias Rosen in Warsaw in 1840.[22] The stimulus for its establishment was a government initiative of 1838 intended to deal with orphans and the needy, many of the latter being elderly. At first this institution was funded to a large extent by some rich and highly acculturated Warsaw Jews; in a later period it was even regarded as motivated by assimilationist goals. The Warsaw Jews were naturally aware of trends in the West, and it stands to reason that the home was modelled after what was considered modern social welfare practice in the West. After a few years, the Warsaw Jewish community began to participate in its funding.

The Warsaw home was intended to provide housing for both orphans and the aged. In the first two decades of its existence, 1,913 orphans and 1,135 elderly found shelter in the institution. In the course of time, however, it appears that more and more attention was given to orphans.[23] In 1910 a separate home was founded in Warsaw for the elderly Jews who had higher education. Its statutes provided for a minimal age of 60 to qualify for admission, and for at least three years of previous residence in Warsaw. Although the requirement for higher education seems to have been unique to Warsaw, the attempt to introduce formal admission standards fits the atmosphere of the time.[24]

The founders of the Warsaw home apparently saw the main function of the institution as providing housing. Thus they did not at first differentiate between the needs of the very young and those of the very old. Although there may have been some benefit in sharing a common kitchen, in other respects it proved more desirable to have separate institutions. Over time, Jews with a

[20] *Jüdisches Lexikon*, i. 253, s.v. 'Altersversorgung'.
[21] On Jewish homes for the aged in the United States, see Zelditch, 'Trends in the Care of the Aged'. I have not been able to find a detailed history of the institution of old-age homes. Some useful information can be found in Gold and Kaufman, 'Development of Care of the Elderly'. The authors note that the first Jewish old-age home in the United States was founded in 1855 in St Louis (p. 272). I am grateful for the assistance of Julie Goldberg of the Brookdale library at the JDC in tracking down this article.
[22] The description of this institution is based on the fine study by Sabina Levin, 'The First Jewish Home for Orphans and the Elderly in Warsaw' (Heb.). Levin quite understandably focuses on the educational programme for the orphans rather than on the services provided to the elderly.
[23] Over the course of its third decade, the institution cared for 981 orphans and 519 elderly: see ibid. 57. [24] *Sprawozdanie za rok 1927—Towarzystwo 'Dom Starców' w Warszawie*, 5.

Western orientation began to view the multi-function home as less than ideal.[25] At the outset, however, this was not obvious and the Warsaw home was not the only Jewish institution to combine care for orphans and the aged. A hostel that provided minimal housing for travellers was founded in Będzin in 1900; in 1905 its mandate was expanded to provide for orphans and the aged, and a year later it was providing services to thirty orphans and ten elderly people. In the course of time the institution concentrated on orphans. At an even later date, in the 1930s, this combination of meeting the needs of the very young and the very old worked in Radom.[26] In Karlin, orphans took their meals in the local old-age home.[27] However, from the late nineteenth century onwards it seems that the separation of orphans and the aged became more and more the norm.

The second home for the Jewish aged to be opened in eastern Europe in a major community was apparently that of Vilna, which was founded in 1864. Until then, Jews in Vilna without housing had turned to a *hekdesh* of two rooms attached to the Jewish hospital. In 1864 a separate home for the aged was founded, with a charter approved by the government. The home housed about thirty residents, and much of its funding came from the *korobka* tax. In the 1870s, and even more so in later years, it received substantial donations from rich Jews in Vilna—mostly highly acculturated—who were also on its board of directors.[28] By 1917 the home occupied a four-storey building with seventy-five rooms, and housing some four hundred residents.[29]

The examples of Warsaw and Vilna, which were among the largest and most influential Jewish communities in the Pale of Settlement, were not followed immediately by other communities. Although records from the period are not complete, we can learn a great deal from Table 4.1, which presents data from a systematic survey of memorial books on the Jewish communities of eastern Europe. According to these data, homes for the aged were gradually founded in other communities, but the real increase in the number of such homes occurred only in the wake of the First World War. Between 1915 and 1920, at least seven homes for the aged were founded, whereas none are recorded for 1910–14.

The establishment of old-age homes was part of a general move towards the institutionalization of assistance for the needy. During the late nineteenth century, an increasing number of institutions for orphans and individuals

---

[25] Evreiskoe kolonizatsionnoe obshchestvo, *Sbornik materialov ob ekonomicheskom polozhenii evreev v Rossii*, ii. 255.   [26] Gutman, *The Destruction of Jewish Radom* (Yid.), 18.

[27] Shohet, 'History of the Jewish Community in Pinsk' (Heb.), 112.

[28] Shemaryahu Levin, *Istoricheskii ocherk razvitiya Vilenskoi evreiskoi obshchestvennoi bogadel'ni*. See also Golomb, *Charity in Vilna* (Yid.).

[29] See Golomb, *Charity in Vilna* (Yid.), 9–11, for a description of the home for the aged.

Table 4.1 Establishment of Jewish old-age homes in eastern Europe, by decade, 1840–1938

	No. homes established	Community
1840s	1	Warsaw[a] (1840)
1850s	0	
1860s	3	Jelgava[b] (1860), Vilna[c] (1864), Pinsk (Karlin)[d] (1865)
1870s	5	Piotrków Trybunalski[e] (1870), Dvinsk[b] (1870), Grodno[d] (1873), Kraków[f] (1874), Brody[e] (*c.*1875)
1880s	7	Radom[d] (proposal) (1881), Równe[d] (1881), Białystok[g] (1882), Riga[b] (1882), Odessa[h] (1884), Bobruisk[d] (1884), Orgeev[d] (1886)
1890s	7	Łódź[e] (1890), Kovno[i] (1890), Buczacz[e] (*c.*1890), Płock[d] (1891), Łomża[j] (1894), Suwałki[d] (1894), Lida[d] (1895), Korzec[e] (1899)
1900s	8	Gomel[d] (1900), Kishinev[k] (1903), Będzin[d] (1905), Kołomyja[e] (1905), Przemyśl[d] (1907), Czernowitz[l] (1908), Wołkowysk[m] (1908)
1910s	6	Włocławek[d] (1915), Baranowicze[d] (1917), Brichany[d] (1917), Kowel[d] (1917), Pruzhany[d] (1917), Ostrog[d] (1918)
1920s	6	Liepāja[b] (1920), Dubno[d] (plan) (1920), Rokiškis[i] (unfinished) (1920), Tomaszów Mazowiecki[d] (1926), Sosnowiec[d] (1927), Tarnów[e] (1927)
1930s	5	Lipkany[d] (1930), Kielce[n] (1930), Turka[e] (1935), Bielsko-Biała[e] (1937), Edintsy[d] (1938)

The years of establishment of the following are unknown: Biała Podlaska,[d] Biržai,[i] Brzeżany,[e] Chełm,[d] Chrzanów,[d] Czortków,[d] Elizavetgrad,[o] Gorlice,[d] Hrubieszów,[d] Khotin,[d] Kobryn,[d] Krzemieniec,[d] Lublin,[p] Lvov,[q] Międzyrzec (Podlaski),[d] Noua Sulit,[r] Panevėžys,[i] Raseiniai,[i] Rēzekne,[b] Rzeszów,[e] Šiauliai,[i] Slonim,[d] Tarnopol,[e] Wilkomir,[i] Włodzimierz (Ludmir),[d] Žagarė,[i] Zdzięcioł,[d] Złoczów.[d,e]

Note: In the rare cases in which there were two old-age homes in one community, the date of establishment of the earlier of the two is recorded. In some instances, the date is not noted explicitly in the sources but can be deduced or estimated from the context or from other information that is provided.

[a] Levin, 'The First Jewish Home for Orphans and the Elderly' (Heb.).

[b] *Recordbooks of the Jewish Communities: Latvia and Estonia* (Heb.), ed. Levin et al., 155 (Jelgava), 85 (Dvinsk), 250 (Riga), 177 (Liepāja), 237 (Rēzekne).

[c] Sh. Levin, *Istoricheskii ocherk razvitiya Vilenskoi evreiskoi obshchestvennoi bogadel'ni*, 56.

[d] The short reference given for each place is to the corresponding communal memorial book, as detailed in Baker, 'Geographical Index and Bibliography', 223–64 (the year is given for communities with more than one memorial book). For Pinsk: i/2. 112; Grodno: 461–2; Radom: 191 (1961); Równe: 373–4; Bobruisk: 48 (1967); Orgeev: 19; Płock: 174 (1967); Suwałki: 109; Lida: 182; Gomel: 195; Będzin: 118; Przemyśl: 240; Włocławek: 623; Baranowicze: 139; Brichany: 16; Kowel: 369 (1959); Pruzhany: 253 (1983); Otrog: 194, 214 (1954), 283, 287 (1960); Dubno: 295; Tomaszów Mazowiecki: 186; Sosnowiec: 257; Lipkany: 139; Edintsy: 214; Biała Podlaska: 313; Chełm: 107 (1954), 373–4 (1980); Chrzanów: 47; Czortków: 166; Gorlice: 67; Hrubieszów: 269; Khotin: 22, 30; Kobryn: 105; Krzemieniec: 105; Międzyrzec: 303 (1952); Slonim: 173; Włodzimierz: 159 (1962); Zdzięcioł: 176; Złoczów: 297.

[e] *Recordbooks of the Jewish Communities: Poland* (Heb.), ed. Dąbrowska et al., i. 189 (Piotrków Trybunalski), ii. 127 (Brody), i. 14 (Łódz, ii. 87 (Buczacz), v. 172 (Korzec), ii. 469 (Kołomyja), iii. 182 (Tarnów), ii. 256 (Turka), iii. 83 (Bielsko-Biała), ii. 110 (Brzeżany), iii. 162 (Rzeszów), ii. 243 (Tarnopol), ii. 219 (Złoczów).

[f] See a detailed history in Żbikowski, *Żydzi krakowscy i ich gmina*, 234–5.

[g] Hershberg, *Recordbook of Białystok* (Heb.), i. 328.

[h] *Sistematicheskii ukazatel' literatury o evreyakh*, 163 (no. 2186); see also Krasnova and Drozdovsky,

'Odesskaya evreiskaya bogadel'nya'.
  [i] *Recordbooks of the Jewish Communities: Lithuania* (Heb.), ed. Levin and Rozin, 521, 540 (Kovno), 650 (Rokiškis), 177 (Biržai), 459 (Panevėžys), 645 (Raseiniai), 661, 665 (Šiauliai), 243 (Wilkomir), 280 (Žagarė).
  [j] *Łomża* (Heb.), 176.
  [k] *Sabah kadishah* (Yid.).
  [l] *Recordbooks of the Jewish Communities: Romania* (Heb.), ed. Lavi, Broshni, and Ancel, ii. 498.
  [m] Lashovits (ed.), *Wołkowysk* (Heb.).
  [n] Urbanski and Blumenfeld, *Słownik historii kieleckich Żydów*, 37 ('Dom Starców').
  [o] Evreiskoe kolonizatsionnoe obshchestvo, *Sbornik materialov ob ekonomicheskom polozhenii evreev v Rossii*, ii. 255.
  [p] Trzcinski, *A Guide to Jewish Lublin and Surroundings*, 16.
  [q] Wiczkowski, *Lwów*, 319.

with various disabilities were established. According to data collected by the Jewish Colonization Society, in 1897 there were at least 126 asylums[30] in the Pale of Settlement.[31] The largest were to be found in those cities that had the largest Jewish populations: Vilna, Berdichev, Kremenchug, Odessa, Elizavetgrad, and Warsaw. Some of these were large institutions even by contemporary standards. The Kremenchug asylum, for example, housed 445 elderly in 1897, and about 3,800 poor used it at some point during the year. Of these asylums, 67 were located in the south-west region of the empire, which included the Kiev district and Volhynia. These regions were both relatively well off and strongly influenced by modernization.

COMMUNAL DYNAMICS AND THE ESTABLISHMENT OF OLD-AGE HOMES

A number of changes in the conditions of Jewish life made old-age homes increasingly necessary. Life expectancy among Jews was apparently on the rise during the nineteenth century,[32] which led to an increase in the absolute number of the elderly, but because this was part of a rapid general population growth within the Jewish community, the proportion of elderly in the total Jewish population did not necessarily go up. At the same time, there occurred a massive migration of east European Jews to the United States and elsewhere. More elderly Jews than in the past had no offspring nearby,

---

[30] I have used 'asylum' as a translation for *bogadel'nya*. The term refers to an institution that provides living quarters to a variety of needy people: the elderly, those unable to work, the poor, and the chronically ill. To use a dictionary translation such as 'poor house' would be imprecise, even though the residents of the *bogadel'ni* were indeed poor.

[31] Evreiskoe kolonizatsionnoe obshchestvo, *Sbornik materialov ob ekonomicheskom polozhenii evreev v Rossii*, ii. 254–7.

[32] On life expectancy see Bloch, 'Vital Events among the Jews in European Russia'. Life expectancy tables are also found in Silver, 'Some Demographic Characteristics of the Jewish Population in Russia', 273, but these have to be used with caution, especially with regard to his data on women.

and this may have increased the number of elderly in need of assistance.[33] However, there is no evidence that residents of old-age homes were those whose children had gone to the United States; it is more likely that these were the elderly most likely to receive financial support from their children.

The real factors behind the growth of old-age homes were connected to attitudinal and institutional change. By the mid-nineteenth century, the *kehilah* (Jewish community) structures in the tsarist empire had been dissolved and philanthropic activity was becoming the main focus of Jewish communal activity.[34] In every period, philanthropists seek to be associated with prestigious institutions.[35] Whereas in previous generations the affluent might have donated a synagogue or founded a study hall, by the late nineteenth century acculturated and affluent Jews wanted something with fewer ties to tradition. A home for the aged combined respectability with modernity in a manner that was devoid of specific religious connotations. Many (though not all) founders of old-age homes were rich and acculturated—a far cry from the homes' residents—and the buildings themselves were often large and prominent. The donors were thus linked quite visibly with their charitable activity, which itself combined commitment to the old with the employment of new and scientific methods.

Significantly, some Jewish homes for the aged published detailed constitutions and programmes.[36] In 1913, for instance, Yehezkel Kotik wrote a model constitution for an old-age home in which it was assumed that such institutions were the only way to assist the aged. This constitution included provisions for a yearly Purim ball and regular inspections by members of a supervisory commission.[37] This document and others do not seem to have been very useful or indeed intended for the use of the residents. Members of the Jewish community were also not necessarily interested in the details of how such institutions were organized. What did interest them was whether these institutions were well organized and operated on modern principles. The image of modernity seems to have been as important as the level of services they actually provided.[38]

---

[33] On the migrations, see Kuznets, 'Immigration of Russian Jews to the United States'. Kuznets cites data illustrating the fact that migrants tended to be young. Among those who did not migrate there was a disproportionate number of older people.

[34] See Lederhendler, *The Road to Modern Jewish Politics*, which describes in detail the main responses to this development.

[35] On orphanages, see Meir, 'From Communal Charity to National Welfare'.

[36] In Suwałki, a printed constitution was published in 1894. See also *Sistematicheskii ukazatel' literatury o evreyakh*, no. 2187; and Kelner and Elyashevich, *Literatura o evreyakh*, nos. 4297, 4448–81.   [37] Kotik, *Instructions for the Members of the Moshav Zekenim Society* (Yid.).

[38] The most recent discussion on this topic is Sperling, 'Der Wandel des jüdischen Sozialwesens'.

It should be noted that in certain communities, residences for the physically impaired—many of whom were no doubt elderly—were set up together with hospitals, or else under their auspices. A city guide to Lvov published in 1907, for example, noted that the *dom starców*, or home for the aged, located next to the Jewish hospital, was also run by the Jewish community.[39] Considering the medical needs of many residents of an old-age home, this arrangement could easily have been seen as the pinnacle of rational planning.

As homes for the aged became more and more common, they apparently began to be regarded as an indicator of a modern Jewish community. Perhaps this is how we can understand the case of Łomża,[40] where a maskilic activist, teacher, and doctor named Feivel Pasmanik established a home for the aged in 1894. The home, which housed four old men and three women, was clearly not intended to solve the problem of the community's aged Jewish population. Instead, it was a symbolic step and as such it justified the effort. The absence of a home for the aged could be lamented as a badge of shame for a community, an indication of lack of civic pride. When writing about Piask, Israel Dayan found it necessary to note defensively: 'Organized institutions for welfare, as we are familiar with them today, did not exist in cities and certainly not in small towns in Poland. Even so, the needs of the elderly were not totally neglected.'[41]

Women were often the organizers and supporters of old-age homes. In more than one case the initiative came specifically from women,[42] as in Płock, where a home for the aged was established in 1891 by several local women. In Brichany, in 1917, Henya Bronshtein established a home for the aged, and in Ostrog the local home for the aged was built by 'the widow of Shamai Sheinberger'. The administration of two small homes for the aged, one in Pruzhany and the other in Noua Suliṭa, was in the hands of local women. Although women had traditionally been involved personally in meeting the needs of the destitute, their entry into organizational life was an innovation in eastern Europe. Until then, areas of activity had been sharply differentiated on the basis of gender, with men responsible for formal institutions. This differentiation was undermined by the modernization of east European Jewish society. In general, new and developing institutional forms such as old-age homes are highly amenable to innovation, in this case the involvement of women.[43]

---

[39] Wiczkowski, *Lwów*, 319.

[40] *Łomża* (Heb.), 176. I thank Rabbi Plitkin from Yeshivat Horev for the reference to this interesting description.

[41] See Dayan on 'Our Town [Piask]', in id., *The Jewish Community in Piask* (Heb.).

[42] For the sources on women's involvement in the establishment of old-age homes, see the memorial books cited in Table 4.L.

[43] See Stampfer, 'Gender Differentiation and Education of the Jewish Woman'.

Old-age homes are expensive to operate, and the need for sources of funding cannot be overestimated. Such institutions are disadvantaged if they have to create their own fundraising structures. Jewish old-age homes were often dependent on support from the taxes that were collected from Jews or from city administrations. In the 1897 count of asylums in the tsarist empire mentioned above,[44] it was noted that there were 116 such institutions in the western provinces of the empire, but only ten in Congress Poland.[45] The reason offered by the authors was simple and convincing: in the western provinces, a *korobka* tax was collected from Jews to be used for communal needs, whereas in Congress Poland there was no such tax and hence no readily obtainable funds. The availability of resources might well have acted as an incentive to establish old-age homes.

In interwar Poland it was not uncommon for old-age homes to benefit from regular support from the civic authorities, although the available data does not allow us to determine the scope of such support. Even more important was the support provided from abroad, either from former residents of a specific community (*landslayt*) or from the American Jewish Joint Distribution Committee (JDC).

The dynamics of philanthropic donations from afar are very different from local support. For distant donors, a main concern is the efficient distribution of funds and supervision over their use. In this context, homes for the aged had a clear advantage over direct support of individual elderly. Direct assistance to individuals required a great deal of bookkeeping, administration, and reporting. Funding organizations—whether the JDC or local government—did not generally have the resources or the desire to get involved in all the necessary details. For them, as for distant donors, it was more efficient to give a donation to a relatively large project that entailed more simple bookkeeping. A home for the aged was an ideal project, since the photographs showing building dedications or elderly residents lined up in front of a home, which were sent to donors (or potential donors) from abroad, provided some evidence that the donation had reached its target.

As a new institution in east European Jewish society, old-age homes fit into modern patterns of charity. Growing acculturation among a new elite of Jewish rich in the modern period generated and highlighted the emphasis on philanthropy and social welfare as opposed to religious institutions.

[44] Evreiskoe kolonizatsionnoe obshchestvo, *Sbornik materialov ob ekonomicheskom polozhenii evreev v Rossii*, ii. 254. A detailed breakdown by region of asylums is found in table 60. Unfortunately for our purposes, it lumps together all types of asylum and does not give a separate breakdown for old-age homes.

[45] Congress Poland was a distinct administrative unit which included many of the Polish lands in the tsarist empire. Legislation that applied in the provinces did not always apply to Congress Poland.

Opportunities to use tax funds or donations from abroad also encouraged the development of centralized or residential institutions. These institutions had a symbolic function in terms of demonstrating both the loyalty of donors to the Jewish community and their commitment to modern and 'scientific' methods. Above and beyond the significantly expanded population of elderly Jews and their concentration in large cities, such institutional and social factors account for most of the growth in the number of old-age homes after the mid-nineteenth century.

It is difficult to assess the extent to which these Jewish homes for the aged met the needs of their constituency. Thus, for example, the establishment of a home for ten aged people in Tomaszów Mazowiecki in the interwar years, or for twelve elderly in Złoczów, is unlikely to have had a major impact on the living conditions of the old people of these towns. Clearly only a very small percentage of the Jewish elderly lived in such institutions; no doubt many more would have been happy to do so. However, measuring the poverty of those who did not find a place in an old-age home is impossible. It is reasonable to assume that needs were great and that the substantial funds invested in old-age homes met only part of these needs. Those who were not fortunate enough to find a place in an old-age home had to get by as best as they could.

If old-age homes were the direct product of need, one would have expected a strong correlation between the size of a community and the year that a home for the aged was founded: the larger the community, the greater the number of old people in need and the greater the resources to provide support—hence, the sooner such an institution would be established. The data shown in Table 4.2 indicate that population size alone is not a good predictor for the establishment of homes for the aged. The homes were not only a new institution but were also only one of several means of addressing the needs of the aged. The establishment of old-age homes thus seems to have been more a product of local initiatives and circumstances, rather than a universal or direct response to need.[46]

It would be a mistake to view homes for the Jewish aged in a stereotypical fashion, as an expression of a decline in responsibility for the aged that had once characterized the Jewish community. Some of them offered superb care. It is true that they were very costly and could assist only some of the Jewish elderly; had the resources invested in homes for the aged been channelled into helping the elderly who lived at home, it would often have been possible to assist more of them, albeit at a lower level of service. Direct aid, however, was not a practical option. Moreover, many donors were acutely sensitive to

[46] There is no question that a comparison of modern patterns of care for the aged among Jews and non-Jews in eastern Europe would be very illuminating. Unfortunately I was unable to find sources for such a comparison.

Table 4.2 Major Jewish communities in eastern Europe *c.*1900 and the dates of establishment of their old-age homes

City	Size of Jewish community *c.*1900	Year old-age home established[a]
Warsaw	219,000	1840
Odessa	139,000	1884
Łódz	99,000	1890
Vilna	64,000	1864
Kishinev	50,000	1903
Minsk	48,000	Unknown[b]
Lvov	44,000	1903[c]
Berdichev	42,000	Unknown[b]
Białystok	42,000	1882
Ekaterinoslav	40,000	
Vitebsk	34,000	
Dvinsk	32,000	1870
Kiev	32,000	
Zhitomir	31,000	
Brest	31,000	
Kremenchug	30,000	Unknown[b]
Kraków	26,000	1874
Kovno	25,000	1890
Lublin	24,000	Before 1905
Elizavetgrad	24,000	Unknown
Grodno	23,000	1873
Czernowitz	22,000	1908
Mogilev	22,000	
Riga	22,000	1882
Pinsk	21,000	1865
Bobruisk	21,000	1884

[a] Where there is no entry in this column there is no known old-age home in the corresponding community. However, it is quite likely that in some cases such a home existed, even though it is not recorded. In general, there is a paucity of sources on southern Russia/Ukraine and Belorussia.

[b] See Evreiskoe kolonizatsionnoe obshchestvo, *Sbornik materialov ob ekonomicheskom polozhenii evreev v Rossii*, ii. 255, where 'well-known' asylums are mentioned for Minsk, Berdichev, and Kremenchug. It is not clear whether this refers to old-age homes or to asylums for the indigent. The book notes that the asylum in Kremenchug housed 445 pensioners and gave temporary housing in 1897 to 3,790 poor people.

[c] See Wiczkowski, *Lwów*, 319.

Sources: In addition to those noted above, see Table 4.1.

the modernity of welfare programmes, preferring to support institutions that fitted their 'scientific' and 'up-to-date' self-image.

In many respects, the interest in homes for the aged was actually indicative of an increased sense of responsibility of the Jewish community vis-à-vis the elderly. The Jewish family per se was not weakening. Rather, organized communities now undertook to supply services that were once left to individuals. The perceived need for homes for the aged reflected not only the increasing number of elderly, but also much higher expectations for their support. Not surprisingly, this process took place in different places at different times, depending on the course of modernization and local conditions. Despite the limited success of homes for the aged in serving a wide population, many did provide an impressive service. Other solutions were not practical, and if the remedy was not as complete as could have been desired, this reflects problems that were far beyond the Jewish community's capabilities.

FIVE

The Pushke *and its Development*

W E CAN LEARN a great deal about a society by paying attention to the
goals to which it allocates charity. The constant support by Jews
around the world of the Jewish community of Erets Yisra'el expresses the
continued ties of the Jewish people to this land.[1] This is well known and
the topic has been well studied. However, less attention has been given to the
fact that it is possible to learn about a society not only from the recipients
of charity funds, but also from the very way in which charity is collected. One
of the most popular methods employed by Jewish charities in recent generations was the *pushke* ('charity box' in Yiddish) which was found in many
Jewish homes.[2] While it may appear traditional, this was an innovation of the
nineteenth century which spread quickly throughout all of eastern Europe.[3]
A careful look at the complicated dynamics behind the simple *pushke* reveals
a great deal about the structure and values of east European Jewish society.

Traditional east European Jewish communities collected money in a
number of ways. Taxation was only one of the standard means. Communities
had to make sure that payments required by the government were met and
that communal facilities, such as synagogues, were kept in good condition.
The needs of individuals were regarded as a very different matter and they
were usually dealt with by voluntary, charitable activities. Women generally
dealt with individual needs by providing assistance, or materials such as meals

[1] On the history of the Fund of Rabbi Meir Baal Hanes [*Kupat rabi me'ir ba'al hanes*], which
was one of the prominent frameworks in eastern Europe for supporting the Jewish community
in Erets Yisra'el, see Rapoport, 'Rabbi Meir Ba'al Hanes' (Heb.). See also Rubinstein, 'The
Booklet "Katit Lamaor" by Joseph Perl' (Heb.). This includes a description of Perl's attempt to
trace the history of this charity. On later developments in support of the Jewish community of
Erets Yisra'el see Hailperin, 'On the Relations of the Councils and Communities in Poland to
the Land of Israel' (Heb.).

[2] The word *pushke* came to Yiddish from the Polish word *puszka*. In Polish it means 'box' or
'charity box'. For various Hebrew translations of this term, see the article on which this chapter
is based: Stampfer, 'The *Pushke* and its Development'. Similar but much larger charity boxes
were found in many synagogues and they were often passed around during weekday services.
This study will concentrate on the home *pushke*.

[3] I was strongly influenced in my understanding of the significance of innovation, including
that of the *pushke*, by Rogers, *Communication of Innovation*.

for the sick or clothing for the destitute. However, many needs required money and this was usually collected from men.

Donations—many donations—had to be collected by charitable organizations which could not resort to coercion. Since few people are eager to part with funds, potential donors had to be convinced to give. People usually made donations because they got something in return, though the payoff was not always clear. However, when donations were made publicly the reward was clear: honour and prestige in the community. Significant donations were usually maximized by a public fundraising campaign. Thus the selling of *aliyot* (the privilege of being called up to the public reading of the Torah), the naming of buildings and institutions in honour of donors, and publicity given to major gifts all encouraged major contributions by providing a return for donations. Smaller donations could not be rewarded in the same way. It was common, for example, to raise funds by house-to-house canvassing or by collecting in synagogues from the men who came to weekday prayers. Neither of these is a truly public act and such donations did not automatically become public knowledge. However, even in house-to-house canvassing donors could be sure that the canvasser would 'spread the word' about the size of the donation. In synagogues, when a coin is dropped into a collection box, others do not see how much is deposited, but it would be clear who put coins into the box—and how often and how many. Often the size of the coin was detectable from the sound that it made as it dropped into the box. For most small donors, the sense of doing a good deed and being able to contribute were apparently a sufficient reward. However, it was also rare to make a substantial donation into the charity box in a synagogue. Collectors for charity and activists, who invested a great deal of time in collecting and raising funds, were also rewarded. They were publicly recognized for their efforts and regarded as honourable and pious for giving their time to a charitable cause. If 'time is money', devoting time to a good cause is equivalent to a donation. The *pushke* was to change much of this dynamic.

The *pushke* was a small box or container with a slit on the top for inserting coins. To make a *pushke* does not require any advanced technology, so the spread of *pushke*s in the nineteenth century cannot be attributed to advances in manufacturing or technology. The innovation of the *pushke* does, however, reflect new charity needs in the Jewish community and changes in the communal make up. In the course of time, the use of the *pushke* also had major consequences for Jewish organizations. Therefore, a historical and social study of this simple and almost 'anonymous' object can deepen our understanding of some of the ways in which Jewish society changed in the modern period.

Use of a *pushke* is simple, but it entails organization and long-term planning. A charitable association prepares *pushke*s and then distributes them without charge in private homes. From time to time, representatives of the association go from house to house and collect the coins that have accumulated in the *pushke*s. In this way, a relatively small group of activists can collect charity from a relatively large group of donors and thus using *pushke*s is efficient. Much charity collection traditionally involves going from door to door, which is very time consuming and worthwhile only when the amount collected at each door is significant. Although wealthy people may have money available at home that is not already set aside for immediate needs, the poor rarely have significant amounts of ready cash which can be given to a charity collector on the spur of the moment. Collecting funds only from the rich meant that a majority of the population was excluded from the charity effort, but regular contributions to a *pushke* made it possible for the poor to accumulate enough money to make it worthwhile for a charity collector to come to their houses a few times a year. Thus employment of a *pushke* increased the circle of donors as well as the total income.

Women were the secret to the success of the *pushke*. Poor males could be tapped with little effort in synagogues by passing a charity box around during prayers, but the use of the home *pushke* had an advantage over collecting money in this way. Most women came to synagogue only on the sabbath or festivals, and thus the contributions were mainly collected from men. Although male donors in the synagogue could be seen as representing family units, having a charity box at home increased the opportunity for others, such as wives, to donate and soon the donations of women made up most of the money collected in *pushke*s. Given the simplicity and efficiency of the *pushke* the obvious questions are why did the *pushke* come into use only in the nineteenth century, and for what purposes was it employed?

Part of the explanation for the delay in the introduction of the *pushke* is tied to the fact that there are inherent limits on its use. One limit is that *pushke*s require local organization and regular collection. A visitor from another location could deliver a fundraising speech to the community, or approach rich individuals, but if his visits to a town or city were not regular, he could not distribute *pushke*s or make sure that any *pushke*s he had distributed were not emptied for another cause. Another limit is that *pushke*s can only be used for constant or ongoing needs, not urgent or occasional causes. The use of *pushke*s requires pre-planning and yields results only after an investment of time and materials. One cannot distribute *pushke*s and start collecting them the next day because it takes time for them to fill up. An additional limitation is that if charity funds are collected by one means for a given goal, people are often reluctant to donate again in a different way for the same goal.

Therefore, when money was collected in synagogue or through public activities for specific local needs, it was difficult to collect for the same purpose, either with *pushke*s or in any other way.

Charities, then, usually had a choice between public fundraising campaigns—which involved donations in public or other public rewards to a donor—and use of the *pushke*. Quite reasonably, the first choice was usually the better one: the returns were quicker and relying mainly on a *pushke* would not have given higher returns. Some of the weaknesses of the *pushke* as a fundraising tool are alluded to in a prayer that it was customary to say when putting a donation in a *pushke*: 'Lord of the world—just as the *pushke* is made so that no one knows what is inside except for the collector who opens it to take out the money, so the heart of a person is hidden—no one knows what another person thinks.'[4] There is no public reward or compensation for donations to a *pushke*. A donation in a synagogue gives honour and the donor can gain respect for his commitment and resources, but there is none of this when a *pushke* is used.

Fundraising campaigns for charity are usually successful only for certain types of goals. Even those who had never heard of the rabbinic statement that the local poor have precedence over the poor from other communities acted in accordance with it. Fundraisers are aware that it is difficult to raise funds in a given community for an institution or need in another community, especially when the local institutions or organizations are trying to raise funds for the same purpose. For example, an orphanage in a neighbouring town will not be able to raise money in a community which is struggling to maintain its own school for orphans, and it may be difficult to convince people to donate money to help the poor in a neighbouring city purchase Passover supplies when there are local poor who need the same help. A campaign for a non-local charity works best when it does not duplicate a local need. There were occasionally cases of this type: for example, communities that were ravaged by fires often turned for aid to other communities, and the same could apply to other disasters—natural and through human agency. These cases required immediate response and therefore, in these circumstances the *pushke* was not useful.

In traditional east European Jewish society there were few permanent charitable goals that were not local in nature. One of the few exceptions was the need to support Jewish communities in the Land of Israel. The members of these communities called on Jewish communities to support them on the grounds that by living in Erets Yisra'el they fulfilled the special *mitsvah* of

[4] I found this prayer in *Shas tekhinah* (Anon., *'Hannah and her Seven Sons'*). I made no effort to determine the date of composition and I am sure that it also appears in earlier editions than the 1904 one cited here.

living in the Holy Land and of observing the special laws that were applied only there. They claimed that donors who supported them could be regarded as having a portion of the fulfilment of these special *mitsvot*—the only way most could fulfil these *mitsvot*, because going to live in Erets Yisra'el was not a practical option for most.

The great yeshivas of eastern Lithuania were another such charitable goal. They were not like the great yeshivas of the Middle Ages, which had been located in large communities and had been communally funded. After the mid-seventeenth century there were no longer yeshivas in the large communities of eastern Europe and most advanced study of Talmud and Torah took place in *batei midrash*, or communal study halls, which did not raise funds. Pious families gave students meals and no teaching staff had to be supported. The new yeshivas—starting with that of Volozhin, which was founded in the early nineteenth century—were not communal institutions, and they claimed to offer a programme of study which was significantly more intensive than *beit midrash* study. Heads of yeshivas could justifiably claim that these new yeshivas did not duplicate existing communal institutions. Since *batei midrash* did not have financial needs, yeshivas were not regarded as competing with them for support. Donors did not 'trade off' the cost of providing meals to local yeshiva students with the donations to central yeshivas because one cost was in kind while the other was in cash.

Yet another non-local charity which was accepted was the hasidic court. Here as well the function of the *admor* or hasidic leader was regarded as without a local equivalent. Thus while pious hasidim may not have supported the orphans or the sick in the town where the *admor* had his court, they were quite generous in supporting the court itself.[5] However, the regular visits to the *admor* and the local hasidic prayer halls (*shtielbels*) offered alternatives to the *pushke*.

The *pushke* came to be used both for support of the Jewish communities of Erets Yisra'el and for the yeshivas. A survey of its history will explain why its use developed, and why this pattern of use of the *pushke* was maintained up until the twentieth century.[6]

*

The development of the *pushke* was tied to significant shifts in the relationships between Jews in eastern Europe and the Jewish communities in Erets Yisra'el which took place in the nineteenth century. Like Jews everywhere, the Jews of eastern Europe had always been interested in the Jewish

[5] Assaf, '"Money for Household Expenses"'.

[6] There were exceptions. In the community of Kelm a *pushke* was used in 1820 to collect money for an elaborate *menorah* for the local synagogue. See Karlinsky, 'Dos shtetl kelm' (Yid.), 144.

communities of Erets Yisra'el and had donated money for their support. However, the link was not an intimate one. Until the nineteenth century, most of the Jews who lived in Erets Yisra'el were Sephardi Jews whose ancestors had come from Spain or North Africa. Their cultural and religious patterns were quite different from those of Jews in eastern Europe. Thus when Rabbi Yosef Karo, a Sephardi Jew who lived in Safed, published his *Shulḥan arukh*, or code of Jewish law, it became authoritative among eastern European Jews only when it was adapted to the Ashkenazi rite by Rabbi Moses Isserles of Kraków. In other words, for Jews in eastern Europe, the residents of Erets Yisra'el were an 'exotic' population with whom there were few direct ties or connections. However, this combination of interest and distance changed dramatically, starting in the late eighteenth century.

There were major waves of immigration to Erets Yisra'el of east European Jews starting from the *aliyah* of a group of hasidim in 1765, and of a group of followers of the Vilna Gaon in 1808.[7] These immigrants did not merge with the veteran Sephardi Jewish communities in Erets Yisra'el, nor with each other. On the contrary, they maintained distinct identities: the hasidim, and the mitnagedim (opponents of hasidism). Both groups saw themselves as extensions of east European Jewry and were regarded as such in eastern Europe. While messianism might have been at the root of these waves of immigration, the realities of life in Erets Yisra'el quickly imposed themselves on the immigrants. Even though they came with the goal of being religiously productive in the Holy Land rather than economically productive, nonetheless they had to find some means of support. The first step in this direction was for the immigrants to organize themselves. Each group set up a structure with clearly defined members and leaders—but organization alone was not enough.

Within a year of the arrival of the first group of hasidim one of their leaders, Rabbi Yisra'el of Polotsk, was sent back to Europe to organize regular support for the hasidic immigrants.[8] His method was to organize *ma'amadot*, or commitments on the part of individuals to donate fixed amounts either on a weekly or yearly basis. This was the preferred method of Rabbi Tsevi Hirsh Lehren, a Dutch Jew who was a central figure in the organized support of the Jewish community of Erets Yisra'el. Apparently the efforts were successful because we know of attempts to divert some of the moneys collected for other purposes. In 1781 Rabbi Yisra'el, Rabbi Shneur Zalman of Lyady, and another rabbi signed a statement forbidding the use of funds collected for

---

[7] A classic study of the immigration of the hasidim is Hailperin, *The First Aliyot* (Heb.). The best source on the immigration of the mitnagedim is 'The Story of the Beginning of the Settlement of the Ashkenazis, which were called "The Pharisees" in the Second Half of the Sixth Century' (Heb.), which was copied from the now lost record book of the *kolel* in Safed and published in Frumkin, *History of the Sages of Jerusalem* (Heb.), iii. 138–57.

[8] Hailperin, *The First Aliyot* (Heb.), 30.

the poor of Erets Yisra'el for local needs. They added an order to all 'volunteers' to commit themselves to a weekly donation for the poor of Erets Yisra'el and to cover all their 'debts' before each of the major holidays. However, they made no mention of a *pushke* and apparently they did not employ this method.[9] After Rabbi Yisra'el died, around the year 1783, Rabbi Shneur Zalman of Lyady took over responsibility for the fundraising efforts, which apparently continued in the same pattern. The text of a denunciation sent by the mitnaged Avigdor of Pinsk to a Russian governor in 1800 provides an indirect indication of the success of the hasidic fundraising programme. Avigdor claimed that the amounts of money sent to Jerusalem had increased a hundredfold—and the traditional precept that the local poor should be helped first had been ignored.[10]

The mitnagedim acted in the same way as the hasidim. The first large group of mitnagedim arrived in Erets Yisra'el in 1808. They were led by Rabbi Yisra'el of Shklov. He was sent back to eastern Europe two years after his arrival in Erets Yisra'el to organize support for his group of immigrants. He took with him a letter signed by all the leaders of the mitnagdic community in Safed. The letter called on the leaders of the communities in eastern Europe to energetically encourage potential donors to make weekly donations to support the community in Erets Yisra'el. It suggested that each community should appoint a special collector to collect donations for this purpose.[11] Rabbi Yisra'el turned for assistance to the followers of the Vilna Gaon and he was not disappointed. The first person he turned to when he returned to Europe was Rabbi Hayim of Volozhin, who was perhaps the greatest of the Gaon's disciples and who had recently founded a yeshiva in his hometown. Their ties were close. Rabbi Yisra'el termed Rabbi Hayim 'our father'.[12] Indeed, Rabbi Hayim stood at the head of the fundraising structure for these communities of mitnagdic immigrants to Erets Yisra'el from the time it was founded, and he maintained an active interest in these communities all his life.[13] One of Rabbi Hayim's final public acts was to send off a public letter prohibiting the reallocation to local causes of funds that had been donated to the Jewish communities in Erets Yisra'el.[14] Rabbi Yitshak, the son

---

[9] See Hilman, *Letters of Shneur Zalman* (Heb.), 9. For information on the term *ma'amadot* and its significance in hasidism, see Rivkind, *Jewish Money in Folkways* (Yid.), 155–6.

[10] Hilman, *Letters of Shneur Zalman* (Heb.), 142–3.

[11] Ya'ari (ed.), *Letters from Israel* (Heb.), 344–5, and see the long introduction to the volume as well.   [12] Frumkin, *History of the Sages of Jerusalem* (Heb.), iii. 131–41.

[13] See the many references to R. Hayim of Volozhin in the index to Malakhi, *Chapters on the History of the Old Yishuv* (Heb.), and the sources he cites.

[14] See Hayim of Volozhin, in Dembitzer (ed.), *Sefer magine erets yisra'el*, 1–2. In the letter of R. Avraham Aveli of Vilna there is a note stating that writing this letter was something R. Hayim did shortly before his death.

and heir of Rabbi Hayim, continued in his father's footsteps and in 1840 he was the leader of the representatives of the Jewish communities of Erets Yisra'el.[15]

One of the novel activities of Rabbi Hayim was to encourage the immigrants to purchase land and to farm it, but this was not out of a desire for productivization. The donors who sent money to support the immigrants were encouraged to feel that they had a share in the *mitsvot* (righteous acts) fulfilled by the immigrants. Therefore, Rabbi Hayim wanted the immigrants to fulfil special halakhic commandments regarding agricultural work in Erets Yisra'el and thus enable the supporters in Europe to have a part, though indirect, in an additional *mitsvah*.[16] This, of course, gave an added incentive to donors. The necessary funds for the immigrants were collected and transmitted to Erets Yisra'el. In a short time, an effective fundraising mechanism was set up by the mitnagedim.

Both the hasidim and the mitnagedim began their fundraising activity in the regions from which the immigrants came and in the circles of their acquaintances. In both groups the goal was to make the support for their communities regular and predictable. To this end they appointed local representatives who would collect the funds for the Jewish communities in Erets Yisra'el and would transmit them via central representatives to their destination. The constantly increasing needs of the growing communities in Erets Yisra'el forced them to expand their scope. Thus, Rabbi Avraham Danzig was sent from Vilna to Germany in 1811 to drum up support there for the mitnagdic communities in Erets Yisra'el.[17] Collection efforts soon covered all of eastern and central European Jewish communities. The importance of the fundraising for both hasidim and mitnagedim and the dangers of competition led them to overcome some of the differences between them. The two sides reached an agreement in 1812 that divided eastern Europe between the fundraisers of the two groups, and the hasidic fundraising organization was integrated into the framework the mitnagedim had set up and based in Vilna. Rabbi Yisra'el of Shklov was one of the signatories of this agreement even though he was a bitter opponent of hasidism—which is an indication of the importance of the agreement to both sides.[18] The willingness to sign an agreement should not be misinterpreted as a peace agreement between hasidim and mitnagedim. Shortly after the agreement was made,

---

[15] See Malakhi, 'On the History of the *ḥalukah* in Jerusalem' (Heb.), and *Chapters on the History of the Old Yishuv* (Heb.), 19.   [16] Ibid. 20.   [17] Ya'ari, *Emissaries to Israel* (Heb.), 759.

[18] This agreement, and a later agreement from 1818, is described in a wall poster entitled *Writing to the New Generation* [Ketov zot ledor aḥaron]. For more details see Frumkin, *History of the Sages of Jerusalem* (Heb.), 141, and Halevi, 'Rabbi Yisra'el of Shklov' (Heb.). See Tishby, 'Anti-Hassidic Polemics of R. Israel of Shklov' (Heb.) for a discussion of R. Yisra'el's opposition to the hasidim.

there were claims, apparently by both sides, that the other side was violating the agreement.[19] However, the fact that there was a willingness to reach an agreement, even if it was not maintained, was significant.

It was in the context of growing interest among east European Jews in the Jewish communities in Erets Yisra'el and increasing needs for support for them that the *pushke* appeared in eastern Europe. It is first mentioned in a letter of Rabbi Dov Baer Schneerson (Der Mitteler Rebbe) written not long after 1813. In it he refers to the widespread use of *pushke*s in homes in Volhynia, Ukraine, and Polesia, and suggests men should put money in a *pushke* before eating a meal. He did not refer to the *pushke* as his own innovation.[20] It must have been a rather recent innovation. In a letter written not long before, Rabbi Asher of Stolin writes in detail about the need to support the residents of Erets Yisra'el. However, he does not mention the *pushke* and instead encourages a weekly donation—apparently to the hands of a fundraiser.[21] The identity of the person who 'invented' the *pushke* is unknown, but it seems it was someone active in the framework of the *kolel*, the religious institution of the immigrants from Volhynia. Apparently the method was adopted by the mitnagedim after the use of the *pushke* spread among hasidim.

The *pushke* was mentioned in a letter written in 1827 by Rabbi Tsevi Hirsh Lehren. He wrote to a supporter in Hamburg thanking him for having set up a charity box in his study hall to collect money for the Jews of Erets Yisra'el. However, Lehren had some suggestions. He wanted his friend to enlist local supporters who would commit themselves to yearly donations to the cause and also place collection boxes in private homes. He stated that in Holland such boxes had been given to those individuals who did not want to commit themselves in advance to a yearly donation of a specific sum. The recipients would put a donation in whenever they were moved to do so. Lehren noted that the income from such boxes was usually higher than the amount to which these individuals had been asked to commit themselves.[22] Lehren did not refer often to such collection boxes in his later correspondence, but con-

---

[19] See Weiss, 'Verdict of Hatam Sofer on the Matter of the Distribution of Money for the People of Israel' (Heb.). See also the letter of Avrahom Sofer, the son of the 'Hatam Sofer', from 1846 on the same issue in Hirschberg, *Zakhor le'avraham*, 29–31.

[20] See the 'holy letters' of the hasidic leaders Admor Hazaken, Admor Emtsa'i, and Tsemaḥ Tsedek in Schneersohn, *Holy Letters* (Heb.), 256. I thank Uriel Gelman for referring me to this important source, which is also cited in the article of Blau, 'The Founding and Development of the Fund of Rabbi Meir Ba'al Hanes' (Heb.), 133.

[21] See the undated letter in Avraham Abish Shur's article 'On the Period of his Residence' (Heb.), 126. The editor notes that it was written in 1812 or shortly after.

[22] Rivlin and Rivlin, *Letters of the Officers and the Administrators of Amsterdam* (Heb.), i. 136. My thanks to Dr Aryeh Morgenstern who brought this very important source to my attention. Ya'akov Lipschitz wrote in his *Zikhron ya'akov* that there was a decision to place in every Jewish house a charity box which was then termed a *shofar* but he provided neither a date or a source for his statement (vol. ii, pp. 30–1).

centrated instead on seeking commitments to regular and fixed donations which enabled him to make long-term financial plans of support for the Jewish communities of Erets Yisra'el. This meant that he focused on enlisting support mainly from affluent businessmen of whom there was no shortage in central Europe. In other words, the *pushke* was not an important tool in Holland.

Despite the ubiquity of the *pushke* in the mid-nineteenth century and later, in the beginning it took time for it to spread in eastern Europe. The *pushke* was not mentioned explicitly in the denunciation that Joseph Perl, who lived in Galicia, wrote in 1829. In this letter, Perl accused the fundraisers for the Jewish communities in Erets Yisra'el of smuggling capital abroad. He mentioned that in many synagogues and Jewish inns there were charity boxes for the Jews of Erets Yisra'el, but he did not explicitly mention the presence of such boxes in private homes.[23] However, he may have been familiar with home *pushke*s. He claimed that Jews were expected to put money in charity boxes before every meal, and that every woman was to donate before lighting the candles for the sabbath and holidays. This strongly suggests that the boxes he was referring to were home *pushke*s, but it is far from explicit evidence. The *pushke* certainly did not replace other fundraising methods overnight. We know that in 1841 an enactment was made in Białystok to send collectors every week to the homes of donors,[24] even though there is no doubt that *pushke*s were already common in many places in eastern Europe at that date.

Already before the middle of the nineteenth century, there are many references to the *pushke* in Jewish sources. Paulina Wengeroff, born in Bobruisk in 1833, wrote that in her parents' house there were two *pushke*s.[25] In an agreement between the hasidim and mitnagedim in 1845 which deals with the division of income from Jewish communities in Hungary there is mention of income from charity boxes in the homes of families and synagogues.[26] In a text from 1852 the home *pushke*s were termed 'the new boxes'. It is not clear if this meant new as a phenomenon in eastern Europe in general, or new to the specific regions discussed in the document—Daghestan, and other regions in Caucasia.[27] In 1852 the 'president' of the Galician *kolel* wrote that charity boxes were placed in the houses of all generous people, and he took this for granted as something obvious and well established.[28] By the beginning of the

[23] Rubinstein, 'The Booklet "Katit Lamaor" by Joseph Perl' (Heb.).
[24] Hailperin, 'Diaspora and the Land of Israel' (Heb.), 719.
[25] Wengeroff, *Memoiren*, i. 118.
[26] See the document edited by Ben-Zion Dinur, 'From the Archive of the Hakham Bashi R. Hayim Avraham Gagin' (Heb.).
[27] Malakhi, 'On the History of the *ḥalukah* in Jerusalem' (Heb.).
[28] See a section from a responsum of R. M. Z. Eitinga cited by Kahana, *Studies in Halakhic Literature* (Heb.), 249. My thanks to Professor S. Z. Havlin for bringing this to my attention.

twentieth century there were more than a quarter of a million charity boxes collecting funds for the settlement of Erets Yisra'el and for the Jewish communities there.[29]

What has yet to be described is how the *pushke* actually functioned. It is simple to say that people put money in the *pushke*. What is less obvious is the stimulus to do so. Most people are not regularly overcome by uncontrollable urges to make donations—even the best-intentioned of people—and this was certainly the case in a population that was not necessarily well off. The key to the success of the *pushke* system is the way it was integrated into Jewish life and practice.

The *pushke* became an effective tool for charity collection because donations to the *pushke* were ritualized and made part of the regular pattern of Jewish life. In the passage from the 1829 letter of Perl cited above, he mentioned the requirement that Jews put a coin in the box before each meal and before lighting the sabbath candles.[30] An additional practice that developed was to make a donation before taking ḥalah, the ritual separation of a portion of dough which a Jewish woman was required to do every time she made bread. In the 1841 Białystok enactment, the collectors were instructed to go from door to door to collect donations when the women were baking bread. However, it was far more efficient to convince women to do the collection work themselves, and to put coins in the *pushke* each time they made bread, as was referred to in the 1845 agreement between the hasidim and mitnagedim referred to above. This linkage was not unique to eastern Europe. In the reports of the *pekidim ve'amarkalim*, or fundraisers for the Jewish community in Erets Yisra'el from 1854, there is reference to the income from the pious women or ḥalah gelt (ḥalah money).[31]

The ritualization of charity giving reached perhaps its highest form in eastern Europe. An entire corpus of prayers was written for women to say when putting money in the *pushke* just before candle lighting. Special prayerbooks for women would give them a choice of various prayers to say on a given sabbath and they could pick the one that best fitted their moods. A Jewish mother could pray that, in return for her doing good deeds, her family would be blessed. By putting money in the *pushke* for the poor of Erets Yisra'el before lighting candles, a woman was able to unite the two good deeds of blessing the holy sabbath and supporting the Jews of the holy land. The combination of prayer, charity, and candle lighting was a drama a woman re-enacted every Friday. Since she could choose which prayer to say, the

[29] *Evreiskaya entsiklopediya*, xv. 523, s.v. 'khaluka'. See also the material Ya'ari included in *Emissaries to Israel* (Heb.), 57–61.
[30] Rubinstein, 'The Booklet "Katit Lamaor" by Joseph Perl' (Heb.).
[31] Rivkind, *Jewish Money in Folkways* (Yid.), 101–2.

resulting ritual was more personal and relevant than might have been anticipated in a fixed ritual. Her family was an audience and this ritual reinforced their awareness of her place in the ritual dynamic of the family. The anticipated consequence of the mother's deeds was the health, happiness, and well-being of the observers—her husband and family. This was, of course, a very different dynamic from the male search for honour among peers inherent in synagogue prayer. Pious acts of males could have positive influences on their individual status and fate, but did not necessarily bring a blessing on the entire family. However, for women to miss a charity donation for a week was to fail to perform a deed that could potentially have a very positive effect on the family. In this manner the most difficult step for a charity collector—to get someone to open his wallet—was solved by a ritual framework, which guaranteed regular weekly donations.[32]

*

At the same time that the *pushke* was utilized for the communities in Erets Yisra'el, it was also used to raise funds for the yeshivas in eastern Europe—and in exactly the same manner. This was not by chance. As noted above, Rabbi Hayim of Volozhin was a central figure in the organization of support for the mitnagdic immigrants to Erets Yisra'el. He was also the founder of an important yeshiva with a novel structure, which was an innovation in many respects. Until his time east European Talmud students had lived in local synagogues, sleeping on benches when the synagogue was empty at night, and eating meals in the homes of pious local families. In the new yeshiva students were given stipends to enable them to rent rooms and pay for meals. The funds for the yeshiva did not come from the Jewish residents of Volozhin but rather from donors all over Lithuania and beyond. In short, while yeshivas in the past had been communal institutions, this one was not. Since it did not rely on communal funding it was necessary for Rabbi Hayim to organize fundraising. He set up a system of local representatives in various cities who collected donations and then transmitted them to the yeshiva.[33] This was very much like the system that was being used at that time to collect money for the Jewish communities in Erets Yisra'el, and it was not by chance since the same personalities were involved in both fundraising activities.

There were good reasons for both the Volozhin yeshiva and the communities in Erets Yisra'el to employ the *pushke*. Immigration to Erets Yisra'el and study in the Volozhin yeshiva did not duplicate local activities. Therefore, for Jews everywhere they were legitimate candidates for support. At the same

---

[32] Ibid. 142 (s.v. 'Likhtgelt'), and 246 (s.v. 'Rabi meir ba'al hanes gelt').

[33] This is described in detail in the first chapter of my forthcoming book *Lithuanian Yeshivas*.

time, both support of residents of Erets Yisra'el and of yeshiva students offered donors the opportunity to share in activities which were regarded as particularly holy—either living in the Holy Land or the study of the Torah on the highest possible level. Both of these had a very strong appeal.[34]

Not surprisingly, one of the earliest sources to mention *pushke*s relates to both the Jewish communities in Erets Yisra'el and the yeshivas. In a travelogue written by the well-known Polish writer Ignacy Chodzko there is a fascinating description of the Volozhin yeshiva in the 1830s. Chodzko wanted to illustrate the importance of the yeshiva for the Jews and wrote that in every Jewish home, especially in small towns, there are two charity boxes, one for Jerusalem, and one for the yeshiva in Volozhin.[35]

Since the same people were involved in raising funds for the Jewish communities of Erets Yisra'el and for the Volozhin yeshiva in the early nineteenth century, there was no competition or disagreements over the distribution of *pushke*s between both causes. When there were legal restrictions on sending money abroad, it was apparently convenient to collect the money for the communities of Erets Yisra'el under the guise of a collection for yeshivas.[36] Complications arose when additional yeshivas began to use *pushke*s as part of their fundraising efforts. The first of these was when the yeshiva of Mir started to distribute *pushke*s. The heads of the Volozhin yeshiva objected and claimed that this was a case of interloping, which is prohibited by Jewish law (*hasagat gevul*). The issue ultimately came to a rabbinical court and the decision given was that all yeshivas had a right to distribute *pushke*s.[37] In the second half of the nineteenth century, the leaders of the Volozhin yeshiva ceased to be central figures in the organization of support for the mitnagdic communities in Erets Yisra'el. The consequence was predictable. In 1876 Rabbi Berlin, the head of the Volozhin yeshiva, wrote that the charity collectors for the communities in Erets Yisra'el had attacked him.[38] While it

[34] Hasidic groups did not use *pushke*s to collect funds for the *tsadik* in the way mitnagedim employed *pushke*s for the yeshivas. Donors to yeshivas were not expected to ever visit the yeshiva, and had they done so they would have had nothing to do there. Therefore the collection of funds from their *pushke*s by fundraisers was a service to the donors, since is saved them the need to travel personally to the yeshiva and hand over their donation. Hasidim were expected to see their 'rebbe' regularly and such visits were seen as appropriate times to make donations to him. Had the money they saved up been collected earlier by fundraisers they would have come empty handed or with less in their hands. This was clearly not desirable. Hence no framework ever developed within hasidic groups to distribute *pushke*s to raise money for the hasidic leader.
[35] Chodzko, *Obrazy litewskie*, 188. I was led to this book by Shatzky's discussion of this material in his *Cultural History of the Haskalah in Lithuania* (Yid.), 181–5.
[36] If we can rely on Rivlin, *Vision of Zion* (Heb.), 86.
[37] Goldenberg, *The Gaon Hayim Yehudah Leib* (Heb.), 8.
[38] See Reines, 'Centres of Torah Study' (Heb.), 28. My thanks to Professor Immanuel Etkes for this reference.

is not clear why they attacked him, in the absence of any other known motives it seems likely that there was some financial dispute between them.

The *pushke* reached America along with the great wave of east European Jewish immigrants in the second half of the nineteenth century. Already in the eighteenth century collectors for Jewish causes in eastern Europe had come to the United States and American donations were important for them even before the great wave of immigration.[39] In the 1870s, the Volozhin yeshiva sent fundraisers to America[40] although for the yeshiva, income from the United States became an important factor only in the twentieth century. Many local institutions in eastern Europe appealed for support to émigrés from their communities in the United States and the *pushke* was an obvious method for them as well. In certain respects, the role of eastern Europe, or 'the old country', for many emigrants was similar to that of Erets Yisra'el for all Jews. Quite naturally many institutions started giving out *pushke*s in American Jewish communities. It was not long before the veteran charities, especially those of the Jewish communities in Erets Yisra'el, began to feel the competition for charitable aid.

The widespread use of *pushke*s by many organizations led to attempts to regulate their use. A public statement signed by Rabbi Yitshak Elhanan Spektor, the rabbi of Kovno and the leading rabbi of eastern Europe, and eighty-five other rabbis was issued in 1887. It prohibited charitable organizations other than those who had long used *pushke*s (such as the Jewish communities in Erets Yisra'el and the great European yeshivas) from using them.[41] Rabbi Spektor reiterated this position in a responsum written in 1888. The questioner, a New York rabbi named Zvi Kantorowitz, had asked whether private charity organizations in Erets Yisra'el could distribute *pushke*s in America. Rabbi Spektor replied in the negative and added that only the central charity organization of the Jewish communities in Erets Yisra'el could distribute *pushke*s.[42] He modified his position a year later to allow other organizations to distribute charity boxes, but on condition that these organizations obtained prior approval from the organization of Jewish communities in Erets Yisra'el.[43] This implied that the yeshivas of Volozhin and Mir were not allowed to distribute charity boxes, though apparently Rabbi Spektor did not have this in mind when he wrote his responsa. In order to clarify the matter the rabbi of Mir, Rabbi Yom Tov Lipman, and the head of the yeshiva in Mir, Rabbi Hayim Leib Tiktinski, wrote to Rabbi Spektor to request clarification in writing. The rabbis from Mir received a prompt response confirming that

---

[39] See Kelner, 'The Beginning of the Organization of the Jewish Communities in the United States' (Heb.).   [40] Rivkind, 'The History of the Volozhin Emissaries' (Heb.).
[41] The text was published by Lunz in 'The Ḥalukah' (Heb.), 38.   [42] Ibid. 49.
[43] Lunz, 'The Ḥalukah' (Heb.), 214.

the veteran yeshivas also had the right to distribute *pushke*s. Similar letters were received from other leading rabbis.[44]

Despite the occasional rivalry between the various causes personal ties between many prominent figures linked to various charitable endeavours continued. The *rosh yeshivah* (head of the yeshiva) of the Volozhin yeshiva in the second half of the nineteenth century, Rabbi Naftali Tsevi Yehudah Berlin, had an important role in defending the 'rights' of the Jewish communities in Erets Yisra'el, and was even an active *hovev tsiyon* (Zionist) for a while.[45] Rabbi Kantorowitz, who was zealous in the defence of a monopoly of the Jewish communities of Erets Yisra'el to distribute *pushke*s in the United States, was also the representative (and fundraiser) of the Volozhin yeshiva in the United States.[46]

The *pushke* was not the only idea adopted by the yeshivas from the settlers in Erets Yisra'el. The very structure of the Ashkenazi Jewish communal organization employed by the east European Jewish immigrants to Erets Yisra'el was adapted for use in the yeshivas of eastern Europe. The immigrants organized themselves in *kolelim*. These were committees who received donations and then distributed them to their members who devoted themselves to study and other holy activities. Thus support from outside Erets Yisra'el was not sent to individuals but to *kolelim* who claimed that they disbursed the funds fairly and efficiently, and also exercised some supervision on the behaviour of the members of the *kolelim*. They were not schools or yeshivas but frameworks for the efficient distribution of financial aid. In Erets Yisra'el *kolelim* were usually organized by common geographic background of their members—immigrants from Galicia in one *kolel*, immigrants from central Europe in another, and so on.

In the late nineteenth century the world of east European talmudic scholarship was in a state of crisis. Once rich men had vied to marry off daughters to promising scholars and offered to support the young couples for years while the young grooms continued their studies. After the mid century, the rich set their sights on more modern young men and at the same time, due to urbanization and other factors, the job market for rabbis became less and less appealing. Young scholars found themselves with no hope of a rich bride or a stable job. The result was that many either had to delay marriage or abandon their studies. To remedy this situation a group of rabbis decided to apply the *kolel* system to eastern Europe. They raised money and founded a *kolel* in Kovno in 1879. Young married scholars were accepted and they were given a stipend to support themselves while they continued their studies.

[44] Portions of this leaflet were cited by Rivkind, 'Dissertation on R. Yitshak Elhanan Spektor' (Heb.).   [45] See Betsalel Landau, 'The Netsiv of Volozhin' (Heb.), esp. pp. 17–18.
[46] On Kantorowitz see Rivkind, 'The History of the Volozhin Emissaries' (Heb.).

They did not necessarily study as a group. Rather, they studied in various study halls in the town and there was loose, but effective, supervision. This framework was explicitly regarded as a replacement for the fathers-in-law that previously fulfilled this role. Donors were encouraged to support what was presented as a unique framework for the training of the rabbinic leadership of the future. The effort was successful, and it was not difficult to recruit students to accept the stipends. What is surprising is that sufficient donors were found to support the programme so that *kolelim* could be opened in other locations as well.[47]

*

The 'blue box' of the Jewish National Fund (*Keren kayemet leyisra'el*) was nothing other than a transformation of the traditional *pushke*. The idea to establish a national fund to purchase land in Erets Yisra'el for Jewish settlement was raised at the First Zionist Congress in Basle in 1897 by Professor Tsevi Herman Schapira. However, a decision to set it up was made only at the Fifth Congress in 1901. Even before the congress was held, articles were published in the Zionist newspaper *Die Welt* on the topic of a national fund. In the issue of 10 August 1900 an article was published discussing the methods to be employed in the collection for the planned fund.[48] The suggestion of the anonymous author/s was to issue stamps, which would be sold in Jewish communities throughout the world—a plan that was ultimately implemented. The intention was that the stamps would be saved by collectors and kept in special booklets. Another suggestion that was raised at the congress was to establish a Golden Book. This was an album that would be kept in Erets Yisra'el containing the name of each individual who donated ten pounds sterling or more to the Jewish National Fund.

There were advantages and disadvantages to the plan for raising funds by means of stamps. A stamp system makes is possible to keep a careful record of income and expenses. It is difficult to embezzle donations when a stamp has to be given in return for every contribution. However, it is expensive to print and distribute stamps, and there is a great deal of paperwork involved in the distribution of stamps. It is complicated and, in effect, it makes donations dependent on the presence of stamps. Both programmes were approved at the congress and the first names were inscribed in the Golden Book on the spot. However, neither method became the source of income that was hoped for. The stamp programme was never very effective as a fundraising tool, and the Golden Book was not much better.

[47] On the *kolel* see the chapter in my forthcoming book *Lithuanian Yeshivas of the Nineteenth Century*.   [48] See Kressel, *The Scroll of the Earth* (Heb.), 24.

The obvious solution was to use *pushke*s, but the Zionist movement was slow to employ this method. In fact, *pushke*s were first employed not by a central Zionist leader but by a resident of the Galician town Nadvorna by the name of Hayim Kleinman. After the Fifth Congress, he decided to go out on his own to collect money for the new national fund. He took a box, put an appropriate sign on it, and placed it in his office. To his surprise he very quickly collected a sizeable sum. This led him to write a letter to *Die Welt*, published on 24 January 1902,[49] announcing his success and encouraging others to do the same. Readers apparently took him seriously, and with growing frequency there were references to the use of *pushke*s for the national fund—but always as a matter of local initiative.[50] *Pushke*s were not mentioned in the first report of the Jewish National Fund in 1903, but in the second report in 1905 they were cited as one of the new methods adopted by the leadership.[51] They did not immediately become the most important method, but by 1939 almost a quarter of a million collection boxes had been distributed by the Jewish National Fund and this was by far the most important means of collecting funds for that organization.[52]

Behind the choice of fundraising methods were political and ideological issues. Stamps appealed not just because they were an accountant's dream, but because there was also a symbolic element to their use. Stamp sales for charity were among the most modern (and successful) means of fundraising in the early twentieth century. They were first employed for general charities in Austria and Holland, and from there the idea spread to Denmark (in 1904) and then to the United States.[53] Very often charity stamps were marketed in government post offices. The concern for order, seriousness, and a sound structure was very strong among the organizers of the Zionist movement. They were sensitive to claims that the movement's goals were unrealistic, and felt that the least they could do was to have practical organizations. For these reasons the very organization of the Jewish National Fund was delayed for some time until all of the questions of its legal status could be worked out. The sale of stamps had the aura of order, modernity, and a quasi-

[49] *Die Welt*, 3/4 (24 Jan. 1902), 13. For biographical details on Kleinman see Kressel, *The Scroll of the Earth* (Heb.), 36.

[50] In *Die Welt*, 3/10 (7 Mar. 1902) there is a report of a *Sammelbüchse* used in Vienna, the next issue contains a report of the use of a *pushke* in Czortków, and in issue 14 there is mention of the use of a *pushke* in Neutra.

[51] See Kremenezky, *Bericht über den Jüdischen Nationalfonds erstattet am VII Zionisten-Kongress in Basel* presented to the Seventh Zionist Congress in 1905. On p. 8 there is reference to new fundraising methods such as *Sammelbüchsen*, *Sammelbogen*, and *Ölbaumspenden*.

[52] Boehm and Pollack, *The Jewish National Fund* (Heb.), 94–5. The amount collected by these boxes was three times as much as was collected by any other means.

[53] Cutlip, *Fundraising in the United States*, 54.

governmental status—if not more. These were excellent reasons to try this method.

It is not easy to find a clear precedent for the Golden Book. That is in itself interesting. It was also quite interesting that some people were ready to pay rather large sums of money to be inscribed in a book that was deposited far away. At first glance, the reward appears disproportionately small in light of the cost. However, it should not be forgotten that the act of inscription in the book was publicized in the Jewish press, so there was a clear 'payoff' for the donation. There was also a symbolic element to the Golden Book. In Jewish communities, a common reward for a donation was an inscription on a wall of a public building or on some permanent object. In this way the memory of the donor's generosity would be transmitted to future generations. One of the minor problems of the Zionist movement in general, and the Jewish National Fund in particular, was that it did not have a place for a plaque. Even when land was bought, one could not nail a sign on the ground. In a sense the Golden Book served as an 'ersatz' wall. It may not have been the intention but it was the best that could be done.

In comparison with the Jewish National Fund's stamps and the Golden Book, the collection box was an uncomfortable reminder of a world the Zionists were rejecting. It was old fashioned, difficult to monitor, and had associations with what appeared to be the least modern elements of Jewish society. However, it worked. To integrate the *pushke*s into the Zionist fund-raising effort it was necessary to eliminate the negative symbolism, or at least to limit it as much as possible. The simplest way to do this was to create a visual distinction between the *pushke* of the Jewish National Fund and the *pushke*s of the yeshivas and the veteran Jewish communities in Erets Yisra'el. An interesting attempt in this direction was recorded in a report of the activities of the Jewish National Fund in Russia in the years 1908—9. According to the report, '7000 boxes were distributed in 200 locations. They were made like the boxes used abroad. However, 857 of the "Moscow" boxes, which have six sides, were also distributed. In total, about 10,000 boxes are in use'.[54] None of these 'Moscow' boxes seems to have been preserved. However, from their description as six-sided, it is clear that they were visually distinctive from others. Why more were not made is not clear, but it is possible to guess that technically it is difficult to make and store six-sided boxes. The ultimate solution was for boxes that were painted in a distinctive colour—blue. With one glance it was possible to see that these belonged to the new world that was being created.

The importance of the *pushke* for yeshiva budgets, for the *kolel*s of the traditionalists in Erets Yisra'el, and for the Zionists is indicative of common features of their supporters. For all the attempts of the Zionists to attract the modern Jew, for many years their appeal, with few exceptions, was much stronger among the poor and traditional than among the assimilating or acculturating rich in central and western Europe. With little support from the elite, Zionist fundraisers found the *pushke* an essential tool to raise funds among the Jews of limited means who were among the strongest supporters of Zionism. This had to done as effectively as possible because of the limited manpower available.

The *pushke* was effective as a fundraising tool as long as it was integrated into a regular pattern of home ritual. By the integration of rituals involving the giving of charity by women the *pushke* found its place in fundraising history. In retrospect it would not be an exaggeration to claim that most of the land purchased by the Zionist movement was bought with the donations of women. Similarly, it was due to the devotion of women and not of men that the yeshivas of eastern Europe continued to exist even when the rich turned their backs on them. It was due to women donors that the *kolelim* in Erets Yisra'el survived and even flourished. Without regular ritual patterns, which made donation not a matter of impulse but a regular part of the weekly routine, such achievements would have been impossible.

Today *pushkes* occupy a peripheral role in almost every fundraising programme. The growing affluence of the Jewish community has made it easier to rely on one-time donations and long-term commitments. The changes in home life make the regular giving of charity in the home a far rarer phenomenon. However, the institutions that were supported by *pushkes* in critical transitional years are still with us today. They survived because in critical years they could rely on the donations of countless women week after week.

SIX

Was the Traditional East European Jewish Family in the Recent Past Patriarchal?

MANY TODAY who rely on popular images of the past would instantly respond: 'Of course, the east European Jewish family was patriarchal!' With equal certainly, nineteenth-century maskilim or 'enlightened' Jews would have answered that it was matriarchal! As David Biale wrote: 'The maskilim . . . experienced their mothers-in-law and, to a lesser extent, their wives as powerful and domineering, they imagined an ideal family in which power implicitly lay in the hands of the husband. Their revolt against the traditional family was a revolt against a perceived matriarchal family.'[1]

Even though maskilim were describing a contemporary reality, we cannot accept their views as the last word on the topic, just as we cannot assume that popular images today are always correct. The maskilim were not always objective and they described mainly what they were familiar with—life in the middle and upper classes in which most of them had been brought up. Biale hints at this by employing the term 'perceived'. Therefore it is not possible to rely uncritically on their views; the topic requires a more careful examination.

It was not just the maskilim who wrote about this. More than a generation later, Ze'ev Jabotinsky, who had a sharp eye and saw through many pre-conceptions, included a revealing vignette in his fascinating novel *The Five*. Jabotinsky used a character, Abram Moiseevich, who in the novel teaches the narrator about the world, to say the following:

In general, you should know, once and for all, about all Jewish households: if something very difficult has to be decided, 'she' is always the one to do it. My wife, Leah, has always been as dumb as an ox, but it would never have occurred to me, let's say, to buy a barge or to sell the house on Slobodka Romanovka, if she hadn't said, 'What do I know? Do what you think'.[2]

[1] Biale, *Eros and the Jews*, 161.
[2] Jabotinsky, *The Five*, 178. However, in his description of the next generation, the power of women was diminished and Marusya is shown as subservient to her husband Samuilo. In other words, modernity can allow young people a free choice of marital partner but may also lead to

This is a description of an east European Jewish family by a man who was intimately familiar with it. It expresses disdain for women, but does not depict a family in which a husband rules.

There are many pitfalls in describing traditional east European Jewish society in the eighteenth and nineteenth centuries, or in describing any society. Among them is the unconscious influence of stereotypes; another is the tendency to 'find' in Jewish society phenomena that are present in non-Jewish societies—even when they are not really there! Perhaps the most important trap is the use of terms without clear definitions or consistent usage. To decide whether the traditional Jewish family in eastern Europe in recent generations was patriarchal it is necessary to consider not only what the reality was, but whether Jews differed from non-Jews and, if so, how. Only then will it be possible to decide if it is reasonable to term that Jewish society patriarchal.

Traditional Jewish family life in the eighteenth and nineteenth centuries was similar to that of previous centuries and it would be difficult to claim that this was a distinct period.[3] It is also important to recognize that there was no single pattern of the Jewish family. There were sharp class differences in eastern European Jewish society, and the cultural and social world of the tailor was very distant from that of the merchant or Talmud scholar. There were also differences that were tied to geography, and Jewish populations in different regions diverged from each other in many ways. It is impossible to take for granted that what characterized hasidim in Ukraine would be equally prevalent among mitnagedim in Lithuania. Similarly, patterns that were found among village Jews were not necessarily found among urban Jews. At the same time, as we shall see, there were characteristics that were common to most traditional Jewish families in eastern Europe.

It is tempting to use literary sources to provide a picture of the Jewish family in eastern Europe but there are certain dangers in doing this. It is important to note that most of the literary depictions of family life, such as those that are found in autobiographies, novels, or stories, reflect life in the middle- or upper-class Jewish family. Most of the authors had received a good education and had the time to write, but these skills and opportunities were not found in all levels of Jewish society. Similarly, the views expressed in the

greater dependence of women on their husbands. It is important to distinguish between the dependence of young people on parents in traditional society, which was not necessarily patriarchal, and the subservience of women to husbands which is more patriarchal.

[3] The best starting point to get a picture of the traditional East European Jewish family is Rosman, 'To be a Jewish Woman' (Heb.), 415–34. His article 'A History of Jewish Women in Early Modern Poland' is also well worth reading. For a rich and suggestive study of women, Jewish and non-Jewish, in a west European community at the same time, see Ulbrich, *Shulamit and Margarete*.

sermons of rabbis—another accessible source—reflect views of another elite subgroup.[4] It is, of course, important to know the views and the realities of elite groups, but this alone cannot be the basis of a description of Jewish society. To depict the features of this society it will be necessary to look further afield.

The first step in such an examination is usually to define the terms and then inspect the evidence. However, in this case there are a number of legitimate and useful definitions of patriarchy. Therefore it may be useful to note some of the characteristics of Jewish family life before looking at the definitions and considering to what degree they 'fit' with the realities of Jewish life.

FATHERS AND CHILDREN

Since the authority of the male head of a family is probably integral to any definition of patriarchy it is necessary to pay attention to the degree of authority the head of the Jewish family held. It is not just an issue of authority over wives.[5] In a study on (non-Jewish) family forms in north-western Europe, Wally Seccombe wrote:

Some combination of the following five prerogatives held by husbands and fathers over their wives and children are generally found in patriarchal family systems . . . a) the right to represent the family group, b) the effective possession of . . . family property, c) supervision of the labour of other family members, d) conjugal rights . . . in marriage, e) custodial rights over children, entailing ultimate authority in their upbringing . . . Note that the two dimensions of authority relations within families, along the lines of gender and generation, are integrated in this definition.[6]

This clearly states that attention should be given to father–child relations and not only husband–wife relations.

In traditional east European Jewish families, authority over children was not monopolized by fathers; mothers also had a great deal of authority over minor children. Until around the age of 12 children were dependent on their parents and the parents were responsible for their children's needs. I have not found any reference in the literature of the period, nor in the research literature, that suggests that fathers had more authority over minor children than did mothers. Fathers often spent more hours a day out of the house than

[4] Thus a text such as the Vilna Gaon's *Alim literufah*, which was a letter he sent to his wife and family on the eve of his departure for Erets Yisra'el, projects a level of expectation from his wife and daughters that says more about the Gaon than about what was common practice in his time.
[5] In the discussion of the term 'patriarchy' below, possible definitions of the term that do not include authority over children will be considered.
[6] Seccombe, *A Millennium of Family Change*, 30–1.

did mothers, and often they had to work far from their homes. In reality mothers usually determined what went on at home, and even when this was in accordance with their husbands' wishes, it does not imply that it was under their husbands' authority.

Certainly gender had an impact on authority. From the age of barmitzvah, many boys did not live at home and therefore were not exposed to the authority of their fathers on a daily basis. Often children from more middle-class homes with scholarly potential left home after studying in *ḥeder* and went on to study in communal study halls, usually in another city. There they lived in the study hall, ate their meals with local families (a system known as 'eating *teg*'), and studied all day. Leaving the home was a form of initiation rite. Parents did not visit their sons often and could not follow closely their advancement in their studies. These youths were totally independent and lived in this way until their marriage. Among the masses the situation was different, but only to a degree. Many youths worked for a set number of years as apprentices after studying in *ḥeder*. While learning a skill, they were subject to the authority of the master artisan. They studied with him and often lived in his home. In most issues, the masters, not the parents, determined what would be done. Upon completing the apprenticeship, the young men did not return home but, instead, married and established their own households, independent of their parents who were often still alive and economically active. Thus the sons of both the poor and the rich could spend more time in their adolescent years under the rule of strangers than of parents. In other words, the Jewish father often had little day-to-day contact with his adolescent sons or control over them, and there was a limit on the potential expressions of authority on the part of fathers.

The situation of daughters was different, but in their lives as well there were few signs of paternal authority. Most daughters were occupied at home helping with household duties and the upbringing of younger siblings. In these activities daughters were under the rule of their mothers. Girls from poor families could learn a skill but did not necessarily live away from home, although some girls were employed as servants and worked outside the home. Thus, in the lives of many—and probably most—girls, there were few daily expressions of their father's rule.

Perhaps the greatest potential for paternal authority can be found in the marital patterns of their children. Until the mid-nineteenth century, childhood ended early among the well-off. Their children married at an early age—in their early teens—with the help of a matchmaker. The use of matchmakers by parents is a clear expression of parental authority.[7] However,

---

[7] It might be that a critical study of matchmaking would discover that for many who were matched up, the parental intervention had a positive rather than a negative impact on the par-

there is no evidence that there was a general social assumption that the father alone determined a match. There were cases when fathers made a match without consulting mothers, but generally mothers had a great deal to say in such matters. In cases of remarriage after widowhood or divorce, parents did not choose a partner for their remarrying children but rather the parties involved made their own choices.[8]

After marriage, the authority of the groom's father did not increase. It was accepted among the rich that after marriage, the young couple would live for an extended period of time in the house of the bride's family (a practice known as *kest*).[9] During this period the father of the bride gained authority and not the father of the groom. The bride's family often lived far away from the home of the groom's father and there is little reason to think that the groom's father could exercise much authority from afar. The young groom's father may have tried to influence his son and even give orders in a letter, but he did not have the means to force his son to do his bidding.[10] The bride and the groom were somewhat subject to the bride's parents, but only for a clearly defined period and their ties were apparently more to the mother than to the father. This is the background to the complaints that Biale cited on the overbearing mother-in-law. The father-in-law had opportunities to influence or to give orders to his daughter and son-in-law, but the contractual nature of the *tenayim*, the prenuptial agreement, determined on a contractual basis how many years of support the couple would receive and under what conditions. The status of the father in this context came not from his being a father but because of the contract and the commitments in it.

Economic issues had a variety of consequences for the authority of fathers among the poor, as noted in previous chapters. Their daughters could not anticipate a big dowry or significant support from parents and therefore poorer Jews married only when they were reasonably certain that they could support themselves. In other words, they married later than Jews who had more money. As a result, even when marrying for the first time they had a say in the choice of a marital partner, and the authority of the poor father in the choice of a marital partner for his children was more limited than among the richer Jews. Most of the poor brides and grooms were not employed by their parents or in-laws after marriage and did not live with them. For a merchant or artisan of modest means it was hard enough to support a family as it was. The addition of another worker in the form of a son or son-in-law did not

ties involved. I know of no study that measures the long-term happiness of couples who married for romantic love compared with matched-up couples.

    [8] See Chapter 3 above.
    [9] See Landes and Zborowski, 'Hypotheses Concerning the Eastern European Jewish Family', 543, and see Chapter 1 above on premature marriage.
    [10] See a fascinating example in Etkes, *Lithuania in Jerusalem* (Heb.).

guarantee an equivalent rise in the number of clients or of income. Instead, many young couples from such backgrounds, who would have been relatively independent even before marriage, migrated in search of a living.

In the words of David Kena'ani, who used a wide variety of sources: 'In these classes they [the poor] always married at a later age . . . they did not take into account factors such as distinguished lineage . . . the concern for norms was weaker, and love in other words, choice of a partner . . . was common.'[11] Kena'ani made a number of important points. He noted that among the poor, the financial, lineage, and scholarly factors that concerned the rich were not important. Often the choice of a partner was made by the parties involved on the basis of a previous acquaintanceship and mutual attraction. A father with few means would have found it hard to exercise authority because he had little to give his child—or to deny them. The poor did not have the resources to employ a matchmaker who would bring them a match from afar. Instead, they found matches close to home, either with local or volunteer matchmakers or on the basis of direct contact between the bride and groom. There were certainly opportunities for candidates for a match to express opposition. If they did not like the suggested partner, it would have been difficult to force them to accept the decision because they were economically independent.

The hounding of youths who had become attracted to Haskalah, or Enlightenment, is a special case in which one generation imposed authority on another. The descriptions of these cases usually concentrate on the cruelty of the tormentors—the father or the father-in-law—but they ignore one small detail. These young men who were spending time reading Enlightenment literature did not work for a living. They lived at the expense of their parents or in-laws who supported them so that they could devote all of their time to the study of Torah. Therefore, when some youths were found 'wasting' their time, their parents or in-laws were angry and reacted harshly. From their point of view, devoting time to the Enlightenment was a form of fraud or abuse of their support. (One can only imagine how donors of a scholarship to a university would react if they discovered that a brilliant student had been given a fellowship but had decided to abandon his or her studies and use the grant money to finance a trip to Goa or Patagonia. An angry reaction would certainly be understandable.) The stories of youths attracted to Haskalah are sometimes heart-wrenching, but they are not significant evidence of paternal authority.

There were (and are) societies in which offspring lived within the framework of an extended family. In other words, there were multigenerational families whose economic well-being was based entirely or to a large degree on joint labour. Such a framework is very conducive to a high degree

---

[11] Kena'ani, *The Houses that No Longer Exist* (Heb.), 60–1.

of authority from the head of the family. However, in east European Jewish society, the pattern of the expanded family was not a factor in paternal authority for the simple reason that multigenerational families were not common among Jews.[12] Multigenerational families fit in with the social realities of an agricultural society or in the lives of the very wealthy in an urban environment. The framework of such a family depends, among other things, on the economic advantages of such a structure and on prosaic factors such as the possibility of constructing a house in which there is room for a number of families. In an agricultural society in which families own land it is not so difficult to build a house with room for a number of families, or to add rooms later. In cities it is more difficult to do so and only the minority of the very affluent could purchase or build a house like this. For most Jews who lived in cities the basic conditions for a multigenerational family were missing. Most Jews lived in small homes or apartments which did not allow for the possibility of building additional living quarters. Most Jews were very poor and could only dream about a big house.

Moreover, there was also no economic advantage in Jewish society for multigenerational families. Among farmers, extra hands always find employment. However, merchants and craftsmen had few tasks to offer family members. In the modern period Jews did not have a tradition of multigenerational co-residence and therefore they also felt no need to make efforts in this direction. Therefore one cannot look for paternal authority in multigenerational families because they were highly atypical. In agricultural societies, such households offered a solution to the question of where older parents would live once they did not have the physical strength for agricultural work. In east European Jewish society, the accepted pattern was for older parents to live on their own. The nature of trade and crafts made it possible to work for more years and not to be dependent on children.[13]

HUSBANDS AND WIVES

The sphere where one could most expect expressions of a patriarchal structure was in relations between the male head of the family and his wife. However, in this area as well, in traditional east European Jewish families male authority could not be taken for granted and male heads of families could not simply force wives to do their bidding. For example, in many societies male authority is expressed in sexual life. However, a Jewish male could not force

[12] Religion was not the decisive factor. There were Jewish societies in urban Muslim environments in which the patterns of an expanded family were maintained. However, the realities of life in a Muslim environment were totally different from those of a European Christian environment and what was common in one setting could be very rare elsewhere.

[13] See Chapter 4 above.

sexual relations on his wife if she did not want them. According to Jewish law, sexual relations during and for a period following menstruation are forbidden. Even a small amount of bleeding leads to a prohibition. Therefore, a woman who did not want sexual relations could always claim that she was in a prohibited period. There were, of course, exceptions and husbands who ignored Jewish law and forced themselves on their wives even when it was prohibited, but they did not enjoy the sanction of Jewish society.

Most men had little real authority over women in religious life. Surprising as it might seem, they usually could not tell women what Jewish law demanded of them and what they should do. In reality, women decided day-to-day questions of Jewish law more than did men. For example, matters of *kashrut* were decided by women; if a woman was unsure in a particular matter—as to whether a chicken was kosher perhaps—she went to the rabbi and not to her husband for halakhic guidance. In other areas as well, such as sabbath and holiday laws, men did not instruct women. There were good reasons for this. Jewish law was not taught in *ḥeder*, and even those scholars who devoted years to studying Jewish texts usually concentrated on the Talmud and its commentaries. Most men, excepting only a small minority of rabbis, therefore had very little knowledge of Jewish law or of the halakhic codes. Both men and women knew Jewish law from observing their parents and peers and not from books.[14] As a matter of fact, most men did not know any more about Jewish law than did women.

Even in areas that were not related to Jewish law it was not easy for a man to come to his wife with demands or to give her orders. Unlike many other contemporary societies, a Jewish woman had a very practical option: to refuse her husband's order and to demand a divorce. In traditional Jewish society in the eighteenth and nineteenth centuries there was a high level of divorce. We do not have any statistical data for the eighteenth century, but the rabbinic literature is full of discussions of divorce and it is not regarded as something exceptional. It may well be the case that there were thirty divorces for every hundred weddings in the nineteenth century and many of the cases of divorce were because women demanded them.[15] Among the factors that contributed to this level of divorce was the simple fact that in eastern Europe it was standard and accepted among Jews that women worked outside the home and not necessarily in the family business.[16] When a woman works in a family business it is difficult to quantify her contribution to the family income and it can be ignored. However, when she has her own business or works for wages

[14] Soloveitchik, 'Rupture and Reconstruction'.

[15] Freeze, *Jewish Marriage and Divorce in Imperial Russia*; and see Chapter 2 above.

[16] The pattern of east European Jewish women working outside the home and not in the family business differed from patterns of medieval Jewish women in Christian Europe, and also from Jewish societies in Muslim lands in all periods. It is reasonable to believe that the reason is

it is easy for her and for others to measure and assess her contribution. The awareness of the economic contribution of the wives limited the authority of their husbands.[17] More importantly, a working woman could assume that if she were ever to be divorced, she would be able to continue working and be capable of supporting herself, whereas a woman who was not working knew that she was dependent on her husband. Therefore, if relations between a husband and a working wife were strained, it was not so difficult for a woman to decide to demand a divorce. Since women's work was often outside the home and not in the husband's business, divorce did not necessarily cause her independent income to drop. The relative economic independence of women and the ever-present option of divorce curbed the ability of husbands to try unilaterally to exercise authority. It should be noted that divorce was common among Jews in every part of eastern Europe and that there were no significant regional differences.

The folk image of the ideal Jewish family did not depict an authoritative husband/father as the head of the model family. There was a popular view in traditional east European Jewish society that the ideal family was one in which the husband studied the Torah all day and his wife supported him. Of course, only in a few cases was this ideal realized. In the descriptions of men who devoted all of their time to study there was emphasis on the fact that women ran the businesses that supported the family. It should not be ignored that the ideal of full-time Torah study assumed that the husband would be dependent on his wife. With dependence like this it is clear that the husband's ability to give his wife orders was rather limited.

It is illuminating to look at expressions of the authority of husbands in Jewish law as it was interpreted in the eighteenth and nineteenth centuries in eastern Europe, even though examining Jewish law does not necessarily reflect the day-to-day realities. The ways in which two interesting laws found in the *Shulḥan arukh* were interpreted in east European rabbinic circles can shed light on the authority of fathers.[18] One of them deals with the authority given to the head of a family to force his wife to perform certain deeds. The *Shulḥan arukh* states that a woman has to do the following for her husband: 'To wash his face, hands and feet, to pour him his drinks and to make his

tied to the willingness of the Christian environment to accept independent economic activity by women as tolerable, in contrast to expectations of 'modesty' that were prevalent among Muslims. However, it may be that there was an additional reason. Steve Ozment notes in his book *Ancestors: The Loving Family in Old Europe*, 23–4, that in the wake of the Black Plague there was a lack of manpower for work in Europe and this brought the entry of women into many fields of economic endeavour. It would be interesting to check if this change in non-Jewish society had an impact on Jewish society that lasted until the modern period.

[17] On this see Becker, *A Treatise on the Family*.

[18] I am grateful to Gershon Bacon for his suggestion to examine these laws.

bed.'[19] This law could have served as a basis for all sorts of demands by men to their wives. However, in all of the responsa literature produced in eastern Europe, there is not one reference to implementation of this law in practice. There were no discussions among scholars on how to implement the law. It is as if this paragraph was erased from the *Shulḥan arukh*. Perhaps a careful search of the literature on customs will turn up a case or two of implementation of this law, but these will be exceptions to the general rule that this law did not enter the world of scholarly discourse.[20]

A far more significant issue is whether and to what degree Jewish law permits violence of husbands towards wives.[21] The most important text for regarding east European Jewish legal stands on this issue is Rabbi Moses Isserles's supplement to *Shulḥan arukh*:

If a man hits his wife it is a sin like hitting a friend and if he is a accustomed to do so, the courts have the right to beat him, to excommunicate him and to whip him in all manners of force and punishment and to make him swear that he will never do so again if he does not obey the court. Some say that he can be forced to divorce his wife if he has been warned once or twice because this is not in the manner of Jews to hit their wives and it is the behaviour of idolaters. All of this is if he starts the dispute but if she curses him for no reason or is insulting to his father and mother and if he warns her and she does not heed him, some say that he can hit her and others say that even a bad wife cannot be hit and the first opinion is the authoritative one.[22]

According to Rabbi Isserles, it may be permissible in certain cases for a husband to hit his wife, but it was not a sweeping authorization. It was permitted only to 'educate' the wife and in specifically defined and limited circumstances; the reason for the permission was not that a wife is subject to the will of her husband. The basic assumption is that violence is generally prohibited unless there is a justified ground for permission. This is not an absolute ban but it is certainly far from the tolerance of violence that characterized contemporary non-Jewish society.[23] Not only is Rabbi Isserles's conclusion interesting but so is the reason he cites for prohibiting violence in most cases. He does not bring a citation from the Talmud or from a rabbinic work but rather states that 'because this is not in the manner of Jews to hit their wives and it is the behaviour of idolaters'. Perhaps he could find absolutely no source in rabbinic literature that could be forced to support his position.

[19] *Shulḥan arukh*, 'Even ha'ezer', 80.
[20] A check in the most comprehensive data base of responsa, *Otsar haposekim*, did not turn up even one case of implementation of this law.
[21] For a full discussion of this issue see the Ph.D. dissertation of Mikhal Wolf, 'Legal Constraints on Wife Beating' (Heb.). Much of Naomi Graetz's book *Silence is Deadly* is on this topic.
[22] 'Even ha'ezer', 154: 2.
[23] Shahar, *The Fourth Estate*, 90; also Grossman, 'Violence towards Women in the Mediterranean Jewish Society of the Middle Ages' (Heb.).

However, it seems more likely that for Rabbi Isserles, the prohibition of violence is so obvious that it needs no textual support. What cannot be determined from his responsa is how much violence towards women existed in Jewish society in his time.

What is significant for issues of patriarchy in the eighteenth and nineteenth centuries is how Rabbi Isserles's position was interpreted and applied. In this period east European rabbis did not vocally support Rabbi Isserles's position that in certain extreme cases violence to a wife may be justified. *Arukh hashulḥan* is a code of Jewish law that reflects halakhic positions current in Lithuania in the late nineteenth century. Its author, Rabbi Yehi'el Mikhal Epstein, referred to wife beating and to Rabbi Isserles's reference to the limited possibilities where violence could be justified.[24] Rabbi Epstein further limited the likelihood of its implementation by adding further restrictions to those of Rabbi Isserles. In the responsa literature of the nineteenth century there is absolutely no statement that reflects understanding or justification of violence to wives.[25] To sum up, there were legal sources with the potential to be used to justify violence but this was not done. Rabbis clearly saw violence as totally unacceptable behaviour.

The Jewish ethical literature reflects, like the legal literature, positions that were widespread in the Jewish elite and teaches more about elite views than about reality. However, the ethical literature, in distinction from the legal literature, was popular among the general community. The wide readership of ethical literature and the reprinting of classic texts demonstrate some degree of identification of the general public with the contents of these works. One can assume that it had some influence on readers and on a wider audience. A check of the ethical literature does not change the picture given by examining the halakhic literature. Ruth Berger dealt with male violence in her book on sexuality, marriage, and family life in the Jewish ethical literature. Her conclusion is simple. She notes that while violence in punishment of children drew support from some authors, and despite the fact that in the non-Jewish society, violence against wives was accepted in certain circles, all of the authors of Jewish ethical literature who referred to violence against women condemned it. There was not one who saw such violence as justified, even in exceptional conditions,[26] and there is no mention of Rabbi Isserles permitting it in certain cases. Again, this is not proof for the absence of violence in Jewish society but it certainly indicates that there was no ideology that justified such violence or even expressed sympathy with it.

It is possible to conclude that in the traditional Jewish society in

[24] Epstein, *Arukh hashulḥan*, 'Even ha'ezer', 154: 18.
[25] See the sources in *Otsar haposekim*.
[26] Ruth Berger, *Sexualität, Ehe und Familienleben in der jüdischen Moralliteratur*.

nineteenth-century eastern Europe, heads of families had only limited authority over adolescent children and even less over married descendants. There
were not many areas in which a husband could force his wife to do his will in
opposition to hers, and there were also no evident regional differences in this
respect. In all of these points, east European Jewish families differed from
most families in other societies in eastern Europe,[27] and apparently to some
degree, they differed from Jewish families in eastern Europe in previous centuries and from contemporary Ashkenazi families in western Europe.[28] However, this is not the case for all of Europe. Recent research has begun to give
more attention to differences in marital patterns in the general European
society and especially to the fact that a unique pattern of delayed marriage
characterized north-western Europe. Among the characteristics of marriage
in this region in the early modern period was 'young persons being close in
age at marriage, or taking charge of selection of their spouses, or saving to
support themselves in households of their own'.[29] In these households,
women had more active roles than in societies with early marriage and men
had less domestic authority.[30] Many of these characteristics would also apply
to Jews. The one exception is delay in marriage but this might be 'accidental'.
Farm workers had to delay marriage in order to first obtain land, but Jews
who worked in trade and as craftsmen could more quickly arrive at their maximum anticipated income and hence marry earlier.[31] The role of medieval
German settlers on Polish urban life and mores should be explored. It is possible that they brought with them values favouring what Hartman terms
'weak families' and that these values were assimilated by the neighbouring
Jews.[32]

[27] The starting point for most studies on family forms is Hajnal, 'European Marriage Patterns'. There are many useful studies on family structure in eastern Europe. Among them see
Blobaum, 'The "Woman Question" in Russian Poland'; Fidelis, 'Participation in the Creative
Work of the Nation'; Żarnowska, 'Family and Public Life'; Melton, 'Proto-Industrialization,
Serf Agriculture and Agrarian Social Structure'; Kaser, 'Power and Inheritance'. For many purposes, the most important general study on women in Poland is Bogucka, *Women in Early Modern Polish Society*. I was unable to consult Żarnowska and Szwarc (eds.), *Kobieta i społeczenstwo*;
Kaser, *Macht und Erbe*, or Karpinski, *Kobieta w miescie polskim w drugiej połowie XVI i w XVII wieku*.
[28] On previous centuries, see Rosman, 'To be a Jewish Woman in the (Heb.). For a detailed
and profound case study of a Jewish community in western Europe see Ulbrich, *Shulamit and
Margarete.*   [29] Hartman, *The Household and the Making of History*, 29.   [30] Ibid. 32.
[31] Hartman sees delayed marriage as a crucial variant. This did not characterize Jews, but
work outside the home did. In a review of Żarnowska and Szwarc (eds.), *Kobieta i społeczenstwo na
ziemiach polskich w XIX wieku*, Basia Nowak summarized Żarnowska's introduction thus:
'because of women's increasing participation in paid employment, gendered division of roles
began to change among all groups of women to varying degrees, and the traditional patriarchal
model was in decline among the intelligentsia, petty nobility, working-class, and peasant communities'. Work outside the home might well have contributed to delayed marriage.
[32] Hartman, *The Household and the Making of History*, 250–6.

This discussion should not lead us to ignore the fact that the status of Jewish men was generally regarded among Jews as elevated over that of Jewish women.[33] In traditional Jewish society in eastern Europe in the modern period, different tasks were assigned to men and women—as is and was the case in every human society. Gender played a major role in determining both status and function. Jews at that time distinguished between the civic realm, in which women did not take part and could not have leadership positions, and the private realm in which women had much to say and do. Scholars were all male and they were regarded as elevated above others. Women could not join this group. However, women were not required to devote all of their energies to mastering rabbinic literature nor were they regarded as failures if they did not. The stigma applied to a poorly educated man did not apply to women. The education that boys received was regarded by both males and females as superior to that of women. However, as we shall see, the fact that men were regarded as superior does not automatically mean that the society was patriarchal.

Two minor but significant expressions of the status of women in Jewish society are worth noting. One is related to Jewish family names. Researchers of these have noted that many of them were created not from men's names but women's. One can point to Sarason, Rivkes, Perles, and many others. This does not mean that in the lifetime of their husbands the women headed the families. There is no evidence for this. However, the adoption of the name of a famous woman, very possibly a widow who could head a family, as a means of identification of her family reflects a reality in which both men and women could be in the centre.

Another indication of the place of women in Jewish society can be found in the aesthetics of Jews in eastern Europe. Males were regarded as attractive if they were thin, had white hands, and wore glasses. These were all reflections of lives devoted to study and perhaps to asceticism. On the other hand, attractive women had full bodies and were strong and active. Their appearance promised work and support. Different ideals are expressed here, but the image of the ideal woman is not one of weakness.[34]

DEFINING PATRIARCHY

It is not easy to define the term 'patriarchal'. One reason is that many use it without defining it and without using it systematically.[35] Reality cannot easily be encapsulated in terms. It has been pointed out that concepts of patriarchy

---

[33] Rosman, 'A History of Jewish Women in Early Modern Poland', shows the complexity of the realities.   [34] Somogyi, *Die Schejnen und die Prosten*, 112–15.

[35] Similarly, terms such as 'modernization' and 'democratization' are used by many often to

and male status did not exist in a vacuum and can be usefully examined in comparison with images of women. Mary Hartman, following the lead of Martha Howell, pointed out that women were 'caught between two gender imaginaries, positioned both as competent and incompetent, as responsible and irresponsible, as trustworthy and untrustworthy'.[36] Howell was describing conditions in early modern Netherlands but this description is equally applicable to the images in eastern Europe. In these imaginaries, there is no semblance of consistency. Definitions are needed, but providing them is not simple.

Most definitions for the term 'patriarchal' fit loosely into two categories. One use is in the context of family and the other is in the context of society at large. A standard dictionary definition defines the patriarchal family thus: 'A social system in which the father is the head of the family and men have authority over women and children'.[37] In this definition, the critical word is 'authority', which in the same dictionary is defined as 'the right and power to command, enforce laws, exact obedience, determine or judge'. According to this definition, among the characteristics of patriarchy is the power of the father to determine how other members of the family will behave and to force them to act as he wishes even if they do not wish to do so. This definition does not emphasize a social, political, or cognitive theory but it stresses behaviour. In other words, it is not statements of authority of the male that determine but deeds. It should be noted that this definition of the term 'patriarchal' relates not only to authority of males over women but also over children.

If this definition is accepted, it is difficult to claim that the traditional Jewish family in eastern Europe in the nineteenth century was patriarchal. As shown above, authority of the Jewish father over his family was limited and far from absolute.

The other type of definition refers to a patriarchal society. In this sense, the term does not refer to the rule of fathers (*pater* in Latin) but to the rule of males, or of some males, in a given society. Sylvia Walby defined the patriarchal society in the following words and her definition is typical for a social definition:

I shall define patriarchy as a system of social structures and practices in which men dominate, oppress and exploit women . . . At a less abstract level patriarchy is composed of six structures: the patriarchal mode of production, patriarchal rela-

present something as good but without offering a clear definition. The meaning of the words often depends more on the speaker than on a dictionary definition, and indeed these terms on occasion are given contradictory meanings.

[36] Martha Howell in Hartman, *The Household and the Making of History*, 102.
[37] Pickett et al. (eds.), *American Heritage Dictionary*, s.v. 'Patriarchal Family'.

tions in paid work, patriarchal relations in the state, male violence, patriarchal relations in sexuality, and patriarchal relations in cultural institutions.[38]

This definition of patriarchy is also not very applicable to traditional Jewish families in eastern Europe in the eighteenth and nineteenth centuries. Since Jewish males were mainly independent traders or craftsmen, there was hardly any patriarchal aspect to the means of production or paid work. The internal rule among the Jews was, of course, limited to males and so were cultural institutions, but with all of their importance they did not determine the structure of the family. There was no male rule among Jews with regard to violence and male authority in sexual life. Therefore this list gives at the most two out of six grounds for identifying eastern European Jewish society as patriarchal, and even these two are weak.

Patriarchy is often linked to politics and political structure. In this context it is important to note that the minority status of the Jews was an important difference between them and non-Jews. This is significant for the link between family structure and the forms of government. John Demos wrote an important and pioneering book, *A Little Commonwealth*, on family life in the Plymouth Colony, which dealt with this issue. The name of the book is taken from a text that reads: 'A family is a little church and a little commonwealth . . . it is as a school wherein the first principles . . . are learned: whereby men are fitted to greater matters in church or commonwealth.'[39]

This is a position that fits many cases. However, Jews were different. The Jews did not see themselves as an integral and natural part of the state and their neighbours did not see them as such. Therefore, for example, the structure of government in a state did not have a deep influence on the Jews. Life in the home did not prepare Jews for roles in the church or in the government because Jews had no roles there. The Jewish rabbinical establishment was not hierarchical in the same way that Roman Catholic Christianity was. Rabbis derived their authority, at least in theory, by being elected by their fellow Jews and they were chosen, again in theory, for their achieved skills. For this reason, in principle one could argue with any rabbi because there was no theory of divine infallibility that applied to rabbis. Therefore, the rabbinate was a poor model for patriarchy. The reality may have often been different and oligarchy may have been the rule rather than the exception, but that reality was not presented as an ideal. True, communal life was limited to males, but its nature was very different from the political ideal that was found among many non-Jewish thinkers.[40]

---

[38] Walby, *Theorizing Patriarchy*, 20.   [39] Demos, *A Little Commonwealth*, p. xix.
[40] Jewish communal life, however, was similar to urban guilds and brotherhoods and this topic merits more research.

If we wish, we can define patriarchy such that it will apply not only to conditions in which fathers or males have authority over women, but to all conditions in which men have status advantages over women. The *Online Dictionary of the Social Sciences* uses a definition of this type:

Literally 'rule by the father' but more generally it refers to a social situation where men are dominant over women in wealth, status and power. Patriarchy is associated with a set of ideas, a 'patriarchal ideology' that acts to explain and justify this dominance and attributes it to inherent natural differences between men and women.[41]

According to this type of definition, almost every non-egalitarian society would be termed patriarchal. If we consider contemporary realities of wealth, status, and power, it is quite possible that every contemporary society today would fall under this category. However, expanding the meaning in this way has a price. If we adopt a definition of patriarchy that includes every situation in which males have advantages over females, we not only lose the linguistic etymology that links *pater* in its original meaning of 'father', but we will also find ourselves without a phrase for that condition in which the father has not only a status advantage but also power and real authority over the other members of his family and can force them to do his will. In other words, expanding the meaning of the term 'patriarchal' creates verbal inflation. Just as money can lose its value, so can a word lose its precision and become trivial without a clear meaning. If every human family pattern or society is patriarchal, then use of the term does not add anything to our knowledge when it is applied to a given society.[42] Similarly, applying the same term to radically different societies creates a sense that there are no significant differences between a society in which a husband can force his wife against her will to

[41] <http://bitbucket.icaap.org/dict.pl?alpha=P>.

[42] Ramazanoglu, *Feminism and the Contradictions of Oppression*, 34–5, writes on 'the over-general use of patriarchy', but her definition is also broad. 'However patriarchy is defined, it is a concept used to attempt to grasp the mechanisms by which men in general manage to dominate women in general. It refers to ideas and practices ranging from the most intimate . . . to the most general economic and ideological factors. It came to mean not only the power of men . . . but also the hierarchical character of male power and the ideological legitimation of this power.' However Ramazanoglu is very aware of the complications that derive from the universal nature of the phenomena inherent in this definition, and of the difficulty to defend it from criticism. If patriarchy is natural, there is nothing to change and little to investigate. However, Ramazanoglu does note the political utility of a claim like this for its users, and that is a good enough reason for her to maintain it. Rich, *Of Woman Born* ,p. xiii, writes that 'on one hand I . . . don't want to let "patriarchy" become a catchall in which specific areas of women's experience get obscured', but, she continues, 'patriarchy is a concrete and useful concept'. For her, the term applies to hierarchies and it is hard to determine what does not come under this category. She has an interesting analysis of the concept in chapter 3 and offers a very inclusive definition, coming to the conclusion that 'the power of the fathers has been difficult to grasp because it

accept his religion or to sleep with him, and a society in which a women can run both a household and a business and a husband thinks twice before raising his voice.

While narrow definitions of patriarchy may not apply to a Jewish society in which husbands did not have a great deal of power over their wives, it cannot be over-emphasized that Jewish society was not egalitarian either in theory or in reality. It is useful to be reminded of the difference between authority and power. Michelle Rosaldo made this point very clearly: 'Women may be important, powerful and influential, but it seems that, relative to men of their age and social status, women everywhere lack generally recognized and culturally valued authority'.[43] She added:

Everywhere men have some authority over women, that they have a culturally legitimated right to her subordination and compliance. At the same time, of course, women themselves are far from helpless, and whether or not their influence is acknowledged, they exert important pressures on the social life of the group. In other words, in various circumstances male authority might be mitigated, and, perhaps rendered almost trivial, by the fact that women (through gossiping or yelling, playing sons against brothers, running the business or refusing to cook) may have a great deal of informal influence and power. While acknowledging male authority, women may direct it to their own interests, and in terms of actual choices and decisions, of who influences whom and how, the power exercised by women may have considerable and systematic effect.[44]

And concluded:

Women gain power and a sense of value when they are able to transcend domestic limits, either by entering the men's world or by creating a society unto themselves.[45]

This was certainly the case in Jewish society. Women had power but no recognized authority. However, since there was power, it complicates the utility of the term 'patriarchy'.

In light of the great difficulty in applying patriarchy to the east European Jewish family, it is noteworthy that so many assumed this society to have been patriarchal.[46] This is natural. The leading role of males in the public sphere, in Torah study, and in ritual matters could blind observers to the role of women in other areas of life and they could easily conclude that male

permeates everything' (p. 57). This use of the term is possible but it has lost all meaning other than as a term that says that whatever it is applied to is in the past or present as opposed to the future.

[43] Rosaldo, 'Woman Culture and Society', 17.   [44] Ibid. 21.   [45] Ibid. 41.
[46] Even Kena'ani, *The Houses that No Longer Exist* (Heb.), 85, wrote about 'a matriarchy inside a patriarchy' instead of simply saying that the Jewish society he was investigating did not fit the standard definitions of patriarchy.

dominance applied to all sectors of society—at least until someone opened a Talmud and noticed that it was printed by the Widow Romm.[47]

One curious factor that may have contributed to a sense that the traditional Jewish family in eastern Europe was patriarchal was the adoption by Jews of an image of their past that emphasized small-town life and an idealized image of family life. This is a general phenomenon that is not unique to Jews. Claudia Ulbrich described this trend in German historiography in terms that fit developments among Jews almost just as well: 'The yearnings and expectations that the contemporary family was less and less able to fulfil were—and still are—projected back into the pre-industrial past',[48] and she went on to describe the creation of a legend, in her terms, of a past household characterized by 'discipline, authority and father rule'.[49] When Jews imagined their past, they assumed their ancestors had lived lives remarkably similar to that of their non-Jewish neighbours. The urbanized gentile descendants of farmers or peasants were aware that in the recent past, their ancestors had lived in more patriarchal frameworks. In a farming society the head of the family owned the land and that was the basis of his power. All the family members worked on the farm under his direction.[50] Sons, married or single, waited for the opportunity to inherit the land. In the peasant household there was ample basis for the authority that is mentioned in definitions of patriarchy and the multigenerational family.[51] However, while this may have been true for the non-Jewish agricultural family, it was not true for the Jewish family. As noted above, Jews had not been farmers and therefore had not come to live in multigenerational families. Such families were rare among Jews.[52] Nonetheless, many Jews unconsciously saw their past as similar to that of their neighbours. It was only natural to assume that if patriarchy was part of the general past, it must have characterized the Jewish

[47] The most widespread edition of the Talmud in eastern Europe was that of the Widow Romm and her sons. She took an active role in all of the publishing activities.

[48] Ulbrich, *Shulamit and Margarete*, 4.   [49] Ibid. 7.

[50] Hartman, *The Household and the Making of History*, 65, and see n. 88 there.

[51] See e.g. Miller, *Transformations of Patriarchy in the West*: 'it was around this [peasant] household that a patriarchalist social order was built' (p. 12); she added 'the inheritance system provided the bedrock of patriarchal authority between the generations' (p. 14). We saw that in Jewish society young people were relatively independent of their parents. Miller also notes that when conditions nullified the dependence of non-Jewish youths on their parents, such as in the years after the Black Plague, the results were immediate: the class discipline of the lords crumbled; fathers lost the power to dictate their sons' future course (p. 7). In others words, when social conditions in non-Jewish society became temporarily similar to those present in Jewish society, the patriarchy that typified the non-Jewish society evaporated. Miller saw a relationship between political rule and family rule in the general society (p. 270), and this again did not apply to Jewish society.

[52] See Chapter 4 above. It should be pointed out that among peasants also the practicality was weakened because of the contribution of women to the family, and it was stronger among

past. In the same way, Jews tended to see shtetl life as having characterized Jewish society in the past, just as village life had characterized non-Jewish life—even though a majority of Jews had always been city dwellers. After all, the shtetl never was as central or as typical as the village had been for non-Jews.[53]

*

It would be an error to claim that there were no truly patriarchal families among eastern European Jews. However, to find them we must look in an unanticipated place—among the families undergoing modernization, thus teaching that modernization does not always lead to the withering away of patriarchalism. Paulina Wengeroff grew up in a traditional family and married a banker who became very untraditional. She wrote:

> Our home was similar to that of many other Jewish families in which the battle of tradition was waged. The man, the breadwinner, has the duty to support his family and therefore he is master. He can request but he is also entitled to command. That was the rule of the day. My husband also began by requesting and when this did not get him what he wanted he *demanded* the fulfilment of his wishes. He became despotic beyond all measure . . . I was compelled to reform myself and my household . . . I had to give up my wig. Despite the most strenuous resistance, I soon had to give up my kosher kitchen and gradually drive the old beautiful customs, one after another, from my house. My heart bled as I watched them leave and I followed them with my eyes for a long, long time.[54]

This case fits every definition of a patriarchal family, and it is not in a traditional society but in a modern and enlightened setting. Instead of the ideal that was accepted in the traditional society of a woman who helps support her family, the bourgeois central European ideal of a 'real man' who supports a family, and a wife who decorates the home, was introduced and internalized. To be sure, the woman was free from work, but as a result she became totally dependent on her husband. From the moment this happened in society, the number of divorces dropped—not because families were happier than previously but because the scope for manoeuvre by women became more limited. This increase in power of the husband has been observed in general in Europe and seen as a characteristic of the early modern period.[55] It should

the affluent (Ozment, *Ancestors*, 48). Ozment also wrote *When Fathers Rule: Family Life in Reformation Europe*, which looks at families in which the father had a great deal of authority, but he describes family structure without using the term 'patriarchal', which does not even appear in the index.

[53] On the phenomenon of the shtetl in Hebrew literature see Miron, *The Image of the Shtetl*; and Estraikh and Krutikov (eds.), *The Shtetl: Image and Reality*.

[54] Wengeroff, *Rememberings*, 208–9.

[55] Hartman, *The Household and the Making of History*, 208. Hartman questions the universality of the phenomenon. See ibid. 214–15.

be pointed out that the bourgeois framework did not add directly to the authority of parents towards children and this is because the age at marriage rose. However, the traditional dependence of children on dowries and inheritances remained as an indirect means for maintaining the authority of parents.[56]

In Jewish society, there was a great gap between the image of the Jewish family and reality. When we look at what actually happened, we see that, according to most definitions, the traditional Jewish family was not patriarchal.[57]

The superficial or casual use of the term 'patriarchy' can distort our picture of the past and warp our understanding of Jewish life. It offers a simplistic view of a reality that was very complex and varied.[58] In many respects, the use of the term 'patriarchy' reflects an implicit acceptance of a chauvinist male view of the ideal social authority of men and their status, and an application of these views to reality. Therefore, this term can hide the voice of women and other members of families such as children or servants. It can erase the memory of the rich contribution of women to the Jewish community. In other words, applying patriarchy to the context of the Jewish community in eastern Europe reflects a high evaluation of status, power, and ceremonies—male spheres—instead of placing a value on reality. In an odd way, this term can express a truly anti-feminist point of view and a position that males are the measure of all that is important.

The view of maskilim, cited above, that Jewish society was matriarchal cannot be dismissed out of hand, even if it is exaggerated. Descriptions of family life generally emphasize the role of mothers in the family dynamics. In traditional Jewish society in eastern Europe, the strongest ties in families were not between fathers and sons or daughters, but rather between mothers and sons.[59] The period of dependence of children on their parents was limited and the ties between mothers and sons were the most intense. This was not because sons were afraid of fathers but because contact with fathers was generally limited. Not so regarding ties with mothers. If we look in sources of the period, it is not difficult to find evidence not only of the central role of mothers in the consciousness of husbands and children, but also the absence of authority of husbands over wives.[60]

[56] On marriage in bourgeois German Jewish families see Kaplan, *The Making of the Jewish Middle Class*, ch. 3.

[57] This conclusion says nothing about the phenomenon in Islamic lands.

[58] For two very interesting studies that show this in detail see Salmon-Mack, 'Marital Issues in Polish Jewry' (Heb.), and Hovav, 'The Religious and Spiritual Life of Jewish Ashkenazi Women in the Early Modern Period' (Heb.).

[59] Landes and Zborowski, 'Hypotheses Concerning the Eastern European Jewish Family'.

[60] Kristina Grish, author of *Boy Vey! The Shiksa's Guide to Dating Jewish Men*, did extensive field research on the topic of Jewish men without any preconceived notions. Interestingly she

As is well known, 'patriarchy' is a very loaded term. Therefore, if there is a concern for precision, accuracy, and objectivity, it is perhaps worth taking the term out of the lexicon of terms used to describe the traditional Jewish family in eastern Europe. It is possible to describe the traditional Jewish family without using the term 'patriarchal'. The avoidance of the term would not be an innovation of Jewish family study. As Claudia Ulbrich puts it:

the concept of patriarchy has lost its central importance in the scholarly effort to unmask gender relationships . . . Yet the traditional images have shown remarkable staying powers, especially since they seemed to be backed by a long scholarly traditional that saw the patriarchally organized family as an unchanging, natural, and fundamental building block of society.[61]

A number of contemporary researchers have also freed themselves from the term.[62] It seems that the application of the term to traditional eastern European Jewish society says more about the speaker than about that society. If this approach is not taken, at the very least it should be noted that what passed for patriarchy in the eastern European Jewish community was quite different from the patriarchy of many other communities—Jewish and non-Jewish.

concluded that today 'in a Jewish home . . . the mother is very dominant . . . the influence of the Jewish mother . . . permeates every area of her son's life'. The quotation is from an article on her by Handwerker, 'How to find a Jewish boyfriend'. Obviously this is not a totally reliable source for broad conclusions and it certainly does not reflect 19th-century realities. Nonetheless this is a relatively unbiased assessment that supports our conclusions about the traditional Jewish family.

[61] Ulbrich, *Shulamit and Margarete*, 5.

[62] Ozment, *When Fathers Rule*, did not use the term, though one could have expected him to do so from the title of the book, nor did Gary Becker in his fundamental *A Treatise on the Family*. For a suggestion on how to avoid using the term see the interesting article by Bloodworth, 'The Poverty of Patriarchy Theory'. I thank Dr Hagit Wolf for the references. A good discussion that summarized the problematic nature of the term is in Seccombe, *A Millennium of Family Change*, 30–1.

PART II

EDUCATION

SEVEN

Ḥeder *Study, Knowledge of Torah, and the Maintenance of Social Stratification*

SCHOOLS HAVE MANY FUNCTIONS besides transmitting knowledge and training in skills. As we shall see, the *ḥeder*, the traditional Jewish element-ary school in eastern Europe, had a variety of such secondary functions. The *ḥeder* encouraged students to go on to become scholars, but it also prepared many to accept a humble place in society and it made a major, though over-looked, contribution to the social stability of the Jewish community. To understand the history of Jewish education and east European Jewish society in the past, it is necessary to have a clear idea of what the *ḥeder* really did and to clarify a number of characteristics of the Jewish community that had a bearing on education.

Concern for status stability or for transmitting status from one generation to another is a characteristic of most human societies.[1] Members of elites want their children to have the same elite status that they enjoy, irrespective of their ability. Various ways have developed to achieve this stability. Status is often, but not always, associated with wealth and political roles, and a number of strategies have developed to pass status on. Transmitting wealth is usually not complicated because in most societies, the right of children to inherit the property of parents is accepted. In western society in the Middle Ages and in the early modern period, stability of wealth was best achieved through land ownership. An estate generated income year after year and offered both income and stability. A less than talented heir could hold on to land and transmit it to future generations while enjoying a yearly income. Political roles were more difficult to transmit, but there were tools for this as well. Concepts of inherited nobility or of 'noble blood' assisted in the transfer of political authority. Such concepts suggested that certain families were bio-logically superior, and this in turn could justify the inheritance of positions of authority and responsibility. Usually nobles were land owners, so wealth and political power often came together in a manner that maximized stability.

---

[1] See Bourdieu and Passeron, *Reproduction in Education, Society and Culture.*

Land ownership and noble rank were not practical methods for east European Jews to achieve status stability. Usually Jews were not allowed to invest in agricultural land and most Jewish wealth in eastern Europe was earned in commerce.[2] Wealth was, of course, very useful, but commercial capital is liquid and unstable and therefore there could be great losses and gains. Conditions were also not ripe in Jewish society for a framework of inherited family status markers, such as titles of nobility. Such frameworks usually come with a state-regulated hierarchical structure that provides the context for the theory of gradation and which can determine who is entitled to use a title, but this was not feasible for Jews in post-biblical times. The inherited status of the *kohen* (priest) and of the Levite was an exception, but it was significant only within ritual spheres. The closest Jewish society could come to a system of nobility was through the concept of *yikhus* or descent from a notable individual. In eastern Europe there were families that were well known for producing leading scholars. However, there were no formal gradations marking different levels of *yikhus*, nor was there unquestioned agreement on who had *yikhus* and who did not. *Yikhus* was also different in nature from nobility. *Yikhus* goes down in value with each generation further removed from a distinguished ancestor, though *yikhus* can be 'replenished' by learned descendants. Gradations of nobility are more effective. The value of a noble title is permanent, irrespective of the number of generations between the current bearer of the title and the first to receive it.

In early modern eastern European Jewry religious authority, with few exceptions, was also not inheritable. Out of principle, most communities would not take the son of a rabbi as a successor to his father and the phenomenon of rabbinical inheritance is very recent.[3] When hasidism arose, the position of *tsadik* was inherited, but the numbers involved were minuscule and it could not become a widely used model. Ordination as a rabbi was not a potential tool for stability because it did not create a special relation to the divine but was only an attestation that an individual had a certain degree of knowledge of religious law. In Judaism there are no rituals that only a rabbi can perform. So even if rabbis could have created a monopoly on ordination for their children, the monopoly would have had limited value and their authority would have been quickly challenged.

[2] There were, of course, exceptions but they were far from the rule. The closest most Jews could come to stability was home ownership or ownership of a building in cities or towns. It is not by chance that a respectable Jewish citizen was termed in Hebrew/Yiddish a *ba'al bayit*, literally 'a homeowner'. Ownership of real estate indeed offers stability but the return on the investment was fixed and offered little potential for growth.

[3] I wrote on this in 'The Inheritance of the Rabbinate', the article on which Chapter 14 is based.

Scholarship and learnedness were potentially useful markers of membership in the Jewish elite. A learned person was learned for life. Moreover, educational achievement was relatively easy to demonstrate. Innumerable Jewish stories about seemingly simple and anonymous individuals who revealed their knowledge in a discussion about Talmud make this point clearly. Thus, for Jews, scholarship could serve as a proxy for the characteristics such as nobility, land ownership, or ordination that gave stable status in non-Jewish societies. Knowledge in eastern European Jewish society was not a 'private' attribute but a public one. Possession of knowledge was publicly demonstrated by the ability to carry on a rabbinic discussion, to cite texts, and to argue a position.[4] As a result there was no need for a central authority to supervise the granting of 'academic' titles or to verify the authenticity of credentials. A probing conversation in the presence of listeners and onlookers was not an insult but part of the social graces of the intellectual elite. Having demonstrated scholarliness, the learned man, whether rich or poor, at home or far from it, could enjoy respect and honour from his Jewish compatriots, and if necessary he could expect aid and assistance from them in accordance with his learned status. His personal status was assured irrespective of the vicissitudes of time. Thus scholarliness could serve as a partial equivalent to the stability that noble rank granted the non-Jewish elite.[5]

This status system was reflected in the ways east European Jews looked at their society. They classified their fellows into two classes: the *sheyne yidn* (literally, the 'beautiful' Jews) and the *proste yidn* (the 'simple' Jews).[6] 'Beauty' for them was not an aesthetic characteristic of physical features but a reflection of the behaviour, manners, and particularly the talmudic knowledge of the 'beautiful' Jew. Wealth did not create 'beauty'. An adult 'simple' Jew, no matter how wealthy he was, could not become 'beautiful' just as a 'nouveau riche' in Western society could never rise above that status. To be 'beautiful' it was necessary to have knowledge of rabbinic literature and the ability to participate in a learned discussion. The 'beautiful' Jews had key roles in most communal decisions and communal leaders were usually drawn from their circles.[7] 'Simple' Jews accepted the leadership role of the 'beautiful' Jews partially because of the power that was often at their disposal but largely because they accepted the view that the scholarly attainments of the 'beautiful'

---

[4] See Chapter 11 below, which deals with questions.

[5] For a good example from an earlier period see Cohen, 'The Story of the Four Captives'.

[6] These concepts are discussed in Zborowski and Herzog, *Life Is with People*, 142–66, and Somogyi, *Die Schejnen und die Prosten*, ch. 5.

[7] On the oligarchic nature of communal life see, for example, Levitats, *The Jewish Community in Russia*, 134–7.

Jews made them superior. In other words, in east European Jewry, knowledge of the Talmud impacted strongly on social status.[8]

The educational system of east European Jewry played an important role in maintaining this knowledge-based status system. Like any other commodity, the value of knowledge lies in part in its rarity. The greater the availability, the less it is worth, and this dynamic operates irrespective of the utility of knowledge. The paradoxical truth is that because study was so important for the members of Jewish society, if the means of acquiring knowledge had been unlimited it would have lost its value. However, limiting access to knowledge would have posed both practical and theological problems. On a practical level it would have been difficult to legislate limited access, especially since it would have come up against the desires of many community members. Moreover, enforcement would have been very difficult. Also, an explicit policy of limited access could have aroused opposition to the possessors of knowledge. They would appear to have 'unfair advantages', and in the long run such an approach might have aroused opposition to the whole religious tradition.[9] Theological issues also would have created difficulties. According to religious tradition the Torah was given to all of the Jewish people and the duty of study was incumbent on all. This would have been difficult to reconcile with limited access to education. These were all factors that supported the almost universal formal education of Jewish boys in eastern Europe.

The issue of access to knowledge was resolved within the standard framework for elementary education in east European Jewry—the *ḥeder*. To understand how Jewish education could be open to all but also function as a tool that maintained social status it is necessary to consider both how the *ḥeder* operated and its 'hidden' reality.[10]

*

[8] See the first three chapters in Ginzburg, *Students, Scholars and Saints*; Heschel, *The Earth is the Lord's*; Zborowski, 'The Place of Book Learning'; and Zborowski and Herzog, *Life Is with People*. The best general introduction to traditional Ashkenazi Jewish culture remains Katz, *Tradition and Crisis*.

[9] The potential for opposition can be illustrated by the consequences of the drafting of Jews to the Russian army that started in 1827. The Jewish communities were assigned a quota of draftees they had to submit and the community leaders had little alternative but to comply. Not surprisingly they drafted from the poorer and simpler elements of society and never from the elite. No attempt was made to present the draft policy as egalitarian. One of the results was a bitter alienation of many of the poor from the 'better' elements of society. See Stanislawski, *Tsar Nicholas I and the Jews*, ch. 1. Limiting access to study probably would have generated the same response, if not a sharper one.

[10] It should be noted that there was an alternative to the *ḥeder* in the form of an institution known as a *talmud torah*. This was a tuition-free institution operated by the community which provided a minimal education for the children of the indigent, so that they too would be able to participate in the synagogue service and fulfil basic religious requirements. It was simply a *ḥeder*

At first glance there appears to be little to understand about the *ḥeder* because it was a remarkably simple educational institution.[11] The *ḥeder* was a private one-teacher school. Studies were conducted in the home of the teacher and he was paid directly by the parents. The organized Jewish community usually did not have much of a role in the functioning of the *ḥeders*. The programme of study consisted of sacred texts. No formal degrees were granted by the *ḥeder*, nor were grades given. The different levels of *ḥeders* were distinguished not by the age of the students but rather by the texts studied.[12] In each *ḥeder* only one type of text was studied. Teachers were not formally trained nor were there any prerequisites for opening a *ḥeder*. In the nineteenth century, no licence from the Jewish community or any other authority was needed to open a *ḥeder*, so anyone who so wished could do so.[13] The decision as to what text to teach was the teacher's, and his decision was determined by his assessment of his own abilities, and by market factors such as demand and competition. The decision as to when a pupil should advance to a higher-level *ḥeder* was not determined mechanically by the beginning of a new school year, but by an assessment by his teacher and especially by his parents that he was ready for a higher level.

Elementary education was not an attractive profession. Salaries were very low because most parents were poor and there were many sons who had to be sent to *ḥeder*. There was also little prestige in teaching little boys. *Ḥeder* teaching was limited to males because Hebrew knowledge was limited to males, but males who could find a more remunerative occupation did so. Therefore, most *ḥeder* teachers entered the profession because they had no alternative and not from a desire to be an educator or because of personal qualifications.[14] *Ḥeder* teaching was, in a sense, a safety net for the

with magnified problems. The classes were large and the teachers perhaps of an even lower quality than poor *ḥeder* teachers. Students in a *talmud torah* had low academic aspirations—and matching low achievements. Since most children went to *ḥeder*, the following analysis will concentrate on it. However, most of the conclusions are applicable also to the *talmud torah*.

[11]   There is a large literature on the *ḥeder*. The best guide to it is Diane Roskies, *Heder*, and one of the best introductions to the subject is Scharfstein, *The Ḥeder in the Life of Our People* (Heb.). An important and neglected source are the articles published on the *ḥeder* in the section 'Sovremennyi kheder' in *Vestnik Obshchestva rasprostraneniya prosveshcheniya mezhdu evreyami v Rossii*, 17 (Nov. 1912), 3–90. An enlightening description of elementary education in one town is Shtern, *Kheyder un beys-medresh*. See also Avital, *The Yeshiva and Traditional Education in the Literature of the Hebrew Enlightenment Period* (Heb.); and Hocherman, 'The Ḥeder' in Jewish Life' (Heb.).

[12]   Shtern, *Kheyder un beys-medresh* provides a detailed description of different types of *batei midrash*.

[13]   At times there were attempts by the government to regulate who could open a *ḥeder*. These attempts had no impact on the social dynamic of the *ḥeder* and so I will not go into them here.

[14]   The situation today is, of course, different because most full-time elementary teachers are women for whom the working conditions are compatible even though salaries are often very

unemployable who in other societies would be welfare recipients. Many *ḥeder* teachers were highly unqualified and were neither learned nor creative.[15] The physical conditions in which they taught were poor, they worked long hours and they always had financial worries. It should come then as no surprise that physical punishment in *ḥeder*s such as whipping and slapping was standard and administered often.[16] While we do not have good statistics on comparative child mortality between boys and girls, it would not be surprising to find that the conditions of study in *ḥeder*s—lack of ventilation, easy transmission of disease, and physical punishment—elevated mortality of boys in comparison with girls. It seems that in the better *ḥeder*s (see below) there was somewhat less physical abuse. There were of course many exceptions to this description, especially among the better-off from whose ranks came most of the writers of memoirs, but one cannot generalize from exceptions.

Ḥeder study began more or less at the age of 3. This was not because Jewish boys were intellectually precocious but for more pragmatic reasons. The best indication of this is that the study day in the *ḥeder* was very long—from morning until evening—even though such a long school day was far longer then practical or desirable for teaching a 3-year-old. However, there was a good reason for the *ḥeder* hours. The study day simply matched the working day of mothers. Like much of elementary education today, one of the basic functions of the *ḥeder* was to serve as a framework for childcare so that mothers could go to work. What complicated matters was that in the highly gendered traditional Jewish society, the teachers of boys were invariably males. Cleaning children who had soiled themselves was seen in that society as a female activity and it was inconceivable to expect a male caregiver or *ḥeder* teacher to take on that responsibility. Therefore, there was an unwritten code that boys began to go to *ḥeder* when they were toilet-trained and this was around the age of 3.[17]

The first level of *ḥeder* study was devoted to learning the mechanics of reading Hebrew. The textbook was the Hebrew prayer-book, though in some *ḥeder*s special alphabet sheets were used initially to teach the alphabet before

low. Were gender expectations today such that only men would be hired to teach young boys, the level of elementary education would no doubt be much lower because many men feel that they have better options. In certain Orthodox Jewish circles today there is no shortage of quite capable male teachers. Many desirable professions require an extended period of formal study, but the generous support for yeshiva students encourages extended years of study. The result is that many leave yeshiva too old to begin to prepare for a remunerative profession and Jewish education benefits because it is one of the few options open to them. However, in traditional Jewish society, formal study ended at an earlier age and there were more attractive options for 'beautiful' Jews than teaching children.

[15] 'Sovremennyi kheder'.
[16] For an entertaining but serious description of physical punishment in the *ḥeder* see Wex, *Born to Kvetch*, ch. 10.　　　[17] For more on this topic see Benedict, 'Child Rearing'.

reading in the prayer-book.[18] There were no primers or texts written for beginning readers and it often took a year or more before a *ḥeder* student was able to read.[19] There were a number of reasons for this slow pace. First, most 3-year-olds are not ready to read and therefore teaching them to read takes more time than teaching older children.[20] Second, there were specific problems with Hebrew reading. The rather primitive way Hebrew is written, with consonants in the form of letters and vowels as scattered marks above, below, and inside letters is confusing. Clearly printed texts are very important for the learning of Hebrew reading. Unfortunately, the well-worn prayer-books that were often used did not always have clear print. However, perhaps the most important reason it took so long to teach children to read was that the pupils did not understand a word of what they were reading. The prayers were in Hebrew and Aramaic but the children spoke Yiddish. Therefore they could not guess the phonetic meaning of letters on the basis of expected content. It would have been easier to start reading with Yiddish texts and then move on to Hebrew. Familiarity with Yiddish would have helped with letter recognition leaving only the Hebrew vowels to be learned. However, in traditional east European Jewish society Yiddish was regarded as the reading language for women; Hebrew was for men. *ḥeder* boys were seen as miniature men and it was not becoming for them publicly to read Yiddish. Of course, *ḥeder* students who learned how to read Hebrew could also read Yiddish but this was an unintended by-product and not a goal.

From a little boy's point of view, mastering the mechanics of reading Hebrew was valuable in and of itself and the lack of comprehension was not necessarily a source of frustration. Most beginning readers in any language are more concerned with the mechanics of reading than the content of what they are reading.[21] Since the prayer-book was in Hebrew, an ability to read made it possible to say prayers along with the adults, and the prayers did not have to be understood in order to be said. This participation in prayer was a milestone for a growing child and was a step towards entry into the world of the adults. Hence, the skill of reading itself had rewards and was a source of personal and family pride.

The teaching of reading in a classic language and not in the vernacular is

[18] On alphabet instruction see Roskies, 'Alphabet Instruction in the East European *Ḥeder*'. An interesting discussion of pedagogic aspects of *ḥeder* study is Haramati, *Methods of Teaching Hebrew* (Heb.), 16–21.

[19] In Israel today, first-grade students start learning how to read after the festival of Sukkot and are expected to be able to read by Hanukah, two months later.

[20] These children were also not ready to study all day—and didn't. Most of their time was spent in play. In principle, most of the *ḥeder* day was supposed to have been spent in review, but little boys had other ideas about using that time.

[21] Readers who are doubtful are invited to sit down with a first-grader and practise reading with him or her. The experience will be enlightening.

not common today, but in its time it was not unique to the Jewish community. In Europe until quite recently formal study was based on the study of Latin texts, while in Muslim lands study is still based on the Koran, which is written in a literary Arabic that is spoken nowhere today.[22] In all of these cases, the difficulties of beginning reading with incomprehensible texts were overshadowed by the value attributed to reading sacred texts.

Writing was not taught in the early nineteenth-century east European *ḥeder*, though it had been standard in Jewish elementary education earlier. Before the invention of the printing press, writing had been an important skill because texts were either dictated to pupils or they copied them and studied from their copies. In those years the ability to write among Jewish males was widespread. However, the teaching of writing complicates education. There is a need for writing materials which are sometimes expensive and always subject to being lost, misplaced, or broken—or even abused.[23] After the spread of print, there was no need for teachers to dictate texts because printed versions were inexpensive and available. Since Jews saw the function of elementary education as exposure to sacred texts and not the mastery of practical skills, the result was a drop in the teaching of writing among Jews—a somewhat unanticipated consequence of Gutenberg's invention.

There was little pressure or need to teach writing in a traditional Jewish society.[24] To be sure, for most east European Jews before the mid-nineteenth century writing was a useful skill, but it was not a necessary one.[25] There was no internal Jewish bureaucracy that required writing in Hebrew. There was also little need to deal in writing with a governmental bureaucracy, and when the need arose, Hebrew was not usually the language of choice in dealing with governmental agencies. Only a minority of Jews needed to maintain business records. The Jewish water carrier or shoemaker certainly did not. The Jewish masses had a limited need for family correspondence and in any case postage was expensive. For the occasional formal document, such as a contract or a marriage agreement, a professional scribe or letter writer was always available.

Parents who wanted their children to learn how to write would arrange with special teachers, known as *shraybers*, to give their children supplementary lessons. The *shrayber* would also teach arithmetic—another skill that was practical for commercial life but not taught in *ḥeder*. The 'message' was clear. The *ḥeder* taught religious and cultural skills but not practical ones. Reading was a key skill for the young Jew because it enabled him to participate in the synagogue rituals. Writing was simply a complication that required paper,

[22] For a very important article on this topic see Eickelman, 'The Art of Memory'.
[23] For details, ask the parent of a first-grader.
[24] For a discussion of this, see Chapter 9.
[25] Hailperin, *Jews and Judaism* (Heb.), 171 and 188.

ink, pens, and much supervision. Therefore it could be left to those who felt they needed it.

Upon mastering prayer-book reading the young boy was ready to go on to the next level of *ḥeder* and *ḥumash* (Pentateuch) with the commentary of Rashi was the text to be studied. The prevailing teaching method in the *ḥumash ḥeder* maintained some significant characteristics of the first-level *ḥeder*. Teaching was still largely mechanical in nature and the texts studied were directly related to synagogue rituals. However, in the *ḥumash ḥeder* comprehension was also a goal. *Ḥumash* was taught through reading the text with the aid of an interpolated oral Yiddish translation that the students had to memorize.[26] In the course of time the text of this translation became fixed and in a sense canonized. As the Yiddish language developed, especially in eastern Europe, the language of this translation became less and less comprehensible to children. Ultimately, not only did the child have to master a text written in a foreign language, but also to learn a barely understood translation which teachers often taught and then translated into colloquial Yiddish![27]

There was logic to this approach even though today a 'foreign' language is usually taught through a systematic introduction to the characteristics of the language and through the use of drills and exercises. Language teaching is quite difficult, as anyone who has tried to do it knows. It is not inherently interesting and the successful teaching of a language requires both mastery of the language and personal dynamism. In general, the less qualified a teacher, the more important and necessary is a structured programme of study. Teaching by rote enabled teachers, who themselves sometimes barely knew Hebrew, to give their pupils some of the tools necessary to understand a Hebrew text.

In *ḥumash ḥeder* the students studied each week the portion of the Torah which was to be read the coming sabbath in the synagogue. Since students, especially beginners, could not master a whole portion in just six days, they simply covered as much of the text as they could and when Sunday came the teacher jumped to the beginning of the next week's portion. This approach was criticized by Jewish enlighteners as being unsystematic and leading to gaps in the child's knowledge of *ḥumash*. Their criticism was groundless and reveals the bias of the critic more than it reflects any understanding of how a *ḥeder* worked.[28] The basic assumption of critics was that the school had the sole responsibility for the transmission of knowledge and that it was the only

[26] It should be emphasized that the translation was not memorized as a flowing text and children would not declaim a chapter of the Torah in Yiddish. It was only learned as an interpolated translation—a translation of words and phrases.

[27] On this translation see Noble, *Khumesh-taytsh*.

[28] On the problem of 'skipping' see, for example, Gamoran, *Changing Conceptions in Jewish Education*, i. 95.

source of knowledge for a pupil. In reality the *ḥeder* student had many alternative sources of information about the deeds of biblical heroes and the biblical narrative that he read about in the Torah. These stories were cited in the conversations of adults the children overheard in the synagogue; they were discussed at home and with siblings; and a *ḥeder* student could always ask his teacher about the outcome of a story that was cut off in the middle. In any case, most of the Torah is not a narrative but rather a collection of laws, and continuity is usually not an issue. Therefore 'skipping' was not a real problem. However, critics were looking for something to criticize and considered only the formal part of education and not the totality.[29]

Like learning to read the prayer-book, the study of *ḥumash* with Rashi's commentary had a number of functions. Since the prayer-book and *ḥumash* were clearly relevant to the child's daily life it was not necessary to convince the *ḥeder* pupil of the significance or utility of his study. He was studying the same texts that adults used with obvious reverence and respect. The study of *ḥumash* with Rashi not only served as a means of learning Hebrew and gaining familiarity with a basic sacred text, but it also exposed the pupil to the midrashic view of the world and to traditional opinions on the role of the Jew in the world. It introduced them to rabbinic methods of thought and textual analysis. When a child was able to read the Torah and Rashi's commentary freely and with comprehension, he was ready to move up to a Talmud *ḥeder*, irrespective of his age, of how much Torah he had studied, or of the season of the year. Students usually began the Talmud *ḥeder* around the age of 10, though there were often wide variations in the age of students since progress from level to level in the *ḥeder* system was the result of 'mastery' of previous stages of study and not based on age.

There were educational critics who found fault with the fact that the entire Bible was not taught, nor was the Mishnah part of the course of study. It could also be noted that Jewish law was not studied. There were very good reasons for the absence of these topics from the curriculum. The claim that the entire Bible should be taught before rabbinic texts was based on an unstated assumption that texts should be taught in chronological order of their writing. Since the Bible was written before the Mishnah or Talmud, and often cited in these

---

[29] The educational realities today are far different. Most parents do not see themselves as competent to supplement what children are taught in school and teachers do not encourage parents to intervene in the teaching of subjects such as language and mathematics. The methods used to teach children are constantly in flux. Therefore, while parents in a traditional society could take for granted that their children were studying the same way they had done, today the only assumption that can be made is that nothing is the same. It is understandable that a person who takes for granted the contemporary approach that gives schools a near monopoly on transmitting knowledge would be troubled by what appeared to be gaps in this transmission. For a parent in a traditional society this concern would be incomprehensible.

rabbinic works, so, critics would claim, the books of the Bible should be taught before going on to later works. This approach, while brilliantly logical on paper, ignores the realities of teaching children—especially children who do not understand Hebrew. Even Hebrew-speaking adults today have great difficulties with books of the Bible such as Job and the prophetic books with their sweeping and brilliant rhetoric. They were certainly exceedingly difficult for young Yiddish-speaking students who had to translate every word and who found it difficult to remember what was written five lines above. Moreover, while *ḥumash* was part of the synagogue ritual, the rest of the Bible was not. Therefore skipping over much of the Bible made a lot of sense to a teacher in a nineteenth-century classroom.

The study of Mishnah presents its own difficulties. The text of the Mishnah is very much like a list of opinions and artefacts. Where the talmudic text tends to use the same words over and over in the course of the talmudic discussion, the concise Mishnah is constantly referring to new cases and facts. In other words the Mishnah presents vocabulary problems. Moreover, the Talmud is inherently more interesting than the Mishnah because it is set in the form of a discussion. It reads as a back and forth argument and generally the Mishnah does not. Of course, in the hands of a gifted teacher the Mishnah and any other text for that matter can be made fascinating for students. However, given the mediocre quality of *ḥeder* teachers and the need to master Talmud before leaving the *ḥeder* (discussed below), the study of Mishnah would have contributed little to *ḥeder* study other than to complicate matters.[30]

Jewish law was also not taught, but for different reasons. It was taken for granted, with good justification, that children would learn from observation at home about the laws and observances prescribed by Jewish law. In a society that was generally observant, it was not necessary to learn traditions from books.[31] In general, the rabbinic elite discouraged the study of law from books and felt that it was better for individuals with questions to turn to a rabbi rather then decide for themselves on the basis of limited knowledge.

In the Talmud *ḥeder* students were introduced to the study of Talmud in the same way they began with the Pentateuch. The teacher simply began with

[30] It is interesting to note that the fervent supporters of the study of Mishnah before going on to the study of Talmud never discuss the possibility of studying other tannaitic texts composed in the same period as the Mishna. *Midrashei halakhah* such as *Sifra* or *Sifrei* are probably more relevant to Talmud study than Mishnah but they are almost never studied. Quite possibly many of the advocates of Mishnah have not mastered the other tannaitic texts.

[31] To teach children about the kosher or sabbath laws in school would be the equivalent of a schoolteacher today feeling a need to teach a normal schoolchild the principles of football. Children may need teachers for geography, but not for football. On the mimetic tradition see Soloveitchik, 'Rupture and Reconstruction'.

a typical talmudic text, translating it word by word until the students 'picked up' both the idiom and thought patterns. There was no systematic introduction to Aramaic—the language the Talmud is written in—nor was there any attempt to provide a structured presentation of rabbinic thought. The idea of starting with a special textbook or sourcebook was unheard of. The beginning Talmud students learned from the same texts as did the most advanced and respected scholars and rabbis.

Testing was done by parents or their representatives. It was a standard practice for a student to be tested on Fridays on the material learned during the week. Since the parents had studied the same material in their youth and in the same manner, it was clear to all what was expected of a boy and what were indications of success. The questions were almost always of comprehension and not of rote recitation of a text. In these examinations, not only was the son being tested but the *melamed*, the teacher, as well. Success meant continued study with him, and repeated failure could initiate a search for a different *melamed*.[32]

There was no formal cut-off point for study in the Talmud *ḥeder*. It was generally accepted that at about barmitzvah age (13), or shortly thereafter, most students would leave the Talmud *ḥeder*. This was not related to the barmitzvah ceremony and it was not the result of legislation or religious law, but a matter of simple economics. As is clear, there was no direct or clear link between the programme of study and the future economic activities of the pupil. The only useful skill learned in *ḥeder*—reading—was learned first. At the age of 13 most boys were responsible and developed enough to begin to work and to contribute to the family income, or to begin an apprenticeship (formal or informal) in order to prepare for the economic responsibilities of adulthood. The only reason that would justify continued Talmud study was if there was a good chance of ending up as a scholar. For those who would not become scholars, to delay work meant loss of income and putting off the start of an apprenticeship. Such a youth would remain dependent on his parents longer and for little measurable benefit. For reasons that will be clarified below it was clear to most 13-year-old boys—and their parents—that they would never be scholars. Therefore most families found that it was logical to end a son's *ḥeder* education at around the age of 13, when he was old enough to begin preparation for practical life.

---

[32] In school systems today most parents are very limited in their ability to choose who the teacher of their children will be. Pity the poor parent who is unhappy with his child's teacher and tries to transfer him to a different one. It is usually easier to change schools than to move a child from one class to another. Today, the teacher is the source of information on the educational achievement of a child and grades are the key to this information. It is not easy for parents to assess achievement independently.

For the minority that continued to study there were various options. Rich parents often hired young scholars as private tutors for their adolescent sons.[33] Some boys went on to what may be called communal or elementary yeshivas. They were similar to a Talmud *ḥeder*, but were on a higher level and excluded students with weak backgrounds in Talmud. Some were private institutions and depended on parents paying for the tuition. However, most advanced study did not take place in yeshivas or with teachers.

For generations up until the late nineteenth century the standard framework for advanced talmudic study had been study in the *beit midrash*, or communal study and prayer hall. Major yeshivas only really became important near the end of the nineteenth century. Perhaps the best known of them, the yeshiva of Volozhin, was founded early in the nineteenth century. However, until the last third of the century it was not a model but an anomaly. It appears that up until the end of the nineteenth century only a minority of the youths who chose to study full-time went to yeshivas. Most chose to continue their studies in one of the many *batei midrash*, or communal study halls, that were found in every community.

In many respects the *beit midrash* offered an almost utopian framework for study. Students in a *beit midrash* were almost totally independent—though within certain bounds. There were no classes or tests and students studied on their own. They could choose to study whatever talmudic tractate they wished. They set their own pace of study and could determine the style of analysis as well. Those who liked mental gymnastics could indulge in them, while those who preferred to deal with the legal implications of the texts studied could concentrate on the way the Talmud was elaborated in later halakhic literature. There was no demand to adopt a standard approach. This system gave maximum freedom to the individual student and wide scope for developing talents and creativity. The absence of formal classes and tests would seem like a dream to many contemporary students. Their parents would find equally desirable the absence of tuition charges or even of a need to support their sons who were *beit midrash* students.

The key to the *beit midrash* system lay in the fact that most boys who went on to *beit midrash* study left home, despite what may appear to us as their tender age, and chose to study in a *beit midrash* in another city. The members of each Jewish community usually provided for most of the material needs of the students in *batei midrash*, albeit at a minimal level. It was the custom for families to invite Talmud students to share in the main meal for one or more days of the week on a regular basis. Thus a student would eat his Sunday meal

[33] Jews living in isolated hamlets in the countryside also hired tutors for their children. The country tutors taught for little more than room and board, and the level of their teaching was correspondingly low and not to be compared with the quality of tutors in rich homes.

with one family, his Monday meal with another, and so on through the week. This practice was called *essen teg* (literally, 'eating day'). A lucky student would arrange families for every day of the week. If he were less fortunate he would find himself on certain days without a family—and without a good meal that day. A truly enterprising student might arrange for more hosts than days, and convince some of his hosts to give him a few coins instead of a meal—leaving him with seven days of meals and a bit of cash.

The *essen teg* system had a number of advantages to it. It was easy to administer because there was almost nothing to administer. Arrangements were made by the students themselves, or by the *gabai* (warden) of the *beit midrash*. There was no need to collect funds or disburse them and there was no drain on the communal treasury. Since the students ate in the homes of the hosts, there was no need to worry about facilities and upkeep. It was usually not too difficult to find willing hosts since householders had a variety of incentives to host a student. They believed that they earned a divine reward for giving meals to a Torah student. Many hosts also enjoyed the company of the students, and saw them as positive role models for their children or, on occasion, as surrogate children. In some cases, *essen teg* was a step towards a match with the host's daughter. Hosting a student was also far from being an anonymous deed and hence it was a source of prestige in the Jewish community, serving as a public display of charity and piety. The housing of students was also taken care of without communal expense and with no complications. Students would simply sleep on the benches in the women's gallery of the *beit midrash* and this solved the problem of their accommodation.[34]

The living conditions of the *beit midrash* students were not easy, but that was part of their experience. Study in a *beit midrash* can be understood as an extended test of initiation in which youths demonstrated their commitment to Torah study. Instead of enduring physical tortures, the *beit midrash* students studied day and night. In this way, they proved to others, and to themselves, the depth of their commitment to study and to the service of God. Improving their material conditions would have denied them the possibility of proving their devotion to others and to themselves.[35]

It should be noted that the system of support, meals with householders, and sleep in the women's gallery of a synagogue was almost identical with the way the vagrant poor were supported by Jewish communities. The community supported young students as if they were needy—even though, as we shall

---

[34] I have done field research on this topic and I can confirm that if one is sufficiently tired, a bench is not a problem at all.

[35] For an article that raises many parallels between Talmud study and initiation rites see Ong, 'Latin Language Study as a Renaissance Puberty Rite'. Note that in the *beit midrash* youths were separated from their families, under the supervision of elders, and lived together—all characteristics of initiation rites.

see, most of them did not come from needy homes. However, since they did not study in their home towns, they could take on a temporary role as a poor youth and become worthy of support. There were many poor Jews who led lives that were just as hard as, or even harder than, those of *beit midrash* students, but the students' condition was different: it was a temporary state that would only last until—at least so they hoped—their marriage. With a good match, they would suddenly be transformed into honourable members of society. In the meantime, living a life of poverty was a test of their devotion and commitment.

*

For many young men, study in the *beit midrash* should have had an irresistible appeal. While the draft law of Nicholas I in 1825 forced Jewish communities to supply the draftees, communal policy was to avoid drafting *beit midrash* students. Not surprisingly, contemporaries reported an increase in the number of Talmud students after the institution of the draft.[36] However, the *batei midrash* were not swamped with students and many candidates remained for the draft. Clearly, had all young men of draft age become yeshiva or *beit midrash* students, the communities that had to meet draft quotas would have run out of candidates. That did not happen.[37] Most young men did not take advantage of study in *beit midrash* because, for most young men, study in a *beit midrash* was not a real option.

There was an unspoken but crucial precondition for study in the *beit midrash*. To merit support a student had to be able to study the Talmud and commentaries on his own. However, as we shall see, most *ḥeder* graduates could not study Talmud independently, and in the absence of this ability they had nothing to do all day in a *beit midrash*. They would also have starved if they had tried. Since householders came to *batei midrash* for prayers and part-time study, the level and achievements of the full-time students were public knowledge. It was clear who was a capable talmudic student and who was wasting his time in the study hall—and it was equally clear who always had an answer to a question and who always mumbled excuses. Householders were only interested in offering meals and support to students who appeared to be promising talmudists. Who would have been interested in supporting mediocrities? Youths who knew that they could not make the grade would not even try to join the students in a *beit midrash*.

Most young men were incapable of independent Talmud study because of the *ḥeder* system—just as the brilliant achievements of the intellectual elite

---

[36] See Shohet, 'Recruitment in the Days of Tsar Nicholas the First' (Heb.).

[37] On this problem in general and the draft in particular see Stanislawski, *Tsar Nicholas I and the Jews*. On the positive influence of the draft on the numbers of *beit midrash* students see ibid. 32 n. 76.

can be credited to the *ḥeder* system. The reason for both phenomena was that *ḥeder*s differed widely in terms of quality,[38] and operated in the context of a complex interplay between teachers and parents. Parents always had a choice of *ḥeder*s and the selection of which *ḥeder* to choose for a child is best understood in a market model. Teachers were interested in acquiring a maximum income along with the best possible working conditions. Understandably, a good teacher could demand higher tuition payments than could an inferior teacher. Parents were interested in getting the best possible education for their children in accordance with the means at their disposal, but parents also had to take into account a number of variables, among which was the quality of the *melamed* (teacher) and the size of the class.

As noted above, parents chose the teachers for their children and paid them directly. If their funds were limited they would invest more in sons who appeared to be talented than in sons who seemed to have only normal skills—or less. The more resources available or the higher the aspirations, the more parents would invest in education and the better the teacher they could hire. All parents wanted small classes and individual attention for their son, but not all could do something about it. However, it was a common practice for affluent parents to seek out the best-qualified teachers for their sons and to pay a premium to teachers on condition that they limit the number of students they accepted.[39] These demands were quite acceptable for teachers because they resulted in smaller classes and better working conditions without a loss of income—and possibly with a somewhat higher one. For the parents this was a way of ensuring more attention for their children and thereby greater progress. The impact on Talmud study was immense. The dialectics of the Talmud can hardly be explained effectively in a rote fashion. The only way for a student to learn to study Talmud on his own is if he has a teacher who really understands what he is teaching, who can transmit this knowledge, and who has the time to give the student individual attention. This is why the following description of *ḥeder* study in an elite circle in nineteenth-century eastern Europe is so significant: 'In 1857 my father sent me to a *melamed* who was good etc. and he paid tuition of seven and a half rubles for six months, on condition that the *melamed* would not take more than six pupils.'[40]

The relative quality and ability of *ḥeder* teachers was a matter of general knowledge in the communities in which they lived. It was usually well known

[38] This fact was usually regarded as obvious by contemporaries and hence not discussed. For references to it see Shtern, *Kheyder un beys-medresh*, 78; Hocherman, 'The *Ḥeder* in Jewish Life' (Heb.), 31.

[39] A contemporary example of this phenomenon is that of parents arranging for day-care for infants. Parents have to balance out available funds with the quality of childcare providers and the number of infants for which a provider is responsible.

[40] Mosheh Leib Lilienblum, cited in Lifshitz, *From Generation to Generation* (Heb.), 74.

whose students made the best progress in their studies and whose did not. Hence a parent's choice of a teacher signalled to the child what was anticipated of him. Boys knew that in certain *ḥeder*s it was expected that the pupils would become learned but that in the others this was highly unlikely. In other words, each knew what was expected of him even if it was never said openly.

Parents who had limited means at their disposal, who were less willing to sacrifice their budget for education, or who had low expectations for their children, ended up sending them to the less capable teachers, who also tended to have larger classes. After all, there is no point in spending extra money on the first stages of education if no long-term difference is expected. Thus, in low quality *ḥeder*s, low expectations of the children were created which, when combined with the worst possible study conditions, not surprisingly were usually fulfilled. With these conditions it is clear why most children failed to master the Talmud.

Even if most pupils did not realize it, *ḥeder* education was a race against time because the *ḥeder* was usually followed by the *beit midrash*. Study there, as noted above, was independent—without teachers or structured guidance—and the communal support was predicated on the fact that the *beit midrash* student was a fully fledged independent Torah scholar. This meant that the entering student had to be able to study the Talmud and the complex literature of talmudic commentaries on his own. This was no small achievement for a 13-year-old. Given the realities of *ḥeder* study noted above, it was impossible for most children to reach this level by the age of 13, or to continue in order to reach it at a later age.

If the function of the Talmud *ḥeder* was to bring the student to the point where he could study Talmud on his own, then the *ḥeder* was not a very successful institution. But it was not alone in its ineffectiveness. The Jewish community as a whole did not do as much as it could to spread knowledge of the Talmud despite all of the talk about the importance of Torah study. Very simple steps could have been taken that would have dramatically increased knowledge and understanding. Surprisingly, tools such as Aramaic–Yiddish dictionaries, or an extensive Talmud commentary in Yiddish or even Hebrew, did not exist, even though they would have been of great aid to students. It certainly would not have been difficult to produce such books. Even classical talmudic dictionaries in Hebrew, such as the *Arukh*, were not generally available.[41] The results were clear. The majority of Jews, such as the pedlars, shoemakers, and tailors, could not study a page of Talmud on their own. They

---

[41] The contemporary phenomenon of Talmud commentaries, such as that of Rabbi Steinsaltz or the Artscroll commentaries which are in the vernacular and which require no major investment of effort to understand, did not have an equivalent in eastern Europe. This was not because of any inability to write such a commentary or lack of printing shops to print one. Pop-

were pious, they said their psalms, they went to hear the midrashic sermons on Saturday afternoons in the synagogues, but they were not themselves learned.

The characteristics of the many *ḥevrot* or study societies devoted to the study of sacred texts reflect the low level of achievement of the masses. *Ḥevrot* were groups of Jewish men who would meet regularly in the *beit midrash* to hear a class given by a learned individual based on a classic Hebrew text. Each *ḥevra* was devoted to the study of a specific book. In almost all Jewish communities the most prestigious of these groups was the *ḥevras shas*, or Talmud study society. Others were devoted to the study of books such as *Ein ya'akov*, a collection of stories from the Talmud, and others to the study of popular summaries of Jewish law such as *Kitsur shulḥan arukh* or to the joint recitation of psalms. Study in a *ḥevrah* did not require independent study skills. All that was necessary was an ability to follow the teachers' explanations. Even so, most Jews did not belong to *ḥevrot* for the study of Talmud but rather to those dedicated to the study of *midrash* or the saying of psalms. This was apparently not out of a lack of interest in Talmud but out of an inability to follow a lecture on Talmud.[42] Of course, the knowledge necessary to follow a lecture is itself much less than what is needed to study independently, but even this was lacking among most Jews.[43] However, this very failure was one of the most important achievements of the *ḥeder*.

To fail students and to make their limitations clear to them is one of the less talked-about functions of educational systems, but the lack of awareness does not make the function any less important. On the one hand, schools try to stimulate ambitions and encourage students to strive for achievement; on the other hand, they have to make it clear to those who are less successful that they will not be able to realize some of their hopes. By stimulating a maximum number of youths to aspire to desirable positions and display their capabilities at an early age a society can identify the most capable individuals for elite positions. However, the more successful an educational system is in stimulating ambitions and in identifying the most talented, the larger the body of frustrated individuals who have tried and failed—and frustration has a social price. Conversely, the earlier the majority 'learn their place', the less frustrated they are likely to be when they grow up. The price of early selection is,

ularization of the Talmud or making it more accessible went against the grain of traditional Jewish society. It will be interesting to see what the long-term impact of these commentaries will be—whether they will spread knowledge or lead to functional illiteracy in Hebrew and Aramaic.

[42] To understand the means by which comprehension was determined, see Heilman's study of contemporary *ḥevrot*, *The People of the Book*.

[43] While no surveys of learnedness can be cited, the relative ignorance of the masses is at the basis of the distinction between the *sheynen* and the *prosten*. On *ḥevrot* see Levitats, *The Jewish Community in Russia*, ch. 6.

of course, the possibility that talented individuals go unnoticed and that there is limited social mobility.[44] However, mobility was not everyone's goal and every approach has its price.

It cannot be overemphasized that there was absolutely no conscious desire among east European Jewry to hold back students whose families were poor, or to deny such students access to knowledge.[45] The impact of the *ḥeder* on social mobility was not discussed, nor was impeding mobility seen as desirable. Mobility is a two-way street but attention, then as now, was usually given to advancing and not to declining. At the same time, since the number of elite or desirable positions is fixed and not elastic, the rise of one is dependent on the decline of another. The phenomenon of tutoring and private lessons today has very similar results to that of selecting a good *ḥeder*. Few parents today who take tutors for their children would say that their goal is to reduce social mobility or to give their children unfair advantages. Parents are simply concerned that their children get the best possible education. It remains to the observer to determine the impact of the behaviour of many individuals.

The educational failure of the *ḥeder* did not result in a loss of Jewish identity among *ḥeder* graduates. It should be pointed out that *ḥeder* study had no impact on Jewish identity. Jews knew they were Jews because of their language, dress, political status, customs, religious practices, and a host of other attributes. What was learned in *ḥeder* may have been quite significant for their future participation in Jewish study, but it was not necessary to form their identities, nor did anyone see the need for *ḥeder* study in order to maintain Jewish identity. Hence failure in *ḥeder* study did not have any clear impact on identification as Jews. For this reason, Jewish society could be rather indifferent about the limited success of *ḥeder* study.

Despite the limited success of *ḥeder* education in teaching Talmud, the *ḥeder* was very successful in teaching one significant fact. All students, successful or not, learned that it is very hard to understand the Talmud and even harder to master all of the rabbinic literature; anyone who did so was deserving of great respect and could not be argued with on his terms. The very possession of talmudic knowledge gave the scholar charisma and this was irrespective of more conventional sources of charisma, such as appearance, bearing, or personality. Charisma of knowledge is best created when every-

---

[44] This analysis is based on Turner, 'Modes of Social Ascent'.

[45] Iris Parush advances the opposite view in her article 'Another Look at "The Life of 'Dead' Hebrew"', 173: 'My thesis is that this society deliberately withheld instruction of Hebrew, and thus prevented Hebrew literature from taking root among a much broader potential readership.' She cites Pierre Bourdieu as providing the basis for her argument. While he is a fascinating thinker, he was not an authority on east European Jewry and cannot be applied without support. Despite her hundred-plus footnotes, I found absolutely no evidence for the claim that this was deliberate.

one has tried to study, just as the charisma of sporting ability gains from near-universal youthful attempts to play sports. Thus, failure in Talmud study could ultimately contribute to rabbinical authority.

The respect for the talmudic scholar may have had wider communal significance in east European Jewish society in the nineteenth century than previously. Traditional communal and religious sanctions were becoming more and more limited. The authority of Jewish communities to impose financial or physical punishments on recalcitrant individuals was often limited. Even when not restricted, the implementation of sanctions did not necessarily contribute to the communal authority and popular respect for the leadership. In the course of the nineteenth century, the formal communal structure lost much of its power in both the Habsburg and tsarist empires and they made the use of formal sanctions even more problematic than earlier.[46] In these conditions, identification of 'beautiful' or learned Jews with the communal leadership could give that leadership added authority. This identification was far from universal and there were many possible options and combinations. However, in considering the impact of the *ḥeder* system, the long-term and indirect impacts should not be ignored.

*

It is now clear that among the characteristics of traditional east European Jewish society[47] were two seemingly contradictory ones. On one hand, education was highly regarded by all Jews; learnedness was one of the critical qualities for membership in the elite and lifelong study was one of the most visible features of that society.[48] For this reason almost all Jewish boys were given an elementary education and advanced study was so strongly supported by the Jewish community that all the material needs of students who went on to such studies were met by the Jewish communities. However, while in many societies education is a means for mobility, traditional east European Jewish society was highly stratified and stable, with little intergenerational social mobility. Membership in the elite was transmitted from generation to

[46] On the nature of communal authority even after the formal abolition of the Jewish communities see Shohet, 'Leadership of the Jewish Communities in Russia after the Abolition of the "Kahal"' (Heb.). Some of the problems of this authority are exposed in Katz, *Tradition and Crisis*, and Abramsky, 'The Crisis of Authority within European Jewry in the Eighteenth Century'.

[47] There are varying definitions of traditional east European Jewish society. I am using the term to refer to Jewish society before it came into intense contact with modernizing tendencies and movements. This would apply to almost all east European Jewish communities at the beginning of the 19th century and to none at the end of the century.

[48] The fullest discussion of this topic that I am familiar with is Goldman, *Lifelong Learning among Jews*.

generation among the leading families. In other words, in east European Jewish society education was ubiquitous but it seemingly did not contribute to class mobility.[49] The key to understanding this situation was the *ḥeder*.

The traditional elementary system among eastern European Jews was one that on the surface offered equal opportunities for all. However, in reality it more or less reproduced in the younger generation the same class divisions of the parents' generation. In this respect the Jewish educational system in eastern Europe resembled the educational systems in many other societies in that it helped to maintain the social order. What is unique and interesting is both the mechanism of reproducing socio-economic class distinctions and the use made of the system. In many societies there were no study frameworks for the masses and advanced study appeared to be open only to the elite. In Jewish society the educational route for advancement appeared to be egalitarian and advanced study was open to all. However, the very freedom of the study in the *beit midrash* and the opportunities it offered for independent personal intellectual growth was the means by which underprivileged or less talented pupils were held back. While this was certainly not egalitarian, it must be remembered that given the costs involved a more extended and more formal educational system was an impossibility under the conditions of the time. Moreover, it would have produced more youths who could study Talmud than could have been supported. This might have had positive results in terms of individual achievement, but also could have led to the collapse of the whole social order of the intellectual elite of eastern European Jewry.[50] The number of scholars the Jewish community could support was limited and the number of rabbinical positions—and rich brides—was equally finite. A greater success in training would simply have created a large population of frustrated young men who were psychologically unprepared to lower their career expectations.

The *ḥeder* system contributed to the balance and stability of Jewish society. It was a conservative tool, even though the popular image was that the educational system was open and every Jewish child could become a talmudic scholar. Jews in traditional east European Jewish society saw the study of Talmud as a means of intellectual mobility, and not just that. They believed that a poor but brilliant Talmud student could become the son-in-law of a rich

---

[49] To the best of my knowledge, the issue of social mobility in east European Jewry has never been dealt with systematically and quantitatively. In the meantime, note that in the 19th century the majority of Jews in eastern Europe were poor artisans, penniless tradesmen, and manual labourers. Even a superficial reading of biographies or biographical dictionaries makes it clear that almost no noteworthy Jews in any areas came from 'the masses'. In the 18th and early 19th centuries members of the elite generally came from elite or near-elite families.

[50] One possible consequence of the universal Jewish concern with the study of text is developed in Bloom, *Agon*.

merchant and thus rise instantly to the top of society. This meant that the religious elite could be regarded as a meritocracy in which membership was based on achievement and not family. Theirs was a status that was both secure and not open to the challenge of being unfairly obtained. Theologically it was sound because it fitted with concepts involving ideas of revelation to the entire community and the universal responsibility to study the Torah. This was effective precisely because the reality was concealed. The system operated with a minimum of organization and this 'secret' no doubt contributed to the strength of the Jewish community even after the abolishment of the formal communal authorities.

Ḥeder schooling began to lose its effectiveness in the middle of the nineteenth century, but the decline was a slow process that went on well into the twentieth century. There was a growing realization that the job market was changing and that there was a need for a formal education that included general studies in order to succeed economically. When this happened, the *ḥeder* was unable to remain in the same form. It was no longer enough to know how to read Hebrew and religious texts—it was now necessary to know how to write, how to read a non-Jewish language, and to learn other skills.

Even after the *ḥeder* was no longer the standard institution for the education of Jewish boys and those *ḥeder*s that remained were transformed, the impact of the *ḥeder* on Jews and Jewish society remained. The belief in study as a means of advancement and that anyone can become learned was not based on fact and observed cases, but these beliefs determined Jewish attitudes and values. Jewish immigrants to western Europe and especially to the United States who grew up with this attitude were quick to take advantage of new educational opportunities offered them, and to reach levels of educational achievement in general studies that could only have been dreamed of in eastern Europe. For many of them, as for their grandparents, status was learning and not necessarily wealth. The results are clear in Western Jewry today.

There are institutions today that call themselves a *ḥeder*. There is no copyright on the word and anyone who wants to use it can do so. However, while called by the same name they do not have the characteristics of the traditional *ḥeder*. They are not in the home of the teacher, the parents do not bargain with the teacher or pay the teacher directly, and advancement is not up to the parents. One might also add that in these institutions that call themselves *ḥeder* there is a lot less violence directed against children than in the past. The *ḥeder* is gone but its heritage is around us in more ways than one.

EIGHT

Gender Differentiation and the Education of Jewish Women

A N ASSESSMENT of the role, function, and extent of women's education in nineteenth-century east European Jewry requires a substantial effort to distinguish facts from images. Our picture of the past is affected, of course, by present-day attitudes and stereotypes, but even at the time, the contemporary reality was seen in light of assumptions based on cultural postulates. There was a variety of images of the Jewish woman and her education, and they were not necessarily consistent. Therefore, pointing out the differences between the realities and the images not only adds to an understanding of women's education in eastern Europe, but also clarifies the value system of the Jewish community in the nineteenth century. It will be necessary to consider the image of women's education as well as relevant quantitative and qualitative data in order to understand the realities of women's education, the way this education was integrated into broader gender classifications, and the implications and consequences of women's education.

THE IMAGE AND FRAMEWORKS OF WOMEN'S EDUCATION

There is a widely held misconception that, in nineteenth-century eastern Europe, almost all Jewish women had a poor Jewish education whereas many received a good general education.[1] A classic expression of this view is that of Zvi Scharfstein, who wrote a number of widely used studies on the history of

---

[1] When I began to study this topic there was little research on it. Jeffrey Shandler generously shared with me the draft of a paper entitled 'Towards an Assessment of the Education of Women in Ashkenaz'. We share many ideas though the scope of his paper is much broader. Unfortunately his paper was never published. This topic has been explored recently in Parush, *Reading Jewish Women*. This is a fascinating but problematic book. Those interested can see my article 'Jewish Women Revisited' and the perceptive reviews by Tova Cohen, 'Information about Women is Necessarily Information about Men' and by Mordechai Zalkin. A superb book that deals perceptively with many of the realities of the lives of both women and men is Freeze, *Jewish Marriage and Divorce in Imperial Russia*. The phenomenon of education in Russia for young Jewish women, often from affluent homes, is explored in the doctoral thesis of Adler,

Jewish education and who stated in the opening to a (short) chapter on the education of girls:

The education of the Hebrew daughter—if we measure education as the degree of knowledge of Torah and books—was on a very low level in our midst. So low as to be a disgrace for the people . . . The Hebrews held that women are just for children and the kitchen and that he who teaches his daughter Torah taught her worthlessness . . . Only the national revival saved the Hebrew daughter from the shame of her ignorance—ignorance from the point of view of Judaism.[2]

A typical portrayal of gender differences in Jewish and general education is that of David Flinker. In discussing education in Warsaw he noted that, compared with the education of boys, the education of girls was backward. At best the elementary teacher would teach the girl to read Hebrew and Yiddish, and with that all the Jewish education of the Jewish daughter came to an end. At the same time:

In the small towns the men would study and acquired a broad and deep Torah education and their wives and daughters were uneducated and absolute boors. However, in the cities in the most recent generations, the girls as well were educated and cultured but their culture was different and alien to that of their parents and husbands.[3]

It is not hard to find justification of such a situation in classical Jewish texts. The classic proof text is 'anyone who teaches his daughter Torah teaches her *tiflut*' (usually translated as indecency or frivolity).[4] This statement suggests that women do not need any Jewish education at all. However, the existence of such statements does not mean that they were accepted, and even if accepted, that they were realized. Students of the history of Jewish education have often tended to see them as a true reflection of reality, but this cannot be taken for granted. It is necessary to check the accuracy of this image by examining the education girls actually received.

A number of frameworks existed in which girls could, and did, study, but there was no standard pattern for women's education as there was for boys. The lack of standardization might well be a product of the lack of interest evoked by women's education. In many locations special *ḥeders* operated for girls. In Tyszowce, a girls' *ḥeder* operated in the same house as the boys' *ḥeder*, but in an adjoining room. The girls were taught by an old widow, Binele 'the

'Private Schools for Jewish Girls'. Rachel Manekin has explored a number of relevant topics regarding the education of Jewish women in the process of modernization. See for example her outstanding articles 'The Lost Generation' and 'Something Totally New' (Heb.).

[2] Scharfstein, *The Ḥeder in the Life of Our People* (Heb.), 127.
[3] Flinker, 'Warsaw' (Heb.), 163.   [4] BT *Sot.* 20a.

rebetsin.[5] The programme of study consisted of prayers, reading and writing Yiddish, arithmetic, and writing addresses in Russian. The textbooks were the prayer-book and three Yiddish texts: *tekhines* (women's prayers), *Tsenah urenah*,[6] and *Nachlas tsevi* (a Yiddish ethical and kabbalistic tract). Sewing was also taught. The young students spent most of their time at play and were called when it was their turn for recitation.[7] Other girls' *ḥeder*s were probably no different.

Some girls were tutored at home. The tutor was often a 'learned' woman who would teach both reading and writing, though at times specialists were hired to teach a particular skill. Inevitably such tutoring was for short periods during the day, probably not amounting to more than an hour. Since it was expensive it was limited to the well-off: 'The well-off who gave any education at all to their daughters limited it to prayer and religious matters. Even they didn't send their daughters to school but they were satisfied with a house teacher and the curriculum was limited to reading and writing in Yiddish.'[8]

Girls' education was practical. Writing was taught by copying business letters rather than authoritative religious texts. Countless Jewish girls began their studies with the deathless words 'I went to Odessa to purchase merchandise', which reflects the utilitarian nature of their education.[9] Their education was seen as the antithesis of that of boys, which was devoted to Torah study—or in other words, to cultural education. This is illustrated in the following anecdote about a little boy who wanted very much to write (and ultimately did): 'In our house it was seen as unnecessary for a boy to learn how to write. My sister was sent to Avrom Note the *shrayber* (writing teacher) but I wasn't. I was supposed to study just *gemara* [Talmud] with the rabbi and not to trouble my head with silly ideas like writing.'[10]

For some girls, the question of where to study was resolved by their being sent to a *ḥeder* along with the boys. The mixing of the sexes apparently was not considered worthy of note or reaction,[11] and the decision to send a girl to a *ḥeder* was usually based on convenience and cost. A *ḥeder* was less expensive than a tutor. As Haya Weizmann-Lichtenstein wrote:

In the town it wasn't customary to send girls to *ḥeder*, rather a *rebbe* [elementary teacher] would come to the house for an hour and teach the girls. In this manner,

---

[5] The term literally means rabbi's wife, though it may have been used for learned women in general.   [6] On *Tsenah urenah* see below.

[7] Shtern, *Kheyder un beys-medresh*.   [8] Zaltsman, *My Town* (Heb.), 45.

[9] Shargorodska, 'Der shura grus' [A Model Letter].   [10] Spektor, *My Life* (Yid.), 159.

[11] This may surprise readers today, given the contemporary concern (or obsession) in certain very Orthodox Jewish circles regarding co-educational education even in elementary grades, but it should be emphasized that a century ago, sending a girl to a boys' *ḥeder* was not considered as having symbolic significance or reflecting an ideological commitment. *Ḥeder*s were not competing with a co-ed system.

they would manage to acquire very little knowledge of the Torah and few of them knew Hebrew. For my older sister Miriam my parents hired a private tutor and he taught her all of the curriculum. However, this was impossible to do for the rest of the daughters because the family was too large. Therefore I was sent to [a boys'] *ḥeder*.[12]

After basic reading was mastered, boys went on to study classical Jewish texts, the Bible and then Talmud, while girls dropped out.

QUANTITATIVE DATA ON WOMEN'S EDUCATION

The clearest quantitative picture of the educational realities of east European Jewry at the end of the nineteenth century is provided in a comprehensive survey of Jewish life in tsarist Russia conducted by ICA (Jewish Colonization Association) at the time.[13] The total number of female *ḥeder* students, whether with boys in a regular *ḥeder* or in special girls' *ḥeders*, was, not surprisingly, low when compared with the number of boys. In 1894, out of 13,683 *ḥeders* (probably fewer than half of the *ḥeders* in the tsarist empire), 191,505 male pupils were enrolled and 10,459 female pupils.[14] These statistics yield a ratio of about one to eighteen. However, this ratio is deceptive with regard to the number of girls *exposed* to education because female students studied for fewer years than males. If we can assume that girls studied at the most for four years and boys an average of nine, the ratio for the first four years would be about one to eight. There was some regional variation, with the ratio of female students three times as high, for example, in the south-west (which included Odessa) as in central Poland.[15]

Despite the various opportunities for formal education for girls it seems that many girls, and probably most, did not get a formal education, and if they did they studied for fewer years than boys. This fits the accepted picture of the education of women. However, if we look at educational achievements and not at schooling then the stereotype becomes problematic. Women as a group were far from being illiterate or uneducated. An indication of the level

[12] Weizmann-Lichtenstein, *In the Shadow of our Roof* (Heb.), 19.
[13] *Recueil de matériaux*.   [14] Ibid. 279.
[15] Ibid. 294–5. It would be premature to attribute this to modern attitudes in the south-west or to differing approaches to women's education. This variation was very possibly due to the fact that many of these *ḥeders* were in small towns where patterns were more fluid and where there were no alternatives for little girls, and not necessarily attributable to a regional interest in reform. Most modernizers sent their children to a very different kind of school—co-ed or otherwise—and not to a *ḥeder*. The attempt at the end of the 19th century to set up a new modern type of *ḥeder* which emphasized Hebrew and was known as the *ḥeder metukan* (reformed *ḥeder*) was a relatively small-scale phenomenon which would not have affected these figures. On this new type of *ḥeder* see Goldstein, 'The Reformed Ḥeder in Russia' (Heb.).

Table 8.1 Literacy and post-elementary education among Jews in European Russia by gender and age group, 1897 (%)

Age group	Literacy in Russian		Post-elementary education	
	Male	Female	Male	Female
1–9	6	5	—	—
10–19	41	30	1	2
20–29	51	28	2	2
30–39	47	17	2	1
40–49	40	9	1	—
50–59	31	6	—	—
60 and over	22	4	—	—

Source: Troinitsky (ed.), *Obshchii svod po Imperii*, vol.ii, table 15 (pp. 134–75).

Table 8.2 Literacy among urban and non-urban Jews aged 10–29 in European Russia, 1897 (%)

Age group	Urban		Non-urban	
	Male	Female	Male	Female
10–19	49	36	33	24
20–29	53	33	48	22

Source: Bureau für Statistik der Juden, *Die sozialen Verhältnisse der Juden in Russland*, 42.

of women's education can be seen by the distribution of Russian-language literacy among the various age cohorts of the Jewish population as recorded in the 1897 census.[16]

Starting from the cohort of men and women born in the 1860s (i.e. ages 30–39), the levels of Russian-language literacy of men and women begin to converge. This suggests an advance in women's education in the younger age groups. However, these data are only for literacy in Russian, whereas much of women's education, as noted above, was in Yiddish.

The levels of elementary ability to read Russian are surprisingly high. It is, of course, impossible to determine how careful the census takers were in accepting statements about literacy. When the data are broken down as in Table 8.2 to urban and non-urban populations, the results indicate that urban populations were more literate than non-urban populations, which makes sense.

[16] Troinitsky (ed.), *Obshchii svod po Imperii*, table 16. In this census, literacy was defined very broadly compared with later censuses, as has been pointed out by Ralph Clem, *Research Guide to the Russian and Soviet Censuses*: 'In 1897 . . . people who stated that they could read were considered literate; in 1926 people were considered literate if they were able to write their last name; by 1959, the questionnaire asked whether respondents could read and write' (p. 167).

Moreover, the gaps were larger between urban and non-urban adult females than among adult males. If the surprisingly high level of female literacy was simply the result of sloppy record-keeping by census takers, the sloppiness should have applied equally to town and country. Hence there is good reason to take the census data seriously.

Unfortunately the census material does not state in which non-Russian language individuals were literate. The questionnaire of the 1897 census did include a question on literacy in any language, which theoretically should have included Yiddish—but apparently Yiddish was not given the status of a language and the census statistics are clearly unreliable on this score. To learn about literacy in Yiddish we need to turn to other sources.

One of the most useful sources on women's literacy is a survey of the literacy of sample groups of Jewish immigrants carried out in 1913 in the United States.[17] It was conducted by a Jewish organization that was interested in dispelling the image of Jews as illiterate, but with a commitment to objectivity as well. In one sample, consisting of a group of 110 women who arrived in New York, 28 women were recorded as illiterate (25 per cent), but of these, eight of them were able to read a prayer-book, leaving only 18 per cent totally illiterate. In a similar study conducted at the same time in Houston, much higher levels of illiteracy for female immigrants were recorded (40 per cent), but this second study apparently did not take into account an ability to read a prayer-book. These data cannot be taken as irrefutable evidence for the educational level of the east European Jewish woman. Migrants to America were not only younger on the whole than the general Jewish population in eastern Europe, but they were also made up of the lower-status elements of Jewish society, were less educated, and less traditional.[18] Hence it would be quite likely that their higher-class contemporaries who stayed behind in the tsarist empire had even higher levels of literacy.[19]

Within eastern Europe the differences were almost certainly not just a question of socio-economic class. There appear to have been significant differences between levels of female literacy in cities and in towns. Studies of Jewish workers in Vilna, Warsaw, and Berdichev in 1913 found that in Vilna less than 1 per cent of female workers surveyed were illiterate, and less than 7 per cent in Berdichev and Warsaw.[20] At the same time Lestchinsky found that

---

[17] See the report *Jewish Immigrants*.

[18] See Kuznets, 'Immigration of Russian Jews to the United States'; Halevy, 'Were the Jewish Immigrants to the United States Representative of Russian Jews?'

[19] These data are of course very revealing about the make-up of the immigrant community. If the sample was typical of the immigrants—and there is no reason to suspect that it was not—it shows that most women who came knew how to read even though most of them came from the 'lower classes' of east European Jewish society and the less traditional element.

[20] Rabinowitsch-Margolin, 'Zur Bildungsstatistik'.

in the town of Gorodishche (in the Kiev region) many of the Jewish factory girls were absolutely illiterate and that almost half of the female population was illiterate, though it is not clear whether this small town was typical.[21]

Given the low figures of school attendance by girls, it appears that most of the literate women learned how to read on their own or with the help of friends or relatives. However, women who learned to read in this fashion were not necessarily drilled in writing, and they received, of course, a less systematic course of study than the women who studied in school. Women who learned how to read informally were not likely to write autobiographies, and therefore testimony about this kind of education is difficult to cite, but the gap between the number of women who read and those who could have gone to school cannot otherwise be explained.[22]

QUALITATIVE EVIDENCE FOR WOMEN'S EDUCATION

It is possible to question the accuracy of statistical data and wonder if there were overstatements or understatements of literacy in Yiddish, or query how representative a sample of the total population was taken. However, there is additional strong evidence for significant literacy among women. A long tradition exists regarding the printing of romances and popular literature in Yiddish directed towards women.[23] To be sure, this literature was read by many men who also found it appealing. What is significant is that addressing these books to women, irrespective of who really read them, presumes a reality in which many women could read and were, in effect, educated—even if they were not recognized as such. As we shall see below, religious literature for women also played an important role in their lives and reading it was seen as significant behaviour. The Gaon of Vilna called on his female descendants to read this literature, apparently instead of frivolous literature, and he took their ability to read for granted.[24] One could argue that his daughters may have been exceptional, but the publicity given to the Gaon's views indicates that they were regarded as role models for the general Jewish population.

[21] Lestchinsky, 'Statistics of a Town' (Heb.), 17–38, esp. 34–5.

[22] Being able to read does not mean that women knew how to write. A survey of signatures on marriage contracts in Warsaw in 1845 and 1860 indicates that only a third of the Jewish men and a similar percentage of Jewish women could sign their names. See Kowalska-Glikman, 'Ludnosc żydowska', 37–49.

[23] For information in English on this topic see Roskies, 'Yiddish Popular Literature and the Female Reader' and 'The Medium and Message of the Maskilic Chapbook'; Weissler, 'For Women and for Men Who Are Like Women' and *Voices of the Matriarchs*; Kay, *Seyder Tkhines*; and Guren-Klirs (ed.), *The Merit of our Mothers*.

[24] See the letter the Gaon wrote to his family on his way to Erets Yisra'el. It was first printed in his *Alim literufah* and often reprinted. This was by no means unique. R. Mosheh Sofer (the

The discrepancy between statistics on schooling and on literacy makes it necessary to carefully consider what the term 'women's education' means. Education usually relates to two important activities. One is the teaching of practical skills which can aid a person in earning a living or being useful in day-to-day life. The other function involves the study of the cultural tradition of a society.[25] All societies have to meet cultural and practical needs, whether formally or informally. The specific determination of what is taught and how is, of course, the product of traditions, needs, and resources.

Among eastern European Jewry, as in many societies, formal schooling (such as the *ḥeder*, *beit midrash*, and the yeshiva)—the most visible aspect of education—concentrated on males and was devoted solely to the cultural tradition of the community. Occupational training for both males and females was carried out within the framework of informal education. Crafts were learned by apprentices on the job under the supervision of skilled individuals. Preparation for commerce or business was also learned on the job, though private teachers for specific skills such as arithmetic were often used. As long as Jews did not enter occupations that required academic credentials or highly technical expertise there was no need to include career preparation in the curriculum. The setting up of commercial and trade schools for Jews starting from the latter part of the nineteenth century with programmes like that of ORT (Society for Manual and Agricultural Work among Jews) were important innovations in the Jewish educational systems. They drew on foreign, non-Jewish models and not on precedents within the local educational tradition.[26] The study of Torah was different because it was not practical, and obviously it did not yield direct economic benefits.

Even *ḥeder*s did not emphasize applied knowledge. In a society that regarded personal salvation, and possibly also group redemption, as the product of correct ritual behaviour, one might have anticipated that the goal of study would be to ensure that males were familiar with all the fine points of the law. This was not the case. Halakhah (Jewish law) was not on the curriculum of either the *ḥeder* or the yeshiva. As with other practical skills, Jewish law was generally learned by example, a system possible in a context where most

Hatam Sofer, 1762–1839) in Pressburg, Hungary (Bratislava), also called on his daughters to read religious works written in Yiddish—but nothing more. See his will, which has been translated into English in Reimer, *Ethical Wills*, 18–21.

[25] This does not mean that education does not have other functions as well. For example, although schools are often expected to encourage certain character or personality traits among their students, in practice these are usually secondary to one or both of the two main functions.

[26] On trade education among Jews in Germany see Eliav, *Jewish Education in Germany* (Heb.), ch. 12. On ORT (Obshchestvo rasprostraneniya truda sredi evreev) in Russia see Shapiro, *The History of ORT*. On vocational training in general see Weinryb, *Jewish Vocational Education*, esp. pt. 2.

Jews observed the law.[27] Since women were not regarded as obligated to study Torah it was easier to justify formal study of secular topics on their part. In a letter written in 1840 Rabbi Elijah Rogoler, the rabbi of Kalisz, claimed that his younger sister (a candidate for a match) was not only beautiful but knew grammar and how to write Hebrew, Polish, and German perfectly, as well as some Russian. Her sister (also a candidate for a match) was described as beautiful too, but no details are provided on her linguistic skills. Apparently knowledge of languages was desirable but not standard, even in circles where provisions were made for their study.[28]

Although males and females were provided with very different frameworks for acquiring literacy education, women were not necessarily inferior to men in Jewish knowledge. Women not only knew how to read but read often. The image of the uneducated woman of the masses coexists with that of the Jewish woman who sat down at home in her chair every Saturday afternoon and read the weekly Torah portion—in Yiddish. It is quite possible that of all the books sold in eastern Europe, the two bestsellers were books specifically intended for a female audience and read only by women—*Tsenah urenah* (often pronounced *tsenerene*), and *tekhines*. The *Tsenah urenah* is a Yiddish text consisting of a free retelling of aggadic material on the Bible. Originally written around 1600 for both men and women, it quickly became the classic women's text. Chone Shmeruk counted 110 editions printed between 1786 and 1900, and he affirms that no doubt there were many more.[29] The regular reading of *Tsenah urenah* was seen as an act of piety and the ability to read it was clearly not seen as exceptional. The repeated reading of *Tsenah urenah* gave a woman a good picture of the biblical narrative as seen through the eyes of rabbis. In terms of knowledge of the biblical narrative, women who read *Tsenah urenah* regularly should have known at least as much of the biblical narrative as a male who had finished the *ḥeder* curriculum.

[27] The tractates of the Talmud that were most often studied were not related to everyday life and even when relevant ones were studied, the halakhic implications and the legal conclusions were often ignored. When questions of practice came up recourse was occasionally taken to written guides, but in most questions of doubt the rabbi was asked. Certainly, convenient summaries of Jewish law, such as Danzig, *Ḥayei adam*, were very popular and many study circles studied them regularly. However, in quantitative terms, the number of circles devoted to popular halakhah was far smaller than those devoted to the recital of psalms or the study of aggadah, Mishnah, Talmud, or similar texts.

[28] See Urbach, 'A Collection of Letters of R. Eliyahu Rogoler' (Heb.), 549. I thank Michael Silber for the reference.

[29] Shmeruk, 'East European Versions of Tse'ene-Rene'. On *Tsenah urenah* see also Turniansky, 'Translations and Adaptations of the Tse'ena Urena' (Yid.). She begins her article by mentioning that *Tsenah urenah* was an 'integral part of the *oneg shabat* (sabbath joy) in every Jewish home in western and eastern Europe and that it was the most popular Yiddish book'.

The custom of having *zogerkes* or prayer prompters for women in the synagogue, who told women what to say and when to cry, could be cited as evidence for female illiteracy and ignorance, but this would not be accurate. An ability to peruse a Yiddish text is not the same as being able to catch the Hebrew of the prayer service, and reading in the quiet of the home is not the same as finding one's place through the din of the women's section of the synagogue.

There were, of course, significant differences between the ways men studied classical Hebrew texts and women studied *Tsenah urenah*. Male study usually took place in the *beit midrash* in the company of peers, and therefore this study was a public demonstration of religious devotion and piety. Males often had additional reasons for studying in public. The many males who were not capable of independent study participated in study societies (*ḥevrot*), and heard regular classes and lectures on classical texts. More advanced individuals who could study on their own had on occasion need for assistance or to consult in order to understand the difficult texts, and therefore preferred to study in *beit midrash*. *Tsenah urenah* was read in the home and it was family members who served as an 'audience' for the woman's study activity. Since *Tsenah urenah* was a Yiddish text it did not present linguistic problems. More-over, since it lacked the status and classical character of a rabbinic book, it could be and was continually updated from a linguistic point of view, as Shmeruk's work points out. This meant that the *Tsenah urenah* was easy to understand and could be studied in private. Perhaps the most significant difference between the evaluation of male study of classical Hebrew texts and female study of *Tsenah urenah* was that only the former was regarded as true study of the Torah, while the latter was merely an act of piety.

The world of prayer also exhibited differences between patterns of male and female behaviour. An examination of the role of *tekhines*[30] makes this clear. *Tekhines* were prayers written in Yiddish and organized around the weekly routine and life cycle of the east European Jewish woman. The *tekhine* literature reflects similar religious values and activities to those of men, but within radically different frameworks. The *tekhines* were read by women individually and usually not in a synagogue; they were not chanted nor said in public. Therefore they were said only by literate women. These women were free to choose which *tekhine* book to use, which *tekhines* to say, and when. Many of the *tekhines* were presented as having been written by women for women, and were adapted to new realities and needs. The covers of *tekhine* books advertised the contents as including 'nice new *tekhines*', even when that was not the case, and a value was placed on their relevance and novelty. All of

[30] On *tekhines* see the important articles of Weissler, 'The Traditional Piety of Ashkenazic Women' and 'The Religion of Traditional Ashkenazic Women'.

this was very different from male prayer. Men's prayers were from the fixed Hebrew text of the prayer-book. The sanctity of male prayers was closely tied to their ancient origins and novelty was disguised. Men prayed according to a ritual calendar and not according to the needs they felt. The writers of male prayers were figures from the distant past, and not individuals with whom one could easily identify. What was common to both men and women was that prayer was said from a written text and that literacy was taken for granted.

GENDER DEFINITION IN TRADITIONAL JEWISH SOCIETY

Women's use of *Tsenah urenah* and the *tekhine* literature instead of the *ḥumash* (Pentateuch) and *siddur* (Hebrew prayer-book) were just two elements of a much wider range of distinctive gender-defined expressions for similar functions.[31] Jewish men and women could be seen as occupying adjacent but different cultural worlds in eastern Europe, in which the expression of a function in one gender was the mirror image of its expression in the other gender. Men and women shared a common spoken language and a common religious/national identity, but much else was radically different. Socially, men and women had no direct relationships unless they had common family ties. In the synagogue or *beit midrash*, the holiest place in the community, the seating of men and women was separated. Men came daily to the synagogue for prayer and study, and often more than once a day, while women came less often and just for prayer. Men belonged to formal associations (*ḥevrot*), whereas social life for women was informal. To a large extent men and women also did not share a literary language. Men were supposed to read Hebrew and, if they could, write Hebrew, whereas if women were literate it was generally in Yiddish. Although Yiddish is, of course, written in Hebrew letters, up until the mid-nineteenth century there was generally no mistaking a book written in Hebrew—that is, directed solely to men—and a book written in Yiddish and ostensibly directed to women, because different fonts or types of letters were generally used for Hebrew and Yiddish.[32] When men gave charity it was usually in the synagogue, while women gave charity into the *pushke*.[33] Even the concepts of beauty were different. The ideal man was a retiring, pale, delicate talmudist, with sensitive hands and long white fingers;

---

[31] This topic has not received a great deal of attention in the literature, and much of what there is has hardly gone past the descriptive. See, for example, Zborowski and Herzog, *Life Is with People*, pt. 2, ch. 4. An example of what can be done by means of careful analysis is Weissler, 'For Women and for Men Who Are Like Women'.

[32] See Weinreich, *Selected Writings* (Yid.), 66. I am grateful to Professor Turniansky for the reference.   [33] On the social history of the *pushke* see Chapter 5 above.

the ideal woman was an active, even aggressive, full-bodied woman with multiple chins.[34]

To be sure, there were many exceptions to this gender division and they did not extend to every sphere of life. Both men and women generally worked and contributed to the family income, so that there was no clear distinction between the males as breadwinners and the women as homemakers as was common in many other societies. The economic conditions did not allow for that. Of course, the women's responsibilities for the home were clear: she was responsible for running the house, even if she was the main breadwinner.[35] Generally, the occupational distribution of men and women was such that there was little direct competition between them. Even in the late nineteenth century when factory work became more common, men and women still did not work side by side in factories.

THE EDUCATIONAL REALITIES OF JEWISH WOMEN

In light of the fact that gender differences often concealed similar functions, it is worth re-examining basic educational institutions among Jews with the intention of distinguishing between image and reality. From this perspective it is clear that in traditional Jewish society, the differences between the educational achievements of boys and girls on the level of elementary education were more perceived than real—just as the differences in knowledge and prayer experience between men and women were more apparent and linguistic than real. Boys spent all day in the *ḥeder*. However, much of their day was spent in play and storytelling, while the *melamed* (teacher) sat down for short periods of time with individuals or groups of two and three.[36] Thus the amount of knowledge a boy acquired in a full day of non-intensive study in a *ḥeder* was not necessarily much more than those of tutored girls who may have studied for an hour or two a day. Women's education was certainly less stressful, which may explain in part why female education was not usually accompanied by the violence which so often characterized *ḥeder* education. It was considered right for boys to be beaten but not for girls—though there were exceptions. Esther Rosenthal-Schneiderman (born around 1900) recalled never being beaten by her teacher, the *rebetsin*, but she got plenty of slaps and pinches from the teacher's husband, the rabbi![37]

[34] Somogyi, *Die Schejnen und die Prosten*.
[35] Michael Silber has found references in literature dealing with Hungarian Jews to men who were supported by their wives and were expected to do household chores (oral communication). I have not found any such cases in eastern Europe.
[36] See the vivid description of Shtern, 'A Heder in Tyszowce', 164.
[37] Rosenthal-Schneiderman, *Complicated Paths* (Heb.), i. 31.

The low pressure and often informal elementary education of women was made possible by the limitations of Yiddish. Among the many virtues of the Yiddish language is that in written Yiddish each letter has one sound and vowels are represented by letters, with the exception of words of Hebrew origin, which are limited in number. In Hebrew, letters also have one phonic meaning, but vowels are represented by dots (often smudgy) in vocalized Hebrew texts and by nothing at all in unvocalized texts—and most printed Hebrew texts were unvocalized. Since Yiddish was the spoken language the beginning reader could anticipate words and sounds from the context. As a result, while it sometimes took well over a year of *ḥeder* study for a little boy to learn how to read Hebrew freely, a young woman should have been able to learn to read Yiddish in a short time—perhaps only a few weeks. Moreover, as soon as she could read she could understand what she read—which was an achievement not every *ḥeder* student reached even after years of study. In short, women had an easier time than men in reaching functional literacy. Moreover, most men did not get much further than functional literacy in Hebrew despite all their years of study. While advanced talmudic study was the goal of male study, it must be remembered that only a minority of students went on to such study.

Women could also go further than reading *Tsenah urenah* to acquire additional Jewish knowledge. A wide number of aggadic texts (texts of the non-legal rabbinic literature) were also available in Yiddish, and even much of the Zohar (the classic kabbalistic text) was, theoretically at least, available in Yiddish. In the early nineteenth century no general works in Yiddish on Jewish law were available, and certainly no adaptations of classical rabbinic texts (such as the Talmud) into Yiddish for women.[38]

There were a few books of Jewish law in Yiddish that were specifically directed to a female audience. These were limited to topics that were relevant specifically to women, such as the laws dealing with kosher food and relating

[38] Works such as *Lekaḥ tov*—a Yiddish crib of selections from the Talmud for *ḥeder* teachers and students, was not part of the woman's library. There was no translation into Yiddish of a comprehensive guide to Jewish law, such as the *Shulḥan arukh*, in the pre-modern period. The creation of popular guides to Jewish law, even in Hebrew, is itself a modern innovation. Danzig, *Ḥayei adam*, a very popular summary of Jewish law directed to non-learned readers, appeared in 1810, while the first Yiddish translation found in the National Library in Jerusalem dates from 1865. On this book see the unpublished MA thesis of Mordechai Meir, 'Rabbi Abraham Danzig'; Goldrat, 'On the Book *Ḥayei adam and its Author*' (Heb.). The first Yiddish translation found in the National Library of Ganzfried's *Kitsur shulḥan arukh* appeared in 1882 (a similar summary published in Hebrew in the 1860s). In short, general guides to Jewish law became available in Yiddish in the second half of the 19th century. On aspects of Jewish law specifically related to Jewish women there were Yiddish publications. See Segal, 'Yiddish Works on Women's Commandments', and Assaf, 'A Responsum against the Writing of Law Books in Yiddish' (Heb.).

to the times when intercourse after menstruation was permitted. The publication of such literature had been a topic of controversy when these books were first printed, and at least one important rabbi in eastern Europe regarded this literature with misgivings and praised women for not relying on it.[39] This was apparently too close to the men's 'territory'. At the same time, since the study of Jewish law—in any form—was not part of the standard *ḥeder* curriculum, there was no significant difference, in fact, in the way most men and women learned Jewish law. What should be noted is that given the amount and variety of sources available in Yiddish, a reader limited to Yiddish could still become quite familiar with most areas of Jewish knowledge.

Women's life contained functional equivalents to male activities that required reading, but these activities lacked the same status. For women these activities were voluntary, whereas for men they were obligatory. However, while women recognized the value of male activities such as prayer and study, men did not place similar value on the parallel activities among women or demand that women devote their time to these activities. The image of female ignorance justified male (and female) views of the inferiority of women, even though the image had little truth to it. The function of limited access to knowledge as a means of social repression was not unique to women in Jewish society. Among men as well, knowledge of Talmud, which was restricted to a socio-economic elite, served as a means of proving to the ignorant masses that they deserved their inferior position in society.[40]

ACCEPTANCE AND REJECTION OF WOMEN'S ROLES IN EDUCATION

In most cases the system of limited formal education for most women was fitted in with the realities of traditional Jewish society in the early nineteenth century. Most women worked, either independently or by helping their fathers or husbands, because their families could hardly make a living otherwise. Moreover they were also burdened by family responsibilities. With a high birth rate and without technologies to save time in housework, even most non-working housewives had few leisure moments or time to study difficult Hebrew texts. An education that trained them to devote hours every day to the study of the Talmud would have been an education designed to

[39] 'It was never the custom to teach women from books and I never heard of such a practice. Rather the known [i.e. relevant] laws are taught by each woman to her daughter and daughter-in-law and recently books of women's law have been printed in the language of the nations [i.e. Yiddish!] and they can read them and our women are energetic in every case of doubt and ask and do not rely on their [book] knowledge in even the slightest matter.' Epstein, *Arukh hashulḥan*, 'Yoreh de'ah', 246: 19.

[40] See Funkenstein and Steinsaltz, *Sociology of Ignorance* (Heb.), and Chapter 9 below.

maximize frustration. Lack of 'school education' was part of a system that functioned to condition women to accept their role in the family and society with a minimum of conflict—just as the fact that most men were unlearned (and knew it!) was one of the ways that led them to accept communal authority. Although most women apparently accepted this role and found fulfilment in the parallel culture that was theirs and which was meaningful to them,[41] that does not mean that all did. The daughter of the famous Yiddish writer Shomer wrote of her mother:

My mother in all the days of her long life bitterly resented the meagerness of her youthful education and cordially despised the three special duties [incumbent on women—candle lighting, ritual bathing, and baking bread in accordance with Jewish law] even if she did, in a manner of speaking, observe them . . . According to my mother, her father spent thousands of rubles on every cause and every charity in the town but denied her a ruble with which to pay for instruction in the Russian or Hebrew she had desired so much.[42]

In her case, economic pressure could not justify the lack of investment in her education and this may have contributed to her frustration.

This dissatisfaction could exist in the circles of the rabbinic elite as well. We learn from an oft-quoted description written by the well-known Rabbi Barukh Epstein about his aunt, the wife of the head of the yeshiva of Volozhin, Rabbi Naftali Tsevi Yehudah Berlin, of events that took place around 1875. Recent research has raised many questions about the veracity of R. Epstein's autobiography but the account seems plausible:

. . . she was worried and vexed about the defiled honour of the women and their lowly status due to the fact that the rabbis forbid teaching them Torah. One time she told me that if Eve (meaning the female sex) was cursed with ten curses, the prohibition of learning Torah is equivalent to all the curses and is even more than all of them. There was no end to the grief. One time, while she was speaking excitably on this subject, I said to her, 'But my aunt, you women are blaming the men for this prohibition when they are not at fault. You yourselves caused this and you are guilty in the matter', and I explained my words. Our sages said (at the end of the second chapter of *Avot derabi natan*) that Torah should only be taught to a humble person. About women, our Sages decided in JT *Shabat* 6, that 'they [women] are ostentatious' meaning conceited beings. If so, isn't it forbidden to teach them Torah because of their character traits, and who is to blame if not they themselves, and why do they complain? She said to me: 'When I have free time I will do research on the word and find out the exact meaning. In the meantime bring me *Avot derabi natan* and I will look for the words which you mentioned from them.' I went and brought . . . and fell right into the trap! In *Avot derabi natan* the wording is as follows: Beit Shammai says: 'A person shall only teach one who is clever, humble and rich'

[41] Zaltsman, *My Town* (Heb.), 47.   [42] Shomer-Zunser, *Yesterday*, 66.

and Beit Hillel says: 'We teach to everyone because there were many sinners in Israel and they started learning the Torah and became righteous, observant men'. As she finished reading these words, she raised her voice in anger and said, 'How did you do this evil thing, or was it because you wanted to trick me that you took the opinion of Beit Shammai as the basis for your word? Every boy who has studied even a little Talmud knows that when there is a disagreement between Beit Shammai and Beit Hillel, the law is in accordance with Beit Hillel, and Beit Hillel permits teaching Torah to everyone!!' . . . As she was in good spirits at her victory over me, she was no longer angry with me, and when she saw that I had taken it somewhat to heart, she comforted me . . . and began to talk about this topic in a general manner . . . I remember that when she mentioned the name of Beruriah, the wife of Rabbi Meir, I told her that a wrongdoing was found against her—that she mocked the words of our Sages, for 'women are light-headed'. In the end she herself was guilty of light-headedness, as is brought out in the story of Rashi on BT *Avodah zarah* 18*b*. She answered me, 'In truth, I know of this legend, but did our Sages find all men guilty because of the sin of Aher, who left the right way [BT *ḥagigah* 15*a*]? Furthermore, Beruriah did not mock with contempt and derision. She only thought that our Sages did not fully understand the rationale of women. According to her view, women are also strong-minded. This was the entire incident and nothing more.[43]

There is no reason to take cases that may well be exceptional or literary inventions as evidence for widespread dissatisfaction among women. Indeed, there were probably as many boys who envied their sisters who were free of the *ḥeder* as vice versa. However, they do indicate the tensions inherent in the educational system for women and the potential for change even in the most conservative circles.

CHANGING PATTERNS OF EDUCATION OF THE JEWISH WOMAN

Changes in women's education can be traced back to early in the nineteenth century. In the two important centres of Jewish modernization in eastern Europe—Warsaw and Vilna—secular schools for girls were founded before secular schools for boys. In 1818 a 'modern' girls' school which taught secular topics was organized in Warsaw and almost immediately there was an initiative to open up a second school for girls. The first secular school for boys in Poland was set up only the following year by Jacob Tugenhold.[44] The first school for girls in the Pale of Settlement was founded in Vilna in 1826. It was successful and continued to function through the 1840s. The famous *talmud*

[43] Epstein, 'Wisdom of Women', 98–100; on Epstein see Rabinowitz, 'Rayna Batya'.
[44] Shatzky, *Jewish Educational Policies in Poland from 1806 to 1866* (Yid.), 210–12. See also Sabina Levin, 'The First Elementary Schools' (Heb.), 78–9.

Table 8.3 Age distribution of Jewish women at marriage in the tsarist empire, 1867–1902 (%)

Year	Age		
	20 and under	21–25	26–30
1867	61	21	8
1885	47	37	8
1902	24	53	15

Source: Based on Rabinowitsch-Margolin, 'Die Heiraten der Juden'.

torah in Odessa was founded seven years later, and the first school for boys in Vilna which included secular studies was founded only in 1841.[45] These developments were, of course, exceptions. However, by the 1860s the traditional patterns of women's education began to erode and increasing numbers of women were studying in the modern schools, public and private, that were appearing, especially in the large cities.[46] The high cost of such an education makes it clear that the female students could have come only from families that were well off—which was not typical for the Jewish community.[47] This shift was related to many factors, of which the most important were probably the influences of 'modern' values and models as well as a rise in the average age at marriage among the upper class of the Jewish community. Whereas the first is generally well known, the second deserves some attention.[48]

In early modern eastern Europe, Jews demonstrated high status by marrying off the children at an early age.[49] Before reaching her teens, a girl from an elite home would become a *baleboste* (homemaker) with all of the duties that it entailed. For her parents this meant undertaking to support an adolescent son-in-law (who often had a very healthy appetite) as well as potential grandchildren for a number of years. For a variety of reasons, this pattern shifted in the course of the nineteenth century, as is shown in Table 8.3.

This rise in the age of marriage created, by the late nineteenth century, a population of teenage girls from well-off families who had to pass time until marriage, and so it was necessary to find legitimate ways for them to spend this time. Study was an ideal solution because it was consonant with contemporary non-Jewish elite views that women's education was desirable. One option for women was tutoring. However, this was expensive and moreover

---

[45] See Klausner, *Vilna: The Jerusalem of Lithuania* (Heb.), 207–8.
[46] See Kreis, 'Russian-Language Jewish Schools' (Heb.).
[47] See Kazdan, *From Ḥeder and Schools to CYSHO* (Yid.), 202. He also brings interesting material on calls for reform.
[48] See Weissman, 'Bais Yaakov: A Historical Model for Jewish Feminists', 139.
[49] See Goldberg, 'Die Ehe bei den Juden', and Chapter 1 above.

was becoming outmoded. Schools were an ideal answer, whether government-sponsored or under Jewish auspices, and the number of women in these schools was constantly on the rise from the mid-nineteenth century.

To justify devoting a few years to study entailed having a sufficiently respectable syllabus. What was to be studied? The traditional rabbinic literacy corpus in Hebrew was regarded as suitable only for males, and Yiddish texts, intended for independent study, were too 'easy' to justify a formal education. There were a number of options. One possibility was to provide a commercial education. This fitted the ideal of the working woman who supported her scholarly husband, an ideal that coexisted with that of the rich merchant and a reality in which many women worked. However, many young women and their parents preferred a cultural education. Such an education was testimony to the wealth of the household. Among the standard elements adopted were the study of French and the playing of piano—both suitably esoteric and non-utilitarian, and valued by the surrounding society as well. At a time when secular studies were traditionally seen in Jewish circles as irrelevant but not evil or harmful, such an education, which was typical for the non-Jewish elite, could easily be seen as not only permissible but even desirable for Jewish women.

However, what men thought general education was about was not always what women found. Even without social contacts with non-Jewish society, a woman who received a general education was introduced to a world, even if only a literary one, which promised not only status but a very different set of values. Women often accepted these values and made radical changes in their lifestyle which led to estrangement from traditional forms of Judaism. Thus by the mid-nineteenth century there was no lack of families in which boys studied Talmud and their sisters French literature, which looked incongruous to later generations who viewed secular studies as evil or as leading to evil. It cannot be overemphasized that only a small minority of Jewish girls grew up in such homes. Nonetheless, this secular situation attracted attention and began to be seen as typical, even though most Jewish homes were far too poor to provide either sons or daughters with higher education.

Although only a minority of women went to modern schools, the number who did was not insignificant by the end of the nineteenth century. In 1899 a survey of such schools in the tsarist empire found 193 girls' schools and 68 schools for both boys and girls (usually in separate classes) as opposed to 383 boys' schools.[50] This yields very different ratios between males and females from the *ḥeder*s. Of the 50,773 students enrolled in such schools, about a third were girls. When population is taken into account, we find that the most favourable ratio of female students to the total Jewish population was in the

[50] See *Recueil de matériaux*, 314, 318.

south (one female pupil for every 109 Jews) followed by the north-west (one per 208) with the least favourable being the south-west (one per 458). The vast majority of the girls' schools were private (172), while of the boys' schools only 187 were private and the rest were government or communal schools. In eastern Europe the cost of tuition of girls in private schools was 50 per cent higher than that of boys. The large number of private girls' schools clearly indicates widespread interest in girls' education and willingness to pay for it along with an unwillingness or lack of interest on the part of the communities or government to invest in women's education. The girls' schools, it should be noted, were not finishing schools with lots of glitter and little content. The academic level of the teachers in the girls' schools was significantly higher than the average in the boys' schools and many of the teachers were women— positive role models.

These figures do not come near to fully reflecting the hunger for knowledge among the Jewish women of the tsarist empire—or their parents. A study in 1894 showed that for almost every girl who applied for admission to a private school and was accepted, another was turned down for lack of space. It was equally difficult for a girl to gain admission to a co-educational school. The highest level of refusals was for admission to communal schools which enrolled mainly males. These schools had the advantage of being inexpensive and also under Jewish administration. Another reflection of the women's desire for an education is the fact that Jewish girls tended to remain in private schools much longer than did Jewish boys.[51]

The pressure for admission to girls' schools in the tsarist empire probably explains the differences between the enrolment of Jewish boys and girls in government schools. Reports from 1898 dealing with public elementary schools in the Vilna and Kiev districts indicate that, in Vilna, more Jewish girls went to public non-Jewish schools than did Jewish boys. About 14 per cent of the female students in the Vilna schools were Jewish while the Jewish boys made up 2.7 per cent. In Kiev the male Jewish pupils outnumbered the females by five to one, but both males and females made up about 4 per cent of the pupils of their respective sexes.[52] One must be careful about drawing conclusions from these data because attendance at these schools was hindered both by administrative hurdles designed to keep out Jews, especially boys, and by a policy that demanded that Jewish children attend classes on the sabbath and on holidays and violate the Jewish sabbath laws by writing.

The situation in Galicia, in the Austro-Hungarian empire, which had a far more effective programme of public schools for Jews than existed in the tsarist empire, was quite different and illustrates the potential for change in an east European Jewish population. Unfortunately we do not have detailed age

---

[51] Ibid. 324   [52] I do not have an explanation for the differences between the two cities.

Table 8.4 Number of Jewish children attending modern elementary schools in Galicia, by type, 1880–1900 ('000)

Year	Government schools		Private schools		Total	
	Boys	Girls	Boys	Girls	Boys	Girls
1880	10.6	18.3	1.9	2.6	12.5	20.9
1890	15.5	29.6	2.6	2.7	18.1	32.2
1900	22.7	43.9	10.3	1.6	33.0	45.5

Note: 'Modern' schools are those with a curriculum of secular studies, including study of the vernacular.

Source: Based on Thon, *Die Juden in Österreich*, 81–8; see also his table 23 on p. 46.

breakdowns of the base population which would enable us to assess the exact percentage of school-age children actually attending school. However, there are rough figures on the age breakdown of Galician Jewry in 1890 (see Table 8.4).[53] There were about 230,000 children under the age of 10 in Galicia in 1890, and 180,000 in the 10–20-year-olds. Thus school-age yearly cohorts were probably roughly 20,000. Assuming elementary schools had six to eight grades, in 1890 the number of school-age children was about 150,000, and roughly 25 per cent of school-age boys and 40 per cent of school-age girls were in these schools. A decade later (assuming no dramatic changes in the size of the cohorts), roughly 45 per cent of the boys were in these schools and 60 per cent of the girls.[54] It is clear that the number of girls who received a modern education was increasing rapidly at the end of the nineteenth century. The masses of the Jewish population still retained traditional distinctions between what was proper for boys to study and what for girls—though this was changing. However, in secondary and higher education, which was directly geared to careers and was common only among the socio-economic elite, the sexual balance was sharply reversed and boys far outnumbered girls.[55]

THE BACKGROUND OF THE STEREOTYPE OF WOMEN'S EDUCATION

The fact that most Jewish women did not study in formal institutions contributed to the stereotype of east European women as having very limited education. Studies of educational history or descriptions of educational realities tend to centre on the development and growth of schools—whatever

[53] I am grateful to Michael Silber for having brought Thon, *Die Juden in Österreich*. to my attention. On education of Jewish women in Galicia see now Manekin, 'The Lost Generation', and '"Something Totally New"' (Heb.).   [54] Thon, *Die Juden in Österreich*, table 23, p. 46.
[55] Thon does not provide data on the sexual breakdown of students in secondary and higher education. However, Michael Silber found that in Hungary boys by far outnumbered girls in

their function. Schools are highly visible institutions and make easy topics for research and description. However, limiting the history of education to schools is justifiable only to the degree that education is concentrated in formal frameworks. For example, in studying American student societies in the eighteenth and nineteenth centuries, James McLachlan found this to be the case in the formal classroom and justifiably claimed that 'the study of the formal curriculum of the early 19th century American College cannot be carried on in isolation from an equally intense study of the students' extra curriculum. To do so produces a completely misleading, in fact, downright false—impression of the history of American higher education.'[56] The same is true for Jewish women's education in eastern Europe.

The conventional image of the extremely low level of women's education in traditional Jewish society can be accepted only if one adopts a very narrow definition of education which limits it to schooling and assumes that a religious text written in Hebrew is significant, whereas one written in Yiddish is not. This distinction is artificial and misleading. To be sure, precisely such an identification of education with schooling was actually held by both men and women in the past. Their attention, like that of later observers, was caught by the fact that, in sharp contrast to the situation among males, few educational institutions were available for Jewish women and those that existed were elementary, poorly documented, and not well developed. However, since only males were really expected to go to school, concentrating on schools means in effect squeezing women into male categories rather than looking at the full educational life of women. Far more significant is the fact that large numbers of women could read and did so, despite the fact that they hardly went to school. They acquired knowledge through reading and in this respect they were more self-sufficient than men, who learned by listening to lectures and sermons. This behaviour was regarded as standard and desirable and not as deviant. It was also not categorized as Torah study, since women studied in Yiddish and mastered different texts from those that men studied. These are not grounds for characterizing the women as uneducated, despite the fact that at the time that is how they were viewed by others and also how they saw themselves. To accept this assessment is to assume that male-oriented values have absolute value and to miss the far more complex manner in which women's achievements were devalued. In short, to understand the past it is not sufficient to rediscover what was known in the past. It is also necessary to point out that which people in the past were not always aware of.

advanced education and there is no reason for the situation in Galicia to have been different. Indeed, had this been the case no doubt Thon would have noted it. See Silber, 'Roots of Schism in Hungarian Jewry' (Heb.), esp. p. 226, table III.8.

[56] McLachlan, 'The Choice of Hercules', 485.

CONSEQUENCES

By the beginning of the twentieth century, women's education among east European Jewry was in a state of foment. Significant numbers of women were exploring new educational frameworks. Traditional patterns, such as the regular reading of *Tsenah urenah* and other religious texts, had exposed women to reading and accustomed them to turn to the printed text as a normal way to knowledge. At the same time, the traditional attitudes that had denied women access to classical Jewish literature had allowed women to read Yiddish *belles-lettres*. For males, reading for pleasure was a problem because, in theory at least, men were supposed to spend as much time as possible on Torah study.[57] Men had to justify not spending time in study either on practical grounds, such as the need to earn a living, or on theological grounds, such as involvement in other pious deeds. Reading literature does not fall into either category. Women, who were not expected to study Torah, did not have to justify how they spent their time and hence their freedom to read for pleasure. Thus, inadvertently, traditional Jewish patterns themselves facilitated change and development in the lives of women. Even in traditional circles, women were easily exposed to new bodies of literature. The Haskalah (Enlightenment) literature and the Hebrew newspaper, which served in the second half of the nineteenth century as agents of change in the intellectual world of men, had their contemporary parallels in the developing Yiddish press and literature which was more directed towards women—and uneducated men.[58] Alexander Zederbaum's influential newspaper *Hamelits*, directed to a Hebrew-reading male public, was outsold in the 1860s by the emerging Yiddish press which originally published works directed to female readers. There is no question that there was a large body of female readers. As Roskies points out in an article on this topic, the Yiddish popular writer Yitshak Meir Dick could boast in 1860 that, after only five years of writing, 100,000 copies of his works had been sold.[59] The whole development of Yiddish literature was possible only because even in traditional Jewish society a high proportion of the female Jewish population was literate, knowledgeable, and accustomed to the written word.[60] The female immigrants to the United States and their daughters displayed an exceptional thirst for education and their educational achievements were far above those of other immigrants.[61] No single factor

---

[57] Katz, *Tradition and Crisis*, ch. 16.
[58] On the Yiddish newspaper *Kol mevaser* see Shmeruk, *Yiddish Literature* (Heb.), ch. 7, and Orbach, *New Voices of Russian Jewry*, chs. 5 and 7.
[59] Roskies, 'Yiddish Popular Literature and the Female Reader'.
[60] The world of the female readership was explored in depth by Niger, *Pages on the History of Yiddish Literature* (Yid.), the section entitled 'Di yidishe literatur un di lezerin', 35–108.
[61] Kessner, *The Golden Door*, 90–1; and see his sources there.

can explain the success of first- and second-generation American Jewish women in the American educational system. However, the fact that in east European Jewish society the ideal mother read regularly and studied from books certainly did not have a negative effect. Here, as in many other cases, a careful consideration of the realities of Jewish life allows for a significant correction of stereotypical views.

NINE

Literacy among Jews in Eastern Europe in the Modern Period

AMONG THE STEREOTYPES common among east European Jews—and among scholars of east European Jewry as well—is the image of the Jews, and especially Jewish males, as literate in contrast to the untutored non-Jewish population.[1] The fact that this is a stereotype does not mean that it is incorrect, but its precision cannot be taken for granted. By considering some of the various meanings of the term 'literacy' and by examining the accuracy of this image we can clarify some of the realities of life in eastern Europe and identify some of the factors that contributed to the success of Jewish immigrants to the United States.

There are many sources that can illustrate how Jews regarded themselves in comparison with non-Jews. The rather rude Jewish folk song 'Shiker iz a goy' (gentiles are drunkards) depicts the drunken non-Jew as a regular resident of a tavern as opposed to the sober Jew who spends his time in the communal study hall (*beit midrash*). The term *a yidishe kop* (a Jewish 'head' or 'brain') implied a quality that was special to Jews. The proverb 'A Jewish women without a *Tsenah urenah* is like a gentile without a pipe'[2] projects the same image. These views are all well known among Yiddish-speakers, which indicates how pervasive these images or stereotypes are, but the fact that a song was well known or a proverb widespread does not prove that everyone shared these views and in many societies contradictory proverbs often coexist. However, if no one identified with these approaches they would not have been preserved and this is true for all folk expressions. The widespread self-stereotype among Jews that they are educated and 'the people of the book' was part of the self-definition of many. Since literacy was part of the Jewish

[1] On the significance of stereotypes in Jewish history see Ettinger, 'The Roots of Anti-semitism' (Heb.). In his entry on literacy in the Russian-language Jewish encyclopedia, Jacob Shabad wrote that at the end of the 19th century 75–80% of Jewish men were literate and about 50% of Jewish women. See *Evreiskaya entsiklopediya*, vi. 756–9, s.v. 'gramotnost''. This is an accurate estimate though it is possible to expand on it, which will be done below.

[2] Kahan, *Jews on Themselves* (Yid.), 4. This booklet is very enlightening about popular Jewish attitudes.

self-stereotype, a study of the realities of that literacy makes it possible to assess the precision of that self-image.

The literacy of the Jews of eastern Europe in the modern period is an interesting topic because, on the one hand, these Jews were heirs to a long tradition of literacy. At the same time they lived in a multilingual world. In that society Jews usually spoke Yiddish to each other, prayed in Hebrew, came into contact with bureaucrats who spoke the languages of rulers such as Russian or German, and dealt with customers and clients who spoke Polish, Ukrainian, Lithuanian, Belorussian, and so on. Most of the latter were oppressed languages with limited possibilities for publication and literary expression. Thus, when considering the literacy of east European Jews, we have to consider literacy in their vernacular (Yiddish), in their literary language (Hebrew), and also in non-Jewish languages. Literacy in the first two categories is significant as a reflection of cultural patterns and exposure to the written word. Literacy in the last category is a reflection both of acculturation and exposure or openness to general culture and society.

Many demographers are in agreement that literacy indicates a great deal about a society and therefore one of the standard indicators employed to describe a population is the degree of literacy. There is a good reason for this. One of the most difficult qualities to measure in quantitative terms is the cultural capital of a society. Knowledge is difficult to count. Measurements of literacy are useful indicators because they reflect knowledge and can also be used to predict potential for development. Changes in levels of literacy can be followed over time and literacy is often seen as linked to the potential for economic growth.[3]

It is not easy to define exactly what is being measured when looking at data on literacy. The term 'literacy' often covers two skills—'reading' and 'writing' —which do not necessarily go together. If one focuses on reading alone it is possible to measure skills: the ability to decipher a word in a familiar context, the ability to read freely, the ability to read an insurance policy, and so on. Reading can have very different functions in different societies and comparisons cannot be made mechanically.[4] Different uses for reading have varying influences on literacy in a society. Writing is also not a simple skill. It does not automatically accompany reading. It is possible to learn how to read without learning how to write, and it is also possible to learn to mechanically copy a text without being able to decipher it. Thus when a person is described as literate it can mean many things and the word 'literacy' has to be used with caution.

[3] For a useful study on the history of literacy see Cipolla, *Literacy and Development in the West.*

[4] Resnick and Resnick, 'The Nature of Literacy'. There is a huge literature on literacy and to survey it here would require a book-length study of its own.

The lack of distinction in the English word 'literacy' between reading skills and writing skills is shared in other European languages. This can be traced to the realities of education in the pre-Gutenberg world. Before books were printed they were very expensive and pupils in schools could not be entrusted with a handwritten codex to use as a textbook. Therefore reading and writing were learned almost simultaneously. One of the first steps of an elementary education was for a pupil to learn how to write, often on an erasable slate. With this skill he could copy down texts that were to be studied. Teachers would dictate texts to pupils and then the pupils would study and review them. This pattern was common both in Christian Europe and the Mediterranean basin. Papyri dating from the third century BCE that contained texts for dictation were found in Egypt, so it is clear that this was not a new phenomenon.[5] Shelomo Goitein was able to reconstruct many aspects of Jewish education in medieval Egypt on the basis of a valuable collection of documents found in an Egyptian synagogue. He distinguished between the ability of children to draw letters and the ability to write freely. He found that not every child was trained to be a professional scribe, but all knew at least how to draw letters though not all wrote freely. The situation in medieval Christian Europe was almost identical with the one Goitein described. Thus Clanchy wrote: 'Although the average medieval reader had been taught to form the letters of the alphabet with a stylus on a writing tablet, he would not necessarily have felt confident about penning a letter or a charter on parchment.'[6] Thus in the Middle Ages knowledge of writing was linked with the ability to read, and hence literacy could be applied to the two skills.

It is natural to assume that the invention of movable type and printing had a positive influence on literacy. The printing press made it possible to develop and distribute popular literature. More books became available for reading and at much lower prices than previously. This encouraged writing in the vernacular, and there were thus many more reasons to learn how to read than in the past. It is not difficult to argue that the printing press is one of the characteristics of the modern period.[7]

Understandably, most research on the influence and impact of the printing press has concentrated on societies in which most of the population was illiterate before the coming of the press. After all, when printing was invented, there were hardly any literate societies. The Jewish community was exceptional because a majority of Jewish males was literate before Gutenberg. There were two key reasons for this condition. The Jewish religion saw study

[5] Marrou, *A History of Education in Antiquity*, 216.
[6] See Goitein, *Jewish Education* (Heb.); Clanchy, 'Literate and Illiterate', 21. Clanchy himself carefully notes that the two skills are distinct.
[7] A useful starting point for literature on this topic is Eisenstein, *The Printing Press as an Agent of Change*.

of the holy texts as incumbent on all Jewish males. In addition, the fact that Jews were usually merchants or craftsmen rather than agriculturists made study more available for young Jews. Jewish children did not have to help their parents in the way peasant children helped theirs. Moreover, Jewish children could easily anticipate the useful applications of literacy and this encouraged them to study.

One interesting difference between Jewish and Christian societies was in the cultural perception of the use of reading skills. For Jews, the function was religious and cultural: one studied in order to gain access to sacred sources. There was no explicit study by children in preparation for economic roles. In much of Christian society study was linked with future career roles, either in the church, or as a clerk, or both. Literacy was seen as a practical skill. After all, one could be a very good Christian without being able to read—something that would have been regarded as impossible in Jewish society. Therefore it is interesting to compare the impact of printing on two neighbouring but radically different societies.

When considering Jewish literacy it is important not to confuse an ability to write in a script with the ability to be a scribe and write a sacred scroll in the special ritual script. The special script used in scrolls is legible to anyone who knows how to read Hebrew, but it is complicated to write. Even though it was a practical skill, it was almost never taught in a school setting. Only those who wanted to be scribes learned the complicated laws of how to write in the special ritual script, and they did this by a form of an apprenticeship with a scribe.[8]

Once there were printed books, Jewish schoolteachers saw little need to teach writing. It was, of course, easier for teachers to work with printed books. Their availability meant that it was no longer necessary to copy the texts studied. The only reason to teach writing was its potential for practical applications in commercial life. However, the explicitly useful was undesirable in the logic of Jewish education. What was important in this system was the holy, and what was not necessary for the sacred was superfluous. Therefore, in most European societies the coming of the book meant an increased usefulness for the skill of reading, which was taught, together with writing, to increasingly large circles of readers—and writers. Among the Jews the coming of the book made it possible to drop writing from the curriculum. Those children whose parents wanted them to learn how to write went to a special writing teacher—a *shrayber*—after or during *ḥeder* hours. This differentiation between reading and writing was not totally unique to the Jews. Some Quakers in England taught reading without writing in their Sunday schools

[8] See Löw, *Graphische Requisiten*, vol. i, pt. 2, pp. 2–3. The late Professor E. Urbach graciously brought this important (and overlooked) book to my attention.

on the grounds that writing was a secular activity and Sunday was holy. In eighteenth-century Sweden there was a royal decree to study reading without writing. What was common to these cases was a sense that the function of reading is for religious purposes—very much as in Jewish society.

Most of the ancestors of east European Jewry were Ashkenazi—Jews who came from the Germanic-speaking lands starting in the Middle Ages. In medieval Ashkenazi society, most Jews—though not all—knew how to read and write. Literacy was essential in a society where most men were involved in trade or moneylending. Thus, in a document of 1377, almost all the Jews of Worms signed their names themselves without using symbols or having others sign for them.[9] In the rabbinic responsa of the Middle Ages there are discussions of what to do with witnesses who are unable to sign their names, but this situation was described as exceptional and not as a daily occurrence.[10] In medieval Poland the situation was different and many of the Jews then were illiterate.[11] However, with regard to more recent times, there seems to be a general agreement that almost every male could read at least prayer-book Hebrew, though with varying levels of comprehension.[12] Almost every boy went to *ḥeder*, and in this respect there was little difference between hasidim and mitnagedim. Since Yiddish was almost always written in Hebrew letters one could assume that anyone who could read Hebrew could read Yiddish.

Until the rise of the Yiddish press most Jews had limited real need for their literacy. There were few forms to fill out and no professional literature. Of course, rabbis needed their knowledge of Hebrew to study sacred texts, and successful businessmen had to keep accounts and correspond, but small merchants and craftsmen often had little need to employ their ability to read or write in their everyday life. As a matter of fact most Hebrew materials were very challenging, to say the least, for most Jewish males. It was necessary to invest years of study to be able to read Hebrew with comprehension, and this was not feasible for most pupils.[13] At the same time, relatively little was published in Yiddish in the first half of the nineteenth century. For many Jews the main utility of reading was in prayer. However, since the same prayers were repeated over and over again, they were said as much by heart as they were read, and even if they were read, who could testify to the precision of the reading?!

[9] Haberman, 'A Testimony from Worms' (Heb.), 229–32.

[10] Kupfer (ed.), *Responsa and Decisions from the Sages of Ashkenaz and France* (Heb.), no. 148, pp. 224–7. I am grateful to Professor Haym Soloveitchik, who brought this source to my attention.

[11] Weinryb, *The Jews of Poland*, 86–7. I thank Dr Michael Silber for referring me to this source.

[12] See e.g. Berlin, *Ocherk etnografii evreiskogo narodonaseleniya v Rossii*, 68–70.

[13] See Chapter 7 above.

Data on the ability of Jewish men in eastern Europe to sign their names can be used as an indication of male literacy, though it must be treated with care. A number of record books of associations dating from the early nineteenth century have been preserved.[14] Of the thirteen founders of a society of water carriers in Minsk, only five could sign themselves. Water carriers were, of course, regarded as very simple people and not highly educated—but one cannot jump to conclusions. One of their first decisions was to purchase prayer-books and Pentateuchs for the synagogue they founded. This might have been a case of people who could read but not write. Among members of a society of craftsmen in Sokołów in 1835, only eight out of twenty-five could sign their names. However, in a society of tailors in Białystok in 1859, thirty-nine signed in a normal way, one signed with a mark, and seven signed with spelling mistakes. The mistakes are interesting. Most involved switching letters that have a similar sound in Hebrew rather than mistakes in 'drawing' the letters. In other words, they are intelligent mistakes that prove, even more than a perfect signature that could have been learned by heart, that the writers were familiar with the alphabet and the sounds of the letters. The only clear conclusion that one can come to from this material is that there were significant differences in different groups of Jewish labourers.

Little is known about the literacy of Jewish women in the past. Cases of literate women cannot be treated as typical or atypical without data to prove it. Women were not obligated to study Torah and usually did not receive a formal education. We can say with reasonable certainty that only a small percentage of women would read and understand a Hebrew text, but the situation with Yiddish seems to have been different. It is easy to learn how to read Yiddish because it is written in a purely phonetic form and without confusing vocalization. The widespread distribution of *Tsenah urenah* proves that literacy in Yiddish was widespread in the nineteenth century.[15] Whether this was a new phenomenon or not is unclear but there is no reason to assume that this was an innovation.

Until the mid-nineteenth century and even later, there were relatively few Jews in eastern Europe who knew how to read texts written in Latin or Cyrillic letters. One can find curious proof for this in an anecdote involving Rabbi Yisra'el Me'ir Kagan (Hakohen). He was a very pious and modest person who wrote a book entitled *Ḥafets ḥayim* on the sins of tale-telling and gossip. One of his biographers wrote that Rabbi Yisra'el Me'ir decided to distribute the book himself. He would go from town to town posing as a bookseller who was selling the book on behalf of the author. By doing so he could encourage people to read the book without 'risking' recognition or

[14] Hailperin, *Jews and Judaism* (Heb.). The sources I use are from pages 171 and 188.
[15] See Chapter 8 above.

fame. For this reason he published his book without including his name on the Hebrew title page.[16] However, in accordance with government regulations the title page does have his name as author in Russian. Despite this, Rabbi Israel Me'ir was able to sell the book in many towns without anyone knowing that he was the author. The Russian part of the title page was simply incomprehensible to the readers of his book, a fact that he had relied on when he embarked on his effort to remain anonymous while distributing it. The anecdote may be apocryphal, though it is a fact that the name of the author does not appear on the Hebrew title page though it does appear in Russian. However, even if it is not true, the assumption of the biographer that readers would agree with him that the Russian part of the title page would be unintelligible is evidence for our claim of their limited knowledge of the Cyrillic alphabet.

A study of how Jews filled out marriage documents in Warsaw in the mid-nineteenth century gives us indications of literacy in Hebrew/Yiddish and in Polish of Jews resident in Warsaw at the time. Stefania Kowalska-Glikman tabulated the signatures on marriage documents in 1845/6 and 1860, which makes it possible to look at changes over time. The author noted that here as well the data have to be treated with caution and we cannot simply use them to come to conclusions about Jewish literacy in eastern Europe because Warsaw Jewry was not typical of Polish Jewry. What is immediately striking is that many could not sign at all. However, it should not be forgotten that in nineteenth-century Warsaw there were very few opportunities or occasions to sign one's name. Therefore, possibly some of those who could not sign could nonetheless read. According to the data in Table 9.1, about three-quarters of the Jewish males could sign in some language. Between 1845/6 and 1860 there was a small increase in the number who could sign in Hebrew and a decline in the number of those who could sign in Polish. The significance of this shift should not be exaggerated. There was probably migration to Warsaw in these years, and the ability of youths to sign may well have reflected their education outside Warsaw and not the cultural climate within Warsaw. The shift in the ability of women to sign appears to be more significant. The percentage of women who could sign in Polish remained lower than that of men, but their share of the total number of women who could sign was greater than the share of the men who signed in Polish.

In the second half of the nineteenth century there were important changes in the scope and character of literacy among Jews. The most important source of data on this period is the census of the Russian empire carried out in 1897. For the purposes of this census, literacy was defined as the ability to read irrespective of the ability to write. Some of these data are presented in Table 9.2.

---

[16] Yashar, *The Hafets Hayim* (Heb.), 107–8.

Table 9.1 Language of signature of marriage documents in mid-nineteenth-century Warsaw, by religion and gender (%)

Language of signature	Jews		Catholics		Protestants	
	Male	Female	Male	Female	Male	Female
1845/6						
Polish	46	11	57	37	86	67
Hebrew	23	13	0	0	0	0
None	27	69	43	63	14	33
Data missing	4	7				
1860						
Polish	44	20	66	40	87	70
Hebrew	29	13	0	0	0	0
None	23	64	34	60	13	30
Data missing	4	3				

Source: Kowalska-Glikman, 'Ludnoscżydowska', table 3, p. 42.

Table 9.2 Literacy in the Russian empire, by religion, 1897 (%)

Religion	Total population		Urban population alone
	Male	Female	
Anglican	86	83	
Lutheran	71	71	
Reform	70	68	
Mennonite	71	70	
Karaite	71	50	
Catholic			52
Russian Orthodox	29	9	46
Jews	49	29	43

Source: Bureau für Statistik der Juden, *Die sozialen Verhältnisse der Juden in Russland*, table 26, p. 42.

It is not easy to explain these figures. Arthur Ruppin claimed that it is inconceivable that half of the males were not able to read Hebrew.[17] He suggested that the census takers did not consider Hebrew or Yiddish as languages for the purposes of the census, or perhaps the Jews assumed that census takers were not interested in Hebrew or Yiddish. Many—Jews and non-Jews alike—did not regard Yiddish as a 'true' language, but as a jargon that could not be treated in the same category as 'accepted' languages. Therefore, it could be claimed that literacy in Yiddish was not true literacy. Boris Brutskus shared this view.[18] He also noted that the census takers were not able to test reading knowledge of Hebrew or Yiddish because they were

---

[17] Ruppin, 'Die russischen Juden', 5.   [18] Brutskus, *Statistika evreiskogo naseleniya*, 47.

Table 9.3 Literacy of Yiddish speakers in the tsarist empire, by age group, 1897 (%)

Age	Urban		Non-urban	
	Male	Female	Male	Female
1–9	9	7	4	3
10–19	47	36	34	24
20–29	53	34	48	22
30–39	52	22	42	11
40–49	46	14	34	6
50–59	37	9	25	3
60 and over	27	5	17	2

Note: The data on literacy were recorded by mother-tongue groups and not by religion or national identification. However, since about 97% of Jews reported Yiddish as their mother tongue, the table in effect records literacy among Jews.

Source: Troinitsky (ed.), *Obshchii svod po Imperii*, vol. ii, table 15 (pp. 134–75).

not Jewish. This might have led them simply to ignore literacy in these languages. It was easier to record people as illiterate than to try to check their knowledge.[19] We have no hard data on what actually happened when census takers went to homes. However, it would appear, on the basis of the reports of contemporaries, that there was probably little consistency with regard to the ways census takers related to literacy in Hebrew or Yiddish, and their reporting cannot blindly be relied on.

The reporting of the 1897 census on Jewish literacy in Russian seems reliable. According to the census, 32 per cent of the Yiddish-speaking Jewish males and 17.5 per cent of the Yiddish-speaking Jewish females were able to read Russian. Brutskus noted that children below the age of 10 were about a quarter of the Jewish population.[20] One cannot expect literacy in any language in this age group. If we subtract the children from the total population of Jews as well as from the Jews who declared that Russian was their mother tongue and then recalculate, we find that 45 per cent of the Yiddish-speaking males and 25 per cent of the females were able to read Russian. In the urban setting the figures were even higher: 51 per cent for males and 31 per cent for females, while for village Jews it was 36 per cent for males and 19 per cent for females. As we see in Table 9.3, there were significant differences between age groups.

A number of other characteristics also stand out from the data in this table. The difference between the literacy rates for men and women was great but it was smaller in the younger age groups. The differences between male and female rates were also smaller in urban areas than in non-urban areas. A

[19] Brutskus, *Statistika evreiskogo naseleniya*, 44.   [20] Ibid. 48–9.

Table 9.4 Literacy in Russian by mother tongue, 1897 (%)

Mother tongue and age group	Total population		Urban population	
	Male	Female	Male	Female
Polish				
1–9	3	2	7	9
10–19	24	14	35	47
20–29	25	11	32	26
All ages	15	7	29	20
German				
1–9	9	8	19	20
10–19	45	39	55	61
20–29	40	31	50	57
All ages	23	13	31	22
Yiddish				
1–9	7	5	11	8
10-19	45	32	55	41
20–29	54	31	58	38
All ages	22	12	26	15

Source: Troinitsky (ed.), *Obshchii svod po Imperii*, vol. ii, table 15 (pp. 134–75).

comparison of literacy in Russian between speakers of various languages is enlightening even though it also raises questions.

The fact that, according to Table 9.4, the level of literacy in Russian among male Jews was higher in the 20–29 age bracket than in the 10–19 age cohort should not surprise us. According to Brutskus,[21] this indicates that literacy in Russian was not acquired in schools and formal education, but rather through informal study or self-study. He pointed out the surprisingly high levels of non-urban literacy among German- and Polish-speakers and he saw this as an indication that study was going on outside of school frameworks. This is supported by the fact that, according to a survey made in 1906, the number of Jewish pupils enrolled in schools where Russian was taught was only a tenth of the number of pupils in *ḥeders*.[22] This fits with the data we have on literacy in Russian among Jewish youths under the age of 10 and with Brutskus's explanation. From Table 9.4 we learn that the level of literacy in Russian of urban Jews was lower than that of German-speaking non Jews. This was due mainly to the high level of literacy in Russian attained by German-speakers in their youth, when relatively fewer Jews had managed to master literacy in Russian. The gap diminished in later age cohorts and after school age. This is when self-study by Jews began to have an influence. The pattern of Jews was similar to that of Poles in the younger ages, but among Poles there was much less of a rise in the later age groups.

[21] Ibid. 52.   [22] *Recueil de matériaux*, 136.

The success of Jews in reaching literacy in Russian without the benefit of formal education was a significant achievement. It indicates an eager interest to learn a new language and a willingness to continue study after leaving school. As suggested above, most Jewish males probably had a minimal ability to read Hebrew and, having learned this skill in one language, they were already somewhat prepared to learn how to read in another.

At the beginning of the twentieth century a number of studies were made of literacy and education in various Jewish groups, mainly of workers. There is a great value to these studies since they were carried out by Jews who treated literacy in Hebrew and Yiddish seriously. They were also aware of the importance of knowing other languages. The first study of this type appears to be a survey carried out in 1901 in Minsk by Boris Frumkin. It surveyed the characteristics of over a thousand workers. The data on literacy are presented in Table 9.5.

It seems that the differences between masters and apprentices were to a large degree a consequence of age differences and cohort characteristics, and not a direct result of the class differences between the two groups. After all, among Jews—as opposed to the situation in many non-Jewish societies— journeymen had, until the twentieth century, good reasons to believe that their dependent role would end and the day would come when they would be masters. To a large extent independence was for them a factor of age.

If this was the case we can come to some interesting conclusions on the basis of Table 9.5. First, there appears to have been a steady decline in the knowledge of Hebrew. The percentage of illiteracy in Hebrew among the younger workers was almost double the level among craftsmen. This decline was sharper among women than among men. If we take into account that Hebrew was learned only in elementary education and only Russian was learned at more advanced ages, we can assume that had this trend continued there would have been a significant and growing inability to read in Hebrew or Yiddish.

Second, while the differences in Hebrew literacy were significant between males and females, the differences between them in Russian literacy were

Table 9.5 Literacy in a group of Jewish workers in Minsk, by language and professional status, 1901 (%)

Status	Literacy in Russian		Literacy in Hebrew/Yiddish	
	Male	Female	Male	Female
Craftsmen (masters)	56	59	87	82
Journeymen	50	52	75	71
Apprentices	59	55	76	66

Source: F[rumkin], 'K voprosu o polozhenii evreev-remeslennikov'.

much smaller. These differences were almost certainly linked to the fact that most boys were sent to a *ḥeder* and received a formal education while girls learned in different frameworks. Third, the data may suggest that the literate population was becoming more and more bilingual. Many of the factors that contributed to illiteracy in Hebrew should have had a negative influence on literacy in Russian. Parents who did not have enough money to send their child to a decent *ḥeder* would have found it difficult to finance an education in Russian. A student who had a learning disability and therefore had difficulties with Hebrew would have probably had the same difficulties with Russian—after all, both were 'foreign' languages for young (and not so young) Jewish boys and youths. The usual 'study route' was to start off in *ḥeder* and to go on to Russian. Therefore, it would be reasonable to assume that most Jewish males who could read Russian, could also read Hebrew.

If that was so we can use the data from Minsk in Table 9.5 to examine literacy in two languages. If we divide the percentages of those literate in Russian by the percentage of those literate in Hebrew we may have a rough approximation of the number who were bilingual. It seems that the share of bilingual literates rose as the cohorts got younger. Of the literate craftsmen, 64 per cent were bilingual, of the literate journeymen, 66 per cent were bilingual, and of the literate apprentices 78 per cent were bilingual. Among women, the percentages were 72, 74, and 83 per cent. In other words it seems that the literate population was becoming increasingly bilingual. This fits the image we have to realities in the past. It is significant because it means that increasingly more workers were exposed to the influence of surrounding cultures and societies by the beginning of the century.

Frumkin also found that there were differences between various crafts. Almost all the brush makers were literate. After them came the metalworkers, carpenters, and furnace makers. The lowest levels were found among trades such as those of shoemakers and bakers. There seems to have been a correlation between better working conditions in terms of salary and working hours, and higher literacy levels. What is not clear is whether the craft influenced literacy, or literate individuals preferred certain crafts, or found it easier to enter more desirable crafts.

It is necessary to be cautious before coming to conclusions with regard to the decline in Hebrew knowledge as shown in Table 9.5. In 1904/5 a survey was made of Jewish library users in Poltava, a Russian city in the south.[23] This city had a population made up of students, craftsmen, servants, and labourers, and not simply householders. Of this population, 65 per cent read only in Russian and not in Hebrew or Yiddish. This is much more extreme then the

---

[23] Goldenberg, 'The People Called Hebrews' (Heb.). I thank Professor Steve Zipperstein for the reference to this article.

Table 9.6 Literacy of Jewish workers in four cities, by occupational group, 1913 (%)

Group and level of literacy	Vilna	Berdichev	Brzeziny	Warsaw
Craftsmen				
Read and write in Russian and Hebrew/Yiddish	54	33	23	38
Read and write in Hebrew/Yiddish	20	11	27	18
Read Hebrew/Yiddish	15	45	45	29
Unable to read	3	0	3	1
Women				
Read and write in Russian and Yiddish	56	28	16	30
Read only Russian or Polish	1	7		7
Unable to read	20	54		

Note: The survey comprised about 760 respondents in Vilna, 410 in Warsaw, 210 in Brzeziny, and 140 in Berdichev.

Source: Rabinowitsch-Margolin, 'Zur Bildungsstatistik der jüdischen Arbeiter in Russland'.

picture Frumkin gave. Of course, the library users were not a random sample that could represent the entire Jewish community of Poltava, and Poltava was hardly representative of east European Jewry. However, these data fit in with other reports we have about a decline in the knowledge of Hebrew.

Sara Rabinowitsch-Margolin made a study of a small sample of workers in Vilna, Warsaw, Berdichev, and Brzeziny in 1913. She did not find a single worker in Brzeziny who could read Polish, and only seven in Warsaw. Of the workers who knew only how to read in Hebrew—about 28 per cent of them—many could read only well-known texts in a prayer-book; they could not read unfamiliar material. In Brzeziny, of those who could read only in Hebrew, no less than about 80 per cent could only read a prayer-book. In Warsaw and Vilna the share of Hebrew-readers who were limited to prayer-books was smaller: in Warsaw it was 20 per cent, and in Vilna 8 per cent.[24] It would be tempting to jump to conclusions about the significance of the cultural environment, but since the samples checked were not large it may well be that these data are more the product of a statistical error and not a social reality. However, they bear examination.

In the same year that Rabinowitsch-Margolin carried out her study, a group of Jewish women in New York carried out a similar study on two groups of immigrants who came to New York that year.[25] It was published as a

[24] The scope of the term 'literacy' is not always clear. Since Yiddish is written in Hebrew characters, any individual literate in Hebrew can read Yiddish. However, since Hebrew texts are generally not vocalized, it cannot be taken for granted that someone who reads Yiddish can also read Hebrew. Almost all men at this time went to *ḥeder* and learned, at the first stage, to read Hebrew. Therefore, it is reasonable to assume that data on male literacy are relevant to reading both Hebrew and Yiddish. For females, literacy usually meant an ability to read Yiddish.

[25] See the report *Jewish Immigrants*.

congressional document in 1914. In their introduction the authors cited the official data on literacy among Jewish immigrants. According to these data, about 17 per cent of the male Jewish immigrants and 33 per cent of the female Jewish immigrants who came to the United States between 1899 and 1913 were illiterate. In 1913 the authors decided to check the statistics for the literacy of immigrants and then to compare their results with the official data.

The first group examined was a group of 1,887 women who arrived in New York. Most were between the ages of 14 and 25. About 15 per cent of them could not read at all in any language. When a control group of immigrants of 130 males and 110 females was examined, 9 per cent of the males and 25 per cent of the females were classified as absolutely illiterate. However, the 'illiterate' males were not so illiterate. All of them were able to read prayers in a prayer-book, but no more than that. The same was true of about a third of the 'illiterate' females. A similar check was made in Galveston, Texas. Two groups were examined. One was of 389 immigrants (351 males and 38 females) and the second of 1,284 immigrants (1,029 males and 255 females). Of the males, 15 per cent were illiterate, as were 40 per cent of the females.

The Jewish immigrants to the United States were far from being a representative sample of east European Jewry. On the one hand, they came from the lowest class of east European Jewish society in terms of social status and they were generally regarded as uneducated. On the other hand, they were relatively young and had a great deal of initiative. Therefore data on their literacy cannot be taken as a precise indication of the level of literacy in east European Jewry as a whole, although it does reveal that significant numbers of Jews in eastern Europe—and not just women—were illiterate or close to it.

The Jewish researchers in the United States compared their records with the data collected by the government officials who dealt with the same groups of immigrants. They suspected the high levels of illiteracy reported earlier might have been the product of misunderstandings or antisemitism. However, they did not find significant differences between their findings and the official data. In one case, the official data even reported a higher level of literacy than the Jewish researchers found. Both the Jewish and the official figures indicated that the 1913 immigrant cohort was more literate than the average of the 1899–1913 immigrant Jews.

The problem that remains is how to explain why the level of literacy reported for Jewish immigrants in 1913 was significantly higher than for previous years. It could be that the cohorts in 1913, or the specific cohorts examined, had higher levels of literacy than the bulk of immigrants in previous years. However, it is possible that the government clerks who recorded data were more careful in considering Yiddish and Hebrew as languages with

Table 9.7 Illiteracy in Poland by religious group, urban and non-urban, 1921 (%)

Religion	Urban		Non-urban	
	Male	Female	Male	Female
Roman Catholic	12	16	27	30
Greek Catholic	26	37	46	55
Russian Orthodox	34	55	62	86
Evangelical	7	9	14	15
Jewish	22	28	35	41

Source: *Rocznik statystyki Rzeczypospolitej Polskiej*, 5 (Warsaw, 1927), 46–7, table 11.

regard to literacy, and circumspect in recording data that they knew would be double-checked, than they were when they knew no one was looking over their shoulders.[26]

There was no general census in the Russian empire between 1897 and the First World War, so the next census data that we can use is from the interwar period. In newly independent Poland, a census was carried out in 1921. It provided literacy data on the population over the age of 10. It is difficult to reconstruct how carefully it was carried out and what exactly the census takers were checking. For example, according to this census a quarter of the urban males and a third of the urban females were without elementary education, and outside urban areas about 40 per cent of the men and 50 per cent of the women were in the same category. On one hand, it seems as if census takers did not always take *ḥeder* education into account; on the other hand, given the general lack of schools for girls, it is difficult to guess on what grounds so many Jewish women were regarded as having received an elementary education. A second census in 1931 followed the first one of independent Poland. It seems therefore that there is some imprecision in these particular censuses and the data in the accompanying tables should be treated with caution.

Tables 9.8 and 9.9 make it possible to follow progress in literacy and note the differences between Jews and non-Jews when both groups are treated as aggregates. These data raise many questions. Szyja Bronsztejn noted that in almost every area the literacy of urban Jews was higher than the literacy of urban non-Jews.[27] The only exception was western Poland, which had been annexed from Germany and whose urban population had received a German education. The question of changes in levels of literacy depends on whether the two censuses were carried out in an identical way or not. I have not found a way to check this. However, the data on illiteracy from 1931 presented in

[26] *Jewish Immigrants*, 146–8.   [27] Bronsztejn, *Ludność żydowska*, 177.

Table 9.8 Illiteracy among Jews in Poland, urban and non-urban, 1921 and 1931 (%)

Year	Urban		Non-urban	
	Male	Female	Male	Female
1921	22	28	35	41
1931	10	17	16	25

Source: *Rocznik statystyki Rzeczypospolitej Polskiej*, 5 (Warsaw, 1927), 46–7, table 11; Bronsztejn, 'Ludnoścżydowska', 176, table 74.

Table 9.9 Illiteracy among Jews and non-Jews in Poland, urban and non-urban, 1921 and 1931 (%)

Year	Jews		Non-Jews	
	Urban	Non-urban	Urban	Non-urban
1921	25	38	19	38
1931	14	21	12	28

Source: *Rocznik statystyki Rzeczypospolitej Polskiej*, 5 (Warsaw, 1927), 46–7, table 11; Bronsztejn, 'Ludnoścżydowska', 176, table 74.

Table 9.10 Illiteracy among Jews in Poland, urban and non-urban, by age group, 1931 (%)

Age	Urban		Non-urban	
	Male	Female	Male	Female
10–14	4	2	7	4
15–19	5	4	9	6
20–24	6	7	10	9
25–29	8	10	11	15
30–39	9	16	15	25
40–49	12	24	19	37
50–59	15	32	24	48
60 or over	28	47	31	64

Source: Bronsztejn, 'Ludnoścżydowska', 180, table 75.

Table 9.10 are reasonable and the concentration of Jewish illiteracy in certain age and residential groups certainly makes sense.

Until the age of 20, Jewish women had higher rates of literacy than Jewish men. This may be due to the fact that in very religious circles boys were sent to *ḥeder* while girls were sent to school, and Hebrew literacy may not always have been recognized. In general, literacy was highest in the younger cohorts and went down with age. This may well be a reflection of the impact of organized education in interwar Poland. The differences between urban and non-urban populations are obvious, but it is not so easy to explain all of the findings. The differences between women's literacy in different regions may have been due to differing opportunities for study. However, most men probably studied in *ḥeder* whether they lived in towns or not. It may also be that there was only partial recording of Hebrew or Yiddish literacy, and that what we see are the differences in the opportunities to study Polish.

In addition to the studies of urban populations, a number of attempts were made to describe the shtetl, or Jewish small town, from a statistical and anthropological point of view. Jacob Lestchinsky described his birthplace, Gorodishche (in the Kiev region), in a study published in 1903.[28] He found that 14 per cent of the Jews above the age of 10 could read Hebrew with some understanding; little more than half of all the Jews (including males and females) could read Yiddish, and about 40 per cent could sign their name in Russian. He also noted that almost all of the males could read, and that more than a third of the women could read Yiddish. He noted that until the Zionists began to be active in the area of education, only one woman knew Hebrew and that there was only one teacher for girls. However, in 1903, after the Zionists had begun to be active, there were still only four teachers for women, and almost half of the girls got no education and were totally illiterate.

A similar study was carried out in 1907 in the town of Krasnopole, which had a Jewish population at the time of 3,100. The data from this study are very precise. It dealt only with the ability to read. According to this study, 93 per cent of the males over the age of 5 were literate, as were 45 per cent of the women. The data from this study are shown in Table 9.11.

Almost all of the sources cited give a picture of literacy at a given time and do not provide information on the dynamics and timing of learning how to read. However, data such as those shown in Table 9.11 suggest that there was growing literacy in Russian though it was not learned in childhood, but by youths and young adults. It also indicates that the gender gaps in Russian-language literacy became smaller and smaller as time went on, while the literacy gap in Hebrew remained. This type of approach can profitably be applied to the first Soviet censuses. The Soviet regime officially treated Hebrew and Yiddish as recognized languages and therefore there is reason to hope that these data, recorded before the Stalinist era, are reliable. The first two censuses, carried out in 1920 and 1926, are not identical in scope but give us a sense of development over time (see Table 9.12).

In both 1920 and 1926 Jews had the highest levels of literacy of all the national groups in the USSR. A Soviet researcher, Ivan Bogdanov, who investigated the phenomenon, attributed this to the urban nature of Jews,[29]

---

[28] Lestchinsky, 'Statistics of a Town' (Heb.). The discussion on literacy is on pp. 34–5.

[29] Bogdanov, *Gramotnost' i obrazovanie*, 132.

Table 9.11 Levels of literacy among Jews in Krasnopole, Mogilev
province, by language and age group, 1907 (%)

Age	Able to read Hebrew/Yiddish		Able to read Russian	
	Male	Female	Male	Female
5–10	74	18	10	8
11–15	88	50	37	30
16–20	80	67	45	28
21–40	79	46	44	17
41–60	74	19	30	6
61 and over	55	20	12	8

Source: L. Rokhlin, *Mestechko Krasnopol'e Mogilevskoi gubernii*, 29.

Table 9.12 Literacy among urban and non-urban Jews in Soviet
Russia, 1920, and the Soviet Union, 1926 (%)

Year	Urban and non-urban combined			Urban	Non-urban
	Male	Female	All		
1920			70	71	63
1926	76	69	72	74	66

Source: Bogdanov, *Gramotnost' i obrazovanie*, 132, 136–7.

but a quick glance at the table indicates that this is not likely. Among every
group there were sharp differences between urban and non-urban populations, but among the Jews the literacy levels were similar. It is more likely that
the cause was a combination of cultural and economic factors.[30]

The census carried out in Ukraine in 1926 gives us a detailed picture
of literacy among Jews and the age breakdown indicates the trends (see
Table 9.13).

Developments in literacy were tied to broader developments of language
use, as can be seen in Table 9.14.

A number of developments are clear here. There was a clear decline in the
number of Yiddish-speakers among the younger cohorts. At the same time
literacy was rising in the younger cohorts. Since the starting point of women
was lower than that of men, the rise in women's literacy was also sharper. The
gap between the literacy rates of men and women was closing. In the Soviet
period after the First World War literacy no longer meant reading a Jewish
language and maintaining contact with a cultural past, but rather reading

[30] See Guroff and Starr, 'A Note on Urban Literacy in Russia 1890–1914'.

Table 9.13 Literacy among Jews in Ukraine, by language and age group, 1926 (%)

Age	Literate in any language		Literate in Yiddish	
	Male	Female	Male	Female
5–9	36	36	22	22
10–14	90	92	64	65
15–19	92	94	65	65
20–24	95	92	65	61
25–29	94	88	65	60
30–34	93	83	67	58
35–39	91	75	68	56
40–44	89	67	70	53
45–49	86	62	70	50
50–54	84	55	70	46
55–59	82	50	71	42
60–64	79	40	71	36
65–69	76	36	69	32
70–74	67	29	67	27

Source: Constructed on the basis of *Vsesoyuznaya perepis' naseleniya 1926 goda*, vol. xi, tables VI, VI-v, pp. 8–11 in the census.

Table 9.14 Command of national language among literate people in the Soviet Union, by national group, 1926 and 1939 (%)

National group	Speaking national language		Reading national language
	1926	1939	1926
Jews	73	40	56
Russians	99	100	100
Ukrainians	87	88	52
Belorussians	72	87	40
Georgians	97	99	98
Armenians	92	89	81

Source: Bogdanov, *Gramotnost' i obrazovanie*, 134.

the language of the general population and hence being exposed to the general culture and integration.

It is a little difficult to explain the relatively low level of literacy recorded for the older cohorts of men. Given the near-universal ḥeder study, most men should have known how to read. Perhaps many men reported that they could not read because they read little and their ability to read unfamiliar texts had 'atrophied'. There seems to be a correlation between levels of literacy among women coming of age in the period when popular Yiddish literature began to flourish. It may well have been that the availability of popular Yiddish literature supplemented the venerable *Tsenah urenah* and served as an additional stimulus for women to learn to read Yiddish. It is no secret that female customers fuelled the explosion of modern Yiddish literature in the late nineteenth century. The availability of interesting material to read was far more effective then the programme of any dedicated *maskil* to bring enlightenment to women. The indications that there was little advancement in literacy levels after the age of 30 fit our view of the importance of widespread self-study in early adulthood.

On the basis of the wide variety of material that has been brought together it is clear that in the nineteenth century there were many Jews—males and females—who were illiterate or functionally illiterate. This certainly contradicts the stereotypical self-image of Jews as literate and educated. We even saw that in recent centuries, ability to write declined among Jews due to the invention of the printed book.

In the course of the eighteenth and nineteenth centuries, the Jewish population in eastern Europe grew at a faster rate than that of the general population. This led to an economic crisis and forced many Jews to enter trades and become manual labourers. These occupations, as opposed to money lending and trade that were common in the Middle Ages, did not require reading and writing skills. In this context, the *ḥeder*, which taught only reading, made excellent sense. Not teaching writing saved money because writing materials did not have to be purchased and classroom furniture could be simpler.[31]

Ḥeder study clearly influenced the dynamics of the Jewish community even though by the end of the nineteenth century study in a modern *ḥeder* may not have provided all the necessary skills as it once had. Some important benefits remained. *Ḥeder* study taught reading and thus inculcated into students a familiarity with Jewish culture. *Ḥeder* study may well have had additional and indirect influences on literacy and study among Jews. The entire phenomenon of self-study of Russian or Polish might well have been possible because graduates of *ḥeder*s had a concept of how an alphabet works and how one reads; all they had to do was to plug in a different alphabet. The rapid expansion of Yiddish literature and the press at the end of the nineteenth century and in the beginning of the twentieth was not preceded by radical changes in education. It could rely on *ḥeder* education for males and a combination of formal and informal education for women.

However, the stereotype, as well as the reality, may have had a significant role and impact on the Jewish community. As noted above, the self-image

---

[31] Diane Roskies discussed this in passing in her article 'Alphabet Instruction in the East European *Ḥeder*': 'The availability of printed alphabet sheets precipitated a pedagogical change. In 18th and 19th centuries *ḥeder* memoirs not a single mention is made of letter writing or tracing preceding reading from a printed Hebrew chart or book' (p. 35).

of Jews as more literate than others has a long history. There were enough literate Jews to allow many Jews to think that the literate ones were the norm, even when this was not exactly the case. This image inspired songs and strengthened self-esteem. However, in the context of the great migration of east European Jews to America it may have had a special impact. Observers have long noted the quick and successful adjustment of Jewish immigrants to the United States, especially in the area of education. Jews advanced more in educational systems than did other immigrant groups, and enjoyed resulting economic and social advantages. Various reasons have been given for this phenomenon, such as earlier experience in urban life, mutual assistance, tendencies to trade, and so on. However, it is possible to add aspirations and self-image to the list.

The immigrants who came to the United States believed in the possibility of advancement through education, and that they (or their children) were capable of taking advantage of new educational opportunities. In eastern Europe poor mothers sang lullabies to their babies about how they would grow up to be learned and scholars. In the Jewish society of eastern Europe this was just a dream. The society was very stratified and few children of the poor could ever master the Talmud. However, in the United States these possibilities became very real. The belief in self-value and capability found an outlet in the public school system. Other immigrant groups did not have this type of self-image and a belief that they had the qualities for success in school. Lacking self-confidence and aspirations, climbing up the ladder was a lot longer and more difficult for them.[32]

Jewish society in eastern Europe was in many respects a literate society. However, it maintained many characteristics of an oral society.[33] The impact of the printed word on Jewish modes of thought has only begun to be studied.[34] The Jewish self-image took a reality and exaggerated it—which is how stereotyping often works—but, once established, the stereotype became an element in influencing the educational goals of Jewish society.

[32] In his fine book *The Golden Door*, Kessner wrote of the Jewish 'respect for education' (p. 173). This could also be termed 'accessibility of education'. Every group respected education; the difference was to what degree individuals—and groups—felt they could succeed. It is hard to over-exaggerate the importance of confidence and self-esteem.

[33] See Chapter 8 above on women's education, which discusses how the cultural world of men was more oral than that of women.

[34] There is still no equivalent of Ong, *Orality and Literacy*, for the history of Jewish thought.

TEN

Dormitory and Yeshiva in
Eastern Europe

THE ESTABLISHMENT of dormitories in many Jewish educational institutions, especially in yeshivas, is a new phenomenon—created to answer new needs in Jewish education. Such institutions did not exist in the pre-modern Jewish communities. Dormitories were found in the past only in Christian educational frameworks. Given the fact that this is such a novelty in Jewish education—and considering its roots—the adoption of this framework in the interests of Jewish education is rather interesting and it is certainly worth a closer look. As we shall see, the history of the housing of Jewish students teaches us more than a little about the history of Jewish education and Jewish society in general.

The decision to open a dormitory is not taken lightly. It requires not only a significant investment of money but also organizational structures which can undertake the responsibility for the dormitory. In other words, if an institution opens a dormitory, there have to be very good reasons for it. There are a number of key questions that should be answered in order to understand the phenomenon of dormitories: first, when were the first dormitories established in Jewish educational institutions and why did these institutions function so long without dormitories? Second, how did this innovation influence Jewish education and how were dormitories received in the Jewish society? Third, did the opening of dormitories convert Jewish educational institutions into what sociologists term 'total institutions'?

*

Analysing the structure of an educational institution sheds light on the basic assumptions of the society that produced the institution, the characteristics of the students, the nature of the educational process, and the resources that were made available to the institution and its founders. A relevant example is the independent housing of university students. Such an arrangement presumes a level of maturity on the part of students. Most university dormitories today function as inexpensive apartments. There is little supervision of the residents or restrictions on their behaviour, and the decision to live on campus or off is usually a financial one. On the other hand, the concentration of pupils or students in a dormitory under supervision and the isolation of the students from families or the neighbourhood reflect a concern that there may be, or is, a conflict between the basic values of the institution and the values of the families of the students or of the surrounding society. When an institution undertakes to provide supervised and concentrated housing for students and accepts the inherent responsibilities of such an arrangement a reassessment of the nature of the social environment has taken place. Opening a dormitory often reflects a decision to shape and influence the character of the student in the institution and not just to transfer knowledge and information.

To avoid confusion, two key terms should be defined immediately. A 'total institution' is an institution for study or work which houses a large group of individuals, all of whom share a single status, who are isolated from the surrounding society for a long period of time and at the same time are under formal supervision.[1] This term can apply to prisons, health institutions, army units, and so on, as long as they meet these criteria. The term 'dormitory', as used in this study, applies to supervised housing under the auspices of a public body which is exclusively for a group of individuals who study in a specific institution. Thus the term does not apply to a framework run by an individual or company for profit, or to housing provided for mixed groups, or for the needy or sick. Certain yeshivas display some of the characteristics of 'total institutions' and this will be discussed below.[2]

In the non-Jewish educational tradition dormitories have long been seen as not only a solution for the housing needs of students, but also as an element in the educational activity of schools and other educational institutions. A dormitory has some of the characteristics of a total institution. It has a regime that demands of the residents some degree of order and adherence to a code of behaviour. That is why for some institutions, living in a dormitory is a requirement for acceptance and participation in the educational programme.

*

From antiquity until the early modern period, communal housing was used in the Christian world for a variety of purposes—not all related to education. Soldiers[3] or members of religious orders who were formally committed to

[1] The study of 'total institutions' has produced a large literature. The basic study is Goffman, *Asylums*. There are some fascinating studies in Samuel, *Total Institutions*. I thank David Assaf for providing me with a copy of Samuel's book.
[2] One of the first to investigate 'total institutions' was Etzioni, 'The "Closed" Organizational Structure'. Unfortunately he dealt mainly with institutions like Youth Aliyah Villages and not with traditional institutions.
[3] Soldiers were not always housed in army quarters or barracks. Very often they were quartered with families under the famous (or infamous) billeting system.

religious or military service were often required not to live in a family framework and were housed in dormitories or an equivalent. In certain societies, servants or slaves who were devoted, not necessarily of their own free will, to the service of a master or family were also often housed in common dwelling quarters which were very similar to dormitories. Those who enjoyed the services of these groups had to provide in return some of their requirements, a basic need being housing. There were also welfare institutions which attempted to provide housing and other services to those in need. The recipients could be the sick, the penniless, travellers, or the mentally ill. These institutions not only met some of the needs of these marginal people but also isolated them from the general society. Possibly the best-known institution of this kind was the leper asylum.[4]

There were almost no dormitories or communal housing facilities in Jewish communities. The Jews did not have armies in the Middle Ages. There were no Jewish religious orders of men or women, nor were there groups of Jews who were sworn to celibacy. Some Jews had servants, but they were limited in number. Jews did not have agricultural estates which can require large numbers of servants or slaves to effectively work the land. Even the richest Jews did not have establishments like the high nobility in Christian society.

The institution in Jewish society which was closest to a dormitory or similar facility was the *hekdesh*, or asylum for needy travellers as well as the poorest local Jews. Indeed, there were great similarities between this institution and non-Jewish asylums for similar populations.[5] The rise of the hasidic movement and the development of the hasidic court, which attracted large numbers of visitors who needed housing, did not lead to the establishment of housing facilities for those who came. Synagogues and other public buildings could offer places to sleep for short periods but generally no formal frameworks for housing visiting hasidim were established. Ad hoc and informal arrangements were usually able to meet the short-term needs of the hasidic courts.

The background of the modern dormitory is deeply rooted in the medieval period. In his well-known book *Centuries of Childhood*, Philippe Ariès noted that in the early Middle Ages dormitories were established for poor university students. It is important to emphasize that at that time universities were religious institutions and therefore poor students were members of religious orders even though they had not yet made binding vows. These students benefited from the donations and legacies of pious donors who contributed money to support worthy young people and constructed buildings to house them. Certainly in the twelfth and thirteenth

---

[4] See Rosen, *Madness in Society*, esp. p. 142.
[5] See Marcus, *Communal Sick Care*; ch. 8 deals with Jewish hospitals.

centuries most university students lived in hostels or private housing which was not supervised. This was the period of the 'wandering student'. Many students who had the necessary resources would travel from institution to institution to study with a variety of teachers and in varied frameworks rather than remain for the full course of study in one institution. Not all were devoted to their studies, of course, and there were many opportunities for those so inclined to indulge in drink and revelry. For students with resources from home, a dormitory was not the ideal solution for housing needs. However, for needy students there was little alternative. As time went on parents began to be aware of the advantages of a more structured learning environment, and the contribution a disciplined framework of study could offer to the educational achievements of their sons. Many affluent parents used their resources and connections to have their children accepted by the dormitories, which led, in the long run, to the displacement of many of the poor from university studies. By the fifteenth century, dormitory accommodation was the preferred framework for study in European universities, and the number of dormitories increased as did the degree and scope of supervision of their residents.[6]

The rise of the dormitory limited contact between students and the outside world of adults and increased the power of school authorities. However, the development of dormitories was a long and slow process, and for generations many students lived outside the framework of dormitory housing —and hence were free of supervision. In the first stage that Ariès describes, the frameworks for housing were separate from the frameworks for study. In other words, dormitories were set up for students, but the residents of these dormitories did not necessarily study at the same institutions. With time dormitories and schools merged so that residents of a given dormitory were all students at the same institution. At the same time, however, many students —often even a majority of non-local students—continued to live outside the dormitory framework. One important reason for the slow expansion of the dormitory system is that dormitories are expensive to construct and maintain. Possibly just as important was the sense that although dormitories were convenient, they were not essential and there was no urgent need to provide such accommodation for all students.

Ariès felt that there was a link between the development of dormitories and the rise of new concepts about the nature of childhood and adolescence. In his view, the increased use of supervised housing was, in effect, an application of the monastic tradition in a temporary fashion to the student population. The function of dormitories, then, was not only to assist students in their studies by providing housing, but also to protect them, through isolation, from the temptations of the street.[7]

[6] See Ariès, *Centuries of Childhood*, ch. 7, esp. pp. 151–3.   [7] Ibid. 169.

Dormitories were widespread in medieval Europe but became the norm only in modern Europe. In France this apparently took place in the eighteenth century. Students in the previous century had usually rented rooms while many found rooms in the houses of their teachers. This guaranteed a degree of supervision but no more. However, in the eighteenth century the number of dormitory schools increased to the point where a majority of students lived in organized housing for students.[8] The same process took place in England somewhat later. Until the nineteenth century student housing in England was left up to the individual's initiative. However, starting in the early nineteenth century, groups of educators began to receive monopolies on the right to provide housing for students, and by the middle of the century most teenage students in England were housed in dormitories.[9] In France this pattern was short-lived and there was a subsequent decline in the share of dormitory students. This reflected a growing desire of many parents to keep their children at home for more years as well as doubts over the efficacy of dormitory education. In England the pattern of education in dormitory schools was longer-lasting.[10] Thus in the European context dormitories developed and changed 'open institutions' into 'closed' ones. In this way students could be sheltered—or so it was hoped—from the influences of the 'street'. However, as we have seen, this was a tendency that could be reversed.

We know relatively little about housing frameworks for Jewish students in Jewish schools in early modern Europe. Yeshiva students apparently rented rooms from householders just as non-Jewish students had done before the dormitories became widespread.[11] By the nineteenth century the Jewish population in Europe was concentrated in eastern Europe and there a new framework for study became popular. The standard framework for the advanced study of the Talmud in this region after the seventeenth century was not the yeshiva but rather the *beit midrash* or communal study hall. Almost every Jewish community had a *beit midrash*, which functioned both as a place for public study and, during prayer hours, as a synagogue. Since these halls were regularly used for prayer, they had the standard layout of a large men's section in front of a smaller section for women.

As noted above, *batei midrash* served a wide population. Some came just for prayer but many householders came to the *batei midrash* for several hours of study every day, which was in addition to time they spent working. This part-time study was usually early in the morning or in the evening. Some studied independently whereas others participated in regular classes.

---

[8] Ibid., ch. 11, esp. p. 267.
[9] On the developments in England see Gathorne-Hardy, *The Public School Phenomenon*, 35.
[10] See Ariès, *Centuries of Childhood*; and Gathorne-Hardy, *The Public School Phenomenon*.
[11] See Breuer, 'The Ashkenazi Synagogue at the Close of the Middle Ages' (Heb.), esp. p. 46.

However, during the day most of those present in the study hall were youths. They studied the Talmud individually without the guidance of a rabbi or teacher and without a fixed programme of study. Talented boys were expected to have mastered the ability to study the Talmud on their own in *ḥeder* or elementary school. The scholarly agenda of the students in the *batei midrash* was based on the inclinations, desires, and ability of the students themselves. In certain respects this may be regarded as reflecting a view that the population that today would be termed 'adolescents' was not necessarily seen as a distinct group that had to be treated in special ways. On the contrary, such students were treated in many ways as adults.

To understand the background of dormitories in Jewish educational institutions it is necessary to review the dynamics of *beit midrash* study which were previously addressed. Most of the youths who studied full-time in the *batei midrash* did not live in their parents' homes, though some of them were married and lived with their young wives in the homes of their fathers-in-law. Early marriage was common among the Jewish elite in the eighteenth and early nineteenth centuries. By living with the parents of the bride, the need to find housing for these young boys was eliminated and there was certainly no lack of supervision of the young husbands.[12] However, most of the Talmud students were unmarried and they lived in the study hall. This had certain benefits for their parents, though they may not have wished to admit it. Jewish homes were often small and crowded. Sending sons off to a *beit midrash* could ease, if only a little, the pressure on space in a home. It certainly decreased some of the pressures often characteristic of adolescent years.

For the students, life in the *beit midrash* was very different from their previous experiences. They spent most of their waking hours in the study of Talmud in the study hall and at night they would simply sleep on a bench in the women's section. The youths did not enjoy comfortable pillows or thick mattresses, but after eighteen hours of study they would not find it difficult to fall asleep.[13] There were no showers in the study hall but students were no worse off than were most citizens because there was no flowing water in private homes. Householders and students alike had to use the communal bath house. Youths would eat their meals in the homes of pious householders who wanted to support young Torah scholars. Thus, with a minimal investment in facilities, communities effectively provided a structure that produced a highly motivated and very knowledgeable scholarly elite. This framework finds no simple parallel in other societies.

Supervision was as important in the *beit midrash* as it was in the university or secondary school. The goal of supervision that was achieved in the dormitories was achieved in *batei midrash* by virtue of the fact that the study and

[12] See Chapter 7 above.   [13] See Chapter 7, n. 34 above.

assiduousness of youths was effectively monitored all through the course of the day by the householders who were constantly coming in and out of the study hall. It was reinforced by the dependence of youths on the daily charity of householders who provided meals to the Talmud students they saw every day in the study hall and whom they deemed worthy of support.[14] Students who were lax in their studies simply would not have been invited for meals. This was possible only because of the assumption in Jewish society that every adult male should devote as much time as possible to study. This in turn was based on the view that study is a religious act and source of merit just as much as prayer or fulfilment of other religious commandments—if not more so. These values were unique to the Jewish community and thus the housing solution which developed in east European Jewish communities was unique to them.

Shemaryahu Levin described life in the *beit midrash* with charm and also understanding. He described the students in the *beit midrash* as passing

the best years of their youth, living under a regime which to the modern student must seem incredibly harsh. Five to six hours of sleep was all that was permitted them. Two hours a day were given to meals and prayers. The remaining sixteen were dedicated to studies. Not all of them were able to endure this terrific discipline . . . [but] they did not dare leave their books. They were ashamed . . . [they] slept in the Synagogue and Study House . . . A regular cushion stuffed with feathers was rarely to be seen among them. They slept mostly on sacks stuffed with hay and straw. Blankets were unknown. They covered themselves with their topcoats. In the winter they used to lie down around the two big stoves at the entrance to the synagogue. In the mornings, they had to get up very early—before the first services began. And it was unbecoming to stop studying before midnight.[15]

There were similarities between the status of Talmud students and the needy in the Jewish community but their status was not identical. Both students and the poor were generally dressed in rags or little better. It was common for needy individuals and needy students to be given meals in private homes. In the case of students, who did so regularly, this was known as eating *teg*. However, the 'right' to sleep in the *batei midrash* was limited to Talmud students. The poor slept in the *hekdesh* or communal poorhouse, but Talmud students never slept there. Thus, within the group of individuals supported by the community, housing arrangements indicated membership in a sub-group.

What helped the Talmud students tolerate their difficult conditions was their awareness that this was a temporary condition. Their hope was to be recognized as a scholar and merit a match with the daughter of a rich man.

---

[14]   This topic was explored in greater detail in Chapter 7 above.

[15]   Levin, *Childhood in Exile*, 258–60. This book provides an excellent description of many aspects of Jewish life in Lithuania.

In such a case a daughter's dowry could be the basis for a successful career in business. During all of the period of study in the *beit midrash* the youths were separated from their homes and under the harsh discipline of the respected householders. In this respect the physical and mental challenge of study in a *beit midrash* was a test of a young student's determination and self-control, and it may well be regarded as a test of manhood before acceptance into the Jewish elite. In fact, the whole process can be seen as an initiation ceremony.

Beit midrash students were free to travel from place to place and to go from one *beit midrash* to another. Thus if it was hard to find hosts for meals in one community, a Talmud student could try his luck in another community. With regard to mobility, *beit midrash* students were similar to the peripatetic medieval university students known as goliards, though one major difference was that in the general society there was no emphasis on independent study as there was in the Jewish community. Thus wandering university students sought out teachers, whereas Jewish Talmud students just needed a community which could provide minimal living conditions. Another difference was that *beit midrash* students did not develop a rich and 'jolly' student life as did the medieval wandering students. Even without the dormitory, the Jewish students were under the constant scrutiny of their patrons, the householders. The goal of Talmud students—a good match—was of course quite different from that of most of the nominally pious Christian students who were already enrolled in religious orders that encouraged celibacy.

There were very good reasons, as we have seen, why dormitories were not employed in the Jewish educational system even though they were widely used in non-Jewish frameworks. They were not really needed and the costs far outweighed the potential benefits.

*

The first real shift in housing arrangements for students was in the yeshiva of Volozhin.[16] This yeshiva was founded around 1803 and it quickly outgrew the ability of the local community to support the students. The increasing numbers of students were too many to be housed in the local *beit midrash*. The founder of the yeshiva, Rabbi Hayim, was able to meet the material needs of the many students who came to study with him by raising funds from the whole region and giving stipends to students. With the money that they received from the yeshiva, students were able to rent rooms with local householders. They paid a fixed amount per month and together with the room, they received all their meals in the house. Despite the fact that this was

---

[16] On Volozhin see the relevant chapters in my book *The Formation of the Lithuanian Yeshiva*. (Heb.)

a radical shift from previous standard practice, it received little attention from contemporaries. It was seen as a minor detail or technical arrangement —contemporaries were much more interested in the size of the yeshiva and the teaching methods of its founder than in the sleeping arrangements of students. The organizational structure of Volozhin was quickly adopted in the yeshiva of Mir. However, the yeshiva of Volozhin was more respected than imitated, and for most of the nineteenth century, most Talmud study continued in the traditional framework of *batei midrash* and Talmud students continued to sleep in synagogues.

Rented rooms solved the problems of housing in the Volozhin yeshiva, but this change did not reflect a new concept of adolescence or a new view of the function of the yeshiva with regard to isolating students or developing their character or personality. Students were still regarded as adults or almost adults. Most of the study in the yeshiva remained independent. Students chose the texts they wished to study as well as the methods and pace of their studies.

In nineteenth-century sources—and they are not few—there are no references to or hints of any attempts to solve the housing problem in Volozhin by setting up a dormitory. Renting rooms was a familiar practice which required no capital investment and Rabbi Hayim was not familiar with any institution with a dormitory which could serve as a model. Hence it is not surprising that a dormitory was not set up in Volozhin—not in the time of Rabbi Hayim and not later.

The arrangement of housing in rented rooms gave students in Volozhin much more privacy than their peers who studied in *batei midrash*, even though the rooms were usually shared by a number of youths. In the rooms students could read literature that they may have hesitated to take into the study hall, engage in conversations that were best avoided when in public, and engage in recreational activities—at least in theory—such as card playing. Such activity was both forbidden and alien to the ethos of the yeshiva, which required investing all possible time and energy to study, but the potential was there. In reality, the vast majority of students used their rooms just for sleeping and no more. They identified with the goals of the yeshiva and had no interest in activities other than study, but the potential for *bitul zeman*, or wasting of time, made it necessary to have a *mashgiah*, or supervisor, who made sure that students used their time in accordance with the aims of the yeshiva. From an institutional point of view this was a structural innovation which, in the course of time, developed in the yeshiva world into a network of salaried staff who were not involved in teaching but in supervision and counselling. This supervision was not foolproof and by the end of the nineteenth century there were active circles of maskilim ('enlightened ones' or modernists) in the yeshiva. This was the result, among other reasons, of the difficulties in supervising students in the privacy of their rooms in private homes. Had a dormitory been in use in Volozhin the social dynamic might have been different.

The first Jewish school dormitories in eastern Europe were founded in 1842—though the Jewishness of the schools is to a certain degree a matter of definition. These were the dormitories attached to the rabbinical seminaries opened by the Russian government in Vilna and in Zhitomir. The schools themselves were founded on the initiative of the Russian Ministry of Education and were modelled, both in structure and content, on Russian schools. Since they were government schools they had substantial budgets at their disposal, so that building a dormitory was possible; moreover, as government institutions there was no question about their legal status. For 'independent' Jewish schools, which often operated without legal recognition, a building such as a dormitory could have led to legal inquiries that might have had problematic consequences.

The establishment of a dormitory in a Jewish setting, especially the one in Vilna, made a big impression on contemporaries. In his book about the rabbinical seminary in Vilna, Ya'akov Gurland described the dormitory in these terms: 'The residents of the dormitory reside in attractive spacious building(s). They are nice and clean and the floors are marble. Servants are at their disposal who do their bidding, their dress is attractive, their beds are comfortable and their diet is healthy.'[17] However, the first dormitories under Jewish auspices to be established in eastern Europe were not school dormitories, but of a somewhat different type. The first true dormitory, founded in Warsaw in 1840, was built as part of an attempt to deal with the needs of the aged and of orphans in a 'modern' way and we have discussed it in Chapter 4 in the context of the history of old-age homes.[18] Apparently a similar initiative was taken in Vilna a few years later, but there are few details about it. In his diary Sir Moses Montefiore mentioned that on 4 May 1846 he visited 'the Orphan Asylum of Mr. Chiya Danzig' in Vilna.[19] This had been founded two years earlier in response to a famine that had struck the region. Danzig had rented a number of buildings to house the starving and gave special attention to their children. However, it is not clear if this institution lasted once the famine was over or whether it was regarded as a temporary measure in a crisis.[20]

[17] Gurland, *Honour of the House* (Heb.), 61–2.

[18] The description of this institution is based on Levin, 'The First Jewish Home for Orphans and the Elderly in Warsaw' (Heb.), which, as I have noted in Chapter 4 above, concentrates on the educational programme for the orphans rather than on services for the elderly.

[19] Loewe (ed.), *Diaries of Sir Moses and Lady Montefiore*, 345.

[20] See Magid-Steinschneider, *The City of Vilna* (Heb.), 218.

An orphanage was founded in Odessa in 1857[21] and orphanages were established in other cities as well.

Both orphanages and old-age homes have a common goal of meeting the physical needs of the residents and therefore they are very different from school dormitories. They are not seen as a means of supplementing the educational activity of a school. This perception was the probable basis for the foundation of the Warsaw institution, which was intended to house both old and young—which in retrospect seems to be a rather bizarre combination.[22] School dormitories are tied to the school year and residents of dormitories are acutely aware of their temporary nature, even though the experience of living in a dormitory can be very intense. During vacations students can return home and during the school year they can dream about returning home. Residents of orphanages and old-age homes have no home to return to and regard their current situation as permanent.[23]

Many of the private Jewish secondary schools that were founded in the Russian empire during the second half of the nineteenth century offered housing to students. These were perhaps not true dormitories, because the institutions were private and the dormitory did not play an explicit role in the educational process. Since parents paid well for this service, the providing institution was probably not able to impose a great deal of discipline on residents, nor impose formal requirements, though we have little information, as will be discussed below, on the realities of life in these 'pensions'. This framework was not a Jewish innovation. The provision of housing was common in non-Jewish secondary schools at the time and the use of the term 'pension' was a clear reflection of the central European model on which they were based. They were welcomed by the government because they were seen as a means of raising the educational level of the provincial aristocracy.

The increased interest in modern education among Jews in the Russian empire in the late nineteenth century and the quotas on acceptance of Jews into public schools increased the popularity of private secondary schools or pensions intended for Jews.[24] These schools played a major role in the Russification (both linguistically and culturally) of Jews. No doubt living away

[21] *Evreiskaya entsiklopediya*, xii. 63.

[22] It may not be as odd as it appears. Considerable efforts are made today to link young people with the elderly, with mutually beneficial results. However, housing them together is not a simple matter.

[23] The history of these institutions is quite interesting and sheds a lot of light on the changing nature of the Jewish community. I have written about old-age homes in 'What Happened to the Extended Jewish Family?'

[24] On these schools see the doctoral thesis of Simeon Kreis, 'Russian-Language Jewish Schools' (Heb.). These schools had been almost totally ignored in the literature until Kreis documented the phenomenon. The discussion on these schools below is based on the data in Kreis's thesis.

from home strengthened this process. These institutions clearly catered for Jewish youths and young women, but there was not usually a serious component of Jewish studies in their curriculum and nothing, or almost nothing, of Jewish content. They often concentrated on preparation for commercial careers and practical studies. The lack of attention to Jewish studies does not appear to be out of a rejection of their Jewish identity but rather reflects a feeling that Jewish identity could be taken for granted. The students in these institutions were clearly not preparing themselves for the rabbinate. Therefore they and their parents would not have felt a need to devote time to the study of rabbinic texts or other Jewish topics.

Thus, while the pensions may be regarded as dormitories, it is not so simple to term the schools 'Jewish schools'. There are many references to the Jewish pensions but I have not found any detailed descriptions in memoirs or similar sources of life in the pension, or of the emotional aspects of study in these institutions. There are many reasons for silence but one may be that graduates of these pensions saw them more as technical rather than as life-shaping institutions and hence felt less of a need to preserve their memory to posterity. These were Jewish institutions in name but not in terms of content.

What seems to have been the first dormitory in a Jewish school to retain and foster traditional behavioural patterns in the setting of a total institution was at a *talmud torah* founded in Kelm in 1866 and later relocated in Grobin.[25] The founder was Rabbi Simhah Zisl Siev, who was a student of Rabbi Yisra'el Salanter. *Talmud torah*s were generally schools for the poorest Jews and they were the equivalent of *heder*s attended by most Jewish boys. However, the *talmud torah* in Grobin was different.[26] It was designed for the sons of established householders. The students studied not only Talmud, which was traditional, and 'ethics' (*musar*), which was an innovation, but also topics necessary for a businessman, such as mathematics and languages. Rabbi Yisra'el Salanter was well known for his belief in the importance of studying ethics and his encouragement of innovation in education, and Rabbi Siev acted to implement the study of ethics in an educational setting.

The *talmud torah* of Kelm/Grobin was founded in a period of accelerating change in the Jewish community. An increasing share of the householder class

---

[25] On this school see Katz, *The Musar Movement* (Heb.), vol. ii, chs. 16–18. The discussion below is based on the sources he cites. For recent study of the Kelm yeshiva see Klibansky, 'Lithuanian Yeshivas' (Heb.), 34–5.

[26] The few sources we have on the school do not explain why it was termed a *talmud torah*. The tsarist government did not encourage private elementary schools which combined general studies and Jewish studies. At the same time, it tolerated traditional educational institutions. At a later period, Zionist schools were called *heder metukan* (reformed *heder*) in the hope that a term that suggested that these schools were simply variations of the traditional institution would save them from being closed. Perhaps R. Siev adopted the same strategy in terming his school a *talmud torah*.

in the Jewish community was abandoning traditional behaviour patterns and rapidly acculturating. Rabbi Siev believed that it is possible to shape the character of a young student through education and create an ethical personality that would remain loyal to what the founders saw as the true Jewish tradition. However, this could only be done in the setting of a total institution that could block out external influences. A dormitory setting was his solution. Rabbi Siev's radical innovations were not accepted by all of the Kelm Jews, and in 1876 the school was moved to a smaller city, Grobin, where it continued to operate for another decade. This school was one of the first organizational signs of the concern in the traditionalist camp for the developments in the Jewish community. What was seen as an extreme condition called for a radical response. But the model of the Kelm/Grobin *talmud torah* was not quickly imitated. It is not clear whether this was for lack of individuals who could take such an initiative because of the expenses and legal complications, or for other reasons.

Increasingly more yeshivas were founded in the second half of the nineteenth century.[27] In these yeshivas, as in Volozhin, students did not sleep in the women's section of the study hall and, instead, rented rooms. However, what had once been a very unproblematic system was now more complex. The traditional practice of renting rooms had been predicated on the assumption that the attitudes and values current in the Jewish community were not contradictory to what was taught in the yeshiva, but in the late nineteenth century there was a great deal of concern over what were regarded as dangerous influences from the 'street'. In small towns the economic impact of yeshivas could be substantial and the head of a yeshiva had a significant influence on what happened in a town, but urban yeshivas, such as those in Kovno (Slobodka) and Vilna (Ramailes), did not enjoy these conditions.[28] It would have been very reasonable for yeshivas to set up dormitories—but they did not, and they also did not relocate to small towns. It is very likely that the reason for this was simply a lack of funds.

One factor that may have mitigated the impact of housing in private rooms and the influence of the street was the difference between the dynamic of study in Jewish society and that in general society. In general society, certainly in secondary school and university, achievement is measured by grades, determined by tests that are taken and papers that are written. The act of

---

[27] This should not be misinterpreted as meaning that there was a great jump in interest in Torah study. The rise in yeshivas was simultaneous with, or perhaps somewhat after, a precipitous drop in the number of students in *batei midrash*.

[28] I know of no study of the economic influence of yeshivas on the communities around them, neither in eastern Europe nor in Israel. A paper that suggests that such an influence could be significant and could serve as a model for such a study is Bamford, 'Public School Town in the Nineteenth Century'.

study, as noted above, is not valuable; only the results matter. The preparation for tests and papers involves individual study which is often done in solitude or seclusion. In Jewish society and in the yeshiva, study was a holy act and it was generally carried out in public. Testing was usually informal and always oral. Students never wrote papers and had no need for private study in libraries. In the view of traditional Jewish society, the act of studying Torah was a holy act, and this meant that the more hours devoted to study, the more merit was achieved. Therefore the Jewish system placed great emphasis on diligence, and frivolous activity (anything which was not study was by definition frivolous) was frowned upon. Even spending time on acts of charity and mercy was regarded negatively. The task of students was seen as to study, and those who did not study were regarded as being responsible for dealing with the problems of the world.[29]

Recreational activities, such as reading literature, and going to plays and concerts, are highly regarded in general society for a variety of reasons. Therefore a non-Jewish institution that wants full control, or almost full control, over individuals can do so only in the framework of a 'total' institution. By controlling housing it is possible to supervise recreational activities as well as study time. In yeshivas, the value and justification of those recreational activities respected in general society were generally regarded as superfluous and frivolous activity and accordingly rejected. Students in yeshivas were strongly encouraged—to put it mildly—to spend all their possible waking hours in the study hall and in the company of their peers and teachers. The result was that there were limited opportunities to 'take advantage' of the freedom inherent in living in a rented room. In various yeshivas and at certain times special supervisors would make the rounds of the students' rooms to make sure that the behaviour of students when out of the yeshiva met the expectations of the yeshiva.[30] Thus a yeshiva could be almost a 'total institution' without going to the trouble of setting up a dormitory for the students. However, 'almost' is often not enough.

There was a long-term demographic development that fitted in well with institutionalized housing for youths. In the pre-modern period, generally only a few children in Jewish families would reach maturity and the level of infant mortality was high. The modern period was marked by rapid population growth among Jews (and other groups), apparently due to improvements in diet and health. The result was that more children reached maturity. The pattern of larger families created stresses on the family structure since there was not a corresponding growth in the size of the apartments and houses of

[29] For a description of some of these points see Katz, *Tradition and Crisis*, ch. 16.

[30] For examples and a fuller discussion see my forthcoming book, *Lithuanian Yeshivas of the Nineteenth Century*.

Jews. This was exacerbated by a rise during the nineteenth century of the age at marriage in the circles of Talmud students. These factors made housing more problematic than in the past. In such conditions, providing housing for even some of the population could help improve the quality of living of part of the Jewish community.

By the beginning of the twentieth century, the pressure and attractions of the heterogeneous Jewish society and of the general society were such as to create a feeling in the traditionalist camp that there were no longer any safe corners.[31] If in the past yeshivas had been institutions which trained a scholarly elite for a traditional society, now yeshivas were seen as a key tool in maintaining tradition in the younger generation. Yeshiva education began to be seen more and more as the standard for the traditionalist circles and not just a framework for the exceptionally gifted as it had been in the past. What had not changed was the physical pressure for space in small Jewish homes with many children. With the new function of preserving tradition and the concern for influences from 'the outside', creating 'total institutions' began to look more and more attractive. Isolation until marriage was seen as a powerful tool against the corrosion of traditional society.

It is not important which institution was first to offer a dormitory. In any case, it is highly unlikely that today we have the data on all the attempts—successful and unsuccessful—to employ dormitories. What is significant is the fact that from the end of the nineteenth century, the use of dormitories in Jewish settings spread. One of the first was that of the yeshiva of Łomża. At the end of the century this was a growing yeshiva, but there were difficulties in finding rooms for the students. In 1899 the yeshiva collected money so that it could expand. A new building for the yeshiva was built and around it small buildings to house diligent students were added.[32] This was not the standard format for a dormitory but clearly a step in that direction.

Another move in the direction of dormitories and 'total institutions' was the opening of cafeterias for students. Food was a basic need, like housing, that had been met until the twentieth century in a non-institutional manner. Students who rented rooms could arrange for meals along with their rooms or could purchase food from street pedlars. However, the most common practice for those who slept in *batei midrash* was to eat meals in the homes of householders, as described above. This practice was never a source of joy for

[31] For an expression of this see Zemba's statement in his article 'The Metivta in Warsaw' (Heb.), 367. Mirsky's book *Jewish Institutions of Higher Learning in Europe* (Heb.) is a very useful compendium for information on interwar yeshivas and therefore, in the interest of bibliographical simplicity, I have used it as the standard source for technical information about these yeshivas. A useful discussion of some of these developments is Luz, *Parallels Meet*.

[32] Rabinowitz, 'The Yeshiva in Łomża' (Heb.), 281. In the Tomkhei Temimim Lubavitch yeshiva, a dormitory and café were built in 1912; see Lurie, 'Lubavitch and its Wars' (Heb.), 69.

Talmud students but it became more problematic by the beginning of the twentieth century. As mentioned before, the poor also ate at the tables of the well-off, and by doing so too, young scholars were putting themselves in the ranks of the lower classes. As long as yeshiva students could look forward to a good match, acting for a while as if they were in the ranks of the poor could be seen as bearable. However, by the end of the nineteenth century the chances of making a good match were decreasing, and with this there was a decline in the belief that the poverty of Talmud students was only a temporary condition. In the past Talmud students, most of whom were from relatively comfortable homes, had 'played' at being poor. When this ceased to be a fiction, eating in householders' homes became truly demeaning. Moreover, at the end of the nineteenth century there seems to have been a decline in the numbers of householders who were eager to host Talmud students. The immediate solution to this problem was to open cafeterias.

Descriptions of cafeterias do not occupy a prominent place in the literature on interwar yeshivas and there was little interest in recording for posterity the date a cafeteria was opened. Attention was given more to the level of study and the quality of the students. Nonetheless, there are references to the topic. By 1907 an attempt was made to open a cafeteria in the Pressburg/Bratislava yeshiva in Hungary/Slovakia, though it began to operate only four years later.[33] In 1919 the Metivta was established in Warsaw. This was a modern yeshiva with a minimal programme of secular studies and a very high level of Talmud study. It was founded by activists who saw rabbinic society in a state of crisis and sought a creative solution. One constructive element of this response was the opening of a cafeteria.[34] This was not the only yeshiva to do so. In the yeshiva of Baranowicze, built apparently in the 1920s, a cafeteria was included as an element of the new yeshiva building,[35] and the same was done in the Lubavitch yeshiva in Warsaw.[36]

In 1924 Rabbi Meir Shapira founded what was perhaps to be the most famous yeshiva in central Poland, Yeshivat Hokhmei Lublin (the Yeshiva of the Sages of Lublin).[37] Dormitory housing was an integral part of the facilities in this yeshiva. The top floor of the central building housed the students. The yeshiva also had a cafeteria which supplied meals to the students. Rabbi Shapira was very concerned about the negative impact of the traditional practice of yeshiva students eating meals in the homes of householders. Some of his closest friends in ḥeder had abandoned the study of Torah, and he felt that this was due in part to the shame they felt eating like beggars in the homes of

[33] Jungreiz, 'Pressburg' (Heb.), 492.
[34] Zemba, 'The Metivta in Warsaw' (Heb.), 377–8.
[35] Ben-Mordekhai, 'Baranovits' (Heb.), 332.
[36] Zeidman, 'Yeshivas of Lubavitch' (Heb.), 348.
[37] See Mandelboim, *The Yeshiva Hokhmei Lublin* (Heb.).

householders. To prevent the dropout of students he felt it was necessary to strengthen their self-esteem. The dormitory and cafeteria were tools to this end. His concern, then, if the description is accurate, was not to create a 'total institution' which would be cut off from society, even though this may have been the practical result. His purpose was to find a means of enhancing the self-esteem of students and his solution created isolation as a by-product. The next year, the heads of the yeshiva in Pressburg/Bratislava also decided to build a dormitory—out of a desire to improve the living conditions of the students and to strengthen their supervision.[38] However, because of a lack of funds, the construction was delayed until the outbreak of the Second World War.

The benefits of a dormitory were no secret. In 1937 the leadership of the well-known yeshiva in Kamieniec Litewski decided to build a dormitory and set out to raise the necessary funds. This effort was cut short by the outbreak of the Second World War.[39] At the same time the Lubavitch yeshiva in Warsaw added a dormitory, but not for all its students—just for out-of-town students.[40] Not all yeshivas were successful in their attempts. In 1932 the Warsaw branch of the Novogrudok yeshivas network was in such dire straits that not only could it not raise money to build a dormitory, but it could not even give students a stipend large enough to cover their meagre rent. The students did not lose hope. Some simply started sleeping in synagogues; other more enterprising students got jobs as night watchmen and slept on the floors of local stores.[41] Dormitories, however, were clearly the way of the future.

*

Dormitories became common in yeshivas for a number of reasons. Although in theory students could have continued to sleep in synagogues, this was no longer regarded as respectable. The only acceptable solutions were to support student rentals of private rooms or to open a dormitory. The growing concern about what was seen as the pernicious influences of the surrounding society added a degree of urgency to the adoption of means to isolate yeshiva students from potential contact with problematic individuals and groups. At the same time, the growing use of dormitories fitted in with a general trend for what appeared to be 'modern' or 'systematic' approaches for dealing with social needs and especially for institutionalization. This was true in many areas. As noted above, the care of the aged began to be seen as best achieved in the framework of an old-age home.[42] The same was done for the sick in the

---

[38] Jungreiz, 'Pressburg' (Heb.), 510.   [39] Zeidman, 'Kamenits' (Heb.), 320.
[40] Zeidman, 'Yeshivas of Lubavitch' (Heb.), 348.
[41] Nakrits, 'The Yeshiva of Novogrudok' (Heb.), 275.   [42] See Chapter 4 above.

framework of hospitals, long before the widespread use of monitors and other specialized hospital equipment which cannot be duplicated in the home. The trend to take care of orphans in orphanages and not in alternatives such as foster homes is also a reflection of this tendency, and other examples could also be given. Dormitories did not usually merit—for very understandable reasons —a great deal of attention in pre-Holocaust eastern Europe. However, they reflected some very basic developments in Jewish society. They illustrate the great sensitivity and responsiveness of traditionalist circles to the major changes Jewish society was undergoing in the nineteenth and twentieth centuries.

ELEVEN

Is the Question the Answer?
The Context and Consequences of an
Educational Pattern

THE ROLE OF QUESTIONS IN EAST EUROPEAN
JEWISH EDUCATION

David Weiss-Halivni, the famous professor of Talmud, was born in the interwar period and spent his formative years in Sighet, Romania. As a young boy he was famous in Sighet as an *ilui*, or precocious genius. Today he is justly celebrated for his amazing memory, but this was not what made him well known as a child. What got all of Jewish Sighet to talk about him were two questions he asked as a 5-year-old in *ḥeder*, or elementary school. The first was somewhat technical, but the second question and its consequences say a great deal about east European Jewish education. In the words of Professor Weiss-Halivni, this question

. . . concerned the manna in the desert. According to tradition, one could sense any taste one desired in the manna, with the exception of garlic. The reason given for the exception is that garlic is harmful to pregnant women. When our teacher recounted this to us, I challenged him, arguing that if the taste of the manna was determined by the selection of the eater, and if the manna potentially contained all tastes, and whatever one desired one had, why couldn't one choose garlic also? If it is harmful to a pregnant woman, let the woman not desire its taste!

The teacher did not know the answer and neither did his supervisor. Weiss-Halivni continued in his description:

The whole town was stirred. A simple question had been asked by a five-year-old and nobody seemed to know the answer . . . the question raised my reputation in town.[1]

As we shall see, this was not a unique type of event in east European Jewish society. On the contrary, it was a direct consequence of a basic characteristic of the educational patterns of this society.

[1] Weiss-Halivni, *The Book and the Sword*, 13–14.

The importance attributed to question asking by children and students may appear to be a rather trivial aspect of traditional Jewish education in eastern Europe. However, attitudes to questions shed light on a number of educational and historical issues, and reflect basic cultural styles. I will try to demonstrate this by comparing the strategies used in two communities—that of east European Jewish society and North African Muslim society—in relation to sacred sources. Ultimately I will try to show how this characteristic of Jewish education may be linked to features of contemporary Israeli life. It is not easy to carry out such an analysis. In dealing with historical questions, it is often easiest to deal with names and dates, or clearly traceable influences. Moreover, making comparisons raises the spectre of objectivity and subjectivity. The attempt to uncover some of the roots of a social pattern is indeed risky, but at the same time it may contribute to explaining phenomena that are not easily quantifiable or reducible to questions of 'who?' or 'where?' At the same time, it is clear there will never be a final word in questions of this type.

While asking questions was a highly regarded skill in traditional east European Jewish education, writing answers—and writing in general—was of peripheral importance. Jonathan Boyarin, a perspicacious observer of Jewish cultural patterns, noted that 'Questions—interrogation of the authoritative text—is the essential pattern of Jewish study . . . It is traditional constantly to dispute and recreate what Judaism is; the loss of that capacity reflects in turn a weakening of Jewish tradition.'[2] Benjamin Harshav refers to an incident in the life of Isidor Rabi: 'When he returned from school as a small child, his mother would ask him: "Did you ask any good question in school today?"',[3] and it is not difficult to find other examples of the emphasis on question asking.

The respect and import attributed to asking questions[4] was closely connected to one of the more overlooked aspects of Jewish education: the special nature of literacy and schooling in the east European Jewish *ḥeder* from the eighteenth to the twentieth centuries. In English, the word 'literacy' refers to two skills: the ability to read and the ability to write. The term is used for the

[2] See the fascinating article by Jonathan Boyarin, 'Voices around the Text'. The quotation is from p. 229.

[3] Harshav, *The Meaning of Yiddish*, 114. The incident took place in the United States but the mother's values were unquestionably those of east European Jewry.

[4] The role of question asking in Jewish culture seems to be more significant than in other cultures and also basic to the culture. A classic expression of this is the famous monologue of Mendele Moykher Seforim which opens *The Little Man* (Yid.): 'How do Jews who meet each other converse? After the first question, Jews really start pouring all sorts of questions on you, like "Where does a Jew come from?", "Does he have a wife?", "Does he have children?", "What is he selling?", "And where is he going?", and more and more such questions, as it is the custom in all the Diaspora of the Jews to ask if you want to appear in public as an experienced man and not just a bench warmer'. Quoted in Harshav, *The Meaning of Yiddish*, 115. The genre of 'question jokes', while familiar in many cultures, was also highly developed in Jewish folklore.

two because, in the western tradition, the skills are taught together in elementary school—as was standard in Jewish education before the invention of the printing press. Manuscripts were always scarce and expensive and Jewish pupils in the Middle Ages, like their non-Jewish peers, had to copy the texts they studied. However, the skill of writing was not intrinsic to Jewish education. In the traditional Jewish education of Ashkenazi Jews attention was concentrated on religious and cultural topics, and was totally separated from practical studies or training which would be relevant for a profession.[5] Practical skills, such as arithmetic, were acquired in other frameworks. After printing led to a drop in the price of books, printed books were quickly adopted in *ḥeder* education and it was no longer necessary for pupils to copy down their texts. This meant that writing was no longer necessary for the study of the standard texts. Therefore the teaching of writing could be dispensed with in the *ḥeder*—and it was.[6] Writing was taught in eastern Europe to those children whose parents had the means and interest to supplement their *ḥeder* education by hiring a *shrayber*. Thus east European Jewish males were generally more fluent as readers than they were as writers.

What is the connection between writing and the importance attributed to questioning? In educational frameworks in which writing is an integral part of the course of study, writing can be a key element in assessing students' achievement and progress. Tests are often written and the grades of written tests, which are ostensibly objective, influence the ranking and evaluation of students. In some educational systems oral examinations are used to measure achievement. This is done in a formal and structured framework of testing. Formal oral testing of this type was common in *ḥeder*s, but in post-elementary study, in *batei midrash* or yeshivas, there were no formal tests at all. Here the dynamic of question asking was the main means of demonstrating knowledge and intellect. This is a totally informal but effective method for students to demonstrate knowledge. In most educational frameworks posing questions is a normal way for a student to clarify something or to indicate to teachers and fellow students that he or she understands the topic.[7] Aggressive questioning and challenging of teachers achieves the same goal. Thus advanced Talmud students demonstrated their talents orally, either explaining complex texts to eager questioners, or by asking questions or pointing out contradictions in the statements of others.[8] A contemporary description of a Talmud class notes

[5] I discuss this in Chapter 9 above.

[6] When exactly this took place is not clear—and it is not important in this context, though it certainly merits a careful study.

[7] See the extended and thought-provoking discussion on the role of questions in contemporary talmudic study groups in Heilman, *The People of the Book*, 141–4.

[8] In some yeshivas, such as Volozhin, there were usually no tests once a student was accepted to the yeshiva. In the cases of tests in yeshivas in the 19th century, the tests were invariably oral.

how a participant asks a question and this is 'a display of his ability to frame an appropriate question'.[9]

The emphasis on questioning certainly fits the texts studied in the *ḥeder*s and in *batei midrash* or yeshivas. Here Jewish law per se was not studied but rather the Talmud.[10] Even when the classical legal codes were opened, it was usually in order to derive commentaries to the Talmud and not to find a simple and clear description of the correct legal views. The Talmud, which was at the heart of the programme of study, is written in the form of series of debates.[11] Since the Talmud was a model for intellectual activity, the study of Talmud naturally encouraged question asking.[12]

However, the study of Talmud also encourages questions in a deeper way. Veteran Talmud students assumed a reality of multiple truths and did not try to seek out the one true explanation or to determine which was the best.[13] When a variety of explanations were raised by commentators on any given text (and this was almost always the case), it was the 'task' of a Talmud student to set out the logic of each explanation and explain how each would answer the 'criticisms' of the other explanations. When an authoritative commentary stated that a question remained open, Talmud students were encouraged to explain why possible answers were not acceptable and thus to prove why the question remained open. The one thing east European Talmud students did not do was to try to decide which commentary was better.

The tendency in yeshivas to explain but not to judge is vividly illustrated in a description by Washington lawyer Nathan Lewin of his difficult adjustment to the Harvard Law School after studying for years in yeshivas. He is quoted as saying:

I really had to unlearn the Talmudic training in order to succeed at the Harvard Law School . . . we'd read a decision from the Supreme Court . . . The main thing that you were learning was to criticize the case: 'Is the decision right? Raise your hand'. And I sat there—what do you mean is it right? . . . How am I supposed to decide whether it's right? I never learned that in yeshiva . . . I would raise my hand, I'd say, 'No, the two cases are reconcilable because there's this little point here and this point there' which would be a terrific *ḥidush* [new idea] in the yeshiva and the rebbe

---

[9] Boyarin, 'Voices around the Text', 227.

[10] This was not the case for all of Ashkenazi Jewry but just those in eastern Europea. In Hungary, for example, apparently a great deal of attention was given to Jewish law.

[11] Recent scholarship has suggested that this appearance is a literary form and that most of the talmudic text is not a transcript of discussions that took place but an artificial construction of such discussions. What is historically true is irrelevant in this context because in the *ḥeder* and yeshiva, the Talmud was perceived as a transcript of actual discussions and hence as a model for intellectual activity.   [12] Boyarin, 'Voices around the Text', 226–7.

[13] For a fascinating discussion of relevant aspects of the talmudic text see Fischer, 'The "Give and Take" of the Babylonian Talmud', esp. pp. 32–53. This characteristic is also explored in Levin, 'Multi-Faceted Logic as a Principal Distinction of Jewish Thinking and Philosophy'.

would say, *Ah! Gevaldig!* In law school, the professor . . . would say 'That's ridiculous' . . . At yeshiva I was being lauded for this, and here at the Harvard Law School they're laughing at me on account of this.[14]

Since questions could be left open, Talmud teachers did not always have to answer every question. After all, the classic commentaries differed among themselves and often raised problems that were left unanswered. Of course, if questions remained open 'too often' a teacher's authority could be undermined. The toleration of questions, and especially unanswered questions, reflected a basic intellectual security of traditional Jewish society. The asking of questions was not regarded as an expression of religious scepticism or doubt. It was taken for granted that even if an answer was not immediately found, yet it existed. As the Yiddish phrase often heard in yeshivas puts it, *fun kashes sterbt men nisht*—'one does not die from questions'. Students were encouraged to live with open questions. There were scholars whose fame came mainly from the questions they asked and not from their answers. It was a challenge to try to answer the questions—and an equal challenge to show why the answer would not have satisfied the questioner.[15] It should be emphasized that not every question was welcomed or considered legitimate. It was questions about the logical explanation of a text that were encouraged. Theological questions or questions that expressed doubt about the underlying assumptions of traditional Jewish belief were not asked in *batei midrash* or yeshivas.

Question asking was one by-product of the oral nature of Jewish education. Of course different schools had different levels of toleration of questions. A poor-quality and insecure *melamed* in an overcrowded *ḥeder* would probably have tended towards rote education more than a better-qualified *melamed* who taught the children of the elite in superior study conditions. Despite variations, on the whole questions were encouraged, especially in elite frameworks which were also models for society at large, and as we shall see, this was for good pedagogic reasons.

SOME ORAL ASPECTS OF EAST EUROPEAN JEWISH EDUCATION AND SOCIETY

The oral nature of male society and of male study in the traditional east European Jewish communities must be emphasized because there was a sharp distinction between image and reality. Male Jewish society was ostensibly a literate society and female society an oral one—but the reality was in many respects the reverse. The literacy of Jewish men had its limits. Men were

---

[14] Wohlgelernter, 'Defender of the Tribe', 18.
[15] Rabbi Akiva Eger's glosses on the Mishnah and the Talmud are a good example.

taught to read Hebrew and in traditional Jewish society it was disgraceful for a man to be seen reading Yiddish. Indeed, on the title pages of some Yiddish-language books it was clearly written that they were intended for women and for men who are like women. Most men read Hebrew prayers every day and this could be considered evidence of literacy. However, education ended after elementary school for most men and only a minority of men could read an unfamiliar text in Hebrew and understand it. Even the use of a prayer-book is questionable evidence for literacy. Prayers were often said by heart and not read—and when read, this was rarely with much comprehension of the meaning of the text. For most men, an unfamiliar passage in a Hebrew text was an insurmountable obstacle, especially since up until the end of the nineteenth century there were almost no Hebrew–Yiddish dictionaries in general use, so that there was no easy way to explicate an unfamiliar word other then by turning to another person for an (oral) explanation. Women read widely—though in Yiddish—so while very literate, their reading and study had low status, as discussed above in Chapter 8.

The realities of Jewish male literacy[16] in eastern Europe fit the concept of 'restricted literacy'.[17] The restriction of study to texts in Hebrew and the low academic level of most *ḥeder*s guaranteed that few would leave the educational system with a mastery of Hebrew.[18] The absence of printed study aids for rabbinic literature, or of popular commentaries in Yiddish on classic texts, meant that most men did not have direct access to the Talmud and to authoritative legal and philosophical literature. While not a secret, this means of restricting effective literacy was not explicit and formal. Quite possibly this phenomenon attracted no attention. Nonetheless, it was effective.

In reality, most Jewish men acquired the bulk of their knowledge orally and not through reading or independent study. In *ḥeder*s children listened to their lessons and did not read independently. Adult males studied regularly in the *beit midrash* or communal study hall in the context of *ḥevrot* or study groups. Members of a study group sat in front of open books, but listened to the text as it was read and explicated and then participated in the discussion— another oral experience. For many men one of the educational highlights of the week was the Saturday afternoon *derashah*, or sermon delivered by a *magid* or preacher in the synagogue or study hall, which was also oral. Even news

[16]   For an excellent survey on a number of key issues in literacy see Collins, 'Literacy and Literacies'.

[17]   Goody uses this phrase in his introduction to *Literacy in Traditional Societies*. Abrahm Stahl uses a similar term—'semi-literate'—in his introductory article 'Historical Changes in the Culture of Israel and their Implications on Dealing with Pupils with Special Needs'. On his use of the term see esp. pp. 13–18. Sydney Stahl-Weinberg uses the same term in *The World of Our Mothers*. Use of the term has been criticized in recent studies for its lack of clarity. See Messick, 'Legal Documents and the Concept of "Restricted Literacy" in a Traditional Society', esp. pp. 45–6.   [18]   I discussed this point in Chapter 7 above.

was spread orally. Newspapers began to be widespread only late in the nineteenth century and the early newspapers were generally in Hebrew. This press was read only by the elite, who transmitted orally to the Jewish population at large those reports in the newspaper that the readers thought worthy of transmission. It took the explosive rise of the Yiddish press to make reading a daily activity for most people. There were few frameworks in which men actually read with the goal of acquiring useful information. What they needed to know, they heard, and there was almost nothing that had to be read. Until there were useful books to read, reading was not necessarily a useful skill. In other words, reading was often more valuable as a sign of being cultured or an indication of status than useful as a practical tool.

I mentioned above that in the oral environment of yeshivas and *batei midrash* in which the educated elite of the Jewish community studied there were no written tests and little or no use of writing for self-expression. Moreover, in these institutions the posing of questions was an important indication of academic level. Indeed, the asking of questions was raised in Jewish society into an art form—a form of mock battle. The study of Torah was even referred to in yeshivas as *milḥamta shel torah'* (the war of Torah) because the students attacked with questions and the teacher fought back.[19] The central role of questions in the educational dynamic of yeshivas is clearly expressed in the following two descriptions of yeshiva life.

A former student of the Volozhin yeshiva recounted in his memoirs a visit to the yeshiva of a famous rabbi, Rabbi Alexander Lapidot of Rasein, who was invited to give a guest lecture even though he was reputed to have made some disparaging remarks about the yeshiva. The students prepared for his visit and as soon as he began to read the text of the Talmud on which he was to base his talk, 'a student stood up and said: "Rabbi, I have a question". The rabbi stopped, heard the question, thought for a few minutes and gave an answer.' This was only the beginning, because the rabbi was soon bombarded with questions.

One of the younger students who was regarded as a genius excelled in questions and asked one as hard 'as a wooden post'. The rabbi was caught off guard, thought for a while, gave an answer, but it was weak and only out of respect did the questioner refrain from saying that it was not a real answer . . . everyone was pleased with the results of the lecture—the rabbi from Rasein now knows what it is to give a lecture in Volozhin and he will remember it for a long time . . . the students who asked good questions were surrounded on all sides, their hands were shaken and they were congratulated on their ability to raise the honor of the yeshiva.[20]

[19] I give a description in my book *The Formation of the Lithuanian Yeshiva* (Heb.), 107.
[20] Epstein, *Ketavim*, 121–2.

This type of behaviour was not necessarily regarded as insulting. A positive attitude to questions is shown by an incident that took place in the famous yeshiva of Telšiai. This famous yeshiva was headed by Rabbi Eliezer Gordon, and his lessons were noted for the intense 'give and take' between the students and their teacher. Students would energetically attempt to contradict the teacher's theses and his responses were equally spirited. The harder the question, the greater the status of the student who asked it.[21] On one occasion, 'the students plotted not to interrupt the lecture of their teacher . . . Rabbi Eliezer began to give the lecture and spoke for ten minutes without a sound from the students. He stopped the lecture and said "I am not used to giving a lecture in a cemetery" and walked out.' Such a response would be rather surprising in a contemporary university where students often sit silently in lectures as they scribble in their notebooks or ask polite questions. Rabbi Gordon was not exceptional. Rabbi Shimon Shkop, who also taught in the Telšiai yeshiva, looked down on students who were quiet, or who had good memories but couldn't ask good questions.[22]

The emphasis on active questioning has remained until today a central and distinctive characteristic of popular talmudic study groups. Samuel Heilman, who studied the dynamics of such groups among descendants of east European Jews in both America and Israel, came to the following conclusion:

questions asked during 'lernen' [study] . . . are the blood and tissue of the activity . . . Through questioning, rules of irrelevance and transformation are evolved and established in every circle. They guide and frame the action. Within the 'shiur' [lesson], they discipline feelings and guide behavior. They include some speakers and exclude others. They also, however, allow for distinctions within the circle. People type themselves according to the type of questions they ask.[23]

There were, of course, exceptions to the emphasis on oral expression in rabbinic society, and they demonstrate the potential of literary means to serve as an alternative to oral measures. One case is the rise to fame of Rabbi Naftali Tsevi Berlin (1817–93), also known as the Netsiv, who headed the famous yeshiva of Volozhin in the second half of the nineteenth century. Rabbi Berlin studied in the yeshiva as a youth and married the daughter of the head of the yeshiva. However, after their marriage Rabbi Berlin apparently failed to meet the academic expectations of his in-laws—and of his wife. The young and apparently depressed young man withdrew from contact with those around him and devoted himself to private study. In the course of time Rabbi Berlin transformed himself into a major scholar known particularly for the broad

---

[21] I discuss this in my book *The Formation of the Lithuanian Yeshiva* (Heb.).

[22] Amiel, 'A Good Day for our Teachers' (Heb.), 42. The theme of the importance of questions was developed by R. Abraham Bloch, who taught in the Telšiai yeshiva in the interwar period; see his *Lectures* (Heb.), esp. 110–13.   [23] Heilman, *The People of the Book*, 140–1.

scope of his knowledge. What was exceptional was how his achievements became public knowledge. Since Rabbi Berlin apparently did not engage in scholarly debates with talmudists in Volozhin, no one knew of his scholarly progress. However, while sequestered in private study he corresponded on talmudic topics with Rabbi David Luria (1798–1855), one of the most respected scholars of his generation. Rabbi Luria was deeply impressed by him and addressed the young Rabbi Berlin with warm words of praise. It was only when the exchange of letters 'accidentally' fell into the hands of Rabbi Berlin's wife's family that he was fully accepted into the family circle, and ultimately called upon to teach and ultimately to lead the yeshiva. However, this was regarded as an exceptional sequence of events in that the young Rabbi Berlin demonstrated his knowledge and profundity in writing and not orally. In the normal course of events it was through the constant oral give and take in the study hall that a budding scholar showed his skills and talents. Perhaps it was not by chance that Rabbi Berlin was not a popular teacher and that he was far more impressive in his written works.

The phenomenon of a literary culture in which oral argumentation was a central activity was, of course, not unique or original to Jewish culture. The same characteristics were found in medieval European universities. Knowledge was demonstrated by students in the framework of the disputation. The following description of an examination in Bologna would have seemed quite familiar to a student in the Telšiai yeshiva: 'your son has held a glorious disputation, which was attended by a great multitude of teachers and scholars. He answered all questions without a mistake and no one could prevail against his arguments.'[24] However, the difference in this case is that answers were emphasized and not questions.

ASPECTS OF ORALITY/LITERACY IN NORTH AFRICAN MUSLIM EDUCATION

To gain a better perspective on the strategies of Jewish education in eastern Europe it is useful to compare them with the approaches of similar societies. Two obvious characteristics of east European Jewish education were the fact that it concentrated on ancient canonical texts and that elementary male education was widespread. In these respects Jewish education was not at all similar to education in Christian societies. Popular and intensive study of an authoritative text was not widespread in medieval Christianity. Direct access to the Bible for the masses was not a goal in medieval Catholicism, and even later, among Protestant groups that encouraged textual study, it was not the original text of the Bible that was generally studied, but rather a translation

---

[24] Haskins, *The Rise of the Universities*, 40.

into the vernacular, and it was usually studied in the context of a school system that gave a great deal of attention to practical matters.

The religious tradition that is probably closest to Judaism with regard to the central role of a classic religious text and widespread education is Islam. In various Islamic societies the Koran was studied by all males and it formed the basis of religious education similar to the way in which the Torah and Talmud were studied among Jews. Of course, not all Muslim societies had identical educational patterns and the Koran was not always studied in the same way.

It is instructive to compare here traditional Muslim elementary education in North Africa in the nineteenth and twentieth centuries with the nineteenth-century east European Jewish *ḥeder*. However, examples taken from Muslim societies in other regions will be cited when relevant.[25] There is no question that there were significant differences between North African Islamic society and east European Jewish society. The Islamic population of North Africa was mainly agricultural whereas most Jews of eastern Europe were involved either in crafts or in trade. The percentage of east European Jews who were urban was higher than that of North African Muslims. The role of women was different in the two societies. In certain ways eastern Europe was more open to modern European influences than was North Africa. Therefore this comparison is not between similar communities, but between communities that have some similarities. It might have been possible to pick communities that are even more similar to east European Jewry, such as North African Jewish communities that share a common religion. However, it is precisely the fact that North African Islam was clearly different in certain respects that makes it possible to examine some of the implications of the differences.

There are also practical reasons for choosing North Africa for purposes of comparison. North African Muslim societies have received more scholarly attention than many other Muslim societies,[26] which means that there is a rich literature on this region. North African Muslims and east European Jews also shared an educational issue. In eastern Europe Jewish schoolboys spoke Yiddish, but had to learn texts written in a different language—Hebrew. Muslim schoolboys had a similar problem in North Africa. Much of the Muslim population did not speak Arabic, but Berber. For them, the Arabic of the Koran was totally incomprehensible. Even the Arabic-speaking population spoke a dialect that was very far removed from the high poetic language and the literary style characteristic of the Koran. Thus for almost all boys

[25] Comparing societies is no simple matter, especially when the person doing the comparison is a member of one of the societies. I have no doubt that despite my attempts to be objective, readers will find points to correct in light of their own experience and points of view. This comparison should be regarded then as the opening of a question and not the final word.

[26] One reason for this is that it is easier to conduct research in North Africa than in some other Muslim societies.

the Koran was an unintelligible text until they mastered its vocabulary. The Koran could have been translated—just as Christians translated the Bible, or the Jews translated the Bible into the Yiddish vernacular for women[27]—but it was not, and hence Muslim boys in North Africa, like Jewish boys in eastern Europe, had to deal with a classic text in the original language. What makes such a comparison between east European Jewish education and North African Muslim education particularly useful is that even though the two societies had similar educational goals and needs, in many respects the educational strategies they employed were polar opposites.[28]

It should be emphasized that the choice of North African Muslim education does not imply in any way that this society was representative of Islamic societies in general, or that conclusions about this society indicate anything about Islam as a religion. In various contexts and times, Islamic societies utilized very different educational strategies.

The first stage of study in North African Islamic elementary schools or *kutab* was to memorize the entire Koran but without making any attempt to understand it.[29] One of the classic studies of Islamic education in North Africa is entitled 'The Art of Memory: Islamic Education and its Social Reproduction',[30] and the title is apt. In the morning, the teacher would write the text of the Koran which was to be learned that day on slates, and during the rest of the day the students would review the verses learned previously and also recite the new verses over and over until they had learned them by heart.[31] Only after a student had learned all or most of the Koran by heart did the study of classical Arabic—a precondition for the understanding of the Koran —begin. This feature was not limited to Morocco. In a study of schools in Mali, which is, of course, not a North African state but strongly influenced by it, an observer found that 'In the traditional Koran school none of the seventy-three students tested had any comprehension of Arabic'. Describ- ing another school, he noted: 'Literacy does not truly begin until the sixth year, the beginning of the "second cycle" in which knowledge of the

---

[27] *Tsenah urenah* is a translation of the Bible with the addition of commentaries, rabbinic homilies, laws, and so on. It was read almost entirely by women See Chapter 8 above.

[28] Many of the customs related to study in the *kutab* seem very familiar to a person acquainted with *ḥeder* life. Practices such as special foods on the first day of study, or gifts to the teachers on holidays are obvious examples. See Zerdoumi, *Enfant d'hier*.

[29] See Bellaire, 'L'Enseignement indigène au Maroc': 'Aucune explication n'est donnée aux enfants sur le Qoran qu'ils apprennent par cœur; le maître qui le leur apprend serait d'ailleurs très embarrassé d'expliquer le moindre passage de ce qu'il enseigne . . . On n'apprend pas le Qoran pour le comprendre, mais pour le savoir, pour le posséder' (p. 425). This was not a local or recent innovation. See Totah, *The Contribution of the Arabs to Education*, ch. 3, 'Curriculum', esp. pp. 48–51, where this is described as prevalent in the medieval period.

[30] Eickelman, 'The Art of Memory'.   [31] Ibid. 493.

Arabic language becomes more important.'[32] A description of elementary education in modern Yemen is no different.[33] Descriptions of traditional education in Egypt are almost identical with those of North Africa both with regard to writing and to the memorization of the Koran. The author of one such study comments that apparently 'Islamic culture, or at least as it is practiced in [the community he studied], emphasizes and fosters rote learning, memory and enumerative procedures', and he adds that 'The resort to rote learning has been the bane of education in modern schools'.[34] This approach was appar-ently related to basic theories of knowledge. In North African Islamic schools

the form of lesson circles conveyed the notion of the fixity of knowledge by minimizing active student contributions . . . no questions were asked during sessions . . . deference and propriety toward their shaykhs prevented their openly raising any issues. Questions had to be placed indirectly, usually in private, so as not to suggest a public challenge to his scholarship.[35]

One consequence of this system is that it did not allow for a scholar to develop in isolation or for an autodidact. The authority of a scholar rested to a large extent on the chain of authority he could call on and not the inherent logic that he could present.[36] In east European Jewish society it was possible, though not common, for a scholar to study in isolation until he was ready to make his mark on the scholarly world, as was suggested above in the case of Rabbi Berlin.

The following description by Shemaryahu Levin of an experience in his childhood would have been unthinkable in a *kutab* in North Africa. He wrote:

No sooner did Motyeh [the *melamed* or Jewish elementary teacher] touch on the subject of Paradise than my tongue was loosened and I began to fire my questions at him . . . If there were two Paradises, one for earth and one for Heaven, did it not follow that there had to be two Gehinoms, two Hells, one for earth and one for Heaven? And why was there no mention of either in the Sacred Book? . . . The questions resolved into a sort of debate between Rabbi and pupil, with the other pupils as an audience . . . They know I would not let Motyeh fool me, and that he would have to give a halfway satisfactory answer or acknowledge defeat . . . He perspired under the cannonade of questions.[37]

[32] Niezen, 'Hot Literacy in Cold Societies', 244–5. With regard to the traditional Koran school Niezen notes: 'The master of the school did not himself wish to participate in the test, so his ability is also in doubt.'			[33] See Messick, 'Legal Documents', 45.
[34] Ammar, *Growing up in an Egyptian Village*, 204.
[35] Eickelman, 'The Art of Memory', 501.
[36] See Colonna, *Les Versets de l'invincibilité*, 282–3. I thank Professor Pesach Shinhar for bringing this fascinating book to my attention.
[37] Levin, *Childhood in Exile*, 134–5. The book is a delightful description of an east European Jewish childhood.

The patterns of study in modern Islam and east European Jewry reflected some of the characteristics of the medieval heritage of each culture.[38] One view of education in medieval Islam saw it as 'the teaching of fixed and memorizable statements and formulas which could be learned without any process of thinking as such',[39] and nineteenth-century Moroccan schools in particular seemed to demonstrate a continuity with patterns in the past and this one in particular.[40] Jewish schools in eastern Europe were dealing with an intellectual heritage of the *peshatim hamithadshim bekhol yom* (new interpretations which are created daily),[41] which implied a constantly growing corpus of knowledge. In other words, one system tends to see knowledge as finite and the other as dynamic. This distinction can be put in different terms. Jewish tradition emphasizes the responsibility and power of the rabbis to innovate and does not necessarily try to base all laws and practices on a divine authority. This distinction between Judaism and Islam was summarized by two scholars of Islam in Iran in the following way: '[The] resolute making of man responsible for the divine word [in Judaism] contrasts sharply with the Islamic dogma that the Koran exists in heaven and that perfect knowledge [for Shi'ites] rests with the Imams', though the authors go on to claim that the differences were larger in theory than in practice.[42] I will return to this distinction below.

Once again it should be emphasized that the distinction between east European Jewish education and Islamic education in North Africa does not necessarily hold for other Jewish and Islamic communities. Memorization is only one of a number of possible options for dealing with an authoritative religious text and the methods employed can shift in the course of time. For example, the Hebrew verb for 'to read' (*kara*) apparently was used in the sense of reading out loud both in the biblical and Second Temple periods, and only later did the personal and individual act of quiet reading become the standard.[43] This stance is very similar to the attitudes to the written text in Islam, but it was not maintained. In the talmudic period there was an emphasis on memory among rabbinic scholars, and the massive oral tradition which crystallized in the Talmud was transmitted by *tana'im* or memorizers who were 'walking books'. Among the Jewish communities in Muslim lands

---

[38] Eickelman, 'Islam and the Impact of the French Colonial System', brings a variety of sources to provide an image of an unchanging Islamic society in North Africa; see p. 222 for the sources. He goes on to criticize the view but it is clear that much indeed was passed on from the medieval heritage. For an interesting discussion of the ties between orality in education and other characteristics in Yemeni Muslim culture, see Messick, 'Legal Documents'.

[39] Marshall Hodgson, cited by Eickelman, 'The Art of Memory', 489.

[40] See Plancke, 'Islamic Education in Tunisia (*c*.800–1574)'.

[41] Rabbi Shemuel ben Me'ir (Rashbam), *Commentary on the Torah*, Gen. 37: 2.

[42] Fischer and Abedi, *Debating Muslims*, 461.   [43] See Daniel Boyarin, 'Placing Reading'.

there was a tendency to emphasize memorization over analysis.[44] However, it is clear that an emphasis on the memorization of texts was not encouraged in east European Jewish education. Of course, in some Islamic societies there was also greater emphasis on comprehension than in modern North Africa. For example, in his classic study on medieval Islamic education, Arthur Tritton cites views that encouraged discussion and saw a value in a broad curriculum.[45]

WRITING, THE PRINTED BOOK, AND EDUCATION IN ISLAMIC SOCIETIES AND EAST EUROPEAN JEWRY

As opposed to the east European *ḥeder* which had abandoned the teaching of writing, in many Moroccan Koranic elementary schools, writing and dictation were at the basis of study because students wrote the texts that they learned by heart.[46] The reason for this was that Jews in eastern Europe and elsewhere had a very positive attitude to the printed book, whereas the response of Islamic societies to print was far more complex. This differing response was on one hand responsible for some of the characteristics of the educational systems in both societies, and on the other hand, it reflected deeper cultural attitudes to the book and to knowledge.

Jews and Muslims generally responded in very different ways to the invention of print. Jews were quick to employ printed books and were excellent clients for publishers.[47] While printing was rejected as a means of preparing cultic objects such as scrolls of the Torah, which are employed in ritual but not for study, it was enthusiastically embraced as a means of providing books and materials for study. In a brilliant paper Elhanan Reiner has pointed out the complex reactions of the Ashkenazi Jewish elite to the coming of the printed book and its impact on Jewish law.[48] While it is very enlightening to

---

[44] Zafrani, *Pédagogie juive en terre d'Islam*, esp. pp. 91–3.

[45] Tritton, *Materials on Muslim Education*. For the emphasis on discussion see p. 7. Tritton also quotes Ibn Khaldun, who states that 'In Algeria and Morocco they teach boys the Koran and some of the different readings but nothing else till they are expert in this subject or fail and as a rule failure in it is the end of learning' (p. 15).

[46] Houtsonen, 'Traditional Quranic Education', esp. p. 491. Writing was not always taught in the framework of Muslim education. In an account of education in Egypt in the 1830s an observer noted: 'It is seldom the master of a school teaches writing; and few boys learn to write unless destined for some employment which absolutely requires that they should do so; in the latter case they are generally taught the art of writing, and likewise arithmetic, by a *kabbanee*.' Lane, *An Account of the Manners*, as cited in Goody (ed.), *Literacy in Traditional Societies*, 262. The *kabbanee* appears to have had exactly the same function as the *shrayber* in the *ḥeder* and it would seem for the same reasons. How pupils in such schools received texts for study is not clear.

[47] Spiegel, *Pages on the History of the Hebrew Book* (Heb.).   [48] Reiner, 'The Ashkenazi Elite'.

consider the varying responses to printing that he analysed, what is clear is that there was no serious attempt to do without printed books.

The printing press was not quickly adopted in Islam, and even while the technology was available in the early modern period, there was no outburst of publications of new texts by the conservative elements of Muslim society— neither in North Africa nor elsewhere.[49] The first major spurt of printing in Arabic was in Italy, which also had a major role in early Hebrew printing.[50] The possession of printed matter was prohibited in the Ottoman empire in 1485 by the Sultan, and only the Jews were allowed to print in the empire. Printing in Arabic and Turkish was permitted in the Ottoman empire only at the beginning of the eighteenth century. In 1728 the Ottoman ambassador in Paris managed to convince the *ulama* (Muslim clergy) to issue a *fatwa* (decree) permitting the printing of books not connected with religion, and somewhat later permission was given for the printing of religious books as well, and the introduction of printing into the Middle East was achieved by Syrian and Lebanese Christians.[51] It was only in the nineteenth century that printing became well established in Egypt.[52] At the same time, scholars in North African Muslim societies displayed remarkable feats of memory and up to the rapid modernization introduced by the French, successfully transmitted the heritage they had received from their fathers.[53]

The reasons for the different responses to printing between Islamic and Jewish societies are not clear. As Bernard Lewis put it, the 'decisive rejection of printing, both when it came from the East and when it was reintroduced from the West, is all the more remarkable when compared with the eager and effective acceptance of paper some centuries earlier'.[54] The reason for the rejection was ostensibly religious. One writer put it thus: 'orthodox Muslims

---

[49] This discussion is based on Pedersen, *The Arabic Book*, ch. 10, pp. 131–41. I thank Professor Zeev Gries, a specialist on hasidism and on many other topics, for the reference.

[50] Printing of Judaica in North Africa is a case in point. Relatively little was printed in Hebrew in North Africa before the late 19th century. In Algiers about 15 books were published in mid century, in Fez 9 books at the beginning of the 16th century, in Cairo 4 books over a long period, and 3 books in Tunis in mid century. (See Winograd, *Otsar hasefer ha'ivri*.) The reason for this is very simple. Jewish communities in the Levant were relatively small and a local publisher therefore had a limited market. In Leghorn (Livorno) (Italy) there was a very active Hebrew press and the transportation ties from Italy to the Levant were excellent. Hebrew printers in Leghorn could easily export and thus they had advantages of scale over local printers. The result was that Leghorn became one of the centres of the Hebrew book trade in Europe and the Leghorn printers supplied the entire Levant with books.

[51] Ahmad, 'The Arabic Printing Press'. See p. 80 on Muhammad al-Jalbi, the Ottoman ambassador, and p. 84 on the role of Christians in the spread of printing.

[52] In addition to Pedersen's *The Arabic Book*, see Roper, 'Faris al Shidyaq', and Atiyeh, 'The Book in the Modern Arab World'.

[53] For a fascinating and extended analysis see 'The Kingdom of the Book', an unpublished Ph.D. thesis by Fawzi A. Abdulrazak.   [54] Lewis, *Cultures in Conflict*, 23.

felt hesitant to adopt it [printing] because the reproduction of the holy
Qur'an by any means other than handwriting or lithographing was objection-
able to them'.[55]

The negative response in Islam to the printed book may be more than a
simple rejection of a novelty because of opposition to any innovation. It may
be tied to the attitude to study in North African Islam, which differed from
the approach to study in east European Jewry. Francis Robinson claimed that
since the oral transmission of the Koran, starting off with the memorization
of the text, was 'the backbone of Muslim education . . . printing attacked the
very heart of Islamic systems for the transmission of knowledge; it attacked
what was understood to make knowledge trustworthy, what gave it value,
what gave it authority'.[56] In his view, 'person to person transmission was at the
heart of the transmission of Islamic knowledge',[57] and printing could
undermine such authority. Indeed, whereas in Jewish tradition the written
text of the Torah (*torah shebikhetav*) was of primary importance, in Islam the
Koran was transmitted in a very different way. 'Still today, reciters of the
Qur'an learn their recitations from oral masters, not from the written text;
scribes write down the text from recitations, not from other texts and students
study with a teacher, never alone with a text. The oral remains authoritative
for the written, not the other way around.'[58] It has been pointed out that this
attitude was present in Jewish society with regard to kabbalah and, significantly, in east European Jewish society such attitudes were widespread only
with regard to kabbalah.[59]

After printing was finally introduced in the Islamic world, there was a
spurt of original responses to modernity and a concomitant rise of religious
experimentation.[60] In Morocco printing was first employed only in 1864 as a
means to 'revive Islam and maintain its tradition', but it eventually weakened
the role of memorization in education and eased the spread of new ideas. 'A
new era began in which independent and creative ideas were more important
and rewarding than writings which served as links in the traditional chain of
authority transmitting divine knowledge from one generation to another.'[61]
Francis Robinson pointed out that the use of printing by the *ulama* in India

---

[55] Ahmad, 'The Arabic Printing Press', 84 Another very interesting study on the topic of
printing in Islam that explains the lag in adoption of the printing press as the result of a complex
of cultural and social factors is Demeerseman, 'Les Données de la controverse'. A thought-
provoking discussion of the lack of influence of Chinese printing on Islam is in Carter, *The
Invention of Printing in China and its Spread Westward*, ch. 15.

[56] Robinson, 'Technology and Religious Change', 234, 235.

[57] Ibid. 237.   [58] Fischer and Abedi, *Debating Muslims*, 105.

[59] See Nasr, 'Oral Transmission and the Book in Islamic Education', 13.

[60] See e.g. Robinson, 'Technology and Religious Change', 246.

[61] Quoted from an abstract of Abdulrazak's dissertation 'The Kingdom of the Book', printed
in *Dissertation Abstracts* (DAI-A 51/01) (July 1990), 263.

was a compensation for the loss of political power and it evolved out of a sense of religious crisis.[62]

The differences in the attitude to the written and later printed book might be related to differences in the models in the cultural heritage of Jews and Muslims, though this is a matter for speculation and it is difficult to test. Moses is one of the paradigms of the ideal Jew. In the Bible he is depicted as a scribe receiving a written record of revelation from God. Writing is a desirable skill and if God chose to write, than the written text is holy. In Islamic tradition, on the other hand, Muhammad is depicted as illiterate. The writing down of the Koran was a concession to difficulties in the oral transmission of the texts and not an ideal. Thus, while the written text of the Koran was indeed treated as holy, it was the oral transmission of the Koran that was regarded as more fundamental.

The question of what was printed was as important of that of printing itself. What books did east European rabbinical culture produce? It published commentaries, collections of sermons, collections of rabbinical responsa, and *ḥidushim* (glosses on rabbinic texts). None of these genres was unique to the region. The genre of the *ḥidush*, or scholarly gloss, was also common both to medieval rabbinic culture and to medieval Christendom. A *ḥidush* involved the pointing out of a difficulty or contradiction in a text and then offering a resolution or explanation. This was developed by the medieval tosafists (commentators on the Talmud after Rashi) and their successors.[63] Their commentaries on the Talmud became classical when they were printed in the *editio princeps* of the Talmud and the study of the Tosafot was at the heart of Talmud study in eastern Europe. The activity of the tosafists paralleled that of the contemporary medieval glossators who had as their goal the harmonization of seemingly contradictory legal texts. The genre of the gloss disappeared in Christian Europe from the time of the Renaissance, but as an intellectual tradition it remained very alive in talmudic study.

What was rare in eastern European Jewish culture was the essay or book that took an idea or theme and systematically developed it. There were no frameworks for young people to develop their skills in this area. It should be remembered that writing an essay is not just a matter of technical skills but rather it reflects a different mode of thinking from the writing of notes. The gloss is a written form of a question and answer. It has an oral character close to the way people speak or converse. Essay writing is different. No one speaks in the form of essays. Writing essays requires skills of integration and analysis, whereas note writing calls on abilities to cite relevant—or seemingly relevant—texts as well as the capability to explain difficult texts or sentences.

---

[62] Robinson, 'Technology and Religious Change', 240–1.
[63] See Urbach, *The Tosafists* (Heb.); Grossman, *The Early Sages of France* (Heb.), esp. ch. 7.

If the skills needed to write essays are not taught and practised, they are not easily learned. Many of the Jewish books published in eastern Europe were oral in character, and this is apparent with regard to the sermons and glosses. However, even responsa have the outer appearance of being a response to a query rather then being an attempt to survey a topic.

There was great encouragement in the east European Jewish communities for the publishing of books and originality was one of the main criteria that gave a book value. A claim to originality was a standard means to acquire status. Indeed, a common criticism of authors was that they attempted to claim originality for themselves though in reality their ideas and points were plagiarized from others. The assumption was that if the author had been creative, he would have merited praise. Jewish authors were often known and referred to by the books they wrote and not by their name. Thus, both in speaking and in writing one could state that the *Mishnah berurah* (a well-known commentary on part of the *Shulḥan arukh*, a major code of Jewish law) said such and such, or that the *Ketsot haḥoshen* (a well-known book on the Talmud) lived in this city or that. In many respects a scholar was an author. In Islamic culture there was far more trepidation about writing and printing new books.[64] In many Islamic communities there was also apparently less use of written documents and a greater emphasis on witnesses than in Jewish communities.[65]

The Jewish educational models in eastern Europe and the society in general seem to have encouraged literary creativity, while in North African Islam the attitudes to creativity were more complex. This difference cannot be superficially related to a dichotomy between oral and literary cultures. To be sure, a system of transmission that emphasizes oral transmission and bases authority on the chain of transmission and not on the logic of an argument naturally tends to limit attempts at originality. A system that is based on the interpretation of a fixed text can measure validity of views not by transmission, but by the degree to which they are convincing as interpretations of the text. However, as we saw, east European rabbinic Jewish creativity was extremely influenced by orality even though it displayed, or tried to display, originality.

Both east European Jewish society and North African Islamic society were challenged by modernity. Each had to deal with a well-developed literary and intellectual culture that came from the outside—German-Jewish Haskalah and Russian and Polish non-Jewish culture in eastern Europe, and French culture in North Africa. However the responses were different. East Euro-

[64] Rosenthal, "'Of making many books there is no end'".
[65] See Messick, 'Legal Documents', 47. Note though that in North Africa legal documents had greater recognition than elsewhere.

pean Jewish society developed both frameworks, such as the modern yeshiva and hasidism, as well as intellectual responses, such as the *musar* movement and Orthodoxy, which served to blunt the challenge of modernity alongside responses that embraced the outside cultures. Although there was great resentment in North Africa of the inroads made by French culture, innovative, institutional, or intellectual responses were apparently slow to develop. This may well have been linked to the structure of Islamic education. In Dale Eickelman's opinion, the traditional system collapsed and he saw social factors as being a partial explanation for the lack of reaction that he observed. However, he also noted that 'since knowledge was considered to be fixed and memorizable, the central ideological problem was that of justifying any change of form or content'.[66] John Damis, who studied the establishment of a new type of Muslim school in Morocco, noted that up to the 1920s, 'At the elementary level, however, Koranic studies had changed very little from their traditional form, due, probably, to the force of inertia. A conservative, inward-oriented society which resisted change in general would hardly be interested in modernizing its Koranic schools.'[67] This, of course, does not mean that there were no responses, but that the scope was limited.[68] It seems reasonable that the graduates of an educational system that encourages questions and creative responses would find it easier to deal with new and unanticipated situations than a system that emphasized memory and conservative responses.

THE HERITAGE OF EAST EUROPEAN JEWISH ORALITY AND CONTEMPORARY ISRAELI SOCIETY

What are the consequences of an education that combines an emphasis on oral expression with comprehension and analysis of texts? The best way for a young scholar to stand out in the traditional east European Jewish educational framework was by developing the ability to make quick retorts, by questioning, and by answering. Such a framework did not necessarily

---

[66] Eickelman, 'The Art of Memory', 511.

[67] Damis, 'Early Moroccan Reactions to the French Protectorate', 16. The rise of the new 'free schools' in response to the French challenge, not surprisingly, is remarkably similar to the rise of novel educational frameworks in east European Jewry in response to the Haskalah (Enlightenment).

[68] For an important discussion of one such response see Merad, *Le Réformisme musulman*. This discussion of the Sallafiya movement offers many points for intercultural comparison. However, it is important to note that the movement did not spread significantly in Morocco and that it was apparently quite localized. I thank Professor Stewart for the reference to this book.

encourage rudeness, but it gave an advantage to aggressive individuals who were quick to make their mark in public discussions.[69] In such a system, quick-wittedness and sharpness were admired skills and, as such, they were imitated. This cultural and communication pattern apparently influenced behavioural structures of their descendants in the United States and Israel.

Few studies have been made of the styles of communication among the descendants of east European Jews. One exception was that of Deborah Schiffrin, who studied patterns of talk among descendants of east European Jews in Philadelphia. She found that arguments were a framework or expression of sociability and noted that 'Argumentative frames, stances and alignments end as quickly and unpredictably as they begin . . . the use of openly competitive forms of talk actually rests on underlying assumptions of cooperation and protection of speaker selves . . . the disagreements . . . seemed to be valued as processes and activities in their own right'.[70] After considering various aspects of the issue, including fascinating anecdotal evidence, she concluded that sociable argument was apparently culturally normative for Jews of east European descent, though she was careful to note that the phenomenon is not unique to Jews.[71]

Similar findings have been made with regard to the dynamics of Jewish families at the dinner table. The distinctive patterns of Jews were vividly presented in Woody Allen's film *Annie Hall*, in which 'the seemingly chaotic, high-involvement style of the first [Jewish] family, where everybody seems to be talking (and arguing) at the same time, contrasts sharply with the orderly formal and smooth conversational ambience of the second [American, non-Jewish]'.[72] Studies of speech patterns of American Jews have apparently borne this out.[73] Itamar Even-Zohar noted that when literary texts written by American Jews are translated into Hebrew, it is often the case that one notes a 'similarity . . . of the semiotic structure of the text, which in concrete terms manifests itself on the level of argumentation (conversation negotiations), patterns of persuasion and influence etc', and he adds that this is not simply a function of the language but also 'of the cultures of which these languages are vehicles of expression'.[74]

[69]   This was not the only avenue for advancement. One exception that quickly comes to mind is that of Rabbi Yisra'el Meir Kagan (Hakohen), the 'Hafets Hayim', who played a major role in interwar Agudat Yisra'el, the international movement and political party of Orthodox Jews. He came to fame after he self-published his book *Ḥafets ḥayim*. He personally distributed the book under the guise of being an agent of the author.

[70]   Schiffrin, 'Jewish Argument as Sociability', 329.

[71]   Ibid. 332–3.   [72]   I owe the observation to Blum-Kulka, *Dinner Talk*, 273.

[73]   See Tannen, 'New York Jewish Conversational Style'. I have not had access to this article but it is cited by Blum-Kulka, *Dinner Talk*, and see the bibliography there.

[74]   Even-Zohar, 'The Role of Russian and Yiddish', 120.

This phenomenon of oral aggressiveness may be more developed among Israeli Jews than among American Jews.[75] Shoshana Blum-Kulka carried out an extensive comparative study of styles of table conversation among Jewish families of east European descent in Israel and America. She found that 'of the two specific Jewish groups . . . Israeli families are higher on the scale of conversational involvement'.[76] She found in Israeli families 'an overindulgence in adversative formats',[77] and she concluded that the Israeli style echoed 'the Eastern European participatory listenership learning styles of the yeshiva as well as the conversational style of Jewish New Yorkers of similar background'.[78]

While difficult to prove, it seems that the inheritance of patterns of argumentation fostered by *ḥeder* and talmudic study in eastern Europe have left their mark on Israeli society. This was stated explicitly by Shlomo Avineri, an astute observer of the Israeli political scene. In discussing the founders of the kibbutzim in Israel he claims that while they were rebelling against their past, 'the modes of their behavior were deeply grounded in the societal behavior patterns of the shtetl, the force of dialectics'.[79] The only quantitative test of this phenomenon which I have found is that of Baruch Margalit and Paul Mauger, who compared patterns of aggression among Israelis and Americans. They found that 'Israelis responded more aggressively [to their tests] on a global level than did Americans', though differences with regard to assertiveness were less conclusive.[80]

Israeli academic life has a reputation for oral aggression which may well draw on the intellectual tradition I have described above. A rather telling demonstration of the 'fame' of this image is in a satire of academic life by David Lodge. He describes a conference in Israel at which the foreign participants spent most of their time having a good time instead of going to the conference. Lodge writes: 'The Israeli scholars, a highly professional and fiercely competitive group, are disgruntled with this arrangement, since they have been looking forward to attacking each other in the presence of a distinguished international audience.'[81] A novelist's description does not prove a phenomenon exists, but it is certainly evidence that the image exists.

Ivan Marcus's vivid description of responses to an academic lecturer in

[75] Consider, for example, Katriel, *Talking Straight*, which analyses a way of speaking that is common in Israel. It should be noted that she sees this '*dugri* speech' as a reaction against talmudic *pilpul* (elaborate argumentation) and not a continuation (p. 18). However, there may be more of a continuation than is apparent. [76] Blum-Kulka, *Dinner Talk*, 274.
[77] Ibid. 277, and see the references there. [78] Ibid. 278.
[79] Avineri, 'The Historical Roots of Israeli Democracy', 7, as cited in Blum-Kulka, *Dinner Talk*, 269. [80] Margalit and Mauger, 'Aggressiveness and Assertiveness', 502.
[81] Lodge, *Small World*, 298–9. I thank Eliot Horowitz for this reference, and for the comment that Lodge must have been in Israel and seen this for himself.

Israel describes a level of oral aggression which apparently was rather different from what he was used to in the United States. He describes the aftermath
of a heated post-lecture exchange of views: 'the audience rose and began to
buzz with excitement. They were talking not about the substance of the lecture, which after all had been of modest consequences, but about the greats,
their teachers and teachers' teachers and what the one had "done" to the
speaker and how he, in turn had fought back.' What caught his eye were
precisely the oral characteristics of argumentation that were common in east
European Jewish society. What should not be ignored is that the lecturer had
been Jacob Katz, of Hungarian origin, and his main critic, Gershom Scholem,
was German. In other words, one should not err and assume that this pattern was unique to east European Jews. However, the acceptance of the
pattern certainly was in line with east European Jewish patterns.[82] To be sure,
the often pugnacious characteristics of Israeli academic discourse are not a
quality unique to Israel—and if it is indeed more developed in Israel than
elsewhere, it is probably for more than one reason.

There may be even more significant phenomena that are tied to the east
European Jewish heritage of question asking. Raymond Cohen considered
two types of cultures in his analysis of the often unsuccessful Egyptian–Israeli
negotiations and relations. He divided cultures into two categories: 'high
context cultures [which] reflect a collectivist ethos, are sensitive to questions
of "face" and shame, and value tradition highly. Low context cultures tend to
be individualist, conscience-oriented, and "modern"'.[83] Cohen found that
Egypt fitted the first category to a large extent, and Israel the second. In his
analysis of the factors that contributed to these characteristics, he noted:

To understand the Jewish style of discourse and argument, it is necessary to start
with the . . . Talmud. . . . Talmud study . . . takes the form of a constant give and take,
query and response . . . between the reader . . . [and the texts]. The tradition of
argumentation in Judaism flows directly from the legalistic style of analysis . . . the
thread of analysis is carried forward by each participant in turn while the others
probe, question and refute his arguments.[84]

The same characteristics that we found were typical of the oral and analytical
nature of traditional study in eastern Europe are here seen to have long-term
consequences. Cohen went on to conclude that:

The tactic of shouting and table-banging, which is an integral part of political life in
Israel, and sometimes makes its appearance in Israel's diplomatic behavior [which

---

[82] See Marcus, 'Last Year in Jerusalem'. This does not mean that scholars in the United
States or the continent are necessarily nicer or more righteous, but that they seem to be more
discreet in their aggression.

[83] Cohen, *Culture and Conflict in Egyptian–Israeli Relations*, 42.   [84] Ibid. 51–2.

he saw as resulting in part from the argumentative patterns of the past], was worse than ineffective against the Egyptians. Diplomats with experience in the Arab World are in no doubt that a loss of temper or display of annoyance is a serious mistake when dealing with the Arabs. Avoidance of confrontation is a precondition of successful business of any kind. Once an Arab is angered and his pride aroused, he becomes immovable.[85]

The sources cited above indicate that many observers find a link between characteristics of the descendants of east European Jews and the cultural patterns of east European Jewry. As one observer put it in discussing Edmond Jabes's Book of Questions, 'Jabes is most thoroughly Jewish . . . [in] his unwillingness to let himself rest comfortably . . . His refuge is the book, not as the source of answers, but as the privileged place of questioning.'[86] However, their emphasis has been more on the consequences than on the causes of these patterns and their propagation. Close attention to the dynamics of *ḥeder* education suggests that patterns of education strengthened the argumentative characteristics of east European Jewish society, if they had not created them, and that the great importance attributed to education among east European Jews also explains how the oral, argumentative patterns were so deep-rooted. Thus it seems that the strategy Jews employed in dealing with sacred texts not only set them off from other societies who were faced with similar problems, but also influenced the ways that future generations lived.

Social phenomena rarely have one cause, and it is almost impossible to isolate factors or to precisely measure their impact. There are societies that delight in questions who have never studied the Talmud, and there are talmudists who have many of the characteristics of high-context cultures. Nonetheless, it seems very possible that the mode of study and the attitudes to the written text in traditional east European Jewish culture had an impact far beyond the schoolroom. Yet the question of to what degree remains open. As Jewish humorists put it, Jews answer a question with a question. But a question is sometimes part of an answer. The first step in understanding social dynamics is to raise some questions, and I hope that has been done here.

[85] Ibid. 59. See also Feghali, 'Arab Cultural Communication Patterns', 358–9.
[86] Jonathan Boyarin, 'Jewish Ethnography and the Question of the Book', 21.

TWELVE

Hasidic Yeshivas in Interwar Poland

THE IMAGE OF HASIDISM as a revolt against the study of Talmud as the major form of Jewish religious expression has long been moderated and amended. It is clear that in many ways hasidism changed the emphasis of study and the texts studied, but the traditional view of study as both a religious and a social act was not supplanted. Many learned talmudists were the product of hasidic households, and the *beit midrash*, or communal study hall, remained an important centre of Jewish life in hasidic communities as in the communities of mitnagedim, or non-hasidic Jews, in eastern Europe.[1]

There is, however, one obvious difference between hasidim and mitnagedim in the second half of the nineteenth century. It is that among mitnagedim, talmudic study was increasingly concentrated in yeshivas,[2] or formal educational institutions, while among hasidim yeshivas were generally unknown.[3] This distinction was stated explicitly in an often-cited responsum of the well-known hasidic rabbi Hayim Halberstam of Sanz. In 1862 he wrote: 'Yeshivas are not found in our land [Galicia] for a number of good reasons . . . rather [young men] sit in groups in the *beit midrash* and they study Torah, Talmud, Rashi, and Tosafot.'[4]

---

[1] See Piekarz, *The Beginning of Hasidism* (Heb.), and Schatz-Uffenheimer, *Hasidism as Mysticism*. An earlier study is that of Joseph Weiss, 'Torah Study in Early Hasidism' (Heb.), a chapter that appeared in 1965. Much is said (and implied) in Idel, *Hasidism: Between Ecstasy and Magic*, ch. 5. A closely related issue is the influence of hasidism on the printing of books. A very useful starting point on this issue is Hayim Liberman's classic study 'Legends and Truth on Hasidic Printing' (Yid.). See also Gries, *The Book in Early Hasidism* (Heb.) for a fascinating discussion of the topic.

[2] For the purposes of this chapter, a yeshiva may be defined as a formal institution for the advanced study of Talmud with a building of its own, a defined body of students, and a constant teacher who gave regular classes. Yeshivas can of course function on various levels. In this chapter the term is applied only to those yeshivas for students aged 13 and over, with more than local fame and students attracted from a wide region. In early hasidism yeshivas were generally unknown.

[3] See the clear formulation by Soloveitchik in his article 'Rupture and Reconstruction', 91. He dates the rise of hasidic yeshivas to the last 30 years. I will claim here that the process had already begun in Poland in the interwar period.

[4] Halberstam, *Divrei ḥayim*, vol. ii, 'Yoreh de'ah', no. 47, p. 33. He also claimed there that the vast majority of Talmud students in Poland in his time studied the simple meaning of the

The distinction between hasidim and mitnagedim with regard to yeshivas disappeared in Poland between the First and Second World Wars, when one of the most striking phenomena of hasidism was the dramatic rise in the number of yeshivas, their ubiquity, and their role in the education (or indoctrination and socialization, if you wish) of the young males of the hasidic elite.[5] Some of these yeshivas were clearly identified with specific hasidic courts—such as the yeshivas of Habad (Lubavitch) and Aleksandrów—while others were identified instead with hasidism in general, such as the yeshivas of the Sages of Lublin (Yeshivat Hokhmei Lublin) and Trzebinia (Chebin). The multiplication of hasidic yeshivas, and the creative solutions they offered to the challenges hasidim thought they were facing, are clear evidence of the creativity and resourcefulness of interwar hasidism.

The Polish hasidic yeshiva did not develop in a vacuum, but had as very visible potential models the Lithuanian and Hungarian yeshivas.[6] Lithuanian rabbis were often employed in hasidic yeshivas, and methods of study that developed in Lithuania on occasion influenced talmudic study in Poland. Some of the characteristics of many Polish yeshivas, such as weekly tests, were also characteristic of Hungarian yeshivas, and this may indicate Hungarian influence. In many cases hasidic youths studied in mitnagdic yeshivas in Poland. This was not discouraged by mitnagedim, and at times it was even encouraged. In the well-known yeshiva Torat Hesed in Łódz, founded in 1909 by the Lithuanian Rabbi Sender Diskin and run in the mitnagdic style, students were required to wear the standard hasidic dress. As a result, in 1929 there were many hasidic youths among the hundred or so students.[7] It is not clear if there were mitnagedim in hasidic yeshivas, but there may well have been some in Yeshivat Hokhmei Lublin. However, despite these models and contacts, we shall see that the hasidic yeshivas were not merely imitations of yeshivas in other places; nor were their founders dependent on importing teachers from Lithuania or Hungary.

The rise of the hasidic yeshiva merits attention in its own right, but it also relates to issues of social communication, responses to changes in technology

---

text. According to him, only the leading scholars engaged in *pilpul*. It is not likely that all of his contemporaries would have agreed with this assessment. On R. Halberstam and this statement see the very illuminating study of Silber, 'The Limits of Rapprochement'.

[5] On interwar hasidism, see especially Piekarz, *Polish Hasidism* (Heb.).

[6] I made an attempt to describe the Lithuanian yeshivas in my book *The Formation of the Lithuanian Yeshiva* (Heb.). On Hungarian yeshivas, see notably Weingarten, *The Yeshivas in Hungary* (Heb.); Friedman, 'Major Aspects of Yeshivah Education'; Fuchs, *Hungarian Yeshivas* (Heb.). See also Mirsky (ed.), *Jewish Institutions of Higher Learning in Europe* (Heb.). A short but interesting article is Ben-Ze'ev, 'On the Method of Study in Hungary' (Heb.). I am indebted to Rabbi Yitshak Dor for the last reference.

[7] See Gelbart, *The Great Yeshiva Torat Hesed in Łódz* (Yid.), 11, 23–5.

and in the media, and the whole subject of social control. Unfortunately almost nothing systematic has been written on yeshivas in interwar Poland as a general phenomenon.[8] The topic of strictly Orthodox Jewish education in Poland and the various experiments involving the integration of secular studies into the curriculum would be well worth studying in greater detail.[9] In this chapter, however, I can only trace the spread of yeshiva study among hasidim.

Yeshivas were important institutions for a number of reasons. For their students, study in a yeshiva was often a formative experience. Many intellectual movements began among these students, and the friendships and influences formed during these years could shape a lifetime. For the *rashei yeshivah*, the leaders of the yeshivas, the institution was also important, though often they also became leaders within the wider community.

Many of the organizational efforts of emerging Orthodoxy were devoted to the development and maintenance of yeshivas, though in the nineteenth century good arguments could be raised against the establishment of yeshivot on the grounds that they were expensive to run and not really necessary. Had yeshivas been crucial for the transmission of talmudic knowledge, investing in them would have been viewed as unavoidable, but they were not a precondition for talmudic scholarship or the training of qualified rabbis. In the early modern period, before 1648, Polish Jewry had been noted for its famous yeshivas but, for reasons that are still not very clear, they disappeared after the mid-seventeenth century, and yet in subsequent generations in Poland there were, nonetheless, many important talmudic scholars. At the beginning of the nineteenth century, the accepted pattern for a young Jew, hasidic and non-hasidic alike, had been to study in *ḥeder* until he was able to study Talmud more or less on his own. Then came independent study in a *beit midrash*. This might be under the ad hoc supervision of local rabbis or scholars who sometimes gave regular lectures or Talmud classes in the *beit midrash*, but where lectures were given they were regarded as peripheral to independent

---

[8] The phenomenon is not unknown. It is referred to in, *inter alia*, Eshkoli, 'Hasidism in Poland' (Heb.), 137. There are, of course, sources on individual yeshivas and on individuals related to yeshivas, but no detailed or general survey. I gleaned much valuable material from Suraski, *Teachers of Torah* (Heb.). The author is not obsessed with citing sources precisely or with clarifying dates—to put it mildly—but nonetheless it is a very useful source. A short but very enlightening article that would be worth translating into English is Wunder, 'Yeshivas in Galicia' (Heb.). There are a number of valuable studies on individual yeshivas in Mirsky (ed.), *Jewish Institutions of Higher Learning in Europe* (Heb.). Perhaps the best place to start reading on the topic is Ben-Zion Gold's memoir 'Religious Education in Poland'. Without footnotes and modestly written, it says more than many scholarly studies. On Lithuanian yeshivas in Poland and Lithuania in this period see Klibansky, 'Lithuanian Yeshivas' (Heb.).

[9] See e.g. Evron, 'The Rabbinate and the Yeshivas in the National Religious Education in Poland between the Two World Wars' (Heb.).

study, to which it was assumed a truly capable student would devote himself in order to master talmudic literature. Through private study of the classical texts, supplemented by reading commentaries and by conversations with learned scholars and occasional lessons, a student could become a *talmid ḥakham*, or recognized scholar.[10] Communal support for Talmud study and the assiduousness of the students ensured the constant supply of candidates for the educational Jewish elite, and it was therefore not at all clear that formal study (in a yeshiva) was necessary.

There were additional reasons for hasidim not to develop yeshivas. The rise of the yeshiva in the Lithuanian context at the end of the nineteenth century seems to have been related to a crisis in mitnagdic society over commitment to talmudic study among the younger generation of the intellectual elite. It was commonly assumed, probably correctly, that study in yeshivas helped prevent young people from abandoning traditional patterns.[11] This sense of crisis does not seem to have been as widespread in the late nineteenth century among hasidim. While in the Russian empire the power of the communal rabbi had been undermined by the institution of 'crown' or government rabbis, the power of the *admor*, or hasidic *rebbe*, appears to have been less in decline in the course of the nineteenth century. Hasidic communities also appear to have been less affected by trends towards modernization than were non-hasidic ones, but this is a topic that merits a separate study.[12] In the absence of threat, or with little perceived threat, there was little incentive to take major organizational steps. As we shall see, this equanimity was to change drastically in the period between the two world wars. An additional potential problem was that a yeshiva could serve as a power base for an aspiring rival to an *admor*, or for rights of succession.

It should be emphasized that the differences between a yeshiva and a *beit midrash* were not always obvious to contemporaries, even though they could have long-term implications. This is clear especially if we compare a yeshiva without a dormitory and dining hall (and most yeshivas lacked these facilities) and a *beit midrash*. It could be maintained that study in a *beit midrash* where a renowned town rabbi gave a regular class was not significantly different from

[10] This issue may sound familiar to those who question the point of hearing lectures in universities when the words of the lecturer could just as easily be read as heard.

[11] This is a central theme in my book *Lithuanian Yeshivas of the Nineteenth Century*. While it is clear to me that there was a sense of crisis at the end of the century, I am not at all convinced that there was a similar sense at the beginning of the 19th century when the first modern Lithuanian yeshivas were founded.

[12] It should be emphasized that in this case perceptions were as important as realities. Even if it could be shown that in the late 19th century an equal number or percentage of hasidim were affected by modernization as of non-hasidim, if this was not generally known then it would not have been acted upon.

study in a yeshiva where a less renowned *rosh yeshivah* gave a regular class. In both cases students ate *teg* and arranged their own housing. The difference was to a large extent one of responsibility. A student in a yeshiva accepted the authority of the head of the yeshiva, and in return expected the leadership to try to meet his needs, both spiritual and material. The responsibilities of a *rosh yeshivah* with regard to his students went beyond those of the teacher, who could walk into a *beit midrash* and then walk out. A teacher in a *beit midrash*, even if he voluntarily involved himself with the needs of students, did so knowing that he was not duty-bound to do so. By accepting responsibility for students, the head of a yeshiva also took on himself authority (and responsibility) with regard to their behaviour and conduct. Thus the transition from a framework of *batei midrash* to yeshivas is not necessarily as dramatic institutionally as it is psychologically. The authority implied within the framework of a yeshiva was a valuable tool in the struggle to maintain the loyalty of students to traditional values and practices.

HASIDIC YESHIVAS BEFORE THE FIRST WORLD WAR

Hasidic yeshivas, like most social phenomena, did not develop overnight. The first were established before the First World War. In most cases they clearly arose out of concern with contemporary developments and a desire to teach. However, they were isolated and their founders were not always persistent. Some were short-lived and were known only locally, while others would close and only reopen after a long break. This suggests that while the founders saw yeshivas as important, they were not necessarily regarded as essential.[13] Almost all were closed during the course of the First World War and the process had to begin almost from scratch in the reborn independent Polish state. Although the pre-war yeshivas had little lasting impact, they indicated the growing sense that institutional or educational change was necessary, even in hasidic circles, and they were evidence of the potential for such change.[14] A survey of key cases shows these tendencies.

Congress Poland

One of the first hasidic yeshivas was established in 1896 in Minsk Mazowiecki (Novominsk, near Warsaw) by the first *admor* of Novominsk, Rabbi Jacob

---

[13] See e.g. the following cases described in Suraski, *Teachers of Torah* (Heb.) on the yeshiva of Rabbi Jacob Weidenfeld in Grzymałów (i. 256, 265); on the yeshiva of Rabbi Sha'ul Zolberman (iv. 208); on Rabbi Tsevi Einhorn in Mstów (i. 280–1); on the yeshiva of Slonim hasidism (i. 178).

[14] Little scholarly work has been written in English on Polish hasidim in the late 19th–early 20th century. An exception is Bacon, 'Prolonged Erosion, Organization and Reinforcement'.

Perlov, who was born in 1847 and had moved to Novominsk in 1872. The *rosh yeshivah* was Rabbi Moses Mass from Siemiatycze, who had been educated in Lithuania but had been attracted to hasidism. The yeshiva was housed in the substantial *beit midrash* of the *admor* and may have had a dormitory and restaurant. In time it was attended by about 200 students. However, the yeshiva seems to have had little fame or influence and it closed during the First World War. After the war, the *admor* moved to Warsaw and the yeshiva was not reopened.[15]

Far better known was the yeshiva of Sochaczew founded by Rabbi Abraham Bornstein (1839–1910), who became famous for his book of responsa, *Avnei nezer* (Precious Stones). The yeshiva was founded around 1883, when Rabbi Bornstein was appointed rabbi of the city. Thus he was rabbi, *admor*, and head of the yeshiva. One of the star students was Aryeh Tsevi Fromer, himself a Sochaczew hasid. Fromer entered the yeshiva at the age of 14 and studied there for five years, becoming very close to the *admor*. When Rabbi Abraham's son inherited the post of *admor* on the death of his father in 1910, he separated the positions of *admor* and *rosh yeshiva* and appointed Rabbi Fromer, then 26, to the latter post. The appointment did not last for long because the yeshiva closed during the First World War.[16]

One of the best-known talmudists in hasidic circles was Rabbi Yitshak Zelig Morgenstern, who became the rabbi of Sokołów Podlaski in his early thirties and founded a yeshiva there in 1899. It was one of the first hasidic yeshivas. He imported Lithuanian talmudists, who had a reputation for sharp-mindedness, and the yeshiva was successful. It was closed in 1906, apparently because of the revolutionary events in that fateful year. Why it was not reopened until after the First World War is not clear.[17]

Establishment of a yeshiva was one of the first steps taken when Rabbi Abraham Mordekhai Alter (1866–1948) of Ger (Góra Kalwaria) became leader of the Ger hasidim in 1905. The yeshiva was named Darkhei No'am (Pleasant Ways), and in a pamphlet published in 1908 Rabbi Alter portrayed it as a means of meeting the crisis of the time.[18] In the course of three years the number of students reached 300. The programme of study concentrated on Talmud, and weekly tests were given to the students. Visiting rabbis at the

---

[15] Suraski, *Teachers of Torah* (Heb.), viii. 180–4; and see *Recordbooks of the Jewish Communities: Poland* (Heb.), ed. Dąbrowska et al., iv. 275.

[16] For a biography of Fromer, see Suraski, *The Last Polish Ge'onim* (Heb.).

[17] Suraski, *Teachers of Torah* (Heb.), iv. 250–1; see also id., *History of Torah Education* (Heb.), 319.

[18] In his *History of the Jews in Warsaw* (Yid.), iii. 362, Shatzky wrote that Yitshak Meir Rothenberg Alter, the first Gerer *rebbe* (d. 1866) was responsible for the foundation of many yeshivas in Warsaw, but these seem to have been small or ephemeral institutions. In any case, they did not have a long-term impact on Talmud study in Poland.

court of Rabbi Alter were invited to give guest lectures to the students and to engage in discussions with them, which provided a means of demonstrating to these visitors the high level of achievement of the students and indirectly of the whole hasidic group. The impact of the institution is reflected in the fact that, according to the yeshiva administration, in the course of three years the students had been tested by no less than 200 rabbis. The yeshiva itself was headed by Rabbi Mendel Alter, the brother of the *admor*. Instead of eating *teg*, the students in Ger were given 'bread in the morning and meat at night' by the yeshiva, and plans were made to build a dormitory and a dining hall for the students, though the outbreak of the First World War prevented their implementation.

Since one of the reasons for the founding of the yeshiva was a concern about the influence of the outside world and not necessarily a concern for improving the quality of Talmud study, it is not surprising that one of the criteria for admission to the yeshiva in Ger was that a potential student should not have been exposed to secular influences or have shown a desire in that direction. Students were not allowed to return to the yeshiva after vacations unless they were explicitly invited to do so, which provided an opportunity to gracefully expel students whose behaviour was not regarded as up to par. The success of the yeshiva was generally recognized and by 1911 a branch was opened in Warsaw. However, the outbreak of the First World War led to its closure.[19]

The first yeshiva of the Aleksandrów hasidim was founded by the *admor* Rabbi Shemuel Tsevi Danziger in 1912. It was located in the *beit midrash*, where young hasidim had previously studied informally. In the yeshiva students ate *teg* as before. The advantage of the yeshiva structure was seen as providing greater supervision. As in Ger and in other hasidic yeshivas there was a regular system of tests. Students were tested every Saturday night, and the examiners recorded their impressions in a notebook that each student kept. The yeshiva was disbanded in the course of the First World War and reopened only in 1925. This time lag suggests that in these years Aleksandrów hasidim felt that yeshiva study was advantageous but not absolutely essential.[20]

Galicia

Perhaps the first major yeshiva in western Galicia was that founded in Bobowa by Rabbi Shelomoh Halberstam (1847–1906) in 1880. There were

[19] See the anonymous *The Great and Famous Yeshiva Institution Darkhei No'am* (Heb.), 10–6, and Suraski and Segal, *Rosh golat ari'el*, i. 222–34.

[20] Makover, *Faithful Shepherd* (Heb.), ch. 2.

about seventy students in the yeshiva in 1888, but little is known about its later development,[21] and it was apparently not long-lived. Rabbi Halberstam's son Ben-Zion (1873–1941) became *admor* in 1905 and immediately set about founding *shtiblakh* (small *batei midrash* usually affiliated with a specific hasidic group) and a yeshiva in Bobowa which functioned until 1914. What led Rabbi Ben-Zion Halberstam to found the yeshiva was clearly the threats from contemporary society in the form of the loss of interest in traditional values and not simply a desire to improve the level of study.[22]

One of the first yeshivas in eastern Galicia was founded by Rabbi Pinhas Halevi Horowitz of Radzyn (Radzyn). The yeshiva, named Torat Hayim, was founded in 1905 in response to the perceived decline of Torah study following the Haskalah. It was carefully organized and a detailed book of *takanot* (regulations) was published. Students were tested weekly and studied Talmud, Torah, halakhah, and ethics, and even—though grudgingly on the part of the administration—writing and some practical skills. Students received a certificate at the end of each period of study, which seems to reflect the influence of the modern school.[23] Needy students were given meals in an organized kitchen and were also housed. The organizers planned to publish an annual volume of the new halakhic insights (*ḥidushim*) of the students. Although this yeshiva did not become important outside its immediate region, it reflects an awareness of the need for yeshivas and the potential for their development, and the model of Radzyn was followed by Rabbi Aryeh Leib Horowitz in Stanisławów in 1906[24] and Rabbi Shalom Mordekhai Schwadron in Brzeżany.

Bełz hasidim had no yeshivas before the First World War, nor to a large extent in the interwar period. Students, called *yoshvim* (literally, sitters), would come to Bełz to study, but there was no formal yeshiva.[25] However, there were Bełz hasidim who established yeshivas. The most important of these was probably Rabbi Abraham Ya'akov Halevi Horowitz, known as the Gaon of Probużna. He founded a yeshiva in the town of Probużna (near Tarnopol in eastern Galicia) after he accepted a position there as rabbi. He

[21] See the newspaper *Maḥzikei hadat* (21 Shevat 5688), 1–3, cited in Wunder, 'Yeshivas in Galicia' (Heb.), 183–4.

[22] Ehrenberg, *Arzei halevanon*, 3. The book includes personal details of the student body, and a detailed analysis of the data might reveal some interesting patterns. There is much interesting material in Goldman and Beigel (eds.), *The Western Light* (Heb.), which is a collection of photographs and documents relating to R. Ben-Zion Halberstam.

[23] See the *takanot* of the yeshiva printed around 1910, *Sefer takanot ushemot haḥaverim*. The book is apparently very rare and the copy in the Jewish National University Library (R80 *A5Z3*) is missing its title page. On this volume see also Wunder, 'Yeshivas in Galicia' (Heb.), 98.

[24] On this yeshiva see the very perceptive analysis of Mondshine, *Hatsofeh ledoro*, 58–72.

[25] See Klapholtz, *The Hasidic Leaders of Bełz* (Heb.), iii. 346–7, for a description of *yoshevim* (yeshiva students) without the use of the term *yeshiva*.

was noted for his long lectures, which implies that the emphasis was less on independent than on guided study.[26]

Regions Bordering on Poland

The Habad (Lubavitch) group within hasidism had a reputation for encouraging talmudic study and knowledge. However, this study was usually carried out in the informal setting of the *beit midrash*. In 1897 the *admor* Rabbi Shalom Dov Ber Schneersohn (1866–1920) established a yeshiva named Tomekhei Temimim (Upholders of Perfection) in Lubavitch. It was headed by his son Rabbi Yosef Yitshak (1880–1950). The programme of study centred on Talmud, but the systematic study of Habad hasidic texts was also introduced. In this respect it differed from many other hasidic yeshivas that were to be founded in the following years. Within some years of its founding, branches of the yeshiva were set up in various locations, changing it from an individual institution into a network. By 1911 there were apparently 300 students aged between 13 and 18 at Tomekhei Temimim.[27] Lubavitch was in the war zone during the First World War and the yeshiva moved first to Rostov and then to Kremenchug. It was then forced to go underground with the communist takeover. The real growth in later years was to be in Poland.[28]

There were parallel developments in Romanian hasidism. The *admor* of Vizhnitsa, Rabbi Yisra'el Hager, founded a yeshiva in Vizhnitsa in 1903 known as Ahavat Yisra'el (Love of Israel). It was the only yeshiva in Bucovina, and Rabbi Hager energetically recruited students. The classes were given by his four sons and other Talmud teachers. In time his sons founded yeshivas in Viszova, Grosswardein (Oradea), Vizhnitsa, and Siret. The *admor* himself tested students every week. Students took the tests very seriously because the results were publicized weekly on a bulletin board in the *beit hamidrash*. The yeshiva was closed in 1914 and reopened in 1922 by Rabbi Yisra'el's son Eliezer.[29]

YESHIVAS IN THE INTERWAR PERIOD

For a post-Holocaust generation it is sometimes difficult to imagine the widespread sense of destruction in the early years after the First World War.[30] There was a general feeling that traditional society had been irreparably

[26] Suraski, *Teachers of Torah* (Heb.), 192–8.

[27] For a detailed study of the yeshiva see Lurie, 'Lubavitch and its Wars' (Heb.). See also the anonymous report in the Lubavitch children's magazine *Ha'ah*, 23 (9 Iyar of 1911), 6, and subsequent issues; *Bericht über Tendenz, Organisation und Verwaltung der von Rabbiner S. D. Schneersohn*, 15.

[28] Zeidman, 'Yeshivas of Lubavitch' (Heb.).   [29] Roth, *Kadosh yisra'el* (Heb.), 48–50.

[30] In *The Politics of Tradition*, Gershon Bacon puts this in a broad context. The superb dissertation of Rachel Manekin, 'The Growth and Development of Jewish Orthodoxy in Galicia'

swept away. The dislocations of the war years had affected hundreds of thousands of Jews. Many, if not most, of the hasidic leaders spent these years away from their traditional seats—whether in Vienna, as was the case for many Galician rabbis, or elsewhere. The migration, poverty, and splitting of families, together with the heady atmosphere of revolution and intellectual change, contributed in many cases to a collapse of traditional authority and to new patterns of behaviour, especially among the hasidic youth. In this atmosphere of crisis patterns of education changed. The once isolated cases of yeshivas established by hasidic courts became the norm, and new organizational frameworks were developed to meet the perceived urgency of the situation.

It would be very difficult to trace the exact sequence of the foundation of hasidic yeshivas in interwar Poland and to provide a full list of these institutions,[31] but the broad picture is clearly indicated by a survey of the main yeshivas founded at the time. It shows that during this period, yeshiva study among hasidim became the norm rather than the exception. What is signifi-cant is not which court was first to develop yeshivas, but the general phenom-enon and the characteristics of the hasidic yeshivas. While hasidic yeshivas were usually sponsored by specific hasidic courts, the students in a given yeshiva were not necessarily all followers of the sponsoring court. Very often followers of one court would study in yeshivas run by other courts.

There was a general sense of crisis among hasidic circles and concern for maintaining the loyalty of the younger generation. Almost every important hasidic court organized study for young people within the framework of yeshivas, both at the seat of the hasidic court and as a network of yeshivas. In this respect the networks paralleled those of hasidic *shtiblakh*.

Interwar hasidic yeshivas were not noted for innovative methods of Talmud study, nor were there, in most cases, innovations in terms of incorporating hasidic values or topics into the study programme. As one knowledgeable chronicler of the history of religious life in Poland put it, the approach of the hasidic yeshivas was to keep to the tradition of *harifut* (sharp-mindedness) and the study of practical halakhah.[32] However, hasidim did break new ground

(Heb.), has much to say on previous developments. The dissertation of Robert Shapiro, 'Jewish Self-Government of Lodz 1914–1939', which is richly deserving of publication, is a fine case-study of this phenomenon.

[31] One of the more telling pieces of evidence for the limitations on our knowledge of a period that is so close to ours is the fact that Goldman and Beigel, the editors of *The Western Light* (Heb.) and dedicated Bobower hasidim, have tried to document each of the Bobower yeshivas, but for at least two yeshivas, which unquestionably existed, they were not able to determine even the names of their heads because not a single survivor, either from the yeshiva or from the town, could be found after the Holocaust. (See pp. 12–13.)

[32] Suraski, *History of Torah Education* (Heb.), 335.

regarding the framework of study. Interwar hasidic yeshivas created unprecedented public ceremonies of ordination which marked the end of a
stage of study. In Lublin there was a celebration in which selected students
were given the title *tsurba derabanan* (literally, one who has caught fire—
by associating with rabbis), which was presumably the equivalent of a
university degree.[33] This innovation resembled the graduation ceremony of
a secular school. It contrasted with contemporary Lithuanian yeshivas, for
example, where little attention was given to halakhah, and where there were
certainly no graduation ceremonies which could imply an end to the course
of study—for the study of Talmud was seen as endless.

There was little interest among staff or students in secular study alongside the study of Talmud. There were generally no secret maskilim (followers
of the Jewish Enlightenment) among the students, as had been the case in
Lithuania. However, the leaders of yeshivas actively employed the print
media. It was very common for the students of a yeshiva to publish a journal
with short talmudic *ḥidushim* by teachers and students, as well as unpublished
materials from previous generations and news of the yeshiva.[34]

Although study in a yeshiva was not necessarily limited to followers of a
given *admor*, hasidic yeshivas were commonly run by the *admor* or by his
designated successor. This policy neutralized the threat that a yeshiva could
serve as an alternative power base to the authority of the *admor*. Moreover,
yeshivas offered respected positions for a designated successor or unsuccessful candidate for leadership.[35]

The hasidic yeshiva was not just a framework for education. It was a
reflection of the power of a hasidic group, it had the potential for the recruitment of new adherents to a hasidic group and, by inviting guest lecturers, it
provided a showcase for the achievements of a hasidic group.[36]

Congress Poland

Yeshivas started reopening in Poland even before the end of the German
occupation. In 1916 Rabbi Yitshak Zelig Morgenstern, the *admor* of Sokołów
Podlaski who had founded the yeshiva mentioned earlier which closed in
1905, announced in the newspaper *Der Yud* the opening of another yeshiva,
Beit Yisra'el, named in memory of his father. The yeshiva was run by his son
and son-in-law. The students ate *teg* and slept in *batei midrash*, but later he set
up facilities for housing and food. Rabbi Morgenstern originally covered the

---

[33] Suraski, *Teachers of Torah* (Heb.), v. 254.
[34] On this see below.   [35] See e.g. the case of Ger mentioned above.
[36] See the description in Suraski and Segal, *Rosh golat ari'el*, i. 232–4. The somewhat cynical
analysis of the social function of visiting lecturers at a yeshiva is mine.

costs himself but went on to raise funds, at first from friends and later, after 1927, in the United States.[37]

The Metivta (Aramaic for 'yeshiva') in Warsaw was founded in 1919 with the encouragement of Rabbi Abraham Mordekhai Alter of Ger and became one of the leading institutions in Warsaw. Students, all of whom were over the age of 13, were divided into classes and given weekly tests. An important innovation was the adoption of a five-year programme of study which included the Bible, eighteen tractates of the Talmud, Jewish law (*Shulḥan arukh*), as well as minimal secular studies such as Polish. With regard to general studies the Metivta was an exception, for in most other yeshivas these were not taught. Their introduction was very possibly the result of a government demand, but the influence of the model of the non-Jewish gymnasium in terms of supervision, testing, and a rational curriculum is very clear.[38] Not all were pleased with the programme, not just because of the introduction of a few hours of secular studies. The well-known rabbi Menahem Zemba was not happy since it emphasized halakhah over depth.[39] His was the response of a traditionalist who grew up in a very different setting.

In 1925 the yeshiva of the Aleksandrów hasidim, Beit Yisra'el, reopened. Already in 1920 the *admor* Rabbi Yitshak Menahem Danziger had called for increased Torah study among his students and for *shtiblakh* to be heated.[40] The *nasi* (president) of the yeshiva—a new title—was Rabbi Avraham Hayim Danziger, the brother of the *admor*. In the student journal of his yeshiva the claim was made that the study of Torah had moved from the *beit midrash* to the yeshiva because of the bad influence of the wider society, and that the yeshivas should be seen as fortresses of faith, once again emphasizing their role as guardians of the values of new generations rather than tools for improved study.[41] The reinvitation system (a postcard sent during the vacation to invite good students to return to the yeshiva) was employed in the Aleksandrów yeshiva, making it easy to exclude undesirable students. The postcard also gave a grade.[42] In Aleksandrów, the practice began (as in other circles as well) to go to the yeshiva at the age of 13, to study there for about three years, and then to continue study in a *kibuts*, a framework for advanced students. In the *kibuts* students studied *Shulḥan arukh* in addition to talmudic studies. In 1931 a dining hall was set up to replace the *teg* system, which was seen as demeaning and also as exposing students to potentially threatening influences.

The son of the *admor* of Aleksandrów, Rabbi Yerahmi'el Yisra'el Yitshak, actively supported the establishment of branches. In 1922 a branch was

---

[37] Suraski, *Teachers of Torah* (Heb.), iv. 250–7.
[38] See Anon., *The Founding of the Great and Famous Yeshiva Metivta* (Heb.).
[39] See Zemba, 'The Metivta in Warsaw' (Heb.), 379. The article makes fascinating reading.
[40] Suraski, *Teachers of Torah* (Heb.), vi. 98.
[41] Yakubovits, *Nehor shraga* (Heb.), 39. [42] Makover, *Faithful Shepherd* (Heb.), 228–9.

founded in Łódz (a place where many Aleksandrów hasidim lived) that was so successful that each class had to be housed in a different *shtibl*. Ultimately in 1932 a three-storey building with a dormitory was constructed, and by the outbreak of the Second World War there were 400 students in this branch alone. Branches were set up in other locations as well, especially in the 1930s. In some towns public tests of students were carried out, which served both as an incentive to study, and as publicity for the yeshiva and indirectly for that branch of hasidism.[43] On religious holidays students from all of these branches would gather at the court of the *admor* in Aleksandrów. This served to strengthen their group consciousness and social contacts, and in order to strengthen this identification, a general council of students in the various Aleksandrów yeshivas was set up.[44] The attempts to respond to the perceived challenges also led to the foundation of youth movements—a clear adoption of the framework so familiar in the secular movements.[45]

Smaller courts also established yeshivas. Such was the case with regard to the *admor* of Piaseczno, Rabbi Kalonymos Kalman Shapira, who is known today for such books as *Esh kodesh* (Holy Fire) and for his writings in the Warsaw Ghetto regarding behaviour under Nazi rule. He inherited the position of *admor* in 1913 at the age of 24, and in 1923 he founded a yeshiva. The programme of study in his yeshiva emphasized preparation for the rabbinate and in 1927 he marked the first graduation of students with a celebration and public ordination. In his yeshiva, as in many others, there was a student publication.[46]

Habad had established a yeshiva well before the First World War, as noted above, but the disruptions caused by the war and the Russian Revolution led to the effective end of Habad yeshivas in their traditional home region. However, after the war there was an upsurge of Habad yeshivas in Poland. A yeshiva was founded in Otwock in 1921, but apparently did not have a great impact. Habad activity was stimulated when the *admor*, Rabbi Yosef Yitshak Schneersohn, moved from Riga to Warsaw in 1933 and almost im-

[43] Yakubovits, *Nehor shraga* (Heb.), 39. [44] Ibid. 46.

[45] The question of youth movements in interwar Poland has been studied extensively for non-Orthodox movements, especially Zionist ones (see e.g. Lamm, *The Zionist Youth Movements* (Heb.)), but hardly any attention has been given to Orthodox, non-Zionist groups. The foundation of youth movements was related to the organization of Agudat Yisra'el and to the desire to create an alternative to movements that were perceived as non-traditional. However, frameworks outside Agudat Yisra'el also recognized the need for such activities. For example, a non-party organization, Tiferet Bahurim was founded in which Stolin hasidim participated. See Israeli (Kula), *The Dynasty of Karlin-Stolin* (Heb.), 338; the claim that the organization was non-party is in the source. See also p. 383.

[46] Zilberschlag, *Memorial Volume for Rabbi Kalonymos Kalman Shapira* (Heb.). On the yeshiva activity of Rabbi Shapira, see pp. 16 and 36. On Rabbi Shapira in general, see Polen, *The Holy Fire*.

mediately founded a yeshiva. The yeshiva was administered to a large extent by the *admor*'s son-in-law, Rabbi Gur Aryeh. Its new building had a dormitory for out-of-town students, which was especially necessary since many were apparently refugees from communist-controlled areas. The yeshiva publicly celebrated the granting of ordination to students in a ceremony called *ḥag hasemikhah* (celebration of ordination).[47]

Eastern Poland

In 1918 the Torat Hesed yeshiva was founded in Baranowicze by Rabbi Mosheh Midner under the guidance of the *admor* of Slonim. It attempted to synthesize Lithuanian and Polish approaches to Talmud study. The Talmud was taught with a concern for depth, clear thinking, logical analysis of the text, and emphasis on the basic ideas of each literary unit. At the same time the yeshiva tried to preserve the hasidic enthusiasm and was a pioneer in developing this synthesis. Rabbi Yosef Mordochovsky was appointed head of the yeshiva, but Rabbi Avraham Shemuel Hirshovitz, grandson of the famous Rabbi Eliezer Gordon of Telz, was brought in from the Lithuanian yeshiva in Telz to be the senior Talmud lecturer. In time a network of branches in other towns was established, and in Baranowicze a dining hall was set up.[48]

In 1922 the first yeshiva of Karlin-Stolin hasidism was established in Stolin. The founder, Rabbi Mosheh of Karlin, took a Slonim hasid to be the *rosh yeshivah*. The stated goal was to attract graduates of the local *talmud torah*. It quickly grew into an institution of about 100 students.[49]

Galicia

The hasidim of Bobowa had set up a yeshiva before the First World War. It had closed in the course of the war but was reopened after it under the direction of the son of the Bobower *rebbe*. In the interwar period there were about 300 students in the main yeshiva, with many others in branches. The students from the branches would come to Bobowa for sabbaths and holidays. By the 1930s the movement claimed that there were about sixty branches and 1,500 students. The centre in Bobowa carefully supervised the activity in the branches and sent out teachers to teach in the branches, which not only

[47] Mirsky (ed.), *Jewish Institutions of Higher Learning in Europe* (Heb.), 348. According to the anonymous report in the pocket calendar published by the Lubavitch yeshiva *Tomekhei temimim* in Warsaw for the year 5697 (1936–37) (Heb.), 11–12, the yeshiva was re-established in Warsaw in 1921, and in 1926 a new building with a kitchen and dormitory space was provided. In 1936 the *kibuts*, or group of older students who studied entirely on their own, and the highest two classes were moved to Otwock. At the time of the report there were about 250 students in Warsaw and eight branch yeshivas, all of which channelled their best graduates to Otwock.

[48] See Weinberg, *Holy Memory* (Heb.), esp. 84–5, 89, 92, 115.

[49] Israeli (Kula), *The Dynasty of Karlin-Stolin* (Heb.), 336.

guaranteed supervision but also gave the hasidic court in Bobowa many opportunities to provide jobs for young talents. A special organization named Tomekhei De'oraita (Supporters of the Torah) was set up to raise funds for support of the yeshivas.[50]

One of the most influential networks for Torah study among hasidim was that established by Rabbi Shelomoh Hanokh Hakohen Rabinowich, the *admor* of Radomsko. On Lag Ba'omer (a minor holiday between Pesach and Shavuot) in 1926 he gathered his hasidim in Kraków and informed them that what the younger generation needed was yeshivas and not *shtiblakh*. He began to set up yeshivas and delegated his son-in-law to develop the system. Since Rabbi Rabinowich was very wealthy he covered many of the expenses of the yeshivas out of his own pocket, but he was opposed to direct publicity of his role in the foundation of the yeshivas. Like others, he actively encouraged the development of a monthly journal, which he thought would stimulate students. The natural competition among students, in his opinion, would stimulate them to study more. On the eve of the Holocaust there were forty-three branches in the network with about 3,000 students.[51]

In Galicia as well smaller hasidic groups set up yeshivas. For example, a yeshiva was founded at the hasidic court in Ostrowiec. The yeshiva, Beit Me'ir, was founded around 1930.[52] There were also yeshivas in Kraków, Przemysl, Rzeszów, Jarosław, Złoczów, Żydaczów, and Turka.[53] In large cities, as in Warsaw, there were a number of yeshivas.[54]

One of the best-known hasidic yeshivas was that of Rabbi Dov Ber Weidenfeld in Trzebinia (Chebin). He was close to many hasidic dynasties, though he was not identified with any particular one. He kept the yeshiva small and did not have more than 100 students. Formal study was at the centre of the curriculum. There were two classes a day, one on Talmud and the other on Jewish law. He did not allow his students to eat *teg*; those who had funds paid for their own meals and were expected to donate towards the meals of their poorer classmates. When Rabbi Weidenfeld accepted a position at the well-known yeshiva in Lublin (see below), the leadership of the yeshiva passed on to his sons.[55]

There remained hasidic groups that had no yeshivas. Bełz was probably the most prominent of the hasidic courts that had no yeshiva. As noted above,

---

[50] Suraski, *Teachers of Torah* (Heb.), v. 78–90.

[51] See Zilberberg, *The Dynasty of Radomsk* (Heb.), ch. 9. He assumes that there were 4,000 students in the network of the Radomsko yeshivas. Suraski, *Teachers of Torah* (Heb.), v. 159–79, also describes the work of the *admor* from Radomsko, though he notes that the total number of students in the network was 3,000.   [52] Suraski, *Teachers of Torah* (Heb.), iii. 98.

[53] These cities are cited in Wunder, 'Yeshivas in Galicia' (Heb.), 9.

[54] See Zemba, 'The Metivta in Warsaw' (Heb.), 378.

[55] Suraski, *Teachers of Torah* (Heb.), viii. 58–145.

there were informal frameworks for study there, but not a yeshiva. Another hasidic group that did not set up yeshivas in the interwar period was that of Lubartów. Rabbi Moses Yehi'el Elimelekh Rabinowitz is reported to have organized students in special *shtiblakh* to study in accordance with a plan he set up. There were Lubartów *shtiblakh*, called *kibuts baḥurim* (a gathering of young men), in a number of locations, including Warsaw. At the same time Rabbi Rabinowitz was on good terms with the leadership of the Yeshivat Hokhmei Lublin and hosted students from the yeshiva.[56] Geography was a factor. A contemporary observer noted that hasidic yeshivas were primarily for students who had left home, but that in interwar Warsaw most of the local Talmud students studied in local *shtiblakh* and not in yeshivas.[57]

Yeshivat Hokhmei Lublin

Unquestionably, the best-known hasidic yeshiva in interwar Poland was the Hokhmei Lublin yeshiva. The story of this institution has been well documented and therefore I will not go into its history in detail, though a systematic critical study is still lacking. This yeshiva was not formally affiliated with a hasidic court, but it attracted the elite of the hasidic yeshiva students in Poland and offered them ideal conditions for studying. It was located in an impressive building in Lublin, and the students were exposed to excellent teachers. However, for our purposes it is important to emphasize that it was not unique as a hasidic yeshiva but simply the best-known one.[58]

Despite the scope and fame of Hokhmei Lublin it, like all other yeshivas in Poland between the wars, suffered from chronic financial troubles. A vivid expression of such funding problems and of the dependence of Polish yeshivas on individual donors is found in a letter written in 1937 by the president of the yeshiva, Mosheh Friedman, to a wealthy kabbalist named Ya'akov Tierhauz. The latter had come to the conclusion, on the basis of kabbalistic texts, that the sabbath should begin on Friday morning at 11.30 a.m. rather than at sundown. This rather eccentric opinion, which meant that each sabbath would last for more than thirty hours, was understandably not very popular, and Tierhauz found it difficult to propagate his views. He then came up with an original idea. He approached the leadership of the Lublin yeshiva and offered to make a major donation to the yeshiva on condition that it adopt his views. Accepting this proposal would have led to many complications, if not a major controversy, but owing to the financial pressures of the yeshiva the president could not turn it down flatly. Instead, he offered to observe two sabbaths

---

[56] David Rabinowitz's introduction to Mosheh Rabinowitz's *Avodat halev*.

[57] Zemba, '*Shtiblakh* of Warsaw' (Heb.), 355–61.

[58] Two of the most recent (though non-critical) works on this yeshiva are Mandelboim, *The Yeshiva Hokhmei Lublin* (Heb.), and Halakhmi, *The Yeshiva Hokhmei Lublin and its Founder* (Heb.).

a year in accordance with Tierhauz's kabbalistic view. However, he would do this only after the donation was made. Apparently the money was not forthcoming, because we have no reports of such a schedule being imposed in the Lublin yeshiva, but the very willingness of the president to consider such an extreme proposal illustrates its desperate straits.[59]

New frameworks were developed in Poland for post-yeshiva study. These were often known as a *kibuts*—a clear echo of the kibbutzim in Palestine. For example, in Warsaw Rabbi Avraham Weinberg set up a *kibuts* in his house for graduates of the Sochaczew yeshiva.[60] Similar institutions existed in Lithuania and were termed *kolel*. As noted above, there was a *kibuts* in the interwar years in Aleksandrów. *Kibutsim* could be tied to a hasidic court or to a yeshiva, but this was not necessary.

POLISH YESHIVAS AND THE MEDIA

A common theme in the writings of hasidim who were involved in the foundation of yeshivas was the view that secular newspapers and literature were a central factor in the falling-away from tradition of the younger generation.[61] An obvious response to this diagnosis was to forbid the reading of such literature—and indeed such demands were made. However, a far more creative response was the publication of alternative newspapers and literature which would divert the readers from what was regarded as dangerous literature. This process had already begun in the nineteenth century with the publication of newspapers such as *Halevanon*. A variation on this approach that became well developed in the hasidic yeshivas of interwar Poland was the publication of journals by the students or administration of a yeshiva.

The publication of journals was justified as a means of encouraging creativity and stimulating students to achieve. However, it was also useful for other reasons. Subscriptions could be a source of funds,[62] albeit minimal, and journals could assist in fund-raising campaigns by serving as evidence for the importance of the institutions that sought funds. They were also a means of advertising the excellence of a yeshiva and the quality of its students—and its leaders. The number of journals published and their timing is an indication of the sensitivity of the hasidic educational institutions to the challenges from within and without. The list of journals published by hasidic yeshivas shown in Table 12.1 should make this clear. Efforts have been made to include only

---

[59] See Mandelboim, *The Yeshiva Hokhmei Lublin* (Heb.), 117–18.

[60] Suraski, *Teachers of Torah* (Heb.), vi. 16.

[61] See, for example, the fascinating volume of Turnowsky, *Truth and Faith* (Heb.), which brought many of the leading hasidic rabbis of the time together with Rabbi Hayim Soloveichik to warn the public to avoid secular newspapers and popular literature.

[62] I thank Meir Wunder for this insight.

Table 12.1 Journals published by hasidic yeshivas in Poland, 1913–1937

Year	Title	Place of publication	Sponsoring institution or hasidic movement
1913	*Hamefalpel*	Kraków	
1921	*Emek halakhah*	Warsaw	Students of the yeshiva Emek Halakhah
1925	*Degel hatse'irim*	Warsaw	Students of the batei midrash
1926	*Ohel mo'ed*	Izbica	
1926	*Or torah*		
1927	*Aseifat gedolim*	Nowy Sącz	
1927	*Beit yisra'el*	Łódz	
1928	*Halevanon*	Gorlice	
1930	*Hakerem*	Warsaw	Piaseczno movement
1930	*Keter torah*	Sosnowiec	Radomski movement
1930	*Kovets talmudi pilpuli*	Kołomyja	The yeshiva Or Torah, Stanisławów
1931	*Beit me'ir*	Kielce	Ostrowiec movement
1931	*Kerem beit shemu'el*	Piotrków	Aleksandrów movement
1931	*Teitsei torah*	Krynki	Students of the beit midrash
1933	*Mekabzel*	Lublin	Yeshivat Hokhmei Lublin
1934	*Beit avraham*	Warsaw	Sochaczew movement
1935	*Hatamim*	Warsaw	Habad movement
1937	*Halapid*	Warsaw	Metivta

Sources: Based on Lewin, *Treasury of Rabbinic Periodicals*, and on data from the online *Israel Union List of Serials* at <http://libnet.ac.il/~libnet/uls/ulsinfo.htm>.

publications of hasidic yeshivas and study circles. One interesting fact that should be noted is that almost all of these journals were published after 1924, the year the *Beit ya'akov* (House of Jacob) journal published by the Orthodox Beit Ya'akov girls' school movement first appeared. Many of the sisters of yeshiva students attended these schools and, while I know of no way of checking whether the fact that young women had a journal was an incentive for young men to call for journals, the timing is thought-provoking

FUNCTIONS AND METHODS OF THE INTERWAR POLISH YESHIVAS

Apart from the sense of crisis there may be subtle reasons that contributed to the adoption of the yeshiva framework by hasidim. The rise of yeshivas was concurrent with the rise of the Beit Ya'akov movement of schools for Orthodox girls, in both cases institutionalizing education for hasidic youth. Their growth came after a rise in the average age at marriage among Jews. In the early nineteenth century, and also much later, marriage in the early teens had been common among the religious/economic elite, but this pattern had almost disappeared by the end of the century. The 'postponement' of marriage among the elite extended the period of adolescence and ultimately required a new framework to provide the supervision and stability which marriage was presumed to offer.

Second, a yeshiva in a hasidic context has the potential for creating difficulties because it could serve as a rival to the hasidic court, as noted above. This problem was often deftly met by integrating it into the system and by staffing the yeshivas with individuals tied to the hasidic court. Indeed, in a period of change the yeshiva could be a useful source of patronage posts. However, hasidic yeshivas could also employ staff who identified with other hasidic dynasties, and would tolerate students who came from other dynasties and remained loyal to them. The yeshiva did not replace the dynamic of the individual ties to an *admor*, and the leaders of yeshivas refrained from heavy-handed demands of loyalty from students or staff, though they could be—and usually were—quite strict when it came to even minimal involvement with what were seen as secular activities.

Yeshivas were, as already mentioned, useful frameworks both for maintaining the status of hasidic groups and for recruiting adherents. Certainly once some hasidic courts established yeshivas, for others to refrain from following suit was to risk losing young hasidim who might be attracted by the social and educational benefits of study in a yeshiva, especially when it promised an end to the 'shame' of *essen teg*.

An important advantage of yeshivas over informal study was in fundraising. The virtues of a *beit midrash* system for Jewish communities—simplicity, reliance on local householders, lack of expenses for teachers, and so on—were a drawback if it was important to look for support outside the local community. Interwar Polish Jewry was impoverished, and it was necessary to seek support in the United States and in other centres of Jewish migration for educational frameworks in Poland. Jewish immigrants who were rapidly undergoing acculturation in the West and were familiar with formal education could readily understand the need to support schools of higher education in Poland and could be convinced to send funds. The *beit midrash* certainly did not fit the Western patterns of formal education, organized study, and certification of completion, but a yeshiva could be made to fit.

The advantages of yeshivas over *batei midrashim* held for institutional support as well. In interwar Poland much of the financial support for education was channelled through the Joint Distribution Committee (JDC) and similar frameworks. Formal educational institutions could provide the necessary documentation to apply for funds, whereas informal educational frameworks were at a clear disadvantage when it came to meeting bureaucratic criteria. Thus there was an incentive to develop yeshivas because not only did they promise an improvement in the educational level but they were also likely to receive financial support.

Hasidic and mitnagdic yeshivas were similar in many ways, and this was only natural given the proximity of the two, as well as the fact that the teachers in hasidic yeshivas were often the product of Lithuanian yeshivas. However, there were differences as well. As pointed out above, hasidic institutions innovated in certain structural areas, such as in providing certificates. The *musar* movement, which was very influential in interwar mitnagdic yeshivas, was not a factor in hasidic yeshivas, which employed hasidism for similar functions.[63] The dramatically innovative approaches to Talmud study which characterized the world of the mitnagdic yeshiva had generally little impact in the hasidic yeshivas. One has the impression that, for the hasidim, the study of Talmud was regarded as extremely valuable but as a means to an end, whether to know halakhah or simply to maintain adherence to traditional behaviour. In mitnagdic yeshivas the emphasis seems to have been more on Talmud study for its own sake.[64]

There were also more symbolic differences between hasidic and mitnagdic yeshivas. Students in hasidic yeshivas continued to wear the traditional dress, while mitnagdic yeshiva students wore modern dress. A quick look at photographs of yeshiva students makes it clear that mitnagdic students usually shaved (using halakhically approved means), while hasidic students grew beards. There also appear to have been differences with regard to the roles of husbands and wives.[65]

It is no easy task to measure the number of yeshivas or students in yeshivas in the interwar period. According to a publication from 1937 there were about 13,000 yeshiva students in the yeshivas supported by Agudat Yisra'el (an international movement of strictly Orthodox Jews founded in 1912) in

[63] See Shifman, *The Dwelling-Place of Torah* (Heb.), 28.

[64] This is a very complex topic with many implications for understanding the intellectual and religious worlds of both hasidim and mitnagedim. However, a careful analysis of these issues is beyond the scope of this study.

[65] It is reported that when R. Meir Shapira (founder of the famous yeshiva in Lublin) visited the author of the *Ḥafets ḥayim*, R. Yisra'el Meir Kagan (Hakohen), in Radun, he refused to stay as a guest at his house on the sabbath. The reason given was that R. Hakohen ate at the same table with his wife on the sabbath, and R. Shapira did not want to upset his routine, implying that R. Shapira would not have eaten at a table with a woman, and that R. Hakohen, out of respect for his guest, would have banished his wife from the table. See Halakhmi, *The Yeshiva Hokhmei Lublin and its Founder* (Heb.), 67. One may speculate that perhaps R. Shapira was afraid that R. Hakohen would *not* banish his wife. However, there are also contrary accounts. The famous mitnaged R. Velvele Soloveichik once went to visit R. Dov Ber Weidenfeld from Poland. Before arriving, one of R. Soloveichik's aides asked an assistant of R. Weidenfeld if it would be possible to ask his wife to leave the room during R. Soloveichik's visit. The quick reply was that R. Weidenfeld would not do such a thing for all the money in the world (Suraski, *Teachers of Torah* (Heb.), viii. 101), and the visit took place despite her presence. These stories are only anecdotes, but they raise issues that merit a detailed study.

the regions of Warsaw, Kraków, and Lwów,[66] which were mainly hasidic, and, including the Vilna region, a total of about 19,000 yeshiva students in all of Poland. Of course, not all hasidic yeshivas were supported by Agudat Yisra'el and some of the yeshiva students counted in the Vilna district were also hasidic.[67] According to a JDC report from 1936, there were about 16,000 yeshiva students in about 170 yeshivas.[68] This figure is a bit lower than the data from 1937, but is basically similar. It seems reasonable to assume that the total number of hasidic yeshiva students was somewhat less than 15,000, and that there were many more than mitnagdic yeshiva students.

What do these figures mean? To try to answer this question we must consider the context. In 1931 there was a total of about 140,000 young Jewish men in the age group 15–19. The younger cohorts were smaller than the older ones: there were about 30,000 19-year-olds but only about 22,000 15-year-olds.[69] If we assume that there were about 20,000 yeshiva students in Poland in the late 1930s, and that yeshiva students were generally aged 14–19, then very roughly the number of yeshiva students per cohort was somewhat more than 3,000. In 1934–5 the number of Jews receiving secondary education was about 30,000, which would be roughly 7,000 students per cohort. Although this figure includes males and females there is little doubt that there were more males in secondary schools, so that one can safely conclude that by the mid-1930s there were far more young Jewish males in secondary schools than in yeshivas,[70] despite the increase in yeshivas and the restrictions on Jewish enrolment in secondary schools.

[66] Chmielewski, 'Stan szkolnictwa wśród Żydów w Polsce', 4–5. Chmielewski cites the following figures: Choreb warszawski 10,077; Choreb wilenski 5,352; Centrala krakowska 2,139; Centrala lwowska 1,190. An Agudat Yisra'el report from the same year (cited by Kazdan, *The History of Jewish Education in Independent Poland* (Yid.), 463) indicated that there were 12,000 yeshiva students in the Choreb orthodox school network in Congress Poland and Galicia. Eck, 'The Educational Institutions of Polish Jewry', 19, cites a different Agudat Yisra'el publication which gives the same figures as Kazdan. These figures are close to those of Chmielewski.

[67] Wischnitzer, 'Documents on the Yeshivot of Eastern Europe' (Heb.), 359, notes that there were 64 students in 1930 at the hasidic yeshiva in Baranowicze. The article was continued in the next issue of *Talpiyot* and was to conclude with a description of the hasidic yeshivas, but the death of the author left the series uncompleted.

[68] Rozenhak, 'On the System of Jewish Education in Poland' (Heb.), 154. Joseph Marcus estimated that there were about 1,000 yeshivas in the early 1930s which educated about 30,000 young men between the ages of 14 and 20. This number probably included transition schools which were past the *ḥeder* level but not what would be called *yeshivot gevohot* ('higher yeshivas'). Marcus, *Social and Political History of the Jews in Poland*, 154.

[69] In a growing population one would expect the size of younger cohorts to be larger than the size of older ones. However, the decline in the size of cohorts in this case was not necessarily a result of a long-term decline in fertility but probably a by-product of the war years, since the 15-year-olds in 1930 were born in 1915 (*Statystyka Polski*, Drugi Powszechny Spis Ludnosci z dnia 9. xii. 1931, Seria C, zeszyt 94a, 42–3, table 15).

[70] Marcus, *Social and Political History of the Jews in Poland*, 149. Of course, there were not

In a generation where yeshivas trained only the elite of the Jewish community and the masses deferred to their leadership, these figures would say little about the future of that community. However, the function of yeshivas was to reproduce a society in a situation where outside yeshivas young men from traditional homes ran a real risk of being attracted to modernizing movements, and the numbers of yeshiva students can give us a clue to the potential size of that society. While the figures we have seen indicate an impressive achievement on the part of hasidic educators under very adverse conditions, they are clear evidence for the well-known fact that traditional Jewish society in Poland was declining in the 1930s.

Yeshivas were very much afraid of the threat of ideas from outside traditional society and made few efforts to attract back to tradition those who had 'strayed'. I have found almost no references in the literature to *ba'alei teshuvah* (those who grew up in a secular world but were attracted to tradition). The one exception is the *admor* of Bobowa, who made special efforts to assist students whose parents were irreligious and hence needed help in order to marry.[71] One story describes how he helped a student who came to Bobowa at the age of 20 without even being able to read Hebrew.[72] It may be that attracting students from non-traditional homes was a common phenomenon but was recorded only with regard to Bobowa. However, this does not seem likely; the policy of Ger to reject a student who had shown any interest in secular studies was probably more common. At this stage yeshivas were seeking not to attract the estranged but to hold on to what they had.

In certain respects, one can regard the hasidic yeshiva as a natural step in the process of the routinization of charisma as defined by Max Weber, and also in the creation of a closed society.[73] While hasidism in the eighteenth century may have been a movement of youth in revolt, in the 1920s and 1930s it was fear of the revolutionary potential of youth that motivated yeshiva leaders. The traditional system of *essen teg* was tenable only in a society in which prominent householders regarded Torah students as fulfilling important roles. With the decline of this assumption, *essen teg* either threatened exposure to non-traditional ideas or required eating at the homes of traditional families of low social status, which undermined the self-image of yeshiva students. It certainly appeared primitive in comparison to the cafeterias university students enjoyed. There was a need for kitchens and dor-

enough Jewish secondary schools for such numbers and most of these students did not study in Jewish schools. On the secondary education of Jews in interwar Poland, see the excellent Ph.D. thesis of the late Jacob Taitelbaum, 'Jewish High School Education' (Heb.).

[71] Goldman and Beigel (eds.), *The Western Light* (Heb.), 31. See also p. 23.   [72] Ibid. 82.

[73] On the contemporary developments—in many respects the continuation of developments that began in Poland—see e.g. Friedman, 'Haredim Confront the Modern City', and his volume *Haredi Society* (Heb.).

mitories if students were to be effectively isolated from the surrounding society. Housing was equally an issue. Sleeping on benches in a synagogue or *beit midrash* was demeaning, but renting rooms and the consequent absence of supervision gave students opportunities for deviant behaviour. Dormitories were the best housing solution, despite the costs and complications. Both dining halls and dormitories could be developed in yeshivas but not in *batei midrash*.

It is well known that many hasidim and mitnagedim adopted a common political programme in Poland between the wars, and were united from this point of view within the framework of Agudat Yisra'el. As we have now seen, this was not the only aspect of life in which the patterns of the two groups converged. The parallel development in the area of education was a creative response to unprecedented change and a vivid expression of the continued vitality of the hasidic movement. While the hasidic yeshivas could not have stopped the whole process of change, they were succeeding to the degree that many of the younger generation of hasidim remained committed to *admorim* and to hasidic behaviour. This process was cut off, and one can only speculate about what would have developed had it not been for the Holocaust.

PART III

THE RABBINATE

The Missing Rabbis of Eastern Europe

THE RABBINATE has long been one of the central institutions of Jewish communal life and, not surprisingly, it is widely regarded as having undergone a major crisis in almost every major Jewish community of the modern period. In Jacob Katz's words, 'the crisis that affected traditional society at the end of our period [the age of emancipation] seemed to many to be primarily a crisis in the rabbinate'.[1] What exactly this crisis was and how it developed is still unclear in many respects. A fair amount of attention has been given to changes in the German rabbinate,[2] as well as to developments in Hungary.[3] However, the east European rabbinate has been relatively ignored, with the major exception of Galicia,[4] even though the Jewish communities of eastern Europe changed radically in the nineteenth century.[5] The impact, or lack of impact, of these changes on the rabbinate is well worth our attention.

The institution of the communal rabbinate[6] came into being in the Jewish communities of Europe in the Middle Ages.[7] It differed in many ways from

---

[1] Katz, *Tradition and Crisis*, 75. On the rabbinate in general see the very helpful book by Schwarzfuchs, *A Concise History of the Rabbinate*. Chapter 11 is entitled 'Many Answers to One Crisis'.

[2] Schwarzfuchs, *A Concise History of the Rabbinate*, discusses many developments in the German rabbinate, as does Sorkin, *The Transformation of German Jewry 1780–1840*, ch. 6: 'Ideologues and Institutions'.

[3] Jacob Katz discusses many issues related to the rabbinate in *A House Divided*. A relevant specialized study is Ya'akov Weiss, *Rabbinate and Community in the Thought of the Hatam Sofer* (Heb.).   [4] Gertner, 'Rabbis and Rabbinical Judges' (Heb.).

[5] One valuable exception is Bacon, 'Prolonged Erosion, Organization and Reinforcement'. See esp. pp. 85–7.

[6] I use the term 'communal rabbi' in distinction to the general term 'rabbi'. The latter is an honorific title that can be applied to any scholar and, in particular, to any individual who was 'ordained' or given the title. Thus there can be many rabbis in one community. A communal rabbi is an individual who was accepted as the recognized rabbinic authority for all the Jewish residents of a given community.

[7] The question of the origins of the rabbinate is an exceedingly complex one which is not directly relevant to our discussion of the rabbinate in the late 19th century. The most recent discussion of this topic is Reiner, 'The Yeshivas of Poland and Ashkenaz during the Sixteenth and Seventeenth Centuries'. The discussion on the rabbinate is on pp. 29–37. See also in the

the frameworks of halakhic leadership in late antiquity. Communal rabbis decided halakhic questions; they generally were given a monopoly on the performance of weddings and divorces, had exclusive rights to excommunicate, and they also preached on occasion. In many communities rabbis were also the heads of local yeshivas. They had access, directly and indirectly, to communal funds and resources and could influence their allocation. Their main functions were broadly defined. They were expected to guide the community on religious issues and often to represent the community. As Jacob Katz put it, the rabbi was the 'exclusive exerciser of the rabbinic functions . . . no other person was authorized to adjudicate in civil and ritual matters or to preach and lecture without his permission or tacit agreement'.[8] Katz added that the communal rabbi 'was held responsible for the integrity of public life'.[9] These were all functions that had not previously been assigned exclusively to one communal functionary or post.

One consequence of the communal rabbinate being one of the most visible and ubiquitous institutions of a Jewish community was that Jewish communities regarded the fact that they had a rabbi and the quality of that rabbi as an expression of their autonomy and status. New communities seeking independence from neighbouring communities actively sought the right to appoint their own rabbi. Communities wanted as talented and as famous a rabbi as possible, and saw his status as reflecting the importance and quality of the community. In Ashkenaz from the Middle Ages on there was a rough correspondence between the significance of a rabbi and the size and fame of the community in which he served.[10] In other words, important rabbis usually were the rabbis of important communities, and important communities made an effort to hire important rabbis.

same volume Cohen, 'On the Character of the Landesrabbiner in Ashkenaz in the Seventeenth and Eighteenth Centuries'. An important discussion of developments in earlier periods is in Yuval, *Sages in their Generation* (Heb.), 398–404. For a good introduction to the role of the rabbinate in Jewish Society at the end of the Middle Ages see Katz, *Tradition and Crisis*, chs. 9 and 17. A more detailed discussion of the rabbinate in a somewhat earlier period is Zimmer, *Harmony and Discord*, ch. 5. See also Baron, *The Jewish Community*, ch. 11 and his many notes; Assaf, 'Studies in the History of the Rabbinate' (Heb.). Much of Lederhendler, *The Road to Modern Jewish Politics* is directly relevant to our topic.

[8] Katz, *Tradition and Crisis*, 87.   [9] Ibid. 90.

[10] This is a practice that is clearly sensed in the literature but difficult to document. Although an analysis of the rabbis rallied in a number of famous controversies would probably make this phenomenon clear, it would go past the bounds of this study. In the meetings of the *va'adim* (councils) of Poland and Lithuania the rabbis of the largest cities were consulted as experts. One could try to correlate between rabbinic authors and the size of the communities in which they lived, but this could be countered with the argument that city residents found it easier to publish than did small-town rabbis, even though in theory the small-town rabbis may have been extremely influential.

Despite the ubiquitousness of the rabbinate in Ashkenazi Jewish communities, it should not be forgotten that the institution of the communal rabbinate itself was in no way essential to Jewish religious life. In this respect there was a basic difference between the authority and function of the ordained rabbi and the ordained priest in the Catholic Church. There are no sacraments in Judaism which can be administered only by an elected rabbi. There is even no absolute need for an ordained rabbi, because ordination itself was a relatively recent innovation. A Jewish layman can conduct a circumcision ceremony, a wedding, or a divorce, and can also bury the dead. All of these acts are equally 'binding' or effective in the eyes of Jewish law if carried out by a simple tailor or by a learned rabbi. However, it was accepted in east European Jewish society that these ritual activities were the monopoly of the communal rabbi, which he could share with others or not—the decision was his.

In most cases the authority of the communal rabbi was not the consequence of his being a part of a complex and formal hierarchy, or by virtue of having been assigned by an authoritative person to the post. His authority was usually based on the fact that he was elected by the local Jewish community. The election process meant that the majority of those voting publicly accepted his authority as the arbitrator of Jewish tradition. This gave the rabbi authority to take initiatives within the Jewish community and also to serve, in many cases, as a representative of the Jewish community to the outside world. The communal rabbi was not necessarily the most learned person in his community. However, having been elected to the position, he had the authority to decide questions of halakhah within the community and fulfil the other responsibilities or prerogatives of rabbis. Personal charisma and scholarly erudition strengthened his position, but without a selection process they alone could not give an individual, talented as he may have been, the status of a communal rabbi.

Some of the responsibilities of the communal rabbi could be assigned to specialists and not all were necessarily his personal responsibility. The task to decide questions of Jewish law was often delegated to *morei tsedek* (teachers of law) or *dayanim* (judges of Jewish law), whose sole responsibility was to give halakhic decisions. Supervision of meat slaughtering could also be assigned to specialists. Giving sermons was also not one of the central responsibilities of the communal rabbi, and *darshanim* or *magidim*—permanent or itinerant preachers—did most of the popular preaching. Traditionally communal rabbis addressed the community as a whole only twice a year, on the sabbath before Pesach (Shabat Hagadol) and the sabbath before Yom Kippur (Shabat Shuvah). What could not be transferred and what was not shared was the fact that only the rabbi was elected. All of the specialists were appointed.

The communal rabbi had both symbolic functions and real authority that derived from his election. In many respects, he personified many of the ideals of the community. Since a rabbi was a symbol of communal values and an active influence on communal events, his selection was in many respects an expression of how the members of a community viewed themselves and their ideals. One understandable consequence was that the selection process of a rabbi was often grounds for bitter internal struggles within the community. Disputes were often totally unrelated to the merits and demerits of a particular candidate, but rather centred on the relative power of different groups within the community and differing opinions as to the characteristics of the ideal Jew.

Despite all the attention given to rabbis and the rabbinate one cannot overemphasize what has long been noted in historical literature: that in traditional Ashkenazi Jewish society the rabbi did not determine the policies of Jewish communities which were not regarded explicitly as issues of Jewish law; nor did all communal decisions depend on his agreement. The true power figures in Jewish communities were the 'secular' leaders. This can be demonstrated very simply. The power to allocate collected funds is the best expression of communal power and in this regard rabbis usually had little to say. It was the elected lay leaders who decided financial and political issues, and they were the ultimate authority in communal questions. Moreover, just as a community could hire a rabbi, so could it fire a rabbi. A rabbi's contract was not for life and there was no concept of automatic life tenure. The rabbi had limited power vis-à-vis the lay leadership, since he had little or no role in their selection. A rabbi could impose a *ḥerem* or excommunication, but it was not imposed lightly and was ineffective when applied against a recalcitrant lay leadership. The rabbi's authority in deciding purely legal issues was generally unquestioned unless there was a legal disagreement. However, most communal issues were regarded as not halakhic in nature and, as such, they were outside the purview of the rabbi.

It is therefore not surprising that rabbinical authority in traditional Ashkenazi communities was usually dependent on the co-operation and support of other elements in the community—notably the *parnasim*, or the lay communal leaders. It is understandable that rabbis tended to support the socio-economic elite from whose midst the *parnasim* had come. They did this by giving honour to members of this group in communal frameworks and by publicly supporting their decisions. This backing was often welcomed by the *parnasim*. If communal leaders had to enforce an unpopular decision, they often found themselves facing opposition from various elements in the Jewish community, and in such cases they needed backing. They could, of course, turn to power structures in the non-Jewish community for support and they did so on occasion. However, they were loath to do this for a variety of reasons. It was usually more desirable to seek rabbinical support, which could often achieve the same results—especially with the threat of excommunication —without a public display of weakness, and without exposing the inner affairs of the Jewish community to outsiders. In return for support, or the potential for such support, the lay leadership supported the rabbinate financially and morally.

The rabbinate was not regarded in the Jewish community as a calling in the same sense as in Christian societies.[11] In the Jewish communities study was the ideal, and talented young men wanted to be learned or at least to be regarded as learned. This did not mean that they had to be employed as rabbis. Rather than make a living from their knowledge they generally preferred to earn a living in business and to devote as much time as possible to study. The virtue of the rabbinate was not in the title or the activities of the rabbi but in the fact that it offered conditions conducive to study. However, the responsibilities of the rabbinate could also be regarded as distractions. To be able to study without such distractions certainly has its appeal. Thus we also find in eastern European Jewry the ideal of the wife who worked to support her husband so that he could devote all of his time to study. Given these realities in eastern Europe one cannot assume that the lack of expressed desire to serve in the rabbinate was a mere pose. In other words, the hesitation expressed about entering the rabbinate seems to reflect a widespread feeling that the rabbinate should be avoided if possible.

Since serving in the rabbinate was not an ideal, many traditional nineteenth-century rabbis felt obliged to justify their acceptance of rabbinical posts. The standard explanation they gave was that they had taken on the rabbinate only after having failed in business, and this because of the need to support a family. Of course, this may well have been mere posturing, or an attempt to demonstrate modesty, but it cannot be dismissed out of hand or in every case.

The realities of rabbinic activity we have described encouraged moderation and consideration of current realities in the process of reaching a decision about halakhah. Since rabbinical authority needed the support of other groups in society, there was a virtue to consensus and compromise. Because of the general agreement on the binding nature of Jewish law, rabbis in the pre-modern period were not accustomed to dealing with individuals who rejected their authority on ritual matters or on principle. Recalcitrance was, of course, a common problem for *parnasim* who wished to collect taxes from Jews who served noblemen, but that was a communal and not a rabbinical problem.

[11] Etkes, 'The Relationship between Talmudic Scholarship and the Institution of the Rabbinate'.

The issues, and the nature of rabbinic authority, were to change drastically in the course of modernization.[12]

THE DECLINE OF THE EAST EUROPEAN RABBINATE IN THE EIGHTEENTH AND NINETEENTH CENTURIES

The rabbinate in modern eastern Europe was apparently not significantly different from the rabbinate in other Ashkenazi Jewish communities up to the eighteenth century.[13] In the following years, many aspects of rabbinical authority changed in almost every country of Europe. During the course of the eighteenth and nineteenth centuries, a number of developments altered the conditions of rabbinic authority in eastern Europe in unique ways, and also made the selection of communal rabbis more complex than previously. Many of these changes contributed to a weakening of the power and status of the rabbinate—a power and status that were not exceptionally strong to start with, as we have seen. Public debate on the rabbinate was often—if not usually—sharp, even though the impact of the debate on the realities of the rabbinate is hard to determine. Although it is difficult to measure the degree of change there were clear expressions of it. Three important indications of a crisis in the rabbinate were the appearance of simony, a great increase in the transmission of rabbinical posts from father to son, and the rise of the crown or government rabbinate.

The sale of rabbinic posts was a controversial issue in the modern period. It both reflected a weakening of the authority of the rabbinate and contributed in turn to an even greater decline in authority as an increasing number of rabbinical positions were sold. Public recognition of the sale of a position means that the holder of that position was not seen as a symbol of the community. The phenomenon is unquestioned. The record book of the Council of Jewish Communities in Lithuania records a decision from 1695 prohibiting the appointment of a rabbi in return for bribes or loans and annulling such appointments when they took place,[14] and it was followed in 1720 by a prohibition on appointments to the rabbinate as part of a condition to a marriage or the trading of rabbinical positions.[15] Such enactments would not have been made had there not been a need for them. The bitter struggle over the rabbinate in Vilna at the end of the eighteenth century—a by-

---

[12] In this context, the disappearance of the *ḥerem* can serve as an indication for the decline of rabbinic authority, though there were also other factors involved.

[13] See Levitats, *The Jewish Community in Russia 1772–1844*, 151–62, for a survey of the characteristics of the rabbinate in the tsarist empire.

[14] Dubnow (ed.), *Recordbook of the Lithuanian Jewish Council* (Heb.), 231, no. 882.

[15] Ibid. 243, no. 913.

product of such a sale—is well known,[16] and it certainly added little honour to the status of the rabbinate. Indeed, the central figure of the dispute and the last rabbi of Vilna, Shemuel ben Avigdor, held simultaneously (apparently by purchase) not only the position of rabbi of Vilna but also the post of the rabbi of Königsberg,[17] rabbi of Danzig,[18] and rabbi of Smorgon.[19] Enactments prohibiting the sale of rabbinical posts were not found earlier in records of the regional councils of east European Jewish communities and this suggests that this was a relatively new issue.[20] However, the fact that we know there was a problem says little about the scope or significance of the problem.[21]

It is certainly easy, from a distance, to criticize simony and the sale of rabbinic posts. However, we cannot ignore the fact that it was the extremely heavy debt-load of communities that made them look desperately for every possible source of income that could help them pay taxes, and selling off rabbinical posts was just one more method of fundraising. The selection of a more or less qualified candidate as a rabbi, and a consequent rise or decline in the quality of halakhic decisions or of rabbinic lectures, probably did not have a significant impact on the quality of life in a community. However, while the sale of rabbinic positions might have solved pressing financial needs, it certainly did not add to the prestige of the rabbinate. Moreover, it was a public suggestion that the quality of a rabbi, and of what he represented, may not be of great importance.

Inheritance of rabbinic posts and the transmission of posts from father-in-law to son-in-law also implies that the quality of a rabbi was not extremely important. This was an innovation that became more common in the late eighteenth century. In the Middle Ages such inheritance of rabbinic posts was proscribed because it was generally recognized that sons and sons-in-law were not necessarily of the same calibre as their fathers and fathers-in-law. Moreover, ties with a local family could complicate the rabbis' responsibilities as judges. Nonetheless, inheritance of rabbinical posts became more and more widespread in the eighteenth and the nineteenth centuries. It does not

---

[16] This dispute has most recently been discussed in Lederhendler, *The Road to Modern Jewish Politics*, 44–6. He cites all the relevant sources.

[17] Magid-Steinschneider, *The City of Vilna* (Heb.), 18.

[18] Klausner, *Vilna: The Jerusalem of Lithuania* (Heb.), 92. His source is not cited but his detailed knowledge of Vilna's Jewish community was unrivalled in his time.

[19] Fuenn, *A Loyal Town* (Heb.), 140.

[20] It would be interesting to see a careful survey of the rabbinical literature on the topic. The extremely useful data base of rabbinic responsa in the *Otsar haposekim* would make such a study feasible. This is a Hebrew-language data base that can be purchased.

[21] Without a systematic study of the rabbinate at the end of the 18th century, which is outside the scope of this paper, it is difficult to come to any solid conclusions about the seriousness of the crisis of the rabbinate at this time or to discover the extent to which there was change as opposed to longstanding problems.

seem that the traditional prohibitions were forgotten but rather that they were abandoned. Communities began to be concerned that voting on candidates for the position of communal rabbi could split the community. As long as communities had fulfilled a role as tax collectors for the non-Jewish authorities, the idea of a communal split was inconceivable, and whoever demanded the taxes would not have tolerated such a situation. However, when taxes began to be collected directly there was a corresponding decline in external pressure on communities to be united and to function effectively. In this new condition, appointing an heir became the ideal compromise. At the same time it reflected a decline in the concern for the level and quality of a communal rabbi. Therefore, transmission of rabbinical posts to heirs should be seen not only as an indication of weakness of the institution of the communal rabbinate, but of the community structures as a whole.[22]

The establishment of the crown or government rabbinate was a critical development of the rabbinate in the Russian empire and it had a long-term impact on the internal rabbinate.[23] The idea behind the new initiative was to supplant the traditional rabbis with a network of rabbis who would be committed to Haskalah and to a degree of integration into Russian society. This initiative was launched by the Russian government in 1835. According to the regulations enacted that year, communal rabbis were required to know Russian and the appointment of rabbis needed the approval of provincial governments.[24] In 1847 rabbinical seminaries were founded in Vilna and Zhitomir to train such rabbis. The government exerted pressure on communities to select graduates of these schools and other individuals with secular knowledge as communal rabbis. Not surprisingly, most Jews regarded these 'rabbis', most of whom where not noted for their talmudic scholarship, as government clerks who had to be appeased but not necessarily regarded as authoritative religious leaders. There was a contradiction between the need to satisfy government demands and a need for traditional rabbinic leadership. The solution that quickly developed was simple. One rabbi was selected by the community to meet the expectations of the government. Such rabbis were termed 'crown' rabbis. At the same time a second rabbi was chosen in accordance with the traditional expectations of the community. The ubiquity of this phenomenon was soon recognized and the term *dukhovnyi ravvin* (spiritual rabbi) developed for such rabbis, a term that was recognized and used even by the government. In effect the crown rabbi usually operated as a government official and wielded relatively little authority within the Jewish community. In many cases, the crown rabbis limited their activities to the recording of vital statistics and to the provision of documentation for passports.

[22] On this see Chapter 14 below.
[23] The best work on the crown rabbinate is Shohet, *The 'Crown Rabbinate'* (Heb.).
[24] On this and the period see Lederhendler, *The Road to Modern Jewish Politics*, 91.

The continued activity and role of 'spiritual' rabbis was not the product of a decision by a representative body of the Jewish communities in Russia. Such a body did not exist in the nineteenth century. It was a universal and spontaneous development based on local initiatives, because only such rabbis could decide halakhic questions which were important for many Jews.[25] The salaries of the 'spiritual rabbis' continued to be paid by the Jewish communities. However, their salaries could not be paid from the official meat taxes (*korobka*) and from 1844 on salaries of these rabbis were generally paid for by donations.[26] In this way, the system of communal rabbis lived on, though not without complications. The crown rabbis were usually not regarded as communal or spiritual leaders, and if they had any aspirations to that role in most cases they were soon disabused of the notion.

There were, of course, cases of talented and conscientious crown rabbis, such as the martyred Rabbi Maze in Moscow, and in certain circles they had a significant influence. The growing numbers of Jews who received a Russian education and who were increasingly integrated into Russian society (or thought they were) no longer had a common language with the Yiddish-speaking spiritual rabbis, and while generally they did take crown rabbis seriously, there were important exceptions. Influence was very much a product of the personal characteristics of a given crown rabbi. However, influential crown rabbis were apparently not the norm even at the end of the century.

Despite the documented limitations in the authority and status of the crown rabbis, the establishment of a framework that was parallel to the traditional system of the communal rabbinate was a public expression of the limited status of the traditional rabbinate. The support given to the crown rabbi by the government and by some of the richer and more powerful individuals in the Jewish community made obedience to the spiritual rabbi a matter of choice, and not something that could be taken for granted or enforced.

THE DISAPPEARANCE OF COMMUNAL RABBIS IN LARGE JEWISH COMMUNITIES

The patterns of the east European rabbinate at the end of the nineteenth century were far from the traditional Ashkenazi model because the community, as a body that collected taxes and had internal authority, had ceased to exist. One of the most striking differences was, as we shall see, that by 1900 many of the largest Jewish communities in eastern Europe did not

[25] Students of modernity in modern Jewish society might well consider the impact of central meat-packing under rabbinical supervision and the sale of checked and 'kashered' meat products as a factor that led to much less dependence of individuals on rabbis.

[26] Shohet, *The 'Crown Rabbinate'* (Heb.), 14.

Table 13.1 Major Jewish communities and communal rabbis in eastern Europe, 1900

Community	Jewish population in 1900	Communal rabbi in 1900	Last year with recorded communal rabbi
Warsaw[a]	280,000	no	1873
Odessa[b]	140,000	no	1890
Łódz	90,000	yes	
Vilna[c]	65,000	no	1790
Kishinev	50,000	yes	
Minsk	50,000	yes	
Lvov[d]	45,000	no	1897
Białystok[e]	40,000	no	1898
Berdichev[f]	40,000	no	
Ekaterinoslav[g]	40,000	no	
Vitebsk[h]	35,000	no	
Dvinsk[i]	30,000	no	
Kiev	30,000	no	
Lublin	30,000	yes	
Zhitomir	30,000		
Brest	30,000	yes	
Kremenchug	30,000		
Kraków[j]	25,000	no	1883
Kovno	25,000	yes	
Elizavetgrad	25,000	no	
Grodno[k]	20,000	no	1818
Riga	20,000	no	
Mogilev[l]	20,000	no	
Częstochowa	20,000		
Bobruisk[m]	20,000	no	1851
Gomel[n]	20,000	no	

Note: Cities where there was shared rabbinate or a split rabbinate are regarded as not having an agreed rabbi of the community.

  [a] Gutman, Netzer, and Wein, *History of the Jews of Warsaw* (Heb.), 70.
  [b] *Jewish Encyclopaedia*, s.v. 'Odessa'.
  [c] The topic of the Vilna rabbinate and the struggles around the person of the last rabbi, Shemuel ben Avigdor, have been discussed widely in the literature. The most accessible source in Hebrew to the topic is Klausner, *Vilna: The Jerusalem of Lithuania* (Heb.). On the rabbinate see esp. pp. 170–1 and other references from the index.
  [d] See the Lvov volume of *Encyclopaedia of the Jewish Diaspora* (Heb.), 428, where it is stated that as of 1897 there were two official rabbis, one for the traditionalists and one for the modernists.
  [e] See Hershberg, *Recordbook of Białystok* (Heb.), i. 177–8. The last rabbi of Białystok, Rabbi Shemuel Mohilever, died in 1898. The leading *dayan*, who had served as acting rabbi before rabbi Mohilever's appointment, continued to serve as the senior judge of the Białystok *beit din* but was not appointed rabbi of the city.
  [f] See Zederbaum, *The Secrets of Berdichev* (Yid.), 78. In the communal budget there is mention of salaries for two *morei hora'ah* and for a government rabbi but not for a communal rabbi. The detailed description of the city also makes no mention of a communal rabbi.
  [g] Levin, 'Ekaterinoslav Rabbis' (Heb.), 113–14, describes a situation in which the city was divided between four rabbis and each served as the rabbi of a district. Death of a rabbi could initiate a rotation of posts.
  [h] See Zinowitz, 'The History of the Rabbinate in Vitebsk' (Heb.), 187. He cites an article in *Hamagid*. He

mentions that Rabbi Zalman Landau left and there was no replacement. This was apparently in the late nineteenth century. Zinovitz adds that this was due to the conflicts between hasidim and mitnagedim.
    [i] *Recordbooks of the Jewish Communities: Latvia and Estonia* (Heb.), ed. Levin et al. There was a split rabbinate in Dvinsk/Daugavpils despite efforts to unite it—a clear reflection of the view that a split is undesirable.
    [j] See Busak, 'Jews of Kraków' (Heb.), 107. He points out that a full successor to Rabbi Shimon Sofer was never found. The 'rabbi' of Kraków in the early twentieth century was Joseph Engel. In the *Encyclopaedia Judaica* (s.v. 'Engel, Joseph') it is pointed out that he had the status of a communal rabbi though he was officially only the *av beit din*—almost but not quite.
    [k] According to the Grodno volume of *Encyclopedia of the Jewish Diaspora* (Heb.), there was no official rabbi of Grodno after 1818.
    [l] Zinovitz, 'The History of the Rabbinate in Vitebsk' (Heb.), mentions in his description of Vitebsk that in Mogilev there also was no rabbi. To the best of my knowledge there is no memorial book for the Mogilev community.
    [m] *Bobruisk* (Heb.), i. 42, mentions that from 1851 on, there were two rabbis in Bobruisk, one for the mitnagedim and one for the hasidim.
    [n] See Cahanowitz, 'Gomel/Homel' (Heb.), 194 and 253 on separate rabbis for 'Ashkenazim' and hasidim.

have an elected rabbi. Moreover, the link between the importance of a rabbi and the importance of a community no longer held. To understand this change and to consider its causes and consequences, it is worthwhile to look at which eastern European Jewish communities had elected rabbis at the turn of the century and which not. Table 13.1 lists the Jewish communities in declining order of size, and notes whether or not they had a *rav ha'ir* or elected communal/spiritual rabbi around the turn of the century. Where possible I noted when the last communal rabbi left his post or died. For some communities there is no information on the rabbi incumbent in 1900. It some cases this absence of information may be due to the lack of a monograph or study of the particular Jewish community. However, it is equally possible that the absence of references to a communal rabbi in a given community may have been because such a rabbi did not exist. What does not exist is not reported.

The significance of the information in Table 13.1 is clear. Out of the twenty-six largest communities at the end of the century, only six are definitely known to have had rabbis and three are more questionable. In other words, by the end of the century a large east European Jewish community with a communal rabbi was the exception and not the usual case. This was not a phenomenon that was limited to the tsarist empire. In the two major Galician communities of Lvov and Kraków,[27] there were also no elected communal rabbis. A little more than a century before, such a situation would have been incomprehensible because, as mentioned above, around the year 1800 there had been a rabbi in almost every community. Equally worthy of note is that the phenomenon of the disappearance of communal rabbis was not discussed as such by Jewish publicists at the end of the century despite the

---

[27] See Manekin, 'Orthodoxy in Kraków on the Eve of the Twentieth Century' (Heb.).

dramatic changes described in Table 13.1. Apparently each case was seen as the product of local factors and was not recognized as part of a broader phenomenon.

THE 'WHEN' AND THE 'WHY' OF THE DECLINE OF THE COMMUNAL RABBINATE

In the eighteenth century it was taken for granted that every community would want a rabbi. Communities that had a rabbi were proud of his knowledge and achievements. Those communities that did not have a rabbi felt inferior. To appoint a rabbi was a declaration of the independence of a new or growing community. It signified that this community was no longer subservient to or dependent on a nearby centre. Therefore, on occasion pressure was exerted on such communities to stop them from appointing rabbis.[28] For growing communities, the desire to have a rabbi was not just an issue of religious concern, but also a matter of communal pride and convenience.[29]

As we have seen, by the end of the nineteenth century the existence of a communal rabbi could no longer be taken for granted; most of the major Jewish communities did not have one. As Table 13.1 shows, the communal rabbinate did not vanish in major communities overnight, nor did it begin to disappear only at the end of the nineteenth century. It was an extended process. In 1793 the Jewish community of Vilna decided to make do without a rabbi as a result of a bitter controversy over the last rabbi, Shemuel ben Avigdor.[30] *Avot beit din*, or judges, continued to be appointed and supported, but their authority was explicitly limited to deciding legal questions. They were not chosen by a public vote and could not aspire to act as representatives of the community. They were halakhic technicians.

To understand why the situation of the rabbinate had changed by the end of the nineteenth century it is necessary to make a systematic analysis of the costs and benefits of the institution. However, it is necessary before that to consider—and reject—some seemingly plausible explanations for the 'missing' rabbis that are inaccurate.

One could claim that the question of whether there was or was not a communal rabbi was often more a question of titles than of substance. After

---

[28] See Dubnow (ed.), *Recordbook of the Lithuanian Jewish Council* (Heb.), 24, para. 916, for a 1720 enactment requiring communities in Lithuania that had not previously had rabbis to appoint a rabbi by the next meeting of the regional council. The reason for this enactment is not given.

[29] See Natanson, *Responsa*, vol. i, pt. 2, p. 11*b*, no. 19, and note the use of the phrase *nitkanu* for competition between communities for rabbis.

[30] For the most recent study in English of this very complex and fascinating dispute, see Lederhendler, *The Road to Modern Jewish Politics*, 44–6.

all, what is the real difference between a rabbi and an *av beit din* (head of a court)? If that was the case, the missing rabbis were not missing at all. There is some truth to such a view. On a day-to-day basis the differences between a rabbi and an *av beit din* were not necessarily significant. Both could decide legal questions and deal with ritual events such as weddings and funerals. However, there was a difference, and it emerged when conditions required authoritative representation of a community. A judge could not make a statement on issues that were not narrowly defined as legal issues. Thus, in crisis situations a judge could also not take an active role in the decision-making process in a community, or speak in the name of the community to outsiders. In short, an *av beit din* could fulfil many of the functions of a rabbi but not all of them.

It could be argued that the absence of rabbis in large communities in 1900 was merely a by-product of technical complications and intensified urbanization—it might be harder to pick a rabbi in a big community than in a small one because it is harder to get large groups to agree on questions than small groups. On close examination this is a weak argument. Indeed, in cities where there were large communities with active and responsible *kehilot* (congregations), such as the larger communities in the early modern period, decisions and selections were made all the time without any sense that size was a problem. With size there may be a sense of anomie and isolation, but the institutional frameworks work—and work well. Insider groups form in cities which influence or control decision making. Indeed, one can argue that the distance of communal institutions from the simple individual in large communities encourages less involvement on the part of the masses, and acceptance rather than rebellion and active opposition. Certainly political institutions in the general community operate very well in large urban concentrations.

Communal institutions are maintained because they justify the costs of their maintenance. In other words, the benefits derived from their operation outweigh the difficulties and strains of maintaining them. If an institution begins to disappear, the cost-and-benefit situation should be considered before going on to other types of explanations. In this case it is necessary to analyse the changing needs of the east European Jewish community in the nineteenth century, as well as the costs and benefits of communal rabbis. Such an analysis can suggest the circumstances in which one can expect the flourishing of the communal rabbinate and the circumstances in which it would be likely to wither away.

In certain respects, there was less need for communal rabbis in large communities than in small ones. As noted above, rabbis are not essential for the maintenance of Jewish ritual. Questions of *kashrut* or sabbath laws can be decided by any knowledgeable man or woman and thus do not require the intervention of a rabbi. All prayer services and rituals can be carried out by laymen or by ordained rabbis who do not have official appointments. However, the distribution of knowledgeable laymen is not even. They are found more in urban centres than in small or isolated communities. Therefore, in small communities, the only real way to ensure authoritative guidance in religious questions was to bring in a rabbi. In larger communities, there was less of a need to import a knowledgeable rabbi.

Large Jewish communities often needed spokesmen to represent them to outside authorities, but this was not traditionally a rabbinical function. In the past this role had been too important to be put automatically into the hands of rabbis. Communal elders tended to keep this function to themselves. Governmental authorities, familiar with the hierarchical structure of the Catholic (and Protestant) churches, often expected to find the same structure among the Jews. They often needed an 'address' to turn to with regard to questions of Jewish law and morality and a rabbi was a natural choice. However, this was not a sufficient reason for each Jewish community to appoint a communal rabbi. The government authorities had hoped that crown rabbis would supplant traditional authorities, so they certainly did not pressure Jewish communities to appoint spiritual rabbis.

The most obvious function of the communal rabbinate was as a final authority for halakhic questions within a community. When any individual can decide religious questions, this creates the potential for communal discord and strife. Where there is a recognized communal rabbi there is no question as to who is authorized to decide such questions. Since communal order is always desirable there is a constant need for clear definitions as to who is authorized to resolve disputes, and for quick and fair decisions in such cases. Indeed, the efficient functioning of the rabbinical courts is widely regarded as having been a very positive factor in the development of commerce among Jews. The fact that cases were tried quickly and fairly was the basis for credit transactions that were critical for commercial dealings. In this the rabbinate contributed to the smooth operation of the community. However, even in this area communities were not dependent on elected rabbis alone. Legal questions could be decided by judges in rabbinical courts as well. Specifically commercial questions were often decided by arbitrators and not by rabbis. Householders with questions could turn to scholars whether or not they had a formal appointment.

There were rabbinical functions that were not filled by judges or arbitrators. The communal rabbi initiated and supervised religious behaviour in the community and also could guide and teach advanced students.[31]

---

[31] On the responsibilities of rabbis see Katz, 'On the History of the Rabbinate'.

However, already by the eighteenth century communal yeshivas had ceased to operate and with their decline the communal rabbinate lost one of the important supports for its authority. While a communal rabbi had exceptional authority as a moral supervisor, this role was seen as peripheral to his main function. The need for someone who would take moral initiatives was recognized, but it alone was not a good enough reason to decide to select a communal rabbi despite all the complications involved.

However, there are also costs to the rabbinate. Salaries are the least of these costs because they can be lowered (and raised), and at all times Jewish communities have found funds for all types of activities—educational, religious, cultural, and so on. However, the price of maintaining an institution does not only involve the expenses which have to be paid but the social cost as well. One of the social costs in the case of the rabbinate was the stresses involved in selection. After all, whenever there is selection there are winners and losers and this holds not only for the candidates themselves but also for their supporters. Selecting a rabbi can easily yield a great deal of bitterness. It is most easily achieved when there is an efficient community organization that is accustomed to making decisions and when there is a common ideology and agreement on the need for an appointment.

The process of choosing a rabbi became particularly problematic in the modern period. As noted above, the government had no interest in the functioning of traditional communal rabbis once the crown rabbinate had been established. The increasing integration of Jews into general commerce meant that cases of commercial law which were brought before a rabbinical court could always be appealed to Russian courts, so that the need for a strong and effective legal system was not a positive factor for the encouragement of the rabbinate.[32] Moreover, as previously mentioned, parties in a commercial dispute could always turn to arbitration even in the absence of a strong communal rabbinate.

The rise of a modernizing upper and middle class that did not identify with the values and ideals of the traditional rabbinate further complicated the selection process. For them, as for traditionalists, a rabbi was a reflection of the ideals of the community, and the kind of rabbi they were interested in was a quite different personality from that which had previously been common. Many modernizers wanted a rabbi with a European education, a modern bearing, and someone who would create a positive impression on the non-Jewish society. The rich and well connected had traditionally run Jewish communities. Now, with sharply different goals from those of the majority of

---

[32] As far as I know, the increasing use of non-Jewish courts in the Russian empire has never been studied systematically. However, it is a key issue and well worth attention.

traditionalists and rabbinically learned Jews, it was increasingly difficult to find candidates that could appeal to all the camps of the Jewish community.

As noted above, usually there was no central hierarchy which could appoint rabbis, nor were there usually regional chief rabbis. Up to the modern period, selection of a rabbi was the decision of the Jewish community or *kahal*. Even when hasidic rabbis involved themselves in the selection process they only suggested candidates for a position. The townspeople still had to go through the election process for the position. The rabbi, then, was 'chosen' by all the members of a community and thus they all accepted his authority. However, his authority was far from unlimited. As mentioned above, the *kahal* employed the rabbi and his activity was seen as one more area in which the *kahal* functioned. If the community was unsatisfied with the rabbi, it was under no obligation to renew his contract.[33]

Communal conflicts were not just a matter of disagreements between modernizers and traditionalists. Even traditional communities faced difficulties in choosing rabbis. In many communities the traditional population was split between hasidim and mitnagedim. Each group was interested in the communal rabbi being chosen from its camp. The choice of the rabbi had little practical impact on the realities of life both in the hasidic groups and among their opponents. However, the selection of a rabbi was regarded as giving prestige to the camp from which he came and an indication of their relative strength.

The disappearance of the communal rabbi was closely related to the decline of the *kehilot* in the nineteenth century. The formal dissolution of the *kehilot* in the Russian empire in 1844 was only one stage. Since selection of rabbis is such a problematic step, it is best done by a functioning body that regularly makes decisions which are binding on the Jewish community. Accustomed to responsibility, to reconciling differences—one might say to parliamentary procedure—and to the ways of reaching decisions, the *kahal* was the natural framework for the task of picking a rabbi. Without a *kahal* there was a greater need for ad hoc frameworks to pick a rabbi and this entailed many complications. It has been noted that in many Jewish communities before 1844 the non-rabbinic leadership was no longer always based on general elections. The draft laws of 1825 which required communities to supply recruits certainly did not attract responsible individuals to seek positions of communal leadership.[34] In the nineteenth century there were many complaints of abuses and monopolization of positions of communal authority

---

[33] Since the rabbi was elected it is therefore understandable why the *kahal* antedated the communal rabbinate. See Reiner, 'The Yeshivas of Poland and Ashkenaz'.

[34] Just as in the case for communal institutions, so in the case for individuals. One cannot assume that the most respected or capable members of a society are the ones who assume lead-

by unqualified or powerful individuals. Thus the formal dissolution of the *kehilot* did not lead to an immediate restructuring of the Jewish communities but accelerated significantly a process that had already begun earlier.

By the end of the nineteenth century the make-up of many communities had also changed. The larger communities in the Russian empire were made up more and more by migrants.[35] It is reasonable to assume that their identification with communal structures was limited in comparison with the ties felt by veteran residents. Having less communal identification, migrants and their children would, of course, feel less of a need to maintain the community rabbinate and sense the importance of having a representative figure. On the other hand, smaller and less economically dynamic cities had a larger local-born population (and greater needs for at least one learned individual), and thus they had enhanced conditions for selecting a rabbi.

Interestingly, the communal rabbinate was declining at the same time in the mid-nineteenth century that supporters of the Haskalah movement were criticizing the rabbinate for being responsible for the sorry state of contemporary Jewish communities. They believed that it was in the rabbis' powers to initiate modernization and to spread modern education if they would only try. The reality, as we have seen, made such innovations almost impossible. The authority of the rabbis was derived from their charisma as bearers and interpreters of tradition. They had no other bases for authority. Radical changes in values and behaviour in the spirit of modernism could only undermine this charisma. For rabbis to initiate such changes would be to undermine their positions with their own hands. It is, of course, rather doubtful that even energetic support from rabbis for these changes would have led to practical results but *maskilim* could always hope. In any case, the critics of the rabbinate attributed to the rabbis more power and authority than existed.

The weakened communities, the internal splits, and the diminished sense of a need for a communal rabbi all contributed to a situation in which the cost of selecting a communal rabbi was regarded as very high. Thus, alternatives such as having no rabbi or letting the rabbinate be inherited were seen as undesirable, but often to be preferred to the trauma of a selection process.

New frameworks developed in the late nineteenth and early twentieth centuries to deal with some of the functions of the *kehilah*. However, these

---

ership roles. There is also a price for leadership. When such positions provide significant economic benefits, power, or status they can be attractive. However, the less to be gained by such a position, the less attractive it will be. A deteriorating *kahal* structure will not attract leading citizens.

[35] I discuss internal migration in my article 'Patterns of Internal Jewish Migration', in which I deal with *guberniyas* (provinces) and not individual cities, but the general trends are clear. It would not be difficult to carry on that study to the local level.

bodies could not select a rabbi in place of the weakened *kehilah*. The decline of the *kehilah* was paralleled by a rise in the role of charitable organizations.[36] Such frameworks could work relatively easily within the framework of Russian law, and philanthropic activity certainly gave status within the community and even without. It seems that such organizations sometimes were assigned the responsibility of disbursing *korobka* funds, funds that in the past had been given out by the *kahal*, but in most cases charity organizations had to raise funds themselves. Fund-raising is a dynamic that encourages consensus and the avoidance of behaviour that can repel donors. Therefore, these frameworks, while possessing status and certainly active, were not necessarily fit for entering the arena of what was ultimately a political question—picking a rabbi. A volunteer philanthropic organization is no replacement for a *kehilah* structure with the authority to tax and with experience in making difficult decisions.

In those communities who chose to make do without a communal rabbi after the death or departure of an incumbent, the absence of a rabbi was not immediately felt. As noted above, communities without a communal rabbi could continue to function as before. In large cities at the end of the nineteenth century there were no shortages of learned laymen or even of ordained rabbis who could be turned to, by those so interested, with questions. There remained rabbis on rabbinical courts and neighbourhood rabbis—the so called *vinkl* (corner) rabbis. The presence of such individuals meant that it was easier to get by without communal rabbis; in a sense it made them more disposable. In smaller towns the situation was often different. Where the rabbi was the only learned Jew, the absence of a rabbi could create an acute sense of loss since there would be no one to monitor *kashrut* and answer religious questions. Such a situation would encourage the selection of a rabbi. Indeed, it is my impression that smaller communities continued to have communal rabbis even after they had become rare in the large communities.

The causes and the consequences of the decline of the communal rabbinate in the large communities are interwoven. The lack of communal consensus made it difficult to choose a rabbi, and the absence of a rabbi made it difficult to create a communal consensus. The result was that the traditionalists or the emerging Orthodox were at a disadvantage in their attempts to struggle with the changes commonly lumped together under the term 'modernity'. The absence of communal rabbis was sometimes a result of

[36] This phenomenon has not been carefully studied. However, I have the impression that often such frameworks replaced the *kahal*. One can point to the 'Tsedoko Gedolo' in pre-Holocaust Vilna, a co-ordinating body for philanthropy very similar to frameworks such as United Jewish Appeal, as such a case, though careful research is needed to decide if this is an example or an anomaly.

modernization, sometimes a contributing factor to modernization, and sometimes had no relation to modernization.

CHANGING CONCEPTS OF THE RABBINATE

At the same time that communities were finding it more and more difficult to pick rabbis, the very concept of the function of the rabbi was changing. If previously the rabbi had responsibilities which were seen as serving the community, in the nineteenth century functions that were far more narrowly defined became current.

One of the richest sources of insights into changing conceptions of the rabbinate among rabbis is the responsa literature (collections of written answers by rabbis to questions of Jewish law), though there are certainly limitations on the utility of this source. This literature was written for internal consumption. As a result it is less polemical than materials prepared for the public. At the same time the arguments and claims raised have to be convincing for otherwise the conclusions of the author—and his authority—can be rejected. A statement in one responsum does not mean that the position expressed in it was universally shared. However, if the same claims appear in a number of responsa, one can draw cautious generalizations. I know of no study of the image of the east European rabbinate in the responsa literature. However, a survey of some of the literature, on the basis of the fine index to the responsa literature at the Otsar Haposekim Institute in Jerusalem, brings to light a broadly held feeling among nineteenth- and twentieth-century east European rabbis that the role of the rabbinate was changing radically in their times.

A responsum written by Rabbi Walkin describes a community that did not have 'a permanent rabbi who was appointed by the city', but rather a learned local householder would 'give them instructions and teach Torah' without payment.[37] Afterwards, the community took as rabbi the grandson of a well-known Galician hasidic *admor* (his name isn't given, nor is the name of the community cited) who knew nothing about deciding questions of religious law. He was given the title of rabbi as an expression of honour for his ancestry and he was assigned income from weddings, barmitzvahs, and similar events. The learned householder continued to decide questions of Jewish law. The 'rabbi' was not idle, and invested a great deal of effort in getting recognition of the Jewish community as an independent body—something in which the householder would not have invested effort. This arrangement worked well until the Russian government expelled all Galician Jews from Poland and the

---

[37] Walkin, *Zekan aharon*, vol. ii, no. 64, p. 79, a responsum written to R. Joshua Soberman in 1932.

learned householder, who had become old in the meantime, was no longer able to carry the burden of being the halakhic authority for the community. The community felt obliged to take another rabbi, but at the request of the 'exiled' Galician 'rabbi', the community agreed to give the new rabbi the title of *moreh tsedek*, or judge, and not the broader title of 'rabbi'. Around 1910 the equally unlearned son of the Galician 'rabbi' and the *moreh tsedek* quarrelled over the rights to the rabbinate of the community. The masses supported the son, while the learned wanted the *moreh tsedek* as their rabbi. What is important to us is that both in the 1880s and around 1910 a community felt a need for a rabbi, as a matter of honour, and what many were looking for was not a scholar or expert in Jewish law but a leader.

The reply of Rabbi Walkin is equally enlightening. He stated that usually a rabbi is not just a leader but is appointed to the post so that he can decide questions of Jewish law. Therefore a rabbi has to be learned enough to fill this function. At the same time, he noted that it was clear that the Galician rabbi was appointed town rabbi not for his legal expertise, but as a matter of 'leadership and honor' and 'to receive for this a salary'. As such, Rabbi Walkin stated, the community distinguished between the two functions of the rabbinate—leadership and legal guidance. He suggested that perhaps they should continue doing so in the future with a rabbi and a *moreh tsedek*. The rabbinate would be a matter of honour and income, but not a legal authority. Rabbi Walkin was quick to express his dismay that an unlearned person had been appointed as rabbi on the grounds that he was a 'holy' man, and stated that he had never heard of such a case before. At the same time, having two rabbis was an intolerable situation that could only lead to conflict. His very practical suggestion was that the son of the Galician rabbi be paid to relinquish his claims to the communal rabbinate.[38] However, as we shall see, such a case was not so extraordinary.

The case of a Rabbi Yosef Aharon Meriles[39] in Bucecea (Romania/Moldavia) and Rabbi Betsalel Dov Weisbach is equally interesting.[40] Rabbi Yosef Aharon had been appointed as rabbi of Bucecea, and he in turn hired Rabbi Betsalel Dov Weisbach as a *moreh tsedek* in Bucecea while he served as rabbi. However, when Rabbi Yosef Aharon suspected Rabbi Betsalel of seeking to usurp his position as rabbi, he fired him. This, quite understandably, became the subject of an extended legal dispute. Rabbi Shelomoh Drimer wrote in his responsum that in his country (Poland/Galicia), and in a number of places, rabbis hired a *moreh tsedek* and paid him a salary out of their own pocket—and thus retained the right to fire him at will. If the *moreh tsedek* had

---

[38] Walkin, *Zekan aharon*, vol. ii, no. 64, p. 79.

[39] On R. Yosef Aharon see Wunder, *Lights of Galicia* (Heb.), iii. 957–9.

[40] Drimer, *She'elot uteshuvot beit shelomoh*, no. 17, written in 1872 in Skala, 10*b*, esp. p. 11*a*.

been hired because of the multitude of questions which were too much for one person to deal with, one could have expected the local community to foot the bill. Since the local rabbis described by Rabbi Drimer paid the *moreh tsedek* directly, it would seem that, in those cases, the *moreh tsedek* was hired because the local rabbi did not want to deal with legal questions. There may have been a variety of reasons for the unwillingness of a local rabbi to deal with halakhic questions. Rabbi Drimer does not enlighten us in this respect and as far as is known, Rabbi Meriles was a learned man. However, it would seem reasonable that, at least in some cases, the *moreh tsedek* was hired because of a problem with the qualifications of the official rabbi.

Rabbi Hayim Halberstam was asked a question about a small town which was situated near a large city.[41] In this small town there had been no cemetery, no rabbi, and no rabbinical court—just a *moreh tsedek*. The smaller community wished to establish a cemetery and wanted all the income from the area served by the new cemetery to go to the local *moreh tsedek* and the local community. The rabbi of the large city objected to this on the grounds that until now he enjoyed honour and income from the small town, and thus he would suffer losses from this new arrangement. Moreover, he claimed, the *moreh tsedek* had a weak personality and could not stand up to evildoers, and as a result, the residents of the small town would no longer be subject to Torah and the commandments. The residents responded by claiming that the rabbi would not suffer significant losses since the local *moreh tsedek* had long received the fees for local weddings. They claimed that their only goal in setting up an independent administration was to build a synagogue and warm ritual bath, and that they ultimately want to hire a learned rabbi who would teach them Torah and instruct them in the correct way of life.

Both the rabbi of the large city and the residents of the small town agreed that there is a distinction between a *moreh tsedek*, who is seen as a technician, and a rabbi, who is expected to be a more charismatic figure ('learned in the Torah') and will take a more active role in communal life. The expectations of a *moreh tsedek* (mastery of the halakhic literature) were clearer than those of a rabbi. On the other hand, the rabbi had a broader range of responsibilities and thus more skills were expected of him.

A responsum sent to a rabbi in Zirowicz dealt with the situation in a city where there had long been two rabbis, one for the Ashkenazim or mitnagedim and one for the Sephardim or hasidim, who employed the Sephardi liturgy.[42] According to the description, most of the halakhic questions (and divorces) were dealt with by the Ashkenazi rabbi. Indeed, the 'Sephardi' rabbi refrained from dealing with all complicated halakhic questions and divorces. When the

---

[41] Halberstam, *Divrei ḥayim*, vol. i, 'Yoreh de'ah', no. 52, p. 78.
[42] Tennenbaum, *Divrei malki'el*, vol. iv, no. 82, pp. 116–20.

hasidic rabbi died, most of the local hasidim preferred to make do with the rabbi of the mitnagedim because it was difficult for them to support a rabbi on their own. However, the brother of the deceased claimed for himself the position of rabbi of the hasidim on the grounds of rights of inheritance. He maintained that it was necessary to have a rabbi who could teach hasidic thought, though the local hasidim claimed that the previous rabbi never did so. The brother was insistent, and since he was not learned enough to fill the role of rabbi, he declared that he wanted to hire a rabbi for a short term to serve the hasidim and in the meantime he would study until he would be prepared for the position.

The reality described here is one in which the rabbi of one group (the hasidim) was not learned, nor did he fulfil any role which could not be done equally well by a rabbi who adhered to the mitnagedim. In other words, there was little difference between the activity of the rabbi of the hasidic community and of the mitnagdic community. The uniqueness of hasidic thought and activity was expressed in the role of the *admor* or *tsadik* and not by a transformation of the traditional rabbinate. For this reason the poor and small hasidic community preferred to make do without a separate rabbi for their community. On the other hand, it had been taken for granted until then that each community should ideally have its own rabbi, even if they got along well. In this community, the ideal of one rabbi for all the local Jews had long been forgotten.

In his response, Rabbi Malki'el Tennenbaum had some rather sharp comments to make on the current rabbinate. He discussed whether it was at all possible to study for a limited period of time and meet the requirements of the rabbinate. In this context he stated that 'today it is enough just to study the codes [and not the more complex Talmud] and know enough to decide halakhic questions since most of the rabbis today are not masters of the *Shulḥan arukh* and the Talmud'.[43] He strongly supported the idea of having only one rabbi for all the Jews in the community on the grounds that this limits conflict.

The opinion that mediocrities can efficiently and reasonably correctly decide halakhic questions was held by others as well. Rabbi Joseph Saul Natanson wrote: 'In our time, when, thank God, latter-day scholars have written guides on every topic, of course everyone who has intelligence and can reason well can determine halakhah.'[44]

*

[43] Tennenbaum, *Divrei malki'el*, vol. iv, no. 82, pp. 116–20.
[44] Natanson, *Responsa*, vol. iii, pt. 3, p. 27, no. 154.

It would be highly exaggerated and incorrect to claim that the decline of the communal rabbinate is what brought on the collapse—if one may use the word—of traditional Jewish society and values in eastern Europe at the turn of the century. However, a simple comparison between the experience of hasidic and mitnagdic populations may show what powerful leadership can do. The many and bitter complaints against the stubborn resistance of hasidim to modernization are testimony to this. Hasidism was not able to roll back the challenge of modernization, but it was able to cut its losses. There were, of course, many socio-economic differences between hasidic and non-hasidic areas which contributed to the differential in modernization between regions. They also make it very difficult to clearly isolate the impact of powerful leadership on the success of hasidism. At the same time it seems reasonable to claim that an absence of strong leadership and organization with the absence of communal rabbis did play a role in the weak response of the traditional camp to the challenges of the time.

The decline in the communal rabbinate may have contributed to a significant phenomenon—the shrinking of the job market for rabbis and the rise of the *kolel* system. As we saw, at the end of the nineteenth century many communities did not wish to hire rabbis. This was exacerbated by the fact that much of the population growth of east European Jewry was in cities, and a neighbourhood rabbi in a city might serve as many Jews as did ten small-town rabbis—but his was only one position. Moreover, city dwellers tended to turn to rabbis less that small-town people. Thus the growing Jewish population of eastern Europe in the nineteenth century did not lead to a corresponding rise in the number of rabbinical posts. Young scholars who were learned in Talmud also found that they did not have the skills, such as advanced general education, necessary to take advantage of the new opportunities for employment for Jews. It was no longer so easy to simply go into trade and hope to pick up the necessary skills 'on the job'. In effect, young scholars found themselves in a very tight rabbinical job market and also frozen out of those occupations which promised the greatest income. This crisis was made more urgent by the drop in numbers of rich people who wished to marry off their daughters to a budding scholar whom they would then support throughout his years of study. The new rich had very different types of sons-in-law in mind.

The radically altered occupational prospects for young scholars was the context for the rise of *kolel*s and yeshivas, both of which provided income-providing frameworks for individuals who would have gone directly into the rabbinate in a different generation. This in turn had an impact on Jewish religious life. Communal rabbis have to deal with laymen all the time and they are constantly encouraged to compromise. On the other hand, *kolel*s give

rewards, both social and financial, to those who practise a particularly rigorous approach to religious life, and there are no incentives in these frameworks
to moderation. Thus the changing occupational patterns could also influence
religious approaches.

   The decline of the communal rabbinate did not mean that rabbinic leadership also disappeared. It remained, but in different patterns.[45] There were
some communal rabbis who exerted great influence. A case that is often cited
is that of Rabbi Yitshak Elhanan Spektor of Kovno. However, it should be
remembered that his fame was due to the fact that he was indeed exceptional.
His role resulted partly from his great talents, and partly from the lack of
accepted communal rabbis in other major cities. However, there were other
rabbis who were very influential, such as Rabbi Yisra'el Meir Hakohen, the
Hafets Hayim, who was rabbi in the small town of Radun, or at a later date,
Rabbi Hayim Ozer Grodzinski, who lived in Vilna but was not the rabbi of the
city. These individuals, or 'super rabbis' as Gershon Bacon terms them, owed
their influence to their charismatic personalities and not to their position.[46]

   With the decline in the communal rabbinate, rabbinic leadership came to
be found more and more among the heads of yeshivas and among *admorim*
or hasidic leaders. *Rashei yeshivah*, leaders of yeshivas, were automatically
influential individuals, if only because they had hundreds of students who
could be counted on to be loyal to them. The *rashei yeshivah* were not bound
by the same influences and restraints as were communal rabbis, and thus the
dynamic of their leadership was applicable to the ideological setting of
the late nineteenth century. In this respect *admorim* were very similar.

   The phenomenon of non-communal rabbis occupying leadership roles in
the traditionalist camp carried over into the twentieth century. If we examine the key figures involved in Agudat Yisra'el, in rabbinical conferences, or in
the traditional wing of the Zionist movement—all measures of rabbinical
importance—it is with few exceptions non-communal rabbis, or communal
rabbis from smaller communities where the communal rabbinate had not
collapsed who played major roles.

   The disappearance of the communal rabbi has, oddly, not attracted attention. It was not a dramatic event nor was it a question of policy. The decline in
the authority of the *kahal* was a precondition for the growth in the number
of communities without rabbis, but it was never the direct cause. The direct
cause usually appeared to be local and different in every case. All of this took
place over a long period. For these reasons contemporaries took it for granted
—if they gave it any attention at all. However, in attempting to analyse what
happened to east European Jewry in the course of the nineteenth century, and

[45] There is a valuable discussion of rabbinical roles in communal leadership in Lederhendler,
The Road to Modern Jewish Politics, 68–83.   [46] On this subject see ibid., from p. 68.

especially to understand the process of modernization, the fate of the communal rabbinate is very enlightening.

Communal rabbis had generally not been very powerful figures in traditional Jewish societies for the real power had been in the hands of the lay leaders of the communities. It was they who had hired and fired rabbis, and not rabbis who appointed the communal leadership. Descriptions of the influence and impact of exceptionally famous rabbis should not be taken as representative of all communal rabbis. Leading rabbis had been charismatic, in one way or another, but the status of most rabbis had understandably been far more limited. Of course, though there were always many more insignificant rabbis than prominent ones, the former received far less attention in the literature of the time and in the memories of subsequent generations than the latter.

The process of Jewish modernization therefore was not a process of liberation from the rule of rabbis (though a struggle against the bonds of tradition was certainly a part of this process), nor is there reason to think that 'the rabbis' could have led the Jewish community forward or in any other direction had they wanted to. The fact that rabbis received so much attention is because they personified tradition. The struggle against tradition needed targets and the rabbis were handy. Tradition was a powerful force, as it is in any society, but this did not mean that rabbis had a great deal of authority beyond technical halakhic issues. There were exceptions. Hasidic leaders—like *rashei yeshivah*—had significant power and apparently some success in resisting the challenges of change in the Jewish communities of eastern Europe during the nineteenth and twentieth centuries. However, these were not communal rabbis. Although the power of communal rabbis was limited even at the height of their authority, developments in the communal rabbinate in modern east European Jewish history are worthy of attention. In this case, their absence was as significant as was their presence in earlier generations.

FOURTEEN

The Inheritance of the Rabbinate in Eastern Europe

THE BEST WAY to become a rabbi on the eve of the Holocaust in eastern Europe was to be born the son of a rabbi.[1] Writing in pre-war Poland, Rabbi Tuvia Yehudah Tavyomi described the situation in these words:

In Congress Poland the tradition was to pass on the rabbinate only to the son or son-in-law of the deceased rabbi (and even this was not a fixed practice and in many towns the sons were not elected) but we never hear that if a rabbi died and left an unmarried daughter, she would transmit the rabbinate to whoever would marry her and it never happened that a rabbinate would be given as a dowry to a daughter. This practice was common in Lithuania and in Volhynia and it was strongly opposed . . . but in our country it was never heard of until very recently.[2]

[1] For a general introduction to the history of the rabbinate see Schwarzfuchs, *A Concise History of the Rabbinate*. On the rabbinate in Europe at the end of the Middle Ages see Katz, *Tradition and Crisis*, chs. 9 and 17, and Cohen, 'On the Character of the Landesrabbiner'. For an earlier period see Zimmer, *Harmony and Discord*, ch. 5. See also Baron, *The Jewish Community*, ch. 11 and his many notes. Bonfil analyses the Italian rabbinate in *Rabbis and Jewish Communities in Renaissance Italy* but makes no reference to inheritance of the rabbinate in Italy and apparently it was not the practice there. On eastern Europe in the early modern period, see Assaf, 'Studies in the History of the Rabbinate' (Heb.), and more recently Reiner, 'The Yeshivas of Poland and Ashkenaz', esp. pp. 29–37. On the rabbinate in 19th-century Russia, see Levitats, *The Jewish Community in Russia*, ch. 8. For a useful introduction to the history of inheritance see Hoenig, 'Filial Succession in the Rabbinate'; Weinberger, 'On Heredity in the Rabbinate' (Heb.); and *Encyclopedia Talmudica* (Heb.), xiv. 346i–73, s.v. 'khezkat serara'. Rabbi Joshua Hutner brought it to my attention. An earlier survey of the halakhic aspects of inheritance is Medini, *Sedeh ḥemed*, vol. viii: *Ma'arekhet ḥazakah bamitsvot*, no. 7, esp. pp. 34–42. *Jewish History*, 8/1 (Spring 1999) was devoted to the topic. The recent publication by Brocke and Carlebach, *Biographisches Handbuch der Rabbiner*, vol. i, gives detailed lists of rabbis for the central European Jewish communities. These data could be analysed to provide a detailed picture of inheritance in central Europe. There is no equivalent for eastern Europe. On Hungary see Silber, 'Aspects of Inheritancee of the Rabbinate in Orthodox Hungarian Jewry' (Heb.). A remarkable recent Ph.D. thesis by Hayim Gertner, 'Rabbis and Rabbinical Judges' (Heb.), contains a prosopographic study of the Galician rabbinate and includes a detailed discussion of inheritance of the rabbinate on pages 243–56.

[2] Tavyomi, *Erets tovah*, no. 6, p. 18. The responsum was addressed to Rabbi Yitshak Edelberg, who became rabbi around 1928; see *Recordbooks of the Jewish Communities: Poland* (Heb.),

This situation would not have surprised the *ge'onim* (religious leaders) of Babylonia (sixth to eleventh centuries CE) or Maimonides (1138–1204). In the *Mishneh torah* Maimonides wrote: 'Not only the monarchy but every position of authority and every appointment in Israel is passed on by inheritance to the son and grandson for ever and this is on condition that the son can fill the place of his ancestors with respect to wisdom and fear of the Lord.'[3] Realities today are not very different. Inheritance of rabbinical posts is almost taken for granted in many contemporary Orthodox or strictly Orthodox Jewish communities. This is true not only in hasidic groups, where inheritance is an integral element of the dynastic system, but in yeshivas and other Orthodox communities as well. It would be tempting but incorrect to assume that there was an unbroken tradition of inheritance of rabbinical posts from antiquity to the modern period.[4] Granted, in many Jewish societies inheritance of rabbinic leadership was accepted. However, as we shall see below, for centuries the standard pattern of Ashkenazi Jewry was quite different. In medieval and early modern Ashkenazi Jewry, inheritance of rabbinic posts was actually prohibited. The situation described by Rabbi Tavyomi was thus the culmination of a long period of 'revival' of the once rejected practice of inheritance and not a direct continuation of tradition. In other words, although contemporary inheritance of rabbinical posts appears very traditional and even archaic, in reality it is also a modern innovation. I shall suggest that it was a practical and reasonable response to changes that took place in the structure of the Jewish community in modern times and that clarifying this development sheds light on the nature of the east European rabbinate and the characteristics of the Jewish community.

INHERITANCE OF THE RABBINATE IN EARLY MODERN ASHKENAZ

In the late Middle Ages and early modern period Ashkenazi Jewish communities were concerned that rabbis might be influenced by family ties with members of their communities. Since the Jewish population of many towns was small, and rabbis often had to decide legal questions which could have great consequences for the individuals involved, steps were taken to try to minimize possible influences on rabbis. One of the ways to do this was to avoid appointing a rabbi who had family connections or bonds of friendship

ed. Dąbrowska et al., iv. 265. Rabbi Tavyomi immigrated to Erets Yisra'el in 1936 (see ibid. 319) and it seems reasonable that he wrote the responsum before he left Poland.

[3] Maimonides, *Mishneh torah*, 'Hilkhot melakhim' (Laws of Kings), 1: 7.

[4] It would be quite interesting and not terribly difficult to trace the interpretation of this text in rabbinic literature.

with members of the community.[5] In many communities this was formalized in the form of an ordinance that prohibited the appointment of a son to his father's rabbinical position. This limitation protected against the negative effects of nepotism. To be sure, Rabbi Moses Isserles wrote in his glosses on the *Shulḥan arukh*:

Sons and grandsons always have precedence before others as long as they fill the place of their ancestors in fear of God and they are [at least] a bit wise (*ḥakhamim ketsat*) and in a place where the custom is to take a rabbi for a fixed period of time or to choose whomever they [the community] wishes (e.g. not just the son), they may do so.[6]

Isserles was torn between the clear statement of the *Shulḥan arukh* in favour of inheritance and the contemporary practice of many communities to prevent this.[7]

Prohibitions on the appointment of sons to the rabbinical posts of fathers were not just paper decisions and they were adhered to in practice. There are cases of important rabbis who were denied appointment to their father's position on the grounds that this would be a violation of these ordinances. Critics of the Ashkenazi rabbinate in the fifteenth and sixteenth centuries attacked the appointment of unqualified individuals to rabbinic posts, but they rarely cited appointments of sons to their fathers' positions as a reason for problems in the rabbinate.[8] Given their critical bent, had such a phenomenon been widespread they would have been quick to condemn it as well. Ben Sasson's classic survey of the social thought of Polish Jewry in the sixteenth and seventeenth centuries cites many criticisms of the contemporary rabbinate, but there were almost no references to inheritance.[9] In the eighteenth century there were new problems regarding the rabbinate in Poland, among them the intervention by nobles in the communal appointment of rabbis.[10] However, these were exceptions in their time and most communities selected rabbis by election. The question of inheritance was not widely discussed.

[5] See Grossman, 'Family Lineage and its Place in Early Ashkenazi Jewish Society' (Heb.), and 'From Father to Son' (Heb.). It is important to distinguish between oligarchies or the concentration of positions of authority in a limited number of families and the view that heirs—and only heirs—have special rights to a rabbinical position.

[6] Isserles, *Hamapah*, 'Yoreh de'ah', *Hilkhot melamdim*, 245: 20.

[7] Simcha Assaf, 'Studies in the History of the Rabbinate' (Heb.), 40. See the vivid description of a case in the introduction of R. Ya'ir Bacharach (1639–1702) to his *Kelalei ets haḥayim* appended to his *Ḥavot ya'ir*. I used the Jerusalem 1992 edition but there are many others.

[8] See Dinari, *The Rabbis of Germany and Austria at the Close of the Middle Ages* (Heb.), 60, and the sources brought together by Shulman, *Authority and Community*, 74–5.

[9] Ben-Sasson, *Reflection and Leadership* (Heb.), 97–8 and 221–8. See also Piekarz, *The Beginning of Hasidism* (Heb.), ch. 10. Piekarz cited an ethical tract (Wolf, *Taharat hakodesh*) which criticized inheritance but concentrated on a related but different issue, the sale of rabbinical positions (ibid. 380).   [10] See Teller, 'Radziwill, Rabinowicz and the Rabbi of Swierz'.

In most Jewish communities in German-speaking lands, inheritance of rabbinic posts was the exception in the late Middle Ages and not at all the rule. In the western branch of Ashkenazi Jewry, inheritance has remained rare up until the present day.[11] The well-known dynasty of the Hirsch-Breuer family in Frankfurt was exceptional.

Inheritance became increasingly common in east-central Europe in the eighteenth century. Rabbi Ezekiel Landau of Prague (1713–93) found it justifiable to call on a community to appoint a son to his late father's post even though the community had an enactment not to appoint the son of a previous rabbi.[12] On the other hand, the need to call on the community to do so indicates that opposition to inheritance was still quite alive. The famous Hungarian rabbi Moses Sofer of Pressburg/Bratislava (1762–1839) came out very strongly in 1820 against inheritance of the rabbinate,[13] but on his death-bed he called on the communal elders to appoint his son as his successor.[14] They did. More or less from then on inheritance of rabbinical positions became standard in Hungary.

It is not a simple matter to trace the timing of the changes or the dynamics of the geographical spread of inheritance in Poland and eastern Europe. It may be that already by the seventeenth century there were differences between the western branch of Ashkenazi Jewry and the east European branch with regard to inheritance of rabbinic posts. In the mid-seventeenth century some Polish rabbis had already given qualified support to claims to the rabbinate on the basis of inheritance. A responsum of Rabbi Sha'ul ben Heschel (d. 1707)[15] of Lvov dealt with a community which had previously made an enactment not to appoint a rabbi who had relatives in the community, but now wanted to appoint the son-in-law of the previous rabbi. Apparently there were enough votes to elect the son-in-law, but not enough to abrogate the enactment. From his answer it appears that he felt that sons of a rabbi should be preferred over other candidates, but he also made it clear that he was aware that this was a controversial stand.[16]

---

[11] Inheritance would have been totally against the grain of the new German rabbinate. See the description in Schorsch, 'Emancipation and the Crisis of Religious Authority'.

[12] See the responsum of Rabbi Ezekiel Landau published in *Kovets beit aharon veyisra'el*, 6/6 (36).   [13] See Sofer, *Sefer ḥatam sofer*, 'Oraḥ ḥayim', no. 2.

[14] On Mosheh Sofer, see Katz, 'Toward a Biography of the Hatam Sofer'.

[15] On R. Sha'ul ben Heschel, see Zunz, *City of Righteousness* (Heb.), 144. On his father, Avraham Yehoshua Heschel, see p. 104. See the text, and the reasons for its insertion, in *Kovets beit aharon veyisra'el*, 6/6 (36) (1991). R. Sha'ul mentions a responsum by R. Moses Isserles on the topic but it does not seem to have been preserved.

[16] In his responsum R. Sha'ul dealt with the problems that can arise if the rabbi has relatives in the community and stated that, were it not for the enactment, the son-in-law could claim the post on the basis of rights of inheritance. He added that his father, R. Avraham Yehoshua Heschel (b. Jacob; d. 1664), who had served as the rabbi of Kraków, had held that worthy sons

Other sources show that inheritance was far from being the standard doctrine in early modern Poland. This is illustrated by an incident in the life of Rabbi Uri Shraga Feibush. This noted Polish Jewish scholar visited the Hungarian town of Alt-Ofen in 1655. The Jewish community took advantage of the visit by a famous scholar and asked him to establish ordinances for the good of the local community. One of his suggestions was to prohibit the appointment of rabbis with family ties in Alt-Ofen.[17]

The best way to reconstruct exactly the spread of inheritance of rabbinical posts would be to check a master list of communities and their rabbis and thus to chart the spread of the phenomenon. Unfortunately, there is no systematic listing of the rabbis of eastern Europe together with their biographies, and certainly no collective biographical study of the rabbinate.[18] In Galicia Hayim Gertner found that in a third of the eighty largest communities in the eighteenth century the rabbinate was inherited, though in about half of these communities inheritance was discontinued during the course of the nineteenth century.[19] He found that, in general, inheritance spread most in the nineteenth century in the smaller communities,[20] and more in hasidic communities than non-hasidic communities.[21] He did not deal with other regions. However, it is possible to get a rough picture of the timing and also of some of the reasons for the acceptance of this practice. Many rabbinical responsa written in eastern Europe deal with various questions that came up with regard to inheritance of the rabbinate.[22] The dates of the responsa and the locations of the questioners and of the responders make it possible to document both changing values and modifications in practice as well. Three key issues were standard themes in the responsa: authority, qualifications, and the right to inherit. Not surprisingly, they have a direct bearing on the nature of the rabbinate in eastern Europe. The following typical examples

should not be rejected from positions. At the same time, R. Shaul assumed that a community had a right to make such enactments.

[17] See Hakohen, *Sha'ar efrayim* (Heb.), who cites the *takanot* (enactments) of Uri Shraga Feibush on p. 41. On Rabbi Feibush, who ultimately came to Jerusalem, see Frumkin, *History of the Sages of Jerusalem* (Heb.), 11, 47.

[18] Such a study could be very valuable and should be undertaken. New resources such as Wunder's multi-volume encyclopedia of Galician rabbis, *Lights of Galicia* (Heb.), and *Record-books of the Jewish Communities* (as yet incomplete), could profitably be used to this purpose. There are some methodological problems as well as gaps in sources which would have to be cleared up in order to do such an analysis well.

[19] Gertner, 'Rabbis and Rabbinical Judges' (Heb.), 244–5.   [20] Ibid. 249.   [21] Ibid. 250.

[22] This led to the creation of a substantial legal literature on the topic of inheritance of rabbinical positions. I found Kahana-Shapira (ed.), *Otsar hashe'elot uteshuvot*, vol. i, to be a very useful starting point. The responsa dealing with this topic are mentioned on pages 135–40. However, the listing there is far from complete. The *Otsar haposekim* data base is a very rich source for this and all of the responsa literature.

from the responsa literature illustrate the approaches to these issues that were common in the modern period.

The first issue, authority, was a complex one. A rabbi's authority was linked to the power of the body that elected him, and therefore responsa dealing with inheritance generally assumed an inability to impose an unwanted rabbi on a community. This is illustrated in the case of a rabbi, apparently unemployed, who claimed that since his father had been the rabbi of a certain community twenty years previously, the position was his by right of inheritance even though the townspeople preferred another candidate. The question was sent to a Galician rabbi, Rabbi Avraham Ze'ev Frankel (1780–1849), and the law for him was clear: if for any reason an heir did not immediately fill the position of his father, he and all other descendants forfeited any future claims to the position. As he explained it, inheritance was only a custom and therefore, in principle, the townspeople had the right to pick a different rabbi. He added that he held this view because only the candidate of the townspeople would be heeded. Rabbis recognized both in theory and in practice that the right to appoint is in the hands of the community.[23]

Second, and equally problematic, was the issue of the qualifications of the prospective successor. No rabbinic authority ever claimed that a totally incompetent son should inherit his father's position. Most legal authorities assumed that when a candidate was sufficiently competent not to make major halakhic errors he should be given the job. If complicated legal cases arose a rabbi could always consult books or more renowned authorities.[24] Supporters of inheritance generally assumed that what was involved was a question of preference for the heir over other more or less equally competent candidates. An example of the potential for complications with regard to competence can be found in a responsum of Rabbi Joseph Saul Natanson (d. 1875) from around 1848. It dealt with the claim of Rabbi Hayim Ya'akov Dominitz of Hussakow to his late father's post and the charges raised by his opponents that

---

[23] Frankel, *Meshiv kehalakhah*, no. 21 starting on p. 40. See on him Wunder, *Lights of Galicia* (Heb.), iv. 274–6. The responsum was addressed to R. Menasheh Rubin with regard to a question about the rabbinate in the town of Łazów. The responsum is not dated but was probably written around 1845 since R. Rubin became *admor* of Ropczyce in 1845: *Recordbooks of the Jewish Communities: Poland* (Heb.), ed. Dąbrowska et al., iii. 351. R. Frankel died in 1849 and this incident is cited by R. Yosef Shaul Natanson with regard to a case that happened around 1845 (see below).

[24] Rabbi Natanson supported the claim of the mediocre son of a great father to the father's post on the grounds that 'in our days, the number of books of Jewish law that have been published on every topic has increased, thank God', so that even a mediocre rabbi will not make errors (Natanson, *Responsa*, vol. iii, pt. 1, p. 27*a*, no. 154). I used the Jerusalem 1973 reprint. These views were shared by others. See Klatskin, *Devar eliyahu*, no. 21, p. 31, who wrote that one of the reasons that the status of Torah is low is that scholars have no honour and minor figures inherit the chair of honour in important cities.

he was unqualified for the position.[25] Rabbi Natanson did not deal directly with the charges, and noted that inheritance should not be automatic and that wisdom was necessary for the post of rabbi. However, he added, he was sure Hayim Ya'akov would merit divine assistance and therefore called upon the community to support his claim. Claims of competence and incompetence were seldom resolved to the satisfaction of all parties. The invocation of divine assistance, as long as there was minimal competence, was one way of ending the series of claims and counterclaims, though it is highly unlikely that everyone was satisfied with this pious hope.

The third problematic issue was finding a legal justification for inheritance. Property can be inherited, but a rabbinical post is not property. What, then, was inherited? One legal scholar claimed that the rabbinate is a commitment to support a scholar, and this commitment is what is inherited and not rights of leadership.[26] This was not totally convincing and, given the questionable legal status of inheritance, there was clearly an incentive to resolve disagreements through compromise and not formal legal decisions.[27] Claims by sons-in-law raised special problems. According to Jewish law, sons-in-law have no rights of inheritance but, in fact, rabbinic posts were often transmitted to a son-in-law. As popular wisdom has it, sons cannot be chosen but sons-in-law can. Grounding the claims of a son-in-law in Jewish law was not

[25] See Natanson, *Responsa*, vol. i, pt. 2, p. 11*a*, no. 17. The case was complex. The candidate, R. Hayim Ya'akov, had agreed to be tested by the rabbi of Przemysl. The results were satisfactory but this was not sufficient for his opponents who then demanded that he be tested by the even more famous rabbi of Dobromil. Here he was less successful. The rabbi of Dobromil (apparently R. Avraham Mordekhai Rimalt) stated that a son should not succeed a father unless the entire community approved, which meant in this case that R. Hayim would not get the post. Ironically, R. Rimalt's son died leaving an infant son. The vacated seat of the rabbinate was filled by a non-member of the family who promised that when the son came of age he would transfer the position to him—and so he did. See *Recordbooks of the Jewish Communities: Poland* (Heb.), ed. Dąbrowska et al., ii. 150–1.

[26] Horowitz, *Tsur ya'akov*, no. 177, p. 217, to R. Avraham of Strelisk. The recipient of the responsum was apparently A. Landman (Wunder, *Lights of Galicia* (Heb.), iii. 690).

[27] Heilprin's responsum, *She'elot uteshuvot ma'aharash*, no. 1, written apparently around 1879, dealt with the claim of R. Mosheh Shapira to the rabbinate of Sassov; see Wunder, *Lights of Galicia* (Heb.), v. 521. R. Shapira had formally signed away his claim to the rabbinate of Sassov but claimed he was pressured into this and therefore his signature was invalid. R. Hailperin replied that this was not a question for a court to resolve but the two sides must get together and work out a compromise. The call for a compromise was practical but it was also a reflection of the weak legal status of claims to inheritance. Similarly, when Ya'akov Yosef Shapira claimed the right to be rabbi of Jagielnica on the grounds that for generations his forefathers had filled that position (see *Recordbooks of the Jewish Communities: Poland* (Heb.), ed. Dąbrowska et al., ii. 279, and Wunder, *Lights of Galicia* (Heb.), v. 499, 527) the response of R. Teitelbaum was to call for a compromise and for financial recompense (i.e. a pay-off) for R. Shapira (see Teitelbaum, *Avnei tsedek*, no. 100).

easy for rabbis and was a constant reminder of the shaky legal basis of rabbinical inheritance.

Rabbis were aware that inheritance could be abused and they could respond vigorously. A case in point involved the widow of a popular rabbi who only allowed a community to bury her husband when it committed itself to appointing the rabbi's son, better known as a businessman than as a rabbinical figure, to succeed his father. The widow presumably was concerned that otherwise her son would never have been offered the position.[28] After the funeral the community turned to Rabbi Joseph Saul Natanson of Lvov (1810–1875) to find out if the appointment was binding. He quickly responded that it was not because it was taken under duress.[29]

THE HISTORICAL GEOGRAPHY OF RABBINICAL INHERITANCE IN POLAND

By the eighteenth century inheritance seems to have been common but not the rule. The case of Lask appears to have been typical. When the local rabbi, Me'ir Getz, died in 1738, his son Elyakum succeeded him. The next rabbi of Lask was Rabbi Pinhas Zelig, no relative, and when he died his son also inherited the position. A local historian commented that while Rabbi Pinchas Zelig's son was not famed for his scholarship, he must have been talented otherwise he would not have been given the appointment. However, he added gently, perhaps the merit of the late Rabbi Pinchas Zelig also assisted.[30] It certainly did not hinder.

---

[28] Natanson, *Responsa*, vol. iii, pt. 2, p. 32*a–b*, no. 117; see esp. p. 32*b*.

[29] In a responsum that deals with a similar case from 1857 from Drohobycz, a complicated situation is described in which the son of a deceased rabbi was apparently 'tricked' out of his inheritance by another rabbi, and upon the death of the latter—who also left a son—the question arose as to which son had the rights to the position. The widow of the second rabbi encouraged her son to claim the local rabbinate, even though he had little interest in actually taking the post. Her motives were clear: she wanted to keep alive the family rights to the position. The resolution is not so important as is the assumption by the parties involved in this case that the position should go on to a son. Natanson, *Responsa*, vol. i, pt. 2, p. 11*b*, no. 19. The concern of mothers for sons, sometimes in opposition to sons-in-law, is not rare in the responsa literature and it may be indicative of some of the family dynamics of the time: see, for example, a responsum from 1917 (Segal-Mishal, *Mishnat eli'ezer*, 2nd section, no. 7, starting on page 112*a*) which dealt with a community in which a sick old rabbi had appointed his son-in-law to carry out his duties. Four years later, the rabbi died leaving a 13-year-old son. The townspeople wanted to retain the son-in-law as rabbi but the widow, apparently more attached to her son than to her daughter, agreed only on condition that the son-in-law would hold the position temporarily and recognize the rights of the son to the position. The question was, was this agreement binding?

[30] Gliksman, *The Town of Lask and its Sages* (Heb.), 10 and 31. I thank Professor Gershon Bacon for referring me to this source.

Until the mid-nineteenth century a rabbi's son could not take inheritance of a position for granted. This is shown both by the questions raised in responsa and by the answers. In one of the earliest Galician responsa on the topic,[31] written in the first half of the nineteenth century, inheritance was presented as a reasonable basis for a claim, but only one factor among many and it could not override the wishes of the community.[32] A contemporary wrote that inheritance by sons was a custom and no more, and therefore did not guarantee a post to a son, son-in-law, or grandchildren.[33] It was noted above that Rabbi Joseph Saul Natanson also emphasized that inheritance was far from being an automatic procedure.[34]

Two leading nineteenth-century rabbis in Congress Poland, Rabbi Yisra'el of Kutna (d. 1893) and Rabbi Hayim Elazar of Kalisz (d. 1889), also stated that a claim to inheritance was valid only with the support of the majority of the community or, at least, of a majority of the scholars, and their opinion was shared by others.[35] However, it appears that the practice was spreading during the nineteenth century. Rabbi Natanson noted:

. . . because of our many sins, many ignoramuses who are sons of rabbis [inherit rabbinical posts] . . . the Torah will disappear since . . . why study since if a scholar is not a descendant of rabbis, of what avail is all of their studies? In our own eyes we have seen that in Eastern Ukraine and Volhynia, there are few legal authorities and also in our country, their number diminishes every day . . . what is the point of being a *posek* . . . [without] the glory of a rabbinical position—however, [today] a rabbinical position is given to the descendants of a rabbis—whether wise or fools. There is much to say on this topic but since just as it is a *mitsvah* to speak out when one will be heeded [so one should keep silent when one will not] because, God have mercy on us, this disease has spread.[36]

In the second half of the nineteenth century, questions with regard to inheritance tended to be related more to questions of implementation or exceptional cases. In other words, it was assumed by all the parties involved that, under normal circumstances, inheritance would be effective. A responsum written in 1862 in Żurawno (eastern Galicia) dealt with the case of

---

[31] For reasons that are not totally clear, there are many more responsa from Galicia on the topic of rabbinic inheritance than from other regions. It does not seem that the problems of inheritance were more severe there than elsewhere or that inheritance was more widespread there. It may be that we simply have more responsa literature from this area.

[32] Frankel, *Meshiv kehalakhah*, no. 21, starting on p. 40.

[33] See an undated responsum of R. Avraham David Wahrman of Buczacz (d. 1841) in his *Eshel avraham*, pt. i, note on *Shulḥan arukh*, 'Oraḥ ḥayim', 53: 25, p. 7. He noted about himself that he undertook not to have a formal appointment and hence his heirs would not have formal grounds to claim his post on the basis of rights of inheritance.

[34] It seems clear, however, that R. Natanson preferred inheritance.

[35] Bornstein, *Avnei nezer*, 'Yoreh de'ah', pt. i, no. 312, pp. 114–17.

[36] Natanson, *Responsa*, vol. iii, pt. 1, p. 27*a*, no. 154. These views were shared by others.

a rabbi's son who sought to supplant his father's successor ten years after the father's death.[37] The author of the responsum rejected the claim on the grounds that it was too late to make a claim but agreed that basically a rabbinic post should be inherited. This same position was expressed in a case from the end of the nineteenth century.[38] Rabbi Hayim Halberstam claimed that the laws of inheritance should apply to rabbinical positions on the basis of law and not just custom,[39] and Rabbi Eitinga of Lvov expressed a similar position in 1877,[40] though in the late nineteenth century the rights of sons-in-law were still unclear.[41] In Congress Poland inheritance became standard. As one scholar put it: 'The practice has spread in the whole world that a capable son inherits his father in the rabbinate.'[42]

From the end of the nineteenth century, inheritance was taken for granted in Poland and responsa dealt more with the implications of inheritance than with the basic question of whether there was a right to inheritance. In 1897 a rabbi intervened to defend the rights of two sons of a deceased rabbi from the encroachment of a brother-in-law.[43] A 1905 responsum[44] dealt with the question of which grandchildren could inherit a position—the children of

[37] Yitshak Horowitz, *Toledot yitshak*, pt. 1, p. 9, 'Dinei shaliah tsibur', rule 1.

[38] In a responsum from 1893, R. Natan Landau wrote to the son of a rabbi who had not received his father's position that in principle he should have received the position, but what was done could not be overturned. Landau, *Kena renanah*, no. 27.

[39] Halberstam, *Divrei hayim*, vol. i, 'Yoreh de'ah', no. 53, p. 80. Rabbi Halberstam dealt with a case where a claim to the post of Radomysl (western Galicia) was made by R. Pinhas Katz, the grandson of a former rabbi (Wunder, *Lights of Galicia* (Heb.), 111, 342). At the time of his father's death, he had been young, and therefore his aunt's husband filled the post. According to R. Halberstam, this was a temporary arrangement and the uncle received the position only in order to preserve the rights of the son.

[40] Eitinga, *She'elot uteshuvot maharyah halevi*, no. 24. A rabbi had died and left two sons. All parties agreed that the question was which of the two sons should get the position. What troubled the rabbi was that R. Moses Isserles saw inheritance of the rabbinate as a custom whereas for him it was a clear case of legal right, and he asked on what grounds custom could overrule legal rights. His answer was that it is possible to make an appointment to a position with the condition that the position will not be passed on as an inheritance!

[41] Orenstein, *Birkat ratsah*. In a responsum of 1873 (no. 123) he rejects the claim that a son-in-law has the legal status of a son and in no. 110 he claims that if a rabbinical contract was given to someone over the protests of a son-in-law, then the contract should override the complaint.

[42] Bornstein, *Avnei nezer*, 'Yoreh de'ah', pt. i, no. 312, p. 121. Shortly after mid century, in Zasław (in Volhynia) the local rabbi claimed that not only did sons have a right to inherit positions, but that in a dispute between the son of the last rabbi and the grandson of a previous rabbi (who had not transmitted his position to his son), that the grandson had precedence over the son. See Aryeh Leib ben Eliyahu (Bolechover), *She'elot uteshuvot shem ariyeh*, no. 7, p. 16.

[43] Yerushalimski, *Be'er mosheh*, no. 10, p. 165. The author, R. Mosheh Yerushalimski, was rabbi of Ostrolenko.

[44] Schwadron, *She'elot uteshuvot maharsham*, pt. iv, p. 73*b*, no. 143, addressed to Rabbi Mordekhai Halberstam of Gribov. Already in his *Mishpat shalom*, no. 237: 16, p. 220, he had dealt with inheritance as a binding principle.

the firstborn son who had chosen not to succeed his father, or the children of the younger son who had actually succeeded the father? Yet another rabbi took inheritance for granted and simply used it as a starting point for an elaborate argument.[45] For one rabbi who wrote after the First World War it was clear that 'the right of the rabbinate is inherited and the townspeople have no right to give the position to anyone else'.[46] Cases, reflecting life, could get very complicated. What were the rights of a rabbi's daughter who had been married to a simple man but, after her father's death, had divorced and remarried, this time to a capable rabbi? Did her new husband have a right to her father's post? This was regarded as an issue serious enough to warrant a fully fledged responsum.[47] In another case, one rather unlearned heir proposed that he would study until he was prepared to succeed his father and wanted the position held for him. This proposal was not rejected out of hand, though the legal decider involved felt the only way to maintain inheritance and at the same time to prevent abuses was to consult with well-known rabbis.[48]

The rights of a minor son were a constant issue, which indicates how much inheritance was taken for granted. Should a community save a rabbinic post for a minor son of a deceased rabbi[49] or for a future son-in-law?[50] In one such case, Rabbi Aryeh Fromer (in one of the last books of responsa printed in Lublin in eastern Poland in 1938) decided in favour of the son. He noted that in his time 'the main function of the rabbinate is to earn a livelihood and it is not a matter of honour—actually a scholar who is not a communal rabbi is even more honoured', and as such his post can be inherited.[51] In other words, the rabbi had become a functionary, and figureheads can inherit positions.

In the twentieth century we find, for the first time in modern Poland, reference to the sale of rights (*ḥazakah*) to the rabbinate. A certain rabbi sold

---

[45]   See Haft, *Divrei ta'am*, no. 105, pp. 184–5.

[46]   Yehoshua Horowitz of Dzików, *Ateret yeshuah*, no. 26, p. 188.

[47]   Klatskin, *Devar eliyahu*, no. 21, p. 31.

[48]   Tennenbaum, *Divrei malki'el*, vol. iv, no. 82, pp. 116–20.

[49]   According to Meir Wunder (oral communication), a rabbi who filled a position until a minor son of the previous rabbi came of age was called a *meineket*, or wet nurse.

[50]   In a responsum written to the rabbi of Makov, mention is made of a town where there was always a rabbi and a *moreh hora'ah* (teacher of instruction), a rabbi who had no communal responsibilities other than deciding legal questions. The *moreh hora'ah* died and a proposal was made to reserve the position for the future husband of the daughter. The rabbi and many townspeople were opposed to the idea but it did have a fair degree of support. In other words, the concept of a rabbinical position as the property of a family had reached a point at which a position could be kept empty and automatically transmitted to a person whose very identity was not yet determined. Tavyomi, *Erets tovah*, no. 6.

[51]   The case involved a situation where a son-in-law 'filled in' while the young son was growing up, but when the son reached maturity the implementation of the agreement was questioned. See Fromer, *She'elot uteshuvot erets tsevi*, no. 103, p. 231.

his rights along with his apartment and promised not to be a candidate for the position. The buyer was duly elected and even received the apartment he had been promised. Simony had not been unheard of in earlier periods, but it had always involved payment to the community. To sell a rabbinic post to a private individual, as any other private property, was an innovation.[52]

Inheritance still had its limits in interwar Poland. A presumptive heir who came to a town with the intention of replacing the incumbent town rabbi on the grounds that he had rights of inheritance was sharply criticized. It was reported that all the rabbis of Poland said that he should either leave the town or agree to a compromise.[53] Similarly, when a growing community wanted to have its own rabbi rather than depend on the rabbi of a nearby town, the request of the community was upheld despite the fact that this meant denying the incumbent rabbi of part of his inheritance.[54]

LITHUANIA AND WHITE RUSSIA

Inheritance seems to have come later to Lithuania than to Poland. One of the earlier responsa of Lithuanian Jews on rabbinical inheritance was written by Rabbi Shemuel Avigdor Tosfa'ah[55] in 1856 to an unnamed community. Rabbi Tosfa'ah ruled that, in general, rabbinical appointments are not inherited. With time the view that inheritance was a right became more common. Rabbi Zekharyah Stern, rabbi of Shavli, held that inheritance should be followed as long as no one had been appointed to the position in the interim.[56] Rabbi Stern explained at some length that since many groups have to be placated in order to elect a rabbi and, in any case, the best candidates were not being accepted, one might as well turn to the son. However, from his responsum it is clear that he was expressing his personal view and not claiming that inheritance was an accepted practice in Lithuania. Even at the end of the century

---

[52] Nebenzahl, *Minḥat yeḥi'el*, pt. iii, no. 38, p. 44.

[53] See Nebenzahl, *Minḥat yeḥi'el*, pt. i, no. 118, p. 153.

[54] The responsum was written in Kołomyja in the wake of the First World War. See Reiss, *Shoshanim ledavid*, no. 2, p. 5.

[55] Tosfa'ah, *She'elot shemuel*, no. 6. The case involved the son of a rabbi who claimed the right to succeed his father after an eight-year delay. The community was split over the issue, though it may be that some of the support for the son was based less on the merits of his case than on dislike for the current rabbi.

[56] Stem, *Zekher yehosef*, no. 18, p. 55. He told the story of the rabbi of Metz, Aryeh Leib ben Asher (1695–1785, the Sha'agat Aryeh), whose community offered a contract to his son on Purim as part of their *mishlo'aḥ manot* (gifts sent on Purim) to him. The response of the rabbi was simple. He tore up the contract and explained, 'if my son will be worthy of the position and if the Metz community does not want to appointment him, some other community will. If he is not, why do you suspect me of favouritism to think that giving him an appointment will gladden me?' While R. Stem felt that this response was laudable, he also held that if all things are equal, sons should be given precedence.

inheritance was still not to be taken for granted in Lithuania. Rabbi Yehi'el Mikhal Epstein (1829–1908) noted that there are views in rabbinical literature that a son has precedence, but he was not familiar with this practice. In his opinion the members of a community should have a free hand in choosing a rabbi and a son has a claim only if he has the same qualities as his father.[57]

However, by the interwar period—and probably earlier as well—inheritance had become standard in Lithuania. Responsa from the period corroborate this. A Lithuanian rabbi in Riga (Latvia) stated, in a responsum written apparently between the wars,[58] that the son of a deceased rabbi can claim—and receive—the position of his father when he comes of age no matter how effective and qualified the interim rabbi had been and no matter what the wishes of the community are. For him, this was obvious.[59]

Lubavitch hasidim, living in neighbouring White Russia,[60] also accepted the principle of inheritance. In a letter written in Lyady in 1903, Rabbi Yitshak Dov Ber Schneerson strongly supported inheritance.[61] This, he wrote, was what the community owed the father in return for his having worked for the good of the city.

ROMANIA

Although not living in a Slavonic-speaking land, Romanian Jews were strongly influenced by developments in Poland and are therefore interesting for comparative purposes. Problems of inheritance came up in the first half of the nineteenth century.[62] In a responsum written apparently in the 1870s or early 1880s, Rabbi Shalom Toibesh, a Galician rabbi living in Romania, wrote that a new and growing community had a right to secede from a veteran and central community, and that this did not violate the right of inheritance of the rabbi of the more veteran community. He pointed out that it 'has been the

[57] Epstein, *Arukh hashulḥan*, 'Yoreh de'ah', 355: 29.
[58] Zelbovic, *Ateret mordekhai*, no. 204.
[59] In a 1932 responsum written by the rabbi of Pinsk, the question was raised about the claims to the rabbinate in a town in which two feuding groups had each appointed a rabbi. The question arose as to the status of the sons of the rabbis on both sides. The rights of inheritance were taken for granted and the discussion dealt mainly with the implications of having two rabbis in one community. R. Walkin was against multiple rabbis and suggested paying one of the rabbis to drop his claims. See Walkin, *Zekan aharon*, pt. 11, no. 64, p. 79.
[60] There was, of course, no political unit by this name in the 19th century. The reference is to those western provinces of the Russian empire which were referred to by Jews as 'Lite'.
[61] Schneerson, Letter.
[62] A responsum written no later than 1856 by R. Aryeh Leib ben Eliyahu (Bolechover), *She'elot uteshuvot shem aryeh*, no. 7, p. 13, dealt with a community that was split over the question of whether the son should inherit the position or not. In his answer, R. Bolechover (d. 1881) wrote that if the heir is not inferior to the other candidate, he has a right to the position.

custom for generations that the son serves in place of his father'.[63] Responsa written at a later date by the rabbi of Czernowitz, Rabbi Binyamin Aryeh Weiss, seconded these views.[64] In Romania as well inheritance had become a standard practice.

The geographic spread of inheritance had been completed by the outbreak of the Second World War. By then it was no longer one option out of several for selecting a rabbi. In most parts of eastern Europe it had become the standard practice. This was even reflected in the halakhic literature of the time. Rabbi Avraham Bornstein of Sochaczew (d. 1910) devoted a major study (sixteen double-column pages) in his book *Avnei nezer* (Precious Stones) to the halakhic aspects of inheritance of the rabbinate. Ostensibly it was written to answer a question as to whether a son-in-law has a right to inherit his father-in-law's position or not. However, from the amount of attention he gave to the question, he clearly felt that the phenomenon was widespread enough to warrant a broad-scale treatment. This was not the only composition devoted to inheritance. In 1928 a Lithuanian rabbi published a separate treatise on the topic.[65] One decade later, a Galician scholar, Rabbi Eliyahu Teomim-Fraenkel (1877–1943), wrote a survey of the opinions that was more than twice as long as that of Rabbi Bornstein. He systematically considered almost every possibility and analysed the positions of previous rabbis.[66] Even though the discussions of inheritance by Rabbi Bornstein and Rabbi Teomim-Fraenkel were published in books of responsa, both of them were basically treatises that filled in the gaps in the existing volumes of Jewish law.

---

[63] Toibesh, *She'elat shalom*, pt. 2, no. 276, starting on p. 99. In 1879 in Iaşi his brother wrote a responsum with regard to the question of the rabbinate in Brăila, Wallachia. After the death of the local rabbi, R. Ya'akov Margolis, some members of the community wanted to appoint an outsider to succeed him instead of his son. The responsum criticized this attempt on the grounds that the rabbinate was a salaried position which gave the rabbi rights to payments for ritual services and therefore if an outsider took the position, he was guilty of trespass. See Toibs, *Ori veyishi*, no. 35, p. 23. Ultimately, the two sons of the deceased rabbi shared the position of rabbi.

[64] Weiss, *Even yekarah*, an undated responsum, continues the saga of the Margolis brothers who shared the rabbinate in Brăila (see no. 2, starting bottom of p. 1*b*; no. 3 starting p. 2*b*; no. 4, p. 3*b*; no. 5, p. 4*a*; 2nd section, p. 66, no. 88). They had a falling out and the younger one claimed to have purchased the rights of inheritance to the rabbinate from yet a third brother, who had not previously been involved. Having ownership of two-thirds of the post he claimed that he should be the sole rabbi. The communal leaders did not know how to resolve this dispute and their suggestion was simply to cast lots; the winner would be their rabbi. The response of R. Weiss was that things should stay as they had been. However, what is interesting for us is the implicit assumption of the communal leaders that whoever would win the lottery would be acceptable, and that this was a reasonable way to pick a rabbi.

[65] Zusmanovits, *Treatise on the Law of Inheritance* (Heb.).

[66] Teomim-Fraenkel, 'Treatise on the Sons of Kings' (Heb.), 140–72.

WHAT WAS INVOLVED IN PICKING A RABBI?

The responsibilities of the rabbi in early modern eastern Europe were as symbolic as they were real.[67] His role was certainly not pastoral nor was he a preacher. It was the task of the *magid* or preacher and not of the rabbi to give popular sermons and to encourage Jews to refrain from sin and do penance. Often the *magid* was not a permanent resident of a community but wandered from community to community, preaching a message of religious revival before going on to the next place. Rabbis often served as judges in both commercial and religious cases but this function was often filled by a *dayan* (judge) or in commercial cases by *borerim* (arbitrators). Most traditional Jews believed that their personal salvation and that of the community as a whole was dependent on the correct fulfilment of halakhah, for which the rabbi was a valuable guide. However, one did not need to be ordained to deal with issues of religious law and most practical questions could be answered by know-ledgeable laymen. The rabbi did have a monopoly on performing weddings and divorces but he was not hired for this purpose. Whatever a rabbi did could have been done by others as well.

The unique function of the rabbi was as a symbolic representative of the community. A community could function without a rabbi but at the price of lacking this symbol of common values. The level and prestige of a rabbi reflected on the self-image of a community and this was a good reason to seek out as talented a rabbi as possible. The common practice for members of a community to pull the carriage of a new rabbi into their town or to 'kidnap' a rabbi from a different community to theirs reflects this attitude.

The symbolic role of the rabbi remained when communities began to split into separate subgroups on the basis of ideology and not wealth or status as in the past. The choice of a rabbi was usually regarded as an indication of relative power of the groups within the community. This was a good reason to take the choice of a rabbi seriously, even if there was no intention to consult with him on a regular basis.

The rabbinate was not necessarily the peak of career aspirations for rabbinic scholars in traditional east European Jewish society. For many young talmudists, the rabbinate was not a goal but a fall-back position.[68] Their ideal was to combine wealth and scholarship, and this was best achieved by successful merchants who could work a few hours a day and devote most of the remaining hours to the study of Torah without the responsibilities and

[67] On this see, in addition to the general literature cited above, Friedman, 'The Changing Role of the Community Rabbinate'. Special thanks to Michal Ben-Ya'akov for bringing it to my attention.

[68] See the perceptive study of Etkes, 'The Relationship between Talmudic Scholarship and the Institution of the Rabbinate'.

distractions of the communal rabbinate, and without financial dependence on householders. A common pattern in rabbinic biographies is a description of how the future rabbi started out in business in his youth and only after failing accepted a paying position as rabbi. Whether this was always true or merely a pose is not important. What is clear is that the rabbinical post was presented as a compromise or an afterthought but, having chosen to serve as rabbis, candidates were concerned about the obvious issues of income and living conditions.

Selecting a rabbi was a complex process. It was expensive to consider a number of candidates, and both budgets and time were limited. Therefore, in practice, the body that selected the rabbi—the *kahal* council, a special sub-committee, or groups within the community—usually considered a limited number of candidates either on the basis of personal acquaintance, regional familiarity, or the recommendation of a famous rabbinic figure. The candidates were invited to visit the community and then the *kahal* made its choice. Despite all the complications, this process would usually lead to the appointment of a better candidate than relying blindly on the son of the previous rabbi.

To sum up, for a community it was desirable but not absolutely necessary to have a rabbi. Selecting a rabbi required an effective communal body and the ability to do so was a reflection of the effectiveness of the Jewish community.[69]

THE CHANGING JEWISH COMMUNITY IN THE NINETEENTH CENTURY

The functions and dynamics of east European Jewish communities in the nineteenth century were not the same as in the early modern period. In 1764 the supra-regional councils (Council of the Four Lands and the Council of the Medinah in Poland–Lithuania) had been disbanded. This ended regional payment of taxes. In 1844 the Jewish communities in the Russian empire were formally dissolved and the local taxes were collected by tax farmers who dealt directly with the government authorities. In the Austro-Hungarian empire, the local communities also lost tax collection responsibilities. Even before the

[69] Accepting the son of a previous rabbi as his successor is just one of a variety of ways in which a community can select a rabbi. In the absence of inheritance, a rabbi was usually selected through some type of competition, either overt or covert. However, there were cases in which a rabbi could even be selected for a community by some authority above the community. The most common case of this type is that of hasidic rabbis, who could on occasion appoint a rabbi to a community that accepted their authority. In the discussion below I will concentrate on explaining inheritance as a means of selection, but parts of the analysis will hold for other means as well.

formal limitation of communal responsibilities there was apparently a decline in the quality of community leadership and there were many reports of abuse of authority. The system of democratic election of communal officials began to break down and in many communities power was concentrated in the hands of a few individuals and families.[70]

The rise of conflicting ideological groups within the Jewish community in the late eighteenth and nineteenth centuries undermined communal structures.[71] The rise of competing ideologies, such as hasidism, mitnagedism, Haskalah, assimilationism, and later Zionism and socialism, made cooperation on communal councils more difficult to achieve than earlier. This complicated the process of selecting a rabbi because the selection process of a rabbi remained a public measure of the power and status of various subgroups in a community.[72]

The legal authority of the rabbinate also declined at this time. More and more Jews, especially the socio-economic elite, turned to the civil courts.[73] This was for a wide variety of reasons, including changes in the economic activity of Jews, increased knowledge of languages, and so on. The establishment of a crown or government rabbinate in the Russian empire, though treated with disdain by traditionalists, contributed to the drop in the status of the rabbinate.[74]

These developments, when taken together, had a major impact on the process of selecting a rabbi. Communities that collect taxes are strong and experienced in making unpopular decisions. As communal responsibilities became attenuated, it became harder for communities to make difficult decisions. Situations such as the need to choose a rabbi could easily end up in an embarrassing stalemate or, even worse, could split a community. Of course, choosing a rabbi's son only limited the potential for a split, but certainly did not prevent it.[75] However, it was a way to avoid a decision which

[70] On the situation of communal organization after the abolition of the *kahal*, see Shohet, 'Leadership of the Jewish Communities in Russia after the Abolition of the "Kahal"' (Heb.). For an excellent introduction to the period, see Stanislawski, *Tsar Nicholas I and the Jews*. Professor John Klier pointed out in a private communication that much remains to be clarified about the status and authority of Jewish communal institutions after the formal dissolution of the *kahal* in the Russian empire in 1844.

[71] On some of the impact on the traditional sector, see Bacon, 'Prolonged Erosion, Organization and Reinforcement'.   [72] See the studies of Gershon Bacon.

[73] To the best of my knowledge this process has never been systematically studied, but it is obvious to any reader of the literature of the period.

[74] The crown rabbinate was a very important phenomenon. See Shohet, 'The Crown Rabbinate' (Heb.).

[75] A vivid example of the potential for a split and the consequence that, once split, communities are difficult to reunite, is that of Ulanov, a small town in the region of Lvov. There was a dispute over the rabbinate in this town apparently in the 1870s and part of the community supported the heir and part opposed him. Both factions appointed a rabbi, and both rabbis

would involve a public acceptance of an ideal, whatever it may have been. In other words, it was not necessarily worth risking a communal breakup in order possibly to get a rabbi who was a little more qualified than an heir.

The phenomenon of rabbinical inheritance and the reasons for it are not at all unique to the Jewish community. Hereditary monarchy has been described as the 'willingness to sacrifice personal ability in the interests of a secure and prompt succession', while 'election . . . surpasses inheritance as a means of providing able rulers; but the inevitable complexity of the electoral mechanism impairs the security of succession'.[76] While in general society in the modern period there has been a trend from monarchy to republican government, in Jewish society the trend was from elected rabbinical leadership to inherited leadership. In both cases it was a reflection of the changing capabilities of the political institutions.

This explanation of the logic of rabbinic inheritance may also explain why simony, or the sale of rabbinical positions, had been widespread in the past even though it was almost universally condemned. Since much of a rabbi's income was from fees for the performance of weddings, the registration of vital events, and so on, the rabbinate could be regarded as a system of tax farming in which the rights for taxes in a given area were sold for a fixed price which was usually paid up front. No one claimed that tax farming was an ideal system and it disappeared as governmental bureaucracies developed. However, in its time it was an effective solution for the desperate communities to raise funds. Explicit simony became rarer as communal authority—and responsibilities—declined, though it was still to be encountered in the nineteenth century.[77]

At the same time that inheritance was becoming an attractive option for communities who found it difficult to make hard decisions, it was also becoming more and more appealing to rabbis. The occupational options for young talmudists narrowed in the nineteenth century. Up until the mid-

claimed to be the true rabbi of Ulanov and each transmitted his position to his son—all this in a community of maybe 1,500 Jews. The same people who rejected inheritance in the 1870s supported it a generation later, so it was probably more a matter of personalities than of principle. Teomim, *Oriyan telitai*, no. 92, p. 64b.

[76] Frederick Watkins, s.v. 'Succession, Political', in Sills (ed.), *International Encyclopedia of the Social Sciences*, xiv. 441–3.

[77] In the 19th century some candidates for a rabbinical post did not 'purchase' the post but instead loaned the community a sum of money (personal communication from Dr Gershon Bacon). Simony in general deserves more attention—and understanding—than it has received. An extended treatment of attitudes to simony in the late Middle Ages is in Ben-Sasson, *Reflection and Leadership* (Heb.), 221–8. My analysis is greatly indebted to the fascinating discussion of corruption in Chwalba, *Imperium korupcji*. Many of the critics of simony ignore the roles and honours given to big donors to universities and charitable institutions. Criticism is sharpest when directed outwards.

nineteenth century young scholars could assume that success in studies would lead to a good match (for example, with the daughter of a rich man) and that the ensuing dowry would provide the basis for a career as a businessman. With modernization, those who could offer a good dowry became less and less interested in talmudic scholars as sons-in-law.[78] Success in business began to depend on the knowledge of languages and general studies, and the new rich began to look for young men with a modern education. This left the rabbinate as one of the few viable occupational options for talmudic scholars, even though the status and income of rabbis appeared to have been low and declining.[79] Rabbis who were hard pressed to raise money for a dowry had a special interest in the option of transmitting a post to a son-in-law. This was not necessarily contradictory to the interests of the communities. The right to transmit a position to a son-in-law is a clear job benefit whose financial value can even be calculated, and deducted from, a salary.[80]

Unfortunately for prospective rabbis, at the same time that the rabbinate became the main occupational option, urbanization led to a crisis in the rabbinical job market. In early modern eastern Europe the number of rabbinical positions had been constantly growing because the number of Jewish communities was always increasing. Population growth led Jews either to migrate to regions which did not have dense Jewish populations, or to seek out smaller urban centres which had no Jewish community or competition. The new communities they founded all needed rabbis. This changed in the nineteenth century. Jews began to move to cities. Urbanization did not diminish the number of Jewish communities but, in the nineteenth century, cities absorbed mobile and 'excess' population so that population growth generated fewer and fewer new communities and posts for rabbis. Rabbis of cities and neighbourhood rabbis could serve populations equivalent to that of several villages or towns. Even disregarding the well-known correlation between urbanization and the drift away from religion and tradition, urbanization was bad for the rabbinical job market.

INHERITANCE IN HASIDIC GROUPS AND IN YESHIVAS

An *admor* (hasidic *rebbe* or *tsadik*) or *rosh yeshivah* was not necessarily a communal rabbi, but a dynamic similar to that of the communal rabbinate led to parallel developments in choosing successors in both hasidic groups and in yeshivas. Dynasties were, of course, common in the hasidic movement.[81] This

---

[78] This forms the background of the foundation of the *kolel*.

[79] See Kaplan, 'In God We Trust'. He discusses the European background in addition to the conditions in the USA.   [80] See Rabinowitz-Teomim, *Seder eliyahu*, 63–7.

[81] This pattern of transmission of authority was regarded by some as yet another sign of the

can be explained as inheritance of charisma,[82] and the same argument could be used with regard to the communal rabbinate. However, there were good reasons besides charisma for inheritance. In his lifetime an *admor* made the major decisions in his court, though he would usually consult senior members of his entourage.[83] However, there was no formal decision-making body in hasidic courts which dealt with questions of policy. Indeed, such a body would have been regarded as an infringement on the authority and role of the *tsadik*. The death of a *tsadik* created a sudden vacuum of leadership and there was no clearly defined and accepted body which had the authority to decide on a successor. This condition almost invited a struggle for the leadership which could be very bitter and lead to splits, with all the negative consequences that involved. Reliance on inheritance could not prevent struggles between sons and sons-in-law, but at least it limited the field of potential candidates and gave a justification for an heir's claims.

Inheritance was not to be taken for granted even among hasidim. Rabbi Hayim Halberstam was once asked to decide who in a family of *tsadikim* had a right to inherit the leadership of a hasidic group. He replied that simple laws of inheritance did not apply because hasidic *rebbes* are different from communal rabbis! In his words:

. . . with respect to the rights of inheritance of honour . . . are the posts of hasidic rebbes in the same category as rabbinical posts? It is known that neither Rabbi Avraham nor his father were rabbis. Their great holiness and their fear of God made their words heeded in the entire region and that is why people streamed to them to study Torah to learn how to fear the Lord. They were also honoured with gifts . . . and they were consulted by many . . . because they had in them the spirit of God. Their prayers and their holy words had results. What can we do if those who come after them don't have this holiness? . . . I do not know how the ability to pray can be inherited.[84]

decadence of post-Beshtian hasidism, though this has been corrected in contemporary scholarship; see Rapoport-Albert, 'Hasidism after 1772'. She refers quite reasonably to the feudal society as a possible model for the dynastic system in hasidism. See also the stimulating discussion in Assaf, *The Regal Way*, 47–68.

[82] This is, of course, a clear echo of Max Weber's discussion as expressed, inter alia, in his papers published in *On Charisma and Institution Building*. For an application of such an approach see, for example, Berger, 'Hasidism and Moonism'.

[83] For strictly halakhic questions, the major hasidic courts (*ḥatserot*) had their own rabbinical courts (*batei din*) which decided halakhic questions for members of the community.

[84] Halberstam, *Divrei ḥayim*, vol. ii, 'Ḥoshen mishpat', no. 32, p. 208. After the death of Yehudah Tsevi Brandwein of Stretin in 1844 (Wunder, *Lights of Galicia* (Heb.), i. 604), his first-born son Avraham (d. 1865) inherited the leadership but a family fight prevented him from getting the clear title to the *beit midrash* of his father. R. Avraham had only daughters and after his death, his son-in-law carried on the dispute with the surviving brothers and their descendants. It was in this context that the question of inheritance rights arose.

Rabbi Halberstam went on to add that the founders of hasidism, the Besht (Rabbi Yisra'el Ba'al Shem Tov, 1698–1760) and the Magid (Rabbi Dov Ber of Mezeritch, *c.*1710), had passed on leadership to their students and not to their children. This statement did not prevent Rabbi Halberstam's descendants from founding dynasties.

Leadership of Lithuanian yeshivas also tended (and still tends) to be handed down by inheritance. There is no question that talmudic scholarship is a learned skill and growing up in the house of a *rosh yeshivah* can help in acquiring these skills. Nonetheless, few sons of top-ranking talmudists are as talented as their fathers. Were intellectual quality the sole criterion for yeshiva leadership it would have been best to seek out a successor through a form of open competition. However, *rashei yeshivah*, like hasidic rabbis, tended to concentrate authority in their hands, and in yeshivas, as in hasidic courts, there was nobody that could take upon himself the responsibility of picking a successor. Here again, turning to a son was sometimes the simplest solution.

Inheritance under conditions of weak communal organization and charismatic leadership was not limited to eastern Europe. It was to be found in Hungary, as noted above, in Frankfurt, and even in New York,[85] and often with very satisfactory results.

*

Inheritance was by no means a perfect solution to the problem of choosing a rabbi. However, as we have seen, there were good reasons for it. It made sense in an east European context, where nobles and kings inherited their status for much the same reasons as the rabbinate was inherited.[86] One alternative to inheritance was not to appoint a communal rabbi at all. However, 'deciding not to decide' was feasible mainly in larger communities in which there was an abundance of learned Jews who collectively could fill most of a rabbi's responsibilities.[87] But there were communities where this was not an option, and for them inheritance of rabbinical positions had an attractive logic and practical advantages. It would have been counterproductive for weakened communities to blindly adhere to open competition for rabbinical posts, and it would have led to negative consequences. One can also question the sincerity of at least some critics. Contemporary critics of inheritance seem to have been disturbed as much by the anti-modernizing stance of many rabbinical heirs and the symbolic implications of their obtaining the post of

[85] One can find the same phenomenon in the household of the neo-Orthodox Samson Raphael Hirsch in Frankfurt or of R. Joseph Lookstein. See Ferziger, 'The Lookstein Legacy'.

[86] The political consequences of the election of the king in Poland, which was one of the few countries in Europe with an elected king, were excellent arguments for the adoption of the system of inheritance.   [87] On this, see Chapter 13.

rabbi as they were by lack of effectiveness. [88] Also, the critics were usually not those who turned to rabbis on a day-to-day basis. For the regular clients of rabbis, as long as a minimal level of competence was maintained, inheritance could be lived with.

Inheritance of the rabbinate reflects the weakness of communal decision-making bodies which were shorn of most of their responsibilities. It resolves the problem of succession in an effective manner, which is why it is so popular. The aura of tradition that comes with inheritance gives added authority to heirs. This should not hide the fact that it is an eminently modern phenomenon and one more expression of the crisis of modern Jewish life.

[88] Even traditional rabbis criticized the innovation. See, for example, 'Der Streit um die Erb-folge', by the martyred Rabbi Dr Joseph Carlebach.

FIFTEEN

The Making and the Maintenance of the Image of the Gaon of Vilna

IT MAY SEEM SUPERFLUOUS at a first glance to try to describe how the image of the Vilna Gaon (Eliyahu ben Shelomoh Zalman 'Kremer', 1720–97) developed. After all, the Gaon, along with the Ba'al Shem Tov (Besht), the founder of hasidism, is arguably one of the best-known east European Jews, and his fame is not a recent phenomenon. In the case of such a famous individual, how can one discuss the development of an image? Therefore, before explaining the process, it is necessary to show why there is a question at all. When this is done it will be possible to deal with the factors that contributed to the image. I will try to show that the image of the Gaon in Jewish society did indeed develop and, in particular, that it has been deeply influenced by printed biographies of him. It appears that were it not for these works, the impact of the Gaon and his place in our awareness of east European Jewish history would have been somewhat different. At the same time this analysis of the development of the Gaon's image is no substitute for a systematic study of his life, and a critical biography of the Gaon is certainly far overdue.[1]

Historians of Jewish history have, quite correctly, taken for granted that the Gaon of Vilna was one of the outstanding Jews in the history of east European Jewry. In a recent study of the Gaon's image in the eyes of his followers, Immanuel Etkes writes: 'Rabbi Eliyahu . . . enjoyed exceptional authority in his lifetime.'[2] There are good grounds for this view. After all, the same was said by Rabbi Shneur Zalman of Lyady who wrote, in a well-known letter to his supporters in Vilna: 'It is said that there is no one in Lithuania who dares not to set aside his views in the face of the views of the righteous Gaon and to openly disagree with him—only in distant lands as Turkey and Italy and most of Germany and Greater and Lesser Poland [do people dare].'[3]

---

[1] Etkes, *The Gaon of Vilna*, deals with many important issues but does not claim to be a full biography. Landau, *The Righteous Gaon of Vilna* (Heb.), was a remarkable biography for its time. However, there are many unpublished sources available, notably the ones cited by Yisra'el Klausner in his various publications and in the Vilnius archives, as I am informed by Mordekhai Zalkin and others. Stern's recent 'Elijah of Vilna' is a major contribution; I do not entirely share his views, but they merit careful consideration.   [2] Etkes, *The Gaon of Vilna*, 1.

[3] Cf. Schneersohn, *Holy Letters* (Heb.), 88. The editor notes that although there are ques-

In the context of Professor Etkes's study the statement is undoubtedly correct. However, the historical reality had additional dimensions. The Gaon was not seen by all as a model for emulation in his lifetime, and he was far from universally heeded or accepted in Vilna.

It should be emphasized at the outset that there is no question about the brilliance of the Gaon, even though, as we shall see, his prominence was not a simple matter in his lifetime,[4] and certain elements of his personality have been overlooked as his image developed. Only some of the Gaon's writings have been preserved, and they undoubtedly are only a very partial expression of his knowledge and intellectual accomplishment. However, they are enough to make it clear that both his scope and depth are possibly unique in recent centuries. If a scholar of the stature of Rabbi Hayim of Volozhin wrote in awe about the Gaon, then it is hard not to be impressed—and in the case of Rabbi Hayim, awe is an understatement. It is also clear that he had a significant impact on patterns of study among the scholarly elite. However, the many references about the Gaon's greatness alone cannot define his role in contemporary Jewish society and his popular image during his lifetime. Most of our sources about the Gaon are from individuals who, like Rabbi Hayim, saw themselves as his students. However, as we shall see, the attitudes of this group were not shared by all his contemporaries.[5]

The Gaon was never elected to an office which provided prestige or a framework for activity, nor did he head a yeshiva or other institution whose continued existence would preserve his memory. After his death, the Gaon's memory was not kept alive by the study of his writings, as we shall see below. The key to the Gaon's prominence was his personal charisma and his influence on some key students, but charisma is a highly perishable commodity. Therefore, an understanding of the process through which the Gaon's image was developed and preserved is a key to a deeper understanding of the society in which he lived and worked.

ASPECTS OF THE GAON'S IMAGE IN HIS LIFETIME

Fame is difficult to measure, but there is clear evidence that relatively early in the Gaon's career he was well known far beyond the bounds of eastern Europe. One reflection of this is that after Rabbi Ya'akov Emden (1697–1776)

tions about its authenticity the letter seems to be genuine. See the editor's discussion on pages 436–7. I thank Nahum Greenwald for the reference.

[4] Apparently relatively little attention was given to the Gaon in the first few years after his death. Much valuable information on this topic can be found in Mondshine, 'Studies' (Heb.). See also Morgenstern, *Mysticism and Messianism* (Heb.), ch. 8.

[5] It would be very interesting to systematically survey rabbinical contemporaries of the Gaon and to see to what degree he was cited, consulted, or relied on. Here silence would be as significant as citation. Unfortunately such a study is outside the scope of this chapter.

had accused Rabbi Jonathan Eybeschuetz (*c*.1690–1764), the rabbi of Hamburg, of being a secret Sabbatean, Rabbi Eybeschuetz turned to the Gaon for support.[6] He included a letter from the Gaon when he published, in 1755, a collection of letters from famous rabbis who supported his position.[7] This was a clear indication of the Gaon's stature even in central Europe. It should not be forgotten that at the time of the writing, the Gaon was only 35 years old. In his collection of letters, Rabbi Eybeschuetz referred to the Gaon with great respect, writing that he had heard that there was in Vilna 'among the scholars of the city a unique individual, the holy and pure righteous one, the light of Israel, master of all the wisdom, with breadth and depth and master of the secrets [e.g. kabbalah] Rabbi Eliyahu who is famous in all of Poland and Berlin and Lissa—wherever he went his greatness is retold', and this description has often been quoted.[8]

However, on careful examination this letter indicates that while Eybeschuetz recognized the Gaon he did not regard him as the most important rabbi in eastern Europe or even in Vilna. The letter is dated 5 Sivan 5755, which is very shortly before the book was published, while the other letters in the book are dated much earlier. This suggests that turning to Rabbi Eliyahu was a last-minute move.[9] Indeed, it turns out that Rabbi Eybeschuetz had appealed previously to a group of scholars of Vilna (apparently not including the Gaon), and this had led in 1751 to the pronouncement of a ban (*ḥerem*) in Vilna against anyone who would speak libellously about Rabbi Eybeschuetz. The Gaon had not been mentioned in that context. Thus, while the appeal to the Gaon can be seen as evidence of his stature, this was apparently only an attempt to supplement the letters of support which Rabbi Eybeschuetz had already received. Had the Gaon's stature been unquestioned it would have been difficult to understand why he was not involved in the early stages of the conflict. While it is possible that indeed this was the case, there is no evidence of this, nor are there any sources that would indicate that the Gaon turned down earlier requests to state his position publicly. This suggests that at the time Rabbi Eybeschuetz thought that the Gaon's support was useful, but that it alone would not be enough to attract the desired public support for his position.

[6] I thank Professor Gershon Bacon for his suggestion to examine this issue. It is interesting that the Gaon apparently took the side of Eybeschuetz, though the wording of his reply is very circumspect. Given the Gaon's later concern for dangerous aspects in hasidism it is curious that he was less concerned about Eybeschuetz. It would seem unlikely that Eybeschuetz would have turned to the Gaon without any previous contact and the nature of this contact would probably influence the response of the Gaon. However, the limited sources we have do not offer an answer to this question.

[7] Eybeschuetz, *Luḥot edut.*   [8] Ibid. 71, 1st edn.; in the Warsaw edition it is on p. 146.

[9] In his letter, R. Eliyahu apologizes for its shortness but not for any delay in responding, which indicates that this was sent shortly after he received the letter.

There was apparently some criticism of the Gaon within scholarly circles even after he had reached the pinnacle of his recognition. This may be learned from the introduction of Menahem Mendel of Shklov (d. 1827) to the Gaon's commentary on the *Shulḥan arukh*, 'Yoreh de'ah'. He wrote: 'may the mouths of those who say falsehoods, speaking of the great *tsadik* in pride and insolence, be stopped up, those who refrain from the true study of Torah . . . who in truth do not want to analyse . . . the bribery that is in their hearts blinds their eyes from seeing directly the truth'.[10] It is not clear to whom these words were directed but the depth of Rabbi Menaham Mendel's feeling suggests that these individuals were not insignificant. If they were not scholars, it is hardly likely that their views would have been taken seriously. Moreover, if these critics were not somewhat learned, they would not have been able to speak out with the assumption that there would be somebody to listen to them.

The Gaon is remembered for the extreme modesty and asceticism of his way of life. Here as well it is clear that the reality was complex. There is no question as to the Gaon's personal lack of interest in material matters. At the same time, rejection of the material had its limits and these limits were to be grounds for complaint and criticism. The Gaon certainly did not live in poverty. Yisra'el Klausner has pointed out that the Gaon received a weekly stipend of 28 zloty, which he did not turn down, as well as an supplement of 18 zloty from private individuals together with the right to live for free in an apartment which belonged to the community.[11] The significance of this income is best seen in the context of the accompanying table of salaries of Vilna functionaries (Table 15.1), which are taken from a study of the Vilna community by Israel Klausner.[12]

The Gaon did not have the highest income of the individuals on the Vilna community payroll. However, his income was near the top and it was several times the salary of minor communal functionaries. The major difference between the Gaon and the others on the payroll is that they had defined responsibilities and were being paid for their work, while the Gaon received his income without filling any communal functions. Although the payment came from the community, the nature of the payment the Gaon received is not totally clear. The Gaon had a very rich relative, Eliyahu ben Tsevi Kremer,[13] who supported the Gaon and his other relatives, and in his will he

[10] Printed in the standard editions of the *Shulḥan arukh*.
[11] Klausner, *History of the Jewish Community in Vilna* (Heb.), 164; id., *Vilna in the Time of the Gaon* (Heb.), 143. Klausner adds the additional source about a supplement of about 18 zloty from private individuals (ibid. 155). See also Bershadsky (ed.), *Akty o evreyakh*, 233, 470, in the complaint (16 Feb. 1786) of Vilna Jews against the *kahal*.
[12] Klausner, *History of the Jewish Community in Vilna* (Heb.). For a similar analysis of the communal finances see Mondshine, 'Studies' (Heb.), pt. 1, 185.
[13] On Kremer see Fuenn, *A Loyal Town* (Heb.), 183.

Table 15.1 Salaries of Jewish functionaries in Vilna, *c.*1785
(Polish zloty)

Position or personality	Salary	
	per week	per year
The Gaon	28	1,456
David b. Simeon, scribe and judge	32	1,664
Rabbi and head of rabbinical court:		
according to contract	27	1,404
in practice	18	936
David b. Yehi'el-Mikhel, judge		1,126
Community doctor	12	624
Cantor	7	364
Shoḥet (slaughterer)	4	208
Watchmen	2	104

Source: Klausner, *History of the Jewish Community in Vilna* (Heb.), 164.

set aside a sum of money for the continued support of the Gaon and his brother. Moreover, Eliyahu Kremer was the trustee of a large estate, that of Rabbi Mosheh Rivkes, which had been given to the Vilna community with the stipulation that the income from the capital be used to support worthy descendants.[14] It is not clear whether this fund was the source of the Gaon's salary or of the supplement, but very possibly some or all of the Gaon's income came from this source—and not from the pockets of the Jewish taxpayers.

An indication of the Gaon's standard of living was revealed in listings of the Jewish residents of Vilna made to provide data for censuses. These records listed 'the [Jewish] inhabitants by street . . . and building',[15] and therefore they are an invaluable resource. It is well known that the Gaon lived in the Fatel house. This was a large building, adjacent to the main synagogue, which had been willed to the Jewish community of Vilna by Mikha'el ben Veitel in 1682.[16] This fits the claim that the Vilna community provided the Gaon with housing. The first listing we have is from 1765. According to this list, the Gaon's household consisted of Eliyahu Zalmanovich, his wife Hannah, son Zelman, daughter Basiah, and maid Nehamah.[17] There was nothing exceptional at the time in having a maid but it was typical of the relatively well-off and not of the poor. It may be noted that in a census listing made twenty years later the household consisted of Eliyahu Zalmanovich, his wife Gittel, daughter Hannah, son Zelman and his wife Rokhla and their

[14] See Landau, *The Righteous Gaon of Vilna* (Heb.), 26.
[15] Tamulynas, 'Demographic and Social-Professional Structure of the Jewish Community in Vilnius', 333.   [16] Klausner, *History of the Jewish Community in Vilna* (Heb.), 71–2.
[17] See the reproduction in the Vilna Jewish newspaper *Jerusalem of Lithuania*, issue 5/6 (73–4) (July–Sept. 1997), p. 2, presented by Izraelis Lempertas.

daughter Freyna.[18] The maid was gone—perhaps because the married son needed the room.[19]

Indirect evidence of the Gaon's income can be derived from the dispute between his heirs and the worshippers of the Gaon's minyan, which arose in the course of setting up the synagogue named after the Gaon (the Gaon's *kloyz*). The plan involved the use of a building which had been purchased by the Gaon. The heirs claimed that it had been purchased by the Gaon out of his own pocket; the worshippers claimed that the Gaon had purchased it with charity funds. Conclusive evidence for either side could not be found, and when the Gaon's heirs swore under oath that the Gaon had bought the property with his own funds, their testimony was accepted. It is, of course, impossible now to determine which side was correct. What can be said is that the heirs' claim appeared to contemporaries to be reasonable enough to be accepted. Real estate in Vilna, as elsewhere, was very expensive and to be able to buy a private house was an indication of some degree of wealth. Apparently, then, the Gaon belonged to the economic elite.[20] This fact was not overlooked by the Vilna Jews.

In many respects the most dramatic expression of the mixed attitudes toward the Gaon in the Vilna Jewish community is in the position taken by the representatives of the poor class of Vilna Jewry in the course of the well-known controversy over the rabbinate of Vilna.[21] In this controversy, the poor were aligned with supporters of the rabbi of Vilna. The communal or *kahal* leadership, who attempted to dismiss the rabbi (Shemuel ben Avigdor) from his position, had the Gaon on their side. In February 1786 the representatives of the masses called on the governmental commission investigating community finances to consider abuses of communal authority, and brought as an example the payment to the Gaon of a weekly subvention. The representatives called for an immediate stop to these payments.[22] This demand was not dropped over the years. During the hearings held in March 1788 on the financial affairs of the community, the representatives of the poor called for the abolishment of the *korobka* taxes on grounds that enough money had already been collected to pay all the communal debts. They also demanded the Gaon return all of the payments that he had received from the community.[23] An extreme and probably atypical expression of the dislike of the

---

[18] Tamulynas, 'Demographic and Social-Professional Structure', 332. This entry is enlightening with regard to the precision of the listing. Hannah was his wife and not his daughter. The census taker took the trouble to record the names correctly but apparently was a bit confused about the relationships. In other words the listing does not appear to be totally accurate.

[19] It appears rather unusual that the married son lived with the husband's family and not the wife's.   [20] Klausner, *History of the Jewish Community in Vilna* (Heb.), 79.

[21] The best source on this controversy is Klausner, *Vilna in the Time of the Gaon* (Heb.). This carefully documented study disabuses the reader of any illusions that communal life was idyllic.

[22] Ibid. 143.   [23] Ibid. 246

masses for the Gaon was the personal attack of Yoel Spektor, apparently a *melamed*, on the Gaon. He claimed that the Gaon received a subvention for no good reason and that there was no legal justification for the grant that he received.[24] Communal controversy is nothing new in Jewish history and such complaints were made in many contexts and against many respected leaders. However, the fact that such charges were raised, and the sequence of events and statements, indicates clearly that awe and respect for the Gaon were far from universal. We cannot measure the number of individuals who shared Yoel's views and there may have been other factors, such as the hasidic/mitnagdic controversy, which played a hidden role.[25] What is important in our context is that such views existed and were apparently shared by many members of the community, while in later years there seems to have been universal reverence for the Gaon.[26]

Impact, which has much to do with fame, is also difficult to measure. The question of the Gaon's place in the struggle against the hasidic movement, which is often seen as a reflection of the Gaon's impact, can be interpreted in more ways than one.[27] On the one hand, it is possible to claim that his initiatives crystallized the mitnagdic circles and stopped the spread of hasidism into Lithuania and surrounding areas. However, it must be remembered that opposition to hasidism began without the Gaon and that the first ban (*ḥerem*) on ties with hasidism was proclaimed in Shklov without his participation. In other words, there probably would have been opposition to the hasidim even without him. Similarly, even in regions that are usually termed 'hasidic', such as Galicia, there were many Jews and famous rabbis in the nineteenth century that were not hasidic. This suggests that even without the Gaon much of Lithuanian Jewry would have refrained from joining the hasidic movement. At the same time it is also significant that despite the active intervention of the Gaon against hasidism, significant circles of Vilna Jewry remained attracted to the hasidic movement and were followers of hasidic leaders. All of this suggests that the impact of the Gaon on the spread of hasidism should be assessed cautiously.

The role often popularly attributed to the Gaon in the formation of a mitnagdic ideology also has to be questioned. While it has been taken for granted that the Gaon created or shaped the mitnagdic ethos, in his brilliant

[24] Klausner, *Vilna in the Time of the Gaon* (Heb.), 153. For similar expressions on the part of Yitshak ben Leib, see p. 155.

[25] I am grateful to Nahum Greenwald (Lakewood) for suggesting this to me.

[26] A similar suggestion was raised by Mondshine in 'Studies' (Heb.), pt. i, p. 199. He noted that the fact that the Gaon left Vilna in order to avoid the pressure of the communal leaders to meet with representatives of hasidism indicates that he was unable to impose his opinions on the communal leadership, or at least one faction of this leadership.

[27] See Etkes, *The Gaon of Vilna*, and Morgenstern, *Mysticism and Messianism* (Heb.).

study of Pinhas of Polotsk, Alan Nadler pointed out that Rabbi Pinhas had worked out a theory of humanity and of man's role in the world which preceded that of the Gaon and in many ways anticipated his views.[28] Nadler does not claim that Rabbi Pinhas alone initiated these views. What he suggests is that the views commonly attributed to mitnagedim and seen as the innovation of the Gaon were actually widely held even before the Gaon started to spread his opinions.

In many contemporary Orthodox Jewish circles there is great interest in the Gaon's customs and the emendations that he made to the liturgy. However, in his lifetime it seems that few of his suggestions were implemented.[29] It was only in Palestine, where at the beginning of the nineteenth century there were no strong communities practising the traditional Ashkenazi liturgy, that immigrants who were followers of the Gaon were able to implement his ideas. In general he is not often cited in the scholarly writings of east European rabbis even though they recognized his brilliance.[30] This silence may well have been because there was little published material to cite, but nonetheless such silence did little for awareness of the Gaon.[31]

There were also some aspects of the Gaon's personality that have been somewhat under-emphasized in biographies and that may well have had an impact on his contemporaries in terms of limiting his influence. The most striking of these aspects is the relationship of the Gaon with the members of his family, and the Gaon's views on how family relationships should be. Today few, if any, would present the Gaon's behaviour as a model, and indeed little is said in contemporary literature about his family life.[32] Rabbi Avraham, son of the Gaon, described his father in the following way:[33]

[28] See Nadler, *The Faith of the Mithnagdim*.

[29] See the discussions on the acceptance of the Gaon's innovation in the section 'Ma'alot hasulam' (Steps of the the the Ladder) in Lewin, *Aliyot eliyahu*; and Betsalel Landau, *The Righteous Gaon of Vilna* (Heb.), ch. 7, pp. 86–107. See also the very important short essay on the topic by Haym Soloveitchik, disguised as a footnote in his 'Rupture and Reconstruction', 110–12 n. 20.

[30] See e.g. Kaminetsky, 'Evaluation and Desire for the Gaon's Commentaries' (Heb.).

[31] In this century there seems to have been an upsurge in interest. Nahum Greenwald suggested that among the factors that should be considered is that R. Yisra'el Meir Kagan (Hakohen) often cites the Gaon in his *Mishnah berurah*, which has become the standard halakhic work (much more than R. Epstein's *Arukh hashulḥan*), and the adoption of the Gaon as an ideal model by R. Avraham Yeshayahu Karelits (1878–1953), the Hazon Ish. One could add that this is related to broader processes described in Soloveitchik, 'Rupture and Reconstruction', and the traditional role of the Gaon's customs in Palestine. This is a topic well worth further study.

[32] See, however, Etkes, who discusses the problematics of tension between study and family life in 'Marriage and Torah Study', and in *Lithuania in Jerusalem* (Heb.). I have noticed a similar phenomenon among rabbis of the *musar* movement, which raises curious questions as to the limits of *musar* behaviour.

[33] The text is found in the introduction of R. Avraham to the commentary of the Gaon to *Shulḥan arukh*, 'Oraḥ ḥayim'.

How devoted he was in his soul to avoid the company of his household and his sons and daughters. He sought only to dwell in the pure fear of God . . . so that he never asked his sons and daughters about their livelihoods or their situations. In his life he never wrote them a letter to ask [about] their health. If one of his sons came to visit him, even though he was very happy—for he had not seen him for a year or two— nevertheless he would never ask them about the situation of their sons and their wives or their livelihood, and when the son had rested for an hour or so, he would urge him to return to his studies.[34]

Rabbi Avraham went on to describe how his father would often leave Vilna to study in isolation. On one occasion the Gaon's son, Shelomoh Zalman (then 5 years old), fell seriously ill just when his father had planned to depart for a period of study in isolation. The Gaon did not change his plans. After a month of intense study he remembered, in the bath house (where he could not think about Torah), that his son had been ill and he immediately went back to Vilna to find out how he was. Both his unwillingness to change plans because of his son's illness and the sudden recollection and return to Vilna were no doubt somewhat bizarre to the Jews of Vilna of his time. The members of the Gaon's family understood this withdrawal as an expression of his commitment to Torah study, and they emphasized that the Gaon needed great willpower to overcome his personal desire to spend time with his children. At the same time their pain seems evident and their efforts to explain his behaviour suggest that they suspected that contemporaries might have found it difficult to understand this type of behaviour, which certainly was not typical of contemporary rabbis.[35]

Similar descriptions of the Gaon's lack of involvement in family matters are found in the introduction to the Gaon's commentary on the Zohar by his grandson, Rabbi Ya'akov ben Avraham. Upon visiting his grandfather, Rabbi Ya'akov noted how his grandfather did not ask him how he and his family were, and he clearly thought this to be unusual behaviour. Aryeh Morgenstern pointed out that this passage was eliminated from the text when it was published. Such 'censorship' is clear evidence of the discomfort felt with regard to this aspect of the Gaon's personality and the desire of later editors to tidy up the image of the Gaon.[36]

The Gaon also had strong views on the place of women in Jewish life that were not typical for his time. In *Igeret hagra* (Letter of the Gaon of Vilna),

[34] The translation is from Etkes, 'Marriage and Torah Study'. No translator is credited.
[35] Ibid. This contains an interesting discussion of the tension between Torah study and family ties, in which the Gaon appears to be an exceptional rather than a typical case. There is a big difference between leaving home for a period of study and being present but inaccessible. It should probably not surprise us that these texts are usually ignored or passed over without much analysis in biographies of the Gaon.
[36] See Morgenstern, *Mysticism and Messianism* (Heb.), 259–60.

which he wrote on his abortive trip to Palestine, he instructed his wife 'to train your daughters . . . The fundamental rule is that they should not go out, God forbid, from the door of the house', and later in the text he writes 'It is also better for your daughter not to go to synagogue for there she would see embroidered garments and similar finery'.[37] Popular stereotypes to the contrary, Jewish women at the time—and not just the poorer ones—had an active role in economic life and often spent much of their days out of the house. To seclude daughters in the house was typical of certain Jewish societies in Islamic lands and this ideal was certainly found in the literature, but it was not at all the accepted pattern in eastern Europe. We know little about what the Gaon's daughters actually did, however, and had the Gaon's ideas been put into practice, they certainly would have been regarded as exceptional. The rabbinic scholars of eastern Europe, many of whom were supported by their wives more than by the local communities, did not attempt to emulate this ideal.

Perhaps it may be possible—and it is only a possibility—to see in the marital matches made by the Gaon's children that the Gaon's place in the contemporary Jewish community was problematic. Money was almost always an important factor in making a match and the Gaon was certainly not a very rich man. However, given the popular image today of the Gaon's place in the Jewish society of his time, and considering that the Gaon was far from poor, one could have anticipated that his children would have married the offspring of the elite of their society. This does not seem to have been the case.

The Gaon had at least eight children. The data on them are incomplete, to say the least, but there is some information on their matches.[38] The Gaon's firstborn child was a daughter who died before her wedding. Almost nothing is known about her, not even her name. His second daughter, Khiena, married Rabbi Mosheh of Pinsk. He did not leave much of a mark in history other than to publish his father-in-law's book *Shenot eliyahu* (The Years of Elijah). The third daughter, Pesiah-Basiah, married Tsevi Hirsh Donchin, son of the *av beit din* of Disna, who also remained fairly anonymous. Yet another daughter whose name has also been forgotten married Yehezkel Halevi of Bobroisk, who also left little impact. The first of the Gaon's sons, Shelomoh Zalman, married Rahel Kissin. In their marriage agreement, the Gaon agreed to supplement her parents' support of the young couple (*kest*), which suggests that her parents were not very wealthy even though money was usually an important factor in matchmaking. Rahel's father was also not renowned as a

[37] Abrahams, *Hebrew Ethical Wills*, 316, 321. (The first quotation was corrected in the light of the original.)

[38] An invaluable source for this is Freedman, *Eliyahu's Branches*. A list of the children is on page 58. Biographical data can be found in the book.

scholar and I was unable to find evidence that the bride had exceptional *yikhus* (illustrious ancestry). Although in eastern European Jewry young couples usually lived with the parents of the wife, this young couple was living in the Gaon's apartment in 1785,[39] which strengthens the possibility that the bride's family was not very well off. The next son, Yehudah Leib, married the daughter of the rabbi of Serhei, who was not known for his wealth or for his scholarliness. He is known only by a *prenumeranten* (pre-publication sub-scription for a book) that he gave. This suggests that he was also not one of the major scholars of his generation. The well-known son of the Gaon, Avraham, married Sarah, daughter of No'ah Lipshitz-Pesseles. A short biography of her father suggests that he was known more for his illustrious ancestors than for his scholarship or wealth.[40] The last child that we know of, Tauba, married Rabbi Uri Shraga of Dubrovna. He published a book, *Menorat shelomoh* (Solomon's Lamp), but he was not a famous figure in his time. The Gaon's granddaughter, daughter of Rabbi Yehudah Leib, was married to the son of Rabbi Avraham Danzig, a well-known Vilna rabbi (author of *ḥayei adam*), but this was a different generation.

It is difficult to second-guess the calculations of matchmakers, especially after the passage of almost two centuries.[41] However, the unremarkable matches that the children of the Gaon made raises some question about the eagerness of contemporaries to create family ties with the Gaon. There are so many variables involved that it would be foolhardy to come to conclusions on the basis of this information alone, but these data fit into the other evidence that suggests that the Gaon's place in Jewish society in his lifetime was more complex than one might imagine. There is no question that the Gaon had a major impact on rabbinic scholarship, but though this was recognized it was not discussed in detail by contemporaries. This fact alone cannot therefore explain his place in the consciousness of later generations.

How, then, was the complex reality of the Gaon transformed into the image of a folk hero whose authority and significance were unquestioned, and who occupied a central role in the memory of Lithuanian and Belorussian Jews? Part, and only part, apparently lies in the way his memory was trans-mitted and, more specifically, in the publication of biographies of the Gaon.

[39] Tamulynas, 'Demographic and Social-Professional Structure', 332.

[40] See Fuenn, *A Loyal Town* (Heb.). According to the description it seems that he was known for his *yikhus* rather than for his wealth. For a biography of R. Avraham see Gottesman, 'Rabbi Abraham, Son of the Gra'.

[41] Nahum Greenwald (Lakewood) pointed out to me in a private communication that the matches made for the children of R. Shneur Zalman of Lyady were also not with extraordinary partners. The stature of R. Shneur Zalman was unquestioned and the obvious conclusion is that it is difficult to prove anything from the work of matchmakers.

BIOGRAPHIES OF THE GAON

Biographies are a key both to our knowledge about the Gaon and to his place in popular consciousness. Some information on the Gaon's life was included in introductions to various books. Biographical data are found in the introduction by the Gaon's son to the 1779 edition of the Gaon's commentary on the Mishnah; Rabbi Hayim of Volozhin wrote about the Gaon in his introduction to the 1820 edition of the Gaon's commentary on the kabbalistic work *Sifra ditsenuta*; and Rabbi Israel of Shklov did the same in his introduction to his own work, *Pe'at hashulḥan*. However, these were not attempts at a systematic presentation of the Gaon's life and their publication is not clear evidence of public interest in the Gaon's person. Books are not usually purchased for introductions and separate biographical publications are more direct evidence of interest.

The first book that can be claimed to have had the intention of providing information on the Gaon was entitled *Ma'aseh rav*.[42] This is a description of the practices of the Gaon together with some stories about him. It was first published in Vilna in 1832 by Yisakhar ben Tanhum. It was reprinted the next year in Lvov and then again around 1840. After that it was not republished until 1856. In the following two years, four editions appeared. The next edition came out only in 1887.

The first full-scale biography of the Gaon was *Aliyot eliyahu* (The Ascents of Elijah), which was published in 1857. It was written by Yehoshua Heschel Levine[43] with supplements from various authors. It was a great popular success. It was reprinted the year it appeared in Stettin and again there in 1861, and in Vilna in 1875, 1881, 1885, and more. This book was a curious innovation in that it was a biography written by a noted talmudic scholar. It was often reprinted and is still in print. This means that it had and has a readership. It was also the inspiration for Mordekhai Plungian's classic maskilic biography of Rabbi Menasheh of Ilya, *Ben porat yosef*,[44] which had a significant impact on the Haskalah movement in eastern Europe.

Aliyot eliyahu was not written in a vacuum. Rabbi Levine himself was an Orthodox rabbi—indeed, one of the early militantly Orthodox rabbis in Lithuania. He was one of the first rabbis to be acutely aware of the significance of the media and was the first to try to publish an Orthodox journal. His first wife was the granddaughter of Rabbi Hayim of Volozhin, and in 1854 he was involved in an abortive attempt to become the head of the Volozhin yeshiva. He was apparently motivated in this venture not by ambition for

---

[42] See Winograd, *Otsar sifrei hagra*, 145–7.

[43] On R. Levine see Stampfer, *The Formation of the Lithuanian Yeshiva* (Heb.) and *Lithuanian Yeshivas of the Nineteenth Century*. For many details on R. Levine see the fine study by Katzman, 'Rabbi Yehoshua Heschel Lewin' (Heb.). [44] See Feiner, *Haskalah and History*, 224–7.

power or fame, but out of a desire to transform the yeshiva into a framework for the training of more 'modern' rabbis who could effectively combat the appeal of modernist movements. Rabbi Levine returned to Vilna following his failed attempt in Volozhin and it was then that he wrote and published his biography of the Gaon. Given his known concern for the religious condition of Lithuanian Jewry, it would seem unlikely that his goal in writing this book was simply to entertain. Far more likely was a wish to exert what he thought was a positive influence on readers.[45] Had Rabbi Levine succeeded in taking over the Volozhin yeshiva and concentrated on teaching and administration, his book about the Gaon very possibly would never have been written, and if so, the 'publishing industry' which developed around the Gaon and the Gaon's fame might have taken a very different turn. Much remains to be clarified about the literary models and goals of the author.

Additional biographies of the Gaon or books with biographical data on the Gaon were written in the wake of *Aliyot eliyahu*. Yehezkel Katznelenbogen published *Sha'arei rahamim* (Gates of Righteousness) with information on the Gaon's practices and works in 1871. Yet another biography, *Se'arat eliyahu* (The Storm of Elijah) by Avraham the son of the Gaon and edited by Shemuel Yevnin, was published in Warsaw in 1878.

The Gaon was not the first Lithuanian rabbi to have a biography written about him. Perhaps the first such case was on a student of the Gaon, Rabbi Zelmele, who was the brother of Rabbi Hayim of Volozhin.[46] What was unique about the Gaon was the number of biographies written about him and, even more significantly, how often they were reprinted. Through these publications the memory and image of the Gaon was preserved and developed.

THE INFLUENCE OF BIOGRAPHIES ON THE PUBLICATION OF THE GAON'S WORKS

The publishing history of the Gaon's writings is a complicated one, but much has been clarified in the complete bibliography of his writings published by Yeshayahu Winograd entitled *Otsar sifrei hagra*. As we shall see, the chronological view of the publishing history is rather enlightening.

The most striking fact about the publication history of the Gaon's works is how little was published and how slowly. In fact, much of the Gaon's literary output was lost because of the slow and unsystematic pace of the publication of his manuscripts. The slow pace was not because of a lack of desire by his heirs and students to bring his writings to the attention of the scholarly world,

---

[45] This is discussed to some degree in Etkes, *The Gaon of Vilna*, 42–5.
[46] See Etkes, 'Immanent Factors and External Influences in the Development of the Haskalah Movement in Russia'; Edward Breuer, 'The Haskalah in Vilna'.

but their task was not easy. The Gaon did not write books but rather notes, which had to be collated and transcribed before they could be printed. This was exceedingly difficult because the Gaon wrote in a cryptic style which was hard to understand.[47] This problem was compounded by the fact that some of the most logical candidates to edit his works—certain of his leading disciples —emigrated to Palestine shortly after his death and it was very difficult to prepare books for publication from a distance. There was apparently public interest in the Gaon's works,[48] and his disciples who emigrated to Palestine did try hard to publish some of the written heritage before they left Lithuania, but they were unable to prepare very much material for publication.[49]

Rabbi Hayim of Volozhin did not deal with the publication of his venerated teacher's works, nor is there any evidence that he tried to obtain handwritten copies of the Gaon's notes on classical texts. Why he did not involve himself is not clear. As a result of the pressures under which the Gaon's students were working, many errors crept into the publications. Of course, mistakes in a text that is cryptic at best make it incomprehensible and its study unrewarding. A student who finds the study of a given text to be frustrating is likely to pick other material for study, and this may have happened in the case of the Gaon's works. It is certainly not clear to what degree the writings of the Gaon were studied in the first generations after his death. It is clear that even when his works were published, it often took years before they were reprinted. This suggests that public fascination with them was limited.

The fitful pace of the publication of the Gaon's works up to the mid-nineteenth century can be documented. Until 1810 about twenty works attributed to the Gaon (not including marginal notes) appeared.[50] This number included new titles and reprints. We know of about fifteen publications in the following decade (1810—20), but only two or three in the next decade. In later years, the numbers began to rise, but the real jump in numbers begins in 1857. In the ten-year period starting in that year, there were no fewer than forty-four publications.

---

[47] See for example the introduction of Menahem Mendel of Shklov to the edition of the *Shulḥan arukh* with the commentary of the Gaon. He writes there that some speak of the Gaon with haughtiness and disdain because they have not analysed the Gaon's sources.

[48] Ibid., 'Yoreh de'ah'.

[49] Dr Aryeh Morgenstern pointed out to me the problems that the disciples had trying to print their teacher's works and in preparing for departure to Palestine at the same time. This point will be developed and documented in a forthcoming study he is currently preparing.

[50] The number of publications is based on data in Winograd, *Otsar sifrei hagra*. This fascinating and valuable resource lists all publications of the Gaon's works, including books that contain sections written by the Gaon and books with his annotations. In counting publications, I only included works that the contemporary reader would have identified as written by the Gaon and not merely that contained a part that he had written.

The uneven pace of the printing and reprinting of the Gaon's works is particularly evident if we concentrate on three 'popular' titles for which one could have anticipated a constant market: the Gaon's commentary on Proverbs, his commentary on *Pirkei avot* (a tractate of the Mishnah which contains many ethical maxims), and his commentary on the Passover Hagadah. The commentary on Proverbs had been selected by the Gaon to be the first of his books to be published,[51] and indeed it was. It was published in 1798 and again in 1815. However, the next two editions were only in 1837 and 1839, and this was followed by another twenty-year gap until 1857. The commentary on *Pirkei avot* was published in 1804 and 1831, and after that only in 1860. The pace of publication of both of these commentaries was uneven and not intensive. The commentary on the Passover Hagadah was printed much more often and it was the only truly popular work which transmitted the Gaon's views. It first appeared in 1805,[52] and was frequently reissued thereafter.

Not only was the publication of the Gaon's works erratic, but it came in spurts. As noted above, in the 1820s only two or three works of the Gaon were published. However, in the two years 1832–3, at least six works of his appeared, and eight more in the next four years, while in the following decade only six appeared. The next and much larger spurt came, as noted above, after 1857. The issue of spurts in publication merits attention. The Jewish population of Lithuania was constantly growing in the nineteenth century, and a growing population means a growing need for books. This alone could explain a long-term rise in publication of the Gaon's work.[53] However, population growth does not explain spurts, which are often in response to events and not to long-term trends. There do not seem to be any major political occurrences, such as shifts in censorship or developments in the publishing industry, in 1832 and 1857 which could explain these spurts.[54] If it is events that we are looking for we must look elsewhere.

Both spurts in the publication of the Gaon's writings came in the wake of the publication of biographies of him. The first spurt came after the publication of *Ma'aseh rav* (1832), and the second after the appearance of *Aliyot eliyahu* (1857). The publication of these books does not seem to have

---

[51] See the introduction by R. Menahem Mendel of Shklov to the Gaon's commentary on Proverbs.   [52] Winograd, *Otsar sifrei hagra*, 97–115.

[53] Zeev Gries pointed out in a conversation that from the mid century on there was a sharp rise in the total number of Hebrew titles published. This process has not been systematically analysed. However, in any quantitative study it is important to allow for population growth and this is often ignored.

[54] A full history of Hebrew printing in Vilna has yet to be written. The most valuable recent publication is Agranovsky, *Stanovlenie evreiskogo knigopechataniya v Litve*, which naturally deals mainly with the famous Romm press. He notes (p. 16) that in the early 1830s there was a significant rise in Hebrew printing in Vilna. It is not clear why there was a concurrent rise in interest in the Gaon's works.

been the consequence of specific events in those years. The composition of these biographies was also not necessarily related to contemporary events. *Ma'aseh rav* was written long before it was published. Rabbi Levine wrote *Aliyot eliyahu*, as noted above, to meet the specific needs of the period and as a response to a specific event. There is no other obvious reason for the sudden interest in the Gaon's work other than the heightened interest which a biography can elicit.[55]

*

Great rabbis have often been known more by their works than by their names. In many Lithuanian yeshivas, the most popular commentary on the Talmud was a book called *Ketsot haḥoshen* (The Corners of the Breastplate) written by a Galician scholar, Rabbi Aryeh Leib ben Yosef Hakohen.[56] It was consulted by many and had a major impact on methods of Talmud study. However, most yeshiva students would have found it difficult to identify the author and little was known in Lithuania about his life. For the users of his works, the name of the book was the name of the author. He was referred to as 'the author of the *Ketsot*' and not by name. There was nothing exceptional about this. Most scholars were referred to by the title of their most famous book and not by name.

Other scholars were talked about by name, but not read. The Gaon seems to have been in this category. As we have seen, there were reasons for this. He left few disciples and a very problematic literary heritage. He wrote enigmatic notes rather than clear and readable comments on the Talmud, so that reconstructing his interpretation of a talmudic text is a difficult and arduous task. For this, and probably other reasons as well, he was not often cited. One consequence of this was that later generations could not even learn of his ideas secondhand. The lack of clear traditions about the Gaon is what made it possible for a wide variety of personalities—from traditional kabbalists to talmudic scholars, and even to modernizers who sought justification for introducing innovations such as the study of sciences and mathematics—to use him as a model and justification.[57]

An indication of the limited visibility of the Gaon's impact can be seen in *Nefesh haḥayim* (Breath of Life) written by the Gaon's illustrious student, Rabbi Hayim of Volozhin. Although there is absolutely no doubt about the formidable influence of the person of the Gaon on Rabbi Hayim, and while

[55] A similar phenomenon—although different in many ways—is the rise of interest in the Maharal of Prague (Rabbi Yehudah Loew, 1525–1609) after the publication of Yehudah Rosenberg's *Miracles of the Maharal* (Heb.) in 1909. See the introduction of Eli Yassif to Rosenberg, *The Golem of Prague* (Heb.), esp. pp. 59–160.
[56] For a biography of the author see Wunder, *Lights of Galicia* (Heb.), iii. 291–300.
[57] See Etkes, 'The Gaon of Vilna' (Heb.).

the ideology of the book, which emphasizes the centrality of Torah study over all other activities, fits the Gaon's views, there are few explicit references to the Gaon in it. A reader who studied the book would come out with few impressions of the Gaon. Without citation, thinkers lose their impact.

The Gaon's works did not have a central role in Lithuanian Torah scholarship in the first half of the nineteenth century. The works of the Gaon that were most reprinted were his commentary on the Passover hagadah and the ethical letter composed for his family, *Alim literufah*,[58] while the market for the scholarly works of the Gaon was very limited. This reality was summed up in the biography of a rabbi who was born three years before the Gaon died. His biographer noted: 'He studied in the true manner as was the approach of the Gaon even though his [the Gaon's] books were not widespread in his youth in those regions.'[59]

If the Gaon's works were not widely studied, how then was his memory preserved? As we saw, in his lifetime the Gaon had a very strong impact on a small circle of individuals close to him and a leading role in the Vilna community and region—though not without opposition. He was regarded with awe among Torah scholars even though there were many elements of his teachings and personality that were not easily accepted by many of his contemporaries. Therefore biographies seem to have had an important role in the maintenance of his memory. However, while they preserved his memory, they also helped shape it. In other words, the Gaon's memory both stimulated interest in a printed biography and was affected by the printed biography of him. In these biographies it was the scholarly aspect of his life that was emphasized and other, and perhaps less convenient, aspects were downplayed or forgotten.[60]

Interestingly, one of the elements that seems to have been under-emphasized—to say the least—in these biographies was the Gaon's opposition to hasidism. It would have been quite reasonable to anticipate that the Gaon's place in Lithuanian Jewish consciousness was a consequence of his leading role in the struggle against hasidism.[61] However, neither in *Ma'aseh rav*, nor in *Aliyot eliyahu*, nor in *Se'arat eliyahu* is there any discussion of the Gaon as a leader of the struggle against hasidism, nor of his involvement in this struggle. No sources are cited and no discussion is included. When these books were published, the traditional and mitnagdic societies had greater external threats to deal with—namely, modernization and its Hebrew variant,

[58] According to Winograd, there were 143 editions of the commentary on the hagadah and 121 editions of his ethical letter; there were 43 editions of his commentary on *Pirkei avot* (Ethics of the Fathers), but no other work was published even 30 times: Winograd, *Otsar sifrei hagra*, 30.   [59] Frumkin, *History of the Sages of Jerusalem* (Heb.), 10.
[60] See Morgenstern, *Mysticism and Messianism* (Heb.), 259–61.
[61] Such a suggestion was raised by Nachum Greenwald in a private communication.

the Haskalah. Very possibly the authors felt that in the face of external threats there was no need to expand on internal divisions.

A comparison with the Ba'al Shem Tov is instructive. Despite the importance of oral communications in early hasidism, most of our knowledge on the Ba'al Shem Tov is derived from a book *Shivḥei habesht* (Praises of the Ba'al Shem Tov) which is a printed volume of stories about him. It was apparently printed not simply for commercial reasons but as part of a campaign by Rabbi Dov Ber to strengthen his claim to succeed his father as the leader of Habad hasidism.[62] The book was extremely popular and six editions came out within the first three years of its publication, which was a clear indication of the potential readership for popular biographies.[63] Despite the unquestioned importance of the Ba'al Shem Tov, it is hard to imagine what our historical memory of him would have been without *Shivḥei habesht*. Books keep memory alive.

Had the Gaon not been as great as he was, no biography could have created his image or reputation. The Gaon was no product of the media. However, in addition to his brilliance and character, many factors strengthened his place in the historical memory of Lithuanian Jewry. His residence in Vilna was one factor and his role in the struggle against hasidism was another. However, it should be clear that the contribution of the printed biography and of the media in general also had an important role which should not be ignored.

---

[62] See Rosman, *Founder of Hasidism: A Quest for the Historical Baal Shem Tov*, ch. 9 and p. 204.

[63] The book had a complicated publication history. It was first printed in 1814, more than 50 years after the death of the Ba'al Shem Tov and after the hasidic movement was already widespread. It was very popular, so much so that it was printed six times in three years. However, it was not printed from 1816 until 1828, and the next time it was reprinted was in 1850. In the 1860s it was reprinted twice, and the next reprint was in 1906. Raphael, 'Shivḥei habesht' (Heb.). A very important discussion is found in Mondshine, *Shivḥei habesht*.

SIXTEEN

The Controversy over Sheḥitah and the Struggle between Hasidim and Mitnagedim

A STUDY OF HOW JEWS once sharpened the knives used in *sheḥitah*, or slaughtering of animals, might appear rather esoteric. However, it is sometimes the case that details that appear rather trivial can have significance that is far greater than could have been expected. In east European Jewish society meat was a central element of the diet, and the observance of the kosher laws was one of the most obvious ways in which Jews were distinguished from non-Jews. Moreover, a rigorous observance of these laws was one of the ways in which individual Jews demonstrated their piety. The quality of the *ḥalaf*, or knife used for *sheḥitah*, is one of the key elements in determining whether meat is kosher or not. During the early days of the hasidic movement, a dispute over the type of knife that should be used—specifically a demand that slaughtering knives be sharpened or 'polished' in a special way—played a major role in the struggle between the hasidim and their opponents. As we shall see, the decline of this dispute contributed to the establishment of a degree of peace, or at least coexistence, between the groups. Therefore, there are good reasons to give some attention to the dispute over these knives.

It is well known that hasidim had special practices related to *sheḥitah*. They demanded that the knives used for *sheḥitah* be 'polished' knives (*sakinim melutashot*), in distinction to the mitnagedim, who vehemently opposed using such knives. In those places where the hasidim were not able to take control over the local '*sheḥitah*', they tended to avoid the products of the communal *sheḥitah* and they would try to set up separate and independent frameworks for *sheḥitah*. Not surprisingly, the special practices of *sheḥitah* of the hasidim occupy a prominent role in the literature related to the demands for excommunication of the hasidim.[1]

---

[1] The most convenient source for texts dealing with the dispute over ritual slaughter between hasidim and mitnagedim is Wilensky, *Hasidim and Mitnagedim* (Heb.). See '*sheḥitah*' in index; also vol. i, p. 26 n. 11.

Various scholars dealt with the topic of the dispute over ritual slaughter and noted that the special *sheḥitah* practices current among hasidim both strengthened the crystallization of the hasidic groups and also sharpened the disputes between them and their opponents. Jacob Katz noted that 'the hasidic slaughterers (*shoḥatim*) were careful to use only well-honed knives—a stringency that served to camouflage their real object, which was to avoid eating together with non-hasidim'.[2] Shmuel Ettinger had a very different view. He claimed that it was actually the mitnagedim who took the step of prohibiting meat slaughtered by hasidim.[3]

Despite the importance of the dispute over the ritual slaughter of meat for the history of the hasidic movement, rather oddly the issue is hardly mentioned in the halakhic literature.[4] Only a few isolated references have survived in hasidic sources. The reason may be related to concerns by hasidim that texts dealing with special practices of ritual slaughter might find their way into the hands of their opponents and be used against them.[5] However, the question remains of why the hasidim would not be interested in a serious halakhic discussion of the use of polished knives.

There is no doubt that economic and social factors influenced the dispute over methods of slaughter. However, they do not seem to be sufficient to explain how the dispute came into being. After all, at the heart of the dispute was a halakhic question and both supporters and opponents of the method should have justified their positions in halakhic terms. Therefore it seems that the dispute warrants a careful examination both of the technology as well as of its halakhic aspects.

The dispute over *sheḥitah* is different in its nature from other disputes between hasidim and their opponents. For example, with regard to the hasidic practice to use a modified Sefardi ritual for prayer, the mitnagedim admitted that the change itself is not prohibited, since it had been permitted for individuals and small groups in the past, such as in the *kloyz* of Brody, but they nonetheless opposed its adoption by the masses.[6] At the basis of the dispute on prayer was the desire of the hasidim to transform a custom of the elite to the practice of the masses. Most of the other disputes derived from the same issue.

The question of ritual slaughter is more complex. At first glance this appears to be another attempt to take the custom of a select few and turn it

[2] Katz, *Tradition and Crisis*, 208.

[3] Ettinger, Review of the Hebrew original of *Tradition and Crisis* (Heb.).

[4] In the *Otsar haposekim* data base there are almost no references to polished knives. The books on the laws of slaughter also do not refer to this issue. See, for example, Greenwald, *Shoḥet and Sheḥitah in Rabbinic Literature* (Heb.); Flekser, *A Halakhicly Kosher Slaughtering Knife* (Heb.).　　　　　[5] Gries, *Conduct Literature* (Heb.), 169, 200.

[6] Wertheim, *Law and Custom in Hasidism*, section 3. See section 9 for his discussion of polished knives.

into the general practice of the community at large. However, unlike other customs which are carried out by individuals and which can be kept in private, changes in customs of *sheḥitah* influence all the community—learned and unlearned alike—because all have to eat from the same butchers' shops. It would have been possible, of course, to have special practices for the slaughter of fowl without having an impact on the community. However, with regard to the slaughter of cows, the matter was not so simple. The meat of one cow fed many households. The rich ate the prime cuts and the poor ate the less desirable ones, but the 'kosherness' of all the cuts was the same. Therefore, those who wanted to be scrupulous with regard to the slaughter of beef could not do this alone. In effect they had to enforce the customs on others. Moreover, both hasidim and mitnagedim took the question of *sheḥitah* and especially the sharpness of slaughtering knives very seriously. Therefore it is understandable that all concerned with Jewish law were interested in the best quality possible of slaughtering knives—and, if the polishing of knives was an obvious improvement, it was not at all to be expected that there would be a dispute over it.

The end of the dispute also requires clarification because very little attention has been given to it. Very often researchers seek out the roots of a dispute and discuss the reasons for its appearance. However, the causes of the decline of a conflict are also worthy of attention. The factors and processes that lead to the creation of peaceful relations say no less about the character of a society than do the causes and reasons that lead to a dispute or to separation. Stories of conflict are more dramatic than are narratives of peacemaking, but they are not necessarily less important or less significant.

THE SOURCE OF THE DISPUTE

The preparation of a slaughtering knife was always a complicated and sensitive issue in Jewish law. The halakhah requires that the knife be as sharp as possible so that the cut will be quick and clean. At the same time the knife has to be straight and smooth. In other words, when looking at the knife from the side there should be no 'ups and downs' on the blade; when looking from the end it should be straight without any sections that protrude to the right or to the left. The knife has to be strong so that it will not be nicked in the course of cutting. However, any step to improve one of these characteristics—sharpness, smoothness, straightness, or strength—risks having a negative impact on one of the other characteristics. For example, making a knife sharper can make it less straight or less smooth. The more a knife is thinner or sharper, the more likely it is to get nicked. There is also a requirement on slaughterers to check their knives and this has to be considered. The standard way of checking knives was for the slaughterer to pass them over his fingernail. If a knife was very sharp, the slaughterer risked splitting his nail during the examination of the knife, and this could possibly lead to his not being careful in the check.

The requirement to use only knives that were sharpened in a special manner was not original to the hasidic movement, and this has been noted by a number of researchers.[7] The issue is referred to in a responsum written by Rabbi Yonah Navon, a resident of Jerusalem in the mid-eighteenth century, and it would appear that the custom had already developed before his time. According to him:

> Here in the holy city of Jerusalem, may it speedily be rebuilt, slaughterers in the past were accustomed to use a sharp knife and were skilled at checking the knife well for nicks even though it was very sharp. Now, in our times there have been questions raised about the sharp knives because expert slaughterers from abroad said that such knives can have defects and it is impossible to check them because they are so sharp. Therefore all of the scholars of the city assembled with the expert slaughterers in the holy city and agreed that no slaughterer will be allowed to slaughter with the very sharp knife. Instead they will use a sharp and smooth knife, in other words, a medium [knife], so that it will not be very smooth, which is a bad knife, and not too sharp because defects are not recognized in sharp knives—as the expert slaughterers from abroad said. This is the current practice in Jerusalem. May the Torah of God save us from error and so may it be His will. I have written this so that the agreement will not be forgotten.[8]

Rabbi Navon died around the year 1760 so it is clear that there is no link between the slaughterers he was referring to and the dispute between hasidim and mitnagedim.

A similar dispute involved Rabbi Natan Adler, the mentor of Rabbi Moses Sofer (Hatam Sofer). In a letter written in 1784 by a member of the Jewish community of Boskovice to Rabbi Natan Mas, a Frankfurt rabbi, the following was reported about Rabbi Adler:

> As soon as he came here, this rabbi terrified us with all types of great terrors from every side and turned most of all to ugly ways of *sheḥitah*, the slaughterer must show his knife to the rabbi every time—both when slaughtering cattle and when slaughtering fowl . . . and after investigation we discovered that he slaughters with a bad and very sharp knife, against the opinion of authorities such as the author of *Bayit ḥadash* and *Siftei kohen*.[9] We never hear such a thing out of fear for the word of

---

[7]   See Shmeruk, 'The Social Significance of the Hasidic *Sheḥitah*'; and Piekarz, *The Beginning of Hasidism*.

[8]   Navon, *Neḥpah bakhesef*, section 'Peri leperi', vol. ii, p. 52, no. 18, para. 7.

[9]   *Bayit ḥadash* is a well-known commentary by R. Yo'el Sirkes (1561–1640) on Ya'akov ben Asher, *Arba'ah turim*, a major halakhic code; *Siftei kohen* is a well-known commentary by R. Shabetai ben Me'ir Hakohen on parts of Karo, *Shulḥan arukh*, another authoritative halakhic code.

God and usually the pressure on the knife and the many back and forth cuts lead to imperfections in the knife. Moreover, this rabbi declared the pure to be impure and permitted the impermissible . . . he spends all his days and years sharpening the knife and checking it without success and for no purpose.[10]

It is known that Rabbi Natan Adler adopted some Sefardi practices, especially ones related to kabbalah, and it is possible that his custom to sharpen knives in a special way is one more of these.[11] However, here as well there does not appear to be any influence of hasidism, but rather a parallel development that was based on the desire to excel in the fulfilment of religious commandments.

THE BEGINNINGS OF THE USE OF
POLISHED KNIVES AMONG HASIDIM

From the early days of the hasidic movement its leaders displayed great interest and care with regard to the laws of *shehitah*. This included careful examinations of knives used for slaughter and concern for the character of the slaughterers—on the assumption that there is a link between the quality of the kosher slaughter and the personal characteristics of the slaughterer. However, there is no evidence for the use of polished knives from the early days of the movement.[12]

The use of polished knives among hasidim began apparently in the time of Rabbi Dov Ber, the Magid of Mezeritch. This can be learned from an undated response written by Rabbi Yehudah Leib of Yanovitz, the brother of Rabbi Shneur Zalman of Lyady. The letter was apparently written to someone who questioned the use of such knives, and this was Rabbi Yehudah's reply:

He made false accusations against the slaughterers who study how to make polished knives as they had been taught by their teacher and their teacher from their teacher up until our first rabbis who invented this, i.e. the famous slaughterers of Mezeritch, whom the holy Magid [some honorifics deleted] kept at his side, and after him, all of the honest ones, his students the famous *tsadikim* who drank in thirst his words, the living word of God. They established the craft and trained many slaughterers and warned them to warn the great and the simple to keep and maintain all that they were taught by their teachers; the main care was given to the polished knife, as our rabbi [honorifics deleted] wrote that a knife that is not

---

[10] The letter was printed as a supplement to Shelomoh Sofer, *Der dreifache Faden*, 157–8. I am indebted to the late Professor Jacob Katz, who brought this letter to my attention.

[11] On R. Natan Adler see Elior, 'Natan Adler and the Hasidic Community in Frankfurt' (Heb.), esp. pp. 36–7, 49, and 52–4.

[12] For example, *Shivḥei habesht*, first published in 1815, appeared when the practice of using polished knives was widespread and well known. Nonetheless, I did not find even allusions to a special technique of sharpening knives in this early book.

polished cannot be sharp, and since it is not smooth enough, it is almost certain that it will make a flawed cut.[13]

More important details on the beginnings of the use of polished knives can be found in a letter of Rabbi Shneur Zalman of Lyady of 1791. He wrote in order to claim that many who used polished knives had nothing to do with hasidism:

In all of the lands of Ukraine and Little Poland and Podolia and most of the lands of Volhynia people eat with polished knives [i.e. meat slaughtered with polished knives] as well as in the great city of Dubno [the residents of which] are not our followers at all and so in Ostrov and Kremenets and Lutsk and other large communities [whose residents are] not our followers at all, and in the Holy Land and many of the Sefardim.[14]

From his words it appears that the practice of using polished knives in *sheḥitah* was often a local custom and certainly not an invention of the hasidic movement. The contribution of hasidism was to spread the custom to additional regions along with the spread of the movement itself.

Near the end of his letter Rabbi Shneur Zalman noted the differences between a regular knife and a polished knife: 'It takes a long time to sharpen a knife and slaughterers do not always have the time. This is not the case with polished knives which can be polished by experts very quickly.'[15] It is clear from his words that 'polishing' is not a separate or distinct act of the slaughterer. Today it is common to rub a knife with a cloth or piece of leather after it is sharpened, but this is not what was referred to in the past as 'polishing'. The term then seems to have referred to a special way of making a knife so that afterwards it took less effort to sharpen it for slaughtering than was the case with the standard knife. In other words, this was a stringency whose goal was to make the work of a slaughterer easier. Other knives, so claimed Rabbi Shneur Zalman Schneersohn, are usually sharp but are not smooth, and this is in contradiction to the halakhic requirement that a knife be smooth. In his opinion this was not a problem with polished knives.

Despite the importance Rabbi Schneersohn attributed to slaughtering with polished knives, he warned his followers:

Far be it from us to speak poorly of those regions who are lenient in these matters. In the generations before us, our ancestors acted in accordance with the lenient view. In these generations, the number of those who are stringent has grown, just as

---

[13] Yehuda Leib of Yanovitz, 'Responsum' (Heb.). See also Hilman, *Letters of Shneur Zalman* (Heb.), 209–11. The responsum was sent to a certain R. Ya'akov. Some have tried to identify him with R. Ya'akov of Smila. See Mondshine, *Migdal oz*, 465. A different version of the responsum was published in *Yagdil torah*, 7/6 (95) (1983), 331.

[14] This responsum has been printed in various places. The more recent and most convenient is Schneersohn, *Holy Letters* (Heb.), 143 n. 61; see also p. 391.

[15] Schneersohn, *Holy Letters* (Heb.), 147.

people are more careful with the laws of new wheat and praying the evening prayer at its correct time etc.

[He added that] I myself have never tried to avoid [eating from] pots [used to cook meat that had not been slaughtered with polished knives]—even pots that had recently been used.[16]

Rabbi Schneersohn returned to this last issue in a different responsum in which he demanded that his followers in Vilna not separate themselves from people who use meat that was not slaughtered with polished knives, even though the use of such knives 'is a great and enormous *mitsvah* which our holy rabbis . . . upheld and truly were willing to make great sacrifices to observe'.[17]

In the writings of Rabbi Shneur Zalman of Lyady and of his brother, Rabbi Yehudah of Yanovitz, there is no detailed description of polished knives, and there is also no detailed description in the writings of those opposed to hasidic slaughtering. In recent years attempts have been made to fill in this gap. Wertheim felt that the main difference between regular knives and polished knives was that polished knives were made out of molten iron, whereas regular knives were made out of forged iron.[18] However, in the sources dealing with the dispute, reference was made only to the shape of the knife and to the method of sharpening, but no mention was made of the material out of which the knives were made. It is conceivable that in parallel to the dispute over methods of sharpening there was an additional dispute over the material from which knives were made, but this has yet to be proven. Moreover, the main sources Wertheim relies on are two commentaries on the *Shulḥan arukh*: *Darkhei teshuvah* (Ways of Repentance)[19] and *Da'at kedoshim* (Holy Knowledge).[20] These were written by later commentators who were not referring to the dispute between hasidim and their opponents but to later disputes.[21]

Another explanation for the dispute was suggested by Rabbi Shalom Duber Levine, who modestly wrote that his explanation, based on an internal Habad tradition, is only a possibility.[22] He explained that the making of a knife begins with a rectangular piece of metal that undergoes a process of sharpening on one side. As a result, when the knife is prepared there is a great area

---

[16] Schneersohn, *Holy Letters* (Heb.), 145. [17] Ibid. 188 n. 5.

[18] Wertheim, *Law and Custom in Hasidism*, 302 n. 1. Shmuel Himelstein, the translator of Wertheim's book, uses the English term 'whetted knives' where I have used 'polished'.

[19] Shapira, *Darkhei teshuvah*. [20] Wahrman, *Da'at kedoshim*.

[21] Wahrman, *Da'at kedoshim*, 'Yoreh de'ah', no. 18: 2, deals with wrought-iron knives but he does not mention polished knives there. He mentions them only in no. 18: 6. In *Darkhei teshuvah*, the commentary of R. Zvi Hirsch Shapira on 'Yoreh de'ah', no. 18: 6, the author clearly does not refer to the original dispute but rather to the use of steel knives. This happened in a later period and will be discussed below.

[22] Levine, 'The Reponsum of Admor HaZaken #7'.

near the edge of the blade that has been ground down and it is difficult to
make this surface totally smooth. However, the situation is different if the
whole process begins with a piece of metal that is made from the beginning to
be narrow on the side that will be the edge of the blade. In such a case less
preparation is needed, the area that is ground down is smaller, and there is less
need to polish. This, according to Rabbi Levine, is how 'polished' knives were
made. It is a very logical explanation. The difficulty with it is that the early
sources do not mention that there was a narrow side in the raw piece of metal
used to make a knife. The sources concentrated on another issue: the thickness of the blade.

The earliest reference that I have found in hasidic sources to polished
knives is in a letter of Rabbi Shemuel Horowitz, the rabbi of Nikolsburg,
to the heads of the Jewish community of Brody. This letter was written as a
response to the excommunication of the hasidim in 1772. He does not explicitly use the terms 'polished knife' but he does write that the hasidim 'excel
in all types of laws of kosher slaughter and in careful examinations of the
knives which are sharp and light . . . and so is the custom in all the regions of
Ashkenaz to sharpen the knives . . . and experience shows that the thinner
the knife is, the easier it is to feel it'. He summarized the point by writing
'the matter of the knives is not an innovation'.[23]

Also Rabbi Yehudah of Yanovitz, cited above, gave particular attention to
the thickness of the knife:

I also recall that when I was in Chernobyl with our teacher, the holy rabbi . . .
Nahum . . . he employed the famous slaughterer Rabbi Lipman who had studied
with the veteran slaughterers in Międzyrzec. He had many pupils and he ordered
them to come to him once a year for a refresher course. He said that the reason was
that the students were not as expert as he was in polishing thinly [*bedakut*] and their
knives were a bit thick and hard to feel.[24]

Other sources mention thin knives together with references to hasidim. For
example, in a biography of Rabbi Shemuel Betsalel ben Shalom Sheftel there
is a description of how he became a hasid in the 1840s: 'There were [among
the hasidim] individuals who went to great expense to be certain that there
would be a hasidic slaughterer who [would] only use a thin knife, because the
mitnagedim supported a slaughterer who would use a thick knife, as is
known.'[25] This statement is similar to an undated responsum written by
Rabbi Aryeh Bolechover to a slaughterer in Kamieniec Podolski. He wrote:

In the generation before us these polished knives were invented, something new
that had never been before and that our forefathers never imagined. Until then

---

[23] See Wilensky, *Hasidim and Mitnagedim* (Heb.), i. 84–8.
[24] Yehudah Leib of Yanovitz, 'Responsum' (Heb.).
[25] Anon., 'Biography of R. Shemuel Betsalel ben Shalom Sheftel' (Heb.), 68.

there had always been thick knives as is still the custom today among Sefardim and in many places in Lithuania. The thick knives are good and attractive after slaughtering [as before]. However, it is hard to sharpen them and to repair them if they become defective. Therefore, in the generation before ours they had the wisdom to invent polished knives that are easy to repair though they also become defective more easily.[26]

A similar terminology is used in the work of Rabbi Avraham David of Buczacz (d. 1841): 'The custom has spread some time ago in a number of places [to use] very thin knives which are termed "polished".'[27] In a book published in 1858 but written much earlier, the author notes: 'Recently the use of polished knives that are very thin has increased.'[28]

On the basis of the material at our disposal it appears that the polished knife was indeed a thin one. Since it was thin it was relatively easy for a slaughterer to sharpen and to achieve a high degree of smoothness and sharpness. However, as mentioned above, such knives are easily nicked and become defective. If this takes place during the act of slaughtering, very complicated halakhic problems arise with regard to the kosherness of the meat. In theory there is no difficulty in checking the knife after slaughtering and proscribing the meat if there is a problem with the knife. However, a great deal of pressure was put on the examiner because proscribing the meat could cause great financial loss to the owner of the cow or the butcher. There was reason for concern that this pressure would lead to approving questionable meat, and that what had started out as a means of achieving a high level of kosherness would have the reverse result. The demands by hasidim for this kind of knife, like the concerns of the opponents, were motivated by a concern for the quality of *kashrut* observance.

THE END OF THE DISPUTE

From the middle of the nineteenth century the dispute over the polished knives waned. In contemporary sources there is no mention of attempts to reach an agreement between the two sides or to a formal agreement designed

[26] Aryeh Leib ben Eliyahu (Bolechover), *She'elot uteshuvot shem aryeh*, no. 3, p. 24. The halakhic difficulties of polished knives are described there. See p. 48: 'Since we cannot turn the clock back to return to slaughter with the thick knives which are good and attractive even after slaughtering and this is a deformation that cannot be corrected . . . Nonetheless it is worth fixing what can be fixed and that is not to sharpen the knife to a sharp point . . . and now you can see that the fingernails of the ancients were better than the bellies of the latter-day scholars, for they used thick knives which are difficult to repair but also do not easily become defective . . . this is not the case with the polished knives of our time which are easy to repair quickly but also become defective quickly in use for slaughtering.' [27] Wahrman, *Da'at kedoshim*, no. 18: 6.

[28] Hakohen, *Minḥat hazevaḥ*, 15, *kelal* 10 (there is a misprint in the text and at the top of the page is written '*kelal* 7'). The identification of 'polished knives' as thin and easily sharpened is repeated in Levine, *The Law of the Sacrifice* (Heb.; 1st pub. 1885); for recent discussions see

to bring peace on *kashrut* issues. The process of mutual acceptance appears to
have happened of its own accord since it was not influenced by any change in
principles on either side. As we shall see, there was a reason for it, and it was
technological.

In the eighteenth century, most slaughtering knives were made of iron.
This was the strongest material available for mass production of knives but it
had a drawback: it was breakable. Steel, made of iron and carbon, was a more
desirable material. However, in the eighteenth century steel was very expensive and hard to work. Steel then was not pure, and there were few varieties of
steel available. The most important developments in the production of steel
took place in the eighteenth century when, in England, Benjamin Henderson
developed a new method for mass producing strong steel at a reasonable
price. This method formed the basis of the famous cutlery centre in Sheffield.
The new methods of steelmaking spread in Germany, and soon reasonably
priced steel knives began to arrive in quantity in eastern Europe.[29] The great
advantage of steel is that it can be sharpened so that it is very sharp without
losing its strength or becoming subject to nicks. Lo and behold, the steel knife
could meet the requirements of all sides![30]

One might have anticipated that, given the inherent traditionalism in the
conservative society, slaughterers and rabbis would have objected to suddenly
switching the knives used in *shehitah* and would have been hesitant about
turning their backs on the materials used by their forefathers. However, this
was not the case. In a guide to slaughterers that came out in Vienna in 1850,
the author wrote that a slaughterer has to have a special knife made out of
good iron that is called 'English Steel'.[31] In the same spirit, another author
wrote:

Now that they have invented ways to make from molten iron select steel and it is a
hard material as is known now, and they make knives with great skill from the select
and expensive steel which even if it is sharpened to a high degree it can also be very
smooth. It has such strength that even the sharp point does not become defective
during slaughtering.[32]

Walman, *Law of Slaughtering* (Heb.), 317–18; Adler, *On the Basis of the Torah* (Heb.), ch 17, esp.
291–8.

[29] I have been unable to find details on the distribution network for steel knives in eastern
Europe and the timing of the spread of the steel knife.
[30] See Lloyd, *The Cutlery Trades*, 31–3. Before high-quality steel knives became easily available, a much-used method for making knives was by forging pieces of steel together. The quality of the results depended on the raw material. Once the new methods of making steel became
widespread, the method of forging was no longer necessary (p. 34). Perhaps Wertheim,
mentioned above, who discussed a transition in the types of metal used, was referring to this
method.   [31] Flaschner, *Zevah mishpahah*, no. 1.
[32] Shapira, *Darkhei teshuvah*, 'Yoreh de'ah', no. 18: 5, n. 40.

In other words, rabbis and slaughterers were quick to adopt technological novelties in order to improve the quality of slaughtering, even though they were abandoning the methods of their forefathers.

It was steel that brought an end to the dispute between hasidim and their opponents. Already in the late nineteenth century, when the classic halakhic code *Arukh hashulḥan* was written by Rabbi Yehi'el Mikhal Halevi Epstein (1829–1908), the dispute over polished knives had become a vague memory. It says there:

> To tell the truth, in our youth we heard (and also saw in some books) that about two generations previously there had been a great dispute between the scholars of Israel with regard to the way to prepare the knife. Some would make the point thin and very sharp while others made it slightly thicker and very smooth but not so sharp. Both sides based their positions on the view that the checking of the knife should concentrate on these particular characteristics. There were those who would even not eat from a meat dish used by the other side. In truth, there is no need to dismiss either method and both laws come from the word of the living God.[33]

ADDITIONAL DISPUTES OVER SLAUGHTERING

Even after the dispute over polished knives had been forgotten, there was never total unity in east European Jewry over issues of *kashrut*. However, the disputes that arose in the nineteenth century did not have a major role in the consciousness of contemporaries and they did not have a significant impact on social unity.[34] The best-known of the latter-day disputes was that which arose, in the first third of the nineteenth century, as a result of an innovation of the slaughterer Rabbi Yitshak of Pilov, a hasid of Przysucha and Kock.[35]

At first glance it seems easy to reconstruct the dispute on the basis of a description in a classic halakhic authority:

> There are two ways to sharpen. One is to sharpen equally on both sides of the knife until the edge is very smooth even though it is not so sharp. This is called the old method of sharpening. The slaughterers in Lithuania . . . and other areas do this until today. The second method is to sharpen the knife on one side until a string of metal called *drot* (wire) is formed. Then one goes over it a few times also on the

[33] Epstein, *Arukh hashulḥan*, 'Yoreh de'ah', *Hilkhot sheḥitah*, 18: 17, p. 49.

[34] The dispute on hasidic *sheḥitah* and its character, which had originally concentrated on the complaints of the mitnagedim about the new customs of the hasidim (i.e. their knives), was transferred in the period of the spread of hasidism, into the hasidic camp, and concentrated on the reliability and quality of the hasidic slaughterers (Assaf, '"The Causeless Hatred is Ongoing"', 490, and see the examples he brings there on pages 485–92).

[35] On R. Yitshak, see Sussman, *Zakhor le'avraham*, 61; and Goldrat, *Minḥat yisakhar*, no. 11, p. 8. I am grateful to the *admor* of Sokolov, R. Mendel Morgenstern, who gave me his time and brought this source to my attention.

second side until the *drot* falls off and it becomes smooth. In this way the edge is very sharp. This is called the new sharpening method and it was invented by . . . Rabbi Yitshak of Pilov. About two generations ago there was a great outcry of the scholars of Israel against this new method for these reasons, i.e. that it is impossible to correctly check it and because it can become defective because of the sharpness and the great thinness of the edge. However in our days, no one complains or doubts this method and every slaughterer in Poland and Galicia and in other places accepts this method of sharpening and it is spreading also in other places and the old has to give way to the new.[36]

What exactly was the innovation of Rabbi Yitshak? According to the above, he would sharpen on one side until it became sharp, and then he would sharpen a bit on the other side in order to take off the metal string that remained on the edge of the knife. Rabbi Hayim Golevski, son of the last rabbi of Brisk, discussed the opposition to this method. In his view the scholars of Lithuania and Galicia objected to the great sharpness of the knives which resulted in their often becoming defective in use. According to him, the innovation of Rabbi Yitshak led to controversies also inside Poland.

Many hasidim in Poland, especially the slaughters of the Kotsk and Gur hasidim, began to use knives that were sharpened on one side. The hasidim of Radomsk did not allow the use of knives sharpened in one side in Sosnowitz. Slowly a dispute developed between the two groups of hasidim. The hasidim of Aleksander also came out against knives sharpened on one side in order to 'turn up the volume'. Of course in Brisk in Lithuania only knives sharpened on two sides were used. This was one of the reasons that the hasidim of Kotsk came out against the author of *Beit halevi* [Rabbi Joseph Dov Soloveitchik (1820–92)].[37]

The memoirs of Hayim Tchernowitz (pseudonym 'Rav Tsa'ir', the 'young rabbi') mention a dispute over *sheḥitah* and apparently refer to the dispute over the method of Rabbi Yitshak of Pilov. Tchernowitz described his grandfather, Rabbi Shelomi Yitshak Drazd, who was a classic mitnaged, and the bitter disputes in his town Sebezh on issues of meat slaughtering. The arguments there were not only between hasidim and mitnagedim but also among the different hasidic groups: 'The hasidic *shoḥatim* had a special way of sharpening the knife involving *zaytlakh* (sides) on the sharp edge and the mitnagedim were opposed.'[38]

[36] Kamen, *Beit david*, no. 18: 5, p. 36.
[37] Golevski, 'Polished Knives' (Heb.), no. 38, 114–15. Golevski noted that the custom in Habad was to sharpen on both sides. See on p. 117: 'When our family and also the grand-mother, the *rebbetsin* were in the summer in the summer home . . . [R. Soloveitchik] said to his family that the double-sided method of sharpening is better but not to make an issue out of this.' This approach is similar to that of R. Shneur Zalman cited above and the point is clear: not every halakhic disagreement leads to a social split.   [38] Tchernowitz, *Memoirs* (Heb.), 104.

There were yet more disputes. Thus, for example, there were legal experts who, out of a desire to protect the knife, required that the place of the cut be shaven before the act of slaughtering. This is mentioned in various legal texts and this view won partial acceptance. In Łomża the local rabbi made a number of enactments and among them was one 'To be certain the neck of cows will be shaven as it should be before the slaughtering and to wash the neck with water'.[39] He justified this added requirement by claiming that experience had shown that sharp and smooth knives polished in the Polish manner are damaged by the hair and dirt on the hair of the neck and there is a danger that the knife would be made defective.

*

The sources that are available do not give clear-cut answers to all of our questions. However, they allow us to reconstruct with some certainty the course of the dispute over polished knives. It appears that a small and elite circle of students of the Magid of Mezeritch adopted a known method to achieve excellence in *sheḥitah*: the use of thin but breakable knives. With the spread of hasidism and the transformation of its customs to the public domain it became clear that the method involving the use of polished knives could offer social and economic advantages to the closely crystallizing movement. The opponents of hasidism were very sensitive to what they interpreted as self-separation from the general community, and as a critique on the practices of others and of their own ancestors. Since there were some real halakhic problems with the new method it was easy to arouse opposition to the use of these polished knives, even though previously the custom had not attracted attention.

The separation engendered by the dispute over polished knives was not long-lasting. Modernization, which presented difficult new challenges to the developing Jewish Orthodoxy, also brought with it a technological innovation —low-cost steel—which brought an end to the conflict. Nonetheless, the patterns of a distinct hasidic method of meat slaughtering were not totally forgotten, but maintained in the form of new disputes, albeit of a more local nature, that were far from the scope and impact of the earlier ones.

Sheḥitah was an area in which it would have been possible to anticipate conservatism. Each change could be interpreted as criticism of the deeds of previous generations, and traditional societies are often very cautious regarding any stand that could be seen as undermining the authority of the past. Moreover, *shoḥatim*, like many other craftsmen, tend to prefer the old and

[39] Tennenbaum, *Divrei malki'el*, vol. iii, no. 41, pp. 67–9. See also Danzig, *Binat adam* (Heb.), no. 11; and Kamen, *Beit david*, p. 36, ch. 18, para. 5.

familiar and are not always eager to learn new and different methods. However, the descriptions of the various changes in methods of knife sharpening and in the materials from which knives were made indicate that both hasidim and mitnagedim were quite willing to adopt innovations. In place of the motto 'the new is prohibited by the Torah', they acted according to the maxim cited by the author of *Beit david* (The House of David), 'the old makes way for the new'.

There is a common opinion that hasidim were more conservative than mitnagedim. In the case of knife sharpening the reverse is the case. Not only in the first dispute over polished knives were hasidim more open to change but also, in the dispute over the method of Rabbi Yitshak of Pilov, the hasidim were the first to accept the new method. If there are still those that think that hasidism was a popular movement whose goal was to free the masses from some of the stringencies of Jewish law, the dispute over polished knives shows us an area in which the hasidim adopted more stringent standards and called on the masses to accept restrictions that had previously been found only among the elite.[40]

An examination of the halakhic aspects of the dispute over hasidic *sheḥitah* helps us understand the ways Jewish law influenced traditional Jewish society in eastern Europe. Alongside social, economic, and organizational factors, it was halakhic issues which were at the basis of the dispute. Those involved in the dispute took halakhic issues seriously and, understandably, their ideas were also influenced by halakhah. Once again we recognize to what degree halakhic and non-halakhic factors intermingle within the lives of the Jews in traditional Jewish society.

[40] For a perceptive discussion of some of these issues see Sperber, 'Hasidism and Stringency in Custom' (Heb.), 126–56, and also 118–19.

Gazetteer of Place Names in Central and Eastern Europe

THIS gazetteer has been compiled using Gary Mokotoff and Sallyann Amdur Sack's comprehensive work *Where Once We Walked: A Guide to the Jewish Communities Destroyed in the Holocaust* (Teaneck, NJ, 1991). We are grateful to Avotaynu as the publishers of that work for their generosity in allowing us to do so. The style of the entries follows their conventions, except that diacritical marks have been added where necessary.

Names of countries have been abbreviated as follows: Bel. = Belorussia; Cz. = Czech Republic; Ger. = Germany; Hung. = Hungary; Lat. = Latvia; Lith. = Lithuania; Mold. = Moldova; Pol. = Poland; Rom.= Romania; Rus. = Russia; Slov. = Slovakia; Ukr. = Ukraine.

Aleksander *see* Aleksandrów Łódzki

Aleksandrów *see* Aleksandrów Łódzki

Aleksandrów Łódzki Pol.; 13 km WNW of Łódz

Alt-Ofen *see* Óbuda

Amdur *see* Indura

Baranovichi Bel.; 120 km N of Pinsk

Baranowicze *see* Baranovichi

Będzin Pol.; 56 km S of Częstochowa

Belorussia part of the tsarist empire in the nineteenth century, later a republic of the Soviet Union (the western half was part of Poland prior to the end of the Second World War), now an independent state (Belarus) between Poland and Russia

Belz Ukr.; 62 km N of Lvov

Bełz *see* Belz

Berdichev Ukr.; 82 km N of Vinnitsa

Berezhany Ukr.; 82 km ESE of Lvov

Biała Podlaska Pol.; 101 km NNE of Lublin

Białystok Pol.; 170 km NE of Warsaw

Bielsko-Biała Pol.; 69 km SW of Kraków

Biržai Lith.; 94 km ENE of Šiauliai

Bobowa Pol.; 82 km ESE of Kraków

Bobroisk *see* Bobruisk

Bobruisk Bel.; 139 km WNW of Gomel

Boskovice Cz.; 38 km N of Brno

Brăila Rom.; 176 km NE of Bucharest

Bratislava Slov.; the capital of Slovakia

Brest Bel.; 163 km WSW of Pinsk

Brichany (Brinceni) Mold.; 202 km NW of Kishinev

Brisk *see* Brest

Brno Cz.; 120 km NNW of Bratislava

Brody Ukr.; 88 km NE of Lvov

Brzeżany *see* Berezhany

Brzeziny Pol.; 21 km E of Łódz

Bucecea Rom.; 120 km WNW of Iaşi

Buchach Ukr.; 94 km NW of Chernovtsy

Bucovina a region now in north-eastern Romania and south-western Ukraine; part of the Austro-Hungarian Empire prior to the end of the First World War and then part of Romania until the end of the Second World War

Buczacz _see_ Buchach

Budapest Hung.; the capital of Hungary

Chebin _see_ Trzebinia

Chełm Pol. 69 km E of Lublin

Chernigov Ukr.; 133 km NNE of Kiev

Chernobyl Ukr.; 101 km NNW of Kiev

Chernovtsy Ukr.; 214 km SW of Vinnitsa

Chervonoarmeisk Ukr.; 88 km SW of Rovno

Chortkov Ukr.; 82 km N of Chernovtsy

Chrzanów Pol.; 38 km W of Kraków

Cluj Rom.; 302 km WSW of Iași

Courland a region in Latvia

Cracow _see_ Kraków

Czernowitz _see_ Chernovtsy

Częstochowa Pol.; 94 km NW of Kraków

Czortków _see_ Chortkov

Dauvagpils Lat.; 189 km ESE of Riga

Disna Bel.; 133 km W of Vitebsk

Dnepropetrovsk Ukr.; 195 km SSW of Kharkov

Dobromil Ukr.; 94 km SW of Lvov

Drogobych Ukr.; 69 km SSW of Lvov

Drohobycz _see_ Drogobych

Dubno Ukr.; 38 km SW of Rovno

Dubrovna _see_ Dubrovno

Dubrovno Bel.; 75 km SE of Vitebsk

Dvinsk _see_ Dauvagpils

Dyatlovo Bel.; 146 km SW of Minsk

Dynow _see_ Dynów

Dynów Pol.; 38 km W of Przemysl

Dzików Ukr.; 56 km E of Lvov

Edintsy (Edineț) Mold.; 170 km NW of Kishinev

Ekaterinoslav _see_ Dnepropetrovsk

Elizavetgrad _see_ Kirovograd

Fürth Germ.; 6 km WNW of Nürnberg

Gadyshi Rus.; a village in the Valdai district of the Novgorod province

Galicia a region that since the Second World War has been part of southern Poland and Ukraine. Prior to 1772, it constituted the southern part of the Kingdom of Poland, then became part of the Austro-Hungarian Empire until the end of the First World War. It was then returned to Poland until the end of the Second World War

Ger _see_ Góra Kalwaria

Gomel Bel.; 277 km ESE of Minsk

Góra Kalwaria Pol.; 38 km SE of Warsaw

Gorlice Pol.; 101 km ESE of Kraków

Gorodishche Ukr.; 142 km SSE of Kiev

Gribov _see_ Grybów

Grimailov Ukr.; 120 km N of Chernovtsy

Grobin _see_ Grobiņa

Grobiņa Lat.; 182 km WSW of Riga

Grodno Bel.; 234 km NW of Pinsk

Grosswardein _see_ Oradea

Grybów Pol.; 94 km ESE of Kraków

Grzymałów *see* Grimailov

Gur *see* Góra Kalwaria

Gusakov Ukr.; 75 km WSW of Lvov

Hrubieszów Pol.; 107 km ESE of Lublin

Hussakow *see* Gusakov

Iaşi Rom.; 320 km NNE of Bucharest

Ilya Bel.; 62 km NNW of Minsk

Indura Bel.; 24 km S of Grodno

Ivano-Frankovsk Ukr.; 114 km WNW of Chernovtsy

Izbica Pol.; 56 km ESE of Lublin

Izyaslav Ukr.; 69 km SE of Rovno

Jagielnica *see* Yagelnitsa

Jarosław Pol.; 32 km NNW of Przemysl

Jelgava Lat.; 45 km SSW of Riga

Kaliningrad Rus.; 586 km SW of Pskov; now in a Russian enclave between Poland and Lithuania

Kalisz Pol.; 94 km WSW of Łódz

Kamenets Bel.; 157 km W of Pinsk

Kamenets-Podolsky Ukr.; 62 km NE of Chernovtsy

Kamieniec Litewski *see* Kamenets

Kamieniec Podolski *see* Kamenets-Podolski

Karlin Bel.; 6 km E of Pinsk

Kaunas Lith.; 94 km W of Vilnius

Kėdainiai Lith.; 50 km N of Kaunas

Keidany *see* Kėdainiai

Kelm *see* Kelmė

Kelmė Lith.; 45 km SSW of Šiauliai

Kharkov Ukr.; 195 NNE of Dnepropetrovsk

Kherson Ukr.; 146 km ENE of Odessa

Khotin Ukr.; 45 km NE of Chernovtsy

Kielce Pol.; 101 km NNE of Kraków

Kiev Ukr.; the capital of Ukraine

Kirovograd Ukr.; 157 km E of Uman

Kishinev (Chişinău) Mold.; the capital of Moldova

Kobrin Bel.; 120 km W of Pinsk

Kobryn *see* Kobrin

Kock Pol.; 50 km NNW of Lublin

Kołomyja *see* Kolomyya

Kolomyya Ukr.; 69 km WNW of Chernovtsy

Königsberg *see* Kaliningrad

Korets Ukr.; 62 km E of Rovno

Korzec *see* Korets

Kotsk *see* Kock

Kovel Ukr.; 126 km WNW of Rovno

Kovno *see* Kaunas

Kowel *see* Kovel

Kraków Pol.; 94 km SE of Częstochowa

Krasnopole Bel.; 95 km SE of Mogilev

Kremenchug Ukr.; 133 km WNW of Dnepropetrovsk

Kremenets Ukr. 69 km SSW of Rovno

Krynki Pol.; 45 km NE of Białystok

Krzemieniec *see* Kremenets

Kutna *see* Kutno

Kutno Pol.; 110 km W of Warsaw

Lask *see* Łask

Łask Pol.; 32 km SW of Łódz

Łazów Pol.; 82 km SSW of Białystok

Lemberg *see* Lvov

Leszno Pol.; 196 km W of Łódz

Liadi *see* Lyady

Lida Bel.; 146 km WSW of Minsk

Liepāja Lat.; 195 km WSW of Riga

Lipkany (Lipcani) Mold.; 208 km WNW of Kishinev

Lissa *see* Leszno

Little Poland the region of southern Poland centred on Kraków

Little Russia in the tsarist period, the region which is now Ukraine

Łódz Pol.; 114 km N of Częstochowa

Łomża Pol.; 69 km W of Białystok

Lubartów Pol.; 32 km N of Lublin

Lubavitch *see* Lyubavichi

Lublin Pol.; 157 km ESE of Warsaw

Ludmir *see* Vladimir-Volynsky

Lutsk Ukr.; 62 km W of Rovno

Lvov Ukr.; 182 km SW of Rovno

Lwów *see* Lvov

Lyady Bel.; 38 km ESE of Minsk

Lyubavichi Rus.; 60 km SE of Vitebsk

Makov *see* Maków Mazowiecki

Maków Mazowiecki Pol.; 69 km N of Warsaw

Mezeritch *see* Mezhirichi

Mezhirichi Ukr.; 45 km ENE of Rovno

Międzyrzec (Podlaski) Pol.; 120 km E of Warsaw

Mikulov Cz.; 50 km S of Brno

Minsk Bel.; the capital of Belorussia (Belarus)

Minsk Mazowiecki Pol.; 38 km E of Warsaw

Mir Bel.; 88 km SW of Minsk

Modliborzyce Pol.; 56 km S of Lublin

Mogilev Bel.; 150 km S of Vitebsk

Moscow *see* Moskva

Moskva Rus.; the capital of the Soviet Union and of present-day Russia

Mstów Pol.; 19 km ENE of Częstochowa

Nadvorna *see* Nadvornaya

Nadvornaya Ukr.; 107 km WNW of Chernovtsy

Neutra *see* Nitra

Nikolsburg *see* Mikulov

Nitra Slov.; 75 km ESE of Bratislava

Noua Suliţa *see* Novoselitsa

Novogrudok Bel.; 120 km WSW of Minsk

Novominsk *see* Minsk Mazowiecki

Novoselitsa Ukr.; 32 km ESE of Chernovtsy

Nowy Sącz Pol.; 75 km ESE of Kraków

Óbuda part of the city of Budapest

Odessa Ukr.; 258 km SSE of Uman

Oradea Rom.; 133 km W of Cluj

Orgeev Mold.; 45 km N of Kishinev

Ostrog Ukr.; 38 km SE of Rovno

Ostrołęka Pol.; 101 km NNE of Warsaw

Ostrolenko *see* Ostrołęka

Ostrov Ukr.; 82 km SW of Rovno

Ostrowiec Pol.; 88 km SW of Lublin

Otwock Pol.; 26 km ESE of Warsaw

Pale of Settlement a region in the western part of the tsarist empire in which Jews were allowed to reside

Panevėžys Lith.; 69 km ESE of Šiauliai

Piaseczno Pol.; 26 km SSE of Warsaw

Piask *see* Piaski

Piaski Pol.; 26 km ESE of Lublin

Pilov *see* Puławy

Pinsk Bel.; 221 km SSW of Minsk

Piotrków *see* Piotrków Trybunalski

Piotrków Trybunalski Pol.; 45 km SSE of Łódz

Płock Pol.; 94 km N of Łódz

Podolia a region in south-western Ukraine

Polesia the region of Belorussia/Poland centred on Pinsk

Polish–Lithuanian Commonwealth a political entity created in 1569 by the Union of Lublin, which united Poland and Lithuania under a common king. It existed until the partitions of Poland in the late eighteenth century

Polotsk Bel.; 94 km WNW of Vitebsk

Poltava Ukr.; 126 km SW of Kharkov

Prague *see* Praha

Praha Cz.; the principal city of Bohemia, later the capital of Czechoslovakia and now the capital of the Czech Republic

Pressburg *see* Bratislava

Probezhnaya Ukr.; 88 km N of Chernovtsy

Probużna *see* Probezhnaya

Pruzhany Bel.; 120 km WNW of Pinsk

Przemysl Pol.; 163 km S of Lublin

Przysucha Pol.; 94 km ESE of Łódz

Puławy Pol.; 45 km WNW of Lublin

Radom Pol.; 101 km W of Lublin

Radomsk *see* Radomsko

Radomsko Pol.; 38 km NNE of Częstochowa

Radomysl *see* Radomysl Wielki

Radomysl Wielki Pol.; 94 km ENE of Kraków

Radun Bel.; 88 km SW of Minsk

Radzin *see* Radzyn Podlaski

Radzyn *see* Radzyn Podlaski

Radzyn Podlaski Pol.; 69 km N of Lublin

Rasein *see* Raseiniai

Raseiniai Lith.; 69 km WNW of Kaunas

Rēzekne Lat.; 88 km NNE of Daugavpils

Riga Lat.; the capital of Latvia

Rokiškis Lith.; 139 km ENE of Šiauliai

Ropczyce Pol.; 88 km WNW of Przemysl

Rostov Rus.; 410 km SE of Kharkov

Rovno Ukr.; 176 km W of Zhitomir

Równe *see* Rovno

Rzeszów Pol.; 62 km WNW of Przemysl

St Petersburg Rus.; the capital of the Russian empire from the eighteenth century until 1918

Sanz *see* Nowy Sącz

Sasov Ukr.; 69 km ENE of Lvov

Sassov *see* Sasov

Sebezh 164 km NW of Vitebsk

Seirijai Lith.; 107 km WSW of Vilnius

Serhei *see* Seirijai

Shavli *see* Šiauliai

Shklov Bel.; 114 km S of Vitebsk

Šiauliai Lith.; 120 km NNW of Kaunas

Siemiatycze Pol.; 82 km S of Białystok

Sighet Rom.; 133 km N of Cluj

Siret Rom.; 146 km WNW of Iaşi

Slonim Bel.; 126 km NW of Pinsk

Smela Ukr.; 133 km NE of Uman

Smila *see* Smela

Smorgon Bel.; 107 km WNW of Minsk

Sochaczew Pol.; 56 km WSW of Warsaw

Sokolov *see* Sokołów Podlaski

Sokołów Pol.; 62 km NW of Przemysl

Sokołów Podlaski Pol.; 82 km ENE of Warsaw

Sosnowiec Pol.; 56 km S of Częstochowa

Sosnowitz *see* Sosnowiec

Stanisławów *see* Ivano-Frankovsk

Stettin *see* Szczecin

Stolin Bel.; 56 km ESE of Pinsk

Stratin Ukr.; 69 km ESE of Lvov

Strelishcha collectively, Novye Strelishcha and Starye Strelishcha, Ukr.; 50 km SE of Lvov

Strelisk *see* Strelishcha

Stretin *see* Stratin

Suwałki Pol.; 114 km NNW of Białystok

Swierz *see* Swierże

Swierże Pol.; 82 km E of Lublin

Szczecin Pol.; 450 km WNW of Warsaw

Tarnopol *see* Ternopol

Tarnów Pol.; 75 km E of Kraków

Tavrida province a province of tsarist Russia consisting mainly of the Crimea

Telšiai Lith.; 69 km W of Šiauliai

Telz *see* Telšiai

Ternopol Ukr.; 120 km E of Lvov

Tomaszów Mazowiecki Pol.; 45 km ESE of Łódz

Trzebinia Pol.; 32 km WNW of Kraków

Turka Ukr.; 62 km WNW of Chernovtsy

Tyszowce Pol.; 107 km ESE of Lublin

Ukmergė Lith.; 69 km NE of Kaunas

Ulanov Ukr.; 56 km NNW of Vinnitsa

Uman Ukr.; 188 km S of Kiev

Vilna *see* Vilnius

Vilnius Lith.; the capital of Lithuania

Vinnitsa Ukr.; 199 km SW of Kiev

Viszova *see* Wysowa

Vitebsk Bel.; 221 km NE of Minsk

Vizhnitsa Ukr.; 56 km WSW of Chernovtsy

Vladimir-Volynsky Ukr.; 71 km W of Lutsk

Volhynia a region of north-western Ukraine. During the interwar period, it comprised the Polish province of Wołyn

Volkovysk Bel.; 163 km WNW of Pinsk

Volozhin Bel.; 75 km W of Minsk

Warsaw see Warszawa

Warszawa Pol.; the capital of Poland

White Russia *see* Belorussia

Wilkomir *see* Ukmergė

Włocławek Pol.; 107 km NNW of Łódz

Włodzimierz *see* Vladimir-Volynsky

Wołkowysk *see* Volkovysk

Wysowa Pol.; 39 km SE of Nowy Sącz

Yagelnitsa Ukr.; 156 km SE of Lvov

Yanovichi Bel.; 38 km ENE of Vitebsk

Yanovitz *see* Yanovichi

Žagarė Lith.; 50 km of Šiauliai

Zasław *see* Izyaslav

Zdzięcioł *see* Dyatlovo

Zhidachov Ukr.; 56 km SSE of Lvov

Zhikov *see* Dzików

Zhirovitsy Bel.; 114 km NW of Pinsk

Zhitomir Ukr.; 120 km N of Vinnitsa

Zhuravno Ukr.; 75 km SSE of Lvov

Zirowicz *see* Zhirovitsy
Złoczów *see* Zolochev
Zolochev Ukr.; 62 km E of Lvov

Żurawno *see* Zhuravno
Żydaczów *see* Zhidachov

Bibliography

ABDULRAZAK, FAWZI, 'The Kingdom of the Book: The History of Printing as an Agent of Change in Morocco between 1865 and 1912', Ph.D. diss. (Boston University, 1989).

ABRAHAMS, ISRAEL, *Hebrew Ethical Wills* (Philadelphia, 1926).

ABRAMSKY, CHIMEN, 'The Crisis of Authority within European Jewry in the Eighteenth Century', in Siegfried Stein and Raphael Loewe (eds.), *Studies in Jewish Religious and Intellectual History, Presented to Alexander Altmann on the Occasion of His Seventieth Birthday* (University of Alabama Press, 1979).

ADLER, ELIYANA, 'Private Schools for Jewish Girls in Tsarist Russia', Ph.D. diss. (Brandeis University, 2003).

ADLER, YOSEF, *On the Basis of the Torah* [Al pi hatorah] (Jerusalem, 1999).

AGRANOVSKY, GENRIKH, *Stanovlenie evreiskogo knigopechataniya v Litve* (Vilnius, 1994).

AGUS, IRVING ABRAHAM, *The Heroic Age of Franco-German Jewry: the Jews of Germany and France of the Tenth and Eleventh Centuries, the Pioneers and Builders of Town-Life, Town-Government, and Institutions* (New York, 1969).

AHMAD, MAQSOUD, 'The Arabic Printing Press in Turkey and the Arab East', *Islamic Culture*, 61/1 (Jan. 1987), 79–86.

ALBIN, MICHAEL, 'The Book in the Islamic World: A Selective Bibliography', in George Atiyeh (ed.), *The Book in the Islamic World: The Written Word and Communication in the Middle East* (Albany, NY, 1995).

AMIEL, R. M., 'A Good Day for our Teachers' (Heb.), in *Sefer hayovel likhvot rabeinu rabi shimon* (Vilna, 1936).

AMMAR, HAMED, *Growing up in an Egyptian Village* (London, 1954).

ANON., 'Biography of R. Shemuel Betsalel ben Shalom Sheftel' (Heb.), *Hatamim*, 1 (1935), 67–79.

ANON., *The Founding of the Great and Famous Yeshiva Metivta* [Mosad hayeshivah hagedolah vehamefo'arah metivta] (Warsaw, 1922).

ANON., *The Great and Famous Yeshiva Institution Darkhei No'am* [Mosad hayeshivah hagedolah vehamefo'arah darkhei no'am] (Warsaw, 1908).

ANON., *'Hannah and her Seven Sons': A New Expanded Shas tekhinah* (Vilna, 1904).

ANON., *Sefer takanot ushemot haḥaverim* [statutes of a yeshiva] (Brodshein, 1909).

ANTIN, MARY, *The Promised Land* (Boston, 1912).

ARBELI, AARON, 'Polish Jewry in the Eighteenth Century as Reflected in the Rabbinic Literature of the Period', unpublished Ph.D. diss. (Dropsie College, Philadelphia, 1961).

ARIÈS, PHILIPPE, *Centuries of Childhood* (New York, 1962).

ARYEH LEIB BEN ELIYAHU (BOLECHOVER), *She'elot uteshuvot shem aryeh* [responsa] (Vilna, 1873).

ASSAF, DAVID, '"The Causeless Hatred is Ongoing": The Struggle against Bratslav Hasidism in the 1860s', *Zion*, 59 (1994), 465–506.

—— '"Money for Household Expenses": Economic Aspects of the Hasidic Royal Courts', in id. *The Regal Way: The Life and Times of Rabbi Israel of Ruzhin*, trans. David Louvish, Stanford Series in Jewish History and Culture (Stanford, 2002), 285–310.

—— *The Regal Way: The Life and Times of Rabbi Israel of Ruzhin*, trans. David Louvish, Stanford Series in Jewish History and Culture (Stanford, 2002).

ASSAF, SIMCHA, 'A Responsum against the Writing of Law Books in Yiddish' (Heb.), in id., *Sources and Studies* [Mekorot umeḥkarim] (Jerusalem, 1946), 249–51.

—— *Sources for the History of Jewish Education* [Mekorot letoledot haḥinukh beyisra'el], 4 vols. (Tel Aviv, 1925–54).

—— 'Studies in the History of the Rabbinate' (in Germany, Poland and Lithuania) (Heb.), in id., *In the Tents of Jacob* [Be'oholei ya'akov] (Jerusalem, 1943).

ATIYEH, GEORGE, 'The Book in the Modern Arab World: The Cases of Lebanon and Egypt', in id. (ed.), *The Book in the Islamic World: The Written Word and Communication in the Middle East* (Albany, NY, 1995).

AVINERI, SHLOMO, 'The Historical Roots of Israeli Democracy'. Second Annual Guest Lecture, Kaplan Centre, Jewish Studies and Research, University of Cape Town, 31 Mar. 1985.

AVITAL, MOSHEH, *The Yeshiva and Traditional Education in the Literature of the Hebrew Enlightenment Period* [Hayeshivah vehaḥinukh hamesorati besifrut hahaskalah ha'ivrit] (Jerusalem, 1996).

AVRAHAMS, ABRAHAM BEN YOSEF, *Zakhor le'avraham* [halakhic work] (Lvov, 1860).

AZULAI, HAYIM, *Ḥayim sha'al* [halakhic work] (Livorno, 1792/5; repr. Lvov, 1886).

BACH, R., *Population Trends of World Jewry* (Jerusalem, 1976).

BACHARACH, YA'IR, *Ḥavot ya'ir* [responsa] (Frankfurt, 1699; repr. Jerusalem, 1992).

BACON, GERSHON, *The Politics of Tradition: Agudat Yisrael in Poland 1916–1939* (Jerusalem, 1997).

—— 'Prolonged Erosion, Organization and Reinforcement: Reflections on Orthodox Jewry in Congress Poland (up to 1914)', in Yisra'el Gutman (ed.), *Major Changes within the Jewish People in the Wake of the Holocaust*, Proceedings of the Ninth Yad Vashem International Historical Conference (Jerusalem, 1996).

BAKER, ZACHARY, 'Geographical Index and Bibliography', in Jack Kugelmass and Jonathan Boyarin (eds.), *From a Ruined Garden* (New York, 1983).

BAMFORD, T. W., 'Public School Town in the Nineteenth Century', *British Journal of Educational Studies*, 6/1 (Nov. 1957), 25–36.

BARON, SALO, *The Jewish Community* (Philadelphia, 1942).

BAUM, CHARLOTTE, 'What Made Yetta Work', *Response*, 18 (1973), 32–8.

BECKER, GARY S., *A Treatise on the Family* (Cambridge, Mass., 1981).

BELLAIRE, MICHAUX, 'L'Enseignement indigène au Maroc', *Revue du monde musulman*, 15 (Oct. 1911), 422–52.

BENEDICT, RUTH, 'Child Rearing in Certain European Countries', *American Journal of Orthopsychiatry*, 19/2 (1949), 342–50.

BENET, SULA (ed. and trans.), *The Village of Viriatino: An Ethnographic Study of a Russian Village from before the Revolution to the Present* (New York, 1970).

BEN-MORDEKHAI, A., 'Baranovits' (Heb.), in Shmuel Mirsky (ed.), *Jewish Institutions of Higher Learning in Europe: Their Development and Destruction* [Mosadot torah be'eiropah bevinyanam uveḥurbanam] (New York, 1956).

BEN-SASSON, HAYIM HILLEL, *Reflection and Leadership: The Outlook of the Jewish Communities in Poland at the Close of the Middle Ages* [Hagut vehanhagah, hashkafoteihem haḥevratiyot shel yehudei polin beshilhei yemei habeinayim] (Jerusalem, 1959).

BEN-YEHUDAH, ELIEZER, et al., *The Complete Dictionary of Ancient and Modern Hebrew* [Milon halashon ha'ivrit hayeshanah vehaḥadashah], 16 vols. (Berlin and Jerusalem, 1908–59).

BEN-ZE'EV, MOSHEH, 'On the Method of Study in Hungary' (Heb.), *Hatsofeh* (5 Kislev 5788), 7.

BERGER, ALAN, 'Hasidism and Moonism: Charisma and Counterculture', *Sociological Analysis*, 41 (1980), 375–90.

BERGER, RUTH, *Sexualität, Ehe und Familienleben in der jüdischen Moralliteratur (900–1900)* (Wiesbaden, 2003).

Bericht über Tendenz, Organisation und Verwaltung der von Rabbiner S. D. Schneersohn in Lubawitsch (Russland) gegründeten und geleiteten Unterrichtsanstalten Tomche Temimim' von dem für die Interessen dieser Anstalt constituirten Centralcomité in Deutschland (Frankfurt am Main, 1910).

BERLIN, M., *Ocherk etnografii evreiskogo narodonaseleniya v Rossii* (St Petersburg, 1861).

BERSHADSKY, S. A. (ed.), *Akty o evreyakh*, Akty izdavaemye Vilenskoyu komissieyu dlya razbora drevnikh aktov, 29 (Vilna, 1902).

BIALE, DAVID, *Childhood, Marriage and the Family in the East European Jewish Enlightenment* (New York, 1982).

—— 'Eros and Enlightenment: Love against Marriage in the East European Jewish Enlightenment', *Polin*, 1 (1986), 49–67.

—— *Eros and the Jews* (New York, 1992).

—— 'Love, Marriage and the Modernization of the Jews', in Marc Lee Raphael (ed.), *Approaches to Modern Judaism* (Chico, Calif., 1963).

BINSHTOK, V. I., and S. A. NOVOSELSKY, *Materialy po estestvennomu dvizheniyu evreiskogo naseleniya v evropeiskoi Rossii za 40 let* (Petrograd, 1915).

BLAU, AMRAM, 'The Founding and Development of the Fund of Rabbi Meir Ba'al Hanes' (Heb.), *Heikhal habesht*, 11 (2005), 127–58.

BLOBAUM, ROBERT E., 'The "Woman Question" in Russian Poland, 1900–1914', *Journal of Social History*, 35/4 (Summer 2002), 799–824.

BLOCH, ABRAHAM, *Lectures on Understanding* [Shiurei da'at] (Jerusalem, 1961).

BLOCH, BRONISLAW, 'Vital Events among the Jews in European Russia towards the End of the Nineteenth Century', in Usiel Oskar Schmelz, Paul Glikson, and Sergio DellaPergola (eds.), *Papers in Jewish Demography 1977* (Jerusalem, 1980), 69–81.

BLOODWORTH, SANDRA, 'The Poverty of Patriarchy Theory', *Socialist Review* (Australia), 2 (1990), 5–33.

BLOOM, HAROLD, *Agon: Towards a Theory of Revisionism* (New York, 1982).

BLUM-KULKA, SHOSHANA, *Dinner Talk* (Mahwah, NJ, 1997).

Bobruisk: Remembrance Book of the Jewish Community of Bobruisk and its Surroundings [Bobro'isk: sefer zikaron lekehilat bobro'isk uvenoteiha], ed. Judah Slutsky, 2 vols. (Tel Aviv, 1967).

BOEHM, ADOLF, and ADOLF POLLACK, *The Jewish National Fund* [Hakeren hakayemet leyisra'el] (Jerusalem, 1939).

BOGDANOV, I. M., *Gramotnost' i obrazovanie v dorevolyutsionnoi Rossii i v SSSR* (Moscow, 1964).

BOGUCKA, MARIA, *Women in Early Modern Polish Society, against the European Background* (Aldershot, 2004).

BONFIL, ROBERT, *Rabbis and Jewish Communities in Renaissance Italy* (London, 1993).

BORNSTEIN, AVRAHAM, *Avnei nezer* [responsa] (Warsaw, 1913).

BOSAK, MEIR, 'Jews of Kraków in the Second Half of the Nineteenth Century' (Heb.), in Aryeh Bauminger et al. (eds.), *The Book of Kraków* [Sefer krakuv] (Jerusalem, 1959), 89–125.

BOURDIEU, PIERRE, and JEAN-CLAUDE PASSERON, *Reproduction in Education, Society and Culture* (London, 1977).

BOYARIN, DANIEL, 'Placing Reading: Ancient Israel and Medieval Europe', in Jonathan Boyarin (ed.), *The Ethnography of Reading* (Berkeley, Calif., 1993), 10–37.

—— *Unheroic Conduct: The Rise of Heterosexuality and the Invention of the Jewish Man* (Berkeley, Calif., 1997).

BOYARIN, JONATHAN, 'Jewish Ethnography and the Question of the Book', *Anthropological Quarterly*, 64/1 (1991), 14–29.

—— 'Voices around the Text', in id. (ed.), *The Ethnography of Reading* (Berkeley, Calif., 1993), 212–37.

BRAYER, MENACHEM, *The Jewish Woman in Rabbinic Literature*, vol. ii: *A Psychohistorical Perspective* (Hoboken, NJ, 1986).

BRESSLER, MARVIN, 'Selected Family Patterns in W. I. Thomas' Unfinished Study of the Bintl Brief', *American Sociological Review*, 17/5 (Oct. 1952), 563–71.

BREUER, EDWARD, 'The Haskalah in Vilna: R. Yehezkel Feivel's "Toldot Adam"', *Torah umada*, 7 (1998), 14–40.

BREUER, MORDEKHAI, 'The Ashkenazi Synagogue at the Close of the Middle Ages' [Hayeshivah ha'ashkenazit beshilhei yemei habeinayim], Ph.D. diss. (Hebrew University, Jerusalem, 1967).

BRISTOW, EDWARD, *Prostitution and Prejudice* (New York, 1983).

BROCKE, MICHAEL, and JULIUS CARLEBACH, *Biographisches Handbuch der Rabbiner*, vol. i: *Die Rabbiner der Emanzipationszeit in den deutschen, böhmischen und grosspolnischen Ländern 1781–1871* (Munich, 2004).

BRONSZTEJN, SZYJA, *Ludnosc żydowska w Polsce w okresie międzywojennym: Studium statystyczne* (Wrocław, 1963).

BRUTSKUS, B., *Statistika evreiskogo naseleniya* (St Petersburg, 1909).

Bureau für Statistik der Juden, *Die sozialen Verhältnisse der Juden in Russland* (Berlin, 1906).

BUSAK, MEIR, 'Jews of Kraków in the Second Half of the Nineteenth Century' (Heb.), in Aryeh Bauminger et al. (eds.), *The Book of Kraków* [Sefer krakuv] (Jerusalem, 1959).

CAHANOWITZ, Y. L., 'Gomel/Homel' (Heb.), in Y. L. Hacohen-Fishman (ed.), *Arim ve'imahot beyisra'el* [Major Jewish Towns], (Jerusalem, 1948), ii. 187–269.

CARLEBACH, JOSEPH, 'Der Streit um die Erbfolge im Rabbinat', *Jeschurun*, 40 (1928), 350–66.

CARLEBACH, JULIUS, 'Family Structure and the Position of Jewish Women', in Werner Mosse, Arnold Paucker, and Reinhard Rürup (eds.), *Revolution and Evolution: 1848 in German-Jewish History* (Tübingen, 1981).

CARTER, THOMAS FRANCIS, *The Invention of Printing in China and its Spread Westward* (New York, 1931).

CHLENOV, YEKHIEL, *Report on the Account of the Money that Came from Russia on Behalf of the Jewish National Fund 1.3.1908–1.1.1909* [Din veheshbon al heshbon hakesef shenikhnas mirusiyah letovat hakeren kayemet leyisra'el] (Vilna, 1909).

CHMIELEWSKI, SAMUEL, 'Stan szkolnictwa wsród Żydów w Polsce', *Sprawy Narodo-wosciowe*, 2/1–2 (1937), 4–5.

CHODZKO, IGNACY, *Obrazy litewskie*, 2nd edn. (Vilna, 1862).

CHOJNACKA, H., 'Nuptiality Patterns in an Agrarian Society', *Population Studies*, 30 (1976), 203–26.

CHWALBA, ANDRZEJ, *Imperium korupcji w Rosji i w Królestwie Polskim w latach 1861–1917* (Kraków, 1995).

CIPOLLA, C., *Literacy and Development in the West* (Baltimore, Md., 1969).

CLANCHY, M., 'Literate and Illiterate: Hearing and Seeing, 1066–1307', in Harvey J. Graff (ed.), *Literacy and Social Development in the West* (Cambridge, 1981).

CLEM, RALPH (ed.), *Research Guide to the Russian and Soviet Censuses* (Ithaca, NY, 1986).

COALE, ANSLEY, 'Introduction to Part III', in Jacques Dupâquier et al. (eds.), *Marriage and Remarriage in Populations of the Past* (London, 1981).

—— BARBARA A. ANDERSON, and ERNA HARM, *Human Fertility in Russia since the Nineteenth Century* (Princeton, NJ, 1979).

COHEN, DANIEL J., 'On the Character of the Landesrabbiner in Ashkenaz in the Seventeenth and Eighteenth Centuries', in Israel Bartal, Ezra Mendelsohn, and Chava Turniansky (eds.), *Studies in Jewish Culture in Honour of Chone Shmeruk* (Hebrew, English, and Yiddish) (Jerusalem, 1993).

COHEN, GERSON D. 'The Story of the Four Captives', *Proceedings of the American Academy for Jewish Research*, 29 (1960–1), 55–131.

COHEN, RAYMOND, *Culture and Conflict in Egyptian–Israeli Relations: A Dialogue of the Deaf* (Indianapolis, 1990).

COHEN, ROBERT, 'Patterns of Marriage and Remarriage among the Sephardi Jews of Surinam, 1788–1818', in id. (ed.), *The Jewish Nation in Surinam* (Amsterdam, 1982).

COHEN, TOVA, 'Information about Women is Necessarily Information about Men' [review of Iris Parush, *Reading Jewish Women*], Journal of Israeli History, 21/1–2 (2002), 169–91.

COLLINS, JAMES, 'Literacy and Literacies', *Annual Review of Anthropology*, 24 (1995), 75–93.

COLONNA, FANNY, *Les Versets de l'invincibilité* (Paris, 1995).

CUTLIP, S., *Fundraising in the United States* (New Brunswick, NJ, 1965).

CZAP, PETER, 'A Large Family: "The Peasant's Greatest Wealth": Serf Households in Mishino, Russia, 1814–1858', in Richard Wall (ed.), *Family Forms in Historic Europe* (Cambridge, 1983).

—— 'Marriage and the Peasant Joint Family in the Era of Serfdom', in David Ransel (ed.), *The Family in Imperial Russia* (Urbana, Ill., 1978).

DAMIS, JOHN, 'Early Moroccan Reactions to the French Protectorate: The Cultural Dimension', *Humaniora Islamica*, 1 (1973), 15–31.

DANZIG, AVRAHAM BEN YEHI'EL, *Binat adam* [halakhic work] (Vilna, 1816, and frequently reprinted).

—— *Ḥayei adam* [halakhic work] (Vilna, 1810).

DAVID OF NOVOGRUDOK, *Galya masekhet* [responsa] (Vilna, 1845).

DAVIS, KINGSLEY and JUDITH BLAKE, 'Social Structure and Fertility: An Analytic Framework', *Economic Development and Cultural Change*, 4 (1955), 211–35.

DAYAN, YISRA'EL (ed.), *The Jewish Community in Piask* [Sefer kehilat yehudei piask] (Haifa, 1988).

DELLAPERGOLA, SERGIO, *La trasformazione demografica della diaspora ebraica* (Turin, 1983).

DEMBITZER, HAYIM NATHAN (ed.), *Sefer magine erets yisra'el* [calls for support for Jewish settlement] (Lvov, 1852).

DEMEERSEMAN, ANDRÉ, 'Les Données de la controverse autour du problème de l'imprimerie', *Revue de l'Institut des Belles Lettres Arabes* (Tunis), 17/65 (1954), 1–46, 113–40.

DEMOS, JOHN, *A Little Commonwealth: Family Life in Plymouth Colony* (New York, 1970).

DIENSTAG, YA'AKOV, 'Eliyahu Gaon: An Annotated Bibliography' (Heb.), *Talpiyot*, 4 (1949), 269–356.

DINARI, YEDIDYA ALTER, *The Rabbis of Germany and Austria at the Close of the Middle Ages* [Ḥokhmei ashkenaz beshalhei yemei habeinayim] (Jerusalem, 1984).

DINUR, BEN-ZION, 'From the Archive of the Hakham Bashi R. Hayim Avraham Gagin' (Heb.), *Me'asef tsiyon*, 4 (1930), 65–71.

DIXON, RUTH, 'Explaining Cross-Cultural Variations in Age at Marriage and the Proportion Never Marrying', *Population Studies*, 25/2 (1971), 215–33.

DORNER, SHALOM (ed.), *Noua Suliṭa* [Novoselitsah] (Tel Aviv, 1983).

DRIMER, SHELOMOH, *She'elot uteshuvot beit shelomoh* [responsa], 4 vols. (Lvov, 1878–91).

DUBNOW, SIMON (ed.), *Recordbook of the Lithuanian Jewish Council* [Pinkas hamedinah] (Berlin, 1925).

DUPÂQUIER, JACQUES, et al. (eds.), *Marriage and Remarriage in Populations of the Past* (London, 1981).

ECK, NATHAN, 'The Educational Institutions of Polish Jewry', *Jewish Social Studies*, 9 (1947), 3–32.

EHRENBERG, ELIMELEKH, *Arzei halevanon* [collection of historical sources] (Jerusalem, 1977).

EICKELMAN, DALE, 'The Art of Memory: Islamic Education and its Social Reproduction', *Comparative Studies in Society and History*, 20/4 (1978), 485–516.

—— 'Islam and the Impact of the French Colonial System in Morocco', *Humaniora Islamica*, 2 (1974), 215–35.

EISENSTADT, AVRAHAM, *Pithei teshuvah* [commentary on *Shulḥan arukh*] (Vilna, 1875).

EISENSTEIN, ELIZABETH, *The Printing Press as an Agent of Change* (Cambridge, 1979).

EITINGA, YITSHAK AHARON, *She'elot uteshuvot maharyah halevi* [responsa] (Lvov, 1893).

ELIAV, MORDECHAI, *Jewish Education in Germany in the Period of Enlightenment and Emancipation* [Haḥinukh hayehudi begermaniyah biyemei hahaskalah veha'emantsipatsiyah] (Jerusalem, 1960).

ELIOR, RACHEL, 'Natan Adler and the Hasidic Community in Frankfurt' (Heb.), *Zion*, 59 (1994), 31–64.

ELIYAHU BEN SHELOMOH ZALMAN (VILNA GAON), *Alim literufah* [ethical letter] [= *Igeret hagra*] (Vilna, 1800?).

—— *Ma'aseh rav heḥadash* [customs], ed. Mosheh Sternbuch (Benei Berak, 1980).

Encyclopaedia of the Jewish Diaspora [Entsiklopediyah shel galuyot], vol. 4/1, *Lwów*, ed. Nathan Michael Gelber (Jerusalem and Tel Aviv, 1956); vol. 9, *Grodno*, ed. Dov Rabin (Jerusalem, 1973).

Encyclopaedia Judaica, ed. Cecil Roth, 16 vols. (Jerusalem, 1971).

Encyclopedia of the Social Sciences, ed. E. R. A. Seligman, 15 vols. (New York 1930–5).

Encyclopedia Talmudica, ed. Meir Bar Ilan, Shlomo Yosef Zevin, et al., 27 vols. (Jerusalem, 1947–).

ENGEL, SHEMUEL, *She'elot uteshuvot maharash engel* [responsa] (Bardejov, 1926).

EPSTEIN, BARUKH, 'Wisdom of Women' (Heb.), in id., *Mekor barukh* [autobiography] (Vilna, 1928).

EPSTEIN, YEHI'EL MIKHAL, *Arukh hashulḥan* [halakhic work] (Warsaw/Piotrków, 1891–1909).

EPSTEIN, ZALMAN, *Ketavim* [Writings] (St Petersburg, 1905).

ESHKOLI, AHARON, 'Hasidism in Poland' (Heb.), in Israel Hailperin (Halpern) (ed.), *Jews in Poland* [Beit yisra'el befolin] (Jerusalem, 1954).

ESTRAIKH, GENNADY, and MIKHAIL KRUTIKOV (eds.), *The Shtetl: Image and Reality* (Oxford, 2000).

ETKES, IMMANUEL, 'The Gaon of Vilna and the "Haskalah": Image and Reality' (Heb.), in I. Etkes and Y. Salmon (eds.), *Studies in the History of Jewish Society in the Medieval and Modern Periods* (Jacob Katz Jubilee Volume) [Perakim betoledot haḥevrah hayehudit biyemei habeinayim uva'et heḥadashah] (Jerusalem, 1980).

—— *The Gaon of Vilna: The Man and his Image*, trans. Jeffrey M. Green (Berkeley, 2002).

—— 'Immanent Factors and External Influences in the Development of the Haskalah Movement in Russia', in Jacob Katz (ed.), *Toward Modernity: The European Jewish Model* (New Brunswick, NJ, 1987).

—— *Lithuania in Jerusalem* [Lita birushalayim] (Jerusalem, 1991).

—— 'Marriage and Torah Study among the "Lomdim" in Lithuania in the Nineteenth Century', in David Kraemer (ed.), *The Jewish Family: Metaphor and Memory* (New York, 1989).

—— 'The Relationship between Talmudic Scholarship and the Institution of the Rabbinate in Nineteenth-Century Lithuanian Jewry', in Leo Landman (ed.), *Scholars and Scholarship in Jewish History* (New York, 1990).

ETTINGER, SHMUEL, 'The Roots of Antisemitism in Modern Times' (Heb.), *Molad*, 25 (1968), 324–40.

—— Review of the Hebrew original of Katz, *Tradition and Crisis* (Heb.), *Kiryat sefer*, 35 (1960), 12–19.

ETZIONI, AMITAI, 'The "Closed" Organizational Structure of Educational Institutions in Israel', *Harvard Educational Review*, 27 (1957), 107–25.

EVEN-ZOHAR, ITAMAR, 'The Role of Russian and Yiddish in the Making of Modern Hebrew', *Poetics Today*, 11/1 (1990), 111–20.

Evreiskaya entsiklopediya, 16 vols. (St Petersburg, 1906–13).

Evreiskoe kolonizatsionnoe obshchestvo [Jewish Colonization Society], *Sbornik materialov ob ekonomicheskom polozhenii evreev v Rossii*, 2 vols. (St Petersburg, 1904).

EVRON, DOV, 'The Rabbinate and the Yeshivas in the National Religious Education in Poland between the Two World Wars' (Heb.), *Shraga*, 2 (1985), 115–29.

EWEN, ELIZABETH, *Immigrant Women in the Land of Dollars* (New York, 1985).

EYBESCHUETZ, JONATHAN, *Luḥot edut* [collection of letters by rabbis in his support] (Altona, 1755; Warsaw, 1890).

FEGHALI, ELLEN, 'Arab Cultural Communication Patterns', *International Journal of Intercultural Relations*, 21/3 (1997), 345–78.

FEINER, SHMUEL, *Haskalah and History: The Emergence of a Modern Jewish Historical Consciousness*, trans. Chaya Naor and Sondra Silverston (Oxford, 2002).

—— 'The Modern Jewish Woman' (Heb.), *Zion*, 58/4 (1993), 453–99.

FELDMAN, DAVID, *Marital Relations, Birth Control, and Abortion in Jewish Law* (New York, 1968).

FENOMENOV, M., *Sovremennaya derevnya: Opyt kraevedcheskogo obsledovaniya odnoi derevni (d. Gadyshi Valdaiskogo uezda Novgorodskoi gubernii)*, vol. ii (Leningrad, 1925).

FERZIGER, ADAM S., 'The Lookstein Legacy: An American Orthodox Rabbinical Dynasty?', *Jewish History*, 13/1 (1999), 127–49.

FIDELIS, MALGORZATA, 'Participation in the Creative Work of the Nation: Polish Women Intellectuals in the Cultural Construction of Female Gender Roles, 1864–1890', *Journal of Women's History*, 13/1 (2001), 108–25.

FISCHER, MICHAEL M. J., and MEHDI ABEDI, *Debating Muslims* (Madison, Wis., 1990).

FISCHER, SHLOMO, 'The "Give and Take" of the Babylonian Talmud: Discourse and the Spirit of Carnival', MA diss. (Touro College, Jerusalem, 1997).

FISHBERG, M., *Materials for the Physical Anthropology of the East European Jews* (Lancaster, Pa., 1905).

FLASCHNER, YA'AKOV BARUKH, *Zevaḥ mishpaḥah* [halakhic work] (Vienna, 1850).

FLEKSER, A., *A Halakhically Kosher Slaughtering Knife* [Sakin sheḥitah kehilkhatah] (Jerusalem 1985).

FLINKER, D., 'Warsaw', in Y. L. Hacohen-Fishman, *Major Jewish Towns* [Arim ve'imahot beyisra'el], vol. iii (Jerusalem, 1948).

FRANKEL, AVRAHAM ZE'EV, *Meshiv kehalakhah* [responsa] (Kraków, 1885).

FREEDMAN, CHAIM, *Eliyahu's Branches: The Descendants of the Vilna Gaon and his Family* (Teaneck, NJ, 1997).

FREEZE, CHAERAN Y., *Jewish Marriage and Divorce in Imperial Russia* (Hanover, NH, 2002).

—— 'The Litigious Gerusha: Jewish Women and Divorce in Imperial Russia', *Nationalities Papers*, 25/1 (1997), 89–101.

FREIMAN, A., *The Arrangement of Betrothal and Marriage after the Conclusion of the Talmud* [Seder kidushin venisu'in me'aḥarei ḥatimat hatalmud] (Jerusalem, 1965).

FRIEDMAN, ARMIN, 'Major Aspects of Yeshivah Education in Hungary', Ph.D. diss. (Yeshiva University, New York, 1971).

FRIEDMAN, MENAHEM, 'The Changing Role of the Community Rabbinate', *Jerusalem Quarterly*, 25 (Fall 1982), 79–99.

—— *Haredi Society* [Haḥevrah haḥaredit] (Jerusalem, 1991).

—— 'Haredim Confront the Modern City', *Studies in Contemporary Jewry*, 2 (1986), 74–96.

FROMER, ARYEH TSEVI, *She'elot uteshuvot erets tsevi* [responsa] (Lublin, 1938).

FRUMKIN, A. L., *History of the Sages of Jerusalem* [Toledot ḥokhmei yerushalayim], 4 vols. (Jerusalem, 1928–30).

F[RUMKIN], B[ORIS], 'K voprosu o polozhenii evreev-remeslennikov', *Voskhod*, 20/39 (21 June 1901).

FUCHS, ABRAHAM, *Hungarian Yeshivas in their Greatness and in their Destruction* [Yeshivot hungariyah begadlutan uveḥurbanan], 2 vols. (Jerusalem, 1978–87).

FUENN, SHEMUEL YOSEF, *A Loyal Town* [Kiryah ne'emanah] (Vilna, 1871).

FUNKENSTEIN, AMOS, and ADIN STEINSALTZ, *Sociology of Ignorance* [Hasotsiologiyah shel haba'arut] (Tel Aviv, 1987).

GAMORAN, EMANUEL, *Changing Conceptions in Jewish Education*, 2 vols., vol. i: *Jewish Education in Russia and Poland*; vol. ii: *Principles of the Jewish Curriculum in America* (New York, 1924).

GANZFRIED, SHELOMOH, *Kitsur shulḥan arukh* [halakhic work] (1st edn. Ungvár, 1864, many subsequent reprintings; 1st Yiddish edn. Lvov, 1881).

GAON OF VILNA, *see* Eliyahu ben Shelomoh Zalman

GARTNER, LLOYD, 'Anglo Jewry and the Jewish International Traffic in Prostitution', *AJS Review*, 7/8 (1982–3), 129–78.

GATHORNE-HARDY, J., *The Public School Phenomenon* (Harmondsworth, 1977).

GELBART, SHMUEL, *The Great Yeshiva Torat Hesed in Łódz* [Di groyse yeshive toras khesed in lodz] (Łódz, 1929).

GERTNER, HAYIM, 'Rabbis and Rabbinical Judges in Galicia in the First Half of the Nineteenth Century: A Typology of Traditional Leadership in Crisis' [Rabanut vedayanut begalitsiyah bemaḥatsit harishonah shel hame'ah hatesha esreh: tipologiyah shel hanhagah mesoratit bemashber] unpublished thesis (Jerusalem, 2004).

GILLIS, JOHN, *Youth and History* (New York, 1981).

GINZBURG, LOUIS, *Students, Scholars and Saints* (Philadelphia, 1928).

GLIKSMAN, MEIR PINHAS ZELIG, *The Town of Lask and its Sages* [Ir lask veḥakhameihah] (Łódz, 1926).

GOFFMAN, E., *Asylums: Essays on the Social Situation of Mental Patients and Other Inmates* (New York, 1961).

GOITEIN, S. D., *Jewish Education in Muslim Countries* [Sidrei ḥinukh biyemei hageonim uve'et harambam] (Jerusalem, 1962).

GOLD, BEN-ZION, 'Religious Education in Poland: A Personal Perspective', in Israel Gutman et al. (eds.), *The Jews of Poland between the World Wars* (Hanover, NH, 1989).

GOLD, JACOB, and SAUL KAUFMAN, 'Development of Care of the Elderly: Tracing the History of Institutional Facilities', *Gerontologist*, 20/4 (Winter 1970), 262–74.

GOLDBERG, JACOB, 'Die Ehe bei den Juden Polens im 18. Jahrhundert', *Jahrbücher für Geschichte Osteuropas*, 31 (1983), 481–515.

——— 'Jewish Marriages in Old Poland in the Public Opinion of the Enlightenment Period' (Heb.), *Gal-Ed*, 4/5 (1978), 25–33.

GOLDENBERG, M. I., *The Gaon Hayim Yehudah Leib* [Toledot hagaon rabi ḥayim yehudah leib] (Warsaw, 1901).

GOLDENBERG, S., 'The People Called Hebrews' (Heb.), *Hashilo'aḥ*, 17 (1907–8), 417–22.

GOLDMAN, BEN-ZION, and AHARON BEIGEL (eds.), *The Western Light and the Lights that it Lit* [Ner hama'aravi vene'erotav shehidlik] (New York, 1991).

GOLDMAN, ISRAEL, *Lifelong Learning among Jews* (New York, 1975).

GOLDRAT, ABRAHAM JUDAH, 'On the Book *Ḥayei adam* and its Author' (Heb.), in Itskaq Refael (ed.), *Sefer margaliyot* (Jerusalem, 1973), 255–78.

GOLDRAT, YISAKHAR, *Minḥat yisakhar* [halakhic work] (Piotrków, 1908).

GOLDSTEIN, YOSSI, 'The Reformed *Ḥeder* in Russia as a Basis for the Zionist Movement' (Heb.), *Iyunim beḥinukh*, 45 (1986), 147–57.

GOLEVSKI, KHAYIM DOV BER, 'Polished Knives' (Heb.), *Yagdil torah*, 5/2 (59) (1981) 114–17.

GOLOMB, TSEVI NISAN, *Charity in Vilna* [Mayse hatsedoke in vilna] (Vilna, 1917).

—— *The Laws of Women: Judging the Feminine Sex According to the Talmud* [Damen-rekht. Mishpat habanos: eyn urteyl iber vayblikhes geshlekht nokh dem talmud] (Vilna, 1890).

GOODY, JACK (ed.), *Literacy in Traditional Societies* (Cambridge, 1968).

—— and IAN WATT, 'The Consequences of Literacy', in Jack Goody (ed.), *Literacy in Traditional Societies* (Cambridge, 1968).

GOSHEN-GOTTSTEIN, ESTHER R., 'Courtship, Marriage and Pregnancy in "Geula"', *Israel Annals of Psychiatry and Related Disciplines*, 4/1 (Spring 1966), 43–66. English abstract (1966), 1–24.

—— 'Mental Health Implications of Living in a Strictly Orthodox Jewish Subculture' (Heb.), *Israel Journal of Psychiatry and Related Sciences*, 24/3 (1987), 145–66.

GOTTESMAN, SHELOMOH, 'Rabbi Abraham, Son of the Gra: His Biography and the Life of R. Abraham, Son of the Gra' (Heb.), *Yeshurun*, 4 (1998), 123–60.

GOTTLOBER, AVRAHAM BER, 'Memoirs and Essays' (Heb.), in Reuven Goldberg (ed.), *Autobiographical Writings* [Ketavim otobiografiyim] (Jerusalem, 1976), 85–108.

GRAETZ, NAOMI, *Silence is Deadly: Judaism Confronts Wifebeating* (Northvale, NJ, 1998).

GREENBAUM, ABRAHAM, 'Contempt for Craftsmen among Jews in Eastern Europe before 1914' (Heb.) [Hazilzul beba'alei hamelakhah beyahadut mizraḥ eiropah lifnei 1914], in Shmuel Ettinger (ed.), *Nation and History* [Umah vetoldoteihah], vol. ii (Jerusalem, 1984).

GREENWALD, J. J., *Shoḥet and Sheḥitah in Rabbinic Literature* [Hashoḥet vehasheḥitah besifrut harabanit] (New York, 1955).

GRIES, ZE'EV, *The Book in Early Hasidism* [Sefer, sofer vesipur bereishit haḥasidut] (Tel Aviv, 1992).

—— *Conduct Literature: Its History and Place in the Life of the Hasidim of Rabbi Israel Ba'al Shem Tov* [Sifrut hahanhagot: toldoteihah umekomah beḥayei hasidei rabi yisra'el ba'al shem tov] (Jerusalem, 1989).

GRISH, KRISTINA, *Boy Vey! The Shiksa's Guide to Dating Jewish Men* (New York, 2005).

GROSSMAN, AVRAHAM, *The Early Sages of France* [Ḥokhmei tsarfat harishonim] (Jerusalem, 1996).

—— 'Family Lineage and its Place in Early Ashkenazi Jewish Society' (Heb.), in I. Etkes and Y. Salmon (eds.), *Studies in the History of Jewish Society in the Medieval and Modern Periods* (Jacob Katz Jubilee Volume) [Perakim betoledot haḥevrah hayehudit biyemei habeinayim uva'et haḥadashah] (Jerusalem, 1980), 9–23.

—— 'From Father to Son: The Inheritance of the Spiritual Leadership of the Jewish Communities in the Early Middle Ages' (Heb.), *Zion*, 50 (1985), 189–220.

—— 'Premature Marriage' (Heb.), *Pe'amim*, 45 (1990), 108–25.

—— 'Violence towards Women in the Mediterranean Jewish Society of the Middle Ages', in Yael Atsmon (ed.), *A Window on the Lives of Women in Jewish Societies* [Eshnav leḥayeihen shel nashim beḥevrot yehudiyot] (Jerusalem, 1995).

GUENZBURG, MORDEKHAI AARON, *Avi'ezer* [autobiography] (Vilna, 1864).

GUREN-KLIRS, TRACY (ed.), *The Merit of our Mothers: A Bilingual Anthology of Jewish Women's Prayers*, trans. Tracy Guren-Klirs, Ida Cohen-Selavan, and Gella Schweid-Fishman; annotated by Faedra Lazar-Weiss and Barbara Selya (Cincinnati, 1992).

GURLAND, YA'AKOV, *Honour of the House* [Kavod habayit] [encomium to school] (Vilna, 1858).

GUROFF, GREGORY, and FREDERICK S. STARR, 'A Note on Urban Literacy in Russia 1890–1914', *Jahrbücher für Geschichte Osteuropas*, 19/4 (1971), 520–31.

GUTMAN, ISRAEL, SHLOMO NETZER, and ABRAHAM WEIN, *History of the Jews of Warsaw: From their Beginnings and Until our Day* [Toledot yehudei varshah—mereishitam ve'ad leyameinu] (Jerusalem, 1991).

GUTMAN, Y. M., *The Destruction of Jewish Radom: A Book of Remembrance* [Dos yidishe radom in hurves: ondenkbukh] (Stuttgart, 1948).

HABERMAN, A. M., 'A Testimony from Worms from the Year 1377' (Heb.), in id. (ed.), *The New and the Old* [Ḥadashim vegam yeshanim] (Jerusalem, 1976).

HACOHEN-FISHMAN, Y. L., et al. (eds.), *Major Jewish Towns* [Arim ve'imahot beyisra'el], 7 vols. (Jerusalem, 1948–60).

HAFETS HAYIM, *see* Kagan, Yisra'el Me'ir Hakohen

HAFT, ARYEH LEIB, *Divrei ta'am* [responsa] (Warsaw, 1904).

HAILPERIN (HALPERN), ISRAEL, 'Diaspora and the Land of Israel', *Ha'olam*, 18/36 (Friday, 29 Aug. 1930), 719.

—— *The First Aliyot of Hasidim to Israel* [Ha'aliyot harishonot shel haḥasidim le'erets yisra'el] (Tel Aviv, 1947).

—— *Jews and Judaism in Eastern Europe* [Yehudim veyahadut bemizraḥ eiropah] (Jerusalem, 1969).

—— 'On the Relations of the Councils and Communities in Poland to the Land of Israel' (Heb.), *Zion*, 1 (1936), 82–8.

—— 'Panic Marriages in Eastern Europe' (Heb.), in id., *East European Jewry* [Yehudim veyahadut bemizraḥ eiropah] (Jerusalem, 1968), 289–309.

—— *Records of the Jewish Council of the Four Polish Lands* [Pinkas va'ad arba aratsot] (Jerusalem, 1945).

HAJNAL, JOHN, 'European Marriage Patterns in Perspective', in David Victor Glass and David Edward Charles Eversley (eds.), *Population in History* (Chicago, 1965).

—— 'Two Kinds of Pre-Industrial Household Formation', in Richard Wall (ed.), *Family Forms in Historic Europe* (Cambridge, 1983).

HAKOHEN, EFRAYIM BEN YA'AKOV, *Sha'ar efrayim* [responsa] (Sulzbach, 1688).

HAKOHEN, MOSHEH AHARON BEN YITSHAK, *Minḥat hazevaḥ* [halakhic work] (Warsaw, 1858).

HALAKHMI, DAVID, *The Yeshiva Hokhmei Lublin and its Founder* [Yeshivat ḥokhmei lublin umekholelo [sic]] (Benei Berak, 1995).

HALBERSTAM, HAYIM, *Divrei ḥayim* [Torah commentary], 2 vols. (Lvov, 1875).

HALEVI, S., 'Rabbi Yisra'el of Shklov' (Heb.), *Sinai*, 3/5 (1939), 30–7.

HALEVY, Z., 'Were the Jewish Immigrants to the United States Representative of Russian Jews?', *Migration*, 16/2 (1978), 66–73.

HANDWERKER HAIM I., 'How to find a Jewish boyfriend', <http://www. haaretz.com/hasen/objects/pages/PrintArticleEn.jhtml?itemNo=605948> (accessed 31 July 2005).

HARAMATI, SHELOMOH, *Methods of Teaching Hebrew in the Diaspora* [Darkhei hora'at ha'ivrit batefutsot] (Jerusalem, 1977).

HARSHAV, BENJAMIN, *The Meaning of Yiddish* (Berkeley, Calif., 1990).

HARTMAN, MARY, *The Household and the Making of History* (Cambridge, 2004).

HASKINS, CHARLES H., *The Rise of the Universities*, 2nd edn. (Ithaca, NY, 1957).

HATAM SOFER, *see* Sofer, Mosheh

HAXTHAUSEN, A. VON, *Studies on the Interior of Russia*, abridged, trans., and ed. Frederick S. Starr (Chicago, 1972).

HEILMAN, SAMUEL, *The People of the Book: Drama, Fellowship and Religion* (Chicago, 1983).

HEILPRIN, ALEXANDER SHEMUEL, *She'elot uteshuvot ma'aharash* [responsa] (Lvov, 1896).

HERLIHY, PATRICIA, *Odessa* (Cambridge, Mass., 1986).

HERSHBERG, AVRAHAM SHEMUEL, *Recordbook of Białystok* [Pinkas bialistok], 2 vols. (New York, 1949).

HESCHEL, ABRAHAM JOSHUA, *The Earth is the Lord's* (New York, 1950).

HILMAN, D. Z., *Letters of Shneur Zalman (Ba'al Hatanya) and his Contemporaries* [Igerot ba'al hatanya uvenei doro] (Jerusalem, 1953).

HIRSCHBERG, Z. (ed.), *Zakhor le'avraham: Mélanges Abraham Elmaleh* (Heb. with French summaries) (Jerusalem, 1972).

HOCHERMAN, YA'AKOV, 'The Ḥeder in Jewish Life and its Literary Representations' (Heb.), *Iyun vema'as*, 2 (1981), 31–6.

HOENIG, SIDNEY, 'Filial Succession in the Rabbinate', *Gratz College Annual of Jewish Studies*, 1 (Philadelphia, 1972), 14–22.

HOLDERNESS, B. A., 'Widows in Pre-Industrial Society', in Richard M. Smith (ed.), *Land, Kinship and Life-Cycle* (Cambridge, 1984).

HOROWITZ, AVRAHAM YA'AKOV HALEVI, *Tsur ya'akov* [responsa] (Biłgoraj, 1932).

HOROWITZ, YITSHAK HALEVI, *Toledot yitshak* [responsa] (Lvov, 1866).

HOUTSONEN, JARMO, 'Traditional Quranic Education in a Southern Moroccan Village', *International Journal of Middle East Studies*, 26/4 (Nov. 1994), 489–500.

HOVAV, YEMIMAH, 'The Religious and Spiritual Life of Jewish Ashkenazi Women in the Early Modern Period' [Ḥayei hadat veharuaḥ shel nashim beḥevrah ha'ashkenazit bereshit ha'et haḥadashah], Ph.D. diss. (Hebrew University, Jerusalem, 2005).

HUNDERT, GERSHON, 'The Decline of Deference in the Jewish Communities of the Polish–Lithuanian Commonwealth' (Heb.), *Bar Ilan Annual*, 24/5 (1989), 41–50 (English summary on p. 149).

—— 'Jewish Children and Childhood in Early Modern East Central Europe', in David Kraemer (ed.), *The Jewish Family: Metaphor and Memory* (New York, 1989).

HURVITZ, NATHAN, 'Courtship and Arranged Marriages among East European Jews Prior to World War I as Depicted in a *Briefenshteller*', *Journal of Marriage and the Family*, 37/2 (1975), 422–30.

HYMAN, PAULA, *Gender and Assimilation in Modern Jewish History: The Roles and Representation of Women* (Seattle, 1995).

IDEL, MOSHE, *Hasidism: Between Ecstasy and Magic* (Albany, NY, 1995).

ISRAEL BEN SHMUEL OF SHKLOV, *Pe'at hashulḥan* [halakhic work] (Safed, 1836).

ISRAELI (KULA), YA'AKOV, *The Dynasty of Karlin-Stolin* [Beit karlin stolin] (Tel Aviv, 1981).

ISSERLES, MOSES, *Hamapah* [glosses on *Shulḥan arukh*]. In almost all editions of *Shulḥan arukh* since 1578.

JABOTINSKY, ZE'EV VLADIMIR, *The Five: A Novel of Jewish Life in Turn-of-the-Century Odessa*, trans. Michael Katz (Ithaca, NY, 2005).

Jewish Encyclopaedia, ed. Cyrus Adler, 12 vols. (New York 1901–06).

Jewish Immigrants: Report of a Special Committee of the National Jewish Immigration Council Appointed to Examine into the Question of Illiteracy among Jewish Immigrants and its Causes, Senate Document 611, 63rd Congress 2nd Session (Washington, DC, 1914).

JOSEPH, S., *Jewish Immigrants* (New York, 1914).

Jüdisches Lexikon, 5 vols. (Berlin, 1927–30).

JUNGREIZ, ISAAC, 'Pressburg' (Heb.), in Shmuel Mirsky (ed.), *Jewish Institutions of Higher Learning in Europe: Their Development and Destruction* [Mosadot torah be'eiropah bevinyanam uveḥurbanam] (New York, 1956).

KAGAN, YISRA'EL MEIR (HAKOHEN), (ed.), *Ets peri* [fund-raising circulars] (Vilna, 1881).

—— *Ḥafets ḥayim* [ethical tract] (Vilna, 1873).

—— *Mishnah berurah* [commentary on *Shulḥan arukh*, 'Oraḥ ḥayim'] (Vilna, 1884–1907).

KAHAN, Y. L., 'How Old are Our Love-Songs?' (Yid.), in id. (ed.), *Studies in Yiddish Folklore* [Shtudies vegn yidisher folksshafung] (New York, 1952).

—— *Jews on Themselves and on Others in their Sayings and Expressions* [Der yid vegen zikh un vegen andere in zeine sprikhverter un redensarten] (New York, 1933).

KAHANA, I. Z., *Studies in Halakhic Literature* [Meḥkarim besifrut hahalakhah] (Jerusalem, 1971).

KAHANA-SHAPIRA, R. M. (ed.), *Otsar hashe'elot uteshuvot* [lexicon of responsa], 7 vols. (Jerusalem, 1971–).

KAHANOV, NEHEMIAH, *Netivot hashalom* [responsa] (Königsberg, 1858).

KAMEN, DAVID, *Beit david* [halakhic work] (Warsaw, 1908).

KAMINETSKY, DAVID, 'Evaluation and Desire for the Gaon's Commentaries in Recent Generations' (Heb.), *Yeshurun*, 6 (1999), 772–80.

KANARFOGEL, EPHRAIM, 'Attitudes toward Childhood and Children in Medieval Jewish Society', in David R. Blumenthal (ed.), *Approaches to Judaism in Medieval Times*, vol. ii (Chico, Calif., 1985).

KAPLAN, KIMI, 'In God We Trust: Salaries and Income of American Orthodox Rabbis, 1881–1924', *American Jewish History*, 86/1 (1998), 77–106.

KAPLAN, MARION, 'For Love or Money: The Marriage Strategies of Jews in Imperial Germany', *Leo Baeck Institute Year Book*, 28 (1983), 163–300.

—— *The Making of the Jewish Middle Class* (New York, 1991).

KARLINSKY, R. HAIM, 'Dos shtetl kelm' (Yid.), in Mendel Sudarshki, Arye Katsnellenbogen and Y. Kisin (eds.), *Lite* (New York, 1951), 1437–52.

KARO, BARUCH (ed.), *The Book of Vitebsk* [Sefer vitebsk] (Tel Aviv, 1957).

KARPINSKI, A., *Kobieta w miescie polskim w drugiej połowie XVI i w XVII wieku* (Warsaw, 1995).

KASER, KARL, *Macht und Erbe: Männerherrschaft, Besitz und Familie im östlichen Europa* (Vienna, 2000).

—— 'Power and Inheritance: Male Domination, Property, and Family in Eastern Europe, 1500–1900', *History of the Family*, 7/3 (2002), 375–95.

KATRIEL, TAMAR, *Talking Straight: Dugri Speech in Israeli Sabra Culture* (Cambridge, 1986).

KATZ, DOV, *The Musar Movement* [Tenuat hamusar], 5 vols. (Tel Aviv, 1955–63).

KATZ, JACOB, 'Family, Kinship and Marriage among Ashkenazim in the Sixteenth to Eighteenth Centuries', *Jewish Journal of Sociology*, 1 (1959), 4–22.

—— *A House Divided: Orthodoxy and Schism in Nineteenth-Century Central European Jewry* (Hanover, NH, 1998).

—— 'On the History of the Rabbinate in the Late Middle Ages', in E. Z. Melamed (ed.), *Sefer zikaron lebinyamin de vris: Benjamin de Vries Memorial Volume* (Jerusalem, 1968).

—— 'Toward a Biography of the Hatam Sofer', in Francis Malino and David Sorkin (eds.), *From East and West: Jews in a Changing Europe, 1750–1870* (London, 1990).

—— *Tradition and Crisis: Jewish Society at the End of the Middle Ages* (1958), trans. B. D. Cooperman (New York, 1993).

KATZMAN, ELIEZER, 'Rabbi Yehoshua Heschel Lewin, Author of *Aliyot eliyahu*' (Heb.), *Yeshurun*, 5 (1999), 742–82; 6 (1999), 700–27.

KAY, DEVRA, *Seyder Tkhines: The Forgotten Book of Common Prayer for Jewish Women*, annotated translation (Philadelphia, 2004).

KAZDAN, ḤAYYIM SOLOMON, *From Ḥeder and Schools to CYSHO: Russian Jewry in Conflict about Schools, Language and Culture* [Fun kheyder un shkoles biz tsisho: dos ruslendishe yidntum: in gerangel far shul, shprakh, kultur] (Mexico City, 1956).

—— *The History of Jewish Education in Independent Poland* [Di geshikhte fun yidishen shulvesen in umaphengiken poylen] (Mexico City, 1947).

KELNER, I., 'The Beginning of the Organization of the Jewish Communities in the United States with the Help of the Jews in Israel' (Heb.), *Shalem*, 1 (1974), 377–426.

KELNER, VIKTOR, and DMITRY ELYASHEVICH, *Literatura o evreyakh na russkom yazyke, 1890–1947 gg.* (St Petersburg, 1995).

KENA'ANI, DAVID, *The Houses that No Longer Exist* [Habatim shehayu] (Tel Aviv, 1986).

KESSNER, THOMAS, *The Golden Door: Italian and Jewish Immigrant Mobility in New York City 1880–1915* (New York, 1977).

KIENIEWICZ, STEFAN, *The Emancipation of Polish Peasantry* (Chicago, 1969).

KLAPHOLTZ, YISRA'EL, *The Hasidic Leaders of Belz* [Admorei belts], 3 vols. (Jerusalem, 1979).

KLATSKIN, ELIYAHU, *Devar eliyahu* [responsa] (Lublin, 1915).

KLAUSNER, YISRA'EL, *History of the Jewish Community in Vilna* [Toledot hakehilah ha'ivrit bevilna] (Vilna, 1935).

—— *Vilna: The Jerusalem of Lithuania* [Vilna: yerushalayim delita] (Kibuts Lohamei Hagetaot, 1988).

—— *Vilna in the Time of the Gaon* [Vilna bitkufat hagaon] (Jerusalem, 1942).

KLIBANSKY, BEN-TSIYON, 'The Lithuanian Yeshivas in Eastern Europe between the Two World Wars' [Hayeshivot halitayot bemizraḥ eiropah bein shetei milḥamot ha'olam], Ph.D. diss. (Tel Aviv, 2009).

KNODEL, JOHN, and KATHERINE LYNCH, 'The Decline of Remarriage: Evidence from German Village Populations in the Eighteenth and Nineteenth Centuries', *Journal of Family History*, 10/1 (Spring 1985), 34–59.

KOCHANOWICZ, JACEK, 'The Polish Peasant Family as an Economic Unit', in Richard Wall (ed.), *Family Forms in Historic Europe* (Cambridge, 1983).

KOTIK, YEHEZKEL, *Instructions for the Members of the Moshav Zekenim Society* [Instruktsies far der khevre 'moshav zekenim'] (Warsaw, 1913).

KOWALSKA-GLIKMAN, S., 'Ludnosc żydowska Warszawy w połowie XIX wieku w swietle akt stanu cywilnego', *Biuletyn Żydowskiego Instytutu Historycznego*, 2 (118) (1981), 37–49.

KRAEMER, DAVID (ed.), *The Jewish Family: Metaphor and Memory* (New York, 1989).

KRASNOVA, EVA, and ANATOLY DROZDOVSKY, 'Odesskaya evreiskaya bogadel'nya', in *Al'manakh 'Moriya'*, 4 (Odessa, 2005); <http://www.moria.farlep.net/ru/almanah_04/01_06.htm> (last accessed 6 May 2008).

KREIS, SIMEON, 'Russian-Language Jewish Schools in Tsarist Russia' [Batei sefer yehudiyim besafah harusit berusiyah hatsarit], Ph.D. diss. (Jerusalem, 1994).

KREMENEZKY, JOHANN, *Bericht über den Jüdischen Nationalfonds erstattet am VII Zionisten-Kongress in Basel (Abdruck aus dem Protokolle des VII Kongresses)* (Vienna, 1905).

KRESSEL, G., *Stories: The Scroll of the Earth* [Korot: megilat ha'adamah] (Jerusalem, 1951).

KULA, WITOLD, 'The Seigneury and the Peasant Family in Poland', in Robert Forster and Orest Ranum (eds.), *Family and Society: Selections from the Annales* (Baltimore, Md., 1976).

KUPFER, E. (ed.), *Responsa and Decisions from the Sages of Ashkenaz and France* [Teshuvot upesakim me'et ḥokhmei ashkenaz vetsarfat] (Jerusalem, 1973).

KUZNETS, SIMON, 'Immigration of Russian Jews to the United States: Background and Structure', *Perspectives in American History*, 9 (1975), 35–124.

LAMM, ZVI, *The Zionist Youth Movements in Retrospect* [Tenuot hano'ar hatsiyoniyot bemabat le'akhor] (Tel Aviv, 1991).

LANDAU, ADOLF, 'Das jüdisches Volkslied in Russland', *Mitteilungen zur jüdischen Volkskunde*, Heft 11/1 (1903), 68.

LANDAU, BETSALEL, 'The Netsiv of Volozhin in the Campaign for the Yishuv in Israel' (Heb.), *Hama'ayan*, 14/3 (1974), 11–23.

—— *The Righteous Gaon of Vilna* [Hagaon heḥasid mevilna], 3rd edn. (Jerusalem, 1978).

LANDAU, EZEKIEL, *Noda biyehudah* [responsa], 2 vols. (Prague, 1776, 1811; many reprints).

—— 'Responsum', in *Kovets beit aharon veyisra'el*, 6/6 (36) (1991), 6–10.

LANDAU, NATHAN, *Kenaf renanah* [commentary on *Shulḥan arukh*, 'Yoreh de'ah'], (Kraków, 1892–9).

LANDES, RUTH, and MARK ZBOROWSKI, 'Hypotheses Concerning the Eastern European Jewish Family', *Psychiatry*, 13 (1950), 447–64.

LANE, EDWARD WILLIAM, *An Account of the Manners and Customs of the Modern Egyptians*, 5th edn. (London, 1871).

LASHOVITS, KATRIEL (ed.), *Wołkowysk: The Story of a Zionist-Jewish Community that was Destroyed in the Holocaust* [Volkovisk: sipurah shel kehilah yehudit-tsiyonit hushmedah basho'ah] (Tel Aviv, 1988).

LASLETT, PETER, 'Family and Household as Work and Kin Groups', in Richard Wall (ed.), *Family Forms in Historic Europe* (Cambridge, 1983).

LEDERHENDLER, ELI, *The Road to Modern Jewish Politics* (New York, 1989).

LEDERMAN, SARAH, 'The Jewish Aged: Traditions and Trends', in Gilbert Rosenthal (ed.), *The Jewish Family in a Changing World* (New York, 1970).

LEIBOWITZ, YITSHAK TSEVI, *Shulḥan ha'ezer* [responsa], 2 vols. (Dej, 1929; Berehovo, 1932).

LÉRIDON, HENRI, 'Effets du veuvage et du remariage sur la fécondité: Résultats d'un modèle de simulation', in Jacques Dupâquier et al. (eds.), *Marriage and Remarriage in Populations of the Past* (London, 1981).

LESTCHINSKY, JACOB, 'Statistics of a Town' (Heb.), in id., *The Jewish Diaspora* [Hatefutsah hayehudit] (Jerusalem, 1961).

LEVIN, J., 'Ekaterinoslav Rabbis' (Heb.), in Zvi Harkavi and Jacob Goldbort (eds.), *Sefer yekaterinoslav-dnepropetrovsk* (Jerusalem/Tel Aviv, 1973).

LEVIN, SABINA, 'The First Elementary Schools for Children of the Mosaic Faith in Warsaw 1818–1830' (Heb.), *Gal-Ed*, 1 (1973), 63–100.

—— 'The First Jewish Home for Orphans and the Elderly in Warsaw' (Heb.), *Gal-Ed*, 4/5 (1978), 55–78.

LEVIN, SHEMARYAHU, *Childhood in Exile*, trans. Maurice Samuel (New York, 1929).

—— *Istoricheskii ocherk razvitiya Vilenskoi evreiskoi obshchestvennoi bogadel'ni* (Vilna, 1900).

LEVIN, VITALIJ, 'Multi-Faceted Logic as a Principal Distinction of Jewish Thinking and Philosophy', in Izraelis Lempertas (ed.), *The Gaon of Vilnius and the Annals of Jewish Culture* (Vilnius, 1998).

LEVINE, JACOB, *The Law of the Sacrifice* [Ḥukat hazevaḥ] (Kraków, 1896).

LEVINE, MORDEKHAI, 'The Family in the Revolutionary Jewish Society' (Heb.), *Me'asef*, 13 (1982/3) 109–26, and 14 (1984) 157–71.

LEVINE, SHALOM DUBER, 'The Responsum of Admor HaZaken #7', *Yagdil torah*, 2/7 (19) (1978), 406–8.

LEVITATS, I., *The Jewish Community in Russia 1772–1844* (New York, 1943).

LEWIN, ISAAC, *Treasury of Rabbinic Periodicals* [Otsar kitvei et toranayim] (New York, 1980).

LEWIN, YEHOSHUA HESCHEL, *Aliyot eliyahu* [biography of the Gaon of Vilna] (Vilna, 1857).

LEWIS, BERNARD, *Cultures in Conflict* (New York, 1995).

LIBERMAN, HAYIM, 'Legends and Truth on Hasidic Printing' (Yid.), *YIVO Bleter*, 34 (1950), 182–208; reissued in expanded form in id., *Ohel raḥel*, ii (New York, 1981), 17–160; Hebrew translation in vol. iii.

LIFSHITZ, TSEVI HIRSH, *From Generation to Generation* [Midor ledor] (Warsaw, 1901).

LIPSCHITZ, YA'AKOV, *Zikhron ya'akov* [memoirs], 3 vols. (Kaunas, 1924–30).

LITWIN, HAYIM, *Sha'arei de'ah* [responsa] (Lvov, 1878).

LLOYD, G. I. H., *The Cutlery Trades* (London, 1913).

LODGE, DAVID, *Small World* (Harmondsworth, 1985).

LOEWE, LOUIS (ed.), *Diaries of Sir Moses and Lady Montefiore* (Chicago, 1890).

Łomża: Remembrance Book of the Jewish Community [Sefer zikaron lekehilat lomza], ed. Yom Tov Levinsky (Tel Aviv, 1952).

LÖW, LEOPOLD, *Graphische Requisiten und Erzeugnisse bei den Juden*, 2 vols. (Leipzig, 1870–1).

LUNZ, ABRAHAM, 'The *Ḥalukah*' (Heb.), *Yerushalayim*, 9 (1911), 1–62.

LURIE, ILYA, 'Lubavitch and its Wars: Chabad Hasidism and the Fight for the Image of Jewish Society in Tsarist Russia' [Lubavits umilḥamoteiha: ḥasidut ḥabad bama'avak al demutah shel haḥevrah hayehudit berusiyah hatsarit], Ph.D. diss. (Jerusalem, 2009).

LUZ, EHUD, *Parallels Meet: Religion and Nationalism in the Early Zionist Movement (1882–1904)* (Philadelphia, 1988(.

MCLACHLAN, JAMES, 'The Choice of Hercules: American Student Societies', in Lawrence Stone (ed.), *The University in Society*, vol. ii: *Europe, Scotland and the United States from the 16th to the 20th Century* (Princeton, NJ, 1974).

MAGID-STEINSCHNEIDER, HILLEL NOAH, *The City of Vilna* [Ir vilna] (Vilna, 1900).

MAHLER, RAPHAEL, *Statistics about Jews in Former Poland* [Yidn in amolikn poyln in likht fun tsifern] (Warsaw, 1958).

MAIMON, SOLOMON, *An Autobiography*, ed. Moses Hadas (New York, 1947).

MAKOVER, YEHUDAH, *Faithful Shepherd* [Ro'eh ne'eman] (Jerusalem, 1990).

MALAKHI, A. R., *Chapters on the History of the Old Yishuv* [Perakim betoledot hayishuv hayashan] (Tel Aviv, 1971).

—— 'On the History of the *ḥalukah* in Jerusalem' [Lekorot haḥalukah birushalayim], *Luaḥ erets yisra'el*, 18 (1912), 81–102.

MALE, DONALD J., *Russian Peasant Organization before Collectivization: A Study of Commune and Gathering, 1925–1930* (Cambridge, 1971).

MANDELBOIM, D., *The Yeshiva Hokhmei Lublin* [Yeshivat ḥokhmei lublin] (Benei Berak, 1994).

MANEKIN, RACHEL, 'The Growth and Development of Jewish Orthodoxy in Galicia' [Tsemikhatah vegibushah shel ha'ortodoksiyah hayehudit begalitsiyah], Ph.D. diss. (Hebrew University, Jerusalem, 2000).

—— 'The Lost Generation: Education and Female Conversion in Fin-de-Siècle Kraków', *Polin*, 18 (2005), 189–219.

—— 'Orthodoxy in Kraków on the Eve of the Twentieth Century' (Heb.), in Elhanan Reiner (ed.), *Kroke–Kazimierz–Cracow: Studies in the History of Cracow Jewry* [Kroke-kazimirz–krakuv: meḥkarim betoledot yehudei krakuv] (Tel Aviv, 2001), 155–90.

—— 'Something Totally New: The Development of the Idea of Religious Education for Girls in the Modern Period' (Heb.), *Masekhet*, 2 (2004), 63–85.

MARCUS, IVAN, 'Last Year in Jerusalem', *Response*, 13/4 (1983), 23–34.

MARCUS, JACOB, *Communal Sick-Care in the German Ghetto* (Cincinnati, 1947).

MARCUS, JOSEPH, *Social and Political History of the Jews in Poland 1919–1939* (Berlin, 1983).

MARCY, PETER, 'Factors Affecting the Fecundity and Fertility of Historical Populations: A Review', *Journal of Family History*, 6/3 (1981), 309–26.

—— L. SANDBERG, and R. STECKEL, 'Soldier, Soldier, What Made You Grow So Tall?', *Economy and History*, 32/2 (1980), 91–105.

MARGALIOT, REUVEN, *Nitsotsei zohar* [commentary on the Zohar] (Jerusalem, 1970).

MARGALIT, BARUCH A., and PAUL A. MAUGER, 'Aggressiveness and Assertiveness: A Cross-Cultural Study of Israel and the United States', *Journal of Cross-Cultural Psychology*, 16/4 (1985), 497–511.

MARROU, HENRI I., *A History of Education in Antiquity* (New York, 1956).

MEDINI, HAYIM, *Sedeh ḥemed* [rabbinic encyclopaedia], 20 vols. (Warsaw, 1891–1912).

MEIR, MORDECHAI, 'Rabbi Abraham Danzig', unpublished MA thesis (Bar Ilan University, Ramat Gan, 2000).

MEIR, NATHAN, 'From Communal Charity to National Welfare: Jewish Orphanages in Eastern Europe before and after World War I', *East European Jewish Affairs*, 39/1 (2009), 19–34.

MEIZLISH, TSEVI ARYEH YEHUDAH YA'AKOV, *Ḥedvat ya'akov* [responsa] (Piotrków, 1903).

MELTON, EDGAR, 'Proto-Industrialization, Serf Agriculture and Agrarian Social Structure: Two Estates in Nineteenth-Century Russia', *Past and Present*, 115 (1987), 69–106.

MERAD, ALI, *Le Réformisme musulman en Algérie de 1925 à 1940* (Paris, 1967).

MESSICK, BRINKLEY, 'Legal Documents and the Concept of "Restricted Literacy" in a Traditional Society', *International Journal of the Sociology of Language*, 42 (1983), 31–52.

MEYUHAS, MOSHEH YOSEF MORDEKHAI, *Bereikhot mayim* [halakhic work] (Salonika, 1789).

MILLER, PAVLA, *Transformations of Patriarchy in the West, 1500–1900* (Bloomington, 1998).

MINOIS, GEORGE, *History of Old Age*, trans. Sarah Tenison (Chicago, 1989).

MIRON, DAN, *The Image of the Shtetl and Other Studies of Modern Jewish Literary Imagination* (Syracuse, NY, 2000).

MIRONOV, B. N., 'Traditional Demographic Behaviour of Peasants at the End of the Nineteenth and Beginning of the Twentieth Centuries' (Russian), in A. G. Vishnevsky (ed.), *Brachnost', rozhdaemost', smertnost' v Rossii i v SSSR* (Moscow, 1977), 83–104.

MIRSKY, SHMUEL (ed.), *Jewish Institutions of Higher Learning in Europe: Their Development and Destruction* [Mosadot torah be'eiropah bevinyanam uveḥurbanam] (New York, 1956).

MITTERAUER, MICHAEL and A. KAGAN, 'Russian and Central European Family Structures: A Comparative View', *Journal of Family History*, 7/1 (1982), 103–31.

—— and REINHARD SIEDER, *The European Family* (Chicago, 1982).

MONDSHINE, YEHOSHUA, *Hatsofeh ledoro* [biography] (Jerusalem, 1987).

—— *Migdal oz* [collection of studies] (Kefar Habad, 1980).

—— (ed.), *Shivḥei besht* [biography of the Ba'al Shem Tov] (Jerusalem, 1982).

—— 'Studies', in *Kerem ḥabad*, 4, pts. 1 and 2 (Kefar Habad, 1992).

MORGENSTERN, ARYEH, *Mysticism and Messianism: From Luzzatto to the Vilna Gaon* [Mistika umeshikhiyut: me'aliyat haramkhal ad hagaon mivilna] (Jerusalem, 1999).

NADLER, ALAN, *The Faith of the Mithnagdim: Rabbinic Responses to Hasidic Rapture* (Baltimore, 1997).

NAKRITS, JUDAH, 'The Yeshiva of Novogrudok' (Heb.), in Shmuel Mirsky (ed.), *Jewish Institutions of Higher Learning in Europe: Their Development and Destruction* [Mosadot torah be'eiropah bevinyanam uveḥurbanam] (New York, 1956).

NASR, SEYYED HOSSEIN, 'Oral Transmission and the Book in Islamic Education: The Spoken and Written Word', *Journal of Islamic Studies*, 3/1 (1992), 1–14.

NATANSON, JOSEPH SAUL, *Responsa* (repr. Jerusalem, 1973).

NATHANS, BENJAMIN, *Beyond the Pale: The Jewish Encounter with Late Imperial Russia* (Berkeley/Los Angeles, 2002).

NAVON, YONAH, *Neḥpah bakhesef* [responsa], 2 vols. (Jerusalem, 1843; repr. 1971).

NEBENZAHL, ALTER, *Minḥat yeḥi'el* [responsa], pt. 1 (Biłgoraj, 1932); pts. 2, 3 (Stanisławów, 1936–9).

NIEZEN, R. W., 'Hot Literacy in Cold Societies', *Comparative Studies in Society and History*, 33 (July 1991), 225–54.

NIGER, SAMUEL, *Pages on the History of Yiddish Literature* [Bleter geshikhte fun der yiddishe literatur] (New York, 1959).

NOBLE, SHLOMO, *Khumesh-taytsh: The Traditional Language of Yiddish Pentateuchal Tradition* (New York, 1943).

NOWAK, BASIA, Review of Anna Żarnowska and Andrzej Szwarc, *Kobieta i społeczenstwo na ziemiach polskich w XIX wieku*, vol. i (Warsaw, 1995), in *Journal of Women's History*, 13/1 (2001), 198.

ONG, W. J., 'Latin Language Study as a Renaissance Puberty Rite', in P. W. Musgrave (ed.), *Sociology and the History of Education* (London, 1970).

—— *Orality and Literacy* (London, 1982).

ORBACH, ALEXANDER, *New Voices of Russian Jewry* (Leiden, 1980).

ORENSTEIN, TSEVI HIRSH, *Birkat ratsah* [responsa] (Lvov, 1889).

Otsar haposekim: otsrot hashut [Lexicon of Halakhic Authorities: Lexicons of the Responsa] (Jerusalem, 2002); digital publication.

OZMENT, STEVE, *Ancestors: The Loving Family in Old Europe* (Cambridge, Mass., 1981).

—— *When Fathers Rule: Family Life in Reformation Europe* (Cambridge, Mass., 1983).

PARDO, DAVID SHEMUEL, *Api zutri* [commentary on *Shulḥan arukh*, 'Hilkhot ishut'] (Venice, 1797).

PARUSH, IRIS, 'Another Look at "The Life of 'Dead' Hebrew"', *Book History*, 7 (2004), 171–214.

—— *Reading Jewish Women: Marginality and Modernization in Nineteenth-Century Eastern European Jewish Society* (Hanover, NH, 2004).

PASCU, S., and V. PASCU, 'Le Remariage chez les Orthodoxes', in Jacques Dupâquier et al. (eds.), *Marriage and Remarriage in Populations of the Past* (London, 1981).

PEDERSEN, JOHANNES, *The Arabic Book*, trans. Geoffrey French (Princeton, NJ, 1984).

PERFET, YITSHAK BAR-SHESHET (RIBASH), *She'elot uteshuvot ribash* [responsa] (Rivo di Trento, 1559).

PICKETT, JOSEPH, et al. (eds.), *American Heritage Dictionary* (Boston, 2000); <http://www.bartleby.com/61/51/P0115100.html>.

PIEKARZ, MENDEL, *The Beginning of Hasidism: Ideological Trends in Derush and Musar Literature* [Bimei tsemiḥat haḥasidut: megamot ra'ayoniyot besifrei derush umusar] (Jerusalem, 1978).

—— *Polish Hasidism: Ideological Trends of Hasidism in Poland during the Interwar Period and the Holocaust* [Ḥasidut polin: megamot ra'ayoniyot bein shetei hamilḥamot uvegezeirot tash-tashah] (Jerusalem, 1990).

PLAKANS, ANDREJS, and JOEL HALPERN, 'A Historical Perspective on Eighteenth-Century Jewish Family Households in Eastern Europe', in Paul Ritterband (ed.), *Modern Jewish Fertility* (Leiden, 1981).

PLANCKE, M., 'Islamic Education in Tunisia (*c.*800–1574)', *Humaniora Islamica*, 1 (1973), 5–14.

POLEN, NEHEMIAH, *The Holy Fire* (Northvale, NJ, 1994).

RABINOVITZ, SHALOM YA'AKOV, *see* Shalom Aleikhem

RABINOWITSCH-MARGOLIN, SARA, 'Die Heiraten der Juden im europäischen Russland vom Jahr 1867 bis 1902', *Zeitschrift für Demographie und Statistik der Juden*, 5/10 (1909), 145–52; 5/11 (1909), 167–73; 5/12 (1909), 177–87.

—— 'Zur Bildungsstatistik der jüdischen Arbeiter in Russland', *Zeitschrift für Demographie und Statistik der Juden*, 9/11 (1913), 153–60.

RABINOWITZ, DAN, 'Rayna Batya and Other Learned Women: A Re-evaluation of Rabbi Baruch Halevi's Sources', *Tradition*, 35/1 (2001), 55–69.

RABINOWITZ, ISRAEL, 'The Yeshiva in Łomża' (Heb.), in Shmuel Mirsky (ed.), *Jewish Institutions of Higher Learning in Europe: Their Development and Destruction* [Mosadot torah be'eiropah bevinyanam uveḥurbanam] (New York, 1956).

RABINOWITZ, MOSHEH YEHI'EL ELIMELEKH, *Avodat halev* [on prayer], ed. David Matitiyahu Rabinowitz (Warsaw, 1927).

RABINOWITZ-TEOMIM, ELIYAHU DAVID, *Seder eliyahu* [autobiography] (Jerusalem, 1983).

RAMAZANOGLU, CAROLINE, *Feminism and the Contradictions of Oppression* (London, 1989).

RAPHAEL, YITSHAK (ed.), 'Shivḥei habesht' (Heb.), *Areshet*, 2 (1960), 358–77.

—— Supplement in *Areshet*, 3 (1961) 440–1.

RAPOPORT, SHLOMO YEHUDA, 'Rabbi Meir Ba'al Hanes' (Heb.), *Yeshurun*, 6/1 (1868) 65–92.

RAPOPORT-ALBERT, ADA, 'Hasidism after 1772: Structural Continuity and Change', in ead., *Hasidism Reappraised* (London, 1996).

Recordbooks of the Jewish Communities: Latvia and Estonia [Pinkas hakehilot: latviyah ve'estoniyah], ed. Dov Levin et al. (Jerusalem, 1988).

Recordbooks of the Jewish Communities: Lithuania [Pinkas hakehilot: lita], ed. Dov Levin and Yosef Rozin (Jerusalem, 1996).

Recordbooks of the Jewish Communities: Poland [Pinkas hakehilot: polin], ed. Danuta Dąbrowska et al., 8 vols. (Jerusalem, 1976–2005).

Recordbooks of the Jewish Communities: Romania [Pinkas hakehilot: romaniyah], ed. Theodore Lavi, Avina Broshni, and Jean Ancel, 2 vols. (Jerusalem, 1969–80).

Recueil de matériaux sur la situation économique des Israélites de Russie, survey conducted by the Jewish Colonization Association (ICA) (Paris, 1906).

REIMER, JACK (ed.), *Ethical Wills: A Modern Jewish Treasury* (New York, 1983).

REINER, ELHANAN, 'The Ashkenazi Elite at the Beginning of the Modern Era: Manuscript versus Printed Book', *Polin*, 10 (1997), 85–98.

—— 'The Yeshivas of Poland and Ashkenaz during the Sixteenth and Seventeenth Centuries: Historical Developments', in Israel Bartal, Ezra Mendelsohn, and Chava Turniansky (eds.), *Studies in Jewish Culture in Honour of Chone Shmeruk* (Jerusalem, 1993).

REINES, MOSES, 'Centres of Torah Study' (Heb.), in Shaltiel Gräber (ed.), *Otsar hasifrut*, 6 vols. (Jarosław and Kraków, 1887–1902), vol. iii, pt. 1.

REISS, DAVID, *Shoshanim ledavid* [responsa] (Kołomyja, 1937).

RESNICK, DANIEL and LAUREN RESNICK, 'The Nature of Literacy: An Historical Explanation', *Harvard Educational Review*, 47/3 (1977), 370–85.

RIBASH, *see* Perfet, Yitshak Bar-Sheshet

RICH, ADRIENNE, *Of Woman Born: Motherhood as Experience and Institution*, 10th anniversary edn. (New York, 1976).

RINGELBLUM, EMANUEL, 'Early Weddings of Polish Jews in the Past', id., *Chapters on History* [Kapiteln geshikhte] (Buenos Aires, 1953).

RIVKIND, ISAAC, 'Dissertation on R. Yitshak Elhanan Spektor' (Review of E. Shimoff's biography of R. Yitshak Elhanan Spektor) (Heb.), *Hado'ar*, 41/24 (13 Apr. 1962), 395–7.

—— 'The History of the Volozhin Emissaries to the United States' (Heb.), *Hado'ar*, 40/11 (14 Jan. 1966), 169–70; 40/12 (21 Jan. 1966), 187–8.

—— *Jewish Money in Folkways, Cultural History and Folklore* [Yidishe gelt in lebensshteyger, kultur-geshikhte un folklor] (Lexicon) (New York, 1960).

RIVLIN, C. H., *Vision of Zion and Jerusalem* [Ḥazon tsiyon yerushalayim] (Jerusalem, 1947).

RIVLIN, Y., and B. RIVLIN (eds.), *Letters of the Officers and the Administrators of Amsterdam* [Igerot hapekidim veha'amarkalim me'amsterdam], 3 vols. (Jerusalem, 1965–79).

ROBINSON, FRANCIS, 'Technology and Religious Change: Islam and the Impact of Print', *Modern Asian Studies*, 27/1 (1993), 229–51.

ROBINSON, GEROID T., *Rural Russia under the Old Regime* (New York, 1932).

Rocznik statystyki Rzeczypospolitej Polskiej, 5 (Warsaw, 1927).

ROGERS, E., *Communication of Innovation*, 2nd edn. (New York, 1971).

ROKHLIN, L., *Mestechko Krasnopol'e Mogilevskoi gubernii* (St Petersburg, 1908).

ROPER, GEOFFREY, 'Faris al Shidyaq and the Transition from Scribal to Print Culture in the Middle East', in George Atiyeh (ed.), *The Book in the Islamic World: The Written Word and Communication in the Middle East* (Albany, NY, 1995).

ROSALDO, MICHELLE ZIMBALIST, 'Woman Culture and Society: A Theoretical Overview', in Michelle Zimbalist Rosaldo and Louise Lamphere (eds.), *Woman Culture and Society* (Stanford, Calif., 1974).

ROSEN, GEORGE, *Madness in Society* (New York, 1961).

ROSEN, RUTH (ed.), *The Maimie Papers* (Bloomington, Ind., 1977).

ROSENBERG, YEHUDAH, *The Golem of Prague and other Wonderful Tales* [Hagolem miprag uma'asim nifla'im aḥerim], ed. Eli Yassif (Jerusalem, 1991).

—— *Miracles of the Maharal* [Niflaot maharal] (Piotrków, 1909).

ROSENTHAL, FRANZ, '"Of making many books there is no end": The Classic Moslem View', in George Atiyeh (ed.), *The Book in the Islamic World: The Written Word and Communication in the Middle East* (Albany, NY, 1995).

ROSENTHAL-SCHNEIDERMAN, ESTHER, *Complicated Paths: Memories, Events, People* [Naftulei derakhim: zikhronot, me'oraot, ishim], 3 vols. (Tel Aviv, 1970–89).

ROSKIES, DAVID, 'The Medium and Message of the Maskilic Chapbook', *Jewish Social Studies*, 41/3–4 (1979), 275–90.

—— 'Yiddish Popular Literature and the Female Reader', *Journal of Popular Culture*, 10/4 (1977), 852–8.

ROSKIES, DIANE, 'Alphabet Instruction in the East European *Heder*: Some Comparative and Historical Notes', *YIVO Annual*, 17 (1978), 21–53.

—— *Heder: Primary Education among East European Jews. A Selected and Annotated Bibliography of Published Sources*, YIVO Working Papers in Yiddish and East European Studies, 25 (New York, 1977).

ROSMAN, MOSHE (MURRAY), *Founder of Hasidism: A Quest for the Historical Baal Shem Tov* (Berkeley, Calif., 1996).

—— 'A History of Jewish Women in Early Modern Poland: An Assessment', *Polin*, 18 (2005), 25–56.

ROSMAN, MOSHE (MURRAY), 'To Be a Jewish Woman in the Polish-Lithuanian Commonwealth', in Israel Bartal and Israel Gutman (eds.), *The Broken Chain: Polish Jewry throughout the Ages* [Kiyum veshever: yehudei polin ledoroteihem], vol. ii (Jerusalem, 2001).

ROTH, NATAN, *Kadosh yisra'el* [biography] (Benei Berak, 1976).

ROZENHAK, SHMUEL, 'On the System of Jewish Education in Poland between the Two World Wars' (Heb.), in Israel Hailperin (Halpern) (ed.), *Jews in Poland* [Beit yisra'el befolin] (Jerusalem, 1954).

RUBIN, RUTH, *Voices of a People* (Philadelphia, 1979).

RUBINSTEIN, A., 'The Booklet "Katit Lamaor" by Joseph Perl' (Heb.), *Alei sefer*, 3 (1977), 140–57.

RUPPIN, ARTHUR, 'Die russischen Juden nach der Volkszählung von 1897', *Zeitschrift für Demographie und Statistik der Juden*, 2/1 (1906), 1–6.

Sabah kadishah: A Collection of Articles and Pictures Dedicated to the 30th Anniversary of the Perlmutter–Klugman Old Age Home of Kishinev [Sabah kadishah: zamlung fun artiklen un bilder, gevidmet dem 30-yerigen yubelay fun keshenever moyshev zkeynim oyfn nomen fun perlmuter-kligman] (Kishinev, 1933).

SAFRIN, YITSHAK YEHUDAH YEHI'EL, *Notser ḥesed* [Commentary on Ethics of the Fathers] (Lvov, 1856, and frequently reprinted).

SALMON-MACK, TAMAR, 'Marital Issues in Polish Jewry, 1650–1800' [Ḥayei nisu'in beyahadut polin 1650–1800], Ph.D. diss. (Hebrew University, Jerusalem, 2002).

SAMUEL, W., *Total Institutions* (New Brunswick, NJ, 1971).

SCHARFSTEIN, ZVI, *The Ḥeder in the Life of Our People* [Haḥeder beḥayei amenu] (Tel Aviv, 1951).

SCHATZ-UFFENHEIMER, RIVKA, *Hasidism as Mysticism: Quietistic Elements in Eighteenth Century Hasidic Thought* (Princeton, NJ, 1993).

SCHICK, MOSHEH BEN YOSEF, *Responsa*, 3 vols. (Munkács/Lvov, 1880–4).

SCHIFFRIN, DEBORAH, 'Jewish Argument as Sociability', *Language in Society*, 13 (1984), 311–35.

SCHIPPER, YITSHAK, 'Die galizische Judenschaft in den Jahren 1772–1848 in wirtschafts-statistischer Beleuchtung', *Neue jüdische Monatshefte*, II: 9/10 (10 Feb. 1918), 223–33.

SCHLESINGER, BENJAMIN, 'The Jewish Family in Retrospect', in id. (ed.), *The Jewish Family: A Survey and Annotated Bibliography* (Toronto, 1971).

SCHMELZ, USIEL O., *Infant and Early Childhood Mortality among the Jews of the Diaspora* (Jerusalem, 1971).

—— 'Some Demographic Peculiarities of the Jews of Jerusalem in the Nineteenth Century', in Mosheh Maoz (ed.), *Studies on Palestine during the Ottoman Period* (Jerusalem, 1975).

SCHMIDTBAUER, PETER, 'Household and Household Forms of Viennese Jews in 1857', *Journal of Family History*, 5 (Winter 1980), 375–89.

SCHNEERSOHN, SHNEUR ZALMAN, et al., *Holy Letters from the Alter Rebbe, the Middle*

Rebbe, and the Admor Tsemah Tsedek [Igerot kodesh me'et admor hazaken, admor ha'emtsa'i, admor ha'tsemaḥ tsedek'], ed. Shalom Duber Levine (Brooklyn, 1987).

SCHNEERSOHN, YITSHAK DOV BAER, Letter, *Yagdil torah*, 2/11 (23) (1978), 642–4.

SCHOFER, L., 'Emancipation and Population Change', in Werner Mosse, Arnold Paucker, and Reinhard Rürup (eds.), *Revolution and Evolution: 1848 in German-Jewish History* (Tübingen, 1981).

SCHORSCH, ISMAR, 'Emancipation and the Crisis of Religious Authority: The Emergence of the Modern Rabbinate', in Werner Mosse, Arnold Paucker, and Reinhard Rürup (eds.), *Revolution and Evolution: 1848 in German-Jewish History* (Tübingen, 1981).

SCHWADRON, SHALOM MORDEKHAI, *Mishpat shalom* [commentary on *Shulḥan arukh*] (Lvov, 1871, and reprinted several times).

—— *She'elot uteshuvot maharsham* [responsa], 9 parts (Warsaw, Piotrków, Satu Mare, Lvov, Seini, Jerusalem, Tel Aviv, 1902–67).

SCHWARZFUCHS, SIMON, *A Concise History of the Rabbinate* (Oxford, 1993).

SECCOMBE, WALLY, *A Millennium of Family Change: Feudalism to Capitalism in Northwestern Europe* (London, 1992).

SEFORIM, MENDELE MOYKHER, *The Little Man* [Dos kleyne mentshele] (Odessa, 1864).

SEGAL, AGNES, 'Yiddish Works on Women's Commandments in the Sixteenth Century', in *Studies in Yiddish Literature and Folklore* (Jerusalem, 1986).

SEGAL-MISHAL, ELIEZER, *Mishnat eli'ezer* [responsa], 2nd edn. (n.p., 1924).

SHAHAR, SHULAMIT, *The Fourth Estate: A History of Women in the Middle Ages* (London, 2003).

SHALKOVSKY, A. A., *Odessa 84 goda tomu nazad i teper'* (Odessa, 1878).

SHALOM ALEIKHEM (pseudonym of Shalom Rabinovitz), *Council of Elders* [Moshav zekenim] (Warsaw, 1922).

SHANDLER, JEFFREY, 'Towards an Assessment of the Education of Women in Ashkenaz' (unpublished paper, 1985).

SHAPIRA, ZVI, *Darkhei teshuvah* [commentary on *Shulḥan arukh*], 7 vols. (Munkács, 1892–1934).

SHAPIRO, LEON, *The History of ORT* (New York, 1980).

SHAPIRO, ROBERT, 'Jewish Self-Government of Lodz 1914–1939', Ph.D. diss. (Columbia University, New York, 1987).

SHARGORODSKA, P., 'Der shura grus', *Filologishe shriften fun yivo*, 1 (1926), 67–72.

SHATZKY, JACOB, *Cultural History of the Haskalah in Lithuania* [Kulturgeshikhte fun der haskole in lite] (Buenos Aires, 1950).

—— *History of the Jews in Warsaw* [Geshikhte fun yidn in varshe], 3 vols. (New York, 1953).

—— *Jewish Educational Policies in Poland from 1806 to 1866* [Yidishe bildungspolitik in poylen fun 1806 biz 1866] (New York, 1943).

SHEMUEL OF AMDUR, *Teshuvat shemuel* [responsa] (Vilna, 1839).

SHIFMAN, PINHAS, *The Dwelling-Place of Torah* [Akhsaniyah shel torah] (Lida, 1910).

SHIMOFF, EFRAIM, *Rabbi Yitshak Elhanan Spektor* (Heb.) (New York, 1961).

Shivḥei habesht [biography of the Ba'al Shem Tov] (Kopys and Berdichev, 1814–15).

SHMERUK, CHONE, 'East European Versions of Tse'ene-Rene 1786–1859', in Lucy S. Dawidowicz (ed.), *For Max Weinreich on his Seventieth Birthday: Studies in Jewish Languages, Literature, and Society* (The Hague, 1964), 320–36.

—— 'The History of the *Shund* Literature in Yiddish' (Heb.), *Tarbiz*, 52 (1983), 325–50.

—— 'The Social Significance of the Hasidic *Sheḥitah*', *Zion*, 35 (1970), 182–92.

—— *Yiddish Literature* [Sifrut idish] (Tel Aviv, 1978).

SHOHET, AZRIEL, *The 'Crown Rabbinate' in Russia* [Mosad 'harabanut mita'am' berusiyah] (Haifa, 1975).

—— 'History of the Jewish Community in Pinsk 1881–1914', (Heb.) in Wolf Ze'ev Rabinowitsch (ed.), *History of the Pinsk Community* [Toledot kehilat pinsk], 3 vols. (Tel Aviv, 1977), vol. i, pt. 2, pp. 5–297.

—— 'Leadership of the Jewish Communities in Russia after the Abolition of the "Kahal"' (Heb.), *Zion*, 42/3–4 (1977), 143–233.

—— 'Recruitment in the Days of Tsar Nicholas the First and the Growth of Yeshivas in Russia' (Heb.), *Historiyah yehudit*, 1 (1986), 33–8.

SHOMER-ZUNSER, MIRIAM, *Yesterday* (New York, 1939).

SHTERN, YEKHI'EL, 'A Heder in Tyszowce', *YIVO Annual*, 5 (1950), 164; repr. in Joshua Fishman (ed.), *Studies in Modern Jewish Social History* (New York, 1972).

—— *Kheyder un beys-medresh* [Heder and Study Hall] (New York, 1950).

SHULMAN, NISSON, *Authority and Community* (New York, 1986).

SHUR, AVRAHAM ABISH, 'On the Period of his Residence' (Heb.), in *Kovets beit aharon veyisra'el*, 2/6 (12) (1987), 115–27.

SIEV, ASHER (ed.), *Rabbeinu Moshe Isserles (Rema)*, (Heb.) (New York, 1972).

—— *Responsa of Rabbi Moses Isserles* [She'elot uteshuvot harema] (Jerusalem, 1971).

SILBER, MICHAEL K., 'Aspects of Inheritance of the Rabbinate in Orthodox Hungarian Jewry' (Heb.), in *Proceedings of the Conference: Heredity in the Rabbinate in Modern Times* [Kenes ḥokerim: hayerushah berabanut be'et haḥadashah] (Ramat Gan, 1995).

—— 'The Limits of Rapprochement: The Anatomy of an Anti-Hasidic Controversy in Hungary', *Studia Judaica*, 3 (1994), 124–47.

—— 'Roots of Schism in Hungarian Jewry' [Shorashei hapilug beyahadut hungariyah], Ph.D. diss. (Hebrew University, Jerusalem, 1985).

SILLS, DAVID (ed.), *International Encyclopedia of the Social Sciences* (London, 1968).

SILVER, JACQUES, 'Some Demographic Characteristics of the Jewish Population in Russia at the End of the Nineteenth Century', *Jewish Social Studies*, 42:3/4, (Summer/Fall 1980), 269–80

SILVERMAN-WEINREICH, BEATRICE, *Kinship Terminology in a Modern Fusion Language*, Working Papers in Yiddish and East European Jewish Studies, 11 (New York, 1975).

Sistematicheskii ukazatel' literatury o evreyakh (St Petersburg, 1892).

SKLAR, JOAN, 'The Role of Marriage Behaviour in the Demographic Transition: The Case of Eastern Europe around 1900', *Population Studies*, 28/2 (1974), 231–47.

SMITH, DANIEL SCOTT, 'Russian Historical Demography and Family History', *Journal of Family History*, 6/3 (1981) 327–33.

SOFER, MOSHEH (HATAM SOFER), *Sefer ḥatam sofer* [responsa], 6 vols. (Pressburg, 1855–65).

SOFER, NAFTALI, *Likutei beit efrayim* [homilies] (Munkács, 1891).

SOFER, SHELOMOH (SALOMO SCHREIBER), *Ḥut hameshulash* [biography] (Munkács, 1893); German edn.: *Der dreifache Faden*, trans. Leo Prijs (Basel, 1952).

SOLOVEITCHIK, HAYM, 'Religious Law and Change: The Medieval Ashkenazic Example', *AJS Review*, 12 (1987), 205–21.

—— 'Rupture and Reconstruction: The Transformation of Contemporary Orthodoxy', *Tradition*, 28/4 (1994), 64–130.

SOMOGYI, TAMAR, *Die Schejnen und die Prosten: Untersuchungen zum Schönheitsideal der Ostjuden in Bezug auf Körper und Kleidung unter besonderer Berücksichtigung des Chassidismus*, Kölner ethnologische Studien, 2 (Berlin, 1982).

SORKIN, DAVID, *The Transformation of German Jewry 1780–1840* (New York, 1987).

'Sovremennyi kheder', collection of articles in *Vestnik Obshchestva rasprostraneniya prosveshcheniya mezhdu evreyami v Rossii*, 17 (Nov. 1912), 3–90.

SPEKTOR, MORDKHE, *My Life* [Mayn lebn] (Warsaw, 1927).

SPERBER, D., 'Hasidism and Stringency in Custom' (Heb.), in id., *Customs of Israel: Origins and History* [Minhagei yisra'el: mekorot vetoledot], 9 vols. (Jerusalem, 1982–2007), ii. 126–56.

SPERLING, ELISABETH, 'Der Wandel des jüdischen Sozialwesens in der zweiten Hälfte des 19. Jahrhunderts in Russland und russisch Polen', in Gotthold Rhode (ed.), *Juden in Ostmitteleuropa von der Emanzipation bis zum Ersten Weltkrieg* (Marburg, 1989).

SPIEGEL, YA'AKOV SHEMUEL, *Pages on the History of the Hebrew Book* [Amudim betoledot hasefer ha'ivri], 2 vols. (Ramat Gan, 1996–2005).

Sprawozdanie za rok 1927—Towarzystwo 'Dom Starców' w Warszawie (Warsaw, n.d.).

STAHL, ABRAHM, 'Historical Changes in the Culture of Israel and their Implications on Dealing with Pupils with Special Needs', in id. (ed.), *Literacy and the Transition to Modern Culture* (Jerusalem, 1973), 9–27

STAHL-WEINBERG, SYDNEY, *The World of Our Mothers: The Lives of Jewish Immigrant Women* (Chapel Hill, 1988).

STAMPFER, SHAUL, 'L'Amour et la famille chez les Juifs d'Europe orientale à l'époque moderne', in Shmuel Trigano (ed.), *La Société juive à travers l'histoire*, vol. ii (Paris, 1992).

—— 'The Controversy over *Sheḥitah* and the Struggle between Hasidim and Mitnagedim' (Heb.), in David Assaf and Joseph Dan (eds.), *Studies in Hasidism* [Meḥkarei ḥasidut] (Jerusalem, 1999).

—— 'Dormitory and Yeshiva in Eastern Europe' (Heb.), in Mordechai Dagan (ed.), *Religious Dormitory Education in Israel* [Haḥinukh hapenimiyati hamamlakhti dati beyisra'el] (Jerusalem, 1997), 15–28.

—— 'East European Jewish Migration to the United States', in Ira Glazier and Luigi De Rosa (eds.), *Migration across Time and Nations* (New York, 1986).

STAMPFER, SHAUL, *The Formation of the Lithuanian Yeshiva* [Hayeshivah halita'it behithavutah] (Jerusalem, 1995; 2nd edn., 2005).

—— 'The Gaon, Yeshivot, the Printing Press and the Jewish Community: A Complicated Relationship between a Scholar and Society', in Izraelis Lempertas (ed.), *The Gaon of Vilnius and the Annals of Jewish Culture* (Vilnius, 1998).

—— 'Gender Differentiation and Education of the Jewish Woman in Nineteenth-Century Eastern Europe', *Polin*, 7 (1992), 63–87.

—— 'Hasidic Yeshivot in Inter-War Poland', *Polin*, 11 (1998), 3–24.

—— 'Heder Study, Knowledge of Torah and the Maintenance of Social Stratification in Traditional East European Jewish Society', *Studies in Jewish Education*, 3 (1988), 271–89.

—— 'The Inheritance of the Rabbinate in Eastern Europe in the Modern Period: Causes, Factors and Development over Time', *Jewish History*, 13/1 (1999), 35–57.

—— 'Is the Question the Answer? East European Jews and North African Moslems: Oral Education and Printed Books and Some Possible Antecedents of Israeli Intellectual Life', *Studia Judaica* (Cluj), 8 (1999), 239–54.

—— 'Jewish Women Revisited', review of Iris Parush, *Reading Jewish Women: Marginality and Modernization in Nineteenth-Century Eastern European Jewish Society*, in *Jews in Russia and Eastern Europe*, 1/52 (2004), 244–8.

—— 'Literacy among East European Jewry in the Modern Period: Context, Background and Implications', in *Transition and Change in Modern Jewish History*, Shmuel Ettinger Jubilee Volume (Jerusalem, 1988).

—— *Lithuanian Yeshivas of the Nineteenth Century: Creating a Tradition of Learning* (Oxford, forthcoming).

—— 'On the Making and the Maintenance of the Image of the Gaon of Vilna' (Heb.), in Moshe Hallamish, Yosef Rivlin, and Rafael Schuchat (eds.), *The Vilna Gaon and his Disciples* [Hagra uveit midrasho] (Ramat Gan, 2003), 39–69.

—— 'Patterns of Internal Jewish Migration in the Russian Empire', in Yaacov Ro'i (ed.), *Jews and Jewish Life in Russia and the Soviet Union* (London, 1995).

—— 'The *Pushke* and its Development' (Heb.), *Katedra*, 21 (Oct. 1981), 89–102.

—— 'Remarriage among Jews and Christians in Nineteenth-Century Eastern Europe', *Jewish History*, 3/2 (1988), 85–114.

—— 'The Social Implications of Very Early Marriage in Eastern Europe in the Nineteenth Century' (Heb.), in Ezra Mendelsohn and Chone Shmeruk (eds.), *Studies on Polish Jewry: Paul Glikson Memorial Volume* [Kovets meḥkarim al yehudei polin: sefer lezikhro shel pa'ul glikson] (Jerusalem, 1987).

—— 'Three Lithuanian Yeshivas in the Nineteenth Century' [Shalosh yeshivot litayot], Ph.D. diss. (Hebrew University, Jerusalem, 1981).

—— 'What Happened to the Extended Jewish Family? Jewish Homes for the Aged in Eastern Europe', *Studies in Contemporary Jewry*, 14 (1998), 128–42.

STANISLAWSKI, MICHAEL, *Tsar Nicholas I and the Jews* (Philadelphia, 1983).

STARR, FREDERICK S. (ed.), *Studies on the Interior of Russia* (Chicago, 1972).

Statystyka Polski, Drugi Powszechny Spis Ludnosci z dnia 9 xii. 1931, Seria C, zeszyt 94a (Warsaw, 1938).

STEM, YOSEF ZEKHARYAH, *Zekher yehosef* [responsa] (Warsaw, 1898).

STERN, ELIYAHU, 'Elijah of Vilna and the Making of Modern Rabbinic Judaism', diss. (Berkeley, 2008).

STOW, KENNETH, 'The Jewish Family in the Rhineland in the High Middle Ages: Form and Function', *American Historical Review*, 92 (1987), 1085–1110.

SURASKI, A., *History of Torah Education* [Toledot haḥinukh hatorati] (Benei Berak, 1967).

—— *The Last Polish Ge'onim* [Ge'onei polin ha'aḥaronim] (Benei Berak, 1983).

—— *Teachers of Torah from the World of Hasidism* [Marbitsei torah me'olam haḥasidut], 8 vols. (Benei Berak, 1989).

—— and A. SEGAL, *Rosh golat ari'el* [biography], 2 vols. (Jerusalem, 1990 and 1995).

SUSSMAN, AVRAHAM B. YOSEF, *Zakhor le'avraham* [halakhic work] (Lvov, 1860).

TABAK, SHELOMOH YEHUDAH BEN PESAH TSEVI, *Erekh shai* [responsa] (Sighet, 1909).

TAITELBAUM, JAKOB, 'Jewish High School Education between the Two World Wars 1919–1939' [Haḥinukh hayehudi hatikhoni befolin bein shetei milḥamot ha'olam 1919–1939], unpublished Ph.D. diss. (Tel Aviv University, 1994).

TAMULYNAS, ALFONSAS, 'Demographic and Social-Professional Structure of the Jewish Community in Vilnius (Based on the Census of 1784)', in Izraelis Lempertas (ed.), *The Gaon of Vilnius and the Annals of Jewish Culture* (Vilnius, 1998).

TANNEN, D., 'New York Jewish Conversational Style', *International Journal of the Sociology of Language*, 30 (1981), 133–49.

TAVYOMI, TOBIAH JUDAH, *Erets tovah* [responsa] (Jerusalem, 1947).

TCHERNOWITZ, CHAIM, *Memoirs: An Autobiography* [Pirkei ḥayim: otobiografiyah] (New York, 1954).

TEITELBAUM, YEKUTI'EL YEHUDAH, *Avnei tsedek* [responsa] (Lvov, 1886).

TELLER, ADAM, 'Radziwill, Rabinowicz and the Rabbi of Swierz: The Magnates' Attitude to Jewish Regional Autonomy in the 18th Century', *Scripta Hierosolymitana*, vol. 38 (= *Studies in the History of the Jews in Old Poland in Honor of Jacob Goldberg*) (Jerusalem, 1998), 246–76.

TENNENBAUM, MALKI'EL, *Divrei malki'el* [responsa], 7 vols. (Piotrków, Biłgoraj, Vilna, Jerusalem, 1891–1976).

TEOMIM, MOSHEH, *Oriyan telitai* [responsa] (Lvov, 1880).

TEOMIM-FRAENKEL, ARYEH YEHUDAH LEIB, *She'elot uteshuvot gur aryeh yehudah* [responsa] (Zholkva, 1727).

TEOMIM-FRAENKEL, ELIYAHU, 'Treatise on the Sons of Kings' (Heb.), in id., *The Inheritance of My Father* [Naḥalat avi] (Biłgoraj, 1937).

THOMAS, WILLIAM, and FLORIAN ZNANIECKI, *The Polish Peasant in Europe and America*, 2 vols. (Chicago, 1918–20).

THON, JACOB, *Die Juden in Österreich* (Berlin, 1908).

TISHBY, ISAIAH, 'Anti-Hassidic Polemics of R. Israel of Shklov' (Heb.), *Kiryat sefer*, 51 (1976), 300–3.

TOIBESH, SHALOM, *She'elat shalom* [responsa] (Zholkva, 1869; several reprints).

TOIBS, URI SHRAGA, *Ori veyishi* [responsa] (Lvov, 1886).

TOLTS, M. S., 'Marriage Rate of the Russian Population at the End of the Nineteenth Century and at the Beginning of the Twentieth Century' (Russian), in A. G. Vishnevsky (ed.), *Brachnost', rozhdaemost', smertnost' v Rossii i v SSSR* (Moscow, 1977).

Tomekhei temimim [pocket calendar] (Warsaw, 1936–7).

TOSFA'AH, SHEMUEL AVIGDOR, *She'elot shemuel* [responsa] (Johannisburg, 1858).

TOTAH, KHALIL, *The Contribution of the Arabs to Education* (New York, 1926).

TRITTON, ARTHUR S., *Materials on Muslim Education in the Middle Ages* (London, 1957).

TROINITSKY, N. A. (ed.), *Obshchii svod po Imperii rezul'tatov razrabotki dannykh Pervoi Vseobshchei Perepisi Naseleniya, proizvedennoi 28 yanvarya 1897 goda*, 2 vols. (St Petersburg, 1905).

TRZCINSKI, ANDRZEJ, *A Guide to Jewish Lublin and Surroundings* (Warsaw, 1991).

Tsentral'nyi statisticheskii komitet, *Dvizhenie naseleniya v Evropeiskoi Rossii za 1867 g.*, Statisticheskii vremennik 8 (St Petersburg, 1872).

—— *Dvizhenie naseleniya v Evropeiskoi Rossii za 1885 g.*, Statisticheskii vremennik 11 (St Petersburg, 1890).

—— *Dvizhenie naseleniya v Evropeiskoi Rossii za 1910 g.*, Statistika Rossiiskoi Imperii 93 (St Petersburg, 1916).

TSEVI ELIMELEKH OF DYNOW, *Benei yisakhar* [homilies] (Lvov, 1910).

TURNER, RALPH, 'Modes of Social Ascent', in Albert H. Halsey, Jean Floud, and C. Arnold Anderson (eds.), *Education, Economy and Society* (New York, 1966), 121–39.

TURNIANSKY, CHAVA, 'Translations and Adaptations of the Tse'ena Urena' (Yid.), in Shmuel Verses, Natan Rotenstreich and Chone Shmeruk (eds.), *Sefer Dov Sadan: Dov Sadan Jubilee Volume* (Tel Aviv, 1977), 165–90.

TURNOWSKY, YISRA'EL YITSHAK, *Truth and Faith* [Emet ve'emunah] (Warsaw, 1911).

TWERSKY, MORDEKHAI DOV, *Emek she'elah* [responsa] (Piotrków, 1898).

ULBRICH, CLAUDIA, *Shulamit and Margarete* (Boston, 2004).

URBACH, EPHRAIM (ed.), 'A Collection of Letters of R. Eliyahu Rogoler' (Heb.), *Kovets al yad*, 6/16, pt. ii (Jerusalem, 1966).

—— *The Tosafists* [Ba'alei hatosafot], 2nd edn. (Jerusalem, 1986).

URBANSKI, KRZYSZTOF, and RAFAŁ BLUMENFELD, *Słownik historii kieleckich Żydów* (Kielce, 1995).

VEBLEN, THORSTEIN, *The Theory of the Leisure Class* (New York, 1899).

VILNA GAON, *see* Eliyahu ben Shelomoh Zalman

VISHNEVSKY, A. G. (ed.), *Brachnost', rozhdaemost', smertnost' v Rossii i v SSSR* (Moscow, 1977).

VOLIN, LAZAR, *A Century of Russian Agriculture* (Cambridge, Mass., 1970).

Vsesoyuznaya perepis' naseleniya 1926 goda, 56 vols. (Moscow, 1928–33).

WAGNER, DANIEL, and ABDELHAMID LOTFI, 'Traditional Islamic Education in Morocco: Sociohistorical and Pyschological Perspectives', *Comparative Education Review*, 24 (1980), 238–51.

WAHRMAN, AVRAHAM DAVID, *Da'at kedoshim* [commentary on *Shulḥan arukh*] (Lvov, 1871).

—— *Eshel avraham* [responsa] (Lvov, 1893).

WALBY, SYLVIA, *Theorizing Patriarchy* (Oxford, 1990).

WALDMAN, KHAYIM, *The Law of Slaughtering* [Torat hasheḥitah] (Jerusalem, 1991).

WALKIN, AHARON, *Zekan aharon* [responsa], 2 vols. (Pinsk, 1931–8).

WALL, RICHARD (ed.), *Family Forms in Historic Europe* (Cambridge, 1983).

WEBER, MAX, *On Charisma and Institution Building* (Chicago, 1968).

WEINBERG, SHLOMO DAVID YEHOSHUA, *Holy Memory* [Zikaron kodesh] [selected writings] (Jerusalem, 1985).

WEINBERGER, EFRAYIM, 'On Heredity in the Rabbinate' (Heb.), *Hatorah vehamedinah*, 9/10 (1958–9), 391–8.

WEINGARTEN, SHEMUEL HAKOHEN, *The Yeshivas in Hungary* [Hayeshivot behungariyah] (Jerusalem, 1976).

WEINREICH, MAX, *Selected Writings* [Oysgeklibene shriftn] (Buenos Aires, 1974).

WEINRYB, BERNARD, *Jewish Vocational Education* (New York, 1948).

—— *The Jews of Poland* (Philadelphia, Pa., 1973).

WEIR, DAVID, 'Rather Never Than Late', *Journal of Family History*, 9 (Winter 1984), 340–54.

WEISS, BENYAMIN ARYEH, *Even yekarah* [responsa] (Lvov, 1894).

WEISS, ISAAC ISAIAH, 'Verdict of the Hatam Sofer on the Matter of the Distribution of Money for the People of Israel' (Heb.), *Moriah*, 8/2–3 (1978), 24–7.

WEISS, JOSEPH, 'Torah Study in Early Hasidism', in David Goldstein (ed.), *Studies in Eastern European Jewish Mysticism* (Oxford, 1985).

WEISS, YA'AKOV, *Rabbinate and Community in the Thought of the Hatam Sofer* [Rabanut vekehilah bemishnat raban heḥatam sofer] (Jerusalem, 1987).

WEISS-HALIVNI, DAVID, *The Book and the Sword* (New York, 1996).

WEISSENBERG, S., 'Menarche und Menopause bei Jüdinnen und Russinnen in Südrussland', *Zentralblatt für Gynaecologie*, 11 (1909), 383–5.

—— 'Der Rückgang der Geburtsziffer bei den russischen Juden', *Zeitschrift für Demographie und Statistik der Juden*, 9 (1913), 53–6.

WEISSLER, CHAVA, 'For Women and for Men Who Are Like Women', *Journal of Feminist Studies in Religion*, 5/2 (1989), 7–24.

—— 'The Religion of Traditional Ashkenazic Women: Some Methodological Issues', *AJS Review*, 12/1 (Spring 1987), 73–94.

—— 'The Traditional Piety of Ashkenazic Women', in Arthur Green (ed.), *Jewish Spirituality*, vol. ii: *From the Sixteenth Century Revival to the Present* (New York, 1987).

—— *Voices of the Matriarchs: Listening to the Prayers of Early Modern Jewish Women* (Boston, Mass., 1998).

WEISSMAN, DEBORAH, 'Bais Yaakov: A Historical Model for Jewish Feminists', in Elizabeth Koltun (ed.), *The Jewish Woman: New Perspectives* (New York, 1976).

WEIZMANN-LICHTENSTEIN, HAYA, *In the Shadow of our Roof* [Betsel koroteinu] (Tel Aviv, 1948).

WENGEROFF, PAULINA, *Memoiren einer Grossmutter*, 2 vols. (Berlin, 1913–19); trans. Henny Wenkart, *Rememberings: The World of a Russian-Jewish Woman in the Nineteenth Century* (Bethesda, Md., 2000).

WERTHEIM, AARON, *Law and Custom in Hasidism*, trans. Shmuel Himelstein (Hoboken, NJ, 1992).

WEX, MICHAEL, *Born to Kvetch: Yiddish Language and Culture in All of its Moods* (New York, 2005).

WICZKOWSKI, JÓZEF, *Lwów* (Lvov, 1907).

WILENSKY, MORDECAI, *Hasidim and Mitnagedim* [Hasidim umitnagedim], 2 vols. (Jerusalem, 1970).

WINOGRAD, YESHAYAHU, *Otsar hasefer ha'ivri: Reshimat hasefarim shenidpesu be'ot ivrit mereshit hadefus ha'ivri bishenat 229 (1469) ad shenat 623 (1863)* [thesaurus of books printed in Hebrew] (Jerusalem, 1993).

—— *Otsar sifrei hagra* [thesaurus of the writings of the Vilna Gaon] (Jerusalem, 2003).

WISCHNITZER, MARK, 'Documents on the Yeshivot of Eastern Europe', *Talpiyot*, 1/2 (Dec. 1950), 157–75; 3/4 (Jan. 1952), 603–18; 6: 1/2 (Mar. 1953), 359–69; 7: 3/4 (May 1955), 739–49.

WOHLGELERNTER, ELLI, 'Defender of the Tribe', *Jerusalem Post Magazine* (27 Jan. 1999).

WOLF, BENYAMIN BEN MATITYAHU, *Taharat hakodesh* [ethical tractate] (Amsterdam, 1733).

WOLF, MIKHAL, 'Legal Constraints on Wife-Beating in the Talmudic Literature and Jewish Law' [Gevulot halegitimiyot shel hafalat koah mitsad ba'al kelapei ishto], Ph.D. diss. (Bar Ilan University, Ramat Gan, 2000).

WUNDER, MEIR, *Lights of Galicia: Encyclopaedia of the Sages of Galicia* [Me'orei galitsiyah: entsiklopediyah lehokhmei galitsiyah], 5 vols. (Jerusalem, 1986).

—— 'Yeshivas in Galicia' (Heb.), *Moriah* (1991), 95–100, 183–4.

YA'ARI, ABRAHAM *Emissaries to Israel* [Shelihei erets yisra'el] (Jerusalem, 1977).

—— (ed.), *Letters from Israel* [Igerot erets yisra'el] (Ramat Gan, 1971).

YAGEL, AVRAHAM, *Lekah tov* [Yiddish collection of selections from the Talmud] (Amsterdam, 1575).

YAKUBOVITS, ALTER YOSEF, *Nehor Shraga: Collection on Behalf of the Establishment of a Fund for Torah and Fear of God, and for the Movement of the Yeshivas 'Beit Israel' and 'Nehor Shraga'* [Nehor shraga: kovets lema'an haramat keren hatorah vehayirah: velitenuat hayeshivot beit yisra'el unehor shraga] (Łódz, [1939]).

YASHAR, M. B., *The Hafets Hayim* [Hehafets hayim] (Tel Aviv, 1958).

YEHOSHUA HOROWITZ OF DZIKÓW, *Ateret yeshuah* [responsa] (Kraków, 1932).

YEHUDAH LEIB OF YANOVITZ, 'Responsum', *Hatamim*, 5 (1936), 33–5; repr. in *She'elot uteshuvot she'erit yehudah* [responsa] (New York, 1957), 202, no. 29.

YERUSHALIMSKI, MOSHEH, *Be'er mosheh* [responsa] (Warsaw, 1901).

YERUSHALMI, YOSEF, *From Spanish Court to Italian Ghetto* (New York, 1971).

YEZIERSKA, ANZIA, *Bread Givers* (New York, 1925).

YUVAL, YISRA'EL, *Sages in their Generation* [Ḥakhamim bedoram] (Jerusalem, 1989).

ZAFRANI, HAÏM, *Pédagogie juive en terre d'Islam* (Paris, 1969).

ZALKIN, MORDEKHAI, *A New Dawn. The Jewish Enlightenment in the Russian Empire: Social Aspects* [Be'alot hashakhar: hahaskalah hayehudit be'imperiyah harusit beme'ah hatesha esreh] (Jerusalem, 2000).

—— Review of Iris Parush, *Nashim korot: yitronah shel shuliyut baḥevrah hayehudit bemizraḥ eiropah bame'ah ha-19* (2001) (Heb.), *Gal-Ed*, 19 (2004), 78–87.

ZALTSMAN, SHELOMOH, *My Town: Memoirs and Sketches* [Ayarati: zikhronot ureshumot] (Tel Aviv, 1947).

ŻARNOWSKA, ANNA, 'Family and Public Life: Barriers and Interpenetration. Women in Poland at the Turn of the Century', *Women's History Review*, 5/4 (1996) 469–86.

—— and ANDRZEJ SZWARC (eds.), *Kobieta i społeczenstwo na ziemiach polskich w XIX wieku*, vol. i (Warsaw, 1995).

ŻBIKOWSKI, ANDRZEJ, *Żydzi krakowscy i ich gmina w latach 1869–1919* (Warsaw, 1994).

ZBOROWSKI, MARK, 'The Place of Book Learning in Traditional Jewish Culture', *Harvard Educational Review*, 19/2 (1949), 87–109.

—— and ELIZABETH HERZOG, *Life Is with People: The Jewish Little-Town of Eastern Europe* (New York, 1952).

ZEDERBAUM, ALEXANDER, *The Secrets of Berdichev* [Di geheymnise fun berditshuv] (Warsaw, 1870).

ZEIDMAN, HILLEL, 'Kamenits' (Heb.), in Shmuel Mirsky (ed.), *Jewish Institutions of Higher Learning in Europe: Their Development and Destruction* [Mosadot torah be'eiropah bevinyanam uveḥurbanam] (New York, 1956).

—— 'Yeshivas of Lubavitch' (Heb.), in Shmuel Mirsky (ed.), *Jewish Institutions of Higher Learning in Europe: Their Development and Destruction* [Mosadot torah be'eiropah bevinyanam uveḥurbanam] (New York, 1956).

ZELBOVIC, MORDEKHAI, *Ateret mordekhai* [responsa] (Riga, 1938).

ZELDITCH, MORRIS, 'Trends in the Care of the Aged', *Journal of Jewish Communal Service*, 34/1 (Fall 1957), 126–40.

ZELIG, SHIMSHON BEN YA'AKOV YEHOSEF HALEVI, *Teshuot ḥen* [responsa] (Dubno, 1757).

ZEMBA, AVRAHAM, 'The Metivta in Warsaw' (Heb.), in Shmuel Mirsky (ed.), *Jewish Institutions of Higher Learning in Europe: Their Development and Destruction* [Mosadot torah be'eiropah bevinyanam uveḥurbanam] (New York, 1956).

—— 'Shtiblakh of Warsaw' (Heb.), in Shmuel Mirsky (ed.), *Jewish Institutions of Higher Learning in Europe: Their Development and Destruction* [Mosadot torah be'eiropah bevinyanam uveḥurbanam] (New York, 1956).

ZERDOUMI, NEFISSA, *Enfant d'hier: L'Éducation de l'enfant en milieu traditionnel algérien* (Paris, 1970).

ZILBERBERG, YEHOSHUA, *The Dynasty of Radomsk* [Malkhut beit radomsk] (Benei Berak, 1993).

ZILBERSCHLAG, DAVID (ed.), *Memorial Volume for Rabbi Kalonymos Kalman Shapira* [Zikaron kodesh leba'al esh kodesh] (Jerusalem, 1994).

ZIMMER, ERIC, *Harmony and Discord* (New York, 1970).

ZINOWITZ, M., 'The History of the Rabbinate in Vitebsk' (Heb.), in Baruch Karo (ed.), *The Book of Vitebsk* [Sefer vitebsk] (Tel Aviv, 1957).

Zohar, trans. Harry Sperling, Maurice Simon, and Paul Levertoff (London, 1949).

ZUNZ, YEHI'EL MATITIYAHU, *City of Righteousness* [Ir hatsedek] (Lvov, 1874).

ZUSMANOVITS, YOSEF, *Treatise on the Law of Inheritance of Posts* [Kuntres mishpat yerushat misrah] (Kaunas, 1928).

Index